PERKIN

Ann Wroe is the Special Features Editor of *The Economist* and has a doctorate in medieval history from Oxford University. She is the author of three previous works of non-fiction, of which the most recent, *Pilate: The Biography of an Invented Man*, was shortlisted for the Samuel Johnson Award and the W.H. Smith Award.

Ann Wroe

PERKIN

A STORY OF DECEPTION

V

VINTAGE

Published by Vintage 2004

1 3 5 7 9 10 8 6 4 2

Copyright © Ann Wroe 2003

Ann Wroe has asserted her right under the Copyright, Designs
and Patents Act, 1988 to be identified as the author of this work

First published in Great Britain in 2003 by Jonathan Cape

Vintage
Random House 20 Vauxhall Bridge Road,
London, SW1V 2SA

Random House Australia (Pty) Limited
20 Alfred Street, Milsons Point, Sydney,
New South Wales 2061, Australia

Random House New Zealand Limited
18 Poland Road, Glenfield
Auckland 10, New Zealand

Random House (Pty) Limited
Endulini, 5a Jubilee Road, Parktown 2193,
South Africa

The Random House Group Limited Reg. No. 954009

www.randomhouse.co.uk/vintage

A CIP catalogue record for this book
is available from the British Library

Papers used by Random House
are natural, recyclable products made from wood grown in
sustainable forests. The manufacturing processes conform to
the environmental regulations of the country of origin

ISBN 0 099 44996 X

Printed and bound in Great Britain by
Bookmarque Ltd, Croydon, Surrey

CONTENTS

INTRODUCTION

THIS BOOK IS ABOUT A MYSTERY. It has remained unexplained for so long that most people believe it has been solved; but not so. And unlike other historical posers, to do with the dates of battles or the terms of treaties or the motivation for invasions, this one is about the most fundamental issue of all: who a man was. When he walked in the world as a young English prince, at the very end of the fifteenth century, almost no one knew whether he was truly that prince, or an impostor. And since his death on the gallows at the age of twenty-five—or possibly twenty-six, for who knows?—that mystery has only grown deeper.

He claimed to be Richard, Duke of York, the younger of the Princes in the Tower. Those princes were presumed to have been killed to make way for their uncle, Richard III, but this young man said he had survived. In this persona, he tormented Henry VII for eight years. He emerged in Ireland in 1491, to be honoured and protected by the courts of France, Burgundy, the Empire and Scotland. He tried three times to invade England, sometimes eluding capture only by moments. He was a political pawn, and also the most keenly sought diplomatic prize in Europe: handsome, charismatic, beautifully mannered, everybody's perfect prince. At the height of his success, he was married to an earl's daughter. But he was officially proclaimed to be—and apparently, in custody, confessed he was—a boatman's son. History now knows him as Perkin Warbeck, the name Henry Tudor delighted to call him.

The mystery of his identity was compounded by the games people played with him. The greatest European rulers of the age—the Emperor Maximilian, Ferdinand and Isabella of Spain, Charles VIII of France— neither knew nor cared who this elegant young charmer was. Instead, they employed him for their own purposes: to unsettle the new King of England and reorder the world to their advantage. All who dealt with him gave him the identity they wished him to have: either the Duke of York, or a conceited upstart from Flanders. It is possible that he was nei-ther. It is also possible that, by the end, even he did not know who he really was.

This book's first purpose, therefore, is to resurrect a marvellous tale that seems on the brink of being forgotten. Its second purpose is to dissect, and call into question, the official cover story. Modern cover stories leave tracks—computer messages, phone logs—by which they betray their nature. Very old cover stories acquire a patina of age and settle into his-tory. So it is with Perkin's confession, which—though largely ignored at the time—is now accepted as true by almost all respectable historians. James Gairdner, the finest fifteenth-century historian of the Victorian age, effected that change by first linking the family details given in the confes-sion to documents in the archives of Tournai, in Belgium. Henry VII hadn't made this family up; so his rival must have been, indeed, just a boatman's boy, cajoled into being a prince (as the confession said) by a group of disaffected Yorkists in Ireland. And that was the end of the story. Most historians of the period now treat Perkin with a certain impa-tience, as a colourful but tiresome diversion on the way to the Triumph of the Tudors. He sparkles for a time but soon blows away, amusing and inconsequential.

Those who look closely find a picture that is deeply perplexing. This young man caused far more trouble, and more nearly upended Henry, than he is usually given credit for. Though he was allegedly attempting an astonishing trick—trying, as a low-born foreigner, to get the throne of England—he proved very hard either to deflate or to expose. The main players, including Henry, behaved towards him in ways that are often dif-ficult to explain. Beyond this, the Tournai family was never linked prop-erly to Henry's captive, nor he to them. Much does not fit in the neat parameters of the official confession, and never has. A different story, per-haps a surprising one, may have been unfolding here. The truth lies somewhere in the details.

Yet catching this character is notoriously hard. He was known to be ungraspable in his own time, like quicksilver or a shooting star. Of the writers who have tried—among them Mary Shelley, Friedrich Schiller and Lord Alfred Douglas—it is possible that no one has captured him except John Ford, whose wonderful play portrays an impostor-prince who believes so completely in his own majesty that he is, in effect, the person he claims to be. In the febrile, casually mendacious and highly coloured world of the late fifteenth century, this young man is almost the perfect exemplar of his time. To write his life, therefore, it is necessary to explore not just late-fifteenth-century politics and diplomacy, but late-fifteenth-century ways of seeing, deceiving and understanding.

Much of this involves putting him in the roles people gave him, or which he gave himself. He was an adventurer, an inveterate wanderer, when real adventuring was prying open the closed husk of the medieval globe. He was a lost prince, at a time when lost kings of all kinds were keenly invoked and regretted. He was a consummate performer, in a world where pageant and display were paramount. He was, as he himself said, Fortune's victim, in an age when all men and women felt the rush of the wheel propelling them to greatness or nothingness. And he was—in one character or another, or both—a deceiver, in a whole world of false appearances. If we look at him in all these roles, as people of the time observed and judged him, we may get a little closer to knowing who he was.

And yet, in the end, the aim of this book is not to stick a name on him. On the contrary, it is almost the opposite: to free him from the tyranny of forced identities. The name "Perkin" is used in these pages only when people would have used it of him, and not otherwise. Thomas Gainsford, whose account of 1618 did so much to make him at the same time lurid and pathetic, was the first to grapple with the idea that his biographers had to use all his names, in all their multiplicity, and then get past them. "Whether I name [him] Peter, or Perkin, or Warbeck, or Prince, or Richard Duke of York, or Richard the Fourth," he wrote, "all is one Man and all had one End." Gainsford was right. He was all these people and, in the deepest sense, none of them.

I sometimes felt as I wrote that this book is not so much about one man as about the human soul: about the "I" that exists apart from the names we are given, the family we acquire or the titles we aspire to. The concept is dimmer to us than it would have been to him. Medieval people pictured the soul as a naked miniature of themselves which, after death, left the body like a candle flame. It glimmered a little in life, and you tried to detect it, but it was hard to catch. Beneath everything that was fastened on this young man, by himself and by others, lay his true self, which was not touched or changed. In the course of retelling and re-examining the story of his life, I hope this book may also uncover a little of that.

Perkin

Prologue: Presence

FACE TO FACE, the two men sat at the window. One was an artist; you could see this from his drab workaday gown, the tablet he held and the way, from long habit, the chalk or metalpoint nestled in his hand. The formalities had been concluded: he had doffed his hat and, holding it to his chest as etiquette required, had knelt to his subject with a few soft words of greeting. Now, as carefully as he might without touching or out-raging him, he was overseeing the way he sat and appraising the light that fell on him.

The young man who faced him was a prince. You could tell this from his clothes: a long gown of cloth-of-gold trimmed with fur, a surcoat of cloth-of-silver, a shirt of exquisite linen and, arranged on his shoulders, chains of briquettes of gold. His black velvet hat bore a brooch set with one large jewel and finished with three pendant pearls. Attendants hov-ered by to hold his gloves, move his chair or, at a nod or lift of a finger, take some murmured message from him. No more credentials were re-quired of him for the moment. These were enough.

His name was already famous. This, as far as the artist knew, was Richard Plantagenet, Duke of York, the second son of Edward IV, late King of England. He claimed to be the rightful heir to the throne now held by Henry VII, and the hoped-for restorer of his father's line. He had been thought dead, murdered as a child with his child-brother in the Tower of London, but now he was alive. He was here, and you could touch him, if you dared touch a young man who was both a prince and a sign of God's miraculous power.

The encounter probably occurred in Malines or Dendermonde in the Burgundian Netherlands, in one of the palaces where the prince was staying as the guest and protégé of his aunt Margaret of York, Duchess of Burgundy. The date was probably the autumn of 1494, though it is not known for certain. Columbus's caravels had already reached, and returned from, the islands east of Cipango across the West Sea. The thrones of France, England and the Empire were occupied respectively by Charles VIII, Henry VII and Maximilian, each in a state of advanced suspicion of the others. Plague had ravaged the western parts of the Empire and had been followed by a spring so cold, under the domination of Saturn and the moon, that vines had frozen and cherry-blossoms had turned to ice on the trees. In London, Nantwich salt was selling for 6d. a bushel and white herring for 2s. 8d. a cord, and an old woman had been burned at Smithfield for nine articles of heresy. The world was composed of nine spheres, nine companies of angels, seven planetary influences, five earthly zones, four elements, four states of existence, four humours (yellow bile, black bile, phlegm, blood) and, at the apex, the perfection of the Trinity, Father, Son and Holy Ghost.

So the two sat, and looked at each other. The prince's gaze was still, the artist's quick, darting from his subject to the sheet of paper he held before him, steadied on a book or a block of wood. The artist's stool was low, the chair of the prince set higher. It could not have been otherwise, for the degrees of social separation had to be preserved. That separation extended to their sense of time as they sat there: the artist's expendable, the prince's precious, belonging to a higher life.

Yet the artist and the young man before him were perhaps more similar than they appeared. Both were engaged in the making of works of art: the prince *princiant,* proving his high nobility by elegance and presence, and the artist endeavouring to show, by sheer skill, that he could make a counterfeit that would live. A counterfeit, as both he and the prince understood it, was a true image, a copy so exact that it could take the place of the living person or the real thing. As a mirror trapped a perfect reflection, so the frame of this portrait could catch the subject in perfect similitude, so lifelike that the figure appeared to breathe, the silk to shimmer and the fur to sink under the hand. Kissing this counterfeit—as you would want to kiss it, or prop it next to you at table—your lips would surely brush living flesh, slightly rough and warm. This mouth, like a mouth in the mirror, could perhaps form words; the hands could move, in their heavy sleeves, in a gesture of courtesy; tears could steal from the sub/ ject's eyes, wet to the touch on the painted wood. A master/painter could move you deeply with a counterfeit such as this.

He would use all kinds of trickery to achieve his effects, as artists were known to do. In common parlance, to "paint" meant to feign; a "colour" was a fiction, an allegory or, at worst, a plain lie, built on a ground of oily untruth as a painter established his colour on the wood. The secret of the best pigments was sometimes common filth, as when urine, lye and alum mixed with powdered brazil wood made the color of a red rose, or when lumps of soot and lye made a beautiful bright wash for the painting of a young girl's hair. Some artists knew, too, about the artificial yellow that could simulate gold, or how to make pretended gold leaf from varnish and Greek pitch crushed in oil. Many a "masterpiece" relied on such tech/ niques. One writer of a painter's guide boasted that he knew how to make "a beautiful ivory which can take a polish and is white and even more lovely than real ivory." Lovelier than the real: the ideal of works of art.

There were many who would say, in the years to come, that Richard Plantagenet was just such a masterpiece: cut from the block in Tournai, sculpted and painted in Burgundy, and then exhibited everywhere. "A curi/ ous piece of marble", Francis Bacon called him. The same verb, *effingere*, was applied to his alleged makers as was used for painting and sculpting in the ordinary way: as if, from wood or silver or white limestone, they had moulded a compelling human form. Nature was easily and busily imitated by those who knew how. At Margaret of York's main wedding feast, in 1468, dry deserts were made of silk and buckram, the waves of the sea of silver/painted wood and the growing grass of wax: all done "from life" and "as lifelike as possible", although this static and shining beauty was nothing but artificers' work. The painted funerary image of Charles VIII in 1498 was so well done wrote the chronicler Jean Molinet, "by subtle art and exquisite pictures, that he seemed actually resuscitated, full of spirit and life." Such skill could no doubt be applied to the making of princes, too.

He sat now with his gold robes falling round him. To gather from those who observed him, he was not particularly tall. Any presence he had did not come from that. Maximilian, who first met him when he was about twenty, called him "a young boy", *ains Jungen knaben*, and Henry VII first described him, two years or so before this portrait, as "the Child". The word "boy", fixed on him by his enemies, meant first of all a churl and a rascal. Yet it also suggested someone suited to diminutives, as well as to manipulation by those who were older and wiser. Both Bacon, writing his story in the 1620s, and Edward Hall, recording it in the 1540s, called him a doll: played with, fought over, carried about, dressed up.

Contemporaries also found two stranger words to describe him. Robert Fabyan, a London alderman who first saw him when he was about twenty-three, called him "this unhappy Imp". The word, usually applied to innocent children, seemed peculiar for a man in adulthood who was, by then, married. It also suggested other images: an urchin, a devil-child, or a creature small enough to hide inside a pitcher or cling to a man's cloak, chattering and harrying him.

The second word was more bizarre. It was used by Bernard André, Henry VII's poet laureate and "royal historiographer", who was blind and never saw the man he was describing. Possibly, then, it came from the circle of the king himself. Recording the campaign in 1497 to drive this presumptuous invader out of the West Country, André referred in passing to *Cornubii . . . unacum papilione suo*, "the Cornishmen and their butterfly." Smallness, lightness, effeminacy and, in William Caxton's version of *The King's Book*, printed ten years before, falseness too. "The liar fareth as a butterfly, that liveth in the air and hath nothing in her guts but wind, and at every colour that she sees changeth her own."

He was certainly embellished, as his age and his station required. Fashion dictated that a young prince in the early 1490s should wear precisely these clothes. He was, and remained, at the cutting edge of elegance. When he was taken up by James IV of Scotland, the king paid for "a great coat of the new fashion to the Prince, with sleeves", and for black hose daringly striped with purple in the French style, the only style worth following. (James had white hose striped with green.) In Stirling at Easter 1496 the prince and his patron, young fellow-dandies, indulged in new hats and fresh lacings for their shirts. Even their underclothes were new, tied up with new ribbons tipped with bright silver tags, as they processed at Mass together.

Now, as he sat for his portrait, every detail cried the latest look.

The angle of his hat was exactly judged; it was not last year's. The neck-opening of his surcoat, one side pleated, the other plain, was unquestion-ably "the new guise", or "the new jet", as he himself would have put it. Cloth-of-gold was the fabric of choice among the tiny elite who qualified to wear it. Silver and gold robes together, as this young man wore them, were the "royalest" advertisement of nobility. Gold chains, the more the better, were so important that in 1491 the Milanese ambassador in France described those worn by the Scottish envoys before he mentioned their horses or their robes. A chain worth £1,000 or more was not uncommon among a king's chief officers. Their value was known and flaunted. Richard Plantagenet wore two long chains carefully arranged in a pattern; the longer one seemed to cross on his chest and may have fallen as far as his waist. Cross-bracing of this sort, like cross-lacing, was almost aggres-sively up-to-date.

Just as fashionably, his blond hair had been brushed to fall in full reg-ular waves to his shoulders. In John Skelton's poem "Magnificence", Courtly Abusion (a hopeless dandy, speaking doggerel French and Flemish) had done this, twirling alone on stage and hoping somebody was watching him:

> My hair busheth
> So pleasantly,
> My robe rusheth
> So ruttingly [dashingly],
> Meseem I fly,
> I am so light
> To dance delight.

"Nesh" was the word for hair like this. A physiognomist, skilled in the science of looking at faces, would tell you that it meant timidity, like the soft-furred hare that started and ran in the field. Soft skin, too, like a woman's, meant a man who was changeable and fickle, susceptible to movement because the denser vapours did not settle in him. The neshness of a man's heart, though possibly good soil for God to work in, was more often a feather-bed in which the Devil lay, tempting him to delicacy and luxury. It was of course unwise, as Aristotle had told the Emperor Alexander, to read too much into one or two signs. But the tenth sign of timidity was also suggested by the pose Plantagenet had struck: "over-lightly moving of colour and semblant, and have semblant to be pensive, and full of thoughts."

As a final decorative touch, the prince's hair had been curled into two quiffs, one on either side of his face. It was not a practical design; if he had tried to do anything active, they would have fallen into his eyes. Some skill would have been needed to achieve this effect. On his first rising, as recommended for princes, his servants would have vigorously washed and rubbed his hair, dispelling the vapours gathered during sleep and unlocking the shutters of the brain. They would next have stretched his hair with hot tongs as he sat by the fire, stiffening it with a sticky paste of resin, egg-white and sulphur, arranging the curls with comb and brush. The freshest gallants fixed them up at night with nets or little presses. Sebastian Brant described the techniques that year in his chapter on Innovations in *The Ship of Fools*, accompanying the printed text with a woodcut of the curled fop, also in wildly cross-laced underwear, gazing at himself in a hand-mirror. Playing with your hair, washing it, trussing and combing it, making it stand out and seem curly, then looking in the glass, were all chief sins of the body that had to be confessed, if you could find a priest handy.

The two fashion-foibles of the age, curling and pleating, were thus exquisitely represented in Richard Plantagenet as he sat there. Such a passion for "curiosities," in Brant's view, drew the soul away from God. Just as dangerously, it led towards that "intricacy of thought" that tried to construct, like a piece of Flemish needlework, a reasoned explanation for the mysteries of the Incarnation or the Sacrament. Plantagenet may never have considered such questions, but his precious curls were quite enough to raise this suspicion about him. He sat still enough not to disturb them; but had you got close to him, as close as the artist was, you might have sniffed—above the herb-and-rosewater perfumes of his recent bath—a more workaday smell, of scorched hair and sulphur.

The pose he had chosen, too, was deliberate. He held his head at the king's angle, slightly dipped to the left, as if attending kindly to someone lower than himself. He had possibly assumed this pose quite naturally, as soon as he sat down. But possibly, too, it had been suggested to him. The look would have been familiar from countless representations, as indeed from his own performances in councils, on balustrades and at formal receptions. It suggested piety, nobility, humility, the benign goodness of the ruling class. The angels, too, had this expression as they gazed on the earth and blessed it in a slightly distant way. It was the ideal look of the age, both in Heaven and on earth.

You could call him handsome; most people did, though his bearing impressed them even more. Molinet thought him "really good-looking", *fort gorgias*, using a word that meant he outshone those around him. The Venetian ambassador to London in 1497 called him *zentil*, "noble", in manners as in looks. Later chroniclers went further. After the off-hand remark of Polydore Vergil, Henry VII's historian, that the young man was *forma non ineleganti* (probably gleaned from people who had seen him) came the assertions of Hall and his followers that he was "of visage beautiful, of countenance demure": like the fifteen-year-old Galahad before his knighting, demure as a dove. Beyond this, Bacon wrote, he had "such a crafty and bewitching fashion both to move pity and to induce belief, as was like a kind of fascination and enchantment to those that saw him or heard him." The looks and manner together made him *amabilis*, lovely and worthy to be loved.

Taken feature by feature, his face was almost a pastiche of what contemporaries admired. The jaw was strongly moulded, with a cleft in the chin. The mouth was delicate and petulant, absurdly fashionable: the lower lip full, with a slight dinted divide at the centre, the upper lip modeled in a perfect bow, even to the little rise at the edges that suggested the suppression of a smile. The nose was well-shaped and in proportion: a nose like this, "rather long and turned up a little", was exactly what Louis XI wanted on his tomb effigy, "the handsomest countenance you can make him," rather than the big hooked article he had in life. Plantagenet's forehead was high, the brows well-shaped, the whole face (smooth and scarcely touched by the razor) regular and open. A sanguine temperament, the physiognomist would have told you: a young man's natural heat fueled with excess of blood and disposed, especially after wine, to laugh, dance and tumble women. In medical treatises the sanguine man was often drawn in court clothes, for courts were the element in which he thrived. He was associated, too, with air, which gave him, like the butterfly, his vitality and levity.

But there was a flaw. It was noticed in October 1497 by Henry VII's envoy Richmond Herald ("a wise man who noticed everything," according to a colleague). Richmond remarked to the Milanese ambassador that the young man had a defective left eye *que manca un poco da strambre*, which lacked a little brightness. For this reason, he was "not handsome," what-ever the assumptions that had gone before. Like his beauty, this defect too passed into the folk memory of him. Bacon's description of his last de-bacle, when he began to "squint one eye upon the crown and another upon the sanctuary," suggested that the strangeness of his left eye was widely known, though only Richmond's observation preserves it in writing.

That eye would have been the next thing the artist noticed, once the general impression of brilliance had settled. Neither the shape nor the colour of this eye resembled the other, and the gaze was slightly mis-directed. The upper lid was creased above it, and under the lower lid, near the nose, was a mark that might have been a scar. Some accident, perhaps, had caused these things, or else he had been born with them. The eye did not seem blind, but its opacity suggested that his vision was dulled. Richmond was right to notice the lack of brightness in it. The artist too, as he drew, could do little to invest it with life. Plantagenet had turned his good side towards him, naturally enough, but the light from the window therefore fell on the most unsettling thing about him.

When faced with contradictory signs in a man you judged him by his eyes, "for they be most true and provable." Strange eyes were danger-ous, and could not be trusted. When a maiden of India with speckled eyes was sent once to Alexander, he found she had been suckled on poi-son that had invisibly envenomed her. A film upon the eye could imply blindness that was spiritual rather than physical: an insufficient knowl-edge of the Creed, or a poor appreciation that the beauties of the world were not lasting.

Eyes of two different lights or colours were even more disturbing. They accounted perhaps for the *veneficium*, the powers of hazardous be-witchment, that Bacon attributed to this young man. Philosophers taught that understanding and affection were represented by the right eye and the left respectively. If these were not in balance, "due and beauteous propor-tion" was offended. When the body politic was thus disordered, the right eye drew up statutes and the left perverted their meaning; the right offered justice, but the left accepted false information; the right made sin-cere and eloquent promises, while the left did nothing to fulfill them. A look that was "single and not turned to doubleness" made the body "fair and light." A double look led to darkness.

You might ask, then (if it was your place to ask), whether this young man was bound for the light or the dark. For the moment, evidently, he was enthroned in hope, but it might not last. Fortune clearly favoured him, but her favour was ever likely to be withdrawn again. In fact it was possible to think, as you looked at him, that Fortune herself had dressed him in his exquisite clothes. She had put on him these stiff, heavy, shining robes in which his natural lightness was weighed down with splendour. She had hung about his neck the chains of a status he might have been happier without; and the heavier the chains, the greater the danger that their sheer weight might crush the life from him. She had placed his hat on his head, giving it a nudge until it was at the very angle worn by Pride, "bonet on side", as he danced in Hell. Then, as a final touch, she had pinned to the brim a brooch so rich that it clearly bore the burden of some sponsor's expectations. She had him then—until, changing her mind like any pretty girl, she began as teasingly to unbuckle him again.

The original of this portrait has long since vanished. It was copied in the 1560s by Jacques le Boucq, a French herald who was making a collec-tion, for a gentleman of Lille, of portraits of notable people. He made his copies in red chalk or pencil; this was one of his red-chalk sketches, *à la sanguine* in French, as if he sought to reproduce the tints of the living flesh. It was done with great care for detail, as not all his drawings were, and with the colour-notes in full. The result was another version, in effect, of the first sketch done by the artist.

This counterfeit was well done; yet, in the deepest sense, it was not true. Like the mirror-image, it was not the person it represented but was somehow dim, removed and secondary. A counterfeit could thus begin to mismatch life, becoming ill-done and crooked. The word contained both meanings. The counterfeit Excalibur given by Morgan le Fay, the en-chantress, to King Arthur looked exactly like his sword, but it was brittle and could not bite steel as Excalibur could. Battle revealed its falseness. Caxton used the word "counterfeit" both for broken walls and for bodies curved with age, fine and straight things fallen out of line. In the poetry of Skelton lurked a character, Counterfeit Countenance, who presided over a whole skewed world of false smiles, gestures, documents and claims. In fact, Skelton implied, this was the real world.

Within five years, Skelton was also to size up this prince who now sat so still and dazzling before the artist. He judged him to be barnyard shit, though dressed up like a peacock. Others were less sure. In 1542, Hall, who had never seen him, used "counterfeit" in both its meanings to describe him. This young man, he wrote, "kept such a princely countenance, and so counterfeit a majesty royal, that all men in manner did firmly believe that he was extracted of the noble house and family of the dukes of York." "All men" was Hall's exaggeration. Yet plenty did believe, or simply did not question; and among them was the artist who was now involved in the task of drawing him.

As he drew, there was a possibility he might uncover the truth of the man before him. He might catch some sense of Plantagenet's soul, his real and eternal self, in his face. The soul was in essence a miniature of him, from the hairs on his head to the nails on his toes; yet it was also divine, God's image in him. However lowly a man was, his soul gave him that nobility. Artists showed it innocent, defenceless and naked as a child, "his right clearness colour of flowers, brightness of sun, figure of man, pleasant as precious stones." St. Bernard saw it as a white lily-flower, delicate and shining, among the thorns and corruption of the world. It was the motivating part and deep nature of bad men as well as good, and its sensitivity to humours made men what they were. In most men the "little soul" lived closed in the breast, but philosophers taught that it dwelt within the brain, spilling out its fiery virtue sometimes to the heart.

Could this reality be caught in a man as he lived? The best artists of the time tried hard to do so. The body, after all, could not obscure the soul entirely. Gross flesh was not opaque, but like a cloud-filled sky or a dark horn lantern through which the brightness of the soul could flicker just a little. In the eyes especially, as through windows, a glimpse of the soul could sometimes be seen. In his *Pilgrimage of the Life of Man*, Guillaume Deguileville described the effect:

> For of the body trust me
> The eyes no very eyen be
> But like to glass I dare well say
> Where through the clear soul is seen
> And outward with his beams bright
> Giveth thereto clearness and light . . .

The soul might also be snared by catching the sitter in some gesture, some semi-private moment in which he revealed himself. The artist might paint him turning, writing, removing a ring, fiddling with a button, so that the face was off-guard and open or, on the contrary, in communion with inward things. Many artists draped curtains behind their sitters, suggesting that they had been suddenly discovered in the private closets where they prayed in church. In the finished portrait Richard Plantagenet was probably meant to hold a white rose, the symbol of his house, which would thus appear to be the substance of his dreams.

Yet Plantagenet's soul remained mysterious. When all was said, the artist had not succeeded in drawing back the curtain. Those eyes, with their long girlish lashes, were fixed on something that was far away. They looked softly, without seeing. At some sudden noise (a shout in the corridor, the window-shutter slamming), you would expect this young man to be startled, even frightened, as his physiognomy suggested. Folk memory made much of this. He was Margaret of York's "dear darling", a timorous creature who often ran away and who, in Thomas Gainsford's favourite phrase, was "exanimated" time and again by the setbacks he encountered. Bacon, too, filled his story with metaphors that suggested both blazing and fading fire and, finally, lack of substance.

Time passed. He heard it by bells striking and calling to terce, prime or evensong. It was the year 1494 of human salvation; and he knew what feast it was, whether St. Gregory or St. John or the Finding of the Cross, more readily than he knew whether it was Monday or Thursday. Even the shortest periods of time were measured by prayers: an *Ave Maria*, half a *Pater Noster*, the regular slipping of beads through the fingers. Yet pressure of time was constant and acute. Contemporary letters made it clear: "I had no leisure", "with you right shortly", "as soon as I may", "written in haste".

An hour, perhaps, had gone by now. Richard Plantagenet's likeness in pencil or chalk had been faithfully committed to paper. The last quick strokes of the fur trim on his robe could be approximations. He had sat a long time at the beck and call of a workman. It was a relief to stand, move and re-establish his authority. A nod would bring the artist close to him, the lord's nod of gentle condescension; and the artist, kneeling again to him, would show him what he had done.

The prince looked on the counterfeit. Or, you might also say, the counterfeit looked on the prince.

CHAPTER ONE

Into Adventure

The beginnings of his story, as he told it, lay deep in the turmoil of the recent history of England. For three decades, to the astonishment of foreigners, the crown had been wrestled back and forth between the Houses of Lancaster and York. Henry V, the glory of Lancaster and the victor of Agincourt, had been followed in 1422 by a child-king, Henry VI, who grew into a saintly fool at the mercy of his scheming lords. England quickly descended into factional warfare, with extraordinary slaughter of the nobility on both sides. In 1460 Richard, Duke of York, claiming descent from Edward III, tried to proclaim himself king but was rebuffed and, in short order, killed. The next year, his son defeated Henry in battle and was crowned as Edward IV at Westminster.

The claims of Lancaster had been blurred by bastardy in the fourteenth century; but those of York, too, were not secure. Edward was king *de facto* but not *de jure*. In recent history, the Yorkist line had passed twice through women; and Henry, besides, still lived. In 1470 Edward IV's great rival, the Earl of Warwick, forced the king into exile in Flanders and brought the befuddled Henry out of prison. The restoration was short-lived. Edward was back within months, gathered supporters in the north, and early in 1471 recovered the crown. For some years afterwards, comforted by this epitome of glorious kingship, the country calmed down. But Edward died in 1483 at the age of forty, leaving in the balance the fate of both England and his two child-sons, Edward and Richard, whose story this young man gave as his own.

He had told it repeatedly, and could do so now if you required it of him, together with the sighs and tears that such a history called for. As a fatherless child of about nine, he and his brother Edward, who was twelve, had been committed to the Tower of London on the orders of their uncle Richard, Duke of Gloucester. Edward was supposed to await his coronation; instead, he had been killed. He himself, however, though tipped for death, had been spared and bundled abroad. He had been forced into wandering "in various countries" without a name or a background that anyone knew, or was allowed to know. In this way, he passed eight desolate years. Towards the end of them, apparently not yet free of aimlessness and poverty, he "spent some time in the kingdom of Portugal."

Meanwhile, his uncle had been crowned as Richard III. His reign was short. In 1485 Henry Tudor, the Earl of Richmond and a sprig of the House of Lancaster, returned from exile in Brittany to encounter Richard at Bosworth. The king was cut down like a dog in the midst of the battle, and his rival was acclaimed as Henry VII in his place. To try to defuse the claims of York, and to dampen England's affection for that house, Henry married Edward's eldest daughter and united their lines. Yet Yorkist claims, true or false, continually dogged him. Every year, risings occurred in some part of England or another. As Henry suppressed them, gradually accustoming the country to his firm and careful rule, the most dangerous claimant of all, this young man, Richard Plantagenet, remained in hiding. He waited only his moment, and the backing of other princes, to cast down Henry Tudor and send him back into the obscurity from which he had come.

So his story stood in most of Europe in 1494. But in 1497, when Henry captured this young man, a different tale eclipsed it. It came in the form of an official confession, already known and publicised in part beforehand, to which he apparently now agreed and put his signature. According to this, he was no prince, but the son of a customs-collector, John Osbeck, who worked up and down the River Scheldt at Tournai, on the border of France and the Burgundian lands. (His own name, though not given in the confession, was established at the same time as Piers Osbeck.) As a very small boy he had been put out to board with his aunt, then sent away to learn Flemish, only to be shuttled back home as war broke out between the local towns and Maximilian, then Archduke of Austria and regent of the Burgundian Netherlands. At the age of nine or ten he went to Antwerp with a merchant of Tournai called Berlo and, almost at once, fell sick. He remained ill for five months, lodged at a skinner's place beside the House of the English Merchant Adventurers. He was "brought from thence", still convalescent, to the market at Bergen-op-Zoom, where he stayed two months at a tavern called The Sign of the Old Man. After that he was hired by John Strewe, a merchant, possibly English, of Middelburg in Zeeland, and then by Sir Edward Brampton's wife, who took him as her page to Portugal. After a year there, restless again, Piers put himself into service with a Breton merchant who took him to Ireland. There, some Yorkist malcontents decided to press him into service as a false Duke of York.

Brampton himself, a Portuguese-born merchant, soldier and royal servant, gave a different version of this young man's life before he had resurfaced as a prince. He told it to Spanish investigators in Setubal, in Portugal, in 1496. Again the boy came from Tournai, the son of a boat-man called Bernal Uberque. He had not, however, gone into trade, but had been placed with an organist in the city. There for some years he had learned *el oficio*, the profession of playing music, especially at the Mass, but eventually he had run away. His age then, according to another Setubal witness who said he had talked to his father, was "fourteen going on fif-teen": still a tender child, by current thinking. He was a *moço* to Bramp-ton, the Portuguese for a servant boy, though once or twice he used the word *rapaz* for him, slang for a youth. Typically for the time, Brampton did not use his name at all. But he too thought that he was called "Piris", or Piers.

Ending up in Middelburg, Piers became an assistant to a man who sold purses and needles. His shop was opposite the house where Bramp-ton's wife was staying, taking refuge from the plague in Bruges, and the boy became friendly with the French children who were kept in her ser-vice. When he heard that they were all going to Portugal, Brampton said, Piers pleaded to go with them and join their family. In the end—almost, it seemed, to stop his pestering—they took him. But he was not with them long before he suddenly announced that he wanted to go home. When next heard of, he was being followed as King Edward's son in Ireland.

All these stories, ostensibly so different, were linked by wandering and jeopardy. The prince had roamed for years, in desperate sadness, in countries he scarcely knew. The boy of the confession had travelled widely under multiple masters, always vaguely discontented, wanting to move on. In Brampton's testimony, he deliberately ran away from Tournai towards the sea; once in Middelburg, he begged to go to Portugal. He desired, his confession said, "to see other Countries". Polydore Vergil thought his poverty and baseness, oppressing him from childhood, had impelled him to wander, like the "land-loper" Henry called him. He longed constantly for the strange and new.

John Mandeville, in his book of travels, described such restlessness as a characteristic of northern Europeans. The moon, the mother of the waters, was their planet of influence, and they wandered as she did, lightly about the world. Unlike the natives of broiling India, stilled by Saturn's dryness and passivity, they could not stay unmoving or uncurious. Possibilities impelled them: of profit, fame, love, escape. Their longing could be summed up in the phrase *per adventure*, which meant, then, "perhaps".

This notion of adventure ran all through life. A young man's sexual equipment was his *denrées d'aventure*, the gear with which he hoped to take a chance with girls. Ordinary men and women "put their honour in adventure" when they picked a quarrel with someone violent or implacable. Merchants were "venturers", their adventure a part-share in the ship in which they hazarded their cargoes and their profits. The precarious foundation of the career of Jacques Coeur, high steward and *argentier* of France, was summed up by the chronicler Georges Chastellain as *galées vagans par les estranges mers*, galleys wandering on foreign seas. The hunt, every man's favourite exercise, was high adventure hazarded in local fields and forests. The deer, bounding into the trees and disappearing, was sent perhaps to lure the hunter into a land he did not know. He followed the quest as he was impelled to, though it might lead to the loss of his hounds, his horse or himself.

Venturers could also be found in every city and down every lane: traveling salesmen, itinerant priests, musicians, ex-students, way-walking beggars, mercenary soldiers dismissed from campaigns. They journeyed in the hope of sudden generosity or a lucky chance around the next bend in the road. Some looked for a new "good lord" whose device they could pin on their hats. They would live by their wits, casting off old ties and loyal-ties, inventing names and histories as needed, and see how far that got them. Such wanderers often carried the tools of a spurious trade, a hal-berd, a rosary or a diploma, in the expectation that some sponsor or some dupe would appear on the horizon. If that hope failed, they would make for the next chance.

A man who put his body or goods in adventure, whether by trade or travelling or claiming a throne, was not entirely without defences. He kept, between his body and disaster, the thin surety of his own talents, like the well-caulked hull of a boat. A free and open heart, dwelling on future possibility and not constrained by what was feasible, was especially dis-posed to receive God's grace and turn adventure to good use. Nevertheless, in general parlance, the word carried more fear than hope. The sense of risk and jeopardy was strong. "Unhappy adventure" was not mishap, but catastrophe: Icarus with his wax wings or Phaeton in his father's chariot, desperately losing control of the bucking and flaming horses of the sun.

II

THE DATE OF THE BOY'S JOURNEY to Portugal, where all the versions of his life met, seemed to be sometime after Easter in 1487. He accompanied the wife of Brampton and possibly Brampton himself, who had come to fetch his wife from Middelburg. Bruges was no longer a good place to be, seething with political unrest, infected with plague and with trade so depressed that "such men as be of any substance . . . steal daily away."

Brampton played down the boy's presence on the trip. He had tagged along, he thought, mostly because he hoped to insinuate himself into Brampton's household. Piers, on the other hand, was thrilled. His ex-citement showed through even in the stiff, fractured phrases of the official confession: "I went into Portugal in the company of Sir Edward Bramp-ton's wife in a ship that was called *The Queen's Ship.*" Whether prince or servant, or both at once, this was his first long voyage.

It was not necessarily an easy one, as Richmond Herald found when he went on an embassy to Portugal in 1489. The party left Southampton on January 19th, but bad weather forced them into Plymouth and kept them there until February 1st. They then sailed again, but the wind was so contrary that they had to make for Falmouth. There they landed "in a great tempest of wind, rain and bad rough weather." Ten days later they attempted to sail again, managing a night and a day before "there was such a great storm of wind and rain that it was a marvel." On February 15th came such a gust of wind that "the said ship took in . . . so much water that she was quite under water and all on one side for a while, and the great sail almost entirely steeped in the sea, and remained so a long time, about a quarter of an hour. And all the ambassadors cried to God, and to all the saints of Paradise . . . "

Richmond had sailed in the winter; the boy sailed later, when the weather should have been kinder. There may have been balmy days, skirting the enormous ocean, with the sun warm on the decks. The smell of Portugal was probably already on the ship, heavy in the perfume of the malagueta pepper Brampton imported. Malagueta grew in the steaming jungles of Cape Mesurado on the Guinea coast, where natives would barter a bushel for a bangle of brass. These "grains of paradise", ground up in wine with sugar, ginger, mace and cinnamon, made hippocras, deeply aromatic and sexually stimulating, which Venus was said to serve lovers on their first visit to her tavern. It was just the sort of thing a fourteen-year-old page might try, having carried it round carefully to the adults with wafers, comfits and ground spices before they went to bed; several steps up from the weak wine and beer he drank routinely, and carrying deep in the beaker the smell of Africa and the Spice Islands.

Yet, according to Brampton, Piers had not found a haven in this household. He had been taken along out of impatience, with nothing particular to offer except, perhaps, a talent for music, and Brampton averred that he did not want him to be either his page or his wife's. When they got to Lisbon, he broke the news to Piers, and seemed to assume he took it badly. Brampton's wife was open to keeping him, but Brampton himself wanted no more French brats. He handed him on.

The handover was so swift that, in Portugal, no one seemed to associate the boy with Brampton, only with his wife. Yet their connection may not have been as slight as both implied. When Brampton gave his testimony, in the spring of 1496, he may well have been seeking to ingratiate himself with Henry VII (who was supposedly going to see it) by stressing how insubstantial the boy was and, especially, how little he himself had had to do with him. Bernard André, Henry's court poet, said Brampton had kept the boy close for a long time, educating him in Yorkist lore. There is no proof of this. But Brampton claimed to know a lot about the boy, including his name, his father's name, his address and his history in general. As for Piers, on this evidence at least, he seemed strangely taken with Brampton, to the point of deciding to leave Portugal when he realised Brampton did not want him.

His fascination was not surprising. Brampton was a most exotic combination of a Portuguese *fidalgo* and an English gentleman: as the patent rolls described him, "knight, *alias* of London, *alias* of Portingale, 'merchant', *alias* 'gentleman', *alias* a godson of Edward IV." He was a wanderer and adventurer par excellence, a Portuguese Jew who had converted to Christianity in England, a member of Edward IV's household and a businessman whose interests, in wool and wine as well as pepper, spanned northern Europe. For a while after 1482 he was captain, keeper and governor of the island of Guernsey, his highest official position, but one that seemed inappropriately static for him. He probably never went there, and was replaced in a year and a half.

His own career, like that of the strange boy he had taken in, had begun with a knock on a door and a change of name. The door he had knocked on, in about 1468, was that of the London Domus Conversorum, the near-empty house in suburban Holborn for converted Jews, where he stayed for about three years. At his baptism in 1472 he was sponsored by Edward IV himself (kings then routinely standing as godfathers to converted Jews), and took his name: Edward, or Duarte, Brampton, in place of Brandão.

The name he had been given before his flight to England was unknown, as was his father's. He was probably the son of a Lisbon blacksmith who may not have been married to his mother, but Brampton preferred to insinuate, like any wandering knight, that he had noble blood. He had gone into exile in England not to better himself, he said, but because he had killed a man for calling him a bastard. He escaped in a small boat with no baggage except a cloak and a sword.

Brampton changed parties and countries as readily as he had changed religion, careful to keep on the winning side. In 1472 he had become an Englishman; in 1479 he became Portuguese again. By 1484— Edward IV's brother Richard now on the throne—he had acquired by royal grant the manors of Faunston, Rusheton, Great Houghton and Sewell in Northamptonshire, including eleven cottages, three crofts, three tofts, stanks, meadows, underwoods and warrens, but it was impossible to see him in such a setting of deep groves, drifting smoke and skylarks. His place was in the exchanges of Europe, or on the world stage that had opened out from Portugal.

He remained consistently helpful to Richard III, though in mysterious ways. In July 1483, not long after the two small princes had been committed to the Tower, he was paid £350 for services unspecified. His estates in Northamptonshire were given to him that year for "good service against the rebels": the Duke of Buckingham and his adherents, who had risen against Richard the previous autumn in the hope, at first, of freeing the princes. Presumably Brampton was either unmoved by their cause or knew a rising was unnecessary. In 1484, he was given £100 a year from the customs for twenty years, "in consideration of services to be rendered by him according to certain indentures" from Easter 1485. Kings by no means always gave their reasons, but these were big rewards. Conceivably, they had something to do with that irritating boy. It is impossible to know for sure.

Richard III's defeat at Henry Tudor's hands in August 1485 either forced Brampton out of England or kept him from returning. Bruges could shelter his ambitions for a time. He had been continually working there not only in trade but on the King of Portugal's business, and within two years he was off again to Lisbon. João II welcomed him with estates, offices and a seat on his council. Back home and richly honoured—not least because he claimed to have been an intimate of English kings—Brampton could begin yet another new life.

Since he was still avoiding England in 1487, it seemed that his sentiments must be firmly Yorkist. But his sentiments were commercial. If he had a Yorkist prince, or the makings of one, in his baggage, it was because it was worth something to him; but the price of Yorkist princes was by then unpredictable, and that of settled monarchs steady. By May 1489, fresh-set in Henry VII's good graces, he was acting as a facilitator for his envoys, including Richmond, in Lisbon, entertaining them "twice or thrice most honourably" in his big house on the Serro dos Almirantes, and generally "doing them all the honour that was in his power."

At that point, by his own account, he had long washed his hands of "Piris." The official confession concurred with this: as soon as Piers arrived in Portugal, "I was put in service to a knight that dwelled in Lisbon, which was called Peter Vacz de Cogna." Pero Vaz da Cunha, as he was called at home, was a knight of high standing at the court of Portugal, one of João II's most trusted commanders and privy to his councils. His family were lords of Tavoa, Sinde, Azere and Pombeiro in the province of Beina, and in 1488 Martim Vaz da Cunha was killed, to the king's great distress, fighting the Moors at Ceuta "like a good knight". Other da Cunhas were international jousters, and were observed by Richmond on that same trip tilting at the court of Spain, after which they danced in disguise with the ladies. It was a mark of Pero Vaz's status that his confessor on one of his naval expeditions was Master Alvaro, one of the most distinguished Dominicans of the day: "a person very remarkable for his life and learning," in the words of Alvise Cadamosto, a Venetian explorer retained at the court, and a preacher to the king himself.

João actively preferred knights of this sort around him, rather than the grandees of the realm. He once famously compared them to the sardines that were landed in their thousands on the salt-flats at Setubal, "so many of them, and very good, and cheap." By tradition, *fidalgos* like Pero Vaz—whom the king expected to be expert athletes themselves—were also charged with the instruction of Portuguese princes in horsemanship, feats of arms and ideals of chivalry. He may have trained his page in these, though all he is definitely known to have done with him was to dress him up like a doll, or like a prince.

Pero Vaz was described in the official confession—in which no one else was physically described—as a knight who "had but one eye." It seemed a strange, gratuitous detail, almost a joke. Knights sometimes covered one eye with a piece of cloth until they had performed some deed of courage or adventure, keeping themselves half-blind for years, but this did not seem to be the connotation in Pero Vaz's case. His one-eye made him sound like a pirate, and there was something of that character in him. The Portuguese courtiers called him "Bisagudo": Hatchet-face.

He also had another side, more courtly and literary, as was required of those close to the king. Garcia de Resende's songbook of the court, the *Cancioneiro Geral*, contained a blithe contribution from him, a "lyrical poem" on the set theme *Cogitavi dies antiquos, et annos eternos in mente habui:* "I have pondered bygone days, and have held the years of eternity in mind." He began, soldier-style, with a blunt statement of the obvious: *Ninguem da o que nao tem,* "Nobody gives what they have not got." He then moved at once to a thought that was paradoxical: that his endless misfortunes, *meus males sem fym*, had given him the woman he loved.

Nobody gives what they have not got
But my endless woes
Made her come to me.

Now I'll laugh at my cares
To hold on to her, my life,
And I'll see them to perdition
Though they're twice as bad.

I'll see the end of you, woes,
Woes that have no end,
For because of you, she's mine!

Inda vos veja acabados
Males, que nam tendes fym,
Poys a vos destes a mym!

The lady, "his life", was probably imaginary, as most were in these contests of poetry. His endless woes sounded more real, and his struggle with them more plausible, but these too were a common literary device. The pain and the love may have been feigned equally, and this, too, was a training he could give.

It is hard to tell how his page got on with him. At first they could barely have spoken to each other, but servants could always be made to understand with a snap of the fingers or a sharp whack with a *cana*, the heavy cane that was used to chastise pages round the court. Piers said in the confession that he had stayed with Pero Vaz "a whole year", which might sound either excited or tired, before he took leave of him. The Setubal witnesses, including Brampton, said Piers stayed with him a good deal longer, until after *las fiestas del señor principe*, the celebrations at the end of December 1490 for the wedding of Prince Afonso to Isabella, Infanta of Spain. There, both at the festivals and "in them", as Brampton said, other courtiers noticed the boy in Pero Vaz's wake. By then, he would have been more than three years about the court. Richard Plantagenet said he had lived for "some time" in Portugal, and implied it was the longest settled period in his wanderings. He went nowhere else, by his account, until he made for Ireland in 1491.

The Setubal testimonies said the same, though "settled" was hardly the word for this kind of life. The court was a movable feast, peripatetic as all courts were: sometimes at the palace on the many-spired hill in Lisbon, raised high above the rubbish-piled streets of the town below; sometimes at Evora or Santarem; more often at Setubal, the king's favourite boating and hunting place, on a wide fish-smelling bay backed by salt marshes and cork and chestnut woods. Wherever he was, the boy presumably did his duties, carrying his master's gloves, holding his stirrup, kneeling to offer him water at meals, in a servant's silence made all the deeper by the fact that he was fifteen and fresh out of Flanders. He did not know this language in which, according to Resende—then a page too, and not much older than he was—his young companions endlessly versified and sighed for the love of girls. He was, or should have been, a nobody.

Two things were necessary, wrote Fernão da Silveira, the king's steward, to succeed at the court of Portugal. The most important was to know how to dress, from the holland shirt to the otter-fur gloves; to look "fair, slim and like a Frenchman" was devoutly to be wished. In that respect, the boy was already interesting. The other vital accomplishment was to be silver-tongued: not just a reciter of poetical conceits, but a storyteller and a self-promoter. Outspokenness was a virtue, but the best of all was to "boast and lie like a trooper", *mentyr de macha mano*. Though da Silveira gave his advice tongue-in-cheek, every young man at court was in competition to be better, or other, than he was. Dissembling was both game and burden. *Nam posso vyuer comyguo, nem posso fogir de mym*, ran another song from Resende's book: "I can't live with myself, and yet I can't run away." One court songster explained that he had lived so long in his self-deception that he did not dare to disabuse himself, in case it killed him.

Nam posso vyuer comyguo, nem posso fogir de mym. But a boy who had already escaped or run away could surely keep on trying, running towards the adventure he thought he wanted or the person he thought he was. In every version of his story, this was why he had come to Portugal at all.

III

FROM THE HARBOUR WALL IN LISBON, where the caravels were hauled up for repair and hammers chinked constantly like birds, the vast Atlantic—the Ocean Sea—stretched out before him. He did not know what lay across it. People said it was India, the furthest limit of the world, or, to the north, the Isles of Orchady. The first islands out there, the Canaries, had been discovered decades before but were still unknown. The only news of them that had reached Flanders was that the people were fierce and hardy and wore the skins of beasts; that a huge, many-branched tree grew there, which caught clouds of sweet rainwater once a day; and that one of the smaller islands contained flowering shrubs whose seeds, if you ate them, could have any flavour you liked: "partridge, pheasant or quail, meat or fish, all you have to do is imagine."

Imagine; and sail on to the west and the southwest, trying not to recall how far away the safe harbour was. He wanted to do this. *I desired to see other Countries*. The churchmen warned him that he should not care to: that the pilgrim soul's longing to break away should be directed only to Heaven, his shining home and haven, not to the illusions of the world. To wish to see other places for their own sake was as foolish and dangerous as to wish to read the hundreds of books now pouring from the newfangled presses. But at the harbour wall it was the great sea, rather than Heaven, that shone and beckoned to him.

The world was round; he knew that. To head in one direction had to bring a man back somehow to the point where he had started. Although it ran contrary to sense to think of men standing on firm ground on the other side without their tunics up over their ears, you could understand it if you watched a fly creeping on an apple. He did not fall off, but the surface curved gently to him everywhere. The flies of Lisbon crept also on oranges, those fruits that so surprised northern boys, from the brightness of their colour to their thick corky rind and the way the fruit fell apart in segments, ornamented with beads of bitter juice. These too came from out there, as far as people knew: from the West Sea, and whatever lay beyond it.

Those who sailed to the west had almost nothing to aim for. Philosophers and poets dismissed it as a place of fading and dying, the reverse of the bright dawn-tinted Orient, and a place where sailors lost heart. Once you were past the Canaries, past Madeira and the Azores, you were in a world of empty sea, the old "green sea of darkness", alone save for the frigate birds and whatever beasts of the deep might find you. But it was also certain that something lay on the other side. Men thought they had seen islands there, heaped up on the horizon like rain-clouds. Antonio Leone, a sailor from Madeira, said he had seen three of them, though more experienced sailors thought these might be the great trees mentioned by Pliny that floated on the sea like islands, their roots encrusted with earth, or Seneca's pumice-stone islands that were blown about by the wind. Canarians had seen one vast, westward island crowned with mountains. They had seen it many times, in both cloudy weather and clear, and always in the same place. On occasion, however, and in the clearest weather, it was not there. There was no explanation. On some days every peak and valley could be picked out, solid rock in the sunlight. Other days showed only the empty and baffling sea.

Whatever these lands were, men had gone in search of them and had not returned. Possibly they had drowned, and their bones had been picked by great fish that bristled with scales like plates of armour; possibly they basked in some terrestrial paradise. The "Authentic Island" of Antilla and the Isle of the Seven Cities lay somewhere in that ocean, already marked on charts, and from time to time objects that might have come from them were found on west-facing shores. Sailors who had been in the Azores reported pine cones washed up on the beaches, although there were no pine trees nearby, and the bloated bodies of two drowned men, "with very big faces, not looking like Christians".

Huge hollow canes had also drifted in, capable of holding nine carafes of wine. John Mandeville said that canes like this grew on the Island of Salamasse, beside a dead sea in which objects, once dropped, were never recovered. On another occasion, one of the King of Portugal's pilots had found a piece of wood "ingeniously worked, but not with iron". Some of these stories came from Pedro Correa da Cunha, captain of the island of Graciosa in the Azores. Doubtless other members of the clan, like Pero Vaz, heard them too. Pedro Correa was particularly excited by the big hollow canes, one of which he showed to João II; he supposed it had been blown by the wind from India.

Columbus, too, leaned on Lisbon's harbour wall when the boy was there, imagining the route that would take him to the Indies and to Cipango, or Japan. The Portuguese had been sailing south for years, and in 1488 Bartolomeo Diaz had reached the furthest cape of Africa. But they had not yet dared to sail far to the west. Columbus would dare, despite the obscurity of his background, his relative poverty and the murmurs that his feats of navigation "in all the known seas" were nothing but false stories. In Lisbon he wrote carefully in the margins of books, especially Pierre d'Ailly's *Imago Mundi*, his comments on the world as he understood it. He noted where pearls were found, where the happiest people lived (under the Arctic pole, where men never died "except from satiety of life"), and how narrow the sea was that separated India from Spain, extreme east from west. His pen occasionally wandered, where there was a spare page, to drawing and meticulously dividing quadrants of circles. In circles creation consisted, as he knew: in the sphere of the earth, in the seven surrounding lower spheres constantly pushed and dragged by the planets, in the eighth sphere scattered with the lights of 1,022 fixed stars. But beyond the *primum mobile*—the ninth sphere, the domain of the shining and crystalline sky—lay stillness, glory, God, the soul's rest.

In 1492 a globe was made in Nuremberg that showed the world as far as it was known. The maker of the globe was Martin Behaim, "Martin the Bohemian," a protégé of Maximilian's, who had been in Portugal in the late 1480s and, before that, in the Burgundian Netherlands. He was apprenticed at the age of seventeen to a cloth merchant in Malines, then bound to a master in Antwerp, from whom he eventually moved away to Portugal: that same common westward urge towards the opening world. Once in Lisbon, trading on some false mathematical credentials, he became immersed in João II's efforts to take accurate readings of latitude. On later evidence, his path may also have strayed across the boy's.

On Behaim's globe—drawn on gores of vellum glued on papier mâché reinforced with hoops of wood—the dark blue sea was reassuringly strewn with islands as soon as there was no discovered coast to cling to. Small imagined isles like stepping-stones crossed the Atlantic, including the Insula de Brazil, the island of Antilla ("a ship from Spain got close to it in 1414") and, usefully central, the Island of St. Brendan, discovered by the saint. On the other side, below Cipango, lay two identical islands "where gold and jewels are". Behaim himself, to judge from a letter he ghosted to João in July 1493 by the hand of a fellow Nuremberger, Dr. Hieronymus Münzer, had no fear of the Atlantic at all. He and his companions, if so commanded, "would start from the Azore Islands and boldly cross the sea, with their cylinder, quadrant, astrolabe and other instruments. They would suffer neither from cold, nor heat, for sailing to the eastern coast they would find the air temperate and the sea smooth." Maximilian himself recommended Behaim to João as the man who could discover "the rich oriental land of Cathay" by sailing west, and urged the king to employ him.

The wilder tales of Mandeville and the *Imago Mundi* were ignored on

Behaim's globe. Only the more reasonable stories—the Three Magi, Prester John, the romance of Alexander—were accepted and recorded, in gold and silver script, by an illuminator. In the islands near Java and Sumatra, instead of Mandeville's yellow-striped snakes and dog-headed men, there were neat notes on cinnamon and nutmeg. No monsters featured on this map except for two sciapods, to fill up space, in southern Africa. Instead, the world was peopled with little groups of men who could easily be bargained with: Russians and Poles in fur hats, Indians hawking powder, fashionably got-up Germans. Only at the top and bottom of his globe did Behaim admit the white emptiness of *terra incognita*. His world was domesticated with neat knobs of mountains and red-roofed whitewashed towns as far across as China; though anyone who read the books would know that these symbols also hid marvels, such as the 1,200 bridges of the Chinese city of Cassay and the garden, concealed at the city's heart, where tame baboons were summoned to be fed by the tinkling of dozens of silver bells hung upon the trees.

The strangest stories were already understood as simple tests for the credulous. You could believe these claims, or you could laugh at them. One of Mandeville's tales involved a type of fruit that grew in the kingdom of Cadissen, near Scythia. When it was cut open, according to local people, "men find therein a beast as it were of flesh and bone and blood, as it were a little lamb without wool, and men eat the beast and the fruit also, and sure it seemeth very strange." Mandeville himself could cap that story: "I said to them that I held it for no marvel, for I said that in my country are trees that bear fruit that become birds flying, and they are good to eat . . . and they marvelled much thereat." Tales of the unconscionable wealth of native kings in undiscovered places were outdone, by Portuguese explorers in Benin and the Congo, by stories of the Great White King of Portugal and his fifty thousand vassals in velvet and jewels.

Some bookmen made it clear that they did not wish to propagate tall tales. The French translator of Virgil's *Aeneid*, in turn translated and printed by Caxton in 1490, refused to include Aeneas's journey to the Underworld because "it is feigned and not to be believed", despite the fact that he had just regaled his readers with the tale of the Minotaur and the Labyrinth. Yet travellers' tales were not always dismissed. In *The Mirror of the World*, also printed by Caxton, readers were admonished not to disbelieve in the marvels of the physical world "until the time we know it to be so or no"; for if God could make the earth so that it hung suspended in the heavens like the yolk in an egg, there was obviously no limit to the strange things He could create.

Besides, despite Behaim, the world was well known only in small patches. To travel widely at all was still unusual; men did not know, or care to know, each other's countries. In 1505 Henry VII's agents in Aragon reported that many gentlemen and common folk "imagine there is no other country but Spain", and in 1498 a Venetian in London re-marked that the English thought there was no other world but England. Although most of them knew this was not so, they had no desire to inves-tigate. It was small wonder that men believed in regions of actual and perpetual darkness, like the lands at the poles or, near Azerbaijan, a coun-try lost in night from which only the crowing of cocks, and occasional cries of men, gave evidence of life and habitation.

Columbus in 1492 set sail with extraordinary countries in his head. His chart showed imagined Cipango, roughly rectangular and three times the size of Spain. Not on his chart, but jotted in the margins of d'Ailly, was an even more fantastic place. Columbus had concluded that, though the earth was round, it was not perfectly so. Instead it was shaped like "the stalk end of a pear" or the breast of a woman with, to the far south, aureole and nipple rising out of the sea. The landmass protruded so far that some thought it touched the circle of the moon, or at least the calmer reaches of the air above the flux and reflux of the atmosphere. That southern pap was the land of all delights, shade trees and continual flowers, palaces of gold. This might well be where his ships were going, if they did not find the land of the Great Khan first.

His voyage was marked by many deliberate deceptions. In trying to explain to his men where they were, and how far they had come, he delib-erately reckoned forty-eight leagues instead of sixty, and instead of twenty "somewhat less", to prevent them being frightened by their distance from home. As they sailed on, seeming to come no nearer to the imaginary islands he had shown on his chart, he said that the currents must have car-ried them off course; they must have left those islands behind. Once landed on the other side of the Ocean Sea, he kept up his remarks about the closeness of the Great Khan although it was clear, as the hamlets of tents or palm leaves succeeded each other, that they were not in a land of great cities at all. As for himself, he tried to soften the strangeness of the scene, with its gaudy flowers and huge trees and multicoloured darting fish, by noting how similar it was to what they knew: breezes like April in Castile, soft shallow seas like the river in Seville, birds that sang like the nightingales of Asturias.

He said, of course, that he knew where he was, but this was not true. The "true north" of the Pole Star and the north of his compass were already out of alignment. His observed latitudes were sometimes out by almost twenty degrees; he might have done better to trust to dead reckoning or, like the frigate birds, to his own instinct. Vasco da Gama, aiming for India, also found that he could not determine latitude properly once he was out at sea. The currents and "secrets of the sea" spoiled the reading of the sun's meridian altitudes, and the Pole Star disappeared. On the heaving deck of a ship, small brass quadrants would not work, and astrolabes gave errors of four or five degrees. The men in charge of observing would sit braced against the mainmast, endeavouring to keep the astrolabe steadily suspended from a finger as they moved the rule against it; and still at the end of the day they would not know how far they had gone, south or west, in the great ocean. Columbus, with his Castilian comparisons, suggested the roughest calculation of all, latitude from birdsong and the mildness of the air.

For all their instruments and careful observations, men still resorted to fantasy. Navigators often did not know which country they were in, what adjoined it, where the rivers led, or what its nature was; but, not knowing, they pretended to. The globe, after all, was confidently covered with named places. Grand claims made with panache were hard to disprove. You, too, could name a kingdom on a map and say you had been there (bringing back with you a leaf, a brown man, a small piece of gold). And you, too, could draw a prince on a map (giving him a turban or a tall hat, seating him cross-legged in a silk pavilion underneath a palm tree), and then—a marvel!—claim to have found him.

IV

PERO VAZ WAS DIRECTLY INVOLVED in the stories of lost or mysterious kings. In 1489, two years after Brampton's boy had joined his service, the one-eyed knight was sent to the Senegal on the King of Portugal's business. Since, by most accounts, the boy was still in Portugal and with him, it is likely that he went too.

Very little of Africa would have been known to him, beyond the usual tall tales. In Tournai (if that was his place) the only hint of Africa had come, on various occasions in the century, with the appearance in town of a wild group of men and women called "the Egyptians." Their leader, "Sire Miquiel, Prince de Latingem en Egypte", appealed for Tour-nai's charity, and received it, with the story that his people were Christians who had been driven from their land by the Saracens. They could not stay more than three days in any town, he explained, because they had to wan-der like pilgrims through the world for seven years before they could return to their country. The Tournaisiens, moved, put them up in the Cloth Hall and gave them bread and beer. But the women, dirty and badly dressed, stole and "spun their fairy tales" all around the town and trained their children to cut purses from people's belts, while the men swindled buyers over horses. In the Cloth Hall, like beasts, "they were not ashamed to do their necessaries and works of nature in front of every-one." The scandalised chronicler who recorded this said they were actually serfs from a town in Germany called Mahode. In Tournai they remained "Egyptians" each time they appeared, and were given herrings and fire-wood with the injunction that no one in town was to hurt them. Eventu-ally, however, the "Grand Count of Little Egypt" was stiffly turned away.

Moving north to the bigger cities, proper Africans were still rarely seen. Madeira sugar—"sugar of Portugal," as it was served at the tables of the Dukes of Burgundy—and pepper, as Brampton shipped it, were the only African goods that were handled wholesale. More muddled and tantalising hints of Africa appeared on the market stalls: ivory, dragon's blood, sticky gums and dried roots, cinnamon bark with its dusty dark smell, brilliantly coloured feathers. Souvenirs came occasionally to north-ern Europe, like the elephant's tusk and foot that were presented to Isabella of Portugal, Duchess of Burgundy, by Cadamosto, who had helped to eat the rest of the creature. (He thought it chewy and tasteless.) The Burgundian Netherlands, like England, contained a few bits and pieces of Africa; but they were for the cabinet of curiosities, and could not easily be joined to make a picture.

In Portugal, that changed. The travel notes of Dr. Münzer, Behaim's ghost-writer, who visited from Germany in 1494, showed what northerners especially noticed there. On the door of the church of St. Blaise in Evora, Dr. Münzer wrote, was the skin of a cobra some thirty palms long, which had been killed with flaming spears. It had colours as varied and beautiful as the stars, scattered with golden spots. "Ethiopian Guinea" was the land it had come from, "and they say it can kill two men with its tail and coils, and that it fights with elephants." In the church of the Franciscans in Lisbon, a big dried crocodile hung in the choir. Both here and elsewhere grew dragon's-blood trees "from the equinoctial regions", curiously spongy and full of tiny veins from which, in March, came bright red blood. On one Sunday excursion to Sancta Maria do Luz, a mile outside Lisbon, Dr. Münzer was shown a pelican's beak ("smaller than a swan's but bigger than a goose's, with a sort of bag for its stomach opening"), reeds from Madeira "as thick as my arm and sixteen palms high", and the skeletons of swordfish, "with saws on their faces two ells long, really hard, that can cut up ships". When he visited Behaim's father-in-law in Lisbon he was given a present of dried musk-glands from a gazelle, with which—as a doctor—he was delighted.

Black faces, too, made Portugal different. In the streets where the boy walked they were common, if no less strange than they had seemed before. Their darkness came in different gradations, from the almost-white Berbers and Moroccans to the near-black Canarians, jumping and hoot-ing and cave-dwelling, and the jet-black Guineans. To the northern European eye—his eye—Negro faces were as far removed as possible from the ideal of beauty. The sun had "discoloured" them. The demons of Hell had such faces, with squashed-up noses and broad grinning mouths, their skin seared by the heat. Their lack of faith made Africans not only live, but look, like brutes.

The land they came from remained as mysterious and frightening as they did. A party of Flemings had landed on the Gold Coast in 1475; the natives feasted on their delicate white flesh, and the next visitors were offered their clothes as barter. Except for exploring Guinea in search of gold, the Portuguese had penetrated little beyond the shore of West Africa. Having set up on headlands the engraved stone pillars topped with crosses that were now being prefabricated in Lisbon, having built the rudimentary forts and established contact with whatever native traders they could find not too far from the shore, they moved on south. Most of the stuff they acquired there could have been found on a beach, or in the trees that lined it: whale amber, pepper, gum arabic, turtle oil. There was little need to go further inland, and every need to press on. Diaz had left behind, at various points down the coast, well-fed Africans in European clothes who were to act as walking advertisements for trading contacts with Portugal. They were not required to speak; like the boy in Lisbon, they were simply dropped among strangers, and made on the shore a sort of solitary dumb-show of unaccustomed elegance.

As they pushed on down the coast, the Portuguese made detours only for the great rivers of West Africa—the Senegal, the Gambia and the Congo—for it was always possible that these huge estuaries marked the first swing of the sea away to the east. Eastward lay the land of Prester John, the Christian priest-king, and the Paradise Terrestre, surrounded with fire flaming to the clouds, from which the world's chief rivers flowed down over gravel crunching with jewels. Portuguese sailors tried these river entries to Prester John's land, though there were reputed to be far more marvels in the land of the Great Khan, which could be reached by going overland. They dared them, too, despite the rumour that the sea approaches to his kingdom flowed over rocks of adamant that sucked out the nails from ships.

Over the years, details of this priest-king had accumulated at the Portuguese court. He was descended from one of the Magi who had come to adore the infant Christ, and his land (in which parrots were as plentiful as gulls in Lisbon harbour) was called Pentexoire, or something similar. He could field an army of as many as a million men, naked or in crocodile skins, to fight the Saracens, and went into battle himself behind three great jewelled crosses of gold. His soldiers had weapons of pure gold, and gold roofed their houses. The precious stones there were so huge (fresh-picked from the gravel brought down by the floods from Paradise) that men made plates and cups of them. It was Prester John's treasure, as much as his faith, that made men long to find him.

His envoys had been seen in Europe. One, called George, had visited Isabella of Burgundy (her elephant's foot perhaps still on display, unless it had begun to stink). Alfonso V of Aragon had received letters from him. Yet this king of mystery had to be more than a humdrum letter-writer. In 1485, ambassadors from the King of Benin reported that whenever a king acceded to their kingdom, a prince called Ogané, from a kingdom twenty moons' journey to the east, would send him a staff and a headpiece of shining brass, "fashioned like a Spanish helmet". More suggestively, Ogané would also send a cross of brass to be worn round the neck, "a holy and religious emblem similar to that worn by the Commanders of the Order of St. John." The ambassadors, however, never saw this prince. He sat behind curtains of silk which, as the envoys left, were raised a little to show the princely foot, a limb so holy that his people kissed it as if it were a relic. By the late 1480s, João and his cosmographers had determined that this ruler must be Prester John. The king decided to check on him, probing the mystery of the cross and the curtains, just as he was to send out envoys later to check on Richard Plantagenet.

The arrival of the fair-haired boy in Lisbon coincided closely with the departure from Santarem, in May 1487, of João's overland expedition to find the dimly glimpsed king in his imagined country. Two men were sent. One of them soon died; the other, a secret agent, crossed the Indian Ocean, went in disguise to Mecca and at last, after seven years, found his king in Ethiopia. Diaz, too, was originally sent out to find Prester John, but after rounding the Cape his sailors would go no further. His fleet came back to Lisbon in December 1488, kingless.

In the same year, however, another African prince arrived in Lisbon. His name was Bemoy, King of the Jalofs, a claimant to a disputed throne who had been forced to flee by his enemies and had appealed to the Portuguese for help. Cadamosto described him as "a tall man, strong and good-looking, forty years old, with a long bushy beard, so that he did not seem a Negro, but a prince worthy of all respect." He and his entourage wore rich Portuguese robes and had been given mules and horses, the necessary accoutrements of princeliness. Yet his skin was blue-black; the hair on his head was short and crinkled, like dry black moss; and his hands when he held them out had pale pink undersides, as if that part only had been touched by God. Of his kingdom, which lay some way southeast of the Senegal River, not much was known except that it was humid and hot, that the people lived on millet grown in silt, and that the summer heat made clefts in the ground so deep that horses could be buried in them.

The arrival of Bemoy, the prince in distress, was extraordinary. The royal residences in Setubal had been hung with tapestries and silk for him, and all lords and nobles were commanded to attend. Pero Vaz would have been there, his page following. The king received Bemoy in the stateroom, on a high dais under a canopy of brocade. Bemoy at once tore off his turban; João, with the typical restraint of civilised and Christian rulers, took two or three steps from the dais and raised his hat slightly.

At this, Bemoy and his men threw themselves on the ground at the king's feet, "making as though they took the earth from under them and threw it over their heads, in token of humility and obedience." João bade them rise and, leaning against his chair, commanded the interpreter to tell Bemoy to speak. The exiled king then poured out his story "with such majesty of person, and with so many effects to arouse pity for his miserable banish-ment, that he was understood even before the interpreter translated his words." The chronicler Rui de Pina thought his speech, with its "swift sighs and many tears", so notable "that [it] did not seem to come from a savage Negro but from a Greek prince, educated in Athens." The force of this piece of theatre was not likely to be lost on other exiled princes, or princes in training.

In order to accommodate himself to his Portuguese allies, Bemoy also agreed to be baptised. This was the occasion for immense celebrations: bullfights, tournaments, fancy-dress balls, astounding displays of horse-manship by Bemoy's men. At the centre of it all, in a special chair set opposite the king's, sat Bemoy himself, with his broad black face and his carefully copied courtesy, perhaps barely understanding what he had done. He had put on proper Christian clothes of hose, surcoat, doublet and robe, with shoes on his feet; he had consented to live, as Christians did, in a house built of stone and roofed with tile, rather than woven of grass. The king had made him a knight in honour of his baptism, and he now possessed a red shield emblazoned with a gold cross and bordered with Portuguese escutcheons. He had a new name, too, João, or John, the name of the priest-king and of the king his godfather. The holy baptismal water had flowed over him, though it did not run down, as on Christians, but caught in his tight curls like dew. At his first Mass he had instinctively knelt and removed his cap as the priest elevated the Body of Christ. But he remained berry-black, ink-black, raven-wing black, with no outward sign that salvation might have been effected in him. In his own country, among his own people, it was always likely that some other Bemoy would appear: imperious, confident, violent, even devilish, his blackness finally overpowering all the grace that had been poured out on him.

Not long after the baptism, João arranged that Bemoy should be restored to his kingdom. It was Pero Vaz, old one-eyed Hatchet-face, who was picked as captain-major to escort him as far as the Senegal. For this "great and costly expedition" he was given twenty armed caravels, a huge force. Delivering Bemoy was only one part, the first and easiest, of Pero

Vaz's task. His further instructions were to establish a fort similar to the one up the coast at São Jorge da Mina, in Guinea, which Columbus had admired. He was also commanded by the king, since "a great part of the land of Guinea was bled of its gold", to tap the gold that came into the markets of Timbuktu and Mombaré, both of them supposedly close to the river in its distant and higher reaches. He was expected, in other words, to stay there for some time. Many soldiers and craftsmen went with him, and a large group of priests (headed by the king's chaplain), with portable altars, vestments, chalices and all that was needed to furnish churches and save souls. Stone had been cut for the fortresses, and lengths of timber planed. There were several big guns on board, and supplies that were intended to last for months.

Leaving Lisbon, the caravels steered south-southwest for two hundred leagues, calling in at Jandia Point in the Canaries and then heading south for the gulf of the Rio de Ouro. This first sighting of the African main-land—the boy's first sighting—showed it "high and flat like a table," until the River of Gold itself, which could be seen from the mast as a lake lying among sandhills. For one hundred leagues after this the coast was treeless desert, though the water teemed with fish. The course was kept to the south to avoid Cape Barbas, where great reefs of rock ran out into the sea and destroyed unwary ships. After this the landmarks were passed in order: Pedra de Galha, a great rock like a vessel under sail; Cabo Branco, with its white hill; the island of Arguim, with a fort and factory where brown-skinned Arabs bartered Negroes and tapir hides for cheap cloths and ker-chiefs; then fifty leagues of desert where, if the ship sailed close enough (though the shallows made this dangerous), you could glimpse gazelles and naked savages on the heat-shimmering sand, pinnacles of wind-weathered rock, camels swaying under blocks of white salt. Beyond this was the town of Oadem, a centre for the Guinea gold trade, where suddenly high palm groves shaded the houses and the Arabs offered, besides gold, sweet dates and goat meat.

The Senegal was now close. The sign of this, on the low deserted coast where men ate each other, was a single grove of palms three leagues from the river. The north bank of the river was forested, and its shallows ran for a league or more into the sea. A wise captain anchored at the palms and considered how to navigate the peculiar tides of the bar, "con-trary to the flow of the tides in Spain". So here, presumably, Pero Vaz lingered for a while and mulled over the tasks he had been given, his page in attendance. They were about fifteen degrees north of the equator, in the searing heat and glare of the dry season in West Africa.

Pero Vaz had been ordered not only to take Bemoy home, but also to push up the Senegal in search of Prester John. This almost went without saying. For at least a decade Portuguese sailors had been looking for this prince along the great rivers of West Africa. In 1485 a band of Portuguese explorers had got ninety miles up the Congo and carved their names on rocks, together with crosses and coats of arms; but some of their number were already dying, and they did not get much further. The Senegal had been passed years before, and men had explored it as far as the Felu cataracts, but it remained a dangerous river. Its mouth was the place where the familiar Berbers, with their milk-brown skin, gave way to the unknown blacks. These blacks were not cowed by bombard fire from the caravels, but swarmed to attack in their dugout canoes, throwing spears and arrows tipped with poison so strong that a wound meant certain death. The river itself was scarcely navigable, turbulent in the wet season and, in the dry, obstructed by rocks and sandbanks. Great "lizards" and serpents infested the waters, and were pecked full of holes by flocks of birds as they swam towards the sea. In tropical waters caravels did not last in any case, but were eaten through by worms and freighted with huge barnacles. Ships like these, riddled with worm-holes, were beached as a warning in the harbour at Lisbon.

For these reasons, as well as others, Pero Vaz seemed to become increasingly uneasy the further he got from Portugal. The climate grew steadily more humid; he sweated in his European clothes. Cloth and woollen garments were believed to putrefy in that heat, unless they were regularly rinsed in the sea. His page would have brought him cool wine and water, waved off the evil biting insects, folded and smoothed his damp sheets. For himself, the African sun would have tormented his pale young skin unless, like one traveller mocked by João, he wore a sunhat and gloves against it. Around him, men were falling ill. The river was known to be rife with fever, the same fever that had caused the coastal fort at Benin to be abandoned three years before. "[Pero Vaz] wanted to go back," wrote Garcia de Resende, "and he was afraid of dying there, because the land was full of disease." He suffered also, perhaps, that different and pervasive sickness: fear of going too far in.

Although Bemoy seems to have done nothing particular to add to the captain's anxiety, the two men fell out with each other. Now they had reached the mouth of the Senegal, Bemoy's home territory, Pero Vaz turned on the prince and killed him. Cadamosto told the story:

> When Pero Vaz entered the river Çanaga with that great power, which amazed all the barbarians of that land, and while he was erecting the fortress (which they say is built in an ill-chosen place on account of the floods of the river), he stabbed Bemoy to death on board his ship, saying that he was preparing a treason. Some maintained that Pero Vaz was deceived in this, and that what chiefly condemned D. João Bemoy to death was the fact that many people began to fall sick, because the place was very unhealthy, and that Pero Vaz was more fearful of having to remain in the fortress when completed than he was of Bemoy's treason.

The crime was treated with surprising leniency when Pero Vaz returned to Portugal. The erring captain was not punished, and João showed his sadness and "great displeasure" only by ordering work to stop on the fortress on the Senegal. Resende thought it showed João's "singular capacity and great piety" that he suffered such a thing. Rui de Pina supposed the captain was excused because "many other people" were somehow involved. The murder, it seems, was seen mostly as an offence against courtesy and hospitality, because Pero Vaz had held Bemoy "in his free power", with no sign of ill-will from him, and yet had killed him.

It may be wondered how much of that distrust, and how much of that casual brutality, had been experienced by the page who stayed with Pero Vaz, however long he stayed. Perhaps the same hand that felled Bemoy on the ship at the Senegal, under the hot blue dome of an African sky, had also struck the boy who waited on him, almost as foreign and unknown. Or perhaps the whole Senegal incident, including the king's inexplicable forgiveness, was coloured by that other charge Pero Vaz had: a boy who, servant though he seemed to be, could not be struck by his master, or by anyone, without some faint imputation of treason.

V

ON WHATEVER TERMS he was with his master, Pero Vaz's boy made an impression in Portugal. Five or six years later, in 1496, he was remembered in the testimonies given to Spanish investigators in Setubal, that favourite retreat of the Portuguese kings. It is peculiar, of course, that he

should have been noticed or remembered at all. He was supposedly nothing but a page, one of hundreds around the court. Yet something had
drawn people's attention to him, and made them identify him as the young
man who was proclaiming, all round Europe, that he was Richard,
Duke of York.

When Ferdinand and Isabella, Spain's rulers, offered the Setubal testimonies to Henry VII, they recommended especially the evidence given
by Rui de Sousa, a Portuguese nobleman and one of the most prominent
figures at court. Indeed, his testimony was all they offered at first, adding
the others as an afterthought. "He knows this business well, and is a person of authority and trust," they told their ambassador in London.
"Having been on an embassy from Portugal to England, he knew the
Duke of York very well. Two years later, he saw this other person in
Portugal."

De Sousa, the Lord of Sagres and Beringuel, was one of João's closest advisers, so intimate with the king that when the two men argued it
was the king, "with very few people" and on a mule, who came to his
house to apologise. "A person of much worth and authority, of good
counsel and lively intelligence, very useful and of great grace and estimation" was the assessment of Resende, who knew him well. Ferdinand and
Isabella knew him too, for he had represented Portugal at the negotiations
with Spain that preceded the Treaty of Tordesillas in 1494. There, after
weeks of argument by de Sousa and his colleagues that pitted the claims
of Portugal against the new discoveries made by Columbus, a line was
finally drawn from pole to pole in the middle of the ocean, 370 miles west
of the Cape Verde Islands, to designate owners for the new world and the
world-yet-to-be-found.

Tordesillas marked the peak, and the end, of de Sousa's diplomatic
career. But he had long been entrusted with talks and embassies of similar
importance. In 1482 he had been an ambassador to Edward IV's court,
renewing the old alliance and explaining to Edward that João now owned
Guinea, despite any pretensions the English might have to exploring it.
Edward was pleased with this embassy and received it with great honour,
including an intimate sighting of his children singing and playing.

Accordingly, at Setubal, de Sousa was questioned first, and was
asked to describe the little Prince Richard he had seen then. He had been
deeply impressed with him, thinking him "very pretty, and the most beautiful creature he had ever seen." He had heard people say since then that

he and his brother had been put in prison, "in a fortress where a tide of water passed by", and that they had been killed. So who, he was asked, was the person who was saying he was the Duke of York now? He was a boy, said de Sousa, a *moço*,

> who came to Portugal with the wife of Duarte Brandon, a Portuguese knight. I saw him walking in the Court of Portugal behind a *fidalgo* who was called Pero Vaz da Cunha, who treated him as his page. When they had the celebrations for the Lord Prince of Portugal [Pero Vaz] dressed him up, and I saw him in a doublet of brocade and a long gown of silk. And after that I knew nothing more of him until now, when I've heard what people are saying about him.

Far from a lapse of two years, as Ferdinand and Isabella supposed, between the little prince in London and the boy in Lisbon, five years had passed. De Sousa, by then an old man who was soon to die, did not seem to "know the business well" at all. His knowledge of English affairs was very misty, his knowledge of the boy even more so. He did not seem to know his name, and gave only two sightings of him.

Yet two aspects of his evidence were intriguing. First, he had noticed the boy as he arrived. In the crowded life of a councillor-ambassador, there seemed no reason for this, unless some buzz had attended him. The buzz may have come from the ship in which he appeared. *The Queen's Ship*, the *Rainha*, was one of the prize vessels of João's fleet: "a most beautiful ship", in Dr. Münzer's view. When he saw her in Lisbon in 1494 she was fully armed, with 36 big bombards and 180 smaller ones, preparing to take two hundred men to Naples. Seven years earlier she was probably less well equipped, but it is still no wonder that the boy, affirming his confession years later in custody, bothered to mention her. The greater mystery is why João had sent her for Brampton and his household, however high "the captain"—as he was called in Portugal—stood in his estimation. They sailed from Bruges in splendour. A boy who stepped from such a ship, sent by the king, was already perhaps proclaiming himself as someone.

De Sousa dropped other hints. He said that Pero Vaz "treated him as his page," as if this was not necessarily the sort of boy he was. A second Setubal witness, Tanjar, a herald of the King of Portugal, gave the same impression. He had seen the boy "living with" Pero Vaz, but did not say he was his servant. And he, too, knew that he had come in the retinue of Brampton's wife, a woman of no particular importance at court. For some reason, the boy was drawing glances as soon as he arrived.

Tanjar gave a clue as to why people might have noticed him: "I never took him for a local, because it was plain to see that he was a foreigner." The difference did not lie conclusively in his fair hair, for there was plenty of racial mixing in Portugal, not least with the Flemings who had been recruited to colonise Madeira and the Azores. The richest men in Lisbon, Dr. Münzer claimed in his patriotic way, were "Germans from Flanders," whose tow-haired children were common on the streets. The queen and Prince Afonso, too, had fair hair, Afonso's so bright that he was said to have "a face like an English child". Something else made this boy different. Tanjar implied that he knew him quite well, though it was not until later—on a visit to Tournai, of which he said he was a native—that he encountered the boy's father and learned his son's name: "Piris, which is Pedro in Flemish." Tanjar seemed not to have known it before, as though the strange boy at court went by some other name and claimed some other background. They had got so close in Portugal, however, that the herald could describe the boy's distinctive features: features that made people say, Tanjar added, that he was the Duke of York.

The boy's clothes, too, attracted a strange amount of attention. Both de Sousa and Brampton commented on the doublet of brocade ("with sleeves", Brampton added) and the long gown of silk ("and other things", said Brampton). Of course the courtiers of Portugal were obsessed with clothes, especially oddities and extravagances, and may have naturally lighted on them. De Sousa, for all his eminence, contributed mostly to Resende's songbook to poke fun at the clothes of his nephew, who had come back from Castile wearing "a big velvet hat which the Castilians call a seesaw":

> Nephew, you look as if
> you've been in Valladolid;
> you're wearing three olive branches on your head!
> But I will forgive you . . .
> . . .
> It shouldn't happen to anyone
> To bear such a weight on his head.

Afonso's *fiestas* had been a special moment in the sartorial life of the court. In 1486, João—austere himself, and believing that austerity would do his subjects good—had passed strict sumptuary laws explicitly forbidding the wearing of silk and brocade "by anyone in the kingdom of whatever condition." They were banned even for the king and queen and on days of *fiesta*, except as trimmings to people's clothes. The law remained in force until the end of the century, with only one exception: in December 1490, for Afonso's wedding, when silk and brocade were provided by special dispensation. This was precisely when the boy was noticed in his finery: at the moment when almost everyone at court was arrayed, just for a few days, in silk and brocade.

Yet de Sousa may well have picked him out for a different reason. The old councillor was renowned as a "maker of plays," *fazedor de momos*—the best ever seen at court, some said. He was thought to be especially good "because he fits so well into this world we're in": that universe of contrived and alluring presentations. At Afonso's wedding, de Sousa had been one of the three court officers who organised the joust-plays, together with Fernão da Silveira, the man who had so warmly recommended the arts of fine dressing and lying. In this capacity he may have remembered the boy at the *fiestas* not just for what he wore, but—since Brampton said he was "in" them—for the part he played. It remains hard to say otherwise why the boy drew, or was allowed to draw, such attention to himself.

Rightly or not, some rumour of fame seemed to hang round him, and may have travelled further than Portugal. While he was there, Anglo-Portuguese contacts perceptibly increased. In 1487–88 Edward Woodville came twice through Lisbon. Woodville, "Monseor Duarte Senhor d'Escallas en Ingraterra", was the uncle of Richard of York and of his sister Elizabeth, now Queen of England. His brother Anthony, Earl Rivers, had been the chief guardian of Richard's brother Edward, and Woodvilles had provided some of the officers, and much of the influence, in Richard's own small household within his father's court. In effect, he had been a Woodville boy. The English visitor, though not counted as important at home and possibly keen to avoid meeting Brampton, who had chased him like a pirate across the Channel in May 1483, was much fussed over in Portugal for his royal connections.

On his way out, coming through Lisbon to fight the Moors in

Granada "out of devotion, and to exalt our Holy Faith," Woodville did not see the king, but he was fêted nonetheless with banquets and celebrations as João's "magnificent and puissant . . . kinsman and friend." On his return, João laid on *toros, canas e momos*, bullfights, canefights and plays, held a feast at which the principal nobles were present, and organized all kinds of pageants, "of which he was very fond, and of which he was a most cunning and careful inventor", just as de Sousa was.

The boy was probably there, walking behind his oneeyed master; and he may also have been the reason Woodville had passed through. The ardent crusader did not need to go via Lisbon to fight the Moors, but could have made landfall in northern Spain without touching Portugal. He was said to have been discussing a marriage between one of João's cousins and a sister of the Queen of England, but it seemed unofficial and halfhearted. On his return Henry VII gave him twenty marks, listing the payment among others for his spies. The king paid, too, for "a Scotsman with a beard" to spy on Woodville for as long as the trip lasted and to send him information in the year that followed.

From that point until the summer of 1491 Henry paid special attention to this distant and friendly country, attention he had not shown before and was not to show again. In subsequent years, Portugal was mentioned only as the place that oranges came from, or swarthy sailors who brought wild cats and popinjays from the new land to the west. In 1488 and 1489, however, fairly generous payments—£6. 13s. 4d., £10—were made every few months to unnamed agents coming from the Portuguese court. The interest reached its peak in Richmond Herald's embassy of 1489, when João was presented with the Order of the Garter, a rare honour, as Henry's "true ally and brother", and in a fivemonth visit by João's ambassadors from December 1490 to May 1491, when they were given costly silver cups with covers as Christmas presents. Prince Afonso's marriage, piracy on the western seas, and Henry's threats of war with France over Brittany explained some of this shortlived interest. They cannot explain it all. Henry had heard something, true or not, and was using his customary instruments to poke and pry.

Richmond himself seems to have gone to spy before he went as an envoy proper. He was sent to Portugal "for certain causes", and apparently alone, in August 1489, before joining the official delegation that left in December. (His August payment was listed alongside that of Carlisle

Herald, who was sent to Bruges, Brampton's town, a few days later.) On the later trip their main business was in Spain, where a marriage was under negotiation. In Portugal their only official errand was to give João the Garter, though they stayed seven weeks, following the court from place to place, enjoying the bullfights and dances, and observing.

Eight years later, it was Richmond who described the young man with the strange left eye as he rode out to give himself up. He gave no indication that he had ever seen him before, though it is not unlikely that their paths had crossed in Portugal. Brampton, as he played host to the envoys, could certainly have passed on information, and others too knew about the boy. As the English party rode into Beja to meet the king, and as they left again, de Sousa escorted them. They rode past a "beautiful high tower" fortified with marble, from which banners flew, cannon fired and minstrels played on "cherumbelles and sackbuts, marvellously pleasant to hear from the height that they were in that tower." The boy, too, may have heard them and craned his neck to see them, as their instruments glinted in the sun. Somewhere among the seven hundred or eight hundred barons, knights and squires who rode with Richmond and his colleagues, among the flags that fluttered all over town or among the dancers in the palace, he may have been observing the representatives of the king who was eventually to hunt him down.

The King of Portugal himself may well have been aware of him, from his arrival in the *Rainha* onwards. João was a man of restless curiosity in every branch of knowledge, from astronomy to artillery, and was also a keen observer of men, whose names and aptitudes he listed in a secret register. Like Henry VII, he was often unreadable, revealing to others neither his thoughts nor his designs. He died, in 1495, before the Setubal testimonies were taken, and never mentioned their subject directly in any correspondence that survives. In 1493–94, however, he sent Behaim the globe-maker as an emissary to "the king's son in Flanders".

Only one person was so described in Flanders at that point: the young man who was saying he was King Edward's son, Richard, Duke of York. Later in the letter in which he described this mission, Behaim explicitly identified him. He had been sent to see "the young King of England, who is at present with the King of the Romans [Maximilian], so that he may live and keep his court there, etc." The casual and unequivocal reference to who the young man was—or who Behaim and

João thought he was—was all the more striking, since Maximilian himself was still not sure.

Officially, the mission was secret; Behaim was ostensibly going to sort out some payments he was owed for sugar. His journey turned out to be as frightening, for him, as any voyage out into the unmapped ocean. As he crossed the sea he was captured and "taken into England, together with my servants and all the money I had to pay my expenses, amounting to 160 gulden." He was then detained for three months "on account of the young king" he was going to see, since tough restrictions had by then been placed on any movement of men or goods between England and the Burgundian lands, where the young man was favoured.

While in detention Behaim fell dangerously ill with fever, and reported that twice he lay with a taper in his hand, lighting the way for his soul to leave the body. At last, a "pirate" took him secretly by night to France. But for that, he might have been imprisoned for many months more. As for the young King of England, Behaim did not find him, any more than he might have found the bearded rulers he had dotted notionally through Africa and the Indies; for Richard Plantagenet in those days was pitching his tent in Louvain, Innsbruck, Vienna or wherever else Maximilian might take him, and was seldom staying long enough anywhere to be pinned down on a map.

Though many in Europe that year were sizing up this young man and promoting his claims for their own ends, Portugal had never played those games. João knew who the King of England was and, being every bit as shrewd and pragmatic himself, had no desire to unsettle him. But in his court, at least, the interest persisted. At the end of 1494, João Fogaça, an officer of the household, sent a list of suggested questions for the chamberlain to ask Dr. Münzer before he returned to Nuremberg. He was to be pumped for news, "fiction or not", of the Great Khan, and then for information of what "the great ones of Castile" were up to in Navarre and Aragon. After those typically Portuguese queries came more esoteric thoughts:

> And you may also ask him,
> just as he leaves,
> which side does the lord of Ravenstein prefer,
> and Madame Margaret.
> Will the prince come, or
> won't he, this summer,
> and what will he do?

And what will he [the doctor] ask?
And what will you reply?

This was certainly the moment when Richard Plantagenet was arranging his invasion of England, when "Madame Margaret"—Edward IV's sister, the Dowager Duchess of Burgundy—was backing him with all her power, and when Philip of Cleves ("Ravenstein"), who had been fighting Maximilian on the side of the rebellious Flemish towns, was still undecided. It seems that some, at least, at the Portuguese court were watching this "prince" or "young king" with more interest than was usually shown in the politics of northern Europe. Unlike their Spanish neighbours, they did not seem to question his claims or to ask who this figure was. They seemed to know.

Sometime in the 1530s João's favourite page, Resende, the songbook compiler and the boy's contemporary, also remembered him. He gave him a verse in his "Miscelanea", in which he listed the notable people and events of his times. Brampton, the brave and invaluable war-captain, was also in the collection, *tam valente capitam | e valer tanto na guerra*, but the two were not connected in Resende's head, at least. Many verses separated them, and Brampton featured, next to Vasco da Gama, in one about famous soldiers. The boy, to Resende, had appeared in Portugal as a character alone and in his own right. Like de Sousa, the poet had no name for him, other than the one he was supposed to have assumed much later.

> *Vimos alcar Branca Rosa*
> *por Rey muytos dos Ingleses,*
> *foy cousa maravilhosa*
> *que em dias e non em meses*
> *juntou gente muy fermosa:*
> *chamouse Rey natural,*
> *a el Rey batalha campal*
> *deu, mas foy desbaratado,*
> *e por justicia enforcado,*
> *por acharem non ser tal.*

We saw the White Rose acclaimed as King by many of the English, and it was a wonderful thing that in days, not in months, he gathered people of the highest birth to him. He called himself their natural King, and gave the King battle on the field, but he

was defeated and sentenced to hanging, because they thought he
was not such a man.

Resende added a comment in the margin: "This boy came to Portugal,
and was a page to Pero Vaz Bisagudo."

It is not improbable that in Portugal the personality of the prince,
whether judiciously hidden or deviously constructed, began to emerge
from the shadows. Indeed, it is almost certain. He had taken courage,
galante contra fortuna; he had breathed in the tang of the sea. At Afonso's
wedding celebrations, the most memorable pageant was a procession of
dream ships. They sailed into the special wooden "fortress" constructed
for the jousts on bolts of cloth that were painted as stormy waves of the
ocean, behind a great swan with white and golden feathers. The ships had
quarter-decks of brocade, sails of white and purple taffeta and rigging of
gold and silk, the whole ablaze with candles and oil lamps. When the
make-believe masters and pilots in silk and brocade swung and climbed
in the gold ropes, with a tumult of shouting and whistling, the mysterious
boy was perhaps among them. Richard Plantagenet unfolded like the
unfurling of the sail, the crack of the boards, and the intoxicating swing
and dip of the ship as it moved, away from dreams, into the open water.

VI

By RICHARD'S OWN ACCOUNT, the decision to leave Portugal was sudden. Sometime in 1491, in the schoolboy Latin of his letter to Isabella of
Spain, *Inde ad Hiberniam navigavi,* "From there I sailed into Ireland." By his
own reckoning, he was seventeen going on eighteen. This was no longer a
child-prince bundled from place to place by his guardians or left in an
anomie of grief, but a young man suddenly in charge of his own life. He
was going to Ireland to seek the protection and help of his "cousins", the
Earls of Desmond and Kildare, who had been alerted by letter to expect
him. (In the seventeenth century, those letters still existed.) Once there, he
would begin to show himself as King Edward's son.

His choice of Ireland was simple. This was a place of strong Yorkist
sympathies, where the lieutenancy of the elder Richard, Duke of York,
Edward IV's father, was fondly remembered. The duke had not tried to
impose English ways on the Irish, as Henry Tudor was doing, but had

allowed free rein to the ambitions of the Anglo-Irish lords such as Desmond and Kildare. Kildare was now Lord Deputy of Ireland, a post notionally held from the English crown; Desmond was the overlord of the southwest, in control of the ports that faced the outlying parts of Europe. Under a law passed by the Irish Parliament, devised when the elder Richard of York was organising his own counterclaim to the English throne, the English king's rebels had immunity in Ireland. This law remained in force, and Yorkist movements had found good purchase even in the part of Ireland, the Pale around Dublin and Drogheda in the east, that was administered from London. So Richard sailed for this useful, half-wild country. He made for Cork, a relatively prosperous and cosmopolitan town in Desmond's southwest: a good place for an aspiring Yorkist prince to go.

According to the confession, Piers went to Ireland too, but by a more tortuous route. After his year with Pero Vaz, he returned to commerce and to wandering. He felt, oddly enough, that he would not see the world with his old master. So he "took licence of him", showing, as with Richard's *navigavi*, the first gleam of independent action. He then put himself into service—the first time he had done so—with a Breton merchant, Pregent Meno, with whom he plied the seas for two or three years. At some undated point, assumed to be the autumn of 1491, they ended up in Cork. Once there, Piers walked the streets dressed like a mannequin "in some silks of my said Master's". The people of the town, deeply impressed with him, decided he must be of royal blood. A group of Yorkist partisans then prevailed on him to be a prince, almost any prince, of their house, so that they might seize back the throne from Henry Tudor. He resisted; they insisted. Once he had agreed, the adventure unfolded inexorably through half the countries of Europe.

Brampton too gave this story of random adventure, but with a very different start. A few days after Prince Afonso's *fiestas*, he said, the boy went down to Lisbon harbour to try and take a ship home. One of Brampton's servants was going back to Flanders, and the boy thought he might go with him. Since Brampton did not want to "take him in as his son", Piers did not want to stay in Portugal any more. Somehow, however, he missed the ship for Flanders. Eventually, he found another that would take him; but it was stopping in Ireland first. He did not mind, he said. It didn't matter to him.

As the ship docked in Ireland, Brampton continued, Piers put on once again the gorgeous clothes he had worn at the *fiestas*. The Irish, being wild people, immediately began to follow him, "and some started to say that he was one of those of Lancaster and others that he was King Edward's son, and so people started to join him, until little by little matters got as they are now."

Brampton's "few days" were probably a longer spell of time. One sailing was missed anyway, and it is not at all sure that the boy did not touch base in Flanders, where rumours of him sprang up that spring. Whatever happened, a ship seemed to drop him in Ireland eventually; and the scene that followed was the same, a boy walking into adulation. Both the confession and the Setubal testimonies stressed the importance of his clothes: the doublet of brocade with sleeves, the long robe of silk. In the English version of the confession it seemed to be pure chance that Piers wore them, or possibly a sales effort by Meno: a good-looking boy advertising his wares, like the sleek and well-dressed Africans left behind by Diaz.

Yet Meno was no silk merchant, and Ireland no place to find buyers. The trade of Bretons with Ireland was mostly in linen, canvas, tin and bay-salt; they took back white-fish and timber boards. Meno's business was in raw wool, fleeces that he had to "bard, clean and clack" before he shipped them. Clacking was the removal from the greasy wool of lumps of mud and dung: not quite the job that a vain and restless boy would have held down for more than two years. Almost certainly he and Meno were together for only one voyage, the one that ended with his mobbing by the Irish.

In the French version of the confession, too, the silks were not Meno's, but Piers's own. Brampton substantiated this. He said that Piers, before he left Portugal, had folded up his finery into a bag and put on "other, old clothes"; then, as the ship docked, he took off his jacket and put on his silks again. The idea of cutting such a figure among the wild men of Ireland came from his head alone, perhaps in imitation of sailors who, preparing to land in some unknown part of Africa, would put on their "gala clothes", as Vasco da Gama described it. It seemed just a bit of crazy attention-seeking, like much of what he did. It was also perilous, because the Irish might kill him for his clothes if they cared to. But he robed himself, and jumped. Homesick though he was for Flanders, he did not mind this detour to Ireland. On the contrary, he seized it as a chance to shine. This was his adventure—wherever it might lead him.

Such stories were all around him. Arthur's knights would stray deliberately from the well-worn path, travelling through unknown regions in a mood compounded of hope and impatience. After a while, strange, chance scenes would begin to appear before them. A hermit praying in a wood; a knight asleep by a stone cross; a shield hung on a tree; a horse saddled and waiting; a woman weeping beside a corpse. If these adventures were ignored, they would come to nothing. But knock on the cob-webbed door, rouse the sleeper, bang on the shield with your own sword, board the ship, and the story would begin, as Lancelot's had:

> And at the last by fortune he came to an abbey which was nigh the sea, and that night he rested him there. And as he slept, there came a voice and bade him go to the sea. Then he started up and made the sign of the Cross, and took him to his harness and made ready his horse; and at a broken wall he rode out, and by fortune he came to the sea. And upon the sea he found a ship that was covered all in white samite. Then he alit and betook him to Jesus Christ. And as soon as he was entered, the ship departed into the sea, and to his seeming it went fleeing, but it was soon dark. . . .

The peculiarity of adventures did not mean that it was wise to evade them. God sent them, each day devising new ones, as He also sent the fresh new hours in which lives could be radically changed. Arthur's court was once shown an adventure of a white hart and a white greyhound pur-sued by thirty pairs of black hounds; they circled the Round Table with such commotion that Arthur was glad when they had gone. But Merlin rebuked him. "Nay," he said, "ye may not leave it so, this adventure, so lightly, for these adventures must be brought to an end, or it will be dis-worship to you."

Arthur's own first adventure had been the most casual of all. As far as people knew, he was a foundling "of no high blood born", handed over to a poor man at the postern gate of the king's castle, a scrap strangely wrapped in cloth-of-gold. Foster-parents cared for him. As a boy of fourteen or so, he went home one day to fetch his brother's sword for the jousting. Finding no one there to deliver it to him, he took instead the sword he found quivering in a stone in the churchyard. It was not difficult to pull it out; he did it again when his father and brother asked him. Then, to his astonishment, he saw them kneel down before him. "Dear father, why kneel ye to me?" he asked. His father replied: "I was never your father nor of your blood, but I wot well ye are of a higher blood than I weened ye were." Within a year the boy was King of England, "by adventure and by grace".

With stories like this ringing in his head, the boy arrived in Ireland. He was a stranger. And there, in a town full of half-savage people, he was suddenly trailed after as though he were a prince. Brampton pictured his followers as a general rabble, but in the confession they were a small, malicious and determined group of more educated men, some of them English.

As soon as they saw him, they cornered him and presented him with a series of challenges. He was Edward, Earl of Warwick, they told him, the son of Edward IV's brother, the Duke of Clarence, the Yorkist with the strongest claim to the throne if Edward's sons were dead. Piers swore that he was not, and kept on denying it. The men did not believe him. The Cross and the Holy Evangelists were brought to him by the mayor of the town, John Lewellyn, "and there in the presence of him and other I took mine Oath as truth was that I was not the foresaid duke's son, neither of none of his blood." The men did not give up. He was the bastard son of King Richard, they told him. Again, "with high Oaths", he swore he was not.

The oaths made no difference. Still the men insisted; and when he hesitated, "they advised me not to be affeared but that I should take it upon me Boldly." He had denied it before God, but he was pushed into this identity and, eventually, a third: that of Richard, Duke of York. The men assured him that they would help him with all their power against the King of England, "and that the Earls of Desmond and Kildare should do the same, for they forced not what party so that they might be revenged upon [him]." *Ye may not leave it so, this adventure, so lightly.* "Against my will," the confession said, he took up the challenge, not denying the name this time but, at some level, apparently accepting it. If they insisted, he would be the prince they wanted.

Brampton's version, again, was different, carrying no sense of coercion. There were no promoters, but instead a natural gathering of simple souls to a boy who walked alone, making no effort to deny their claims for him. Both of these were tall stories, but they carried for those who heard them a true Arthurian ring: chance encounters, instant claims, immediate counterclaims, the ready invocation of the Cross and the sense, so strong in the legends of Arthur, that a man who fitted requirements might be put to the test long before his name had been properly established.

From the point of view of the Yorkist partisans, according to the confession, the arrival of this paragon was even more startling. They found a ship docked in the harbour and a striking young man wandering in the street. He wore silk, a whole long gown of it that floated and shone about him. This was a country in which the loyalty of Irish chieftains was bought by Henry Tudor with lengths of green and blood-red woollen cloth; but the boy wore silk. Brampton mocked at the way the Irish had run after him "because of that little bit of brocade". But the arm clothed in white samite rising from the lake, or the ship sailed in silk that Lancelot saw on the sea, was not more shocking than this apparition. Silk was so precious that it was used, in England at that time, mostly for laces and ribbons. No one below the rank of knight could wear it. It was so magical and precious that it was supposed never to decay, and in royal Wardrobe accounts it was paid for by the ounce, as if the stuff could be compacted in the hand like gossamer. A boy dressed in silk was a challenge that could not be ignored: as, Brampton implied, the boy himself knew.

The Yorkists of the confession guessed his quality without knowing who he was. They did not care. He looked worth taking up, and they pressed him. Typically, too, he tried to resist them without revealing who he was. He told them only who he was not, leaving intact the mystery of his background and his name. This, of course, only inflamed them all the more. They pestered this strange boy; he brushed them off, or tried to, presumably speaking in French, the language of courtiers and palaces. Then came the ritual set-piece: the boy, in his astonishing clothes, kissing the processional Cross that was thrust slantwise towards him, then kneeling to touch and kiss the Gospels, his golden hair falling forward, confirming even at the supreme moment of denial the possibility of everything he might be, or might be made to be.

Another story had begun like this, when Tristan at fifteen had been dropped in Cornwall after his kidnapping by merchants from Norway. He was left there alone on the shore, an unknown boy with his fair hair curling in locks to his shoulders, in a robe and mantle of magnificent brocade interwoven with slender cords of silk, "and so well cut to his handsome figure that fine clothes have never been cut better by man or woman." The first people he met on the road, two pilgrims, were immediately captivated by him, and especially by the splendour of his clothes. "Good God," they mused, "who is this boy and where is he from, that has such beautiful manners?"

Tristan was royal: the orphan son of a knight and a princess, hidden and fostered for seven years, then trained abroad for another seven in all the skills befitting a prince. But he was also, as he was to remain, a consummate dissembler. He told the pilgrims he was a Cornish huntsman lost in the chase, "and somehow, I don't know how, I rode out of touch with both huntsmen and hounds." He told those huntsmen, however— proceeding "very subtly to fabricate his story" and speaking, like Piers, in French—that he was a merchant's son from Parmenia, "seized with an urge that ceaselessly nagged me to go into foreign lands." His true story was that he had been lured on board a merchants' ship and carried away by strangers, for "they resolved that if, by some ruse, they could get him away they would reap great profit and honour from him."

Strong echoes of the story of Tristan could be heard in the official story of Piers. Yet for those who distrusted or scorned it, there was a precedent in history as well as legend. It came, appropriately enough, from Flanders. Twenty years after the mysterious disappearance of Baldwin IX, Count of Flanders, in 1205, a hermit came to live in a wattle hut by a fountain in the forest of Glançon, not far from Tournai. He had once been a minstrel and a conjuror, but had decided on impulse to embrace the holy life. As he begged one day in the local town, "by adventure asking bread for God," a knight approached and prostrated himself before him. "Lord, I recognise you," he said. "You are truly the Emperor Baldwin." The hermit denied it, saying that he was just a poor man; but the more he denied it, the more the knight insisted it was true. In the end, the bewildered hermit let himself be taken to the knight's house. There, installed most reverently and surrounded by noblemen who assured him that he was just like Baldwin, he began to soften to the prospect of imposture.

The false Baldwin turned out badly. Though he prospered for a while, making glorious entries into Lille, Ghent and Tournai with his long white beard flowing over his purple robes, he was constantly caught out by questions. The Bishop of Senlis asked him when and where he had done homage for Flanders and married Marie de Champagne, Baldwin's wife; the false Baldwin, of course, could not answer. He claimed that his memory was fading, and tried to avoid conversation. Rather than talk to Louis VIII, the King of France, he fled by night, leaving his servants to find his bed empty. He lived for a while in hiding, allegedly in Burgundy, but was exposed before long as a juggler-trickster—a *jongleur*—called Bertrand, from the village of Rains near Vitry-sur-Marne. When he was arrested he confessed his imposture freely, but emphasised that he had played the part of Baldwin at the instigation of others. It had never been his idea. Everything had unrolled from that chance moment in the street, as he begged for bread and, with unaccountable devotion, a knight fell down at his feet.

Some at least of those involved in the story of the kidnapping in Ireland would have known of the conjuror-hermit who played Baldwin, the most famous case of its kind in northern Europe. They would have been aware, too, of how the story ended. Bertrand was dragged on a hurdle and hanged, with his body nailed on a gibbet between the corpses of two dogs. Ravens and kites, faithful denizens of the landscape of perilous wandering, flew down to feed on what remained of him. But nothing adventured, nothing gained; nothing risked, nothing won.

The ship sailed, and left him: Richard, Duke of York.

CHAPTER TWO

Imagined Princes

*T*he imagining of Richard, Duke of York, the second son of
Edward IV, did not begin in 1491 when Pregent Meno's boat
reached Cork. It began with Richard's birth, in the mind of his
father. A child was not put on the earth clothed, comforted or with possessions; even a king's son came in naked and destitute, relying on God for
grace and on his father for his substance. All through his childhood he
toddled, or trotted, towards a model of princeliness and power that was
carefully laid down for him.

Given the frailty of human life, the imagined end would possibly
never be achieved by nature. Imagination itself was a strange and fragile
thing. Few people knew for certain in which organ it resided, whether in
the heart or the brain, but it was known to vary with the humours in
man: grim, sad or cheerful according to the blood, phlegm and bile that
coursed in him. It was affected by climate, geography, excessive dryness,
the softness of the skin. Good and bad angels shaped it. In the brain it
grew like spiders' webs, trapping images and sensations in a private treasury and holding them up to thought. So Edward, like any father, treasured and considered the image of his second son.

57

Prince Richard's birth went unnoticed in the chronicles. Such care-lessness with record-keeping was not unusual. His sister Katherine and brother George had no known birthdays either. The date was later tenta-tively set as August 17th, 1473, at Shrewsbury, near the borders of Wales.

In the birthing chamber he was laid in a gold-painted cradle canopied with cloth-of-gold under a tiny scarlet blanket trimmed with ermine. He probably puked on this, like any little prince. Cradle-bands laced from silver buckles held him safe and still, and swaddling bands, bound tightly as far as his chest, kept the tiny limbs straight. "Rocksters," hired only to do this, tipped him gently from side to side when he cried. Outside the cradle he was cared for by a wet-nurse. In 1502, when this nurse was old and poor, Richard's sister Elizabeth remembered "the woman that was norice to the Prince brother to the Queen's grace" and sent her three and a half yards of cloth for a gown.

As a baby, Richard was seen at once in terms of the man he would grow into. At baptism, still so new that basins of warm water stood at the chapel door to wash the birth-blood from him "if need be," the prince was expected to hold his lighted candle as he was carried to the altar to make offering. He was viewed with anticipation and impatience. The bundle in the crib was already a long-limbed adolescent sprawled on a bed; his little penis, undoubtedly assessed, was already a getter of powerful lords. Foreign envoys would admire him naked, and send descriptions home.

In May 1476, when Richard was about two and a half, Master John Giles was being paid for his good service in instructing him in grammar. "Grammar" meant the Latin sort, out of the *Ars grammatica* of Donatus, every small prince's first headache; at this stage, such lessons were mostly intended to teach him how to say his prayers. In 1477 he was given rooms of his own, including a council chamber. The allocation of firewood for "my Lord of York" in the Household Ordinance of 1478 (twenty bun-dles of tall wood, eight faggots, four bundles of coals) implied that there were several fireplaces to keep burning. No one else was given coal, sug-gesting special warmth for him; and he alone received no candles, suggest-ing that when dusk fell it was bedtime, naturally enough.

The prince was not yet five. He had a chancellor, Mr. Molyneux, an attorney, Andrew Dymock, a treasurer, a council, his own seal, and sev-eral servants to lay out his clothes and make his fires. We know the names of two of these: John Rodon and Thomas Galmole, "gentleman". His chamberlain was Sir Thomas Grey, a banneret and knight of the body to the king. It was Grey, unless he was thought too elderly for these duties, who dressed and undressed Richard, sat naked with him in the bath and, on public occasions, brought him out in his best robes to be fawned over by visitors.

Until he was seven (at which age, the textbooks said, it was advisable to remove boys from the company of women), Richard would have spent much of his time in the company of his mother, Queen Elizabeth, and his six sisters, five of them older than he was. That was where Rui de Sousa saw him in 1482, singing with his mother and one of his sisters. "He sang very well," said de Sousa, besotted. He would also have passed long hours in his own chambers, as his elder brother did, following the minimum requirements for his education that had been laid down by his father. Edward IV considered that all small boys should have an early start to the day, with Mass, followed by grammar, music or "other training exercises of polite learning". They were "in no wise to be suffered in idle-ness, or unvirtuous occupation". The human child, like a green branch, was only tender for so long; as he was bent, so he grew.

His brother Edward, the king-to-be, was always treated with more elaborate care. The 1473 regulations drawn up by his father for his household insisted that he should hear all the divine service every holy day and that, as he ate ("his dishes borne by worshipful folks and squires hav-ing on our livery"), he should have noble stories read to him. Servants were to speak only of honour and virtue in his presence, and his "dis-ports," or games, might be only those "as behoveth his estate to have expe-rience in." Most of this, however, would also have applied to Richard. Edward's bed-curtains, when he was three years old, were drawn at eight o'clock at night. Very probably, Richard's were too.

It was hard to exaggerate the preciousness of these children. As long as the wet-nurse suckled them, her food and drink were carefully tasted. They were not only watched in bed, by servants deputed to stay awake all night, but were constantly attended by doctors. Weapons were never to be drawn in their presence, or rough words exchanged. They were to be sheltered from brawlers, backbiters and dice-players. Again, there was the notion of tender plants: an idea underlined in the king's illuminated books by the arms of Edward and Richard painted in the borders like growing things, entwined with acanthus leaves and flowers.

Richard's bevy of older sisters undoubtedly petted and teased him.

Edward seems to have been more solemn company, already "most skilful in letters for his years," but with him, too, Richard played, until at the age of ten his brother was moved away to Ludlow. The chronicler of Croyland Abbey described the court as filled with "those most sweet and beautiful children", as if even the casual visitor would find them skipping round him. The "disports" of the household rules were never specified, but de Sousa saw Richard play-fighting, again very well, with sticks and a two-handed sword. Caxton's 1474 edition of *The Game and Playe of the Chesse* mentioned that royal boys should be taught to swim, joust, play with axe and sword and, most strangely, "spring and leap", as if even natural exuberance could be codified.

Sometime around 1482, Richard was portrayed in glass at Canterbury exactly as his father had imagined him. The little prince, in a crown and a cloak with an ermine collar, knelt at a prie-dieu before seven scenes from the life of the Virgin. His back and neck were remarkably straight, his hands clasped as piety required. His real age was perhaps five or six, but his body was that of a slim adolescent who was already responsible and reasonable. His pose was that of filial obedience. He would have knelt like this to his father whenever he encountered him, asking for his blessing, since that touch on his bowed head was a sign that his father's shaping continued and an admission that he needed it. Edward IV's letters as a child to his own father, the previous Richard, Duke of York, acknowledged how vital that daily benediction was: "through which we trust much the rather to increase and grow to virtue, and to speed the better in all matters and things."

Yet it was not only training, or parental will, that shaped a boy. The planets too affected him, sometimes to such a degree that earthly instruction made no difference. The *Secreta Secretorum*, of which Edward IV had a well-thumbed copy, told the story of two sons. One, born to the King of India, was sent by his father to learn science in the greatest university in the land. Yet "the great will of the father, and the great business of the doctors might fasten no wit upon him." He wanted only to be a metal-forger; he had been born in such a constellation that "he had no other grace". By contrast, another boy was born in a poor weaver's house "in the planets of Venus and Mars, in the degree of Gemini with Balance", with no star uprising that was contrary. As he grew, his father and mother tried to teach him weaving, but the threads simply tangled in his hands. All their beating and "scouring" made no difference; his stars de-

termined that the boy, though a weaver's son, would know heavenly wisdom, and would become at last a governor and counsellor of kings.

So, when all was done that could be done, Fate could still play
games. The soul could be mismatched with the body, so that a boy could
never grow into his parents' dreams for him. The king's son could go to
the forge, black-handed and sweating, swearing like a workman, while
the weaver's son moved to the palace. Any father hoped never to encounter this. But there was no denying that the whole process of imagining a boy—looking at him, letting his image lodge in the cobwebby skin
of the brain, holding it up to the light of reason—was as hazardous as
bringing him, squalling and bloody, into the world in the first place.

As Edward's "right entirely beloved" second son grew in virtue, honours
were steadily loaded on him. This was done as much for his father's sake
as for his own, to fix in lands and titles the glory Edward had won in battle. Richard's role, in his father's words, was to stop the glory gliding
away. He had been "called into existence" for that reason.

When he was about nine months old his father made him Duke of
York, girding his son's tiny waist with a sword and placing on his head a
cap and circlet of gold. Solemn jousts were held in celebration. By 1478
he was being called Earl Marshal of England, an honour that included
the right to hold, in a small uncertain hand, a golden stick ringed at each
end with black and adorned at the upper end with the king's arms. In
May 1479 he became Lieutenant of Ireland, on condition that he did not
meddle with the disposal of vacant archbishoprics.

Richard's titles did not only make him more illustrious. They turned
him, in effect, into a collector of fees for his father's treasury, and consolidated in him, a little boy kneeling in obedience, the power that would
otherwise have gone to a less subservient local lord. He also became a figure with legal authority to make requests or witness deeds, but usefully
without the maturity to make legal trouble. And so, from the age of four,
he witnessed acts and charters. Before long he was nominated to become a
Knight of the Garter, the highest order of chivalry, and on August 17th,
1480, probably his seventh birthday, he took delivery of his regalia: the
Garter itself, "richly wrought with silk and gold", a blue velvet cloak
lined with white damask, a blue silk sash with gold buttons. The blue
cloak would have swamped him; there were seven yards of it, almost as
much velvet as would have been ordered for a man. A child vested like

this, in glory, was supposed to feel his own soul moving with "strength sensible" in parallel with his father's. He himself would begin to want honours, as he would also begin to want the wonders of Heaven.

Some years before that, Richard had already taken his biggest step into the adult world. He was married at the age of four—his soul by then endowed with at least some stirrings of reasonable virtue—to Anne Mowbray, aged five, the heiress to huge estates in Norfolk. This marriage, from its first mooting, brought more titles to him: Earl of Nottingham, Earl Warenne, Duke of Norfolk, Lord of Segrave, Mowbray and Gower. By arranging the Mowbray marriage, with a family who were treated locally as princes, Edward was again making use of his son to procure that glory for himself.

Contracts to join tiny children in marriage were common practice among princes. All Richard's brothers and sisters were similarly precontracted. The wedding itself was usually understood to be years away, "when both shall have reached nubile years". There was no waiting for nubile years in Richard's case. The little heiress and "the high and mighty Prince Richard, Duke of York" were married, in January 1478, with the full panoply of church and state. Edward organised the wedding jousts, the many-course banquet, the furnishing of St. Stephen's Chapel at Westminster "with tappets of azure colour, inramplished with fleurs-de-lis of gold curiously wrought," the largesse of gold and silver money thrown out to the crowd. So many attended that the man who recorded it, to his irritation, could not see who was who as the last course, of sweets, wine and spices, was carried "marvellous reverently" to the freshly laid tables.

This was Richard's wedding, but he was barely noticed. The recorder did not mention him. His bride, bringing all her land to the king's private domain, was the centre of everyone's attention. Under the golden canopy, in his miniature bridegroom's robes of white damask, he would presumably have kissed this unknown little girl and placed a ring on her finger. He did what the adults required of him. No unmannerly incidents were recorded at the wedding or at the banquet afterwards. When Henry VII's second son, Henry, was invested as Duke of York at the age of three in 1494, he had to be carried a lot, and at one stage he was placed on a table like a trophy so that he could see over people's heads. It is likely that Richard, too, spent much of his wedding as a small, tired boy in arms. The white robes would not have stayed white for long.

There was of course no question of consummation, though this too was imagined. The issue of Richard's body, particularly male issue, was confidently anticipated in the charters that granted his titles to him "and the heirs of his body coming". Richard, Duke of York was both a child and an adult, already a landowner and administrator, girded with swords he would grow into and married to the girl whose womb he would quicken, if God willed it. Each title he acquired—including that of hus-band—was like another cloak, adding substance to the shadow and warming the body into stronger, healthier life.

But life could not be taken for granted. God too had His plans, as a common prayer of the primer, one of the first taught to noble children, neatly understood.

Domine Jesu Christe, qui me creasti et redemisti et preordinasti ad hoc quod sum: tu scis quid de me facere vis: fac de me secundum voluntatem tuam cum misericordia.

O Lord Jesus Christ, who created and redeemed me and preor-dained me to what I am, you know what you wish to make of me; of your mercy, make of me what you will.

In 1479 Richard's brother George died, still a baby; in May 1481 his sister Mary, aged fifteen, was also wrapped in waxed cloth and placed, in lead, in the ground. The next November his wife, aged eight, followed her. She died at the palace in Greenwich, where possibly she and Richard had kept some sort of formal company together, eating, reading or dancing as partners; but she did not play boys' games. Three barges conveyed her body to Westminster, where she was buried in a chapel ded-icated to St. Erasmus, the patron saint of pregnant women. Like Mary, she had been imagined with a line of small replicas kneeling behind her. Yet nothing had come of her marriage save that, by the king's strong sleight of hand, most of her lands had been passed across to Richard.

So far, the little prince himself had kept growing. He seemed to shoot quite fast, so that by the age of seven his orders for new clothes of velvet and figured satin were outpacing his brother Edward's. According to Sir Thomas More, who never knew Richard but, early in the next century, wrote a highly dramatised version of his life, he was a frail child, often ill; yet in 1480 he was invested as Lieutenant of Ireland for another twelve years, as though his father was confident of his strength. The Wardrobe accounts allow a glimpse of the little lieutenant out riding, in a gown of green satin lined with purple velvet and black sarcenet, on a horse saddled and harnessed with crimson velvet and "velvet upon velvet" green cloth-of-gold. "A very noble little boy," Rui de Sousa called him.

Certainly his health was by now less fragile than his father's. Edward IV's licentiousness had caught up with him. The loud, vigorous, gorgeously clad figure at the centre of Richard's life—hunting, dancing, clapping men's shoulders, fondling women's waists—had become corpulent and slow. His lovely face had grown puffy and sometimes apoplectic. To mount a horse was now an effort. He ate, often alone at the board, with a physician in attendance and an array of dietary powders, including emetics, spread out in front of him.

One day the king came back to Windsor, went to bed and did not get up again. No one was sure what was wrong with him. His water gave no clues. Some said he was furious at various diplomatic disappointments, including the implosion of his marriage plans for his eldest daughter, or overcome with melancholy. Others said he had acute indigestion from eating too much fruit on Good Friday. Possibly, thought Dominic Mancini, an Italian observer, he had caught cold while fishing on the river. Edward loved the water: but there was to be no more boating.

Soon the king could not sit up, or keep any position save lying on his right side. Mounds of pillows and cushions supported him: pillows of finest holland or linen from Rennes, bolsters stuffed with duck-down, cushions of figured velvet of every dark colour, crimson and viridian and night-blue, tasselled with gold. In the Wardrobe these were kept, as his clothes were, with little fustian bags of aniseed and spices. He would have smelt of these, as also—to the small boy nervously seeking his blessing by the great curtained bed—of the sticky perfumes that shaped his hair, and sickness, and sweat.

Within a few days, on April 9th, 1483, the image of the dying king on his pillows was replaced by others. First his body was laid out on a board in the palace at Westminster, naked save for a cloth from the navel to the knees, while the lords spiritual and temporal and the mayor and aldermen of London came to view it. The body was bowelled, balmed, sered, or wrapped tightly in waxed cloth, wrapped again in Rennes cloth secured with silk cords, wrapped again in tartryne tied tightly, wrapped again in cloth-of-gold, and taken away to St. Stephen's Chapel, where it lay in state for eight days. This was presumably where Richard would have seen it, disconcertingly still, the corruption working underneath the wax.

The body was then placed in a coffin covered with black cloth-of-gold worked with a white cross; above it was a canopy of cloth imperial fringed with gold and blue silk. Alongside the coffin, inside the hearse, "there was a personage like to the similitude of the king in habit royal crowned with the crown on his head, holding in the one hand a sceptre, and in the other hand a ball of silver and gilt with a cross-pate." This personage, its face carved in wood and then painted with open eyes, went in procession with the corpse to Windsor, in a royal carriage covered with black velvet. The habit royal it wore was a surcoat and mantle of estate, "the laces lying goodly on his belly", just as, within the coffin under the layers of tartryne and linen, the great clumsy lacing showed where the king had been cut open and eviscerated.

Another image of him was left. Above his tomb, on the north side of the altar in his glorious unfinished chapel of St. George at Windsor, his coat of mail was hung. It was gilded and covered with crimson velvet embroidered with the arms of England and France, on which the lions were picked out in pure gold and the fleurs-de-lis in pearls. The coat hung, alongside his banner, still suggesting the bulk of the man who had worn it, as though the gorgeous king had left his carapace behind.

At his tomb, the most obvious prayer for a son to make was the first and simplest:

> *Pater noster*
> *qui es in caelis*

(but his soul was not yet in Heaven, only in Purgatory, where he needed every earthly prayer possible to keep him from the claw-fingered devils who would try to drag him down)

> *sanctificetur nomen tuum*
> *adveniat regnum tuum*

Edward's will—at least in the version drawn up in 1475, when Richard was about two—envisaged his second son at the age of sixteen enfeoffed with the castle and manors of Fotheringhay, Stanford, Grantham and Bolyngbroke. His inexorable improvement and enrichment continued, but Edward had already imagined too far. Whatever he hoped his son would be had died with him, as the idealising soul stepped away from the laggard, struggling body. His will existed on paper; he had spent his last conscious hours, it seems, trying to revise it. John Russell, the Bishop of Lincoln, mentioned with pity "the inextricable cures, pensivenesses, thoughts and charges wherewith [the king's] wise and forecasting mind was hugely occupied and encumbered, afore his decease." But the sense of uncertainty that hovered over every will had deepened and darkened. From now on Richard, Duke of York, carefully constructed for more than nine years, began to disappear.

II

AFTER EDWARD'S DEATH, his eldest son was supposed to become king. The date of his coronation as Edward V had been fixed for June 22nd, 1483. On that understanding, food for the banquet was ordered in and lengths of blue velvet and crimson cloth-of-gold were purchased for the new king's riding robes and those of his retainers. On June 5th, dozens of letters were sent out under the young king's seal to the men he intended to make knights. In all the ceremonial, the king's younger brother Richard was expected to be important.

Yet on April 30th, Edward had been intercepted on his way to London and taken to the Tower by his uncle Richard, Duke of Gloucester, and Henry, Duke of Buckingham, in a manner that showed they were assuming control. Edward's escorts, Lord Richard Grey and his governor, Earl Rivers, both of them from his mother's Woodville side, were arrested on grounds of plotting "to subdue and destroy the noble blood of the realm". At the beginning of May, Queen Elizabeth, understanding that the tide was turning against her and her family, fled into sanctuary at Westminster with Richard and his five sisters. There, surrounded by the furniture she had managed to bring with her, the queen sat "alone alow on the rushes all desolate and dismayed", and wept.

If these images were true—they were More's, darkly imagined—they would have left their mark on Richard. Yet he stayed no more than six weeks in this exile-household before the Cardinal Archbishop of Canter-bury, Thomas Bourchier, came on June 16th to take him, too, to the Tower. The archbishop argued that Edward was missing his brother and that the boys should be together. Richard was also needed for the corona-tion, assuming it was still to happen. His mother, More wrote, refused to let him go because he had been ill. Bourchier insisted, saying that by keep-ing him in sanctuary his mother was implying that he had committed a criminal offence.

Throughout speech and counterspeech, in More's version of the story, Richard stood silently beside his mother, at one point holding her hand. It seemed that the queen would never give in; but then, quite sud-denly, she capitulated. They could take "this gentleman". She kissed him, blessed him and, in tears, delivered him to the archbishop and his officers. Richard, too, was crying. He was escorted through the corridors as far as the door of the Star Chamber, where his uncle Gloucester, now Lord Protector of the kingdom, took him in his arms, kissed him, wel-comed him "with all my very heart" and seemed to comfort him.

From there, Bourchier and Sir Thomas Howard conveyed Richard downriver to the Tower. He was in a squadron of eight barges, paid for by the Howards; More said that the Thames was full of boats. These, and the press of armed men round Westminster—thousands of them, by one estimate made that week—might have excited a nine-year-old as much as frightened him. At any event, a contemporary description of Richard's journey ended on a brighter note, as if a small hand had been placed con-fidently in a larger one: "and so [he] departed with my lord cardinal to the Tower where he is blessed be Jesu merry."

Perhaps he was. The word "merry" meant mostly to be in good health, mental and physical; that remark may have meant no more than "he is all right". Yet Richard seemed, on the rare sightings of contempo-raries, to be a lively child who liked playing and singing. That was why Edward needed him. The elder prince, in striking contrast, was portrayed as mired in sadness that seemed to sap his well-being: "heaviness" against Richard's lightness, the token of good health. Dr. John Argentine, who was with him in the Tower, allegedly told Mancini that Edward, "like a victim preparing for sacrifice", was getting ready for death by daily confes-sion and penance for his sins. More repeated the story: after a little while in the Tower, "the prince never tied his points, nor aught wrought of him-

self, but with that young babe his brother, lingered in thought and heaviness." The doctor would have recognised this as the influence of black
bile and bad angels, terrors dwelt on so obsessively that they were almost
bound to take shape in the world, as well as in the mind.

Dr. Argentine was possibly also the source of a heartbreaking scene
described by Jean Molinet, writing at the court of Burgundy. The elder
boy, he wrote,

> was unsophisticated and very melancholy, aware only of the ill-will
> of his uncle, and the second son was very joyous and witty [*spir-
> ituel*], suited and ready for dances and frolics, and he said to his
> brother, wearing the Order of the Garter, "My brother, learn to
> dance." And his brother answered: "It would be better if you and
> I learned to die, because I believe I know well that we will not be
> in this world much longer."

Such stories could well have been apocryphal. The princes were easily
sentimentalised in their captivity, and those who retailed their fate round
Europe often barely knew their names. In distant Malines, Molinet called
Richard "George", confusing him with an uncle or a brother who was
already dead. Yet the clear thread of their characters persisted, sombre and
debonair. It was Richard who made Edward happy, to the extent he could
be happy. Because he was in the Tower too, all was not books and devotions. He put on his Garter of gold and silk, and danced.

The boys were also outside playing. The London chronicler Robert
Fabyan, writing some time later, reported that in the late summer or early
autumn of 1483 "the childer of King Edward" had been seen "shooting
and playing in the gardens of the Tower by sundry times." As far as he
was concerned, they were never seen again. Richard, Duke of York was
caught in that moment, in the sunshine, aiming his bow, running to the
target, plucking out the arrows, running back, aiming again, shouting,
jumping. His bow was possibly strung with silk and kept in a velvet case
of murrey (dark crimson) and blue, York's colours, with his badge on it;
his father had given bows like this to guests when they went hunting,
together with arrows tipped with gold. These "convenient disports and
exercises" had once been part of his progress towards ideal princeliness,
between the noble and improving stories and the first antiphon of evensong. Now they were the last sure glimpse of him, any nine- or ten-year-
old, running on a lawn and aiming at nothing beyond a butt of straw.

. . .

Less than a week after he had been taken to the Tower, Richard had been removed from the legitimate blood-line of Yorkist princes. The occasion was a sermon preached by a friar, Dr. Shaw, under the great canopy outside St. Paul's, at the instigation of Richard of Gloucester as Lord Protector. A few days later, Parliament enshrined the arguments in law. Edward IV, it appeared, had been contracted to marry Eleanor Butler before his marriage to Elizabeth Woodville. That union was therefore invalid, and the children bastards.

No evidence was offered by Dr. Shaw. Eleanor herself was dead, and could neither confirm nor refute the story. But such things were readily believed of Edward. He had apparently promised to marry Eleanor so that he could immediately bed her; that sounded in character. Dr. Shaw also suggested, for good measure, that Edward himself had been a bastard, the result of an affair between Cecily of York and a common soldier of Rouen called Blaybourne. This seemed preposterous, but George, Duke of Clarence, Edward's wayward brother, was also said to have put such a story about; and Charles the Bold of Burgundy, Edward's brother-in-law, often called him "Blaybourne", in fits of rage, long before Dr. Shaw preached his sermon. According to either line of argument— Edward's dalliance or Cecily's—Richard of Gloucester, Edward's only surviving brother, was now the rightful king.

He took charge, as Richard III, on June 26th. From that date, Richard of York and his brother had no official standing. Their bastardy meant that they could inherit nothing from their father; it involved, therefore, the removal of the titles he had given them and their distribution to others. On June 28th John Howard, a Mowbray heir and a kinsman and friend of the new king, was given the titles of Earl Marshal and Duke of Norfolk. On July 19th, Richard III's son, Edward, was made Lieutenant of Ireland. By March 1484 "the king's kinsman William", another Mowbray heir, had received the family title of Earl of Nottingham.

No reference was made in the patent rolls, even in passing, to the boy who had held these honours immediately before. Although bastardy was often openly acknowledged, and although the deposed child-king Edward was referred to occasionally in the rolls as "Edward the Bastard", or "Edward, Bastard, late king", his brother Richard vanished. Even the appointment of one of his servants, Thomas Galmole, to another post contained no mention of the little duke he had once served. All that remained unaltered was that in Bury St. Edmunds, in Suffolk, the chantry and guild of the Most Sweet Name of Jesus continued for a while to pray for Richard as though he were a prince.

Little of this dissolution would have been noticed at the time. Richard had carried out none of the official duties attached to his titles, acting always through deputies; so when Howard appeared as Duke of Norfolk at Richard III's coronation on July 6th, carrying the crown, this seemed suitable and unremarkable. The Norfolk title, a dream attached to a child, was now in legitimate adult hands, just as the gorgeous silks and velvet half-gowns ordered for Edward V's crowning had now been altered for broader adult backs.

None of this meant for certain that Richard was dead. He was nobody worth mentioning, and could presumably have stayed in that empty quarter for a while. But the silent record strongly suggested that the boy, as well as the prince, was no longer in play. Mancini reported that summer that the princes were seen day by day "more rarely behind the bars and windows [of the Tower], until at length they ceased to appear altogether." The patent rolls followed the small fading faces. In 1489 another entry, revising the Howard claims to the Norfolk estates, stated unequivocally that Richard had died.

This was less than firm proof. Possibly the Howards were expressing their impatience with the prevailing uncertainty about the prince's fate. A large land claim was at stake and, as it happened, Richard's bastardy had by then been reversed on Henry VII's order and by Act of Parliament. Although there was no word or sight of the little prince, he could not be counted out of the picture unless he was dead. His death was therefore declared, whether true or not. It had been recorded too, in general terms but explicitly enough, in the Act of Attainder (conviction for treason) passed against Richard III by Henry in 1485, after Richard had been killed at Bosworth. In that act, Richard was accused of "shedding of infants' blood". There was no need, by this stage, to say who those infants were.

From the summer of 1483 many commentators, not all with favours to seek or axes to grind, were freely imagining the princes' deaths. Mancini (who implied that the princes had disappeared before he left London in mid-July) reported that he had seen men break into tears when Edward's name was mentioned, already suspecting that he had been killed. The Chancellor of France, addressing the Estates General in January 1484, emphasised the horror of murdering boys who were already long-limbed and strong. The Croyland chronicler mentioned a rumour, current in August and September 1483, that they had died "by some unknown manner of violent destruction." In Bristol, the town clerk simply noted in the margin that "this year [September 1483–September 1484] the two sons of King E. were put to silence in the Tower of London."

The further the story travelled, the more bizarre the deaths became. A Castilian visitor to England, Diego de Valera, thought the princes had been killed with herbs while their father was away in Scotland. In France, there was a rumour that they had fallen into the moat of the Tower and been washed out to sea. In Portugal, Rui de Sousa heard that once the boys had been imprisoned, "they bled them, and they died from the forced bleeding." Fabyan's Great Chronicle mentioned London whisperings, after Easter 1484, that they had been poisoned, drowned in malmsey, smothered with feather-beds.

Hindsight or ignorance coloured many of these stories. But the consensus at the time, insofar as consensus can be plucked from what survives, was that the boys were dead, though it was not clear how. Margaret of York, the princes' aunt, maintained that "everyone" thought so. Brampton called their murder "the worst evil in the world", as though the world knew. As to who had done it, the strongest motivation plainly belonged to Richard of Gloucester, the man who was now king. He shared, with his brother, a family trait of ruthless efficiency. Yorkist kings did not leave their rivals to inconvenience them. They hunted them down, as Edward IV after his victory at Tewkesbury had sent soldiers from Wales to hunt down the Earl of Pembroke and his nephew Henry Tudor before they could slip across the Channel; or they killed them, as Henry VI had been murdered in the Tower, quite probably, some thought, by Gloucester, his wounds bleeding afresh as he was laid on the pavement at St. Paul's for all to see.

Yet Richard's guilt was not entirely clear. Against it, there were the ties of blood and loyalty and the loving words at the door of the Star Chamber; besides the fact that the princes, once bastards, were already put aside by Act of Parliament. Perhaps the murderer, or at least the motivator, was not Gloucester but Buckingham, who had been so thick with the Protector at the time of Edward's kidnapping. The Croyland chronicler hinted at it, noting that it was Buckingham who had first suggested putting Edward in the Tower. Several European chroniclers suggested it, Philippe de Commines writing that Buckingham had done the deed himself on Richard's orders. The "Historical notes of a London citizen" stated it flatly, saying that "this year [October 1482–October 1483] King Edward the Vth, late called Prince Wales [*sic*] and Richard Duke of York, his brother . . . were put to death in the Tower of London by the vise [advice] of the Duke of Buckingham."

Certainly Buckingham's mixed political emotions, seeking power both for Richard and for himself, could cast him as either the murderer of the boys or their protector. It was a case of which role would advance him more. In the autumn of 1483 he was associated with a rash of rebellions in the south and west that were intended, it appeared, to set the princes free. Two months or so later the rebels switched their efforts to an attempt to install Henry Tudor, since news had come that the boys were dead. Whatever his aims, Buckingham seemed to know what their condition was. At first, they were alive; by the end of the year, they were somehow removed from the picture.

Yet there was no firm evidence that they were dead, as there is still none now. Two centuries later, when the bones of two children were dug up in the Tower, they were generally accepted as those of the princes, but forensic tests were not conclusive. At the time, there was no proof of death at all; only strong suspicions. The appointment, for example, of a new mastermason and masterjoiner "at the king's command" at the Tower in July 1483 may have implied new men to make coffins and holes in walls, or nothing of the kind. In the same month, Richard III sent out a warrant to try "certain persons of such as of late had taken upon them the fact of an enterprise, as we doubt not you have heard." This cryptic conspiracy may have had to do with trying to free the princes, or not at all. People of that time, too, were careful not to leave paper trails. The reappointment of Robert Brackenbury as constable of the Tower for life in March 1484, "considering his good and loyal service to us before this time, and for certain other considerations especially moving us", perhaps raised eyebrows then, as it does now. Richard himself never produced the boys, the easiest way to refute the rumours. Instead, he railed against "false and contrived inventions".

This may well have been bluster. Alternatively, it may suggest that he had done something else with the boys, short of killing them, that he was unable to explain. Niclas von Popplau, a Silesian visitor who met

Richard in 1484, heard the rumour that he had killed the princes, but added: "Many people say—and I agree with them—that they are still alive and kept in a very dark cellar." In the same year, Brampton received his large and unspecified rewards from the king. In January 1485, James Tyrell, a royal officer, was listed for a payment of "as many sacks of wool as shall amount to the sum of £3,000 sterling . . . to sell for his use and profit", apparently in thanks for services in Flanders "for divers matters concerning greatly the king's weal." They must have concerned it very greatly; the sum was enormous. Yet the idea that Richard would store up trouble for himself by keeping potential rivals alive seemed, and seems, extraordinary.

The notion that the boys still lived was therefore a minority opinion. Yet the hope flickered. A certain optimism could surface in the bleakest circumstances. In 1471, after the Earl of Warwick had been killed at the battle of Barnet, ambassadors were reporting that the rumours of his death were untrue and that, on the contrary, he was in some secret place waiting for his wounds to heal. Richard II, murdered in 1399, was supposed to have escaped to Scotland, and poor Edward II, sodomised with a burning poker, to a monastery in Italy. In secret places, those who had been marked to die rested and drew breath. Even Charlemagne's horse Bayard, thrown into the Meuse with a millstone round his neck, escaped to go on running, his pale mane flickering, through the woods of the Ardennes.

Polydore Vergil said it was fairly common report that the princes had gone to "some secret land" and survived there. As the shock of Glouces-ter's takeover subsided, it was possible to hope that the worst act of vio-lence had somehow been avoided. In 1484, Elizabeth Woodville reached an accommodation with the king. This suggested to some that he could not have killed her sons, but that on the contrary Elizabeth knew that one was alive, or both were. The princes had perhaps been smuggled out of the Tower and shipped across the sea, as Gloucester himself and his brother George, at much the same ages, had been sent to Utrecht for safety by their mother in 1461. Alternatively, they had been taken to some northern castle and then, after Richard's defeat at Bosworth, had fled to Europe with other political refugees. Perhaps their Woodville relations had rescued them. Thomas More remarked that Elizabeth Woodville, in sanctuary, was desperate to try to smuggle her younger son abroad but had no time to arrange a time, place or people to help. Precisely for this reason, Richard had surrounded the sanctuary with armed troops on land and boats on the river, to prevent a prince escaping.

Yet, unlike the murders, the flight of the princes did not seem to be pictured in any detail at the time. When, in 1490, rumours spread in London that the younger boy had turned up in Flanders, the whispers were not followed by speculation as to how he had arrived there. He was simply there, as if by magic. Somehow, too, his brother Edward, always less resilient and shadowed by death, had dropped away. The young man who eventually reappeared as Richard claimed that his escape had been singular in every sense. Edward had been killed in the Tower but, by a miracle, he himself had survived. Sometimes a human agent was posited; often it was the simple work of divine power, "God's might," as he put it in 1496. In the same document he described how, God touching him again, he had "graciously escaped & overpassed as well by land as by sea" all the traps that Henry Tudor had laid for him. When standards were raised in Richard's name in the West Country in 1497, they showed a small boy escaping by himself: from the tomb and from the jaws of a wolf, marvellously spirited away.

It seems true to say that his survival and revival were neither widely believed in nor hoped for. The English did not mythologise this missing prince as they had mythologised Arthur, *rex quondam rexque futurus*, the once and future king. He was not expected to rise again from the misty Isle of Apples, the gray-eyed boy who pulled the sword fiercely and lightly from the impossible stone. Nor, like Frederick Barbarossa, was he supposed to slumber in some hidden place until his people needed him. In certain half-wild pockets of England there was a tendency to dream this way, and in 1499 Henry's astrologer, William Parron, mocked those who believed that Richard of York had returned: they were like the Cornishmen waiting for King Arthur, he said, or like the Flemings who believed that Charles the Bold was still alive, though his head had been shattered in the snow at Nancy more than twenty years before. Such dreams were not general. They were for the credulous only: people who believed in things never known, corpses rising again or their dead ash, blown in the wind, somehow assuming a prince's shape.

Nevertheless, when Richard reappeared, as some believed, prognostications came with him. Bernard André claimed that false prophecies about him were scattered far and wide by charlatans, blinding simple minds; illusions spread by devils, Vergil thought. In 1493 a priest who was expert in prophecies, Thomas Ward, joined the resurrected prince at his court in Malines. Presumably, Ward wrote verses predicting glory and kingship for him. Well past the end of the new Richard's brief career the priest continued to write more, slipping him a book in prison to encourage him in dreaming.

None of those prophecies has survived, but undoubtedly some were plays on the heraldic devices of the little prince: the falcon in the fetterlock (the fetterlock snapped apart, the falcon flying) or the White Rose of York blossoming again, while the Tudor dragon slunk bleeding away. Stray Yorkist sayings that had applied to his father were probably recycled. Several such prophecies mentioned an alliance with the Scots against the "sinful" English, which Richard was to seek. Another, called "The Lily, the Lion and the Son of Man", had the Yorkist hope allied with an emperor against the French. Again, the resurrected Richard was to tread that path, as though the prophecies themselves shaped the way he went.

Yet his name was not ideally suited to the prophecies of his house. The Yorkist hero, "the true heir, God's chosen", was almost always called Edward, pitted against an accursed Henry, *Henricus maledictus*, who had usurped the throne. The third Richard had not been meant to reign, and the second Richard, a poor substitute for Edward his father, had always seemed weak and ambiguous in prophecy, symbolised by an ass. The forecasts may have shifted, therefore, away from Richard's name and towards his resurrection. In some prognostications a dead man "that no man saw born, nor no man shall see buried" was supposed to appear, disappear for a while "where no man shall find him" and then emerge "to execute judgment in his father's house". In another version, he had been twice buried and would reappear, to reign gloriously, after seven kings had brought England to destruction. The colour of this prophecy was clearly Yorkist, but it was vague enough to be reworked for any circumstance: a king exiled, a king killed, the second coming of Christ.

It was vague enough, too, to apply to a wandering and characterless child whose only fame was to have cheated death. For Richard, like his brother, was less a king-in-waiting than a lost boy. Both were *innocentes*, pure beings who had left no mark on the earth. That same wistfulness tinged a semi-prophecy given by Molinet, probably based on his own sighting of Richard Plantagenet in Malines in 1493:

J'ay vu filz d'Angleterre
Richard d'Yorc nommé,
Qu l'on disoit en terre
Estainct et consommé,
Endurer grant souffrance;
Et, par nobles exploitz,
Vivre en bonne esperance
D'estre roy des Angloys.

I saw a son of England called Richard of York, who they said was dead and eaten up in the earth, endure great sufferings; and, by noble deeds, live in good hope that he would be king of the English.

It was not the English who hoped he would be their king. It was Richard himself; and though there was a measure of confidence and even triumph over the rumours of death and the "great sufferings", the next stage was tentative. He hoped they would accept him. He lived in that hope. But the "noble exploits" were part of the future dreaming, the feats that would draw attention to himself, and he had not yet performed them. For those who believed, he would restore the House of York and, with it, just laws and good governance in England. But Molinet's verse gave no tantalising detail of the sort that prognostications usually contained: the king actually seated on the throne, his sceptre extended over the waters, his enemies trampled, the biblical peace of lions and lambs lying down together in the flower-enamelled grass.

Molinet had touched on a truth. The English did not hold Richard Plantagenet, Duke of York, in their hopes or imaginations. He had made no impression on them: no deeds of arms, no laws, no exercise of political skill, no public appearances to speak of. Mancini had described Londoners weeping for Edward, not for him. In most minds, he was an unformed child whose reappearance on the scene—if he could possibly reappear, shaking out of his hair the dust and worms of death—would mean only the return of faction and disorder. The imagining of Richard of York, the perfect prince, had been the project of a small circle only. It was a circle even more ardent, but almost as small, that took on the project of imagining him again.

III

WHO RECONSTRUCTED HIM? According to the official confession of 1497, two men in particular. One was John Atwater, a merchant who was twice mayor of Cork; the other was John Taylor the elder, a former servant of Edward IV's brother George, Duke of Clarence. Taylor is difficult to disentangle from his son John Taylor the younger, a minor court official for Edward IV, former hosier and, for four years, controller of customs for all the main ports of the West Country. Presumably they worked together much of the time. At several points of the story a Taylor hovers in the background, though Atwater was the more consistent and more committed friend.

Henry VII himself blamed both men, though not equally, for helping to set up his tormentor. When Atwater was captured in 1499 the king described him, in a letter to Louis XII of France, as "the first mover and the half-inventor", *le premier motif et inventeur de meitie*, of the imposture. Geronymo Zurita, a late-sixteenth-century chronicler of Aragon, said Atwater accepted and confessed it as he died: he was *el primer inventor de la representacion*. Wherever the confession went, the story spread: a big role for the sometime mayor of a small town in a country that was, in every sense, off the edge of Europe.

Yet Henry, in his punctilious way, had called Atwater only the "half-inventor". There were others to blame. When Taylor the elder was captured in France, also in 1499, the Milanese ambassador reported— probably deriving it from Henry—that Taylor was the man who had suggested taking the feigned boy to Ireland "when he first declared himself the son of King Edward". The ambassador added that he thought the king would rather have Taylor in his hands than 100,000 crowns, for to track him down, when the conspiracy had long since collapsed, would prove that Henry never forgot and never gave up. In the end, however, he did not execute Taylor, preferring to imprison him and pardoning his son. The confession made him a bystander in Cork, not one of those who actively accosted the boy. In the king's mind, the blame for setting Richard Plantagenet in motion did not lie with Taylor as much as with Atwater; and it did not lie with Atwater, in its origins, as much as with someone else entirely.

The motives of Atwater would have been uncomplicated. He was a merchant, a local worthy and an instinctive Yorkist. Taylor the elder, too, was described as "a creature of King Edward's", a fanatical Yorkist who would favour any sprig of the White Rose. But his preference, as it happened, was not for Richard, Duke of York. As one of Clarence's servants his first loyalty was to Clarence's son, Edward, Earl of Warwick, who had been kept in royal custody since the execution or murder of his father in 1478, and who was now in Henry's ward in the Tower. Taylor had been involved very early in conspiracies about Edward. According to Clarence's attainder for treason, the duke had wanted "to cause a strange Child to be brought into his Castle of Warwick, and there to have be [sic] put and kept in likeness of his Son and Heir," while his real son was sent "into Ireland, or into Flanders, out of this Land, whereby he might have gotten him assistance and favour against our . . . Sovereign Lord." Taylor was sent to get little Edward, then aged about two, to convey him out of the country, but failed in his errand. There was no further word of the "strange Child", or of where Clarence had hoped to find him. But it was another instance of a vogue for smuggling innocents abroad, where they might grow until they were dangerous.

Taylor seemed to be forgiven his part in this "false and untrue entente". By late 1478 Edward IV had made him a forester and bailiff on the Clarence lands in Worcestershire. His son was employed at court as a yeoman of the chamber and then, in 1481, appointed to the post of surveyor of customs and subsidies in the ports of Poole, Exeter, Dartmouth, Plymouth, Fowey and Bridgewater. The job was an important one, carrying the power to examine all port records and seize ships and their cargoes. By 1482, Taylor the younger was also keeper of the seals of the subsidies and ulnages of cloth in Devon and Cornwall, and in 1485 his father was made keeper for life of the king's park of Morelwood in Gloucestershire.

This, however, was the apogee of the Taylors' official favour. Sometime after the Yorkist debacle at Bosworth, both were replaced in their jobs, Taylor the younger within four months. His replacement, James Boneython, was explicitly rewarded for services to Henry in Brittany in the years when he had waited to invade. Sidelined by new loyalists, under a cloud for incompetence, Taylor seemed to linger in England nonetheless, and in 1489 was granted a general pardon for reasons unspecified. His father, however, had already fled to Rouen in Normandy. There, in Edward IV's birthplace, Taylor the elder was plotting again to put Edward, Earl of Warwick, on the throne of England. His ambitions were enormous for the sort of man he was: ex-servant, ex-bailiff, now expatriate. But in the hope that politics might blow his way again, he had also made his services available to the King of France. If Charles VIII wanted to make trouble for Henry, Taylor was there in Warwick's cause.

Edward, Earl of Warwick, was a figure almost as shadowy as Richard, Duke of York. He was a year and a half younger, born in February 1475, and had lost his mother even earlier than he had lost his father. His lands were managed for him, by Taylor the elder among others, and his only legal personality was that of an incapable child. Since much of his life had been spent in confinement, he was unknown to the English at large. Before Bosworth, he was at Sheriff Hutton castle in Yorkshire. After it, for a short strange spell, he was with other "young lords" and ladies, including Edward IV's daughters, in the care of Henry's mother, before Henry moved him to lonely residence in state apartments in the Tower. He seemed seldom properly involved at court, or in the company of other children. Although Edward IV had taken some responsibility for him after the death of his father, no trace survives of him in the Wardrobe accounts of 1480 except a payment for five different pairs of shoes, double- and single-soled: signs of a boy who was growing fast, like a straggling plant, though hardly ever exposed to the light of day.

In 1484, after the death of his own son, Richard III had for a time named Warwick as his heir. In 1485, certain grants of offices suggested that he had changed his mind to John de la Pole, the Earl of Lincoln, another of his nephews. There was said to be something not quite right with Warwick, some feebleness of mind. Vergil famously remarked that he could not discern a goose from a capon. The young man who emerged in reported conversations in 1499—rare sightings in an almost unrecorded life—was naïve, querulous and childlike, always needing to have things explained to him and doing nothing on his own initiative. At one point, a short sword was put into his hand; he accepted it as though he had no notion of its purpose. Conspiracies to make him king were concocted in his presence, and he let them proliferate with barely a word. A dangerous stranger was introduced to him; almost at once Warwick shook his hand, calling him "my special friend". It was not surprising that Richard III should have decided that this poor simple creature could not be King of England.

But others imagined it. In the days after Bosworth there were whispers of plans to make Warwick king, which explained why Henry put him under closer ward and, perhaps, why special spies and inspectors were stationed at the largest ports to check on what, or who, was being taken from the kingdom. In April 1486 Humphrey Stafford hatched a plot on the rumour that Warwick had been set free in Guernsey and taken to Flanders, and his followers were indicted for shouting Warwick battle-cries. A wild gathering in May in Highbury, near London, featured a standard with a ragged staff, Warwick's badge. Then, later that year, a boy of about ten appeared in Ireland who was said to be Warwick himself, escaped from the Tower.

As it emerged, though the story was cloudy, the boy had been trained by an Oxford priest. Two Yorkist lords—Francis, Viscount Lovell, and the Earl of Lincoln—had given him their backing. According to Vergil, his instructor had thought for a while that he might pass him off as Richard, Duke of York, also escaped from the Tower (some said) and in concealment in England. But in 1486 Prince Richard's death, so much more likely than his survival, still seemed to hang too heavily over the idea of reviving him. Although Henry had Warwick in his own prison and could easily disprove a counterfeit, Clarence's son still made a more plausible focus for conspiracy.

The false Warwick was taken to Ireland and crowned in Dublin on Whit Sunday, allegedly with a diadem that was borrowed from a statue of Our Lady. That done, the mayor of Dublin carried him round the city in his arms. The Earl of Kildare promoted him, and an impressive roster of bishops, abbots, lords and officers of the Irish Pale gave him their support. Coins were struck in his name at the mints of Dublin and Waterford. The child-king, called Edward VI—since Edward V, though never crowned, was deemed to have reigned for two months or so—issued edicts through his keepers, Lovell and Lincoln, and in June 1487 the trio invaded England with a force of Irishmen and German mercenaries. At Stoke, near Nottingham, they took the field against Henry. Lincoln, the possessor of a genuine claim to the throne, was killed; Lovell, at first supposed drowned while trying to swim the Trent, fled away to Flanders. The boy, named as Lambert Simnel—whether or not he was—was captured and packed off to the king's kitchens, later to rise to the position of falconer.

In the annals of imagined kings, this boy advanced further than Richard Plantagenet ever did. He felt the holy chrism on his forehead; the Milanese ambassador reported in 1497 that Henry, out of respect for the sacred unction, thought he might make a priest of him. He wore a crown, even if a borrowed one, and faced his enemy on the battlefield. Yet the materials out of which this prince had been made seemed deeply unpromising. Simnel was pronounced to be the son of an artisan, variously a barber, a joiner, a tailor, a baker or an organ-maker. His background was provincial England. It was said that he looked the part, with a certain natural elegance, and he had been trained for a while. Yet his presumption worked mostly because he was required to be nothing but a puppet, a boy carried aloft, spoken for and acted for by lords at the forefront of his cause; and because his supporters, especially in Ireland, would have flocked to a Yorkist figurehead if it had been painted on a board, immobile and mute as the real Warwick often was.

As proof of this, they continued to embrace the false Warwick even after Henry had produced the real earl from custody. He was eleven. He was brought out of the Tower in February 1487 and made to walk to St. Paul's, perhaps the longest walk he had done in some years, to hear Mass. There, as he had been instructed, he showed himself praying. After the service, he talked to people in the nave of the church. Yet when news of this display reached Ireland, Simnel's supporters insisted that the boy in St. Paul's had been a fake. Though their own imagination might be "spurious and empty", as Vergil mocked, it was also hard to break that imagination down.

The defeat at Stoke did not change this. Nor did a second public display of Warwick in London, this time walking beside Simnel, on Relic Sunday in July. A Yorkist prince loitered now in many people's heads, dangerously re-created. Whoever he was (the fantasies shifting as necessary), he gave hope of a restoration. Molinet, writing in Burgundy about the plots of 1486, described how the House of York had been tall, splendid, built in such majesty that its glory shone through the seven climates of the world. But it had toppled so suddenly that hardly a wall or pillar still stood from which it could be raised again *en royale convalescence*. All that remained was one curling sprig of foliage from the royal stock, a tiny plant creeping among the ruined stones. But sprigs could grow. Branches would begin to form, then buds, until eventually the mended stones would make a triumphal arch hung thick with roses, shining, barbed and white.

Henry, too, sensed this continued movement of the ground. He was said to have ordered at Stoke that the Earl of Lincoln should not be killed, for through him "he might have known the bottom of his danger", In the parliament held five months after the battle, a court was set up to inquire into "compassings, conspiracies and imaginings" to murder the king within the royal household itself. He wrote also to the pope, asking Innocent VIII to censure the Irish prelates who had sanctioned Simnel, so that others would not "attack us thus flagitiously for the future". Irishmen swearing allegiance to Henry in 1488 were enjoined to let him know of such dangers "without delay or feigning". And all this time the king's spies and agents went back and forth between England and Portugal.

The story Henry was trying to counter, of fatherless princes surviving in secret, was very like his own. He had been born in 1457, at Pembroke Castle in Wales, to a mother of fourteen whose husband, Edmund Tudor, had died three months before. From both father and mother he had received a portion, no more, of royal blood. His mother, Margaret Beaufort, was descended from John of Gaunt, Edward III's third son, by an illegitimate line; his father's mother had been Queen Catherine of France, the widow of Henry V. For fourteen years Henry had remained in Wales, obscurely enough, bound perhaps for a local marriage and modest estates. But as the Yorkist dynasty came to power in England, and the Lancastrian line was slowly extinguished, he had become the sole remaining male heir of his house. The Yorkist ghosts he now faced, whoever they were, were political replicas of his own child-self, both as vulnerable and as dangerous.

Hounded overseas in 1471 after Edward IV's victory at Tewkesbury, Henry had taken refuge with his uncle Jasper Tudor at the court of Duke Francis of Brittany. He was treated kindly there, but his exile dragged on for years, becoming increasingly hazardous as the Yorkist kings, well aware of him, tried to winkle him out. As Brittany grew more unstable with the duke's illness and madness, Henry was forced to appeal to the French king's pity too. Only this, and the unpopularity of Richard III, emboldened him to invade England. His long banishment had left marks on him: caution, suspicion, pragmatism, a self-sufficiency that bordered on friendlessness, and a lasting preference for the French language and

French style of kingship. This made him, to some degree, a reserved foreigner in his own kingdom, where his Yorkist-Plantagenet rivals seemed to display, spuriously or not, an idealised native purity and openness and grace.

His mother, despite her misgivings, had agreed that he should be sent abroad but covertly kept in touch with him; so mothers, too, required watching. During the Simnel uprising, Elizabeth Woodville had been sent to a convent and her estates confiscated in the apparent belief that she was sending, or might send, financial help to some shadow-prince beyond Simnel. If that shadow-prince was Richard of York, there was peril here for Henry. Before the end of 1485 he had reversed Richard III's bastardisation of Edward's children in order to take the princes' eldest sister, Elizabeth, as his wife. The language was uncompromising. He had overturned Richard's "false and malicious imaginations"; he desired that the statute should be taken off the rolls, annulled, cancelled, burned and utterly destroyed, and that the matter should remain "for ever out of remembrance and also forgot." By this act, suppressing one memory and awakening another, Henry himself had contributed to the revival of Richard of York. He knew as much; his new act was not to be construed as "in any way hurtful or prejudicial to the act of stablishment of the Crown of England to the king and to the heirs of his body begotten." Yet it was. Instead of the wraithlike bastard boy, there was now a ghost with a claim: crowned, ermined, waiting, like his image in the Canterbury glass.

The spring of 1489 brought a rash of vague scares and stirrings, besides a serious revolt in Yorkshire for which Henry was forced to raise levies up and down the country. The grievance appeared to be taxation, but Henry could never be sure that more secret efforts were not afoot. Feigned, contrived and forged tales, as he described them, dogged him constantly. Henry did not say what these stories were, as Richard III never had; people knew. Yet their focus was shifting. Interest was moving away from Warwick, who was easily accounted for, to Richard of York, long lost sight of and still feared.

In January 1491 Sir Robert Chamberlain and Richard White colluded at Barking to levy war against Henry and adhere traitorously, as their attainder said, to Charles VIII of France. Chamberlain, a strong Yorkist, had been with Edward IV on the ship that had brought him back from exile in 1471; for some years he had been under house arrest and under bond for his loyalty. White was described as a "gentleman" from Norfolk. These two and several others, though apparently conspiring for Charles, were tracked down to Hartlepool in the northeast, a leapingoff point not for France but for Flanders, where Richard of York was now rumoured to be.

Henry, desperate to know where they were going and why, sent Sir Edward Pickering with more than one hundred horsemen to extract the rebels from St. Cuthbert's sanctuary, where they had taken refuge. He also told the Bishop of Durham, who had protested faintly about this breach of privilege, that he wished to be "certified particularly and by parcels of all such writings and goods as shall be found in their caskets, males, trunks, or in other their carriages." The bishop himself was not to be trusted, for he had been greatly favoured by the Yorkist kings and had been an associate, too, of John Argentine, the princes' doctor, who possibly knew what had become of them. The Hartlepool operation was expensive: Pickering spent £140 6s. 8d. on it, though the king had advanced him only £40. But Henry found all he needed, for Chamberlain and eighteen accomplices, including his two sons, were safely brought to London and attainted without trial. Chamberlain was beheaded in March, though the rest were pardoned.

What Chamberlain had been plotting was not clear, but there was "talking in secret wise" in London that he had been trying to slip away to Richard, Duke of York, preserved by Edward IV's sister, Margaret of York, the Dowager Duchess of Burgundy. Her protégé would later confirm it; in 1496, Richard claimed Chamberlain as one of the men who had died for him. The attempted journey from Hartlepool to the duchess's court at Malines, in Brabant, pointed to another inventor, reviver or protector of Richard, Duke of York; and not merely one among several but, in the king's view and most others', the first and foremost. Only a year after Richard's reappearance, Vergil said, Henry knew that it was Margaret who had raised him from the dead.

Margaret had been born in 1446 at Fotheringhay, the third daughter of the previous Richard, Duke of York. Her four brothers, two of them kings, had predeceased her; her husband, Charles the Bold of Burgundy, who had taken her as his third wife, had been killed by the Swiss in the winter of 1477 as he foolishly besieged the town of Nancy. He left in jeopardy, and in unaccustomed misery, a swath of territory that contained some of the most prosperous cities of Europe—Antwerp, Ghent, Brus-sels, Bruges—and stretched from the Somme in the west to the Rhine in the east. It covered Brabant, Limburg, Friesland, Zeeland, Hainault and Luxembourg, as well as Flanders; but "Flanders" was where Henry and his officers imagined Margaret to be, and the place from which his troubles came.

After Charles's death, Margaret was the chief support of her step-daughter Mary of Burgundy, fighting to keep Mary's rich inheritance out of the hands of the King of France. After 1482, when Mary—who had married Maximilian—died in a riding accident, Margaret devotedly ful-filled her duties as godmother and protector to her children. She had dowry properties to keep up at Malines, Binche, Rupelmonde and else-where; she pastured cattle, shipped wool, rebuilt palaces, sent charity to prisoners and the poor, and lent her patronage both to new religious movements and to the new art of printing. Beyond all this she had the usual diplomatic headaches of a widow, without much freedom of action, in a half-foreign land surrounded by predatory powers; and, many said, a penchant for political schemes she should have left alone.

In particular, she longed openly for the restoration of the House of York to the throne of England. On its face, there was little dynastic logic to this. A Yorkist princess, her niece Elizabeth, was now Henry's wife and (after two years' delay) the properly crowned Queen of England. By raising up male claimants, Margaret was endangering what little prestige and glory her family still had there. Yet she herself suggested that Eliza-beth's status did not count. Her family, she told Isabella of Spain in 1493, had "fallen from the royal summit". Their only hope lay in a "male rem-nant" who could recover the throne "usurped by this most iniquitous invader and tyrant" and could restore, without dilution, the name of York again.

Bernard André, Henry's poet laureate, repeated frequently the cur-rent court opinion that Margaret spent her time thinking up "new and unheard-of outrages" to damage the king. Like Juno hurling storms at Aeneas, she lashed and railed against him. "Spite never dies," André wrote of her in his high-heroic *History of the Life and Deeds of Henry VII;* "a woman's anger is eternal." In the original, the words *quia aeterna est mulieris ira* were underlined (the only underlining in the work), and the word *Nota* was written in the margin. It was not Henry's writing, but it would have been his thought. In a letter to Gilbert Talbot of 1493, his first surviving mention of the conspiracy of the resurrected Richard, he blamed Margaret from the opening sentence for "contriving" and maliciously setting "another feigned lad" on him. Henry may have blamed Taylor and Atwater for the first staging in Ireland; the conception and birth, sometimes in those terms explicitly, he blamed on Margaret, and continued to do so even after the confession produced another story. "It is well known how the thing was done," said André, needing to say no more.

She was an easy scapegoat, as all women were. Hate and spite were presumed to be their only weapons, and few could decorously defend themselves. Yet, to judge by Margaret's own words, there was no scapegoating in this case. Her loathing of Henry was manifest, as was her approval of any movement that might dethrone him. She had helped Simnel in 1487 with money and men and, immediately before, had given shelter at her court to Lovell and Lincoln, his promoters. When they failed, it was natural for her to try a better instrument. Vergil caught the hint of alchemical creation, saying that she had "made a man" through whom her hatred could express itself. Edward Hall, embellishing Vergil, caught it too: Margaret, "intending to cast white sulphur to the new-kindled fire, determined clearly to arm and set forward pretty Perkin against the king of England with spear and shield, might and main."

In Margaret's case, the imagining of princes had a particular poignancy. She longed for children, but produced none. Before her marriage to Charles in 1468, her husband-to-be had announced to the magistrates of Valenciennes that she was "ideally shaped to bear a prince". But she was not, and Charles moved on to other projects. Two years into their marriage, in June 1470, the couple were so rarely together that suppers *à deux* caused surprise to the keeper of her household accounts. In 1473 they were together twice, from January 24th to the 28th and on April 12th. While Charles, with his insatiable desire for glory, engaged eternally in wars (as Philippe de Commines put it), Margaret dedicated herself to the saints who could help to set in her womb the tiny figure of an heir of Burgundy. She prayed to St. Waudru, whose belt protected women in pregnancy, and to St. Anne, whose three marriages had surrounded her with a glowing crowd of children. Offerings were made to St. Colette, the patron of miraculous births, who had also raised a dead child to life, and to St. Margaret of Antioch, who protected women in labour. On four occasions between 1472 and 1476 she made a pilgrimage to the shrine of

Our Lady at Hal, whose intercessions were supposed to quicken the barren. Nothing helped her.

Her mother had been gloriously fertile, bearing twelve children. Her
brother Edward and his wife had filled the English court with pretty
babies. Margaret's child remained all that was hoped and desired of her
while her husband lived, and she too was depicted in her prayer-books in
the fashionable shape of the time, with the swelling girdle of a mother-to-
be. Possibly there were miscarriages; possibly, too, a child was born dead.
The Burgundian records show no sign that she ever "took her chamber",
or ceremonially withdrew from public life in the last weeks of pregnancy.
But for some reason, in mid-February 1473, Margaret went away alone to
the little palace-cum-hospice of St. Josse-ten-Noode, at the edge of the forest of Soignes outside Brussels. Her habit in those years, when she had
charge of her stepdaughter Mary, was to stay with her continually, usually
in Ghent, with rare trips of a week or two to Brussels or Malines to catch
up with administration. Her journeys to shrines to pray for a child would
take a day or two, at most. Yet she stayed at St. Josse for two months, not
returning until April 12th, and on her return Charles came to meet her,
exceptional though this was.

Ten-Noode means "need" or "affliction". Philip the Good, Charles's
father, had built this *maison de plaisance* among the vineyards mostly as a
place for rest or recuperation from illness. Both the local wines and the
waters that flowed there, near the source of the Maelbeek, were supposed
to have curative properties. Our Lady, too, had appeared more than once
in the forest among the tall stands of beeches, leaving the sweetest perfume
behind her, and hermits had been drawn to pray there alone. Margaret followed them, as far as a duchess could. Though she had been "faring well"
in early February, in Sir John Paston's opinion, all was not well now.
Something traumatic had happened to her, needing exceptional treatment
and a long recovery, and it is not unlikely that it was the loss of a child. A
dead child born perfect, however, would still have been acknowledged
and baptised. This baby—if baby there was—was perhaps unformed
still, and the accident kept quiet. One later rumour suggested the birth,
around this time, of a secret love-child. But Margaret would never have
borne a living child, especially a son, while Charles was alive, and concealed him.

Malicious French tongues had spread a tale, almost certainly false,
that she had been "somewhat devoted to love affairs" (in fact, a *putain*)

before her marriage to Charles. More and more people knew this, wrote the Milanese ambassador to France in July 1468, and "in the opinion of many she even had a son." The story was so current in Bruges, he went on, that Charles had ordered anyone caught spreading it to be thrown into the river. In short, Margaret was not deemed infertile, and the notion of a secret son already flickered round her. Yet by 1477 the death of her husband, if nothing else, had consigned her to childlessness.

From that point on, her imagination and her deep affection were linked to other people's children. In 1478, as godmother to Philip, Mary of Burgundy's son, she carried him at his christening (his long train of crimson cloth-of-gold trailing after him), and later undressed him in public to prove he was a boy. In 1481 she rewarded the Malines receiver for his good services by lifting his tiny, slippery child naked from the holy font of baptism. Almost her last duty, in the first years of the next century when she was close to death, was to care for the little prince, her step-great-grandson, who was to become Charles V. For the decade or so before, and possibly much longer, she also seemed to have placed her hopes in someone else's child.

Vergil thought that Margaret herself had discovered the boy. Having searched with her spies for years for an ideal candidate, she found one, "not unhandsome in appearance, quick to learn and very cunning." He spoke English already, Vergil claimed, as well as other languages. Building on this perfect base, the duchess gave him an intensive grounding in family history, mythology and duty. How he came to her attention, and what his history was, remained a mystery. "By chance she came upon him," Vergil wrote. "Tournai" was all the background he was given, although this was a French city with which Margaret had no obvious connection. His wanderings had drawn a veil across his life. He might as well have been the snow-child in *Les Cent Nouvelles Nouvelles*, conceived, so his lying mother told her husband, when she ate a sorrel-leaf crusted with snow in the garden in winter. The husband, distrusting this tale, took the boy on crusade with him and reported that, in the heat of the desert, he had melted away.

The same sense was often there in the historians' accounts of Margaret's creation, a false and pretty thing that could not possibly last long. Nonetheless, they imagined that the boy was trained hard. Vergil described Margaret teaching him methodically about "English affairs and the lineage of the House of York," enabling him easily to deceive the world. Yet women were inefficient by themselves, and Margaret lacked besides one part of the knowledge necessary to make this prince: recent experience of both England and her brother's court. She had been back home only once since her marriage in 1468, and then for just a few months. André therefore asserted that Margaret needed "light and worth-less" part-players to help her. One was Stephen Frion, a former secretary to the Dukes of Burgundy who became, apparently on Margaret's recom-mendation, French secretary to Edward IV and Richard III. He was so good that both Richard III and Henry VII automatically reappointed him, on a salary of £40 a year. But his loyalty did not last. By November 1486, his pay now in arrears for more than a year, he was moaning so loudly about "importable costs and charges" that Henry ordered the money paid "so that we may hear no further complaint of him in that behalf." The gesture did not mollify him. Margaret worked on him, André said, until at last—"infected by the woman's poisonous sugges-tions"—he left the service of Henry and began to paint (*effingere*) the image of Edward IV's younger son on a boy whom he and his co-plotters had found. It is possible that he had been Margaret's agent all along, and remained so as long as she thought necessary.

André did not say who Frion's co-conspirators were; there were a lot of them, and it would take too long, he said, to list these scoundrels man by man. The boy they had found, a native of Tournai called Peter, had been educated "in this region" by "Edward, a Jew supported in baptism by King Edward"—Brampton, a tiny gleam of accuracy. By "this region", André meant England; he later said specifically that the boy had been trained there, and added that the plotters "then pretended he had been brought up in various countries." No other source, save André, gave all this plotting and painting. But certainly Frion left Henry's service, rather precipitately, in 1489, just after heading a mission to France and without collecting the Michaelmas instalment of his salary. He was apparently working now for Charles VIII, although there is no sign in the accounts that the French king ever paid him. In the summer of 1492 he went to Ireland, on Charles's behalf, to pick up Richard Plantagenet, perhaps a young man he already knew. By then, in André's opinion, the work of transformation had long been success-fully accomplished by Frion and his gang. Margaret's involvement was mostly to encourage this boy, by alternately bullying and loving him, to imagine that he was Richard.

Charles VIII apparently told James IV of Scotland that Richard of York had been "preserved many years secretly" by Margaret. She herself hinted that this was so. In 1495, in a letter to the pope in which she pleaded for Richard's claim to be given apostolic recognition, Margaret gave as a parallel example—the only one she cited in a long and rambling letter—the story of the child-prince Joash from the first Book of Kings, snatched away from those who would kill him "and secretly brought up in the house of his aunt". Margaret did not quite have this story straight; little Joash, though indeed rescued by his aunt, had in fact lain hidden for six years in "the House of the Lord", the Temple, not in his aunt's house. The idea of secretly bringing him up was also missing from the Old Testament version. Margaret seemed to have absorbed this story to make it her own. Possibly, it reflected what she herself had done.

Jean Molinet, as he chronicled the court of Burgundy, did not endorse the rumour that Margaret was creating or concealing a prince. But he kept open the notion that a prince had survived. Margaret, he wrote, had lost her brothers, her husband and her nephews. Most had died by "hard swords"; but of her nephews, only one was "snuffed out and dead". The other, presumably Richard, was merely "a prisoner":

> *J'ay veu haulte princesse*
> *D'Yorck de grant renom,*
> *De Bourgoigne duchesse,*
> *Marguerite avoit nom,*
> *Perdre par dures glaves*
> *Ses frères, son mari,*
> *Ses nepveux, l'ung esclaves,*
> *L'aultre estainct et péri.*

In 1486, a payment occurred in Margaret's household accounts at Malines for eight flagons of wine "to the son of Clarence from England". Since Simnel never went to Margaret's court, this was perhaps another prince, Warwick or Richard, in preparation. It is possible that the Simnel plot was always intended as a first test of the Yorkist waters; certainly, when it failed, Margaret was undeterred. After Stoke, as after Bosworth, she opened her court to refugees fleeing from England.

With other players, too, she had connections. She knew Brampton, who was active in Bruges and whose service included financial dealings with the Habsburgs as well as her brother's business. She could have arranged her protégé's placement in his household and even, as Hall supposed, a voyage with her "new invented Mawmet", her new doll, to Portugal. (Brampton himself never hinted in public testimony that she had been involved with him, but it would hardly have served his cause to do so.) Portugal had close blood-links to Burgundy through Charles's mother, Isabella, the great-aunt of João II, and Charles at moments of passion spoke of "we Portuguese" as though he was one. Maximilian's mother, too, had been Portuguese. In this friendly but distant place, removed from all pressing European conflicts and probably, on balance, still faintly Yorkist, a prince or quasi-prince could be safely held for a while. Brampton may deliberately have waited at Bruges to hear the outcome of Simnel's invasion, and taken the boy away with him as soon as that hope disappeared.

By 1488 Margaret was also in secret negotiations and correspondence with James IV of Scotland. On November 4th of that year, only five months after the young king's accession, an embassy of forty-two exiled Yorkists—including Richard Harliston, a former governor of Jersey, and the undrowned Lovell—was sent by Margaret to see him. Safe-conducts had been granted both to them and, provisionally, to "all other English persons whom they may draw to their cause." In early December Margaret sent another letter to James, carried by "an English herald" who was attached either to her or to an English prince who was taking shape behind her. The exchange of letters became regular, and from 1489 they were carried from Flanders by Rowland Robinson, a Durham man and old Yorkist servant who was later closely allied to Richard Plantagenet. In the same year Margaret was receiving messages, via Scotland, from Ireland, where Richard was to make his public reappearance. By 1490, a year before he landed there, she was actively spreading the rumour that he was still alive.

It is more than likely that she was organising something. If so, it was with great secrecy and circumspection; nothing was committed to paper, and nothing would be set publicly in motion without the approval or acquiescence of rulers more powerful than she was. Yet it seemed plausible enough to contemporaries that her hands were busy. Moreover, this was a woman who well understood the dynamic of acts performed in secret, whether benevolent or malevolent. Her distributions of rye to poor tenants on her Binche estates in Hainault were made by secret deliveries, so that the recipients of her charity would not know who had helped them. The action was the more powerful, and the more deserving of credit in Heaven, because its source was concealed and its effects imagined at a distance. So it could be with princes, too.

IV

IN OCTOBER OR NOVEMBER 1491, all these half-secret movements seemed to come together. The moment was right. For much of that year and the two years before, Henry VII had been helping the Duchess of Brittany to make war on France. Brittany, a vassal-state of France, had sheltered Henry when he was in exile—though France, too, had helped him. In gratitude, he had now packed Brittany with English troops and archers. But by the autumn of 1491 Charles VIII was clearly on the brink of overpowering the duchess by military force and offers of marriage. Henry, claiming that the French king "threatened the destruction" of England too, got a huge fleet ready and raised a tax from Parliament to wage full-scale war against him. Charles now had a lively interest in unsettling Henry and had, at his court, restive English agents fired with the same ambition. If Margaret wished to exploit this moment, she, too, could join in.

Charles made his first moves that summer, sending two ships to Scotland in June or July to fetch an embassy from James "to treat and communicate on certain matters touching the weal of the king and his kingdom." The leader of the French contingent was Alexander Mony-peny, Seigneur de Concressault, an expatriate Scot who was one of Charles's intimates. He was sent to discuss "great matters" with James, and was authorised to stay for at least six weeks. These "matters" were almost certainly the favouring of a Yorkist attempt against Henry.

While these ships were on the sea, one "Mr. George d'Annebar, an English knight" came in some haste to Charles from Dieppe, "wishing urgently to speak to him about the services he could do for him, as much in getting rid of the English who are in Brittany as in other matters concerning England." Despite the mangled spelling, or possibly the false name "Dunbar," this sounded like Sir George Neville, hot from Scotland, where he had been in April. Neville, a bastard scion of the line that had produced Edward IV's great rival, Richard Neville, Earl of Warwick, had been banished from England. His "other matters," like Monypeny's, probably concerned the putting up of a Yorkist claimant, true or false.

By at least September, Charles began to equip an expedition to go to Ireland on the same business. Two vessels were made ready: a ship of 100 tons, the *Mary Margot*, and a smaller craft, the *Passerose*. These were manned by up to 140 soldiers and sailors, who were to wear surcoats and carry shields marked with the red cross of St. George, *à la devise d'An-gleterre*. Thus accoutred or disguised, they were to take John Taylor the elder "and other Englishmen in his company" from Honfleur, in Nor-mandy, to unspecified harbours in Ireland and England. Taylor and his men were provided with brigandines, or coats of mail, helmets, bows, quivers, bombards, muskets and standards. The whole expedition cost Charles £1,737 *tournois*, a little less than he had spent on Monypeny's voyage.

In great excitement, Taylor passed news of the venture to his friends in England. On September 15th he wrote to John Hayes, a fellow-Yorkist and, like him, a former Clarence servant of long standing. Six years before, Hayes had been made receiver of the late duke's West Country estates on behalf of Edward, Earl of Warwick. He had also been charged to collect fees for Henry from lands in the West Country "late belonging to certain rebels of the king", and had been appointed deputy to Sir John Fortescue, overseer of the royal wine-cellar, in the ports of Exeter and Dartmouth. He preserved, therefore, a wide web of southwestern contacts that might be made active again. Taylor, calling himself "your old acquaintance", addressed Hayes with a servant's defer-ence. But he had extraordinary news to tell him, that Charles had embraced their quarrel.

> . . . Sir, ye shall understand, that the King's grace of France, by the advice and assent of his Council, will aid and support your Mas-ter's Son to his right, and all his Lovers and Servants, and take them as his friends, both by Land and by Water, and all they [*sic*] may be well assured safely to come unto France, both Bodies and Goods, and such as have no Goods they may come hither and be relieved, if they be known for true men to the quarrel; and over that, he will give help of his own Subjects, with Ships, Gold and Silver, to come into England . . . and the King and his Council say they will ask nothing in recompense, but to do it for the wrong he did, in making Henry King of England, and for the good will

he oweth unto the Son of your Master, for they be near of kin. . . . Sir, ye shall hear by other friends, Sir, the convenable time of help is come, and therefore now endeavour yourself, and put to your hand, and spare for no cost, for there shall be help in three parties out of Royaume, but here is the place most meetly for you. . . .

Taylor, fizzing with the plot, urged Hayes to show the letter to "your Master's Son's friends", to get those friends together to help, and to "make labour unto my Lady Warwick", the earl's grandmother, to write to the King of France encouraging the enterprise. In this, Taylor was over-ambitious or out of touch, for the Countess of Warwick had died the year before, leaving the orphan earl with no close relation but his sister. He needed French help more than ever.

Hayes, who did not get this news until November 26th, treated it with due caution. He did not question the bearer, but told him to go, and threw the letter into the fire. Somehow, it survived to incriminate him; he was arrested, charged with misprision (concealment of knowledge of treasonable acts) and forfeited his lands, goods and offices. On the other side of the Channel, however, the expedition had already gone ahead as planned.

Charles, when commissioning the ships, did not seem to have passed on the purpose of this voyage to his captains. It was understood to be open-ended; they could take two months over it, if need be, until they found the right place at which to land. Taylor, on the other hand, his head still full of Warwick, claimed to know exactly what the king intended. He saw the venture as the first leg of an invasion, to be reinforced by armed help from Ireland and Scotland (the other two of the "three parties out of Royaume") and to reach its climax with Warwick's release and enthronement. No doubt he expected Hayes to be laying the ground at home. In that, of course, he was disappointed.

The end of the voyage was not recorded anywhere, but the official confession suggested in any case a quite different scene. In that version of events, Taylor and his companions were simply in Ireland in the autumn of 1491 when Piers, out of nowhere, suddenly arrived. Nothing had been planned. They had not been meant to meet, and there was no indication of any French-backed expedition. Two Irishmen, Atwater and Hubert Burke, from the ruling family of Connaught, had joined Taylor, together with Stephen Poytron, another Englishman. When they stumbled on

Piers, strolling glamorously in the street, they saw his potential immediately, but so did everyone around them. The Yorkist plotters merely joined in, adding their ideas to the general tumult of interest in him. Far from being trained in anything, the Piers of the confession came to Ireland as a blank sheet, to be cut into shape or painted in the colours his sponsors thought they wanted.

According to this version of the story, Richard, Duke of York was in fact their last choice for the character he should play. The people of Cork, predictably enough, thought the boy in silk from the Breton boat "should be the Duke of Clarence's son that was before time at Dublin." But Taylor, for all his interest in a Warwick plot, did not pursue this idea, perhaps because one false Warwick was enough. Instead, a different scheme took wing. Poytron, together with Atwater, accosted Piers and told him, with emphatic oaths, "that they knew well that I was King Richard's bastard son."

The confession said that this was the role Piers first agreed to be trained for. He was to be taught, presumably, that "proficiency in all good manners" which is almost all that history records of King Richard's bastard son, John of Gloucester. John's claim was a weak one, but as the illegitimate son of the last king he had a slightly stronger title than Henry had. He had been treated, too, as a Yorkist prince, lodged in palaces and clothed in silk jackets, and had been maintained for a while by Henry himself on a pension of £20 a year. Piers could probably pass for him already, for all anyone knew. It was only "after this"—after they had played with the notion of making him John—that his sponsors decided he should be Richard of York, "because King Richard's bastard son was in the hands of the King of England." As he was.

Henry, in his letter to Talbot in 1493, gave the same impression, though in a different order, of the late appearance of Richard of York in the planning of the "great abusion". The boy's first identity, he wrote, had been Richard III's bastard son; "after that", the son of the Duke of Clarence; "and now the second son of our father, king Edward the Fourth, whom God assoile." *And now.* His identity could have been changed even after the boy left Ireland; it was just a whim, the last in a series of rash and ridiculous inventions.

As Henry would later present it, the "invention" of this boy came fairly close to alchemy. Like the various practitioners he paid from time to time for their experiments with powders and their demonstrations of "multiplying", so the Yorkist plotters, lacking anyone authentic, tried to manufacture gold out of dross. They believed, as Henry liked to believe, that the process was possible in principle. According to a treatise on alchemy of 1477 that Edward IV had among his books, Ramon Lull, the Catalan philosopher, had once succeeded in making four ladies of silver and four knights of gold, bearing on their robes the story of their transformations:

> Of old horses' shoes, said one, I was iron;
> Now I am silver, as good as you desire.
> I was, said another, iron fette from the mine;
> But now I am gold, pure, perfect and fine.
> Once was I copper, of an old red pan,
> Now I am good silver, said the third woman.
> The fourth said, I was copper, that grew in filthy place;
> Now I am perfect gold, made by God's grace.

Some similar persistent experimentation with rubbish seemed able to produce princes, at least in Flanders and Ireland.

The official confession implied that it took a lot of labour. Piers Osbeck, fresh from the boat, had to be made a plausible Englishman before he could be made a prince. "[They] made me to learn English," the confession said, the first essential act. By this account—so different from Vergil's, where he was fluent years before—he already spoke a little. He had gone to John Strewe's in Middelburg "for to learn the language" (presumably, though not certainly, English), and had then lain sick for months beside the House of the English Merchant Adventurers in Antwerp, where the sound of the language outside the window might slowly have become familiar. When he was approached in Cork he understood what people were saying to him, and seemed to know enough to protest that what they were saying was wrong.

Brampton, however, implied at Setubal that "Piris" spoke only French. In Middelburg as a runaway he had sought out French children as friends, and he tagged along too with French-speakers in Portugal. In 1494 the Earl of Kildare, who had flirted very briefly with him, remarked indignantly in a letter to the Earl of Ormond that he had been accused of comforting, aiding and lying with the "French lad". This may well have been how the boy appeared to him in Ireland, as yet unschooled. On the other hand, it may have referred to the principal power,

France, that was then behind him; or, since Kildare was trying hard at that point to content the king's mind, as he put it, it may have been an ingratiating reference to Henry's own dismissive term for him, *le garçon*.

Piers said he did not want to learn English, but was forced to "against my will". Resistance would have made the learning sulky and slow; presumably it went in somehow. Yet it may have been a strange sort of English, all the same. He was in Ireland. His chief Irish sponsors, Atwater and the Anglo-Irish Earl of Desmond, would have spoken quaint and heavily accented English; Kildare, although a virtual king in Ireland and among the most anglicised of the Irish rulers, was barely literate, signing his name with a rough "G. E. of K". These lords employed priests and secretaries endowed with proper education, but still one that was far beneath the standards of the court in London. The Yorkist plotters were aiming very high, and with difficult material.

They themselves would have been little better educated than the Anglo-Irish lords, and their speech provincial. Foreign supporters of their new prince might not care or notice if he spoke like a Devon bailiff, but Englishmen would. In his preface to the *Eneydos*, Caxton noted how much speech differed from place to place in England: so much so that a London mercer, asking a woman for eggs sixty miles away in Kent, could not make her understand until his companion asked her for "eyren". England was a patchwork of different usages and accents where the language of princes, delivered "in polished and ornate terms craftily", was not to be heard outside the court.

The teaching of court English to Piers, therefore, would have been something of a miracle. But miracles occurred. Goodness knows, even magpies could be taught phrases of *politesse;* and James IV in 1493 discovered that, if you confined a dumb woman with her infants to the empty island of Inchkeith in the Firth of Forth, they could turn out speaking something that was very like good Hebrew. Many poets of the time wrote in an English so heavily Frenchified and Latinised that it could usefully disguise more basic errors. Stephen Hawes, a groom of Henry's chamber, thought he made his groom's English noble by using words like "respeccion," "facundiously," "finishment" and "solacious". Perhaps others would have thought so, too, had Piers tried.

He would have had to be trained in manners, too, and again from scratch, before the more delicate and detailed remembering of Richard could begin. His sponsors "taught me what I should do and say," he said in the confession. According to that document he had already learned, at most, the conduct required of a page. He knew to keep his nails clean, not to spit across the table, not to jiggle his feet or turn his back on people. Besides that, he had perhaps learned how to make conversation (though not with his betters, to whom he did not speak), and how to do something entertaining, such as play the lute or sing. He was not completely unpolished, though almost so.

A servant could be turned into a royal herald in a matter of days; it had been done before. Philippe de Commines related how in 1475 Louis XI had seized on *un varlet*, a simple servant, put a herald's tabard on him, and sent him into Edward IV's camp to deliver a speech on Louis's behalf. The man seemed, in Commines's opinion, not up to the job at all, "fit neither in stature nor in aspect", although he could express himself "tolerably enough". He was also terrified at the proposal, and fell down at Commines's feet begging not to be sent. Commines tried to persuade the king to employ someone "more proper", but Louis would not. Over a night and a day Commines and the king instructed the man; a coat of arms was made up for him, an escutcheon was borrowed, his boots and his cloak were fetched and, with a final briefing, he was sent into the English camp. There he acquitted himself so smoothly, to everyone's surprise, that Edward dismissed him with a present of four nobles, and Commines did not report that the imposture was detected. But that was a piece of play-acting of, at most, a few hours' duration, requiring no change of language and only a few degrees of separation on the social scale. It was easy compared with what was required of Piers.

Again, his sponsors could hardly help him. The roughness of Kildare's manners, when he visited London, astonished Henry VII's court. (Among other things, he took the king by the hand; talked bawdy to him; and told him, with liberal "beJaysuses", three unflattering tales of the Bishop of Meath "as though he were among his fellows in his own country", reducing the king and his company to gales of laughter that he could not understand.) Desmond had had to be forced, by Richard III, to abandon his warrior's cloak and leggings for proper doublets and hats. Atwater was of the merchant class, presumably not without intelligence, but with no knowledge of the maze of etiquette in which princes moved. The same was true of the other hangers-on in Ireland mentioned in the confession. None could have taught Piers as he needed to be taught.

Nonetheless, against these odds, the confession said the plotters took him and princified him. Geronymo Zurita described the last, essential part of the process: "They called him Richard, and proclaimed him as Duke of York, and gave him hope that they would put him in his kingdom of England, which legitimately belonged to him if he was who he said he was." Much of the instruction might have been difficult; but the infusion of a little hunger, the waving before his eyes of a king's life, could have made the boy warm to the project on his own. "Why kneel ye to me?" cried the teenage Arthur, astonished, as Sir Ector and Sir Kay fell to the ground before him. With every day that men knelt to him, waited on him, laid out his clothes and made up his fires in that Irish winter, Piers could enter a little deeper into the prince's part. "How very pleasing it must be to a human creature," ran one of Henry's books, *L'imaginacion de vraye noblesse*, "when he realises he is of noble generation and of ancient lineage, for . . . those sprung from a noble line are more inclined than others to be courtly, debonair, frank and virtuous." When his imagination thrilled to his nobility, the alchemy was performed.

This arduous experiment, however, may never have occurred, for the opening scene on the quayside at Cork was probably quite different. When lords entered towns, either as rulers or as guests, the clergy and town officers would come out to meet them. They carried, typically, the town Cross and the relics, to which the visitor knelt in veneration, and holy water, with which he was asperged. The officers of Cork may well have been there to receive Richard Plantagenet in this way, with honour. The oath sworn by Desmond to Henry five years later strongly implied that he had "received" the young man on his arrival in the town, but was not to do so in future. Certainly this was as likely as the thought that the officers would come, with their holy articles, to sort out a quayside argument between some Englishmen and a ship's boy.

Taylor's French ships, too, bobbing in the harbour with their red-and-white panoply as the boy arrived, had gone there for some purpose. They were not an invasion force; the soldiers and sailors were there to defend and manage the *Mary Margot*, and only Taylor and his nine companions were meant to land. Looked at closely, they seemed more ceremonial than warlike. Taylor's small band was an armed escort for someone royal, or presumed royal: carrying standards, with special helmets and breastplates for four of them, and imitating, with their bows and quivers, the elite archer corps that guarded Charles himself. Stowed in the hold was a single suit of precious white armour costing £49 *tournois*, much like the armour ordered the next year by Henry for his war with Charles. This was gear for a prince, whether real or imagined.

In his letter to Isabella, Richard explained that he had gone to Ireland from Portugal for a purpose. Henry too, in his letter to Talbot, kept a sense of purpose in the journey. "At his first into Ireland," the king said, the feigned lad "called himself" a Yorkist prince, no forcing necessary. Pregent Meno was arrested at sea for having "conveyed" him, as though he was his servant and under orders to make trouble. James Ware, an Irish historian of the mid-seventeenth century, said many asserted that the young man had openly "carried himself" as Richard, Duke of York, when he arrived in Cork, and that the citizens had joyfully received him. His letters had preceded him, and Richard told Isabella that his "cousins" had recognised him. There was nothing random about his coming, and no confusion, either, about his name.

The prince who had come to Ireland was not necessarily a real one. He could still be a contrivance, a young man merely trained to look, speak and act the part. But authenticity had never been the point of the plots that had multiplied since Bosworth. Whoever he was, men immediately ran after him, as Brampton said: an authority he could hardly have enjoyed if he had come to Ireland as a simple foreign lad. Immediately, they pinned their hopes on him and saw him, in their minds, enthroned. And he, with a prince's smile, accepted their devotion.

V

IN THE EVENT, the reimagining and the remembering of Richard, Duke of York were not so far apart. If the real Richard was alive, he had been stripped of his titles, taken out of England and concealed abroad in a process that was much like death. For safety's sake, he had been made to stop looking and behaving like a prince. And he had been made to forget. This was Richard Plantagenet's own version of what had happened to him. He had lost everything, he told Isabella, and the connection with royal blood had been severed; he had become a hollowed-out child whose only occupation was wandering and weeping. Like the human soul fallen from Heaven, grieving for it knew not what, he drifted through the world oblivious of the fact that he had ever been a prince.

In a speech that was given to him by Vergil, ostensibly delivered in

Scotland in 1495, the resurrected Richard told his listeners that he had been obliged for a long time "almost to forget myself", *ego vero per aetatem mei ipsius fere oblitus*. In the end, a slow unfolding, he had begun to know what he was; but he had forgotten so deeply that he had needed strong prompting in order to remember. "At last, when I had been thoroughly taught what I was," he became himself again. The word Richard used was not *quis*, but *qualis*; he sought to recover not who, but what sort of man, he was. Having been tasked so hard to forget his name and back-ground, he could not remember even that fundamental.

It could be argued, of course, that any effort of forgetting which he had been forced to make had not been applied to a prince's life at all. Instead, it had quietly obscured his life as an organ scholar or a boatman's boy. Perhaps this was the identity he had had to bury in darkness, forget-ting his low manners, his rough friends and his father's quayside lan-guage. Insofar as he remembered it, it could become the prince's other life, entered into for a time like a station of Purgatory and then, by God's grace, left again. The central task was the same: to forget utterly the tiny acts and feelings that might betray him until he was allowed to be himself again, whoever that person was.

Deliberate forgetfulness of the self was usually a sin. The churchmen called it *acedia* or *caecia cordis*, heart-blindness and loss of inward sight, applying it especially to a man's obliviousness of where he had come from in order to exalt himself. The boat boy's *acedia* was oiled with ambition and vainglory, but the prince's would have been allowed for a while, as long as it did not slip as far as wanhope or despair. The line between self-forgetting and madness induced by grief was a very fine one. A woman in mourning was often said to be "out of herself", and only after a little time would be "set in her mind" again. In 1486 the friends and family of Thomas Langford, who by continuous "vexations" had been "put from his remembrance and mind", tried to organise, if they could, his "finding of himself". By Richard's own account, he had needed much the same sort of gradual persuasion.

In order to live as a prince, he needed either to remember himself or to be remembered by others. The word meant reassembling: fragment by fragment, he would be remade, as Christ had commanded His disciples in the upper room to remember His Body in the wine and bread. The process was always an effort. Somehow the image had to be summoned from the back of the head, where Memory kept a cobwebbed and ramshackle cupboard of past things, before it could be imprinted in the heart, as in a book. Henry VII promised Ferdinand of Spain that he would keep all secrets communicated to him "in the shrine of his heart", both a place of careful keeping and a library of imprinted confidences. This was where Richard Plantagenet needed to be reassembled: in Yorkist, and in English, hearts.

The act of remembrance was an antidote both to absence and to death. By writing of lost loved ones, thinking of them, repeating their name in prayers, they came alive. In Skelton's poem "Philip Sparrow," a girl mourning her pet bird brought him to life merely by embroidering him, stitch by stitch, onto a piece of silk; with the last dip of the needle, the bird flinched and bled. A counterfeit prince, too, could be made that way, reassembled with each stitch and brushstroke into the figure of the real one. And perhaps in a while, if you pricked the young man who walked the world as Richard, he too, in some mysterious way, would stain the needle with Richard's blood.

Remembrance and imagination were in any case perilously close. Imagination drew partly from objects that were remembered, while memory could conjure up pictures that were imagined. Georges Chastellain once found himself on the brink of a dream, *entre-oublié*, forgotten and forgetting, still in his clothes and half-dozing on a bench a little before dawn, "and with my imagination full of impressions of the day that had passed, afterthoughts beginning to rise into my spirit." Memories had become imaginings. Conversely, Earl Rivers in his *Cordyal* asked readers to fix the vile images of Hell in their memory, although as yet they had traversed that dreadful place—scalded by fire, frozen by unendurable cold—only in imagination. Their hearts would now be stamped with Hell as if they remembered it; as if they had travelled there in unconsciousness or dreams, like the shivering heroes of the books they read.

Richard Plantagenet, newly remade, could do the same. When prompted, he remembered another life; or perhaps he only imagined it, by repetition fixing it so deeply that he believed he remembered it. He was made to repeat his life-story often, especially by Margaret when she later publicly displayed him: a sign of careful and deliberate imprinting. Those who talked to him were impressed and convinced, Bernard André said, by the details he could recall of his life as a prince. "He showed plainly," he wrote, "and rehearsed from quick and easy memory all the times of Edward IV, and all his servants and household officers, as if he had been brought up there and knew it from earliest childhood. And he added, besides, circumstantial details of places, times and persons, with which he very easily swayed the fickle minds of those men." Vergil agreed: the young man was trained "so that afterwards he might readily remember everything, and convince everyone by his performance that he was a child of the House of York." It is not clear whether these alluring memories were fetched from the back of his head, or from the red and beating book of his fresh-imprinted heart.

Almost any Yorkist refugee who crossed the new prince's path, from his re-emergence onwards, could have brought him memories of the court if he needed them. These need not have been sophisticated but, more convinc-ingly, the sort of thing a small boy would recall. He needed to know his brother's games, his sister's teases, the names of horses and servants. He would need pocket descriptions of family acquaintances, from retainers to archbishops, to tie to the people he might meet. He would need rooms and gardens. Though some supporters would be happy to demand no details from a memory that might be uncomfortably fragile, others would insist on them. The prince would have required help as much as the boat boy, for, as he said, he had purposely emptied his mind of the faces and scenes from his previous life. Those eight desolate years came in handy. You might well not have been able to tell, had you caught him in some hesitation or mis-take, whether it was exile or falseness talking.

The sort of memories recorded by Bluemantle Pursuivant, one of Edward's heralds, at Windsor in 1472 would have set him in good stead. Bluemantle noted the white silk tents over beds and baths, the nightcaps of ginger and syrups, carpets underfoot and, in the park, grazing bucks glee-fully set upon by the king's wild packs of hounds. The chambers of the queen—chambers where Richard spent much of his time—were noisy with games of ivory ninepins and indoor bowls. Some Yorkists would have seen Richard's marriage, some the funeral of the little girl he had kissed before the altar. Some could describe the gold head of St. George in the king's chapel at Windsor, or the fabulous gold Virgin that Edward had bought for £160 in 1478, sitting with Jesus in her arms on a cushion of silver under a pavilion of gold set with rubies, sapphires and pearls. Esteemed vistors might have seen the king's books of Josephus and Livy and the Trojan Wars, the heavy leather covers opening like a box, with their great ornamented clasps, to show the close-ranked helmeted soldiers fighting and bleeding.

In June 1478, when Richard was four, someone had brought a lion to court. Did he remember that muzzled sinewy beast, or the thick chain that held it? In the same year, one of the bedrooms was hung with new tapestries showing the story of Noah. Did he remember the animals two-by-two, the rainbow, or the dove with the olive branch, in silk knots under his small patting hands? At his wedding jousts that January, Earl Rivers had appeared as St. Anthony the hermit, with a hermit's house made of black velvet, complete with bell-tower and windows and a gar-den fenced with gold trees, all built into his livery and that of his horse. The bell in the bell-tower even rang; could a boy forget that?

Among those who were associated with him in Ireland or before it, several had their own memories of the court of Edward IV. Taylor the younger had been there as a yeoman of the chamber, probably as a very young man. The Black Book described his duties as "to make beds, to bear or hold torches, to set boards, to apparel all chambers . . . to take messages." He had to watch the king "by course," on a rota, at night as he slept, fetch drink and blankets for him, and possibly let in paramours. Commines, doing similar duty once for the Duke of Burgundy, had to walk up and down the room with him while the duke was assailed by night thoughts. Taylor would also have known the king's favourite dogs, which shared the chamber; one of the chamber pages' jobs was to clear up "defaults of hounds". These scenes could easily be shifted from his memory to the receptive mind of a boy, until he too believed that he had seen, through an open door, the gorgeous figured velvets laid out ready, or had dragged a dog away by its studded collar from the damask hangings of the bed.

Stephen Frion, too, who may have known the boy for some time before he came to Ireland to find him, had memories to pass on. From him, the resurrected Richard could piece together the style and personali-ties of the royal secretariat and details of visits by ambassadors. The single letter of Frion's that survives, dating from 1480, when Richard was six or seven, also mentioned a huge boar's "tooth" Edward had just received from Louis XI of France ("the biggest that was ever seen, one foot and three fingers long and more than two fingers wide"). It came with "the dried head of a beast like a wild stag, done up in the most marvellous way you ever saw." Frion said he had no idea what these strange presents signi-fied. To a small boy, they may have meant nothing more complicated than hunting, and finding, monsters in the deep French woods.

André suggested, however, that the young man's "memories" had come from a different source. "Whatever I told you so readily of bygone signs or times," he had him confess to his followers, "I kept all that in my memory from when I was very small, for I was the little servant-boy of a former Jew, the godson of King Edward . . . in England, and my master was in the most intimate circle of the king and his children." The "former Jew," of course, was Brampton. The boy had not only been his servant, but by André's account—written for Henry—had lived with him at court in close association with the king's children, including the little prince whom he was to impersonate.

Brampton, of course, would have denied all this. Yet he could not deny that he and the boy had known each other at least a little; and if they had ever lived together as father and son, as Brampton said the boy had wanted to, there was plenty that "the captain" could have told him. Besides his boasts of the battles he had helped Edward win and the rebels he had sent packing, Brampton had memories of his service as an usher of Edward's chamber, two stages or so higher than Taylor the younger was. As such, he was often abroad fetching "stuff" at huge expense for the king's Wardrobe, including, in 1478, seventy-seven yards of black velvet. He also lent Edward large sums of money and probably received, in per-son, his military commands; he revelled in the king's sponsorship at his "standing-up baptism" and was close enough, he implied, to feel the king's back-slapping cordiality and to glow at his least familiarity. It is hard to know how intimate he really was. But he knew enough, for certain, to add precious fragments to the store of the page who waited on his wife.

The pieces, then, were there to be assembled. Nor was it difficult to fix such scenes in a young man's imagination as something he himself treasured and remembered. The techniques were laid out explicitly in devotional works of the time. By reading such books as St. Bonaventure's *Mirror of the Blessed Life of Jesu Christ*—found then in most literate house-holds, as well as in Margaret's library—Richard could learn how to enter, by contemplation, into another world and another life, that of Jesus. He was asked to make himself "present in his soul" in the stable at Bethlehem, drawing close as Mary wrapped her Child in the kerchief from her head and washed Him with milk from her full and aching breasts. He was made to see, "as though . . . with bodily eyes", the livid lacerations on Jesus's back after the scourging, and how He shivered with cold as He tried to find His clothes. This was true imagination, as St. Bonaventure said. This was the "oneing and knitting" of his soul to Jesus.

At times, he was asked to do more than observe and suffer with the characters. He himself had to enter into the story. After the death of Jesus, as Mary, John and Mary Magdalene wept at the foot of the Cross, St. Bonaventure enjoined him to comfort them, "praying them to eat some-thing, for they were still fasting . . . and so taking their blessing / go thy way." So, summoning his courage, he could walk up to them (Our Lady in her blue robe of constancy, her face still swooning and pale, the Mag-dalene with her disordered red hair). He could touch them, on a shoulder or the hem of a sleeve. They would turn to him; they would speak to him, just a few words, for him alone, as he knelt among the dry stones on the hill of Golgotha. Of course, this conversation had not truly happened as the world would understand it. But why did his heart move as it did, if he had not been present with them?

In the case of Richard Plantagenet, there was one scene in particular that he was obliged to see in his soul and re-create for those he was trying to persuade. This was the moment of his escape, the moment when he had not died. No other person's memories could help him here; in effect, he was alone. It might be supposed that he would revel in this, laying out images of the greatest pathos before his astonished listeners. Yet nothing that survives suggests that he dwelled on what had happened in the Tower.

The most detailed account appears in his letter to Isabella of Castile in 1493. Letters of this sort had been written to most of the rulers of Europe: to Maximilian, to the kings of Denmark and Scotland, and to anyone else in power who could help. Each of them went out with a cover-letter from his protector of the moment. Richard himself implied that he sent many from Ireland in the eight months or so he was there, from the autumn of 1491 until the summer of the next year. One certainly arrived in Scotland: in March 1492 the king paid £9 for letters from "King Edward's son and the Earl of Desmond." The story in them would have been the same as the one Isabella heard.

Most gracious and excellent Princess, my most noble Lady and cousin, I commend myself entirely to your majesty.

When the Prince of Wales, eldest son of Edward King of England of pious memory, my very Dear lord and father, was put to death, a death to be pitied, and I myself, at the age of about nine, was also delivered up to a certain lord to be killed, it pleased divine clemency that this lord, pitying my innocence, should preserve me alive and unharmed. However, he forced me first to swear upon the sacred body of Our Lord that I would not reveal [my] name, lineage or family to anyone at all until a certain number of years [had passed]. Then he sent me abroad. . . .

The letter began abruptly enough, almost shockingly, with Edward dying, but then moved immediately away. At no point, then or later, did Richard seem to describe how his brother had died. In his proclamation of 1496 he omitted him entirely. The verb used in the letter for the killing of Edward, as for his own near-murder, was *extinguere*, to quench or snuff out a light: a word suggesting neither swords nor blood, though not so specific as to mean suffocation. His brother, the shadow, died bloodlessly. His death was to be pitied, *miserandus*, but the unemotional gerund suggested a duty of pitying rather than spontaneous tears. It was as if Richard had neither witnessed nor imagined this death, nor felt for the brother who had suffered it. No adjectives of either love or grief were applied to Edward. In a few words, he was gone.

Richard himself was described only a little more clearly. All that was given was his age, "about nine," *nonum fere agens annum*. There should have been no "about" about it; but in a letter of this sort, intended mostly to arouse compassion, pinpoint exactness was unnecessary. Vagueness was a virtue: blurring faces, blurring times and places, as if the whole picture was seen through tears. He, or rather the Latin secretary, used *fere* again a little later, to explain how he had wandered "for about eight years." Fuzziness about his own age was suspicious, but may not have sown such doubts at the time. It could be attributed to disorientation as well as to deceit, or could be considered merely normal. Age was ignored for the most part (or guessed at with a casual "or thereabout") except in the case of the very young, the very old, or kings dying. Robert Fabyan thought Richard was about seven when he went to the Tower; Dominic Mancini thought he was eight. By those standards, Richard Plantagenet's letter was accurate enough.

The matter of his age disposed of, the letter began to race on. He was handed over, Richard wrote, to "a certain lord" to be killed. This, one might suppose, was the most terrifying moment of his life. It was dismissed in a few businesslike words, with no sense of where, when or why the events had unfolded. The story was perhaps assumed to be famous by this time, too famous even to mention the Tower. The lord to whom Richard was delivered, Edward's murderer, seemed set to kill again, but softened at the sight of Richard. He was evidently someone in high authority, but it was impossible to work out exactly who he was.

These particular details, Richard implied, had not been forgotten (as so much had been) but suppressed. The "certain lord" had made him suppress them. He had done so roughly: the word *adegerit* suggested physical pushing, and the whole scene was dark, overlaid with fear and obscurity. All that glimmered in this letter was the moment when the lord's face changed from murderous intent to pity, and the moment when the pyx or monstrance containing the Sacrament was brought for the boy to kiss. That in itself implied that he was hustled somewhere else, or that a priest came, but the imagined scene did not change: the boy, the lord, Christ's Body, the dark. At some point, Richard hinted, when "a certain number of years had elapsed," he would remember and reveal everything about this scene. But not yet.

It is not known for certain that he ever disclosed it in detail. Yet bits and pieces survive, in the chronicles of Burgundy and the Low Countries, that may be fragments of the story as Richard Plantagenet told it round Europe. The "Divisie-chronicle" of Holland, Zeeland and Friesland, written down around 1500, contains this passage:

> some say that Henry Earl of Buckingham killed only one child and spared the other which he had lifted from the font [that is, he had been his godfather], and had him secretly abducted out of the country. This child was called Richard, and after being in Portugal he came into France to King Louis the Eleventh [*sic*] and from there he secretly came into Brabant to Lady Margaret his aunt.

Molinet, at the Burgundian court, and Commines, at the French, also mentioned Buckingham's involvement, though not as the murderer-abductor directly. And Molinet produced, uniquely, stories from the Tower. In particular, he gave a remarkable account of the boys' encounter with the men sent to kill them, perhaps derived from a scene he had heard Plantagenet describe—after 1492, or possibly before it—in the state rooms at Malines.

> The elder son was asleep, and the younger one was awake, and he sensed something bad was happening, because he started to say: "Hey, brother, wake up, they're coming to kill you!" Then he said to the officers, "Why are you killing my brother? Kill me and let him live!"

Dr. Argentine may have passed on some stories, but not this one. This was a scene only one of the boys, or one of the killers, could have described with any plausibility. Somehow, it had reached the court of Burgundy, and with Richard playing the hero's part. His brave words to the killers were already famously moving: they were the same as those given to the Virgin in popular meditations, as she upbraided the Jews for wounding Christ and asked them, instead, to kill her. The "learn to dance / learn to die" story may well have come from the same source: the witty little dancing prince, alongside his "unsophisticated" brother, now stirring his audience to sympathetic tears.

Diplomatic correspondence did not allow flights like this. Yet as the story of Richard ran on in his letter, it began to gather pace. He was sent abroad "with two men who were to guard me and govern me", escorts who did not sound entirely benevolent. And so, "an orphan deprived of the King my father and the King my brother, exiled from the Kingdom, stripped of my native land, my inheritance and all my fortune, having fled through great dangers I led my miserable life in fear and tears and affliction, and for about eight years I lay in hiding in various countries. . . ."

Conveniently enough, some might think, he was not allowed to say who his guards and governors were. In any case, they disappeared from his life when "at length, one of those who governed me died, and the other was sent back to his own country, and I never saw him again." This implied that one of his guardians was not English and was still under outside orders, but the veil was so completely drawn that even these clues were uncertain. As it happened, the reward given to Brampton in 1484 for "services to be rendered by him according to certain indentures" was also made, in the same form on the same day, to "Christopher Colyns, esquire". Colyns had been, like Brampton, one of Edward IV's gentleman-ushers; he was also a draper and a collector of tonnage and poundage in the port of London, who might have known how to get goods, or boys, secretly out of the port and abroad. In November 1486 Henry pardoned him, three years before he pardoned Brampton; but Colyns ("late of the county of Kent, late citizen of London") seems still to have been wandering outside the country.

Richard himself implied that he did not know who these men were, just as he had no idea which countries he was passing through. The only certainty was that, "scarcely out of childhood", he was now alone. He was also desperately sad and poor: as poor as the Lancastrian exiles Commines saw, begging barefoot and barelegged for bread in Flanders in the 1460s, and poorer than Henry had been as he faced "a thousand deadly dangers" in his fourteen years of exile in Brittany. Richard could not cap "Henry Richmond, the evil grasper of the kingdom of England", as he called him, in length of absence; but he could cap him in indigence and in pervasive sadness.

No more about the great escape was mentioned in Richard's letter. He offered his readers a story that might have seemed, to many, too sketchy to be true. It is possible, though, that more fragments survived not only in the continental chronicles, but in the plausible speech to the court of Scotland that Polydore Vergil gave him later. Vergil never saw the letter to Isabella, though it is possible—since he asked the Scottish king personally for documentary help with his history—that he was shown Richard's first letter to James. In any event, the story he made Richard tell was remarkably similar to the one that was sent to Spain.

I think you are not unaware, O King, of the misery which befell the issue of Edward King of England, the fourth of that name. In case you do not know, I am his son, saved from slaughter by the beneficence of most high and almighty God. For my father Edward, when he was dying, appointed as guardian of his sons his brother Richard, Duke of Gloucester, whom he hoped to make more attached to his sons the more he loaded him with favours. But alas, to my misery, it happened otherwise than he imagined. That man was not the guardian of our line but almost its extinguisher. Behold, suddenly the cruel tyrant, seized with ambition to be king, ordered that my brother Edward and I should be killed together. But the man who had been given the unspeakable task of murder-ing us, pitiful innocents that we were, loathed the abominable deed as much as he feared not to do it. Being thus in two minds, at last, in order to satisfy the tyrant and in part escape the blame, having murdered my brother, he saved me, and allowed me to leave the country with only one servant to keep me company . . .

Beyond the striking similarities, several details diverged. The reference to Gloucester was new; but this was probably Vergil's addition, since the resurrected Richard, perhaps diplomatically, did not mention his uncle in anything that survives. The "certain lord" was now merely a man, *ille;* there was no oath of secrecy, and only one companion who was sub- servient to the boy. This man was described later, Vergil "reporting" Richard, as "a loyal household servant of Edward his father", narrowing the field a little and raising again the shadow of Brampton, if you assumed the rescue to be true. As always, however, that was a large assumption.

Neither the letter nor the speech saw any dynastic purpose in Richard's rescue. He was saved out of simple pity, then abandoned, as if he had no usefulness to those who had pitied him. This was sad, but also inexplicable. Why should he be saved, if his brother was killed? How had he been taken from the Tower? If he was truly a prince and a claimant, whose claims people knew, how was it that he had been left for eight years to wander alone? Looked at hard, the story was unconvincing on all those points. But you could also argue—if Yorkist sympathy inclined you to— that this letter, in its very artlessness, was the authentic voice of a trauma- tised young man.

At the moment of his emergence in Ireland, no work seems to have been done on the details of his past. The imaginations of Richard were limited to what was necessary, no more. The story was still crude. But the most important point of his letters was a different one. More than any- thing, he had to establish himself as the second son of Edward IV. Whatever authority he claimed to have came from his father, not from himself. Deprived of his father, he wrote, forbidden even to remember him, he had been reduced to nothing. The repeated invocation of Edward in these letters and the heavy, almost physical, sense of him were the first steps towards the remembering of Richard: as if the coat of golden chain-mail that hung above the dead king's tomb, covered with crimson velvet, embroidered with the arms of England and France in gold, rubies and pearls, stirred with the limbs of a prince who was now old enough and strong enough to put it on.

He and his sponsors sent out the letters, and waited.

CHAPTER THREE

Evidence of Things Seen

Richard Plantagenet's months in Ireland were spent in half-hiding. Despite that, Henry had already been sneaking vicarious glimpses of him. He knew he was there, by naval intelligence, as soon as he arrived, and confidently told the pope that the French were behind him. At this point all he knew of the young man himself, according to Vergil, was that he was saying he was Richard, Edward's son. Henry had no idea whether this was true, but the very claim may have made him ill; his apothecary's payments that autumn were seven times higher than usual.

Accordingly, he took no chances. On December 7th, 1491, John Ismay was sent to check on the readiness of ships between Southampton, Land's End and Bristol; the next day, a force of two hundred soldiers was dispatched under Thomas Garth and James Ormond to "suppress the king's rebels" in Ireland. That same month a ship sailed to catch Meno, who had "conveyed the Child" (Henry's words, and apparently his emphasis) across the sea. In February the *Margaret of Barnstaple*, "among other vessels", fitted with guns, several barrels of gunpowder and 110 men armed with bows and bills, was deployed to "go on warfare" along the Irish coasts. Spies kept Henry supplied with extra soundings and sightings.

Around June 1492, an invitation came from France promising Richard—as he told Isabella—help and assistance against the "criminal usurper", Henry Tudor. It was late in coming, but all the more welcome because his supporters in Ireland, warier now than when Simnel had appeared, had failed to coalesce. The invitation was accepted, and some-time in late June or July the new-fledged prince was fetched by Stephen Frion and Louis de Lucques, one of Charles VIII's chief naval captains. As Richard put it, they came "with many ships and a great company" to "call me forth". Henry, in London, would not have been surprised. "The French are so on the watch to increase their power by any villainy," he had written that January to Ludovico Sforza, the Duke of Milan, "and what mischief the French are machinating against us, or what snares they are laying, we pass over in silence."

Charles viewed the sponsoring of Richard Plantagenet as the ulti-mate prop of his defences against England. For much of that year, well aware of the vast fleet that Henry was assembling on the south coast and the English armies gathered to defend Brittany, he had been raising heavy taxes to fortify his own coasts and the castles on his borders. Armies had been recruited too, including mercenaries from Switzerland. As he explained in his tax-raising letters to his people, Charles felt surrounded by enemies on every side, especially by "our old enemies and adversaries the English", who would not hesitate to undermine him by malice or sheer force. The last part of his war strategy, as he explained it in a letter of September 30th, had been to get several warships ready and send some to Ireland, to bring the Duke of York to France. "And both this and all the other things concerning the security of our kingdom have put it in such good order and provision that the English and our enemies will not be able to put anything over on us, for which may our Creator be praised." In Richard, Charles had a rival to Henry who could, perhaps, topple him; or, at the least, make him beg the French for terms.

So Charles hoped. But for much of 1492 he was not sure what the prince in Ireland amounted to, and bided his time. It is probable that Tay-lor the elder, sent the previous autumn, had reported that Richard was not as ready to launch his claim as the king supposed. At the beginning of June, in Dieppe, an Italian merchant who was being pumped for the usual news of England—how many ships ready, what tonnage, how

many men, what Henry intended—was asked what the English were say/
ing about "King Edward's son who is in Ireland". His answer, based as it
seemed to be on quayside chat in Portsmouth and Southampton, was not
encouraging. "They talked about him more before than they do now," he
said. "Some said [then] that he wasn't there at all, others that he was the
son of King Edward's brother. Anyway, for the moment they don't
bother with him much." Perhaps, if the English themselves were not
bothered, the King of France should not be.

Nonetheless, in the end Charles brought him over, braving the
English ships and the roving German pirates. Béraud Stuart d'Aubigny,
an expatriate Scot who was Charles's chamberlain and one of his coun/
cillors, welcomed the prince at Honfleur, the port from which Taylor had
departed. As Richard arrived Honfleur was being strongly fortified, with
two towers and a gate, against the English; and here was Charles's other
defensive ploy, a slight young man whose arrival was described as a
descente, just like the *descente* expected any day by Henry on Calais. The
word implied that he came in armed strength, and the record confirmed it.
He was surrounded with *ses gens*, usually men/at/arms, as well as atten/
dants and servants, and Charles had to send out orders that these particu/
lar "English" were not to be attacked without his leave.

D'Aubigny was probably picked, as he had been picked to escort
English ambassadors the year before, because he was "well used to English
ways." He also brought with him, no doubt, a contingent of the king's
Scots Guard, of which he was made captain the next year: a dazzling
troop mounted on white horses, in white surcoats embroidered with gold
and silver. The "waiting for [the duke's] coming" and the reception cost
well over 500 *écus*, for Charles sent additional "men to provision them",
seemingly surprised by their numbers. The young man who disembarked
thought he was in Heaven, Vergil wrote. He now had kings among his
friends.

He found shelter in France for about five months. Almost nothing is
known of what he did there. For the time he was at court, d'Aubigny's
pension was increased from £2,300 to £3,000 *tournois*, perhaps conceal/
ing duties performed for him. Richard's chief minder, however, was
Alexander Monypeny, who had been sent to Scotland by Charles the
summer before. His father, William Monypeny, had long been in the
diplomatic service of the French kings, "enjoying the highest authority
and foremost about his Majesty", as one ambassador described him. Dur/

ing the secret negotiations for a marriage that never was between Charles, then dauphin, and Edward IV's daughter Elizabeth, Monypeny was said to be the only man admitted, besides the English herald, to the intimacy of the French king's chamber. For foreigners, the family could hardly have been closer to the royal designs.

The intimacy of Charles's chamber was presumably offered to Richard too, though it is not certain. The king was twenty one when his guest arrived in France; sweet natured, but not yet capable, Commines said, of understanding state affairs at all. This may have explained both his invitation to Richard and his quixotic decision, within three years, to invade Italy and press his claim to the kingdom of Naples. He was sickly, almost deformed, and with an energetic taste for curiosities. Small dogs overran his apartments, ripping the cloth of gold curtains on his bed, and parrots and white blackbirds, hung with little bells and coloured ribbons, fluttered on perches near the ceiling. In the palace at Plessis he had a giant aviary in which canaries flew and sang. The cages of his singing birds were dressed in bright green silk to look like trees. In many ways, Richard Plantagenet in France was such a creature, hung with ribbons and bright colours, learning to sing but not yet to be risked outside his gilded cage.

Nonetheless the stay in France, short though it was, provided a space in which the prince could be consolidated. He had already built a net work of diplomatic contacts by dint of the appeals sent out from Ireland. A letter to Ludovico Sforza that December from the Milanese envoy in Vienna showed that "the son of King Edward" was being talked about at Maximilian's court, and was thought to be on his way to Augsburg; per haps the King of the Romans had invited him. Envoys came to visit from Burgundy, where Margaret was preparing for him, and from Scotland. The employment of Monypeny and d'Aubigny so close to him showed clearly the continuing interest of the Scots. To them, too, he was "King Edward's son".

A tiny court had formed around him. It seems to have contained the Taylors, father and son, Frion, George Neville and Anthony de la Forsa, the young son of a famous Yorkist diplomat. At this stage Frion may have been Richard's chief counsellor as well as his secretary, although he did not stay with him past December. Month by month, more refugees joined the newfound prince and more visitors came through, presenting their cre dentials and, at the same time, assessing his. He was still a strange and sur

prising figure, but one who was accruing power. According to a later letter from one of Henry's officers, "when he was in France at the king's
court he made himself be called Plantagenet." There was authority in that
"made himself be called", as if the motivation came from him. Given
such confidence, it was hardly surprising that Charles "affirmed" to
James IV that this was Edward's son. Already, nine months away from
Cork, this young man had the hauteur of a prince.

That in itself would have commended him. The first view of
Richard Plantagenet was not necessarily a clear one, but a general impression of suitability. He was "either true or plausible", in the nimble
diplomatic language of the time. Georges Chastellain saw this in Philip
the Good of Burgundy: he was instantly a prince by *semblant, effigie, image*
and *figure*, sheer appearance. And this was often all that was required. If
the heart was uplifted, as general impressions of nobility or beauty always
vaguely stirred it, there was no need to investigate further. It was enough
to be able to apply to Richard Plantagenet, as to a far-away city or a gold
cup, the adjective "rich" or "fair", without testing how thick the metal
was or whether, on closer inspection, the shining towers and spires would
dissolve into the air.

In the *Secreta Secretorum*, Aristotle's supposed book of advice to
Alexander, princes were advised always to show themselves in rich and precious clothing "of the most strange cloth that can anywhere be found".
Tiny stitches and shifting colours, as on a piece of gold-embroidered satin,
were cause for astonishment. At the court of Burgundy, Charles the Bold
was said to have a passion for being seen as extraordinary and strange:
haute magnificence de coeur pour être vu et regardé en singulières choses. A king or
queen who appeared "uncuriously adorned"—like Louis XI in his old
grey coat, with a lead badge in his hat—had lost, with robes and jewels,
the dignity of royalty.

Impassiveness, too, was expected of kings. By appearing still as stat-
ues, they summed up the unchanging dependability of their laws; they
were true, veritable and steady, as God was. Solemnity, or "sadness", was
also expected, alongside the stillness. The Milanese envoy Raimondo
Soncino, given audience in 1497, found Henry VII standing quite still,
leaning against a chair upholstered in cloth-of-gold. He found his presence "wonderful". The Venetian ambassador Andrea Trevisano saw him
two weeks earlier in the same pose, "leaning against a tall gilt chair".

Throughout Trevisano's presentation of his credentials Henry stayed standing and did not stir, possessing his throne in steadiness, as a king should.

Soncino noted also that the king wore a "most rich" collar, with four rows of large pearls and jewels. Gems of uncommon beauty clearly distinguished not only princes from people, but princes from princes. Henry understood this as well as anyone, seeking out—as one way among many of bolstering his fragile claim to the crown—rare jewels of great price. In 1504 alone, his bill for jewels was £30,000. The king's gems were "attended" when he went on his journeys, wrapped in careful packaging of soft wool, and the palace rules of 1494 stipulated that on grand occasions he should put on his most precious jewels himself, no purely temporal man touching them.

Richard Plantagenet, the wandering prince, could not compete with this. But at some point, probably in France, he acquired the code-name "The Merchant of the Ruby". The stone carried some association with him, not implausibly because he wore one—perhaps as the jewel in his hat-brooch—as the gift of someone who cared for him. That brooch too you could try to interpret if you cared to, as people interpreted Philip the Good's black hat, strewn all over with huge pearls like tears, as a sign of grief for his wayward son. Richard's three pendant pearls, perhaps, were tears for the father, mother and brother he had lost. But a ruby would have drawn most attention to him. Beyond its intrinsic virtues—an inextinguishable light that glowed in darkness, the power to protect a man from losing blood—the ruby was understood to hold the kingship among jewels. It was the stone of the sun, which, as it rose, was always described as red rather than gold. Both the Great Khan and Prester John were said to light their palaces with dozens of rubies, set into pillars and walls. On the island of Macumeran, according to John Mandeville, the ruler was obliged to wear a ruby about his neck, "for if he beareth not the ruby, they would no longer take him for king." Isabella of Spain seemed to take this to heart, covering herself, according to Richmond Herald, with rose-red balas-rubies the size of beechnuts and tennis balls. Yet one ruby alone could make that point strongly enough.

In the ever-moving royal court at Amboise, Vincennes, Moulins or Bois Malherbes—as later at Malines, Innsbruck, Vienna, Edinburgh and

Stirling—Richard Plantagenet gave the required impression. He was liv' ing in the royal apartments and the royal hunting lodges, eating, dancing, hawking and hearing Mass alongside the king's young cousins, or the king himself. They greeted him as one of them, with the usual "caressing demonstrations". Like them, he would have spent long hours outdoors, seeking the fresh air that doctors recommended to stir the king's stale humours and make him stronger. The very sight of Richard then, mag' nificently mounted, hounds at his heels and hawk on wrist, showed the world that he was noble. He wore the glittering clothes of a prince, unless he was in shirtsleeves, hose and slippers to play tennis, a sport Charles loved. The king's courtesans were also available to him. At night, the sheets on his bed—"white sheets and soft", an unspeakable luxury— carried scents of violets and red roses from the royal laundry. Charles called him "cousin" and, in proclamations to his people, styled him the Duke of York without equivocation, "true heir to the realm of England."

This prince had courtiers and soldiers round him. When he went through the streets of Paris, merely a few months out into the public view, he rode attended by a guard of honour, probably part of the king's Scots Guard, under Alexander Monypeny. Advisers huddled with him in cor' ridors, suggesting important and secret business. Servants held his stirrup when he dismounted, half-knelt to give him letters, tasted his wine before he drank it, took his cloak from his shoulders and draped him in it again. This was how a prince was treated and how he was judged: by the num' ber of his horses, the crowd of his attendants, how he disposed them and gave them their orders, and whether they kept their faces continually turned towards him "with reverence and honour and obedience."

Yet, as Richard complained to Isabella, all this rich regard did not translate in the end into active French help for him. Charles would not help him against evil Henry "at all". That realization came brutally in November 1492, when England and France made peace. Henry had decided, after all, not to go to war to defend the autonomy of Brittany. In October, having crossed the Channel with his army, his minstrels and his Spanish fool, he laid siege to Boulogne, but he did not mean it. The two kings pledged their skin-deep amity in a treaty at Etaples on November 3rd. Richard Plantagenet's presence at Charles's court was not acknowl' edged in the main body of the treaty. Instead it was implied in a separate codicil of December 13th, in which each side promised not to help or shelter the rebels or traitors of the other. Vergil felt sure, however, that it was Henry's "sniffing" of Edward's resurrected son that had caused him to sue for peace.

So Richard left Paris. Hall said he sneaked away by night, giving Monypeny the slip and taking advantage of the darkness, because he feared that the French king would give him up to Henry. Among those who signed the codicil for Charles was d'Aubigny, who had first greeted and protected him when he arrived from Ireland. But the king probably gave Plantagenet the nod directly, for his delivery had never been part of the peace talks, and Bernard André thought his cause was safely thriving there. Charles saw to it that everywhere he stayed had a means of escape, a specially constructed staircase leading from his chamber window to the garden or the street. Richard may well have gone by such a way. He may also have needed to disguise himself: perhaps in a long black gaberdine of Catalan leather, of the sort Charles was seen wearing in the rains of the year before. Thus hidden, somehow, he made his way east to the Burgun-dian lands and to Margaret.

There, the crises that had followed the deaths of Charles the Bold and his daughter, Mary, were six or seven years in the past. The burghers of Ghent and Bruges, having resisted and even imprisoned Maximilian, had come to accept him as their regent. Prosperity and peace were return-ing, and with them a genuine enthusiasm for Maximilian's young son, Philip the Fair, about to enter his Burgundian inheritance. With the duchy now governed, in effect, by Philip's council, Margaret could more often turn her attention to other things: to her own estates, to reading, to praying, and to working with proper diligence to restore the House of York to the throne of England. Her best chance was approaching.

II

ON ALL SIDES, by this time, there was an interest in looking at Richard Plantagenet. But it was not always easy to see him. This was not just because he himself was elusive, slipping from country to country, but because it was often hard to get a good light on the subject. People longed to see almost everything more closely and more clearly. Their greatest desire, after peace, was for brightness, something better than the hazy and secondary illumination of the world.

Artists increasingly filled their paintings with the effects of light on faces, objects, walls and water, on metal vessels and the folds of clothes. Light softened, rippled, chiselled and burnished. The best poets, too, described it with the intricacy of jewellers. William Dunbar, at the Scottish court, wrote of roses touched by the morning sun until they sparkled like rubies, each bud scattered with brilliant beryl-drops of dew. These were no longer flowers, but gems crystallised into fiery brightness by the effect of ordinary light. Above them, the shining heaven was scaled in silver like the iridescent side of a fish, and gold light outlined every leaf and branch of the overhanging trees. Both Chastellain and John Lydgate made the centrepieces of their dream-stories pavilions of glass or temples of "celestial clearness", as bright, Chastellain wrote, as if divine light had been infused in them.

When dreams and imaginings could be so sharply illuminated, it did not matter that Bernard André, who wrote the boy's story for Henry, was blind and never saw him. He carried him in his head, lit by remembered sunlight that was gaudier than life. André, describing himself explicitly as another Homer who would "clarify and resist the darkness", wrote his history as scenes from classical mythology performed against the rocks and seas of a half-infernal world. Long before he encountered the young man who called himself Plantagenet, he saw him on that well-lit stage, part monster and part moth.

The subtle machinery of the eye itself was often apt to go wrong, and babies were carefully born into darkened rooms, as obscure as the world itself, to stop them squinting in the light. But defects of sight went uncorrected for the most part. Though spectacles were in use, their lenses of quartz or white beryl distorted as much as they clarified. The Venetian ambassador Zacharia Contarini, who visited Charles VIII in June 1492 when Richard Plantagenet was about to appear, remarked that the king's large white eyes evidently made him see badly, but he seemed to take no measures to help himself. The letters he snatched from Contarini could be inspected well enough, if he held them close; so too could Plantagenet, if he went nose-to-nose with him.

The poor-sighted accepted, therefore, that the world was unclear. If they read a lot, and as old age "bade them good morrow", it would become cloudier still. William Caxton complained that his eyes were dimmed from looking too much at white paper, and in 1473 Thomas Betson, still young, complained that writing letters by candlelight made his eyes ache. At the age of forty, at just the moment when he was required to appraise the "feigned lad" in person, Henry VII himself could sense that his eyes were failing. "I beseech you to pardon me," he wrote to his mother, "for verily, madam, my sight is nothing so perfect as it has been, and I know well it will impair daily . . ."

Starved of light, you took your book or letters to the window. The building projects of princes often included reglazing, in an attempt to bring in modernity in the form of brightness. When Edward IV made repairs to the Prince's Wardrobe in Old Jewry, most of his improvements were the mending or replacing of glass. Glass windows like these, heavy and beautiful when compared with the horn or oiled linen in the windows of the poor, were so valuable that they were moved, in their wooden case-ments, from house to house. The effect of sun shining through them was still new and extraordinary. The rooms of Paradise itself were "clarified and depured" with glass. Lydgate's poem "The Life of Our Lady" gave as a metaphor of the Incarnation the sunlight piercing brightly, but with-out harm, through panes of beryl or crystal. It was possibly only in those years that a poem of star-crossed young love could reach its climax in the line "Through the glass window shines the sun."

Yet the brightness these windows supplied was merely relative. People still longed to see "without coverture or without glass": that is, clearly. Windows were mullioned or diamond-leaded, divided into small panes of thumb-thick greenish glass that were pocked with imperfections. Even glass that was plain and functional admitted a light that was usually dim, as if filtered through veils of water. In Flemish portraits of the time the windows were often opened—first the box-like shutters, then the full panes—or else dispensed with completely, in favour of the light of day.

The hankering to see more clearly did not end when night fell. Poets still tried to describe what they saw. Lydgate wrote of the face of a slovenly servant shining "like barked leather" in the light of a candle. If matters were important enough, you could make yourself discern the tini-est details by torchlight, as when Charles VIII examined a night delivery of forty-nine falcons and had each one described to him. Beaks and talons, cuffs and pinnons, the lie and shade of feathers, were inspected under light as fretful and alive as the birds themselves. Charles sent two back as unsatisfactory.

In royal palaces, interior lighting had become more and more elabo-rate: sconces on the walls, sixty-light candelabras hanging low from the roof-beams, massed candles on the tables. At the grandest ceremonies, candelabras were combined with mirrors to double the effect, astonishing the crowd as they saw their own faces, reflected small, high up among the flames. Some "disguisings" or masked dances were held in giant lanterns where, behind "panes" of white lawn, hundreds of lights illuminated the scene. A small army of men with ladders was employed to light and extinguish them.

The night lighting for Margaret of York's wedding had been especially elaborate, and by day too she showed the contemporary fervour for seeing clearly. In 1491 and 1492 she had been paying particular attention to the light in her palaces. At Binche, her favourite retreat in the hills of Hainault, windows were made "to look out on the garden", "to look towards the fields", "to give light in *la grande salle*", and proper glass-makers were employed for the first time to glaze them. In her palace at Malines, the reception hall was now lit by a long wall of windows installed on her orders.

By this light, with the eyes of a woman no longer considered young, she could indulge a passion for illuminated books of exquisite detail and beauty. In the margins of her prayer-books, small wild flowers— pimpernels, pansies, violets, forget-me-nots—were painted as if they had been plucked from the stalk and laid on the paper, casting a shadow. Flies and butterflies visited them, their wings overlapping the borders of the pictures as if, with the flick of a finger, they might fly off again. To portray nature with such fidelity was a sort of magic, like the act of creation itself. Skelton called such images "envived pictures well touched and quickly", so real that they appeared alive. The daisy in particular—the marguerite, Margaret's own flower, the symbol of womanly virtue and constancy— featured in the margins of her books, growing in little blue-and-white pots or laid fresh-picked on the page. Though she might be childless, her flowers flourished everywhere, touched quickly from paper into life.

Her books also included, in the same minute detail, pictures of her as she saw herself and wished others to see her. Almost invariably, she was praying: in the square before the church of St. Michael and St. Gudule in Brussels, in her chamber at Malines, or in her private oratory where, in the background, one of her many greyhounds scampered down the hall. In one book she was pictured, in cloth-of-gold and helped by her attendants, performing the seven corporal works of mercy in the streets of Malines. She placed bread in the hands of an orphan boy and of a cripple on crutches, who tried to raise his hat to her. She gave water to a pilgrim from a silver flagon, lifting the bowl to his lips herself and looking on gently as he drank. She proffered shirts, money and comfort to the imprisoned and the sick. As she did so, her subjects barely noticed her, walking past or loitering in the distance with their eyes on the sky. Margaret was doing these things not just for show, but for Jesus, who stood beside her and, at the last, would come to judge her, gazing intently at her from His shining throne in the clouds, as the smoke rose that would consume the world. In that last conflagration, all the illusions of the world would disappear: her rich clothes, her books, her palaces, the vanities she craved and the curiosities she pursued, reduced to the dust and nothingness they truly were, if she could see them clearly.

In a book that was written at her request soon after her marriage, the risen Jesus came to visit her in her chamber. Margaret saw this "beatific and uncovered vision" quite suddenly, as she prayed. All was otherwise as normal: the stone floors neatly swept, the scarlet covers drawn up on the nuptial bed, the morning light streaming through the latticed windows. A greyhound in a gold collar slept at her feet, nose on paws. Margaret herself, in a black steepled headdress and black-figured cloth-of-gold, knelt on a prayer cushion. And there was Jesus before her. He had just risen from the dead, naked under a crimson cloak, still carrying the triumph-banner of the Cross, red on white, with which He had climbed from the tomb. The banner fluttered in the breeze of His arrival, and rays of golden light shone from Him.

By these signs she would have known Him; but He was showing her the marks of His wounds, to make her sure. His left hand, held out towards her, bore the print of the nails, still fresh and welling with red blood; she looked at it in rapture, knowing this was the evidence that counted. The disciple Thomas had said he would not believe "until I see the marks of the nails in his hands, and put my finger into the place of the nails, and put my hand into the hole in his side." A week later, the disciples again behind locked doors, Jesus appeared and commanded Thomas to touch Him in just that way. Thomas, doing so, immediately declared: "My Lord and my God."

Now that Jesus was before her, Margaret was unsure how best to welcome Him. She wished only to gaze on Him in contemplation; but the court was pressing and she was too busy, among "the curiosities of the world", quietly to enclose herself with Him. All she wished was that He might "illumine my interior eyes, that is, the faith and reason and consideration of my soul." So He instructed her. She was to lay out for Him the table of her heart, spread with the meat of understanding, the bread of pain and the wine of tears. That done, she was to make ready the bed of her heart in which she was to lie with Him, "in purest chastity and pure charity", receptive under the scarlet covers to everything He was to say to her.

She should look, Jesus told her, at the glory of God, "who has imprinted such sweetness and loveliness in precious stones and grass and flowers, and who has put in a little part of the body of man, that is, in the faces of some, such great beauty." She was to gaze on the torments of Hell (yes, Margaret told Him nervously, she already understood that the fires there "are as different from worldly fire as worldly fire is from a fire painted on a wall"). Most especially, she was to contemplate Jesus Himself on the Cross, and the wounds He had suffered for her sake. The lance-wound in particular—which Jesus also showed her, the crimson cloak slipping down around His waist—was a sign so deep and important that it led on, in Margaret's devotions, into seven other signs of the love of Jesus. It was a bleeding Lure to draw her heart, a Treasure to redeem her, a Well of grace, a Tavern to slake her thirst at the rim of His opened flesh, a Bed in which to rest, a Shield to defend her, and a Tree of Life in which she could enter, frail as she was, to burrow deep into the red sap of Jesus's love and let the bark grow over her.

Jesus had risen from the dead to walk into her chamber with all the signs of His Passion, which was her redemption, visible upon Him. He had come in so softly that Margaret's dog had continued to sleep in the middle of the polished floor. The tiny details of His wounds and His face were so precious that she was careful to avoid them as, at the beginning of her prayers, she kissed the painted page. Instead she kissed the blue hangings of the bed until, after a time, the colour was worn away. She had seen the signs, as Thomas had; and she had believed, as anyone would who had been so close to the very Son of God.

When Richard Plantagenet came to her court in the winter of 1492, that same deep contemplation of proofs was turned, she claimed, on him. It was in that newly glazed reception room at Malines, as the December light lay dully on the fields and woods of Brabant, that she saw a young man who called her "aunt" as he knelt to her, the mud of his travels still on him.

The next August, when he sent his letter to Isabella of Spain, Margaret sent one too, a step-by-step description of how she had come to know him for who he was. Her letter was passionate, almost to the point of disturbance. Vergil described her as "scarcely of sound mind" for joy when she thought her nephew had returned. The letter, dictated eight months later, showed that the emotion had not faded.

What she told Isabella was not necessarily true. She had a vital argument to make, which she would not have hesitated to bolster with lies. God would understand and forgive the imperative, as He did (in His great mercy) daily and hourly around the courts of Europe. Yet the letter, truthful or not, still laid out the sort of authentication that was expected in such cases. Though she herself may never have examined Richard—knowing all along who he was—Margaret had to prove she had been sceptical, as Isabella herself would have been. The two women were much the same age, Isabella just five years younger. Both presented themselves as competent, strong and not easily fooled, the antithesis of what most men expected.

Like her nephew that same day, sitting at the same table in the palace of Dendermonde, Margaret wasted less than a line on greetings and preliminaries. She came straight to the point:

> Last year, the Earls of Desmond and Kildare, the chief lords of Ireland . . . wrote to me that the second son of Edward, late King of England, my most beloved brother, by name Richard Plantagenet, Duke of York—who everyone thought was dead—was still alive, and was with those earls in Ireland, safe and held in great honour. They affirmed this with letters reinforced with their seals and with a sacred oath. They prayed that I might be willing to bring help and assistance to this same Duke of York by the law of necessity and blood, and promised that they would also help him themselves. These things seemed to me to be ravings and dreams.

Deliramenta et sompnio similia. Not just a joke, as so many people were to describe it, but delirium, of the sort that made sufferers from the sweating sickness throw off their stinking sheets and cry for cold water, though it killed them. The news from Ireland could not possibly be true. Margaret, too, had thought Richard Plantagenet was dead, as "everyone" else did. Her busy contacts with London in 1484, when her chaplain, her commercial agent and her envoys had all been there, had not informed her otherwise, or so she implied. Ravings and dreams.

Nonetheless, Desmond and Kildare had affirmed this with letters sent under their seals. Although this seemed obvious, it was worth reporting. Seals identified the senders and bound them to their words, as clearly as if their owners had appeared and spoken. Princes who had emerged from nowhere, with no seals of their own, depended on those of others to authenticate them. That was why Plantagenet's first letters to James IV of Scotland had been written jointly with Desmond, and why, according to Margaret, he did not write to her himself, but let Desmond and Kildare do so for him. From a distance he had no way of proving who he was, save through their seals and their words.

Lacking a seal, he might have sent a token of some sort. Small personal objects—a ring or a jewel—would often be slipped inside letters, but this private language could not be understood unless the parties knew each other. "I received a token from you," wrote Thomas Betson to his beloved, "the which was and is to me right heartily welcome, and with glad will I received it." He sent another mysterious token to Elizabeth Stonor, "the which your ladyship knowth right well." The person receiving the token had to be able instantly to place it on the sender's body: the ring warm on the finger, the Agnus Dei medal pinned to a shirt or nestled among the chest hairs. Again, Plantagenet's exile had presumably deprived him of even such small and precious things. Margaret received no token from Ireland to convince her, save the fact that the boy was held "in great honour" there. The messenger who brought the letters had perhaps said more; letters often begged the recipient to give full faith and credence to the bearer, who would "open and declare" more details. But even if he did, this faint gleam of other people's recognition was not enough for her.

Desmond and Kildare had also confirmed their letters with "a sacred oath". Since neither man had ever seen the little Duke of York, they had no way of identifying the young man in their care. Oaths were as cheap in Ireland as they were elsewhere. Nonetheless, Margaret claimed that they had brought in God, compellingly and boldly. They had also talked solemnly of "necessity and blood", ties that should have bound her to this young man sight unseen. She refused to be moved by such appeals.

But the claims were building steadily round Richard Plantagenet, if that was who he was. And he was moving closer.

> Afterwards this Duke of York was received by the King of France, just recently in France, as the son of King Edward and as his cousin. And I sent certain men who would have recognised him as easily as his mother or his nurse, since from their first youth they had been in service and intimate familiarity with King Edward and his children. These men too with a most sacred oath affirmed that this man was the second son of King Edward. They cursed themselves with great oaths if he should turn out otherwise, and were ready to endure every torment and great physical pains of every kind.

Margaret gave no indication who these men were. She could have meant any of the refugees from Edward IV's household who were now in Europe. The men she had sent, she implied, were as physically close to the subject as it was possible to be. Simply to have seen the little Duke of York, or to have known his father, was not enough this time. The knowledge required was instinctive, mother-love or nurse-love: as deep as the sort that came from carrying and kissing a child, seeing him naked, knowing the smell of him, distinguishing his cry in the dark.

Armed, as Margaret claimed, with knowledge that went this deep, her envoys reported that they had recognised the prince and knew him for certain. As might be expected of old servants and retainers, they offered themselves up to every sort of torture for his sake, clinging wildly and devotedly to the reality of this young man, Edward's son. The sacred affirmations—most sacred, a notch higher than Margaret had received before—were now multiplying. There were "great oaths" too, not holy but vernacular and emphatic, like the "high Oaths" Piers said he had sworn to the plotters who had pestered him in Ireland. The noise of Richard was dinning in Margaret's ears. She was on the brink of believing, but still she had not seen him with her own eyes.

More than a year after the first signs in Ireland, Richard Plantagenet came to her palace in Malines. This was how she described his appearance to Isabella, dictating the words—with stops and starts, for translation by the secretary—on that August day, as Richard sat listening beside her. *At last*, the passage began. *Tandem ipse Dux Eboracensis ex Francia ad me venit.* After all the rumours and half-proofs, the pitch of excitement was almost audible. Here he was.

> At last the Duke of York himself came to me out of France, seeking help and assistance. I recognised him as easily as if I had last seen him yesterday or the day before (for I had seen him once long ago in England). He did not have just one or another sign of resemblance, but so many and so particular that hardly one person in ten, in a hundred or even in a thousand might be found who would have marks of the same kind. Then [I recognised him by] the private conversations and acts between him and me in times past, which undoubtedly no other person would have been able to guess at. Lastly [I recognised him by] the questions and conversations of others, to all of which he responded so aptly and skilfully that it was manifest and notorious that this was he who they thought had died long ago.
>
> I indeed for my part, when I gazed on this only male Remnant of our family—who had come through so many perils and misfortunes—was deeply moved, and out of this natural affection, into which both necessity and the rights of blood were drawing me, I embraced him as my only nephew and my only son.

Perhaps none of this was true; perhaps all of it was; perhaps it was a seamless mixture of truth and lies. On the one hand lay all the suggestions and rumours that she herself had contrived him: that she had been following his movements in Ireland day by day and hour by hour, as Vergil said, and had been waiting in deep anxiety and grief to receive her creation back from France. On the other hand came this impassioned account of an extraordinary surprise. She had not hidden him from his enemies or played any part in his wanderings, a story she might have told without reproach if she had wanted to. Instead, there was the shock of recognition. He had suddenly appeared from nowhere in Ireland and was now, just as suddenly, with her.

If she had made him, it was still some time since she could have last seen him. Five and a half years had passed since he had left Flanders with Brampton, and no firm evidence suggests that he returned. In that time, he had changed from a child to a young man marked by experiences she could only guess at, and latterly by the clear understanding that he was a prince at the head of a cause. Whether or not her account was true, she responded to him with turbulent emotion and love.

Her feeling seemed summed up in that last phrase, *my only nephew and my only son*. The secretary's Latin had no linking conjunction: Margaret had embraced him *velut unicum nepotem: velut unicum filium*, as if she struggled to improve and emphasise the words that tumbled out of her. To call him simply her nephew did not do justice to the closeness of the bond. The ties of necessity and blood that the Irish earls had mentioned were now moving in her, drawing her, as if she could not fight them.

Richard Plantagenet was, of course, an orphan now, the son of no one left living. Elizabeth Woodville had died in June 1492, still in the convent at Bermondsey to which Henry VII had confined her. In that sense, Margaret could present herself as his mother by substitution, as she called herself mother to Mary of Burgundy, to Mary's children and sometimes to Maximilian. But it went deeper. Margaret intended *eundem nutrire atque alere*, to bring him up and cherish him, as if this nineteen-year-old was still a little child to be suckled (the literal meaning of *nutrire*) and held close.

Feelings this strong were acknowledged in the contemporary and near-contemporary tellings of the story. André imagined Margaret calling her nephew "my most beloved"; Hall thought she called him her "dear darling", a phrase plucked from a lullaby for a child.

> Lullay my liking, my dear son, my sweeting,
> Lullay my dear heart, my own dear darling.

She received him, he said, as if he were "newly cropen out of his mother's lap again," an astonishing newborn suddenly in her arms. Political sponsorship did not need to go so far, and never had in Simnel's case. Though Henry considered these young men as two of a kind, this one was different.

Margaret had in fact seen the little Duke of York, but during a single visit to England, and long ago. She admitted it: the word *olim*, in times past, occurred three times in four lines. As it happened she had seen him twelve years before, when she was thirty-four and he was seven. She had been in England for three months, from June to September 1480, staying not at the royal palaces but at the Coldharbour in Thames Street, which her brother had refurbished for her with green silk and sarcenet. From time to time, she saw the little prince. On July 20th there was a banquet in her honour, out at Greenwich, to which presumably Richard came. On August 17th he probably celebrated his seventh birthday, appearing a little later in his new green and purple robes and in his Garter regalia. His aunt may well have seen him in that flowing blue cloak, with the blue silk sash and gold buttons.

But she implied she had seen him more often and more intimately than that. They had talked and done things together privately, and these they both remembered. Since Margaret claimed that their shared memories were so vivid, it is odd that both of them agreed, in deeds drawn up in 1494, that the date of Margaret's visit had been not 1480, but 1481. Dates, once again, went astray in the drama. They had met and talked; that was what was important.

What had passed between them? Perhaps she, or he, could remember or imagine something: a short walk in a garden, a solemn speech of welcome carefully rehearsed, a little greyhound stroked on a lap. They might have looked together through the pages of the Hastings Hours, supposed by some to have been brought by Margaret to London in her luggage, and admired the pictures of Maytime drunkards revelling in boats, or men and women scrambling for sacks of money that were tipped down the margins of the page, or souls being carried up to Heaven like bareback riders by their angels, flying past the deep-blue orb of the world with its dust of golden stars. On the last page, now worn and stained as if much looked at, gray-furred wild men ran down from their caves to fight a knight who was half sea-monster, a helmet and cuirass riding on seaweed. All through the book the painted flies buzzed again, with their gauzy wings and pinpoint eyes, tempting the squashing finger of any small boy.

The resurrected nephew could also bring memories of his own. They might have been of the ship called the *Falcon*, his own device, in which Margaret had come from Flanders; the ceremonial barge in which she had gone down the Thames, attended by twenty-four officers in jackets of murrey and blue; the new tapestries of Paris and Helen at the Coldharbour, the Trojans bristling with arrows and spears as Helen was carried off; or the huge shining horse Aunt Margaret was given by his father, caparisoned with a saddle of blue and purple cloth-of-gold with a fringe of blue and purple silk tipped with Venice gold, on which she had ridden away. And if those sightings were not there—her protégé waiting, like the image crafted by Pygmalion, for her to animate him with the breath of his own life—she could step in, take his hand, and provide them for him.

III

MARGARET RECOGNISED HIM not only in these fragments of memory, she told Isabella, but by "signs": many, many signs, unique and particular. Perhaps unsurprisingly, she made no attempt to describe what these were. They seemed to be an accumulation of little things attached to him directly: as small, perhaps, as the way he turned his head or expressed irritation. If he was false, Margaret's vagueness was just as well. If he was real, it could be taken for an overwhelming sense of him she could not describe: that shock of the heart. "Sir, what is your name?" asked Galahad of Lancelot, the father he had never known; "for much my heart giveth unto you."

Yet proper, visible signs were needed also, to point to the truth of who he was. However strongly Margaret or others believed in Richard Plantagenet, these physical proofs needed to be inspected, seen again and again, to sustain the faith of those who followed him. Columbus seeking Cipango had not seen land, but had assured his sailors by signs that it was there: drops of rain that fell without wind, sandpipers in flocks of forty, drifting vegetation that bore "something like fruit." For days, sailing on and on, these sightings sustained them. Christ Himself had left a sign of this sort, His own body in the form of bread as sustenance and life. Men and women could never get enough of this sign as it was elevated by the priest, lifted high and clear and without obstruction, backed by curtains so that its whiteness shone. They believed in Him and in their salvation effected through Him; but to see this truth, in the form of the bread on which angels feasted, was a daily necessity as urgent as bread itself.

For Yorkists who sought such physical proofs, Richard could provide them. He claimed to have three "hereditary" marks on his body that could be recognised by anyone who had known Richard, Duke of York. Maximilian, for one, seems to have been convinced by the *trois enseignes naturelz*, *qu'il a sur le corps*. Richard was prepared to show these marks to anyone, Maximilian reported: to the princes of the great houses, to everyone who had known him as a child, even to Henry himself "if the opportunity were only given him," to prove that his claim was true. They were his "special" proofs. He could, of course, prove his authenticity to them in more general terms. Merely by appearing "in proper person" and "show[ing] our selves openly unto you," as he said in his proclamation of 1496—riding past, perhaps not even dismounting, but glittering—he could confound Henry Tudor "and all his false sayings". But if they demanded more, he had his marks.

It is not entirely clear what they were. Maximilian's letter, which might have said more, has disappeared. At Setubal the herald Tanjar also mentioned three *señas* observed on the boy in Portugal: a mark on his face under his eye, an upper lip that was slightly raised or prominent (*el beso alto levantado un poco*) and another mark *sus los pechos*, on his breast. From these marks, Tanjar said, "people said he was the Duke of York." Two of them appeared, and were perhaps even emphasised, in the portrait that was done of him. Yet Richard's own boast suggested that his special marks were not immediately apparent. He had to reveal them by taking off his clothes—unless, at the tennis court, you could catch a glimpse of the breast-mark underneath his open shirt. Nor, by the sound of it, were they acquired or cosmetic features, though sometimes these were accepted when there was nothing else to go by. In 1477, when the body of Margaret's husband Charles was found at Nancy, dug out of the caked snow after several days, his face was so gnawed by wolves that he was recognised only by his Italian valet, who knew him by his long fingernails, and by his Portuguese doctor, who knew him by his scars.

The Yorkists who joined Richard Plantagenet in France or Flanders needed to test his signs with particular care. Foreigners might accept the bright surface, but Englishmen could not leave it at that. "Clear inspection and whole intellection" were necessary, not least because of the risks they had taken in leaving their country and adhering to this young man. Unlike Charles or Maximilian, they were not so highly placed that they could play political games unpunished. Nor was this a puppet-child, like Simnel, with nobles in his vanguard, whom no one needed to see; he himself was their leader. Charles had required him merely to be plausible as a charming creature round the court. These Englishmen required him to be plausible as their lord and their king.

So they examined him, looking at him with the hard, frank stare that was accepted between people who were about to pledge loyalty to each other or transact some kind of business. Some, if sufficiently close in rank or familiar to dare, might have taken his hand too and held it for a long time, for the true form and shape of things had to be discerned by touch as well as sight. "Avising" was the word for this. It implied deep concentration, as when Charles the Bold had avised Margaret on their first meeting: taking her hand as he scanned her face for "a tract of time", stepping back a little and then forward, thrusting his dark wolfish face into hers. He was informing himself of the full possibilities of this person, as he might have pressed the flanks of a horse or walked the bounds of a piece of property, assessing what advantage they could bring him.

Courtiers and commoners alike wanted and needed to see their kings this close, if they dared. Admitted to the royal presence, envoys sent back the tiniest details of the faces they had observed. Henry VII's envoys stared keenly enough at the young Queen of Naples to see wisps of brown hair showing through her kerchief and her nose "a little rising in the midward, and a little coming or bowing towards the end"; although they could not quite detect, as he commanded, whether her breath was sour or sweetened with musk and rosewater. Other envoys came close enough to King Ferdinand of Spain to notice that he was "somewhat lisping in his speech, the cause thereof we think is of a tooth the which he lacks before." Henry himself could be identified, it was said, by a tiny red wart, no larger than a pinhead, a little above his chin. To look more minutely than this you would need the eyes of a lynx, peering through all "outward accidents" to the true prince underneath the surface.

Edward IV consciously played to the longing of his subjects to observe him. Often, Mancini wrote,

> he called to his side complete strangers, when he thought they had come with the intention of addressing or beholding him more closely. He was wont to show himself to those who wished to watch him, and he seized any opportunity that the occasion offered of revealing his fine stature more protractedly and more evidently to onlookers. He was so genial in his greeting that if he saw a newcomer bewildered at his appearance and royal magnificence, he would give him courage to speak by laying a kindly hand upon his shoulder.

When Yorkist refugees examined the young man in Malines, therefore, they would have demanded more than the marks that he could show them. Most especially, they wanted him to be like Edward. More gloriously even than most kings, Edward had shone at the centre of his court: "the sun, the rose, the lodestar, the sunbeam, the lantern and the light," as one of his servants wrote inconsolably after he had gone.

Several of the new conspirators had been his servants too, and had got very close to the late king. Sir Robert Chamberlain and Sir Gilbert Debenham had sailed back to England with Edward from exile in 1471; they had seen him not merely in majesty, but queasy, anxious and wind-swept, in his travelling clothes. Stephen Frion had taken dictation from him; Thomas Ward, a sometime colleague of Frion's who possibly joined the conspirators at his prompting, had been Edward's doctor, palping the puffy whitish body under the robes and taking his urine. All these men sought some sense of him again: not vaguely, but keenly and closely.

Sons of rulers, especially rulers who had been loved, were naturally expected to resemble their fathers and were endlessly compared to them. Georges Chastellain, describing Charles the Bold, could think only that his face was rounder than his father's, his complexion darker, and his eyes, light as an angel's, "his father's living image" perfectly reflected. Dr. Shaw saw in Richard of Gloucester "his father's own figure . . . the very print of his visage, the sure undoubted image, the plain express likeness of the noble duke, whose remembrance can never die while he liveth." People led before the newfound prince in Malines searched in just this way for the "print" and "favours" of Edward, and many may have found them. To judge by the only contemporary likenesses of the king, in some ways the young man was strikingly like him. His face was the same shape, as were his chin, jaw, mouth and nose, and the same curious crease of bone ran from his right eye up to his brow. Artistic convention accounted for some of that, but not all of it; no similar features, save strong chins, linked the portraits of Edward and his brother Richard III.

Other aspects of the young man's face did not suggest that he had Edward's blood in him. Edward's eyes were very different, set in pronounced lids with lower brows; his upper lip was long; and his hair was brown, rather than fair, though he had sired a crowd of fair-haired children. (At Elizabeth of York's coronation, observers had marvelled at her yellow hair falling loose down her back.) Most strikingly, Edward had been over six feet tall, commanding, broad-chested, room-filling, where the boy who claimed to be his son was still childishly slight at the age of twenty. "Of invincible courage, and the handsomest prince my eyes ever beheld," said Commines of Edward, though he thought him a little gone to seed when he saw him at the Anglo-French peace talks at Picquigny in 1475. "His thoughts were wholly employed upon the ladies, hunting, and adorning his person." Certainly the adorning of the person was there in the young man, and perhaps the easy amorousness also. He would only have had to curse like Edward ("By God's blessed Lady!") to start a pulse of recognition in his hearers, as he would only have had to fall on his knees to say the Angelus, the prayer Elizabeth Woodville had wanted to be said three times a day in England, to kindle thoughts of the mother who must have tenderly instructed him.

To see Edward in Richard Plantagenet entailed catching and dwelling on certain things, rather than others. There was no perfect match. Nonetheless, a resemblance was recognised then that can still be seen now. The Irishmen and others who accosted the boy in Cork, according to Henry's story and the confession, insisted that he must be some sort of Plantagenet. Most of them could not have known what a Plantagenet looked like, but their recognition was meant to add authenticity to the story. Henry himself implicitly admitted it: the face looked right. "He looked somewhat like the Duke of Clarence," said Molinet, who could not possibly have known that. It was there in the young man who called himself Plantagenet, some sort of Yorkist look.

Later historians floated the idea that the newfound Duke of York might have been a bastard of Edward's, a memento of some fleeting love affair on one side or other of the Channel, but contemporaries did not think so. Certainly the young man at the court of Burgundy was too young to have been a souvenir of Edward's exile there at the end of 1470. Possibly he was the fruit of some casual liaison elsewhere. But bastards were usually recognised and usually quiescent, accepting their status and grateful for whatever position they could get. Besides, those who saw the resemblance between Edward and Richard Plantagenet in the 1490s seem to have accepted it as legitimate, in every sense. They had many motives for doing so: defiance, dynastic loyalty, love, hate, gratitude. Fired by all these, they laid the ghost face on the living one. The print and favours Yorkists found in Richard were what they longed to see: Edward in remembrance, living.

This seems to have been Richard Harliston's case. Harliston, Edward's governor of Jersey for fifteen years, had resolved to hold the island for York after Bosworth and, though attainted of treason and sub-

sequently pardoned, went on to fight for the young man whom he supposed was Richard. A Jersey chronicler in the next century, struggling to
explain such a risky course of action, wrote that Margaret

> had so skilfully arranged matters that several servants of Edward
> IV, and the most loyal ones at that, believed and were persuaded by
> her [that the two sons of King Edward were still alive] . . . among
> whom Harliston firmly believed it to be true, that the said child
> [Richard], to avoid the fury and rage of King Richard his uncle,
> had found a way to escape and come to Flanders; and he aban-
> doned his office of captain and went to Flanders thinking to give
> help to the child of Edward, who during all his life had been his
> good lord and master.

The first leap of faith was the hardest, to picture Richard out of the
Tower and alive. After this, the process was uncomplicated, an act of
piety for the king he had loved. Yet Harliston, with his life in the balance,
would hardly have made such a decision if the young man himself had
failed to persuade him.

Nor would Robert Clifford, who joined Richard Plantagenet in
Malines in 1493. Clifford had known both Edward IV and Richard,
Duke of York, and at close quarters. As a young man, a minor officer at
court, he had been the most ardent of Yorkists, and had been among the
first to sign up for Richard's wedding jousts in 1478. He had received his
prize for the best "tourney without" from a little bride who sat under a
canopy with a notably pretty little boy, in yards of shining silk, with a
bridegroom's crown pressed down on his fair hair. Clifford himself was
dressed then, as he had fought, in full Yorkist colours of murrey and blue,
on a horse caparisoned with those colours "inramplished" with suns and
white roses. This was presumably not his only sighting of the little
prince, but it may have been the most memorable, even if sweat and exhil-
aration blurred the look of him. Presumably he still had his prize, an
"M" of gold for "Mowbray", set with an emerald, to remind him of the
emotions of that day.

When Clifford saw the young man in Flanders, he immediately
believed that he was of royal descent. *Iuvene viso*, Vergil said, he was convinced: as soon as he saw him, and apparently by sight alone. Hall said he
knew him to be King Edward's son "by his face and other lineaments of
his body"; John Stow thought it was "gesture and manners" that con-

vinced him. Having seen and believed, Clifford then wrote letters of credit and confidence to England, affirming what he saw. He also spread the word in Calais, telling a lady of the town that this was King Edward's son. The man who reported this remark, then deputy lieutenant of Calais, felt the force of this bald observation: "Never words went colder to my heart than those did."

Frank testimonials like Clifford's were rare. Too often, people who could have made the comparison—favourably or not—did not do so. In Setubal, disappointingly, Brampton was not asked whether the new-found Richard of York resembled the old one. But Rui de Sousa was. He had reported enthusiastically that the little prince he saw in 1482 was *un muy gentil mancebete . . . muy lindo y la mas hermosa criatura.* Was the person he had seen in Lisbon, the one who now said he was the Duke of York, anything like that wonderfully "noble" and "pretty" little boy? "No, because the other one was very beautiful."

What made the young man in Malines less handsome may well have been his discoloured eye, mentioned as a sign by nobody, but undoubtedly noticed, as King Ferdinand's tiny cast in the same eye was noticed when he smiled. Presumably, too, that eye could instantly prove or disprove Plantagenet's claim to be the prince. If he was an impostor, his promoters had therefore taken a calculated risk in choosing him; but if the general look and manner of Edward's son were right, small physical flaws or differences could be explained away. Perhaps in his long years of wandering someone had beaten him, prince though he was.

All these were, in any case, proofs positive. Vague as the marks may have been, they went uncountered by proof that Richard, Duke of York was dead. Without this, the young man's pretensions could never be quashed entirely, no matter how sceptically the claims and the signs were received. When Isabella got Margaret's letter, she wrote back pointing out "such doubts about him", but this cold water had no effect. Margaret simply said "that she would never write anything to them about him again"; the defiant embrace of the protégé, the toss of the head. As the Easter anthem *Christus Resurgens* demanded of the Jews, "Let them either produce Him buried, or adore Him rising." Until the body of the little prince was produced, nobody could say that Plantagenet was indisputably a fake. Maximilian found this a powerful argument. As he wrote in ruminative mood, justifying his belief in Richard, Duke of York many years later, "nobody had seen him dead."

A corpse was essential. In April 1471, after the battle of Barnet at which Richard Neville, Earl of Warwick, and his brother had been killed, Edward IV had the bodies of his two great enemies brought to St. Paul's: "and in the church there, openly showed, to all the people." They lay there for three or four days. Margaret herself, in a letter written that year to her mother-in-law, Isabella of Burgundy, explained how important this had been. Her brother had heard "that nobody in the city believed that Warwick and his brother were dead, so he had their bodies . . . laid out and uncovered from the chest upwards in the sight of everybody."

Henry VII could not produce, and was never to produce, the body of Richard, Duke of York. Faced with death and silence, he could do no better than anyone else. Undoubtedly he wanted to. This, after all, was the man who wrote to Pope Julius II that the best way to save the Church and confound unbelievers was "to seize with a strong hand the most holy sepulchre of Christ from the hand of the infidels, and exhibit His presence corporally."

Without bodies, there could still be a murder story. People still lived—among them James Tyrell, now an officer in Calais, Sir John Howard and Dr. Argentine, now one of Henry's physicians—who could probably have produced one. Henry did not seem to ask them, although for a time, in 1486, Tyrell was under subpoena to reveal what he knew about certain other policies of Richard III "touching imprisonment and coercion". Perhaps the king presumed, as was true, that most people shared his own opinion. Richard of York's death was the fundamental, unspoken fact against which to judge the absurdities that pestered him.

There are hints that he tried to trace the possible movements of the princes. In the early spring of 1494 Thomas Lyneham was paid 66s. 8d. "for an inquisition and investigation of certain evidence, charters and muniments belonging to the domains of Middleham and Sheriff Hutton and for his expenses in bringing the same to the king and his council." These two northern castles, where Richard III had lived and Edward, Earl of Warwick had been kept for a while, were places to which some said the princes had been taken and, perhaps, spirited away again. But Henry seemed to find no clues there. In default of physical proofs, the main argument expressed by his envoys was the one Margaret had mentioned: everyone knew Richard was dead, and it was madness to think otherwise. Henry instructed his envoys, Vergil wrote, to say that Richard had been murdered with his brother in the Tower many years before on the orders of their uncle. *Sicut in confesso erat*, the fact was beyond doubt; *nemo homo nesciebat*, there was no one who did not know this. To assert otherwise was "completely absurd" and "the height of madness", since Richard III would in no way have safeguarded himself by killing one boy and not the other.

Yet Henry at this stage offered neither witnesses nor proofs. Only his envoy Somerset, who proposed in 1495 to show Margaret and Maximilian the chapel where Richard was buried, tried to back up the story with evidence that could be seen and touched. Somerset's bluff, however, was not called, which was just as well, since neither he nor Henry had any tomb to show. Molinet was taken in, saying that the boys had been given "royal obsequies" after King Richard's death, but few followed him. No funerals would have been held with more pomp and show than those of the princes if Henry had discovered them. There could also have been false tombs and false bones, the ossified remains of any poor children wrapped in rags of velvet, as the presumed bones allegedly appeared when they were found in 1674. Any of these would have helped the king. Yet none could be as convincing as the stiffening bodies, still recognisable, laid out naked from the waist up as Richard Neville's had been, "to show the people"—thereby rendering as cold, and as dead, any lingering hopes the people may have had.

IV

HAVING DECIDED TO HELP HIM—having been unable to refuse him— Margaret now had to determine how to do so. She had no resources, she told Isabella, but was a poor widow as bereft as Richard was. She hardly knew where to turn. Her first action, tantamount to declaring war on his behalf, was to organise through Philip's council the issue of letters of marque, allowing Flemish merchants to take reprisals against English ships. But to raise the money and armies needed to win back a kingdom was clearly beyond her: "for after so many slaughters of our most unhappy house . . . what help, what aid remains in me?" For the moment, she had to make her protégé a king in other ways, by polishing him and giving him the tokens and trappings of royalty.

Richard "kept his magnificence", as Molinet put it, first in the Hôtel de Bourgogne in Malines, which Margaret had placed at his disposal as soon as he arrived, and later at the Hôtel des Anglais in Antwerp, the House of the Merchant Adventurers. This house stood in Bullinckstrate, or Wool Street, beside the Old Bourse: a substantial building on three floors, with a fashionably stepped façade, three entrance doors and half a dozen large windows for each floor on the street side. Inside were several chapels, though the Merchant Adventurers, when they left in the summer of 1493, were careful to take with them the "jewels and stuff" with which the chapels had been decorated. Bare rooms with stripped-down altars, at least at first, heard Richard's prayers for the success of the enterprise.

Outside the House of the Merchant Adventurers he displayed his arms, also provided by Margaret: an escutcheon quartered with the royal arms of England and France, the three lions and the three lilies. (He preserved, as all English kings did, a largely spurious claim to France based on territories long since lost.) Beneath the shield, written out in full, were his titles: *Arma Ricardi principis Walie et ducis Eboraci, filii et heredis Edouardi quarti, nuper Dei gratia, regis Anglie et Francie, domini Ybernie*. Molinet reported that this shield, "displayed as a public and common spectacle where so many very illustrious princes were passing, so many grand persons and merchants from different countries", astounded some people. Two of those offended, English supporters of King Henry, rode up one night to throw a big pot of mud and "other filth" at it, meaning to mock and degrade not only the arms and the titles, but, with them, the young man who flaunted them. Clumsily, they splattered the door rather than the shield, and Richard's protectors burst out and gave chase. The culprits got away, but an innocent bystander was killed in hot blood during the pursuit. He had felt, Molinet wrote, the rough sharp-stinging thorns of the White Rose defending his arms: or rather of Margaret's and Philip's men, defending them for him.

One of Maximilian and Philip's most trusted officers, Huc de Melun, governor of Dendermonde and knight of the Golden Fleece, was put in charge of Richard's affairs, "running the whole business". A big house at Dendermonde was also made available to him, and it was from here that he wrote to Isabella, pressing his newly provided signet ring, engraved with lions and lilies, into the warm red wax. De Melun took command of Richard's personal bodyguard, thirty halberdiers in the Yorkist livery of murrey and blue embroidered with the white rose: exactly the outfits that Margaret's bargemen had worn when they had escorted her by water from London. That glorious Yorkist scene, Margaret's last sighting of England with her house at the apogee of its power, was now revived in Richard.

The badge of the white rose that surrounded him had become his personal possession, as it had been Edward's. On the king's accession, a chronicler had dreamed of the garden that might be made in England "with this fair white rose and herb". Margaret now wanted her protégé to walk in that image from day to day. Round the court, at her insistence, Richard was called "the White Rose". Molinet too followed her orders, working the metaphor with delight. "The rose bush that symbolised England," he wrote, "was heavy at that time with double roses, some of which were carried by the king and some, white ones, by Richard of York, and their thorns were scratching each other." Envoys and merchants visiting Flanders picked up the image too. Caspar Weinreich, a Prussian merchant trading with Flanders, referred in his Chronicle simply to "the White Rose" who, in the summer of 1494, sprang up against the King of England; Adam Abell's vernacular chronicle spoke of the "White Rose" who arrived, apparently fresh from Margaret, in Scotland; and the only time Raimondo Soncino called the Duke of York "the White Rose" was when he was writing to Milan from Bruges in the summer of 1497. Richard was the prince on whom the hopes of York depended, and Margaret did not let him forget it.

Edward IV's white rose had come with a motto: *confort et liesse*, comfort and joy. Margaret's White Rose was quite likely to have kept the motto of the man he claimed as his father. Such a tag was even more appropriate to him, the prince restored to his people, as Jesus at His Nativity had brought God in person to mankind. He had scarcely been recognised, a poor frail child who had formed in His mother's womb as quietly as dew on the April grass. "Who have you seen, shepherds? *Quem vidisti?*, ran the teasing Christmas antiphon. Surely not a king? Yes, truly, a king: comfort and joy.

The white rose was Margaret's device also, occurring on her jewels and belts, on her wedding crown and in her books. By sharing it with him, their stems were twined together and their common stock made obvious. White roses also proclaimed their dedication to the Virgin, whose flower this was, and placed their enterprise under her protection. By then, it was almost a secret code between them, like the "White Rose" letters later sent from him to her: a code everyone knew, as they knew the Ragged Staff was Warwick and the Eagle was Stanley. These badges

themselves—for which men plotted and fought, fastening them on their hats or stamping them on their spurs—summed up the character of a dynasty, its strength, its forbearance or its craftiness. If Richard Plantagenet was now the White Rose, the symbolism to a certain degree overtook the name and the face. It transfigured him.

But two could play at roses, as England knew. Henry VII's red rose, or his new Tudor rose of Yorkist white and Lancastrian red, were badges of triumph that were being carved on the king's palaces and leaded in his windows, sewn onto his liveries and painted in his books. His buckhounds had red roses, fleurs-de-lis, crowns "and other our badges" enamelled on their gilt collars. Sick men and women in the London hospital he founded lay under green-and-white coverlets, his colours, embroidered with the red rose. Henry's court poets described a garden of Tudor roses being planted in England, barbed and seeded proper, as the genealogists insisted, and guarded by the Richmond greyhounds and the Beaufort portcullises, the other devices of his family. Against these the White Rose in Malines was sometimes equal: Edward's swelling and aggressive flower, its branches stuck with thorns. More often, however, the symbol mirroring Richard's fortunes, it seemed decorative and almost powerless. It could prick and scratch, as when the degraders of Richard's escutcheon had been roughly chased away. But its beauty had not yet made the point that this was a badge to fear.

Behind these outward signs, the prince himself may still have needed working on. The chroniclers reported that Margaret made her protégé repeat again and again, in public and private, the tale of his wonderful escape and of his wanderings, smoothing it with repetition and turning it by long familiarity into his own life. Vergil said, as André did, that these stories were the chief reason people believed in him.

In general, few public utterances were required of princes. Much of the ceremonial was conducted without words. A man knelt to his prince, was motioned to rise, was beckoned to come closer or take up another position, and was grateful for any remark that was made to him. When the prince turned his back, he was tired of him and, wordlessly, expected him to leave. Meals were consumed largely in silence, though minstrels might play or improving books might be read aloud to the diners. Richard, however, had to speak more than most, since so much of his pulling power lay in his story.

His public recitals were presumably both in French and in English, raising again the question of how well he spoke either. A prince's claim to speak a language often meant little: Maximilian boasted that he had picked up Bohemian from peasants, Spanish "from messages in letters" and English from archers. Sycophantic servants would ensure that their masters believed they were fluent, even if they could do no more than drop a stray phrase into a conversation. Again, Richard had to do considerably better than that.

Certainly, at first, his English was not much needed. In France he could have spoken French to almost everyone, including Alexander Monypeny, his guardian-in-chief, without incurring comment. (For his part, Henry VII in England conducted much of his business, and confessed, in French, feeling more at ease in this than in English.) Northern European princes spoke French as the normal language of royalty, the mark of a civilised man, and shouted it on the tennis court and the hunting field. French had been the language of the books of chivalry and romance that Edward IV had acquired for the instruction of his sons; French words had given Richard, Duke of York his first images of knightly adventure, as his servants carefully carved and served his meat.

The working language of the court of Burgundy was also French, written and spoken. Margaret's estate accounts were in French, as were all the books she commissioned for her library. She prayed in it, as well as using it for impatient memoranda. Yet she also kept her English going. When Caxton presented her with the first printed quires of his translation of the *Recueil des Histoires de Troie*, Margaret checked them through and found "a fault in mine English which she commanded me to amend." The fault, Caxton surmised, came from his clumsy Kentish mannerisms; he had learned to speak and spell broad Wealden English, rather than the polished court version the duchess knew.

If an English prince, risen from the dead, had come to Margaret's court, he would have had to speak English on at least some occasions to her and her visitors, however Frenchified he might appear from day to day. She could not have carried on the promotion, or the deception, without it. And it seems that her protégé rose to the occasion. André claimed, for Henry's ears, that the boy had been brought up in England; Vergil said he already spoke English when Margaret found him. In the confession, he learned it twice over. All this suggested his English was so good that it needed accounting for. No slips in English were laid against him afterwards, although this would have been a simple way to expose and mock him, and despite the fact that even native speakers could get mixed up when they had lived some time among foreigners. After eight years in Bruges, Caxton in his French-Flemish phrase-book was beginning to drop Flemish words into his English: "It en is not", from the Flemish *het en es niet*, and "spoil the cup" from *spoel*, meaning "rinse". He may not have noticed, but Englishmen would.

Only two pieces of evidence give a hint of what this young man's English sounded like. In September 1497 Richmond Herald, who was probably a native of southern France and who worked mostly in French at Henry's court, described him as "well-spoken". He seemed to mean in English, though that is not completely certain, and the young man might naturally have fallen into French with him. If it was English, Richmond was a poor judge of that; he was said to have turned down the job of Garter Herald in the mid-1490s because he could not speak the language well enough. By "well-spoken", he probably meant a gracious manner of speech in which the graciousness, rather than the grammar, impressed him.

A second clue comes from October 1496, when a letter was written by "Richard of England" from Edinburgh. The beautiful hand, strikingly close to the finest hand of Edward IV's secretariat, was not his, belonging probably to the scrivener Nicholas Astley, who was in his service; the well-bred English spelling was Astley's job, too; but the elegant English itself and the almost overzealous punctuation, in an age that largely ignored it, were strongly suggestive of the way Richard had spoken as he dictated. The phrasing of his proclamation to the people of England, probably written a few weeks before, was very similar. There were few English people around him at this stage in his career, none of them—Sir George Neville partly excepted—of quality; and there were none, as far as we know, whose English was like this.

> Right trusty and our right entirely well-beloved, We greet you heartily well / Signifying unto you that we be credibly informed of the great love favour and kindness, that ye in time past showed unto our most dread lord and Father King Edward the fourth, whose soul god rest, With the sage / and politic counsels, that ye, in sundry wises, full lovingly gave unto him, whereby he obtained, the advancement and promoting of his matters and causes: wherefore ye stood right much in the favour of his grace. / Desire and heartily pray you, to be from henceforth unto Us: as loving / faithful and

kind Counsellor and Friend: as ye were unto our said Father, in showing your good and discreet minds for Us, in such matters and causes, as by your great wisdom ye shall seem best to be moved / for our weal / comfort and relief / and that it will please you to exhort move and stir / our lovers and friends / to do the same / and that We may understand, the good heart and mind that our most dear Cousin the King of Spain / beareth towards Us. / And in your so doing / you may be sure to have Us / as loving a good lord. unto you / or better, than ever was our said lord and Father. And any thing: that ye shall of reason desire of Us / that may concern the weal of you, and of our right trusty and well-beloved servant / your son / Anthony de la Forsa: which hath full lovingly, given his long attendance upon Us / in sundry Countries, We shall with good heart / be ready / to accomplish, and perform the same / When it shall please almighty god to send Us unto our right / in England; and that it may please you, to give credence unto your said Son of such things as he shall show unto you. / And our lord Jesu preserve you in all honour joy and felicity, and send you the accomplishment of your noble heart's desire.

The style this letter most closely resembled in the graceful musicality of its phrases was that of Earl Rivers, poet-philosopher and knight-errant, who had overseen the education of Edward, Prince of Wales. That was the standard: as literate as England could produce.

His handwriting, too, looked English, though high-class French-men and Burgundians—including Archduke Philip and the Binche receiver—could also produce hands much like this. Since no sample of his writing survives from before August 1493, it is hard to tell what improvements, if any, were made to his hand in Malines. By then it was impressive, often hard to distinguish in size or fluency from the hand of the notary or the secretary. His "Richard" was signed in the same way as almost any other English Richard of the time: a V-shaped "R", a trailing "y" (never "i"), a loop on the final "d". His signature did not change through his career, though it got more confident. The first surviving example, on the letter to Isabella, was small and cautious; the one on the letter from Scotland was deliberately larger and freer, a bold prince's hand. To have fine and plausibly English handwriting, if he was a fake, showed extraordinary care in his fakers, since princes wrote so seldom that any vaguely educated hand might pass muster. Maximilian, for example, said that people were amazed by his own good handwriting, and James IV's signature, from a highly cultured man, was a child's scrawl. If his handwriting did not prove Plantagenet was authentic, it nonetheless showed the meticulousness with which he had been created.

His manners, too, seemed perfect. Moving as he did among royalty, he could not have got away with less. Envoys noted, in detail, the dispositions and words of princes when they first met them. They recorded whether they had smiled, stepped forward, nodded, drawn the envoy confidingly aside or made any other gesture of graciousness. If the visitor was near in rank, there was careful hat-work to be done: the velvet bonnet nudged, half-lifted, sometimes removed completely and held flat against the chest for as long as was honourable and fitting. At table, precedence in sitting down and taking water to wash was very keenly noted. The meetings of princes with favourite envoys sometimes entailed small comedies of stirrup-holding and elbow-taking, or were complicated by national fashions in kissing. The giving of gifts, often meant to be spontaneous, could lead to long *combats de generosité* in which the recipient protested his unworthiness and the giver, with increasingly sharp-edged courtesy, forced them on him.

Richard Plantagenet seemed to fit flawlessly into this world. A tiny detail of his manners emerged in 1496 in Scotland, when he approached and politely saluted a Burgundian captain who would not speak to him. He observed thereby the first rule of courtesy, that a man should be eager to greet others first, and showed besides that he had learned to imitate Edward IV's confident and easy accessibility to ordinary people.

There were no recorded mistakes, save one that was apparently mentioned by Giles, Lord Daubeney, Henry's chamberlain, in October 1497. When the young man called himself Plantagenet in France, Daubeney wrote, he said it was his baptismal name, "and that the second son of King Edward was so called. And by this it appears that the whole affair was a lie and an abusion." This, sent across to Calais with the confession, seemed to be the best that Henry and his officers could do. At one point, he had got his name wrong. Yet many may neither have noticed nor been bothered. Erasmo Brascha, the Milanese ambassador in Flanders, reported a conversation in which Richard told him that "Ireland had held him for its lord before he went to France." The remark seemed utterly cas-

ual and confident, as well as embellished, since Ireland had done no such
thing. Brascha relayed it straightforwardly, feeling no urge to question
whether this young man was really so exalted. He took him for a prince
as, by now, he was.

Margaret's next necessity was to seek out new sponsors for him. Richard's
letter to Isabella claimed that by this stage, late August 1493, "envoys
offering friendship and confederation" had come to him from Denmark
and Scotland, and that "great nobles of England," banished by Henry,
were also seeking him out. But the most vital man to persuade was Maximilian, King of the Romans: not only Margaret's lord and her stepson-in-
law, but potentially the most powerful ruler in Europe. That very month
Maximilian's father, the Holy Roman Emperor Frederick III, had been
suddenly carried off by a surfeit of ripe melons and cold water; and the
whole sprawling territory of the Habsburg empire, stretching from the
North Sea to the Dolomites to the borders of Hungary, had fallen at last
to his son's charge.

Maximilian was thirty-three, getting into middle age: magnificently
athletic, intellectually omnivorous, aquiline, jut-jawed, and distracted by
ambitions as various as the lands he ruled over. From well before his
father's death, he had been deeply embroiled in trying to consolidate the
interests of the Empire. In particular, he wavered between mending
fences with France and fighting to regain the territories on his western border, a land-claim going back to Charlemagne. In 1490 he had opted for
peace of a sort, concluding a treaty of marriage between his little daughter
Margaret and Charles VIII; but within a year Charles had broken that
treaty and sent Margaret home. Maximilian did not forget the humiliation. Worse was to come, for in November 1492 Henry VII, a possible
and intermittent friend, suddenly made peace with Charles. The treaty left
the King of the Romans, as one Prussian merchant put it, "sitting
between two chairs". Maximilian, incensed at this betrayal, now began to
look for ways to take revenge on Henry. As it happened, Margaret had
just the instrument he needed: a young man whose hopes had also been
dashed by the Treaty of Etaples. As long as Maximilian had been toying
with an English alliance, she had hesitated perhaps to push her White
Rose forward. Now she could.

In November 1493, therefore, it was arranged that Richard should go to Frederick III's funeral in Vienna. (The old emperor's body, brought slowly down the Danube from Linz on a funerary barge ablaze with lights, had lain for fifteen weeks in the cathedral while his far-flung subjects made their way towards him.) Richard went with Duke Albrecht of Saxony, Maximilian's uncle, and Albrecht's son Duke Henry. Already, however, he appeared to have little need of chaperoning. On the evening of November 6th, a Tyrolese official called Ludwig Klingkhamer caught sight of him as he came into Vienna. The grand entourage was travelling in three carriages, presumably one each, containing also their luggage and changes of clothes. With at least four horses to each carriage and thirty mounted attendants to each lord, this made a considerable procession. Klingkhamer thought the young man with Albrecht and Henry was "a king from England"—indeed, he thought he was Margaret of Burgundy's "own brother", or Edward IV himself.

The party had to wait a while for Maximilian, who had business to finish against the Turks; but on the Wednesday after St. Katherine's Day, November 25th, he received Richard in audience. Into his reception hall, crowded with princes and ambassadors (as an officer reported back to Nuremberg), came "a young lord"

> who claims to be the rightful next natural heir to the kingdom of England. He had Bruno, his spokesman [Ludovico Bruno, Maximilian's Latin secretary], make a formal speech in Latin, an *oratio*, as the learned men would say: how he was deprived of his kingdom by the pretended King of England who currently ruled there, and how they were unjustly keeping it from him by force, although it was his by right and nature. For this reason he was desperately unhappy, and by telling his story he was begging [Maximilian] for his gracious advice, help and support, that he might not be utterly abandoned. In the same manner he asked the princes and the ambassadors to support his request before His Majesty with their prayers.
>
> The chancellor, Dr. Konrad Sturtzel, answered him in Latin on His Royal Majesty's behalf and with the advice of the princes and ambassadors. His Imperial Majesty was delighted to see in person the prince who had just been announced and glad that he had arrived in good health. And he was very sorry for the adversity he had met, or might meet. But as the matter was so important and so serious, His Royal Majesty wanted to think it over, take advice, and

then give an answer. And if [the prince] found any shortcomings in his lodgings, anything that was not arranged to his pleasure, His Majesty would give orders that it should be put right.

They exchanged these speeches and then took leave of each other.

Ten days later, on St. Nicholas's Day, December 6th, the visitors converged for Frederick's funeral. The setting was the Stefankirche in Vienna, in which, Molinet reported, 8,412 Masses had already been said for the emperor in the weeks when his body had lain there. The atmosphere in the cathedral was so thick with incense and candle-smoke that it was difficult to breathe, and the open sobbing of mourners added to the heaviness of the air. It was late in the day, and the background gloom of the Stefankirche was reinforced by black drapes that fell from the vaulting to the floor. Almost eight hundred candles, each of them repelling a demon from the corpse and lighting the way for Frederick's soul, burned in sconces on the columns and the walls.

A wooden chapel, built for the occasion, stood in the centre of the church with 346 candles blazing around it. Inside was the emperor's coffin, covered with white damask and then with black silk embroidered with a great cross of gold. Laid out on the coffin were the symbols of Frederick's power: his sword, his sceptre, the imperial crown, the golden orb. The Herald of the Empire, in a surcoat of cloth-of-gold, stood before it, and around it were forty-eight monks in black hooded capes, heads bowed, with flaming torches in their hands.

The cathedral was filled with nobles from every corner of the Empire, and beyond it. Their precedence, both in seating and in the offertory procession, had been arranged with exquisite care by nearness of blood and degree to the dead emperor. For this first Mass, "Richard, son of Edward, king of England" was on the socially lower left-hand side of the coffin, among the representatives and ambassadors. He was not with Maximilian, or Albrecht of Saxony, or the archbishops. Yet he had ridden to the cathedral in the most distinguished group, headed by Maximilian and the representatives of the Kings of France, Hungary and Sicily; and as everyone stood in the church, there were dukes and bishops enough on his side. The man who went ahead of him in the offertory procession was Georges Lucq, the commander of the Teutonic Order and the Duke of Lorraine and Bar. After him came at least two lords, a canon and a count. Since so many princes had sent representatives rather than making the long trip themselves, his presence in person was noted in the official record. It is strange, in view of later opinions about him, to see him listed as "King Edward of England's son in person" and "King Edward's son of England himself", but so he appeared: the real thing, rather than the proxies that others had sent.

At the Mass of Requiem the next day, he did better in his ranking. That service included a long eulogy (an *exclamation*, Molinet called it) by Jehan Perger, a distinguished poet, noting Frederick's victories and his journeys to all the Holy Places "where Our Saviour walked with His precious feet." After this, the lords of the sixteen counties, dukedoms and provinces of the Empire offered at the hearse their banners, helms, shields and torches, and each province led a horse, caparisoned with livery and shying from the blaze, as far as the platform of fire. This time Richard found himself alongside Henry of Saxony and Albert, Duke of Bavaria, the emperor's son-in-law, both right-hand-siders of the day before. After the presentation of the horses he and the other mourners, in order, walked up to do reverence and make offering again. He did so with two of Archduke Philip's representatives, one on either side of him. They laid their purses of money on the coffin, on which Frederick's imperial robes were now arranged, and knelt for a moment among the jewels and lights and paraphernalia of gold, as if caught inside a treasure-box of flame.

If you had watched King Edward's son then, he would have been equally aware that he was being watched. He might have wept a little, stirred by the tears of those around him. His devotion, like his sorrow, was part-sincere, part-show; *oraison très-dévote par semblant*, as Chastellain remarked of Louis XI as he knelt and prayed, for a very long time, before the holy oil at his coronation. Merely to be part of such a scene, on such a scale, worked to Richard's advantage, even if he was barely distinguished in the richness of the crowd. More or less from that moment, Maximilian adopted him.

The new emperor's second-wife-to-be, Bianca Maria Sforza, the daughter of the Duke of Milan, adopted him also. On January 20th she reported to her father that "the son of King Edward" had brought her a letter from Maximilian and a declaration of his own cause, delivered orally in his name as Bruno had delivered it at that first audience, from Jason Maynus and Baltasar Pusterla, Maximilian's chief rhetoricians. Both the written form of the declaration and a copy of Maximilian's letter were sent on to Ludovico Sforza. Bianca Maria had received this appeal "most properly", her father told her. From Richard's point of view, his salesmanship had now reached Milan.

His place at Maximilian's court was soon established. On December 14th, and again on March 17th, he was a witness among other dukes to Maximilian's grants of privileges. But March 16th saw a far more impressive sign of favour. On that Sunday in Innsbruck, exactly a week after the marriage of Maximilian and Bianca Maria (when, according to the Milanese envoy, he was showering her with presents and "they were sleeping together daily"), Maximilian had determined that they should go to Mass together, Bianca Maria dressed in the German fashion and wearing the beautiful crown he had given her. This was, in effect, their ceremonial displaying of themselves after their marriage. A huge company went to the church, filing in behind the unsheathed imperial sword carried by Georg of Polheim: gouty Sigmund of Tyrol in a litter, the Duchess Katarina "covered from head to foot in pearls", Bianca Maria in her crown. The new Queen of the Romans was accompanied by Albrecht of Saxony and Christopher of Baden; Maximilian's escort was the son of King Edward of England, alone. "[Cardinal Peraudi] and four bishops read the Mass," the envoy went on. "There was glorious organ-playing, with trombones and horns, and the singing was outstanding. At the banquet, sitting with the King of the Romans and the queen, were Cardinal Peraudi, Archduke Sigmund, the Duke of Saxony and Richard of England. Queen Bianca behaved most charmingly . . ."

So, clearly, did Richard. He sat there as Edward's son, in his proper place at the top table, accepted. His Englishness Maximilian and Bianca Maria had to take on trust, since Maximilian admitted that he could only understand, not speak, the English he had learned from those archers. Richard's claim, for the moment, could not count on explicit help from them. But they did not question his credentials as a prince. In his later autobiography, the *Weisskunig*, Maximilian remarked that nobility was as obvious as a clear and precious stone, or as a fine fruit with a delicate flavour: it shone from a man, or left a perfume about him, that could be recognised at once. It probably did no harm that Maximilian also found fair hair, like his own, "peculiarly beautiful".

In the further reaches of Europe, in the shadow of the Alps, which prince this young man might actually be did not matter particularly. In terms of diplomatic games, it did not matter whether he was truly a prince or not. But that he was a prince, in his entrance and dismounting and walking and talking, was not doubted by those who met or saw him. It was because he was so plausible, as backer after backer discovered straight away, that he could be so useful.

Once Richard had returned to Flanders with Maximilian in the summer of 1494, there was no lack of opportunities to parade and shine. In mid-August he rode into Malines with Maximilian, Bianca Maria and the young Archduke Philip, making his joyous entry alongside them. All along the streets, hung with rich cloths and tapestries, stood painted stages showing live captioned tableaux from the Bible and classical mythology; there were dances, jousts and fireworks. On the 18th, the imperial party entered Antwerp to an even more sumptuous welcome. Molinet described it: it was night time, and the town was so full of flambeaux and lanterns, with so many wax torches fixed to the gates, bell-towers and houses, that it seemed as if the whole place was on fire.

Similar wonders were conjured up on the evening of September 10th at Louvain, in Brabant, when Philip took his oath as the new lord. His friend Richard, Edward's son, escorted him, sitting on a special dais draped with cloth-of-gold beside Maximilian, the Duke of Brunswick, Albrecht of Saxony and the Archbishop of Mainz, as the privileges of Brabant "at great length, and in German" were read out to the archduke. Trumpets and clarions then sounded "a fantastic fanfare". At the princes' back was the town hall, pinnacle upon pinnacle of vaulting stone chiseled like lace and floodlit with torches; before them was a crowd in which each person held a candle, like a burning sea of souls beneath the sparks of the stars. Edward's son shone too, and the gold on him blazed, the lights and the dark both flattering and obscuring him.

Molinet recorded him again on the evening of October 5th, once more in Antwerp, at Philip's grand entry as Duke of Brabant. As usual, the two young men rode in together. The streets had been hung again with tapestries and silk, and "stories" had been installed both inside and outside the town. Among these "new, singular, joyous entertainments" was a castle, six or seven feet high by as many wide, hanging in the air, with subtle machinery inside it that let off a shattering noise as the arch-duke passed, making everyone jump. But the firm favourite, "the one to which people gave the most affectionate glances", was the story of the Three Goddesses, "and you saw them naked, and real live women."

Philip, aged sixteen, was the star of this show, the new Duke of Brabant coming into his inheritance. An "imitation angel" hung in the air
above the marketplace, its wings lit up with fireworks, bringing him a
sword in token of his sovereignty. But Molinet noticed particularly
Richard of York, "really handsome", *fort gorgias*, shining in splendour,
surrounded *pour triompher* by his own courtiers and twenty archers in
white-rose livery. The chronicler recorded him on the grand platform outside the town hall at around ten the next morning, after High Mass, as
Philip took his ducal oaths before the people, and gold and silver coins,
like bright rain, were thrown down on the crowd.

Molinet, writing this scene in later years with the young man's confession before him, claimed to be already uneasy about this Prince of
England. Richard of York was perhaps just another clever contrivance, a
castle in the air. Yet at the time neither he, nor most other people in town,
could prove that by observing him. In the pageant that was Richard, there
was an impression of expense, gilding and good workmanship that was
perfectly satisfactory at a general or even a closer glance.

Henry VII, Molinet added, was astonished at the "state, honour,
upkeep and favour" shown to Richard by the Burgundian court. The
magnificence and exaltation in themselves, as Polydore Vergil said,
"dressed up the lie in the likeness of truth." The young man, so patently
glorying in his honours and his title, both believed in himself and drew
others to believe. Henry's envoys reported that Richard was enjoying himself as he pleased, with plenty of people to support him in his hopes of
the crown and a growing crowd of recruits to help him win it. Yet his foreign favourers did not know for sure that this young man was the Duke of
York. As Molinet said, they hoped he was.

From time to time, unnerving visitors from England tried to pull the
pageant prince apart. In September 1493, Henry sent Sir Edward Poynings and Dr. William Warham to tell Margaret, with her White Rose
beside her, that this prince of hers was both *sordido genere* and a cooking-
pot boy, and was nothing but the fruit of her own monstrous pregnancy.
Margaret, furious, "would have done all kinds of injury to William,"
Vergil wrote, "if he had not taken care of himself." The next year,
Garter Herald came to tell Philip and Margaret that Richard, again present and *princiant* in his stillness and his gold, was *fils d'ung vilain*, a base
man's son. On that occasion, too, the envoys were rebuffed and their
observations dismissed as evidently ridiculous.

A third incident occurred in the spring of 1495, when Sir Charles Somerset, Henry's cupbearer and the captain of his guard, arrived in Brabant on a mission to Maximilian. Somerset was an impressive figure, the English equivalent of Monypeny or d'Aubigny, who usually went at the head of an elite guard of one hundred royal archers. He was also the bastard son of Henry Beaufort, third Duke of Somerset, which gave some edge to the exchange that followed.

The English envoy was shown into the receiving chamber to find everyone together on the dais, Richard at Margaret's side. Invited to approach, Somerset bowed to Maximilian; bowed to Margaret; bowed to Philip; but made no sign of reverence to the other person there.

Margaret bridled instantly, unable to hold back in the fierceness of her anger. "It seems you do not recognise my nephew Richard," she told Somerset, "since you do not deign to bow to him."

"Madam, your nephew Richard is long dead," Somerset replied. "And if it would please you to lend me one of your people, I will take him straight to the chapel where he is buried."

At this point, Richard interjected. He was amazed, *merveilleusement estonnez*, that Somerset should think him dead. When he was enthroned in his kingdom, he told him, which he hoped would be soon, he would not forget those words; while he, Somerset, *vilain menteur*, base-born liar, would most painfully regret them.

Somerset apparently did not answer, and this seemed to be the end of the interview. If he had not gone to Malines with his mind made up and his story straight, nothing would have suggested to him that the young man he looked on was not a prince. He was on a dais beside princes, beautifully dressed, and he had spoken for himself with controlled flashes of anger; for that "marvellously astonished" showed that he was certainly angry, or feigning to be. *En princiant, [il] tenoit ses gravitez*, said Molinet; he kept a solemn and impressive princeliness, as Aristotle recommended. If any aspect raised a doubt, it was perhaps the way Margaret leaped in at once to defend him, as if her sense of his honour and his identity was stronger than his own. Yet even that protection, by the dowager duchess and the doyenne of the House of York, might have confirmed the title he was claiming.

Some chroniclers thought he was frightened and demoralised whenever Henry's envoys came to Malines, relying on Margaret to argue for him and sometimes to bundle him bodily from the room. Though the mockery made her furiously angry, Richard himself was terrified. The truth seems otherwise: he knew the forms and rituals and, by carefully observing them, he could defend himself. As long as Margaret was physically beside him, however, she saw that task as hers.

For much of his time at her court she also seems to have kept him close and apart from other people. It is easy to believe that though few were admitted to Margaret's study—green velvet on the table, purple taffeta on the walls, a writing desk of solid silver and, behind a grille, the beautiful books laid out—he was often allowed there. He was her secret, the one she was perfectly happy not to share with Ferdinand and Isabella if they sniffed at it; he was her prize, to be produced for those she felt she could trust to support him. His public appearances, like any prince's, were carefully staged and controlled. When Robert Clifford went to Malines, Vergil said, it was Margaret who persuaded him on his arrival that everything he had heard about Richard of York was true. She offered him the proofs herself. Only later did she show him "her" Richard, as though he were a tableau arranged in an antechamber, a young prince snatched from Hell to Heaven, with the scroll of his life-history falling from his hand.

V

THROUGH ALL THE PROPS AND PAGEANTRY the idea gradually emerged that Margaret's White Rose was not merely a prince, but a king. In 1493 he seemed still shy of making the claim directly. The wording on his escutcheon made him "prince" and "duke" only; his letter to Isabella, though filed away by the secretary with the remark "from Richard who calls himself King of England", made him "cousin", no more. Yet even this betrayed the first inklings of kingship. "Cousin" did not mean just the thin relationship of blood that existed between Richard of York and Isabella, going back to Philippa of Lancaster, the sister of Henry IV, but the general courteous sense in which all rulers were "cousins" across Europe. He had ended the letter with an almost cheeky *bene valeat*, "Hope you're well," rather than the usual elaborate commendation to God. As of right, he kept company with kings and considered himself one of them.

Margaret's letter, too, traded on this theme. She asked Isabella to make our case to your husband . . . so that once he, together with your Excellency, has recognised this man as a kinsman bound to him by laws of blood, he may do whatever he can to send him favour and help. For if, by divine assistance, he should recover his inheritance (which, with the help of the nobles of England, we hope may happen), he guarantees and promises that he shall be bound by even greater closeness, alliances, deference and love to your Majesties and Kingdoms, than was his father King Edward in time past.

Richard's escutcheon, his signet and his seal already made play with the royal arms of England. Soon he had his own royal money, too. In 1494, silver *gros* coins were minted for him, apparently in some quantity as specie for his eventual invasion. They bore no king's name; that, perhaps, was still a step too far. But the obverse carried the legend *Domine Salvum fac Regem*, "God save the King", from the ninth verse of the twentieth psalm: a motto that Edward IV had adopted as his own. It also bore within a tressure of five curves the royal shield of England, surmounted by an arched crown, flanked by a crowned rose and a crowned fleur-de-lis. The reverse carried, within a tressure of four curves, another rose, another lily, an arched crown and a lion of England: lots of royal symbols, as if he and Margaret could not decide which they most wanted.

Another lion of England marked the beginning of the legend on either side. The legend on the reverse was a prophecy, *Mani, Teckel, Phares*, a shortened form of God's warning to Belshazzar written on the wall by the shining hand: *Mene, mene, tekel, upharsin*. Here, on a silver groat, was a sharper challenge to Henry Tudor than Richard Plantagenet ever managed to deliver in person. *Mene*, God hath numbered thy kingdom, and finished it; *Tekel*, thou art weighed in the balance and found wanting; *Upharsin*, thy kingdom is divided, and given to the Medes and the Persians. Or to me.

The device on his seal made the same uncompromising claim. It bore, under the royal arms, the inscription "Secret seal of Richard IV, King of England and France and Lord of Ireland." By 1494 he was sealing documents, and signing them too, as a king. He was now *Rychard d'engleterre* (another echo of Margaret, who signed herself *Marguerite d'engleterre*). His secret seal, used only for documents of the greatest importance, showed the royal arms of England and France again, under an arched crown. The crown enclosed more fleurs-de-lis, and crowned lions holding ostrich feathers.

His actual claim to the throne was never argued out in detail on paper, either by himself or by others. He claimed it by simple right of blood, as Edward's son. Had you challenged him (having moved beyond more basic questions of identity), he would probably have produced a version of a famous roll of genealogy commissioned by Edward IV around 1470. This roll, scattered all over with white roses, golden crowns and the fetterlock of the Dukes of York, traced Edward's claim to England back through his father, Richard, Duke of York, who was son and heir of Anne, daughter of Roger Mortimer, Earl of March, who was son and heir of Philippa, daughter of Lionel, the second son of Edward III. It then moved back further still, in a heavy red line punctuated with red circles and boxes, through the Norman kings, the Saxon kings, the pre-Roman kings, Arthur and the sons of Noah, and ended in Eden, where Adam and Eve in their leafy aprons ate the apple under the tree.

Edward had claimed the throne *de facto* in 1461—his predecessor, Henry VI, being both in custody and judged incapable—by seating him-self on the marble chair in Westminster Hall. He claimed it also *de jure*, calling his father, Richard, Duke of York, "king in right of the realm of England". Having inherited the kingdom like a piece of property, as his father's "vray and just heir", his title was then assured by the lords in council and by the acclamation of the people as he sat on the King's Bench in the royal cap and robe, with the sceptre in his hand. He later claimed it again from the throne in Westminster Abbey, with St. Edward's crown on his head, while the congregation saluted him as just, legitimate and true. On the two days following, he kept wearing the crown so that people should see him and know that it was his. As he wore it at St. Paul's on the second day, a representation of an angel descended and censed him: God's power directly flowing from Heaven to the House of York.

Yet the Yorkist claim was shaky. It not only passed through women, but lacked the recent continuity of the Lancastrians in Henry IV, Henry V and Henry VI. Edward had won his crown in 1461 only by removing that last Henry, the reigning monarch, from the throne that was his. In 1470, under the threat of a Lancastrian restoration engineered by the Earl of Warwick, Edward himself had been forced to flee the country. Charles the Bold, who sheltered him, signed a statement in 1471—when

Edward was barely out of the door—declaring himself heir through his mother, Isabella of Portugal, to all the possessions of Henry VI, and promising to make good his claim as soon as possible. In 1475 he remarked to a Milanese ambassador that "Edward was afraid of him, in fact hated him, on account of his claim to the English crown." His own title, Charles bragged, was much better than Edward's. There was an argument in this, as well as a reminder of the others who waited if Edward stumbled.

After his victory at Barnet in 1471, Edward gave out that his title now rested on reason, the authority of Parliament and his triumphs on the battlefield. Yet in 1485, at Bosworth, that claim of victory in battle passed to Henry Tudor. God (who controlled the disposition of such things) had approved him, rather than the blood of Edward. Henry had had the *Te Deum* sung on the field of Bosworth and immediately afterward, the sweat of battle still on him, had exercised his royal prerogative by knighting eleven of his followers. Richard's battle coronet, plucked in legend from a hawthorn bush, became one of his devices, with the branches growing through it to become his own dynastic flowers. His victory at Stoke two years later showed God's continued blessing of his rule, and the battle-standards he had carried then were dedicated in thanks to Our Lady at Walsingham. The image of himself he ordered for his tomb was "in manner of an armed man", of wood plated with fine gold, in full armour, sword and spurs, "holding between his hands the Crown which it pleased God to give us, with the victory of our Enemy at our first field."

Sanctified victories apart, Henry's title was considerably weaker than that of the pageant-king across the Channel, if the pageant-king's claim was true. His descent, after all, was by illegitimate line from John of Gaunt, the third son of Edward III. To England's crown, as Richard III put it, "he hath no manner of interest, right, title or colour, as every man well knoweth; for he is descended of bastard blood, both of father's side, and of mother's side." Although the Beauforts, who made up much of this bastard blood, had been legitimised, doubts remained as to whether or not they were banned from holding the crown. Only the result of one battle, not particularly noticed outside England, proved to anyone that Henry should have been king.

He himself acknowledged the weakness of his claim by bolstering it from other quarters. In December 1491, just after he had heard of the surfacing of Edward's son in Ireland, Henry wrote the pope a letter that begged him "firmly to support our rights and claims, and not to give ear to the fictitious complaints and accusations of our enemies." If popes could not help him, legends might. He claimed a mist-shrouded pedigree from Cadwallader, the last British prince to have hegemony over Britain ("Saint Cadwallader", in André's estimation), and kept his red fire-breathing dragon as one of his devices. At the banquet that followed his coronation, the king's champion rode into Westminster Hall—a riot of red roses, dragons and green-and-white Tudor fringes—on a horse entirely caparisoned with Cadwallader's arms. In that same pedigree, Henry's kingly title was traced back as far as the Trojan Brutus, who was said to have ruled over Britain in the Dark Ages. His propaganda claimed that even his enemies were forced to acknowledge it. André's Margaret, stiffening the spine of her beloved nephew in Malines, sneered at Henry's line as "that Trojan blood".

The king's ancestry then passed through Arthur. Henry, to double-prove the point, had named his eldest son after him and had especially engineered his birth to take place at Winchester, the alleged site of Camelot, where the real Round Table hung on the cathedral wall. One of Henry's greyhounds was called Lancelot; his favourite oath, "By the faith of my heart", uttered with both hands pressed to the breast, was Lancelot's favourite also; in court poetry and pageant he ruled over "Britain", Arthur's country. Keen attention was paid to the prophecies of Merlin that the true heir of the Celtic kings would come from Wales, as Henry had done, to rescue England from the tyrant. Welsh harpers and rhymers were paid for the genealogical comfort they gave him.

Yet Arthur had been chosen king merely "by adventure and by grace". More solid and more contemporary proofs were needed too. As often as he could, Henry associated himself with Henry VI, his father's half-brother, whose sanctity was attested since his death by miracles, and who was said to have picked the young Henry out as a "lad" destined for greatness. Most vitally, he had married Elizabeth of York, thus yoking to himself the title of her house as well as Lancaster. He was adamant, however, that his claim did not reside in his wife, and made sure that Parliament recognised his own title, entailed upon "his most royal person", before it incorporated hers. The reason for this, Bacon thought, was that he knew her claim might not stand because her brothers, or one of them, might have been saved and alive.

Two more devices were used to reinforce his claim. One was to date his reign from the day before Bosworth, in order to turn his opponents that day into traitors against their king. His rewards to those who had served him in the battle talked of "the recovery of our realm of England", as if he was merely taking back what was his. The second device was to obtain from the pope in March 1486 a bull of anathema and excommunication against all rebels, present or potential. This was powerful medicine, as Henry told the pope the next year. A man called John Swit had mocked the papal bull, asking aloud, "What signify the censures of Church or Pontiff? Don't you see they have no force?" "When he pronounced these words," wrote Henry, exulting in the story, "he fell dead upon the ground, and his face and body immediately became blacker than soot itself, and shortly afterward the corpse emitted such a stench that no one could come near it. This really happened, Most Blessed Father, and if we hadn't been certain of it we wouldn't have written to you." There could be no clearer sign of God's approval of Henry and his censure of those who threatened him. And yet, despite it all, Henry could not disguise that he had come to England as an adventurer and usurper.

In October 1494, as Richard Plantagenet in Antwerp paraded his murrey-and-blue halberdiers, played with his seals and handed out his insulting silver groats, Henry organised his most direct riposte to him. He created his own little Duke of York in his son Henry, then aged three. Young Henry's titles included Earl Marshal and Lord Lieutenant of Ireland; his colours were blue and tawny (close enough), his badge the white rose as well as the red. The four challengers in the "jousts of peace" that followed wore cognizances of the queen's livery, murrey and blue, on their helmets. At Henry's institution his father went crowned, wore his state robes and stood under his Cloth of Estate in the Parliament chamber, sparkling and utterly royal, to receive the obedience of his new knights.

Margaret's White Rose could not compete with this. But he still had his claim to argue. He had no fear of bastardy now, since Richard III's act against Edward's sons had been reversed by Henry himself. Papal anathemas burdened him, but the pure right of his title meant that he could not possibly be struck to the ground, scorched and twitching, as John Swit had been. A dispossessed king could not be a rebel. His route *de jure* was clear, obstructed only by "Henry", or "Henry Tydder" (deliberately made title-less, like a peasant), "who illicitly occupies England."

When Margaret and Maximilian wrote letters to the pope on Richard's behalf, they made no argument for him other than the right of blood. Margaret's letter, written by her lawyer on May 8th, 1495, was a passionate statement that the pope had been deceived in his acceptance of Henry's arguments, especially the request for excommunication. Rightful heirs, the letter ran, should be allowed to hold their kingdoms in peace; if "tyrants without sufficient title . . . sprung from adulterous embraces" usurped them, nothing should prevent the true heirs recovering their right. Though Henry, by marrying Elizabeth, was trying to secure the succession of his children, "the most illustrious lord Richard" had the only legitimate claim. It went "against the necessity of nature" if his subjects, his friends and especially Margaret could not intervene to restore him. To recover his throne was "an act of piety", both in himself and in others. Margaret's lawyer made this appeal "on behalf of my most illustrious lady, the most illustrious lord Richard, the whole House of York, those adhering to him and those who will do so, those who follow him, his dependents and those who will be drawn into connection with him. . . ." This was almost becoming a claim by acclamation.

Yet Richard's arguments were still made by others rather than himself. It was not he who wrote to the pope advertising the justice of his cause, but his two chief sponsors. His letter to Isabella was much thinner on the subject of his legitimacy than Margaret's was. She apparently also wrote several times to John Morton, the Cardinal Archbishop of Canterbury, to tell him that her protégé was King Edward's son. ("But truly he is not reputed the son of King Edward in this country," Morton said he replied to her, with an old man's dryness.) It does not appear that her White Rose ever wrote to Morton himself. The churchman, then in his mideighties, had been Edward IV's Master of the Rolls and had been promoted by him; but he was now extremely close to Henry, too close for Richard to dare a direct approach.

Without Margaret physically behind him, his statement of his claim always seemed more timorous. His proclamation of September 1496, when, as Richard IV, he finally invaded England, reduced his case to mere phrases here and there. Henry Tudor had seized the crown "unto us of Right appertaining", and had then tried to divert Richard's subjects from "the duty of their allegiance"; but Richard, once restored, would reestablish the laws of "our noble progenitors, Kings of England". These were not byzantine lawyers' arguments, but simply right speaking: "right and nature", as he had told Maximilian.

And right could be used. Now that Margaret had her claimant, she could make him work for her in more selfish ways. She had her own claims to pursue, and could extract from her White Rose promises to restore her to her proper rank in England. Her chief worry, one that did not cease to agitate her, was that Edward IV had never finished paying her dowry: 81,666 gold *écus*, almost half, was still owing. After Charles's death, she could not claim several of her Burgundian territories until the dowry was paid in full. Importuning letters to Edward got her nowhere; he appeared not to care that she was "one of the poorest widows, deserted by everyone, especially by you", or that the King of France "does his best to reduce me to a state of beggary for the rest of my days."

Margaret had claims too to Hunsdon, a fine manor house in Hertfordshire of which she was particularly fond, and unexploited rights to ship 860 half-sacks of wool a year into the Low Countries and "through the straits of Morocco", the standard term for unrestricted trade. On top of this, she was owed for money paid to Lord Lovell and the Earl of Lincoln for promoting the Simnel rebellion. Her king, once seated in Westminster Hall or crowned in the Abbey, the angel censing him, could give back everything; he could make her a powerful English princess again, in exchange for everything she had made him.

The deeds in which he promised to do so were drawn up in December 1494, in Antwerp, not long before the planned invasion of England, which had been set for February. They filled six protocols. The final instruments themselves do not survive, but the notary's drafts do. They were jotted down in French, presumably the language of the discussion that produced them, and show how exhaustively the promises were teased out and rewritten until Margaret was satisfied with them. They are also a picture, one of few we have, of sponsor and protégé working together, two years after he had been taken publicly under her wing in Malines.

It seems that his statement of his claims was still being refined. He was Duke of York, not king, and each form of words for his relationship to Edward was slightly different. At the beginning of the first document, the words *vray heretier et successeur du royaume d'engleterre*, "true heir and successor of the realm of England", were squeezed in as an afterthought in the margin. In the sixth deed, the word *vray*, true, was missed out and had to be inserted. The sense that he would mark the beginning of a dynasty that would endure was still cloudy: in several of the deeds, the words "and our heirs" or "and their property to come" were inserted as an after-

thought to bolster his personal obligations. There was, however, a reference at Margaret's dictation to the Yorkist effort that had preceded his.
The purpose of the 1487 rebellion had been "to recover the kingdom of
England for our line" and "to kick Henry out of it." The perpetrators (as
the Antwerp notary, a Fleming, misheard them) had been "the lords of
Lincol and Louvet, our cousins", but they were clearly not meant to be its
prime beneficiaries. Their effort was part of a continuum that was reaching its apex with his own plans.

The smoothest parts of these documents were those that dealt with
the relationship between Richard and his "very dear and well beloved
lady," Aunt Margaret. No deletions or amendments were needed to Margaret's "great love" and "perfect kindness", nor to his own gratitude: "We
have no doubt that, if it is the pleasure and permission of God that we
may see our kingdom again, it will be through the good favour, help and
diligence of her and her good friends, for which we do not know how to
thank her enough." As a rather peculiar act of gratitude, he made her a
present of the castle and town of Scarborough on the bracing coast of
Yorkshire, a town that Richard III had particularly liked and visited, and
whose liberties he had extended.

There was no doubt who was the moving force behind these deeds,
despite Richard's assertion of "our free will and desire, without constraint". Margaret's determined sense of wrong shone through them, as in
the insertion made after her statement of her wool-shipping rights: "from
which she has profited not at all, or hardly." Richard was getting the deeds
notarised "as it pleases our aunt," and was committing himself to these
obligations as she and her council would advise for the best, "without
deception". He promised to restore her rights or pay her money "at her
will and pleasure", not his own, and bound himself by papal censures to
do as she requested. In the case of the dowry, about which she cared so
deeply, he divested himself of any legal recourse if he failed to pay. At one
point, a wordy phrase describing when he would restore her rights, once
he was king, was replaced with the single word "immediately". This was
exactly the tone of Margaret's letters to her officers: "Don't fail", "No
later than the end of this week", "No more excuses".

The last deed of all was more personal. Richard spoke less as a king-
to-be than as a nephew, acknowledging a private debt to Margaret of
8,000 gold *écus* for supporting and equipping him for his invasion of
England. At almost every point, he—or Margaret—used the first person

singular, which was then corrected to the royal first person plural. The etiquette of kingship, like his title, looked unsettled, as if he, or she, could not yet put that social distance between them. Perhaps they could not.

> We, Richard, Duke of York, legitimate son of the late Edward of happy memory, last of that name King of England, and true heir and successor to the Kingdom and Crown of England, Recognise and confess by these presents a duty and loyal obligation to my very dear and well-beloved Aunt Madame Margaret of England, Duchess of Burgundy, blood-sister of my said late lord and father, in the sum of 8,000 gold écus of the coin and mint of the King of France, above and beyond the other sums of money that We ["I" deleted] owe her and for which sums We are ["I am" deleted] obligated to her in previous instruments, the which sum of 8,000 gold écus aforesaid is not included in these preceding obligations, but arises as much from money lent and money spent by her for Us ["me"] and our ["my"] affairs, as from responses and obligations she has entered into in her own name on our ["my"] account towards certain persons and for certain particular business of ours ["mine"], of which we do not wish to make further declaration here, and We are well pleased and satisfied with it all.

When all the rewriting was done, and the deeds redacted, "the most Illustrious Lord Duke" signed them and sealed them. The chief witness was Robert Clifford, who had also been chief witness to the shape of Plantagenet's body and the features of his face.

One more document remained for the king-to-be to sign. This one was drawn up partly on his own behalf, as a last will and testament before his invasion of England, and partly on behalf of Maximilian, who also had claims to pursue. The King of the Romans had insisted for some time that he had a claim to England, as Charles the Bold did, through Isabella of Portugal, his first wife's grandmother. At Malines on January 24th, 1495, a portentous document was therefore drawn up in the name of Richard, King of England and France, Duke of York, Lord of Ireland and Prince of Wales, granting England to Maximilian, his son Philip and their heirs, if Richard should die without legitimate male issue.

This extraordinary statement had been at least ten weeks in the making, with the first draft sketched out at Vilvoorde, near Brussels, on November 9th. The final version opened with the royal "We," *Nos*, trailing huge curlicues down the margin and about to sprout with leaves. Next, his claim: "It is incontestable that the dominions of our late Lord and Father Edward, King of England and France, Duke of York, Lord of Ireland and Prince of Wales, have devolved on us by virtue of our legitimate right." This was his inheritance. Those who occupied it at present—for some reason, they were plural—were "iniquitous usurpers".

After this came laborious expressions of respect for Maximilian, confidence in his virtues, careful reflection on his own part "bearing in mind the value of this transfer", and assurances that although he might be thought under age (seeming again to be unsure precisely what that was, but hovering around twenty), this was a spontaneous, not a forced, donation. The imperial secretary had ended his text with a colon and a quick curving line, indicating where Richard should sign; and in his usual neat hand, now fluid and confident, he did so, *Rychard d'engleterre manu propria*.

The French formulation was presumably for Margaret's and Philip's benefit; the second document he signed in Latin, *Richardus Angliae rex. man. prop.* This may have been the first time he had signed himself "King of England." *Manu propria* was the proper style for business or formal letters signed by kings. Richard's *propria* sailed out into the margin, beyond the ruled pencil line that kept the text contained, and there had obviously been a pause, betrayed by the slightly higher placing of the word, while he wondered whether or not to cross it. The pause, one assumes, was not about *propria* itself, and the question of whose "own hand" this was.

Underneath his signature Richard drew a monogram, as kings did. Twice he took the pen down, then up, making loops, before he finally made a horizontal stroke through the whole thing, looped it, and finished with twirls until his ink ran out. The first downstroke wavered a little, betraying uncertainty about the pattern he was to make, for it is likely that he had never drawn one before. Monograms could not be done quickly. They had to be the same each time, as Henry made sure his were always the same: tiny emblems of the steadiness of kingship.

The usual signs and tokens accompanied this transfer of England to Maximilian. It was done in Margaret's oratory in the palace at Malines, with the Holy Scriptures laid open for Richard to touch and kiss before four witnesses. The document acknowledged that this had been done. On a separate slip of paper two inches wide, fed through slits in the document, red wax was puddled with a candle to take the impression of his seal.

The second-ranking witness, watching as her White Rose drew his king's monogram first on Maximilian's copy, then on Philip's, was Margaret herself. The moment could be judged a triumph for her. Her prince and Maximilian had combined their interests, and, at least on paper, the throne of England had come considerably closer. Yet there was still a sharp distinction between the settled and confident authority of Maximilian and Philip and the nebulous "powers" that Richard was transferring to them, "with all the rights attached to any title, whatever it may be, and whatever rights may be added to them in the future." The deed itself was described as a *donatio, cessio, translatio sive quocunque nomine conspexi possit*, "a donation, handing-over, transfer, or by whatever name it can be described". No document of such terrifying vagueness could have issued from an English chancery. Nonetheless, Richard had recited it aloud, or read out the vital parts of it, in the full character of a king. Besides the clothes, the jewels, the attendants, the deportment, he had now taken on—for himself or for others—a king's cares: enemies, dynastic solicitude, the necessity of fighting, and the risk of failing.

CHAPTER FOUR

Fortune's Smile

round 1494, when Richard Plantagenet was travelling back with Maximilian through Austria and Germany, Albrecht Dürer drew the goddess Fortuna with a sprig of sea holly in her hand. Dürer was twenty-three, three years or so older than Richard. He drew Fortuna often in those years in the landscape Richard now knew: naked or dressed like a rich burgher's wife, her head bandaged or her hands full of horse-harness, strolling past steep-roofed houses or looming in the clouds with the peaks and woods of the Tyrol spread out far beneath her. His "Little Fortune" of 1494 was a particularly disturbing figure. She was naked, round-shouldered, heavily pregnant, and trying to keep her balance on the little globe under her feet. She also seemed blind, holding out the sea holly (which symbolised luck in love) like a weapon whose leaves could cut and draw blood.

Fortune would have been on Richard's mind as much as she was on Dürer's. Those who claimed to be kings were well aware of Fortune's keen interest in them, as she turned with a wink and a kick the great wooden wheel on which they rose and fell. The going up was easy: they scrambled on eagerly, naked and bareheaded, gradually acquiring robes, crowns and sceptres as Richard was starting to acquire them. At the top of the turn they sat for one giddy moment, enthroned. But asses' ears were already sprouting on their heads, pushing off the crowns, and they tumbled down as full-scale donkeys, bare-arsed and braying. Fortune, impassive, kept turning. As the wheel's rim touched the earth, more would-be kings climbed on.

She danced with men, too. A powerful verse from a poem attributed to Skelton described how Fortune had lured Edward IV into the whirling, senseless round with her. To do so was not difficult. At the Christmas and New Year disguisings she could easily have taken the floor with him, elaborately masked and in the bright deceiving clothes in which it was impossible to tell one woman, or one man, from another. Edward, like Henry VII after him, loved these games of extravagant concealment. In Skelton's poem, Fortune sniffed her perfume ball, tossed it in the corner and drew Edward on:

> She took me by the hand and led me a dance,
> And with her sugared lips on me she smiled;
> But, what for her dissembled countenance,
> I could not beware til I was beguiled. . . .

Richard Plantagenet's Fortune was cruel and alluring in just these ways. In his formal transfer of England to Maximilian in 1495 he described (not in his own words, but solemnly reciting in Latin, one hand on the Scriptures) how men reeled under her blows. "Exposed to her attacks", "up against a blind opposition", all they—and especially he—could do was have faith that Divine Providence would eventually "brush aside these blunders". In Bacon's version of one of Richard's speeches, collated from much that he actually wrote, he described himself as "tossed from misery to misery and from place to place", like Fortune's tennis ball.

But he was also aware, as young men were renowned to be, of Fortune's importuning and seductive side. He was reported to have said much later, at the moment when he gave himself up, that for two years he had longed to escape from his troubles, "but Fortune had not allowed him." To those who wondered why he kept going, when going on made no sense, this was his answer. The girl with sugared lips had drawn him, amorously and imperiously, into her great deceiving dance.

Henry VII's attitude to Fortune was different. He too had been her plaything to much the same degree: exiled to Brittany, forced at one point to flee through the woods in disguise, battered by storms on his first attempt to land in England. Yet since 1485 she had been kinder to him. He could attribute to her steady favour (as well as to the Virgin, who always heard his prayers) his landing at Milford Haven, his victory at Bosworth, his marriage, the birth of Arthur, his victory at Stoke. Although Fortune could never be depended on and could be forestalled only by patient planning—such as doing his most vital business on Saturdays, his lucky day—Henry did not seem to feel he was her victim, as his rival did. He was always on the watch for her, one envoy said, and he often challenged her, energised more than dismayed by the risk of fighting. The names of the royal ships he built for the 1497 campaign, sparked by Scotland's support for the feigned boy, were the *Mary Fortune* and the *Sweepstake*. Astrologers, whom he consulted regularly, seemed to keep him ahead of most of the hazards that lay in wait for him.

Henry was also a devoted gambler, betting—and often losing—large sums at cards, dice, tennis and shooting at the butts. His love of tennis was unsurprising, for it was seen as a game that enabled a man to win against Fortune by sheer dexterity, strength and talent. If Richard saw himself as the hapless ball, Henry was a player, skilfully engaged. An Italian treatise on "the Ball Game" exhorted players to think of the court, closed in on all sides by walls and barriers, as "nothing more or less than this troublesome world":

> But we should be calm and tense, not expose ourselves too much, not be too daring or too timid, have our eyes and hands alert for defence, and, when the blows come, overhand, back-hand, open-hand, at the volley, at the bounce or at the half-volley, endeavour cautiously to return them as soon and as best we can, so that the adverse blows of Fortune do not strike us.

Whole afternoons were spent in the long grass alleys at Sheen and Windsor, ratcheting the bucking crossbow or batting leather balls, with the flat of the hand, into the hazard or the chase. Whole nights, too, were spent at a table with tricks, trumps, sleight of hand, and close advisers who would lend him money. The card games of the time proclaimed their danger in their names: Flux, Plunder, Pillage, Triumph, Condemnation, Honors, Cuckoldry, Torment, Who Wins Loses. For those tired of cards, there was a game called *Totum Nihil* (All or Nothing), played with a four-sided disc that was spun like a top. On the night before the surrender in person of the lad who called himself Plantagenet—the night when, as Raimondo Soncino put it, Henry had at last made himself "perfectly secure against Fortune"—he wagered, and lost, the biggest sum he had ever risked at cards.

Yet no one was secure, least of all a king. Human life was a progress through ambushes and shadows, across ground made "slippery and lubric" by the goddess herself, and disaster could not always be prevented. The warnings were hard to read. In 1497, the year the mawmet from Flanders made his most determined attempt on England, Londoners were alerted to trouble of some sort by a mysterious "Spanish" sickness and, at St. Neots, by a storm of hailstones as large as plates "which beat down the corn standing that it came never to good." Strange weather—thunder in the small hours of the night in December 1500, a great night wind in June the next year—was always "wonderful" to the London chronicler, a matter for awe and speculation. Molinet, Dürer and Maximilian all noted, with a mixture of fascination and fear, the swarm of little crosses that appeared at Liège in 1501, in houses and churches and on the clothes of women, "really strongly imprinted, and not with the least artifice, as they would be if portrait painters had done them." Molinet could not decide whether the crosses were *feints ou saints, approuvées ou reprouvées, veritables ou variables*, but waited for some disaster to occur. Maximilian, in his magpie way, collected the cross-imprinted kerchiefs and aprons and deduced that they meant war against the Turks.

The sky seethed with doubtful signs as the wind blew and, at night, stars moved. In 1472, the year of Richard of York's generation, a comet was sighted that lasted for almost two months. It changed constantly, at first shining with a long white flame of fire, then dwindling to the size of a hazel-stick, then quenched-out and dark. The chroniclers did not try to guess what it meant. The next year, Richard's birth-year, saw aches, fevers and bloody flux, cutting men down as they worked in the harvest fields. A little stream near St. Albans called the Womere, or Woe-water, surged high and flooded, as did others at Lewisham and Croydon, and a headless man called out "Woes! Woes!" between Banbury and Leicester. This meant dearth, pestilence or battle, depending on how troubled the water was and how long the man was heard crying. Since no one was quite sure, it was safest to take these as warnings "for amending of men's liv, ing": to repent, and avoid sin in future, in case calamity sprang suddenly from the water or the air.

England by then had been through four decades of political upheaval. Things had quietened down, and in fact all through the strug, gles between York and Lancaster the violence had been localised, doing little to deter the self-improvement of gentry and tradesmen. Commines thought the wars had been remarkable for leaving England so undam, aged. Yet nervousness persisted just below the surface. Deep into the os, tensibly peaceful reign of Edward IV, the world was still sometimes "right queasy" and "all quavering" to the comfortable Paston family, landowners in East Anglia. There was no knowing where it might "boil over next".

Henry's main objective, when he became king in 1485, was to estab, lish a sense of continuity and tranquillity through settled rule. But his arrival did little at first to settle stomachs, since he came accompanied by an illness, the sweating sickness, that no one had seen before. This distem, per was not seated in the veins or the humours, but sent a malign vapour directly to the heart. The treatments that seemed most obvious—cool air, cold water—often killed the victims. Although the outbreak disappeared as quickly as it had come, people were left wondering what it meant. Per, haps the king would sweat and struggle too, or the whole kingdom would.

In the decade since, Henry had governed with remarkable care and circumspection. Self-sufficient as he was, and suspicious of the motives of others, he gathered power mostly to himself and to a circle of intimates who were often self-made men. His favoured institutions were his own council and special tribunals under his control, such as the court of Star Chamber, to which even the most powerful magnates could be sum, moned without fear of defiance. The great houses of England, weakened by decades of fighting and often now headed by minors, could in any case be largely bypassed or ignored. Repeatedly, in the hope that the lesson would be remembered, Henry's statutes stressed that his subjects owed loy, alty first to him, rather than to any local lord. They also emphasised hon, est dealing, a necessary restoration of trust. In 1493, a law was passed against idlers and malingering beggars; in later years Henry issued a strong new coinage, including a pound-sterling coin with his face in pro, file, and standardised weights and measures stamped with his name and his arms.

In all these ways, elements of disruption and uncertainty were removed from English life. Yet Henry's subjects, while appreciating this, had not yet taken to him by the mid-1490s. Though often affable, with a love of music and a keen eye for pretty women, he did not have Edward IV's common touch, and displayed an anxiety for amassing money that coarsened to sheer greed as he grew older. He had still not managed to outlaw the dangerous bands of fighting men retained by local lords, largely because he needed them for his own armies. His skill at keeping England out of foreign wars was acknowledged, but England itself was not yet resigned to the new dynasty that Henry represented. The pretenders that dogged him, though he scorned them as foolish children, consumed much of his attention and his energy; and all through his reign, the queasiness lingered. Around 1503, a group of his officers in Calais seemed by no means sure that Henry's son would succeed him. It depended, said several, on "how the world turned".

The king's insecurity, like other people's, was constantly fanned by rumour. People despised "flying tales" yet nonetheless repeated them, and almost every important story arrived in fragments of steadily hardening speculation. In 1456 came a rumour that Lord Beaumont was slain, "and my Lord of Warwick sore hurt, 1,000 men slain, and six score knights and squires hurt; and nothing true, blessed be God." When Katherine of Aragon landed in England in 1501 the news was hailed as "tidings of certainty . . . albeit that many times fleeting rumours ran that she was landed sundry times before." By contrast, several months elapsed before certain news of Richard III's death at Bosworth reached the court of France.

Accurate reports were further hampered by bad roads and heavy seas. When Henry travelled, he needed guides to help him in the trackless countryside round Guildford and Bath; road-clearers went ahead of the royal convoy, together with scouts who checked for signs of plague. In 1497, important letters sent by Ferdinand and Isabella were lost at sea, and others that survive from near that date are heavily stained with sea-water. ("None of the other letters you mention in your last have arrived. Please always send duplicates." "Don't send the treaty by land courier. The roads are insecure." "Sent the dispatches to Flanders, but they were probably forwarded in the ships that were driven to Ireland by bad weather.") Whenever Richard Plantagenet changed his bolt-hole it was weeks, sometimes months, before the crowned heads of Europe could find out where he was. Even Henry lost track of him occasionally. He paid £5. os. 10d. in the autumn of 1495 for "letters about rumours" of his whereabouts, a hefty sum for unsubstantiated news.

Henry had a sharp suspicion of flying tales. He was known to be "hard of credence" and slow to move; Soncino said he was "cautious, and reflects deeply all his proceedings." He would not allow himself to be disturbed by news that lacked confirmation, but would send his servants to check that the rumour was true. "If ye knew King Harry our master as I do," said Sir Hugh Conway, speaking in Calais around 1503, "ye would be wary how that ye brake to him in any such matters, for he would take it to be said but of envy, ill will and malice." Henry also insisted on knowing the names of informants, to test their motivation Only then, when he felt as assured against lies and surprise as he could be, did he take action.

The most worrying rumour of all took no time at all to cross the sea. The story that Richard of York was alive leaped out of France and Flanders into England, "blazing and thundering over", in Bacon's words. Reports arrived from travelling Yorkists and in letters written directly by Richard or his sponsors, asking for help. From the spring of 1493 these were being received in London; gradually, they spread to the furthest reaches of England. Conspiracies blossomed after them, Vergil wrote, like the leafing and flowering trees.

Each man who received the news (no women are specifically known to have done) had to decide on his answer. First of all, he had to determine whether to believe this flying tale, or leave it well alone. The whole of England, Vergil said, was split into rival parties by the news of the resurrected Richard, with every man poised between hope and fear, profit and peril. Some, who had lost their jobs or offices with the new regime or had suffered an uncomfortable change of master, had little to lose by supporting the risen prince. Many were in a more difficult position. To believe this tale, and to act accordingly, would involve hazarding comfort, money, office, property and reputation: in short, everything. The reward for picking the winning card would be new power and preferment, with luck; the penalty for losing would be disgrace, attainder and death. Blind Fortuna, teetering on her globe, now rolled above their heads.

II

POLYDORE VERGIL FOUND a mixture of motivations among the Englishmen who cast their lot with Richard. The most fervent, he claimed, were lost souls, *perditissimi*, sanctuary men and outlaws who were pushed by poverty or bribes to join him. Among the better class of his supporters, many were foolish dreamers and risk-takers. Some, royal officers and servants, believed that Henry had not adequately rewarded them. Certain people longed genuinely for the restoration of the House of York. Others simply wanted excitement, novelty and change. So said Vergil; though it is hard to believe that many in the England of the mid-1490s truly wanted that.

His description, as cutting as one would expect from Henry's historian, was nevertheless largely true. From the start, the English conspiracies in favour of Richard Plantagenet had no focus save, vaguely, him. No one man organised them. They grew organically, on a small scale, in different corners of England, nudged along sometimes by local knights but more often—especially in London—by freeholders, minor royal officers, priests or schoolmasters. The cells began, and remained, as largely unconnected groups of the like-minded. Many of those involved have no known history beyond their indictments for treason. They are merely names, united by little more than random, often foolhardy, acts and by a longing for the past. The story of these plots is a journey deep into the undergrowth of unconverted Yorkist England.

At the core of the conspiracy were people who had been at King Edward's court. Their motivation was loyalty to the house and the regime, sometimes reinforced by land-ownership or marriage and now sharpened immeasurably by the shift of power, offices and land to the party of the red rose. In Richard's intimate circle, Frion, Ward and Taylor the younger had all been Edward's servants; Frion had probably been Margaret's too, from well before the business of princes. Anthony de la Forsa was the son of a veteran diplomat, Bernard de la Forsa, who had done Edward's negotiating with Spain; George Neville had been an esquire of the body to Richard III and had married the widow of Earl Rivers.

As early as February 1492 one of Edward's yeomen, or attendants, of the chamber was hanged at Tyburn for treason, presumably an old servant spreading word of the resurrected prince. Richard Harliston had also been a yeoman of his chamber before becoming governor of Jersey. Later indictments mentioned Edward's bow-maker; a servant of Richard's sister Elizabeth of York; and William Daubeney, the clerk of Edward's jewel house. James Tyrell, with his mysterious services for Richard III, was now employed out of the country; but Sir Thomas Tyrell, his first cousin, who had been a chamber-servant of both Edward IV and Richard III, fomented Yorkist plots at his house in Hampshire. He was also the nephew of Elizabeth d'Arcy, the long-serving mistress of the nursery for Edward IV and his queen. That was how close the connec-tions went to the court and the little prince.

Up and down the country, other old Yorkist servants and receivers of Edward's favour rallied to the cause. One web centred on southwest Suf-folk. Sir Robert Chamberlain and Sir Gilbert Debenham, both knights of the body to King Edward, were landowners there from the Mowbrays, Anne's family. For both these reasons, they extended their loyalty to Richard, Duke of York. Debenham had been pardoned for "treasons" in March 1486, becoming a knight of Henry's body and keeper of the Irish mines, but had clearly not reformed. Richard White, who had conspired with Chamberlain earlier but had escaped hanging, naturally joined the "new" (or possibly old) conspiracy; two other Whites who joined, yeo-men of Suffolk, may have been relations.

Far to the north another web was woven in the Cumbrian fells, where the Skeltons, who held lands by grant of Richard III, had been conspiring and rebelling ever since Henry had appeared. Edward Skelton, "gentleman" of Carlisle, had joined the cause of Simnel, fought at Stoke and fled to the court of Burgundy. Once the new prince was in place, Skelton plied back and forth between Malines and England, helping to foment conspiracy. From Cumbria this northern web reached into Durham, where George, Lord Lumley (who had married one of Ed-ward IV's illegitimate daughters), plotted with, and won a pardon for, Rowland Robinson, the errand-boy between Richard and Margaret.

Yet another network centred on Calais, which was something of a nerve-centre between English Yorkists and Margaret's court, as well as a bastion of spying. Out of Calais came Sir Thomas Thwaites, the trea-surer of the English garrison by Henry's appointment, and Sir Robert Radcliffe, the keeper of the gates. Thwaites had been Edward's chancellor of the exchequer and, in 1475, his secretary of war. He was also one of the royal officers, in his jacket of murrey and blue embroidered with the white rose, who had escorted Margaret down to the sea by barge at the end of her visit to England in 1480.

One particular circle of conspiracy was inspired not only by loyalty to Edward but also by affection for Edward's mother, Cecily, Duchess of York. Cecily still lived, now in her late seventies, in deeply devotional retreat at Berkhamsted in Hertfordshire. Several of the most fervent adherents of the new White Rose came from close by. Robert Clifford lived at Aspenden; his father-in-law, William Barley, lived at Albury, together with the Bramptons, Thomas and John. All these (the Bramptons being no relation to Duarte Brandão, but solid Englishmen) arrived at Malines together in June 1493. Thomas Brampton, like Thwaites, had attended Margaret in 1480 in his Yorkist livery. Barley, like Thomas Tyrell—whom Barley placed in charge of several of his manors while he was away on Richard's business—had connections to the royal nurserymaids: women who, as Margaret said, would have known the prince without thinking.

The Berkhamsted influence spread further. A priest from Aspenden, Bernard Oldham, also went over to Malines. Robert Leybourne, the Dominican prior of King's Langley, six miles from Berkhamsted, was condemned for his part in the conspiracy in 1495. Richard Lessy, dean of Cecily's chapel and steward of her household, became a chief conspirator in England. In 1495, Cecily in her will (of which he was executor) assigned him money to pay whatever he owed the king in fines for his treason: "and if that [he] cannot recover such money as I have given to him . . . then I will he be recompensed of the revenues of my lands to the sum of 500 marks at the least." No other debt so troubled her. When Lessy was bound to the king for his loyalty—put under surety and the threat of fine if he should misbehave—nine other esquires and gentlemen of Berkhamsted were named with him, four of them members of Cecily's household. They may well have shared his sympathies.

Cecily's will contained several other names close to, or connected with, the plots around her resurrected grandson. She left her carriage, horses and harness to Richard Boyville, who had been bound for his loyalty with Lessy and had served Margaret in Malines. She left her best down-feather bed to Alexander Cressener, a relative; his son Thomas was later condemned for his part in the conspiracy. Another legatee, Anne

Lounde, who received "a little buckle and a little pendant of gold . . . a little girdle of gold and silk . . . and a little round-bottomed basin of silver," may have been related to William Lounde, the priest who became Richard's chaplain and chancellor. The network centred on Cecily strongly suggests that Margaret, who wrote to kings, popes and cardinals on behalf of her White Rose, wrote of him to her mother too, stirring some quiet hope there.

A large number of conspirators were clergy, "sounder in body than in mind", Vergil thought. They included the Dean of St. Paul's, William Worseley, a renowned doctor and preacher; the provincial of the Dominicans, William Richford, "outstanding in his knowledge of sacred literature", according to Bernard André; the prior of the Order of the Knights of St. John of Jerusalem, John Kendal; the pastor of St. Stephen's Walbrooke, Dr. William Sutton, "a famous divine", as well as an executor of Elizabeth Woodville's will; and the Abbot of Abingdon, who had been involved in half-cocked Yorkist plots before. Priests had a particular grievance against Henry. Since 1489, ex-clerks or those without papers had been made subject to the ordinary criminal law for serious offences, and were being branded on the left hand with an "M" for murder or a "T" for theft, like laymen. This may have disposed them to support Henry's rival, but their chief motivation seems to have been the usual one: old loyalties to York.

Since few indictments survive, it is often unclear what these conspirators did. André said that the big names, including the churchmen, sent money to Flanders or passed along cash given secretly by others: a clue that, as Henry feared, the "names" were only the tip of the trouble. Of necessity, the conspirators moved with great care. Much of their communication was by secret signs and codes. A cryptic language of Yorkist conspiracy was already well established. Taylor the elder's letter of 1491 mentioned unspecified words that had passed between the plotters "at the Black Friars, when ye were at your breakfast", and "in Stokingham Park, when Sir John Halwell hunted therein". They also used secret handshakes: "Sir, ye remember, that the token between you and me is, that such as I shall send unto you, shall take you by the thumb, as I did you, when ye and I went up out of the cloister into St. Peter's Church, and by that token ye should be assured of all things, and fear nothing." Later Yorkist secret tokens included silver-tipped laces, bent ducats, pairs of gloves and holy pictures, sent wordlessly between the conspirators. Letters to supporters were written in tiny characters, then folded so small that they could be hidden in the palm of a hand.

Most of the plotters in the early 1490s kept what was called "a foot in two shoes", working for Richard Plantagenet but performing, without tremors, the offices that the king or their immediate masters expected of them. This was only prudent, for there was no knowing how solid the young man "beyond the sea" would turn out to be. Nonetheless, letters came that had to be answered. Several of the attainders for conspiracy involved receiving messages from Richard and, worse, writing back.

In early February 1493 such a letter reached Sir Gilbert Debenham at his house in Westminster. On the 10th, Debenham and Sir Humphrey Savage drafted a letter to send back with Richard's messenger. Debenham said he would come as soon as possible to help Richard prepare for war. Savage, meanwhile, would stay in London to await Richard's coming. Both, in the standard language of their indictments, promised to do all in their power to comfort and assist him and to overthrow the king. By May 20th, Savage was in consultation with another group, including Robert Bulkeley, one of Henry's yeomen of the chamber, and two monks from Westminster Abbey, John Grove and William Graunt. They agreed to get war-gear together, including "bills" (small halberds, somewhere between a spear and a battle-axe) and brigandines, or coats of mail. The presence of Bulkeley suggests an attempted infiltration of Henry's household through the menials who made the king's bed and packed up his regalia, possible assassins.

At some stage, Henry's sergeant-farrier, the "well beloved" servant who was marshal of his mares and foals, was pried away too. His name was William. The last recorded payment to him, in January 1492, was for "the leechcraft of a horse of ours" and the careful leading of the horse, once cured, from "le Studde" near Warwick to Eltham in Kent. The king's last grant to him, of a tenement in Warwick, occurred in March 1493. By the year's end William had joined the plotters and gone across the Channel.

This was still a London conspiracy, but by the summer of 1493 letters from Richard were getting further afield: to Suffolk, and to Roger Harlakenden in mid-Kent. Harlakenden, receiving on July 6th a missive "desiring, moving and arousing him" to join the cause, wrote back the same day, agreeing to help Richard "in all that he desired against the king." He was probably typical of the rare country gentlemen tapped by Richard: the most important man in Woodchurch, custodian of the church keys, with his own pew in the church and a house large enough to contain a private chapel. His household servants joined the cause with him. His neighbours, however, disliked him and kept their distance from his treasons.

Meanwhile, another cell was forming not by letters, but by word of mouth. On January 12th, 1493, Robert Clifford and John Ratcliffe, Lord Fitzwater, had a long talk about King Edward's son at the "Syon house" in Windsor, possibly a house connected with the strongly Yorkist Sion foundation at Isleworth, some way downriver. Fitzwater was Henry's steward of the household—an intimate and influential post—and had been high steward at his coronation. He had also, however, been one of Edward IV's esquires of the body, once warning Edward privately at dinner that he was about to be assassinated. As a result of what Clifford told him, Fitzwater agreed to get an armed force together, five hundred men arrayed for war, to help Edward's son "in whichever part of the country he entered". He made this offer with some warmth, saying he was willing to forgo the services of these men for the rest of his life in order to make Richard king. It seems that Clifford had made contact with the risen prince, who had only just reached Malines from France, and was already strongly proselytizing for him. On January 14th, he agreed with Fitzwater that he should go to Richard, tell him what they were prepared to do for him and urge him to make war on Henry.

Clifford was to prove the key figure in the English conspiracy, a rare link between otherwise self-willed groups of plotters. He was not without bravery. At Richard of York's wedding jousts he was among the first to sign up and fought "with ardent courage," though he won his prize for "prudent behaving": having dislodged a rib of his opponent's armour, he took no advantage of this to do him further damage. Yet Vergil thought there was nothing of firmness in him and, in general, Clifford nailed his colours to safe masts. Before Bosworth, he had been a forthright Yorkist. After it, he became Henry's chamberlain of Berwick, on the Scottish border, and was given some of the lands that Lovell had forfeited. At Stoke, he fought for the king against Yorkist rebels and was knighted on the battlefield, as George Neville was. Later that year, he helped to carry the canopy over Elizabeth's litter at her coronation. Between 1489 and 1491 he was frequently in Brittany, at first as the captain of a company of archers and later as one of Henry's envoys.

In that second capacity Richmond Herald went with him, and his report catches something of Clifford's difficult, imperious character. At Southampton Clifford turned down the ship Richmond had ordered, saying it was "too small for his person" and pulling rank—by means of a warrant sealed with the king's privy seal—to get a vessel four times as large and elegantly furnished. The wind was contrary, but Clifford nagged the sailors first to depart, then to put into Guernsey and let the ambassadors off, and then (the envoys safely on shore) to chase the French warships they had encountered. He refused to take risks or be made a fool of. On the embassy itself he let Richmond do most of the talking, while he himself listened, sized up his interlocutors and, where necessary, retired with them for private conversations. At the end of their trip Richmond came home early with a report to give the king; but Clifford stayed, up to something.

In the spring of 1493, his secret conversations were not limited to Fitzwater. On March 14th he was talking again about the young man who said he was Richard, this time in Sir William Stanley's house at St. Martin-in-the-Fields, near Charing Cross. This was then outside the city, a slightly risky and under-built place, though Stanley's house was no doubt impressive. By now Clifford had probably been back to Malines to transmit the plan he had made with Fitzwater, and had returned even more fired up, convinced that he had kissed the hand and knelt at the feet of Edward's son. He would have needed this enthusiasm to dare approach Stanley, the biggest fish of all.

Stanley was Henry's chamberlain, the man who controlled the appointment of all household officers, the ceremonial of state and, most especially, access to the king in his private apartments. He was therefore as close as any man could be to Henry, a ruler who deeply distrusted both political intimacy and the presumed prerogatives of high birth; and he was, within these limits, pre-eminent at court. He had won Bosworth for Henry by belatedly bringing in his three thousand troops on his side, and it was he who had crowned him, in the field, with the battle coronet plucked from the hawthorn bush. Yet Stanley had been a Yorkist for much of his life. Henry VI had charged him with treason, and two years later, in 1461, Edward IV in victory had knighted him. He had also been

Pencil sketch, c. 1560, of a portrait of 'Richard, Duke of York', c. 1494

Richard, Duke of York:
Canterbury stained glass, c. 1480

Edward IV: engraving from an edition of Livy, 1472

Edward IV: later copy of a portrait of c. 1475

Margaret of York, c. 1470

Margaret of York greets the risen Jesus, c. 1470

Signature from the letter to Isabella, August 25th 1493

Signature and monogram from the 'will', January 24th 1495

Monogram from his proclamation of 1496

Top: Silver *gros* coin of Richard IV, 1494
Bottom: Copper 'Vive Perkin' jeton from Tournai, after 1497

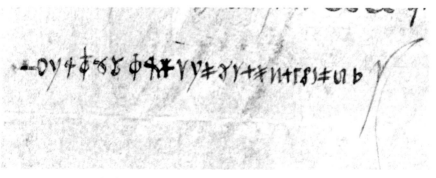

His secret code, from a Burgundian warrant for payment of March 10th 1495

Paying Margaret back: the first page of the draft protocols of December 1494 steward of the household at Ludlow of Edward, Prince of Wales. It was hardly surprising, therefore, that he wavered at Bosworth. His betrayal of Richard III proved no deep conversion, but simply a tendency to follow the way the wind was blowing.

Stanley was also related to Henry by marriage, since his brother Thomas, Earl of Derby, had married the king's mother. He had expected to reap particular favours from this tie, especially the earldom of Chester, but Henry did not rule in that way, preferring to keep the crown apart from the factionalism that Stanley represented. As it was, he had been made constable of Caernarvon, justice of north Wales and lord cham‑berlain, for which he drew a salary of £100 a year. He had extensive estates in Cheshire, bringing in £3,000 a year from rents and fees, and in his castle at Holt, on the Dee in north Wales, he was rumoured to have money, jewels and plate valued at more than 40,000 marks. In short, he was one of the wealthiest men in England.

Yet Stanley was still unsettled. In the first Parliament after Bosworth he had sent a nervous petition to Henry, fearing that Richard III's grant of lands and manors to him was "not sure and sufficient in law". Confirmed in part in those, and compensated for the rest, he still seemed distrustful, and apparently felt that Henry's rewards were not enough for what he had done. Such edginess, a sense of coolness on the other side and "not feeling quite in grace", was a common court affliction. Vergil thought that Henry detected his resentment, was put out by it and "relaxed a little his affection for him", increasing Stanley's unhappiness. During the Simnel rebellion, according to one tale, he had dressed his men in the rebel colours, and once again his forces had been late to engage on the king's side. Among all that finery in the castle at Holt he still kept a Yorkist souvenir, a girdle clasp decorated with part of a livery collar of gold with suns and white roses. Had Fortune smiled differently, he might have worn such a collar again.

His conversation with Clifford on March 14th was probably not the first he had heard of the resurrected Richard Plantagenet. As Humphrey Savage's uncle, he may have been aware of the whisperings in that house and the rustle of letters passing. Robert Bulkeley too, the royal servant with whom Savage was plotting, was related to Stanley by a series of marriages. The servant at the chamber door, made bold by blood‑intimacy, could murmur to the chamberlain, and the infiltration of Henry's household could become extraordinary.

When Stanley and Clifford talked, they agreed that Clifford should cross the sea, enter the service of Edward's son and help him with prepa/ rations for invading England. Stanley himself would do nothing yet. He would wait for "a certain private sign they used between them", and whenever Clifford sent such a sign he would leap in with all his power to assist the war effort. The attainder called these "promises" made by Stan/ ley. It is unlikely they were anything as firm as that, at this stage or later. The only charge that seemed to be laid against him was a remark, made in the course of talking to Clifford, that "if he knew for sure that the young man were King Edward's son, he would never bear arms against him."

Clifford set out for Malines on June 14th, accompanied by William Barley and others from the Berkhamsted circle. He was to spend the best part of seventeen months in association with the White Rose, leaving behind the wife who had thoughtfully sent him "horses, harness and stuff" when he was on service in Brittany. His presence in Calais late in 1493 suggests that he was also on official business for the king from time to time. He kept his feet in two shoes. Reports and visits were meanwhile made to Stanley. During those months Clifford seemed to work his way deep into Plantagenet's confidence, so that by December 1494 he was one of the witnesses to the protocols that were drawn up with Margaret. Rob/ ert Fabyan said he was "by such favour . . . taken in with him" that he came to know all such friends as the doll/prince had in England.

Stanley, meanwhile, waited for the secret sign they had agreed be/ tween them. He remained imperturbably at the centre of Henry's court, showing nothing of the disaffection in his mind. Fabyan gave a glimpse of him on Twelfth Night in 1494, when Clifford had been six months at the court of the White Rose. On the day of the festival Stanley sat alone, as lord chamberlain, at the high table in Whitehall, "keeping the estate for the king, and was served as the king should have been in many points." In the evening, at eleven o'clock, he was in Westminster Hall with all the court to see the disguisings. They began with a man from the king's chapel, dressed as St. George, riding into the hall followed by "a fair vir/ gin attired like unto a king's daughter, and leading by a silken lace a ter/ rible and huge red dragon, the which in sundry places of the hall as he passed spat fire at his mouth." The allusion was to England's peril and Henry's valiant protection; André, too, portrayed the feigned boy in Flanders as a monster hissing out flames. After the dragon came courtiers and ladies, "all costiously and goodly disguised," who danced for "a large hour" before the assembly. In the midst of this entertainment, where so much was not what it seemed and where the sixty dishes that made up dinner were served by breathless courtiers still masked with gold spangles, Stanley sat with a worm of deception in his own heart.

There were other such scenes. One involved Thomas Langton, Bishop of Winchester, who in October 1494 assisted in full pontificals, with mitre and crosier, at the institution of little Henry Tudor as Duke of York. For a year, and possibly longer, Langton had been part of a cell centred on John Kendal, the prior of the Order of the Knights of St. John of Jerusalem in England. It included Dr. William Hussey, Archdeacon of London, Thomas Tyrell and Sir James Keating, prior of Kilmainham and head of the Order of the Knights of St. John of Jerusalem in Ireland. Keating had supported Simnel, but had been pardoned. He had held his ecclesiastical posts in Ireland for well over a decade, and from this vantage point he passed on information about Richard Plantagenet from an early stage in his reappearance. He then joined him at Malines, and relayed news from there. Kendal also kept an agent, Guilhem de Noyon, a brother-knight of his order, permanently in "the parts of Flanders" to tell him how Richard's affairs were going, and these reports were sent on to Langton and the others.

The cell was well concealed. One scene, and a snatch of conversation, showed it in operation. It took place at Christmas in 1493 or 1494 at Tyrell's place, a fine house at Aven in Hampshire. Kendal and Langton were visiting, and Kendal chanced to remark that "King Edward was in this house in the old days." True, Tyrell replied: "and he made good cheer in the old days, and I hope, if it pleases God, that his son may make as good cheer as he did." His son; no hesitation. Tyrell also boasted that his house had been built with money from France, "and he hoped soon to have enough to build another one just as nice." That too had a Yorkist gloss, for Edward had wrung a lot of money out of France by threatening a war, and many hoped that his son might do so after him. All in all, more than enough treasonous talk for a Christmas gathering.

Kendal himself was a curious figure, part rover, part soldier, part huckster. He raised money for his order by selling indulgences, printed by Caxton, for a national crusade to rescue the island of Rhodes from the Turks. In 1485 he acted as ambassador for the Master of Rhodes, and tried to relieve the Turkish siege of the island by shipping in oil and wine. By 1487 he was also a sort of errant ambassador for both the pope and the

King of England. The Venetians thought highly of him, voting him money in the Senate to replace his "most excellent" horse when it was stolen, but his actions on behalf of his order—from handling funds to launching land claims—were often suspect. Some of the money he raised in these dubious ways may well have gone to Richard Plantagenet.

The doings of Kendal's circle were frequently bizarre. Much of this activity was exposed when one of his agents, Bernard de Vignolles, made a confession in March 1496 in Rouen. The original document has *La confession de Bernat de Vignolles* in Henry's hand on the back, suggesting that he took possession of it personally. It made good reading, for this was schoolboy stuff: pranks, tricks, ointments and disguises, though deadly serious in intent.

The core of de Vignolles's testimony involved a plot to kill Henry, his children, his mother, and anyone else who was close to him. This seemed to require the services of an astrologer, someone able not only to mix secret ointments but to tell the best time to apply them. When Kendal and Dr. Hussey were in Rome in 1492 (Plantagenet being only just in France, and his cause very young), the archdeacon was sent to find such a star-gazer. The first one he came across, a Spaniard called Radigo, could not help, but a second Spaniard, Master John Disant, was willing. In order to prove his credentials, Master John arranged the murder— probably with counterfeit sugar—of a servant of Gemes, brother of Bajazet II, the Emperor of the Turks, who was then in Rome in papal custody. But the money the Englishmen left the assassin "by banker's bill" was not enough, and for some time the project hung fire.

Eventually, de Vignolles was sent to nudge Master John along (as well as to silence the first astrologer, who had been gabbing of the plots). Master John thought matters might proceed more quickly if he came to England; de Vignolles was afraid he would be recognised, but Master John volunteered "to come in the habit of a friar, and since he was missing two teeth, he would make two others of ivory, the colour of his own; and he would come by sea, to be on the safe side, and say he was going to St. James of Compostella." So the astrologer, disguised as a friar, carrying deadly stuff, perhaps disguised as sugar, was to make a false pilgrimage on behalf of a young man perhaps disguised as Richard, Duke of York. That made sense.

In the end, Master John stayed in Rome; he too was short of funds. But before de Vignolles left, the astrologer gave him a little wooden box containing ointment. This ointment, he told him, should be spread along and across any doors through which the king passed, "and if this were done it would cause the persons who bore the greatest love for the king, to murder him." Apparently it worked by twisting minds towards violence, rather than by killing on contact, but by this time de Vignolles wanted nothing to do with it anyway. Back in his lodgings he opened the box, only to find such a vile and stinking mixture that he threw the whole thing into the latrine. Compunction seized him on the way home; Kendal wanted this stuff, after all, and was expecting to receive it. So de Vignolles bought a similar box from an apothecary and filled it with a mixture of dry earth, water, quicksilver (also bought from the apothecary) and soot scraped out of the chimney, until it was the same colour as the ointment the astrologer had given him. Why he went to such trouble to reconstruct something that Kendal had never known or seen is impossible to say; but the counterfeit had to be perfect, even if no one but the counterfeiter would appreciate how perfect it was.

Eventually, back in England, he delivered the box to Kendal. The prior would not touch it; he was galvanised by de Vignolles's description of how it worked, "that it was very dangerous to touch it if you wanted to do something bad with it, and he would be in great danger if it stayed twentytwo hours in the house." Kendal ordered him to throw it away somewhere far from the building, where it would never be found, and de Vignolles did so.

That seemed to be the end of the plot to assassinate Henry. Kendal decided to concentrate on the cell's main business, finding money ("stones", or inverted triangles, in their makeshift code) for the Merchant of the Ruby, their codename for Richard Plantagenet. He was certainly looking for funds in 1494, though the letters on the subject that survive, written in dreadful Italian spiked with worse Spanish, date from two years later. This one was sent to de Vignolles, who had probably already jumped ship.

> On the 15th of this month I received your letter written at Rouen and I understood that you've found two merchants at Rome who are used to selling stones, who were very pleased to meet you and would gladly know if you want to get some of these things. I'm well pleased with all this and would like them to go to Brother Guilhem de Noyon, who can be found three or four miles from Aire and Douai in the Pays d'Artois. I pray you to go there your

self to assess the perfection of these stones and then to come back here immediately. And when I've heard from you that the thing is certain, they will immediately be told of my decision through you, and in one way or another we'll find a way to conclude the business to their satisfaction. . . . The bearer has been badly delayed on the road because he was held up for twelve days at Portsmouth. . . .

If . . . you do not find Brother Guilhem at home, leave the merchants there and go and find Brother Guilhem at Bruges or wherever he may be. At any rate, he won't be far away. Nothing else comes to mind at the moment. I've given the present bearer three [inverted triangles].

How de Vignolles was supposed to find Guilhem, at no fixed address in Artois, is hard to imagine. A letter sent two weeks later by Kendal to Guilhem himself said that Bernard had been sent to find "his little brother" Guilhem "in Rouen or in the interior of Picardy", an even wider area to search. Such plots seem hardly serious; and it was typical of Richard Plantagenet that his subscribers included, alongside the serious and devoted, enough worthless charlatans to suggest that he might be one himself.

While Kendal was doing all this, he was also one of Henry's trusted servants. Far more than Fitzwater or Stanley, who had done little but promise to help, he walked an astonishing tightrope between the king in England and the young man across the sea. In the same year as the astrologer-search through the back streets of Rome, Kendal helped to negotiate the Treaty of Etaples, which obliged Charles VIII to stop assisting Henry's rebels. He was also a fairly regular member of Henry's council. It is true that he got into a scrape or two. In 1492 he was in trouble for publishing papal bulls preferring him to the priorship of St. John's, which was then vacant, without the king's permission; and at a council meeting in 1494, in Henry's presence, he was proclaimed deserving of "grievous punishment" for making a false claim, by means of a false deed, in the council itself, *absque verecundia*, without shame. Kendal's whole career was conducted *absque verecundia*.

His circle, however, with its distinguished divines, its sprinkling of country gentry and its access to cash, should have been one of the more useful for Richard Plantagenet in England. The newly formed prince needed people of this sort. The cause was lamentably short of lords like

Fitzwater, who could raise men, and of merchants, who could raise money. Fitzwater was the only lord who committed himself to the cause. (André, Molinet and Richard himself said there were many more "great men" involved, but named no names.) Among his supporters who were charged with treason, only three were active merchants, and only Maurice Seles, a goldsmith, represented the higher-earning echelons of London trade. Taylor the younger had been a merchant, but plotting had taken him over; John Heron, later Richard's right-hand man, had been a mercer in London, but had fled the city with his debts unpaid.

The presence of more such adherents, however, is shown by other London pardons: of a knight, two "gentlemen", a vintner and four drapers, all drawn into Richard's plots. It is also suggested by the bonds for allegiance, like Richard Lessy's, that Henry demanded from subjects he did not trust. In the early 1490s the number of these increased dramatically, as Henry endeavoured to keep Yorkist murmurings in check. The £1,000 bond in 1493 of Sir Ralph Hastings, whose steward, William Lounde, had already decamped to Malines, was typical. A group of acquaintances, including a fishmonger, an armourer, a goldsmith and a London alderman, pledged themselves to meet his bond in the sum of £50 or £100 each. All were required to appear before the king and his council at regular intervals. In the same year, however, Hastings himself stood guarantor for 1,000 marks of the bond of John Hayes, the man who had received Taylor the elder's letter from Rouen. The guarantors might promise "faithful behaviour as lieges," but they were sometimes of the same political sympathy as those who were being punished. They helped them for that reason. Among those, for example, who stood surety for the allegiance of John de Lysa, "that he would not associate with the king's traitors and adversaries in Flanders, or lend them his aid", was Thomas Barley, gentleman of Hertfordshire, whose brother William was already in Flanders, and in deep.

So the conspiracy was growing, cell by cell, with only limited evidence that the cells connected. Vergil mentioned a "general decision" to send Robert Clifford and others to Flanders, and spoke of the conspirators as one large group. The legal records give a different impression, of small inward-looking clusters with no wider organisation. Yet as soon as Clifford had confirmed from Malines that this was Edward's son, some concerted effort was made to spread the word. Hall, writing fifty years later, said Clifford's "letter of credit and confidence" was published by the other conspirators, so that people would know the rumour was true.

The beginning of 1494 saw a flurry of publicity. In the first week of February one group, consisting of Thomas Bagnall, John Heath, John Scott, Alex Singer, John Kennington and others, "made and fabricated . . . various bills and writings, rhymes and ballads concerning seditions and treacheries and uprisings as much against the king as other nobles of his council." Of the five named, four were yeomen; the rhymer, and per-haps the sole writer-down of these spoofs while the others thought them up, was probably Kennington, a schoolmaster. All but Bagnall were Londoners, and were said to have supported the king's enemy in Flanders "for many days before". On the 5th, they pinned up their poems on the door of St. Benedict's in Gracechurch Street, near London Bridge, on the Standard at Chepe and on the doors of St. Paul's. They had not ventured far from home (St. Benedict's, by the herb market, was probably their local church), but they had done their part.

Three days later, in the parish of St. Andrew's Holborn in the Lon-don suburbs—and for some days beforehand elsewhere—a group of conspirators also agreed to spread word of Richard Plantagenet "in vari-ous towns and counties of England and in all the towns along the sea-coast." This was to be done very subtly and artfully, Vergil said, so that the rumour could not be tied to anyone in particular. The man picked for the job was Edward Cyver, known as "English Edward", a hat-maker from Northampton. He and several others, perhaps with yokes of spuri-ous bonnets slung across their shoulders, were to find out how people were thinking and work to shift their sympathies from Henry to Richard. When the survey was done, Cyver was to report back to Richard on the readiness of England to receive him.

How far English Edward got is not recorded. But an exhaustive doc-ument, the charges brought by an oyer and terminer commission—one specially charged to deal with cases of treason—after Richard had tried to invade, shows how widely the network of supporters extended by the spring of 1495. The first six names on the list came from Warwickshire, Norfolk, London, Surrey, Ashton-under-Lyme and Kent: in short, from all over England. Two of them, Henry Mountford and John Corbet, both "captains" of Richard's forces, were sons of people of standing who themselves had kept a prudent distance. Henry Mountford—who had taken one hundred men to Ireland three years before to help squash Plan-tagenet's supporters, and had been rewarded by the king as his "trusty and well-beloved knight" for service both there and, earlier, in Brittany—was the younger son of Sir Simon Mountford of Coleshill in Warwickshire. (Thomas Bagnall, the ballad-maker, had also come from Coleshill, signs of a tiny Mountford cell.) Mountford *père* was a knight-commissioner of the shire and a guest at the ceremonies where little Henry Tudor was cre-ated Duke of York. He also bought one of the Caxton-printed Kendal indulgences, touching on another circle of conspiracy. On receipt of Richard Plantagenet's letter he had sent him £30, somewhat less than the standard present Henry VII gave to visiting ambassadors. He entrusted the money to his son Henry to deliver, not seeming to wish to make direct contact himself. John Corbet was the son of an "honest" grocer of Lon-don, who owned Corbet's Quay on the Thames: a rich man who also kept apart from such unnecessary risk.

Even more striking were the names that followed those of Richard's captains, the foot-soldiers of his invasion force. Almost all were yeomen or labourers, and they came from some of the remotest spots in England. Thomas Slater and John Martindale came from the fells of Kirkby-in-Kendal in Westmorland. Yorkshiremen came from Whitby, Ripon, Rip-ley and Sherburn-in-Elmet, possibly places where the northern rebellion of 1489 still found an echo. The west of England yielded soldiers from Bristol, Taunton, Hereford and Chipping Campden. Having heard the rumour of Richard's survival (in the village street, in the fields, in the wool-clipping shed), they appear to have taken individual decisions to help him. That help included making their way to Malines, when many of them had never seen the sea before, and leaving their wives—as Clif-ford had left his—to manage affairs at home.

Vergil was not surprised at this; any field labourer, or worker in some humdrum job, would be only too pleased to join up and get the chance of plunder. Some, perhaps, were simply strong-armed by their masters. The masters, however, trod carefully, preparing the ground in England but keeping their heads down. They sent Richard letters, telling him they were waiting and would help him when he came. It was mostly the young and headstrong, like John Corbet, or the poor, like Henry Lount, labourer of East Sutton, who took their bodies across the sea and offered to fight and die for him, the greatest risk of all.

III

AS THESE CONSPIRACIES GREW, Henry watched them with his usual keenness. His network of spies was superb, and was bolstered—as Edward IV's had been—with the newly invented system of "posts", or mounted relay-riders, placed along the roads. In 1497 Henry's postal service in the West Country ensured that letters could reach Woodstock from Devon, a distance of more than one hundred miles, in a day. These gave extraordinary speed to a system already staffed with the sharpest eyes and ears. "As for such tidings as ye have sent hither," the Earl of Oxford told John Paston in 1487, "the king had knowledge thereof more than a seven-night passed." He made certain he did.

Looking through Henry's account books, the range of nebulous helpers is impressive. "To two men that came from Ireland", "to a black friar a stranger", "to an Englishman of the French king's guard", "to two monks spies", "to a spy that dwelleth in the West Country", "to a fellow with a beard a spy in reward". Two more clerics, Brother John of the Dublin Franciscans and Master James Norwich, trained in theology, were sent to spy in Ireland when the "Child" was there. Heralds such as Richmond, Rouge Dragon, Carlisle Herald and Bluemantle Pursuivant were constantly on spy-business, Bluemantle sometimes with six other people in a kind of undercover progress. Lowlier court officers were sometimes sent too, such as "Guilhem, one of the shakebushes [beaters]", sent to Flanders "in our especial message" in 1496. At many points, trumpeters were employed to gather information. These, like the heralds one or two notches above them, were ideally suited to spying: close to the elbows of important people, yet also faceless functionaries who might not be thought to be listening or watching, though almost all were.

To this crew of people, usually invisible and nameless ("flies and familiars", as Francis Bacon called them), were added others who passed on scraps to Henry as part of their daily work. Top officers in Calais had a separate budget for spying, as did the keepers of other castles nearby. In 1503 instructions went to Sir John Wiltshire, then controller of Calais, to get in touch with "Messire Charles", a French spymaster, and use his agents to descry the intentions of the king's rebels. He could recruit any-one to get information "in any manner", and the king would pay them. He was to make a list of the rebels' names and give it to one of Henry's heralds, and was to do his best to turn the servants of the chief man he was spying on, promising each of them the king's pardon on condition that "he will declare those whom he knows . . . on his coming to the king." These methods exactly were used against the newfound prince in Flanders.

Professional diplomats, too, had a brief to spy. All Henry's envoys had this colouration. There was no spy so good or safe as an ambassador, said Commines; if the other side sent one over, he recommended sending two back. Other princes' envoys were never to be trusted, yet they should all the same be lodged handsomely and given attendants who could, in turn, spy on them, while preventing fickle and mutinous people from re- sorting to them with news. Dr. Rodrigo Gonzalez de Puebla, the Spanish ambassador in London, remarked that his lodgings in a city monastery were "the most public place in the whole of England", so crowded were they with foreigners, "sharp spies" and king's officers trawling for infor- mation. He trawled in turn, assiduously. For his part, Henry had a habit of giving his most private briefings to envoys—flattering them deeply by "opening his whole heart clearly and completely", as they supposed—out of doors, riding in the parks or gardens of his palaces, where no spy could overhear them unless he lurked in the trees.

These ambassadors were public figures with public duties to per- form; they mixed with other envoys, were well known to the rulers whose courts they visited, and smoothly delivered their official statements. Yet their more vital job was to observe and report anything of interest. When William Warham went to Malines in the summer of 1493 he overstayed his visit by ten days, somehow eking out his expenses, to watch how Mar- garet's protégé was treated. The officers Henry sent in 1494 and 1495 are known to have given the king such reports. Their work involved nothing difficult or undercover, but simply mingling and looking.

Such men were also usually given a last page of instructions, un- monogrammed and unsigned, that assumed they would delve deeper than the usual *tres affectueuses recommendations*, catching the king or some chief councillor "on his own", "in secret", or "when you see some con- venient moment". Richmond Herald, Henry's usual envoy to France, was once told that if the subject of the feigned lad and his latest sponsor did not naturally arise, he should "endeavour by all proper means to give occa- sion to such remarks", after which "he may reply that as far as that busi- ness is concerned the king cares nothing about it, and it is the least of his worries." As well as showing the king's bravado, the envoys could also use these private moments to intimate a nastier side.

The most useful people of all, perhaps, were officers whose standing was deliberately ambiguous. One such was François du Pon, one of Henry's French secretaries, who was employed for him from May 1488 to 1494, and probably later, "in the parties beyond the sea". His service involved keeping close to Maximilian, "to abide with him during a cer-tain season, and to advise us", sometimes performing some particular "charge and hasty errand", at others simply attending on him for as long as Henry required. Du Pon was never said to be on an embassy, and his pay, £10 a month, was only one-third of what proper ambassadors like Warham received. He was so permanently hanging round the court of the King of the Romans, doing "good service . . . there daily unto us", that he had to be paid not with cash from the Exchequer but by payments sent out with unreliable German merchants, or by letters of exchange drawn up by Florentine creditors in London.

November 1493 found du Pon in Antwerp, writing to Henry to complain that Herman Ryng, the Cologne sable-merchant assigned to pay him, "hath but late done to be delivered . . . 20 pounds sterling in ready money." From his address, it appears that his brief had not been to follow Maximilian or the feigned boy to Austria. That job had been given to the better-qualified "John Stoldes, alman", who had been "sent into the parties of Almayne . . . for certain great matters touching the weal of us and this realm". (Exceptionally, the warrant for Stoldes's payment was written twice, "and [we] be greatly desirous of his speedy coming again", added Henry, writing in December.) But du Pon, too, had uses. In July 1493—a moment of intense anxiety in Henry's relations with Bur-gundy—the faithful Frenchman had been sent again into the parties beyond the sea with four horses, intended as a present. The king wrote that du Pon was to be paid a reasonable sum of money to get the horses well-bitted, bridled and stabled. No word was said of whom this present was for, or why, which was in itself unusual. It was most probably a pres-ent for information, and about one subject in particular.

In all these ways—through diplomats, heralds, lieutenants based abroad, snoopers recruited locally and at home—Henry spied on "the lad who makes himself out to be Plantagenet". He began early, but the galvanising moment, Polydore Vergil said, was Clifford's departure for Flanders, and Henry's conviction that the nobles of England were about to embrace the conspiracy after him. The marginal notes in André show how, at this stage in the boy's career, the king acknowledged his *subtilita*s, *astutia, malicia* and *calliditas*, a dangerous and slippery intelligence. Henry had to show very quickly that he could expose and thwart him. He followed two main lines of subversion: first, combing northern Europe to find out who his tormentor was, and second, burrowing into his household at Malines, to find out who supported him and to peel them away.

It was vital to pin a name on this boy—almost any name, and fast. An invention would have troubled nobody on moral grounds. Political expediency could reorder the world, if it was essential; and it was essential. The deception, Vergil said, had to be quickly recognised as such by everyone, or new upheavals would occur. Henry had done the same with Lambert Simnel, using the name early—whether true or not—and persisting with it, until its lightness and silliness turned the threat into a joke. If you could name the Devil when you saw him, you could make him disappear.

The king's agents fanned out through all the cities of Flanders and northern France, searching for the boy's home and his parents and promising rewards for information. Vergil also said that Henry wrote to "friends", presumably the other kings of Europe, asking them to do the same. The young man's own friends were hard to find, since he had apparently travelled so incessantly since childhood that very few people knew him. Yet when the spies reached Tournai they stopped searching, discovering that he was remembered there. Before that moment, Tournai "in France" had probably meant no more to Henry than the place his tapestries and carpets came from, delivered by the Grenier brothers, Jehan and Pascal, and confusingly measured in "ells Flemish". From then on, the city was to feature much more than he wanted in his thoughts.

By the summer of 1493, probably before Clifford had reached Malines, and as du Pon was busy with his equine presents beyond the sea, Henry had assembled a plausible alias for Margaret's White Rose. He was, he wrote to Gilbert Talbot in July, "another feigned lad called Perkin Warbek, born at Tournai, in Picardy". The "feigned" was added later, stressing the point. In August 1494, in a set of instructions issued to Richmond before he went on embassy to France, Henry emphasised that "the person who calls himself Plantagenet and the son of the late king Edward" was of no consanguinity or kin to him, but "the son of a boatman called Werbec, as the king is duly assured."

How had he come to know this? According to Richard Plantagenet, in his royal proclamation of 1496, he had made it up. The king had just "surmised us falsely to be a feigned person giving us nicknames, so abusing your minds". These nicknames showed Henry's "malicious" brain at work; they had not necessarily sprung from any researches he or his agents had done. In any case, Richard went on, it was evidently a false story. If he had been a fake, he would have been easily exposed; Henry would have had no need to bribe people to leave him, because they would never have stayed. "Every man of Reason & discretion may well understand," Richard sniffed, "that him needed not to have made the foresaid Costages and importune labour if we had been such a feigned person as he untruly surmiseth."

As he pointed out, Henry had done much more than call him silly names. The king

> as soon as he had knowledge of our being alive Imagined, Compassed and wrought all the subtle ways & means he could devise to our final destruction [and] also to deter & put us from our entry into this our Realm hath offered large sums of money to Corrupt the princes in every Land & Country and that we have been Retained with / & made importune labour to certain of our servants about our person / some of them to murder our person / and other to forsake & leave our Righteous quarrel and to depart from our services . . . and to bring his Cursed and malicious intent aforesaid to his purpose / he hath subtly and by Crafty means levied outrageous and importable sums of money upon the whole Body of our Realm to the great hurt & impoverishing of the same. . . .

In the speech attributed to him in Scotland, Richard mentioned that his nemesis had also bribed, corrupted and exposed those who had befriended him and taken him in during his years of exile. Some years later Edmund de la Pole, an undoubtedly genuine Yorkist claimant, confirmed that this was Henry's *modus operandi*, complaining to Maximilian that the king was "[practising] in all quarters and with all kinds of people whom he can corrupt with gold and silver to destroy me."

Vergil thought Henry's "friends" among Europe's rulers had provided most of the information he needed to trace his young tormentor, and certainly they sent him some. The king gave the impression, however, that he had also done much foraging on his own account and at his own expense. His August instructions to Richmond Herald, now much damaged, mentioned three sorts of overseas sources for the young man's life, all of them people very close to him. First, Henry had heard from "those who [are acquainted with] his life and conduct [*gouvernement*]", presumably from watching him in Malines. Second, he had questioned "some others his companions, who are . . . at present with the king". Third, Henry mentioned "others . . . beyond the sea, who have been brought up with him in their youth, who have publicly declared at length how . . ."

No trace survives of these long declarations, nor of the board, lodging or rewarding of the "companions" who came to England. Ambassadors did not notice them, and Henry himself did not otherwise refer to them. That does not mean they did not exist. "A certain French spy coming from overseas" was sent on from Westminster to Henry at Kenilworth in July 1493, the very month in which he wrote to Gilbert Talbot with, at last, the boy's name. For whatever snippets he provided the spy was paid 30 shillings, a handsome sum for spying, and was then fitted out with new clothes, from bonnet to boots, for the journey back.

Yet it is possible that the Tournai discoveries did not derive from any of these sources. Other useful people had reverted to Henry, bringing with them information about the boy; and it is likely that Henry had been gathering this, piecemeal and secretly, even before the boy's emergence in Ireland. Edward Brampton seemed to dodge back to England for a while in 1488, staying almost incognito at the Domus Conversorum; in 1489, the year he played host to Richmond Herald in Portugal, he was given a general pardon, "provided that the said Edward produce sufficient security in the King's chancery for bearing himself as a faithful liege should bear himself towards the king's person and majesty." Such a rider on a pardon was unusual, suggesting that Henry wished to make double-sure of this wandering "knight, alias of Portingale". The official confession, as it eventually emerged, mentioned Brampton's wife but not Brampton himself, perhaps by arrangement, and contained very little that might obviously have come from him. But he remained in good standing, and in the autumn of 1499 (now billed as an ambassador of the King of Portugal) was still enjoying exemptions from customs duty in the port of Southampton.

Pregent Meno, the Breton merchant who had brought the boy to Ireland, had also changed sides. He had been captured in December 1491, having been followed from Cork, by a ship called the *Anne of Fowey*. Yet he does not appear to have been punished and eventually reaped rewards, presumably for information or for a mouth kept shut. In April 1495 he was given a grant of £300, to be paid in instalments of £30 twice a year, from the customs on wool, hides, wool-fells, lead and tin going through Dublin and Drogheda. In 1496 he was made an English denizen, a privilege granted to no more than half a dozen people a year and those mostly in high places, such as Henry's chief legal adviser, also a Breton, and his Norman confessor. In May the same year Meno was granted "licence to buy, within one year from that date, thirty sacks of wool from any seller of wool in England", and to "transport [them] to any part of the world free of customs or other dues", a generous reward for nothing in particular. An entry in March called him the king's servant rather than, as usual, "merchant".

From November 1494 Meno was also holding military posts in Ireland. In March 1496 he was made constable of Carrickfergus castle, with six men under him, and captain of a company of archers. Carrickfergus was ideally placed, far north and opposite Galloway, to intercept intrigues on the feigned boy's behalf between the Irish and the Scots. Meno was also paid often alongside Henry Wyatt, Henry's commissioner in Ireland, for loans made to messengers carrying the king's letters. Wyatt's other life was espionage, mostly in Scotland, and Meno too preserved a secret life for which Henry continued to pay him. "Petit John Pregeant the Breton", or "Petty Jean Meno", was being rewarded at 40 shillings or 66s. 8d. a time until 1497, probably for spying.

Henry since his exile had an affinity with Bretons, and used them widely for undercover work. Their mobility, in ships plying the feigned lad's tracks between Ireland, France, Flanders and the West Country, was especially useful. An undated slip of paper in the handwriting of John Heron, who kept the king's private accounts, mentioned the large sum of £95. 6s. 8d. paid to eight Bretons, two of them heralds; another herald was paid "to convey them to the sea side". Exceptionally, the total of their payments was enclosed in a rectangle of neatly stitched white silk thread.

In the autumn of 1497, at the last moment, the feigned boy's official confession was topped up with more crumbs from Bretons across the Channel. They had no names, as befitted shadows.

For Henry, a prudent and even obsessive manager of money, the expense of employing so many men abroad was cause for keen regret. But he had no choice. If the boy was to be crushed, he had to be exposed as a fraud and detached—by whatever means Henry or his agents could devise— from the foreign powers who favoured him. In theory, this might not be difficult to do. As Henry knew, the European leaders who supported his rival were dallying with Fortune too. For this reason, their favour was as treacherous and qualified as any other kind.

Every ruler waited to see how the world turned, and changed his loyalties accordingly. Treaties would be signed with great pomp and solemn oaths one year, only to be annulled by deals concluded with a rival party the next. After the AngloFrench peace treaty of 1475, as Commines complained, "scarce anything was performed that was promised . . . but their whole business was hypocrisy and dissimulation." Ferdinand and Isabella, having signed the Treaty of Medina del Campo with Henry in 1489 (setting out, for the first time, the details of the proposed marriage between their daughter Katherine and Prince Arthur), subsequently had their signatures cut out with a pair of scissors. No compunction was felt at abandoning "our most dear and wellbeloved Cousin" if some more profitable arrangement suddenly emerged elsewhere. On bases no firmer than this ("smiling with mouth and teeth", in the current phrase), Richard Plantagenet's support in Europe had been carefully constructed.

His letter to Isabella of August 1493 mentioned eight rulers who seemed to be on his side. Of these, by the end of 1494, only Margaret seemed immovably secure; and she, as he often mentioned (having evidently heard it from her time and again), was "only a poor widow, who does not have the resources to help me". Bernard de Vignolles's testimony confirmed that Richard was looking elsewhere for money because he had no hope of finding it in Flanders, and Ferdinand and Isabella also thought that Margaret's *ynportunidad* eventually drove him to leave.

This was not how it appeared to Henry. Bernard André said that Margaret had poured out treasure and impoverished herself to help "this mean fellow". ("Not very good sense," he added. "Everyone just laughs in mockery to see her throw away so much money like that.") She had even stripped herself of her rich girdle on his behalf, an implication of sexual wantonness as well as improvidence. Yet the sums Margaret spent on her White Rose were modest compared with those she spent on others. The protocols of December 1494 implied that much more than 8,000 crowns had been raised for him, but even twice that was less than the 20,000 crowns Margaret had spent on Philip's gold chain at his chris-tening. And every crown of it was understood to be lent, not given. By 1494, having recovered or been recompensed for the lands she had lost in the wars in Flanders, she had money to lavish on Richard's enterprises if she had wanted to. Moreover she could do so secretly, with no need to declare her spending in her accounts. But, with her usual shrewdness, she seems to have kept the money close.

Other friends, too, were shaky. James IV of Scotland was in frequent touch, but the depth of his friendship had not yet been tested. In Ireland, the Earls of Desmond and Kildare were being worked on by Henry and his officers. Desmond was holding out, but Kildare—having lost his position as lord deputy in 1492 on account of his Yorkist flirtations—had been issued in 1493 with a general pardon at his own "urgent entreaty". By the end of 1494, after a final surge of plotting with the Irish chiefs and with Scotland, he was pleading once more for royal favour in England. (He had never done anything with the French lad. Never.) The King of Denmark seemed to go no further than sending envoys to Richard. Duke Albrecht of Saxony continued to show kindness, but he, too, was short of funds to spare. That left as the main props—besides Margaret— Philip the Fair of Burgundy and his father, Maximilian.

Philip was only fifteen in 1493, four or five years younger than Rich-ard. The two were natural companions at Malines, where Philip kept his own court and governing council. Since the death of his mother, Mary of Burgundy, when he was four, Margaret had in effect become his mother, although from the summer of 1494 Philip was also the ruler to whom she was bound to defer. The dowager duchess saw to his education and chose his playmates for him; and since she considered both these young men as her children, they were virtually brothers.

In some of the most memorable events of Philip's young life Richard was beside him, the closest in age and rank, another king's son as far as most men supposed. He was with him at Cologne in June 1494 when Philip hugged and kissed his father after months of absence, telling him, like some little ambassador, "My Lord, you are very welcome." He rode beside him that August at Malines and saw him make his first knights, tapping each candidate two or three times on the shoulder with a sword, in the church of St. Peter at Louvain in September. They proba-bly played chess, a court craze, together, perhaps using Margaret's finest set, which had pieces made of glass.

Philip, young as he was, could live with the risks his friend repre-sented. Moreover, his father and Margaret were insistent that Richard should be helped to win the throne of England. But neither Maximilian nor Margaret governed the Burgundian Netherlands, where Richard was now so fêted and protected; Philip did, through his council, and his councillors were much less sure. The region depended on raw wool imports from England for cloth-making, its chief source of income. But trading relations had soured as soon as Plantagenet had arrived in Malines, when Margaret had organised the letters of marque that autho-rised attacks on English ships. In the months that followed, as her favour to him increased, so too did the risk of English economic reprisals.

The whole Burgundian territory was recovering, besides, from the years of internal war that had followed the deaths of Charles the Bold and his daughter. Commines, writing at the start of the 1490s with the contempt of a Burgundian who had sold his soul to France, thought he had never known a people so miserable and desolate—punishment, he thought, for past hubris and lascivious behaviour in bath-houses. Con-temporary records for the city of Bruges showed the extent of the misery: the fields around the town ruined and still uncultivated, menaced with wolves, while fishermen on the coast were terrorised by pirates and raiding gangs, some English and some French. The last thing this region needed was the cessation of trade with England. However much Philip was inclined to help his friend, the advice of his council was to drop him.

Henry sent his first envoys to protest in July 1493, when Poynings and Warham came with their story that Richard, Duke of York, was no prince, but base-born, and had assumed the name and persona of a boy who was dead. At the end of "a pleasant and a luculent oration", as Hall called it, Warham added the strikingly nasty coda that Margaret had given birth to this creature when he was Philip's age: a leggy and long-haired young man, cropped out of her womb after crouching there for fifteen years, scrambling up immediately to do battle with kings, and the second such child she had borne in a matter of years.

According to Vergil, Philip and his councillors debated for a long time whether or not the young man they were harbouring was indeed this freakish fairground apparition, or Edward's son. At last, Philip seemed to buckle; he told Henry's envoys that, out of respect for their king, he would not support this claimant or his followers any more. But he said he could do nothing to stop Margaret, who was sovereign in her dower lands. This was untrue, since her power was subsidiary to his; Philip could order her to cease if he wanted to. But he did not want to because, despite the smooth words, he did not mean to drop Richard. Young as he was, he had learned to deceive like a prince already.

Henry, grasping this immediately, broke off trade in September. English merchants were given fifteen days to leave the Low Countries, and the English wool mart at Antwerp was abandoned. No more con-tacts were allowed between the merchants of the Burgundian territories— especially Flanders—and England, save sales of wool through Calais. Henry talked loudly in September of "our great voyage over the sea", war-noises. He also demanded a surety of £20,000 from the German merchants of the Hanseatic League that they would not ship illicitly to Philip's territories, a ban they frequently ignored. In October there were riots in London, apparently against Hansa profiteering during the embargo. In April, all Flemings were expelled from England.

Philip's councillors, though dreading the economic damage, agreed that the archduke should respond in kind. In May 1494 Philip imposed a counter-embargo: by a decree in his name and Maximilian's, all imports of English cloth into the Burgundian Netherlands were banned. This was tightened still further in January 1495, just a week before Richard signed over England to Maximilian, by letters patent from Philip and his father that revoked all special licences and proclaimed the ban again. As for Richard himself, he lorded it in the great house in Antwerp that the English merchants had left empty.

Meanwhile, Henry's envoys continued to spread their accusations of trickery and deception. In July 1494 Garter King of Arms, the most dis-tinguished of Henry's heralds, arrived at Philip's court with the details, or some of them, that Henry had gathered the year before. The young man they were calling Richard, he told them, was a native of Tournai, "the son of a bourgeois of the town, and whatever celebration they were mak-ing of him, they would be deceived in the end." When he said this to Margaret, "she said the contrary, and gave the herald no credence, and he was in grave danger of prison, but was released because it was his master

King Henry who had made him learn those words." Undeterred, Garter went out into the streets of Malines and proclaimed "in front of ten or twelve officers, kings of arms and heralds" that Richard was a *patelineur*, a wheedling trickster and a base man's son, and that Henry had certain proof of it. This, too, Philip's council heard and pondered.

In March 1495 Somerset came, with his bold statement that Richard's tomb could be inspected by anyone who wanted. Philip was beside Richard and Margaret then, sitting a few feet away. He was quite close enough to see how they took that claim, whether their colour changed, and how strongly they reacted. It was said you could always tell fakers because their virtue did not last: their shows of piety or emotion passed too quickly, just as false gold discoloured and false emeralds broke. Plantagenet's behaviour seemed consistent enough, restrained always by ritual salutations and good manners. But there again, as Vergil remarked, "there is no deceit more deep and secret than that which lurketh in the dissembly of understanding, or under some colour of courtesy."

Even those who now thought they detected a deception were not entirely sure what sort it was. All the words Jean Molinet applied to Richard when he wrote later, from *patelineur* to *piperie*, cheating, and *traffiquer*, to deal falsely, implied not someone who had taken on a false life, but someone who sold false wares. When this prince displayed himself in Malines or Antwerp he was on the same footing as those who hawked fake relics, bloodstained rags or gray pieces of cow's bone, or sold fresh handfuls of straw from the stable at Bethlehem. His natural companions were bakers who put dust in their bread, or priests who trickled oil or wine by subterfuge down the face of the local saint to produce miraculous sweats. They might seem convincing in themselves, professionals at their calling, but what they offered was worthless. "All is not gold that outward showeth bright," wrote John Lydgate; "a stockfish bone in darkness giveth a light."

No more is known of the story that Garter Herald shouted in the streets of Malines. But the fragments Henry was accumulating about the boy included the assertion, true or not, that he had travelled with a merchant. He had evidently learned young how to swindle, as merchants so often did: weighing false, giving deceptive patter, swearing great oaths to the quality of his wares, showing them fast or in the dark. Details emerged too, at this stage or later, of the boy's employment at Middelburg in a haberdasher's shop. That shop sold mostly needles and purses, but haberdashers also filled their shelves with pretty and frivolous junk: play-ing cards, combs, mirrors, brooches, painted cloths, glass beads, hatpins, laces, tin-foil, jewel-boxes. In the 1480s and 1490s trinkets like these came into England mostly on ships from Flanders, especially from Middelburg and Antwerp. They were often the goods of wandering salesmen and peddlers rather than fixed shops, and the rootlessness of their sellers—like Richard Plantagenet's—was yet another reason for suspecting and dis-trusting them.

More than anything, the quacks and tricksters sold promises. This potion would cure the whooping cough; that bracelet would win a girl's heart; this little card, pressed into your hand by a wandering friar and printed with the implements of the Passion of Christ, would spare you 32,755 years of the torments of Purgatory. Richard of York made similar great promises, all the time, by many accounts. In 1494, he was promising Maximilian a glorious invasion of England. Later, he made the same promise to other people, and lured in followers with offers of fresh-minted money. With the promises went copious lies about influence and friends in high places. As his prospects waned, so the claims were to become more extravagant. The haberdasher's boy was apparently in part-nership with Fortune, selling typically meretricious stuff: "precious jew-els" shaken in a tray, which, if you looked at them in daylight rather than the half-dark, turned out to be bits of tin and glass.

But the doubts Henry's envoys had sown were not conclusive. Though the young man's claim could now be described as a manifest lie, there was still, Vergil admitted, a "face of truth" on it. He was playing his part with such skill that "he was praised to the heavens, as possessed of every quality and virtue and the very model of his forebears." For this rea-son, no other name was fastened yet on Richard at the court of Burgundy. All through these incidents, Molinet still called him either Richard, or the White Rose. The Tournai clue was apparently ignored, although a jour-ney of only sixty miles would allegedly have turned up people ready to recognise him, call him Perkin, and hug him with parental tears. The simple imposture in the form Henry had it, the "great abusion" that lured people in as with a stage performance, did not seem to be laid at his door. Those who distrusted him at Philip's court levied charges against him that were vaguer and more general: that he was a deceiver, in some way still to be established, and that the claims he was making somehow did not match him.

So Philip did not give up Richard, and Henry did not believe for a moment that he had. Richard, after all, remained in Malines until the summer of 1495, raising money and men, and his chief adviser and protector remained Huc de Melun, on Philip's staff at a salary of 2,000 francs a year. André made a three-headed monster out of Margaret, Maximilian and Philip: the dragon Geryon, a multicoloured creature hanging half on and half off the northern coast of Europe, who in turn spawned a fire-breathing monster-child that tried to make war on England. Sometime after the attempt, Henry wrote icily to Philip—who was complaining about incidents between English and Flemish seamen—that the "great injuries" done to England had given the king, and all Englishmen, every reason to attack him.

Nonetheless, in other rooms and at other times, Philip's councillors assured Henry's envoys that the archduke had ceased to support the Duke of York. The ruse was one that others followed. Richard Plantagenet had nuisance value, and several European rulers wanted to see how far, and how profitably, Henry could be annoyed. It was quite possible to irritate the King of England without going to the extreme of putting up a pretender to his throne, but the opportunity seemed heaven-sent. Several of Henry's tormentors seemed genuinely to like the revived Duke of York, but they, too, would have been prepared to drop him as soon as the experiment ceased to pay. It was not only Fortune, though she got the blame, who could toss a man aside like a perfume ball.

The chief of these experimenters was, and remained, Maximilian. Even before his split with Henry over the peace made with France at Etaples, he was said to appreciate the usefulness of keeping the English king "in a state of suspicion". Richard claimed to have had early offers of help from him. By April 1493, when Maximilian's wounds were raw, Carlo Barbiano passed on the rumour, current at the French court, that Maximilian intended to try "to make king of England the boy who calls himself the son of King Edward, who fled thither, and give him his daughter [Margaret] to wife . . . in order to make perpetual war on France." A portrait of Margaret survives from a few years earlier: a sulky little girl with her father's nose, fingering her crystal prayer-beads in a window. Had matters turned out differently, she might have been Richard's wife.

At that point, however, Maximilian had not even met "the boy". There is no sign of those early ambassadors that Richard boasted of. As

Maximilian remembered it later, in the years when he had made his peace with Henry, he had not been especially enthusiastic to meet him anyway. "The son of King Edward came to the White King," he wrote (using his customary poetic persona), "and asked for help. He told him that he wanted to inherit his father's kingdom and reminded the White King of the alliance that the White King had had with his father concerning him and his children, of whom he was one. The White King complied with this request." Maximilian said that he took up "the young boy" because he and Henry, for the moment, were not getting on. "The White King was not very keen on this," he added, "as he was well aware that the matter was not very solidly founded. For he knew well that the New King [Henry] was highly agreeable to his people." The contemporary report of their first meeting in Vienna substantiated that, of course; Maximilian had said he would "think it over".

Yet he warmed to the young man quickly, and as quickly made him part of his plans. By December 12th, 1493, two weeks after their first meeting, the Milanese ambassador reported that Maximilian was already working on a "compromise" between Edward's son and Henry, "but the King of England remains mistrustful"—unsurprisingly. The King of the Romans had a natural sympathy for Yorkist causes, stemming from his affection for Margaret ("the old lady") and his gratitude for friendship shown to him in his struggling days by Edward IV and Richard III. He once explained that he recognised no obligation to Henry, only to the Duke of York, and felt himself obliged 'for his honour and that of the Empire" to maintain him for a time, "principally because of the friendship he had with King Edward his father". After a while, however, his reasons shifted to the usefulness of having an English prince at his beck and call, both against France and in general. In any case, he liked this fairhaired boy with his extraordinary tales. Increasingly, full of enthusiasm for his "new king", he called him his kinsman.

Henry found it impossible to believe that Maximilian aided and favoured "such a deception" with any sincerity. It was "derogatory to the honour of any honourable prince", he thought, to encourage the *garçon* in Flanders. Such a course would add nothing to his reputation and bring him "even less profit". "And the king is very sure that the King of the Romans and the people of standing [*gens de facon*] over there know all about the deception, and that what he does is because of the displeasure he felt, and still feels, at the treaty and agreement made by the king with [the King of France]." That was certainly a part of it. Another part was Maximilian's wish, mentioned as a secret aside by Henry to Richmond Herald in March 1496, for "another king in England whom he can use to help himself and put in [our] place to help him succeed in his business." These malevolent attitudes, Henry thought, were very different from a conviction that he was backing someone genuine.

In fact, Maximilian never knew for certain who the "young boy" was, but it would not have been in his character to admit it. He was con/vinced that he knew matters hidden from others, including the true inward nature of the men he met. He called this "the secret knowledge of experience." As his father had dabbled in the innermost composition of things, leaving behind a treasury of alchemical books and (people said) two chests full of lumps of gold from his experiments, so he himself had laboured to understand perfectly the secret nature of mankind. He had even presupposed the existence of hidden stars, "as yet undiscovered and unknown", that might have effects on human beings. If anyone came to him with some request, as Edward's son had come, he never refused him without looking first into his life and character. He would wait, too, for the favourable moment to help him as laid out in the stars. His Master of Secret Instruction said that, on these occasions of high decision/making, he did not call Maximilian a man; he called him "Time", for his pupil had gone so far beyond the limits of ordinary men that his master had nothing more to teach him.

But still Maximilian looked at the fair/haired boy he had decided to favour, and wondered. In September 1494, two months after Garter Her/ald had spread around Malines his stories of Richard's past, the King of the Romans began to make inquiries of his own. He was still in Malines, in the thick of the rumours. He did not appear to check in Tournai, but he asked Philip of Nassau—a member of Philip's council—and the Pro/vost of Utrecht to find out from designated Englishmen, and from mer/chants doing business in England, "what people in England think about the Duke of York, the late King Edward's son, and what people are say/ing." The request was scrawled wildly on a small piece of paper with more scribbles in the margin: "those doing business in England", "what/ever others they may best find in England", as the inquiry widened in Maximilian's mind. When they found out, they were to write him a detailed report. Perhaps he meant mostly to test whether sympathy was running in Richard's direction before the planned invasion; but their brief was clearly also to find out who people thought he was. Even Maximilian in his note made a mess of it, writing what looked like "the Duke of Charles" before crossing "Charles" out and putting "York" above it.

Maximilian's firmest statement of belief came in September of the following year, when he wrote to Pope Alexander VI in support of Margaret's appeal, made four months before, for the reversal of the sentence of excommunication passed on Richard and his supporters. Her plea had evidently gone unheard, and it seems that new condemnations had been issued. These were "surreptitious and frivolous," said Maximilian. Richard was "the born son of Edward, the legitimate and true deceased king, and it is evident that he has an excellent right [*optimum ius*] to that kingdom." The prince and Margaret were both "violently injured and aggrieved" by the excommunication; justice and conscience demanded its reversal. Firm enough. Yet Pope Alexander might have noticed that no tag of courtesy, such as the usual "most illustrious", was applied to the Duke of York, whereas it always was to Margaret; her nephew floated curiously free from the weight of royal etiquette. The words "legitimate and true" were also applied to King Edward, rather than to Richard. On the first mention of the duke, Maximilian threw in a potted version of his story: "who, lest he should be put to death by the occupiers of the kingdom, has hitherto often hidden himself, wandering over the world as an unknown exile." Yet the Aragonese chronicler Zurita said he also gave out a different version: that Richard was "the son of King Edward, who had taken shelter in the land of Flanders", with no wandering to speak of.

He also retailed a third, completely different, story. According to Erasmo Brascha, the Milanese ambassador to the court of Burgundy, Maximilian told him in February 1495 that Robert Clifford (Richard's "chief man", as Brascha put it) had "divulged" that "this Duke of York was not the son of King Edward, but is the son of the Dowager Duchess of Burgundy and the Bishop of Cambrai."

Brascha had been close to Maximilian for a while, handling the transfer of Bianca Maria's dowry, and was thus in a position to hear confidences. This one was almost certainly untrue, though when Brascha wrote next to Ludovico Sforza he thought it worthy of a letter by itself. A child born to Margaret in 1473 or 1474—apparently the years in question—would have been assumed as Charles's, despite the dead state of their marriage, not hidden away as an embarrassment. There is no sign, moreover, that Margaret ever gave birth to a child that lived. Yet rumours that she had had love affairs, and a bastard son, had been current before her wedding: most of them coming from the court of France, where Brascha had recently been an ambassador.

As for the Bishop of Cambrai, it is not clear which one was meant. The old one, John of Burgundy, who had died in 1480, was a noted rogue whose funeral had been attended by thirty-six of his illegitimate children. The present one, Henri de Berghes, was the chancellor of the Order of the Golden Fleece and a councillor of the Burgundian court: a man of unimpeachable virtue, who had been Margaret's court chaplain and confessor for more than a decade. She and he led lives of such shining chastity, to all appearances, that there was a delicious irony in the idea that they had sinned carnally together. Yet something—a sense, perhaps, of unusual closeness between Margaret, Cambrai and the boy—also gave the rumour wings, and had unloosed the gossiping tongues of the Burgundian court.

Maximilian did not say that he believed the story. But he was happy to repeat it with no disclaimer, as if it scarcely mattered whether York was authentic or not. And it did not matter. Maximilian knew all about the doubts, and sponsored him despite them. Brascha continued his report of their conversation: "His Majesty also told me that the said duke will proceed for the present to Ireland, where he has strong connections."

The King of the Romans had taken a chance on Richard, and was determined to cling on. He seems to have done so out of enjoyment of the dare—the thrill it gave him, and the annoyance it caused others— as much as anything else. In his chaotic life, crammed with personal administration of a sprawling empire from dozens of different places, there was little time to think or to live with the customary grandeur of princes. Many of his memoranda were scribbled on writing desks set up in bare rooms in his hunting lodges, and his meals might be mouthfuls of bread and cheese taken in the open air. In one year, 1493, he was levying troops to take on the Turks in Inner Austria; in the next, he was trying to organise his protégé's invasion of England. He lived frenetically, on impulse, and his *Prinzen von York* was one of those impulses: alluring to some people, senseless to others. Sport, too: a prince hunting for a throne while his enemies, far better armed, hunted him.

Maximilian's greatest joy was the chase, in all conditions and all weathers. Molinet described him once hunting in Lombardy, "dressed like a poacher . . . his [councillors] in damask and satin, carrying halberds, his courtiers carrying pikes, clothed in three colours of silk, really well turned out." Up in the mountains, searching for chamois and wild boar, Maximilian enjoyed the contrast even more: himself, the emperor, with crampons on his shoes and a haversack on his back, balancing a nine-foot javelin in one hand, exposing himself to every danger while his scared servants ran back home. In the *Teuerdank*, his imaginary romance of his journey from Styria in 1477 to marry Mary of Burgundy, he fell into scrape after scrape and, by a hair's breadth, survived. He chased the chamois to a sharp peak never reached by men before; then he slipped, bending all his shoe-spikes save one, but that one held and saved him. He hunted wild pigs over thin ice, and the ice broke, but he scrambled free. A wild stag ran at him; he caught his spurs in the brush and fell, discharging his crossbow, but it killed the stag rather than himself. Rocks were thrown at him, and missed; guns exploded, but he had leaned back in time; boats tried to ram him, but he swung away nimbly on a rope. Small wonder that he liked the idea of a prince who had slid away from murderers, been spirited from fortresses, disguised himself in rough clothes, wandered among awful dangers and, more than once, evaded betrayal by his own friends.

Richard of York was also, like him, an *umbzotler* (the slang word was his own), a traipser around from place to place. In the early summer months of 1494 they were travelling for a while together, living on sauerkraut and sharp cheap wine as they wended their way from castle to castle between Vienna and Brabant. Once there, they hunted together in grand style. In late August 1494 Molinet described a hunting party of Maximilian, Bianca Maria, Philip and Margaret "taking their solace" in the wooded groves around Malines, Antwerp and Brussels. Richard was by then so close to all of them that he is certain to have been included. By Maximilian's standards, this was soft and relaxing stuff, so easy that the women were with them; and his prince, too, was soft, wonderfully pliable to work with. If he succeeded, Maximilian had a ready-made alliance with England. ("He can then order York about exactly as he likes," in the words of the Venetian ambassadors to Germany.) If his protégé, having succeeded, died childless, Maximilian stood to gain the English throne himself; in a matter of months, the papers would be signed and sealed. If he failed, Maximilian could drop him as easily, and with as little compunction, as a trail that had gone cold in the woods around Malines. This was the theory. In practice, having accepted Richard's claim, there was a tie through Margaret, his children's godmother, that became a bond of honour. Fondness, too, got strangely in the way.

Maximilian, famously impecunious, never gave York much money; hunting was said to absorb what little cash he had. But he lent him some of his best military captains; provided him with a knot of highly placed imperial supporters such as Ludovico Bruno, his Latin secretary, who had first declared York's cause to him in Vienna; and put pressure on both Philip and Albrecht of Saxony to support him with men and ships. Uncle Albrecht was a trusted lieutenant, who had fought for Maximilian both in Burgundy and against the Hungarians. Philip was, for the moment, a dutiful son, accepting the destruction of his country's trade on the understanding that his father's new king would win England. His household was so enmeshed with his father's, with many officers shared between them, that he had little choice but to follow wherever the wild schemes led.

With a mixture of nagging, encouragement and procrastination, Maximilian kept Richard Plantagenet in play on the European stage. In 1494, Charles VIII invaded Italy; the outrageous adventure united Europe against him, but it could not unite effectively while Maximilian and Henry were enemies. To get England into the Holy League that was forming against France, Maximilian had to be made to drop his Prince of York. He refused, and his first reason was disarmingly simple. York was doing well, he said. He was going to win England. Maximilian's impatience to pit his prince against Henry was so intense that his spokesman was already saying in May 1495, two months before an invasion was attempted, that the Duke of York had taken the field against him.

From the point of view of *Realpolitik*, the risk Maximilian was taking was bizarre. Many rulers of Europe thought him flighty, silly, exasperating, irresponsible, and never more so than in his championing of Richard, Duke of York. Perhaps he was just a fool as his father had suspected, finding him so doltish and silent as a child that he thought he might be a mute. Maximilian was surely just allowing himself to be beguiled and enchanted, as princes often were by the flattering liars they attracted to their courts. "He is very fickle," Machiavelli wrote of him later: "he takes counsel from nobody, and yet believes everybody. He desires what he cannot have, and leaves that which he can readily obtain;

therefore he always takes contrary resolutions, and lives in a constant state of agitation." "Why should we deal with him?" sighed the King of Hungary; "he is so inconstant, starting so many things and finishing nothing." And his trademark was so often trickery: a puppet-prince one year, then "counterfeit and new-forged strange coins . . . called Roman groats . . . far of less value than men take them for", with which, Henry complained, Maximilian deceived and damaged Englishmen a few years later. "How I wish," Henry once sighed, "that the emperor would not undertake any enterprise except after mature consideration."

Beyond Henry, it was the Spanish sovereigns, Ferdinand and Isabella, who found Maximilian hardest to deal with. His scattiness was the reverse of their own practicality and clarity of purpose. Ever since their marriage in 1469 and their respective successions to their kingdoms (Isabella to Castile in 1474, Ferdinand to Aragon in 1479), these two had worked tirelessly to create in Spain the sort of peaceable, modern, centralised state that Henry was striving to build in England. By 1494, the Jews had been expelled or converted and the last Muslim kingdom, Granada, had been conquered by Ferdinand for Christ. With the voyages of Columbus, Spain's horizons were opening to untold riches over the western ocean. Yet sharp irritations had sprung up closer to home.

Charles VIII was the chief of these. When he invaded Italy in 1494, Ferdinand and Isabella were appalled. They were desperate to keep French ambitions in check (those ambitions threatening, in particular, disputed territories on their own northern border) by organising the Holy League with Maximilian and Henry both inside it. To make that possible, they needed to detach Maximilian from the Duke of York; but they did not know how. They had had a plan to win over Philip and silence Margaret by proposing that the archduke should marry their daughter Juana; with Juana as the new archduchess, Margaret's place at court would be diminished and she would lose her influence. Henry, sceptical at first, grew to love this idea, urging it again and again on Ferdinand and Isabella until they had brought it to conclusion. They had fewer good ideas for dealing with Philip's father—though, with typical self-confidence, they thought they knew him well enough to effect a reconciliation with Henry, and often offered to do so.

In the Spanish sovereigns' view, as in Henry's, it was scarcely credible that Maximilian should support "him". (Ferdinand and Isabella could seldom quite say what "he" was: not a duke, not really a man, but a sort of roving pronoun.) The King of the Romans was giving "him" not only favour but also *autoridad*, as Zurita pointed out, from his very interest in him. This was so clearly a ruse on Maximilian's part that it had to collapse as soon as it looked unprofitable; when he clung on, they were dumbfounded. This business was just a joke, Isabella wrote to de Puebla in London. The word was *burla*, one of her favourites: gibe, taunt, hoax, mockery. She often applied that word to "him", though his claim was not quite the biggest *burla* in the world; that, she told de Puebla in 1496, was the story that she and Ferdinand had lately sent an ambassador to talk to the King of France. They would never talk to the King of France. Nor, for that matter, would they have anything to do with "him". A letter to de Puebla of July 20th, 1495, made that last point more than clear.

> As for what you say, that the King of England complains greatly because we have written letters to him who calls himself the Duke of York, who is in Flanders, from which much favour has come to him, tell him that we assure him that we have never written such letters. Once, a long time ago, when we were in Barcelona, he wrote us a letter and the Dowager Duchess Margaret wrote us another, asking us to hear the facts of his case and thereby recommending him, and we never replied to him, not one thing, and we wrote to her explaining that there were such doubts about him . . . and we never wrote any more to her about him nor to anyone else. Because we believe that business is a joke and we won't favour such a thing in any way at all, especially since it hurts the King of England. . . . If the King of the Romans or the archduke his son helps him in any way, we will help our cousin the king against him.

Fine words; yet Henry, though he once said they were the only princes in Christendom he trusted, did not trust them. He complained to de Puebla that the Spanish sovereigns were up to their necks in the business of "him of York". They snapped back that this remark was "like everything else that comes out of France": false, in other words. "You can swear to him and assure him," they told their ambassador, "that we don't know a thing about him and we take no pleasure in him . . . This business is a joke, as we really believe it is, and as you know it is, and as you heard us say when you were here. About this matter there is nothing more to say."

Yet, having said that, their resolution wavered. As de Puebla wrote to them in July 1495, "if the King of the Romans clings on to York, it will really make it hard to achieve what your Highnesses desire." At around the same time, a less dismissive message about York was sent from their high-nesses to Gutierre Gomez de Fuensalida, their ambassador in Germany:

> We were rather displeased that [the King of the Romans] has tried to do so much for the Duke of York. Although we don't believe he has done it with the intention of causing us trouble by it, it cer-tainly has caused us trouble, because it's on account of the Duke of York that we don't have the King of England [on our side] against the King of France, and the King of the Romans doesn't have him either. And for that reason he should stand back from him . . .

So the Duke of York hovered at the edge of their calculations, another title and another claim: sometimes with his ass's ears, but as often vaguely crowned and intimidating. As he became more dangerous to Henry, he gained in authenticity. He became "he who calls himself the son of King Edward", or, as their letter to Fuensalida showed, "the Duke of York" proper. He was also entered as the Duke of York in their list of cipher codes for "the pope, the emperor, kings, and other persons of the blood royal". He was DCCCCVII, 907, between Margaret of York and King Alfonso of Naples. Though they mocked him publicly, in secret they gave him the status he accorded himself, at least provisionally.

This was not a sign that they thought he was authentic. Since the name that rulers and envoys were calling him by was a royal one—and since, despite Henry's discoveries, no other name was in circulation—his natural place was among the crowned heads. The Duke of Milan was in the same quandary. In the mid-1490s, his ambassadors in England were writing to him only of the Duke of York, and he was reduced at one point to asking Maximilian whose side he should take in this struggle of English princes. Yet Soncino said he himself had also told him, several times, "that this movement was thought puerile by everyone". York was a joke; but his very name made Henry afraid, and could induce him to do what other princes wanted.

De Puebla told the Spanish sovereigns this, and described how con-versations touching on "the boy who calls himself Plantagenet" called forth from Henry his most emotional outbursts and his wildest suspicions of other people's motives, including theirs. The Spanish sovereigns were in the middle of protracted negotiations with Henry about the marriage of Prince Arthur with their daughter Katherine, another means to limit and frustrate the King of France. Discussion of Katherine's dowry was especially difficult; the English king was demanding too much. If his position suddenly looked less secure and his claim less legitimate, Spain would have the stronger hand. The "joke" was clearly no joke to Henry. "By the faith of his heart," as he cried to de Puebla, he was "mortally sorry" for the plots that were being woven round this boy. "Although he argued that he was make-believe," wrote Zurita, "he was terribly worried about him."

The sovereigns of Spain never shared Maximilian's personal interest in the Duke of York. They were thus far honest in their dealings with Henry, that they never made contact with DCCCCVII directly. It was true enough that they did not answer his letter to Isabella, filing it away instead with a sceptical remark ("from Richard, he who calls himself the Duke of York") scribbled on the back. But they began to understand the lure of him, and play with it, while at the same time assuring Henry that his interests were their only care.

At the bottom of it all, they badly wanted Henry to prevail. But in the mid-1490s, despite almost ten years of wise and shrewd rule since Bosworth, neither he, nor they, believed that his throne was secure. For years, they had nagged him on that score. In July 1488, their commissioners had remarked that it was surprising they should consider giving Henry their daughter at all, "bearing in mind what happens every day to the Kings of England". At least the greatness and prosperity of Spain, they went on, "would do much to make impossible what has happened so often, and still happens, to the Kings of England." They would not let it drop. Moreover, for several years afterwards, Ferdinand and Isabella continued to think that way.

They were far from alone. As Philippe de Commines so constantly said, the disposal of events, and especially of battles, was out of men's hands. Fortune misled men, and God ordained what would befall them, according to criteria that no man could understand. This was just what the Spanish sovereigns had been hinting at: Fortune, blind or careless, whirring her wheel between Henry and the boy, letting the silly joke ride perhaps to the summit, while the anointed King of England—like so many just before him—teetered, tripped and fell.

IV

By the summer of 1493, the king's suspicions and fears were being fanned almost daily. Indemnities owed to Scotland by the terms of a truce had not been paid, and on July 6th Henry remarked that "plain and express war" might break out if the money was not sent "in all haste possible". On the 9th he fretted to his treasurer that his ambassadors to the King of France, Thomas Ward and Matthew Baker, "have been far longer time with our cousin . . . than was thought" and asked him to forward Ward another 100 marks. He may have suspected that Ward was slipping from his grasp, about to flee to Flanders. His "express mind", as he put it, was to try to bind him to his service. Both in the north and from the south, his enemies seemed to be regrouping. Henry's uncharacteristic use of "express" in both these warrants showed how close to panic he was.

Most of all, as his letter to Gilbert Talbot of the 20th showed, he expected invasion from Flanders: "captains of estrange nations" descending on England, whipped up by Margaret's malice and her promises, to claim estates there and to put her feigned lad on the throne. He asked Talbot to be ready to go to war at a day's notice, "upon any our sudden warning". Typically, many others would have received the same letter at the same time. Henry was also sending knights and carefully picked troops to guard the coasts, the ports "and all roads and footpaths", taking no chances. Talbot was to get eighty mounted men ready, "as many spears, with their custrells and demi-lances, well horsed, as ye can furnish, and the remainder to be archers and bills." As he wrote, the king was at Kenilworth, a favourite summer hunting palace in Warwickshire, with twelve gunners in attendance.

Two days later Henry commanded all the ships of war under the east-coast naval captains to be coppered and victualled at Orwell, on the Suffolk coast, and sent to sea. He also wanted "due search" made of the Thames, Sandwich, Ipswich and ports between, to see what vessels were there and whether they should be made ready. Five ships, including the *Bonaventura* and the *Mary Walsingham*, had already been rigged forth to do "service of war" for six weeks, "forasmuch as we be determined with God's grace to advance unto the sea in all haste". The other warships were to follow. Orwell was particularly important because it lay between Flanders and Scotland, a good place "to rancontre [engage] our rebels and their complices in their sailings to and fro." The letter ended with a plea to his treasurer and under-treasurer "to advertise us with all speed in every behalf."

This peril did not go away; indeed, it grew. The trade embargo imposed a few months later made Henry no more secure, for these desper-ate policies hurt England as much as they hurt the Burgundian cloth-towns. Meanwhile, the boy was increasingly fêted there. But Henry's private terrors were not for public display. As the king gave Richmond his instructions in August 1494, he brushed the danger off. Charles had sent letters to warn Henry that Maximilian was determined to help the boy who said he was Edward's son "with people, favour and all he possibly can", and to that end "had arrived in Flanders with a considerable force". Charles offered Henry all the help he could think of against this imminent danger, but Henry waved his offer away. The boy was no threat to anyone. The abusion was manifest and evident, "just like the other one the Duchess of Burgundy concocted, when she sent Martin Swart [Sim-nel's German troop-captain] to England." There was no lord or man of standing in the kingdom of England who did not know that perfectly well. It was notorious. There was no doubt at all that his subjects held the boy *en tres-grand desrizion*, "and not without cause." Besides, England was in "as good and peaceful obedience as it has ever been in the memory of man".

Henry already knew, from his spies at home, that most of this was untrue. Despite his cautiousness he had a habit, when excited or panicky, of overstating his case. Ambassadors were surprised, at times, to find him almost giddy with happiness or gratitude when he received them: con-stantly taking his hat off, making extravagant shows of devotion. When-ever Henry was afraid he would not be believed, he multiplied his claims. ("This really happened, Most Blessed Father, and if we hadn't been cer-tain of it we wouldn't have written to you.") As later events made clear, he was never as certain of the Tournai story as he said.

Moreover, beneath his bluster, he took the threat of invasion seriously. He had already sent out warning letters on July 21st 1494 to all the east-coast ports. The town officers of Grimsby, on the Humber, kept the one they received:

HR

Trusty and well beloved, we greet you well. And so it is as we be credibly informed that our cousin the King of Romans is come to Malines, or else shall be there; wherefore, as it is said, our Rebels take courage, and do prate and say that within this our Realm be certain persons which will not long tarry from them, but go unto them in haste, upon knowledge of the coming of the [King of] Romans foresaid; and inasmuch as, be it so or not so as it is before written, good policy adjudgeth we should provide for the worst; Therefore we will and charge you that ye have sure and continual await upon all manner of vessels within your offices, and in espe⁄cial within the creeks and in other small rivers able to pass crayers or boats to the sea, that no manner suspect person be suffered to pass, but that he be attached, and thereupon with the demeaning and ground of his suspicion be safely sent unto us. . . .

Yet Henry told Richmond to inform Charles that he was perfectly confi⁄dent and calm. He was grateful for the French king's "honourable offers" to get Breton and Norman ships ready, under orders to leave immediately if Henry wished it, "because the business could be sudden"; he was glad, too, that Charles was turning down requests from his subjects to join the boy's invasion force (and, the damaged document seems to say, promising to kill those who did so). He took these offers as the fruit of "good and cordial love." On the other hand, they were not really necessary. "The business of the *garçon* is of so little worth and value," he told Richmond, "that the king does not intend to put the subjects of his brother and cousin to any pain or labour on that account or to give them that trouble. . . . He would do so if he needed to." As for the idea that Maximilian would help this boatman's boy invade England, "the king can't believe at all that he or any other prince would want to do such a thing."

Four months on, in the instructions given to Richmond in Decem⁄ber, Henry's bravado continued unchecked. "Thanks be to God, the king . . . is in good health and prosperity of body, and is also as well loved and obeyed in his kingdom as ever a king has been in England." Even Ireland was looking better: "Affairs there are progressing as well as he could wish for." As for the feigned boy, "It appears each day more than the last, to every person, where the said boy comes from and who he is." Small flick⁄ers of unease showed only in the secret page of Richmond's instructions, or what now remains of it:

Then in case the king's good brother and cousin . . . those being around him . . . should give any impression in words about the King of the Romans . . . and the boy who is in Flanders, the said Richmond may reply as he did on the other trip. And he will say that the king fears them not, because he knows that they are inca' pable of hurting him or doing him injury.

Henry knew well that they were not incapable of hurting him. Yet by that stage, at the end of 1494, the king's defiance was better founded. The difference was made by his agents, who laboured constantly behind the scenes to undo the English hopes of the young man in Flanders. The apparent discovery of who he was had little effect, since Henry—for rea' sons best known to himself—gave this almost no publicity until his tor' mentor was captured. But the other prong of Henry's undercover work proved devastating. His spies, working both in London and inside the court in Malines, eventually destroyed the conspiracies in England. By the time the king gave Richmond his instructions that December, his enemies at home were on the brink of elimination.

The first cracks in the English conspiracy appeared very early. By April 1493, barely two months after the cell had been formed, Humphrey Sav' age and Gilbert Debenham "and other our rebels and traitors" had fled to sanctuary at Westminster. They had almost certainly been fingered by John ap Howell, who had brought them the letter from Richard in Febru' ary and received Henry's pardon in March.

Although Savage and Debenham were apparently still free to come, go and recruit—two monks of the abbey were in the circle by May— Henry had his eye on them, and was perhaps merely playing with them to glean more information. (William Graunt, one of the monks, had been charged by the king with feeding them.) It seems these plotters had not yet done anything, since a warrant of April 20th spoke only of "murders robberies and other such inconveniences as would by likelihood ensue" if they remained unrestricted. For this reason, the king invoked papal bulls allowing him to keep them "more straightly" in sanctuary. He became, in effect, their jailer, paying 10 shillings a week for each man's keep to the archdeacon and the "kitchener" of the abbey. If Savage and Debenham were still conspiring, they were fools; and yet they were doing so, by all accounts.

Executions of conspirators occurred as early as that May, when "four men, all fastened upon an hurdle" were drawn from the Marshalsea to Tyburn and hanged. The London chronicler did not say what this was for, but Fabyan called it treason. Sometime that summer—that season of high nerves at Kenilworth—Henry had issued letters, with the advice of his council, covering him for all necessary acts against traitors. In the autumn, when crowds of apprentices attacked the Hanseatic merchants' headquarters at the Steelyard in London to protest against Hansa profiteering during the trade embargo, Henry seemed to think this had treasonous colours too. The mayor and brethren of the city were asked to make diligent inquiries of the "rebels"—a word used specifically for those opposing the king—and to take their information to the king's council, "that the king might thereof sufficiently be informed".

In February 1494, barely a week after nailing their ballads and rhymes to the church doors, Thomas Bagnall and his circle were caught. They managed to flee to the sanctuary of St. Martin's le Grand beside St. Paul's where, on the 12th, "Sampson Norton, knight, Simon Digby [the constable of the Tower] and Henry Winslow, knights, and others came with swords, bows and arrows" and dragged them out, save Bagnall, who protested. His desperate statement, in an untidy scrawl on a small piece of paper, survives with the indictment:

> he sayeth that [he] is a sanctuary man of St. Martin's [interlined] / the sanctuary place beside Chepe / and was taken out of St. Martin's against his ["my" deleted] / will / [interlined] by master Sampson and other and Master Digby being present / and prayeth thereto to be restored ["permitted" deleted] and acknowledgeth the treason whereof he is arraigned

After the dean and chapter had interceded for him, citing the inviolability of sanctuary, Bagnall was committed to the Tower. The others, though they pleaded not guilty, were hanged on February 26th. Two more men were hanged that day, Robert Bulkeley and "a Dutchman" who was probably one of Richard's agents. Bulkeley's uncovering had been sudden. As late as February 3rd he had been one of Henry's "well-beloved servants", about to share with two others a reward of £12 for his services; by the 24th, "it is now that the said Bulkeley is unpaid of his part of the said sum . . . by reason of his rebellion." His hanging and beheading two days later would have been Savage's and Debenham's fate too, if they had not fled to sanctuary.

In the course of the year Henry arrested most of the prominent churchmen who supported Richard, including Worseley, Richford, Lessy, Leybourne and Sutton. Among the laymen arrested were Sir Simon Mountford (for his £30 donation), Lord Fitzwater (for his promise of armed men), Radcliffe, Thwaites, Daubeney, Thomas Cressener and Thomas Astwood, the young steward of Marton Abbey. It is not known who these men's accusers were or, in some cases, exactly what they had done, but any contact with "Flanders" would have placed them under immediate suspicion. Apparently harmless dealings with someone who had been in trouble—as slight as going up to him and wishing him good day—could also tar a man with treason.

Henry had gained his evidence about the English conspiracies largely by infiltrating Richard's household. It was probably not difficult to do. The White Rose gave no impression of being particularly careful in his choice of counsellors and friends, but seemed to take eagerly and gratefully to anyone who expressed support for him. Many of those who were close to him, such as Stephen Frion and Thomas Ward, had been Henry's faithful servants not so long before. (John ap Howell too, the Welsh letter-carrier, may have been Henry's man.) Even young Anthony de la Forsa, whom Richard was to praise in 1496 for serving him "full lovingly" in many countries, was being rewarded by Henry as late as April 1494 for "divers causes us specially moving". His reward, 10 marks or £6. 13s. 4d., was the same as another made to him the year before for some unspecified usefulness. In Vergil's version of the first speech Richard made in Scotland, he remarked with almost childlike surprise that Henry had encouraged people to be friends with him and then, under cover of friendship, they had "searched through all the secret things".

Molinet told the story of the infiltration, placing it in 1494. Three *grans personnaiges d'Engleterre*, he wrote, turned up one day at the court of the King of the Romans, who was then at Malines, where Richard was. They sought refuge there because Henry had banished them from England for supporting Richard's cause, which they considered to be pressing, lawful and just. Richard received them lovingly and made them his chief counsellors, "so much so that nothing was done, openly or covertly, that did not pass through their hands." These three worked so hard, by sending reports "and in other ways," that the greatest men in England began to subscribe to Richard's quarrel and promised they would help him to invade.

Molinet, possibly using Richard's own estimates, reckoned there were more than forty of these nobles, among them "the great chamberlain of King Henry", and that they pledged a total of 40,000 florins to advance his cause. As a proof of intent they sent him their seals, which Richard passed, as usual, to his confidants. At that point the confidants wrote secretly to Henry, asking him to order them home, for it was time to go. When the king's messenger arrived, hotfoot from Calais, the three men immediately bagged up the seals, saddled their horses and "without taking leave of Richard", a gross discourtesy, rode like the devil through the back-country to Béthune, Calais and England. The bag of seals was delivered to Henry, and all Richard's most prominent supporters in England could now be identified.

Who were the three men? Not figments of Molinet's imagination, certainly. Letters sent by Henry to Calais on October 22nd, 1494 mentioned the surrender, apparently in Calais, of "three of our rebels that have forsaken the feigned lad and will now submit them unto us to have our grace and pardon." They were not *grans personnaiges* in the king's book, merely shipwrecked malcontents of the usual sort who resorted to Malines. Nor did Henry suggest that they were spies; but it is likely that they were, and that the man they had chiefly been working on was now about to turn.

According to Fabyan, after the best part of two years in close proximity to the young man in Flanders, Robert Clifford had "seen by many likelihoods that it should not be he, whom he was taken for." A long stay with Richard had somehow disabused him. He was still there in October, when the three men decamped with the seals; indeed, he was still there in December, when he witnessed the protocols drawn up by Richard and Margaret. Very soon after that, he left Malines and fled to England. A courier "brought the tidings" on December 19th, and was paid £3 for his good news.

Some thought that Clifford, too, had been a spy from the start. The rumour was rife in his own day, and there is certainly something disquieting about him in the early months of 1493: closeted with Fitzwater in Windsor, conniving with Stanley in Charing Cross, drawing the chief players one by one deep into treason. Perhaps those fervent claims to see

Edward's face in the young man had been nothing but entrapment. But Vergil did not think so. "It is certain," he wrote,

> that the plot did Robert no good and did great damage to his name . . . so that afterwards he was very little in the king's good graces, and was not free of blame. He was a very keen partisan of the House of York. From the beginning of the affair he went over to Margaret in order to hurt Henry, and it appears that he mistakenly believed that Peter was Richard, Edward's son.

One small incident also suggested that Clifford was not Henry's man. Sir Richard Nanfan, the deputy-lieutenant of Calais, said that when he had told the king how Clifford was spreading news of Edward's son around the town, "his Highness sent me sharp writing that he would have the proof of this matter." Most contemporaries thought that Clifford had been a true believer, and that his friends had to intercede hard with the king to purchase his pardon and restore him to grace. Only once they had succeeded did he dare to come back. Vergil took a simpler line: Clifford had been worked on with promises of a pardon and of high rewards, and so he turned. Such were the inconstant and contradictory purposes of men.

His victim's own reaction is worth noting. In his proclamation of 1496 Richard referred to Clifford without bitterness or, indeed, characterisation at all, merely saying that he "and others" had "verified and openly proved" the extent of Henry's corruption of his closest servants. The lack of condemnation perhaps implied that he still considered Clifford an ally for the future. That, as so often, was a bad misreading.

Clifford seems to have been back in London, and singing to Henry, by late December. Some of Henry's spies had deliberately left Flanders with him to keep him under observation. His servant Richard Waltier came back too, but William Barley and the Bramptons did not. Vergil said it took Henry's agents another two years to loosen Barley: "he would hear nothing of returning then, but . . . later he came to his senses." He was attainted in 1495, and was not pardoned until July 1498. In the autumn of 1497, however, a "Master Barlee, the Englishman" showed up in Scotland: still Richard's servant in some obscure capacity, despite his son-in-law's defection.

When Clifford himself arrived in England, the king's private accounts show that he was arrested, and rewarded, at more or less the same time. The arrest may have been for show, but it took three men to "bring up Sir Robert Clifford", as a prisoner, on January 9th, 1495. The expression was doubly curious because both he and Waltier had been pardoned on December 22nd, almost as soon as they reached England. Prisoner or not, on January 20th Clifford was given "by the hand of Master Bray" (Reginald Bray, already gaining infamy as one of Henry's chief fiscal agents) the astonishing sum of £500 for services rendered.

The king, who had returned to Greenwich for Christmas, decided after the festivals to shift his court to the Tower. He did this so that those called in for questioning would think nothing amiss, but could be immediately incarcerated if necessary. There Clifford, abasing himself before Henry, told the king what he knew. He may have divulged, as Maximilian said he did as soon as he got to England, the story of Margaret and Cambrai—just possibly the reason he was disabused, if he was disabused at all. Yet Henry did not need that. What he needed was Clifford's list of contacts, especially high contacts, in the vicinity of the English court itself.

Among those who were soon to be arrested, attainted or executed, it is not clear how many were specifically betrayed by Henry's prize informant. The conspiracy had already imploded, with numbers of the knightly or clerical members in custody, by the time Clifford, desperately excusing his behaviour, threw himself at Henry's feet. But his list included many names, Vergil said; and the first among them, naturally, was Sir William Stanley's.

By all accounts, Henry was deeply shaken to find his chamberlain involved. Here was a man closer to him than almost any other, privy to his secrets and "next to his body", bound by battlefield loyalty and holy ties of marriage. Until indisputable evidence was produced, the king would not believe the accusation. Or so he made it seem. In truth, just as Stanley had dissembled his satisfaction with Henry and his rewards, so the king had dissembled his confidence in him. An anonymous informer in the next reign suggested that Henry may have known about Stanley's dabblings two or three years before he acted. The late king, he said, "would handle such a cause circumspectly and with convenient diligence for inveigling, and yet not disclose it, to the party nor otherwise, by a great space after, but keep it to himself and always grope further, having ever good await and espial to the party. I am sure his Highness knew of the untrue mind and treason compassed against him by Sir William Stanley and divers other great men . . . and kept it secret, and always gathered upon them more and more." As he had done, indeed, and was still to do, with the feigned boy.

Stanley, even at the moment of his arrest, seems not to have taken the plunge. He was waiting for Clifford's signal to act, which had not come. (Many other conspirators, Hall said, were waiting for it too, and were concluding from Clifford's silence "that they were by a little & little dampnified and hurted.") Stanley may well have wanted to see the young man for himself before he made a commitment. He also needed to be sure that prominent rulers, especially Maximilian, were truly behind him; hence the importance, as Henry had pointed out, of Maximilian's return to Malines in August 1494 with Richard firmly in his company. Stanley gave no hint of his dangerous thoughts, even sitting on the commissions that indicted Thomas Bagnall's accomplices in February 1494 and "English Edward" Cyver in September.

Had he, in fact, done anything? He had made his remark about not bearing arms against Edward's son, but Vergil judged this a sign of *mala voluntas*, ill-will towards Henry, rather than outright treason. (Hall thought melancholy made him say it.) He had agreed to send Clifford to Flanders. Molinet said he had also been among those who had sent their seals and promised money; André, too, said Stanley had pledged to use his "great heaps of money" to defend the young man and bring him to the throne. He had not got near to taking out of storage the two brigandines, covered with cloth-of-gold, that he kept at Holt. But this was still "rebellion" in Henry's book.

Many other rebels, in London and elsewhere, were arraigned at the Guildhall at the end of January 1495. There was no suggestion of trials. Molinet said that Henry simply showed them the incontrovertible evidence of the seals they had sent to Richard, at which, "bitterly ashamed and confounded", they confessed their treasons. Radcliffe, Mountford, Daubeney, Cressener and Astwood were condemned to die. The first three were beheaded on Tower Hill on February 4th; Cressener and Astwood were spared because they were young, a popular decision with the London crowd. On the same day Thwaites and Lessy were attainted for misprision, knowledge of treasonable acts. The next day Robert Holborn, a shipman, and Hans Troys, another "Dutchman", were hanged, cut down alive and beheaded, this time at Tyburn. A Breton called "Petty John" was hanged there on the Friday. Molinet reported that twenty-four "rich merchants" tried at this point to flee to Richard's protection in Malines, but were seized at sea and hanged "shamefully". This story, with its hints of untold wealth and the cunningly inflated idea that Richard could offer royal protection to anyone, may have come from the camp of the White Rose himself.

Assigning Stanley's fate took a little longer. He was arraigned over two days, February 6th and 7th, before the King's Bench in Westminster Hall, and was executed a week later. His first plea, unusually in such cases, had been not guilty, though Vergil thought he had almost proudly admitted his offence to Henry. In any event the justices overruled him, and on February 16th, at around eleven in the morning, Stanley was beheaded on Tower Hill. He died without recanting, apologising or explaining, to the bafflement of the London chroniclers. Fabyan, writing seven years later, especially marvelled that Stanley had lost his huge wealth, position, lands and fees "for a knave that after was hanged"; and "not he alone, but many other" had fallen for the same deception.

For Henry, Stanley's execution was the strongest possible signal of intent. He would kill anyone, no matter how close their blood or office might be to his own, who took the feigned lad's side. Having done so, he then paid the £15. 19s. for his chamberlain's burial at Syon. He also allotted £31 to his servants for their wages and horsefodder, and gave £10 to Stanley himself, apparently to tip his executioner for the hopedfor mercy of a swift and single stroke. After this, moved as Bacon said by "the glimmering of a confiscation", Henry seized Stanley's treasure. At Holt the king's commissioners missed nothing, from lead piping to old cushions and saucers in the pantry. They noted whether the sheets and carpets were "good", "right good" or "somewhat worn", and observed where bits of gold trim had fallen off the bedhangings. The wine cellar, disappointingly, was empty. In Stanley's private closet they found a counting board, a crossbow, various phials of medicinal waters and a set of builtin pigeonholes for his letters and bills; in "the high wardrobe" they found his scarlet Parliament robes and his Garter robes still hanging, royal rewards to him. The commissioners' speed suggested that Henry was searching for information as well as gold; but there was nothing in Stanley's houses to incriminate him except the Yorkist girdleclasp, and that was broken.

The fate of John Ratcliffe, Lord Fitzwater, the only other lord involved, was curiously different. He had been arrested on February 22nd, but was not convicted of treason until October or November. Even then, Henry "of his most special grace" did not have him executed. Instead, Fitzwater was committed to prison for life in the castle of Guisnes, near Calais. He was beheaded in Calais more than a year later, in November 1496, after attempting to escape by bribing his keepers. Hall said it was widely supposed that he intended to go "to Perkin." His detention and beheading across the Channel were meant perhaps to deter other members of the Calais garrison, which had produced two traitors, or to show through Calais and further into France how fully Henry had crushed the conspiracy. Fitzwater, however, did not recant what he believed, and it is possible—since he was executed for other offences as well as the escape—that he had not altogether finished plotting.

If the clergy had not been able to claim their privilege, there would have been yet more executions. Worseley, Richford, Sutton, Hussey and Leybourne were sentenced on January 30th and 31st to be hanged, drawn and quartered with the rest, but naturally were fined instead. Worseley had to pay £1,000. All were eventually pardoned, though Worseley not until June and Hussey not until July. Lessy, at first sent to the Tower, was also pardoned, released, fined and placed under bond. In subsequent years, Worseley was repeatedly bound to the king for his loyalty.

The clearest image of how the conspiracy passed, like a shadow, across one life emerges from Worseley's account rolls. The scholarly dean had kept a merry household beside St. Paul's, flowing not only with claret and "Roundeletts of sweet wine called Malmsey", but with beer brought in from the landlord of the Hart's Horn. His servants went clad, as Henry's did, in fashionable medley and tawny cloth; Thomas Shaw's wife kept him in freshly laundered linen; and his accounts (for "various things and stuff" on "various sheets of paper") evinced a certain blitheness. Then, in the roll for 1495–96, the tone abruptly changed. The wine bill plummeted, from £22. 7s. 4½d. to £3. Under "wages and fees" Worseley was now paying £10 a time to Reginald Bray and Thomas Lovell, Henry's financial enforcers, and to Simon Digby, the constable of the Tower. To John Heron, keeper of Henry's privy purse, he paid £135 "into his hands at Westminster" for the bond of allegiance now imposed upon him. Payments appeared for several journeys by boat up the river to Sheen, answering Henry's orders to appear; for meat and fish "bought for the dean when he was in the Tower of London", where he and his servants were kept for sixteen weeks; and for bribes and presents for the members of the King's Council Learned in the Law, who seem to have heard his case. The next roll, in which all the fines were repeated, contained Worseley's first recorded medical expense, a pot of ointment. It would not have been surprising if he had fallen ill. Fabyan claimed that Richford and Leybourne, despite their pardons, died shortly after their trials for sheer shame at what they had done.

Some laymen, surprisingly, escaped death. Debenham and Savage seem to have stayed in sanctuary for good, with Henry continuing to pay for their keep. Stanley's bastard son Thomas, possibly also betrayed by Clifford, was imprisoned in the Tower. The possibility of recantation may not have been offered to anyone, although Richard in his proclamation mentioned some who had "dearly bought their lives". Henry, who was often merciful, intended in this case to make harrowing examples.

In the midst of these punishments came a few last, wild tremors of conspiracy. People continued to scribble out treasonous rhymes and writings about the king and to put them up in public places. Those words "soon stuck in their windpipes", Vergil said. Another group, "as if stripped of all fear", openly bragged that Henry's days as king were numbered, because from hour to hour they were waiting for the Duke of York to come. Henry hanged them, and their imitators slowly grew quiet and obedient.

Curiously, the Kendal cell stayed almost untouched. The Bishop of Winchester continued in his office. Kendal was put in bond for his loyalty for a mere £100, received a general pardon in 1496, was made a justice of the peace for Essex and Middlesex and went on writing in his dreadful Italian. The lay members, too, were not apprehended, though Thomas Tyrell had said as much, or more, to damn himself as Stanley had. It is possible that Henry spared some of the guilty, in this cell and others, in the hope that they would prove useful to him later.

As for Clifford, he was rewarded yet again by being appointed master of the king's ordnance in August 1495, backdated to Easter, on 2 shillings a day and a salary of £100 a year, the same sum Stanley had enjoyed. Subsequent records show that he was not paid very regularly, and neither were his gunners, but tardy payments were a hazard of working for this king, and Clifford was soon so busy that he was scarcely to notice. Vergil may have been right that he was never quite in grace again; but, as with Pregent Meno, Henry had once more performed the trick of transforming a close acquaintance of the feigned lad into a bastion of his own defences, well-mortared with rewards. In this strong state, having bought off, hanged or beheaded any Englishman who threatened him, he awaited whatever the boy and his promoters would try to do next.

V

NEWS OF CLIFFORD'S BETRAYAL crossed the Channel early in January 1495. From the 3rd onwards, warning letters were going from Malines to Bergen-op-Zoom and Zeeland, on the coast, where forces had begun to gather for the invasion of England. The urgency, almost panic, behind these messages (sometimes sent *a toute extreme diligence*) sounded like Margaret, though the messengers were sent from Philip's household. Everything was secret. On the 8th, news came of an English ambassador in Brussels; on the 16th, Philip sent a messenger to his father "with certain letters that the King of England had recently written to various towns round here". On later occasions, Henry took pleasure in marking his triumphs against the feigned lad with flurries of propaganda across the Channel. One of those letters of January doubtless reached his rival, like a personal blow to the heart.

It would have taken time for Margaret's White Rose to grasp what had happened to his hopes in England. When the news sank in, Vergil said, he was devastated with grief. Yet he may have tried not to show it or believe it, all the same. In a defiant phrase in his 1496 proclamation, Richard declared that his friends had been murdered because Henry "stood in dread" of them. Other friends, who had been scattered or had fled to sanctuary, were possibly still waiting to help him if he invaded. Besides, Maximilian, Philip and Margaret were still firmly behind him. "He determined," Hall wrote, "not to leave the hope and trust that he had conceived in his mad head to obtain the crown and realm of England."

Yet the executions of early 1495 put his plans back sharply. Originally, his invasion of England had been set for February 22nd, which explained why his "will" was drawn up in January. The collapse of his network in England spoiled those calculations. Richard's preparations for victory or death, "given the uncertainty of human destiny", had to be shelved until the summer, together with the expectations of his backers.

The invasion plans were treated by Maximilian and Philip as "secret affairs" or, more graphically, "certain secret affairs of our own pleasing of which we do not wish to make further declaration here." Money borrowed for Richard by Maximilian from Simon Longin, his treasurer, was to be laundered secretly through the treasury at Lille, "for this time only", as he said each time, though "without any counterfeit or dissimulation". The largest loans, of £6,800 (for a ship), £4,000 and £2,000 *tournois*, were authenticated not just with Maximilian's signature but with a secret code that looked half Greek and half Egyptian. The ship-loan warrant had a long line of twenty-four such characters, so random in their appearance that it is hard to believe they meant anything. They were written in a hand smaller and more careful than Maximilian's, though in the same ink and clearly at the same time. Since Maximilian had already signed, he had no need for code. It may well have been the Secret Project himself who took the pen afterwards and drew, like a schoolboy, squiggles, loops, thetas, double-crossed crosses and musical notes, until he could not think what crazy sign to draw next.

In answer to outside inquiries that spring, Maximilian was either indifferent or coy. His envoy Naturelli told the Venetian ambassadors in May that he was "not involved in it at all", but that the Duke of York "had taken the field against the king under the favour of the archduke." A month later, in June 1495 (the invasion force still far from ready), Maximilian let drop that "he was informed of the proceedings of the Duke of York," who was already attacking England, and intended to send him reinforcements. By July 11th he had to admit that he could not get to the imperial Diet he had called at Worms, let alone help the Venetians against the Turks, "because he was impeded by the burden of much expenditure, and by having to dispatch the Prince of York, the new King of England, for the defence of his right." Years later, in the *Weisskunig*, Maximilian continued to hedge. "[The White King] sent some of his people, but in small numbers," ran the text. The gloss (also by Maximilian) said that, on the contrary, "the White King's men then came to his comfort in great numbers."

The imperial estates knew better than most that Maximilian had been driving the enterprise for months. In early 1494, he had instructed the government of Tyrol to find 16,000 florins as countersecurity for a loan to be raised through George Gossenbrot, his financial agent in Antwerp, "for the young King of England for the conquest of the kingdom." A fleet and troops were mentioned, but the Tyrolers refused. Their report of the following November, courteous but firm, explained why:

> We asked Gossenbrot . . . to come to us and describe [the situation], and we assessed with greatest care whether we could find some way to comply with your wishes as we have always been willing to do before. And we find that George Gossenbrot cannot underwrite the amount your Majesty demanded. . . . Also we feel that your Imperial Majesty had this project put into your imagination with little reason, and that something has been demanded of you that will bring damage to yourself and the whole German nation. Therefore your Majesty should not go deeper into this matter, as we cannot help you any further.

In March 1495 Maximilian tried to sell the cause in a slightly different way to the Diet at Worms, telling them that since Richard's claim to England was much more valid than Henry's, he would make a better ally in the essential war against France. These words, too, left his listeners unmoved.

Money proved hard to raise generally. Margaret gave 8,000 crowns intended, as both Richard and Maximilian said, to cover the provisioning of the whole invasion force. More money was found by Guilhem de Noyon and the Kendal circle, perhaps working on Margaret's behalf, through Daniel Beauviure, a Catalan, in Bruges. Beauviure advanced 9,000–10,000 francs. John Kendal and his agents tried to amass their own "stones" for the enterprise. James Keating, the most committed to York's cause, was accused by Kendal that year of selling or pawning a piece of the Holy Cross and various other relics and jewels from his priory in Ireland, probably to float Richard's fleet. Richard also raised money on his own account, apparently on the surety of nothing more than his name and his seal, from Paul Zachtlevant of Amsterdam. Zachtlevant, looking at the young man as he signed and sealed the papers before him, thought this signature was a good enough guarantee.

In the end, despite the Tyrolers, Maximilian contributed a fair amount of money. The total borrowed from Simon Longin by himself and Philip for "secret affairs" in the early months of 1495 alone was around £15,000 *tournois*. Not all of that would have gone for the invasion, but much of it would. He also ordered Philip to supply four cannon from the Burgundian arsenal. The document in which this request was contained told its own story. Maximilian passed on to Philip on June 17th a list of twenty-one things to do, including stationing troops on the border with France, helping his father "finish off" the war with the Duke of Guelders, getting new seals made and employing a few messengers who could speak German, "including Topping van Loo and Perequin Fon-taine, whom the king knows." Number nineteen on the list was the only order touching the invasion. "Concerning Monsieur d'York, who wants to make his journey, the king desires that [the archduke] shall deliver to him four pieces of artillery to make the said voyage in case this is required." It was York who was pushing for this invasion; Maximilian already had plenty on his plate.

Nevertheless, he spread the net wide to raise funds for him. Philippe de Commines, in Venice as an envoy in April 1495, was shown letters sent from Bruges and Worms to Flemish and Florentine merchants, ask-ing for loans "for the going into England of him who calls himself the Duke of York" (Commines's wording). Most especially, month after month, Maximilian nagged Albrecht of Saxony by letter to get the money together and organise the ships. To dispatch the Duke of York was Albrecht's "mission", Maximilian told him, and he particularly wanted to get the finance tied up before Passiontide and Easter. "I realise there's a bit of a lack concerning York's business," he wrote early that spring:

> firstly that you apparently haven't found any money in the several places we told you about. We ask you to note that we've written to you . . . with further instructions about which merchants should give this money, as doubts seem to have assailed you. . . .
>
> You now tell us that the Zeeland tax-collector doesn't want to give you the tax money that had been agreed. We entreat you in all earnestness not to get dazzled or misled by his supposed reasons and delays, but to negotiate with him anew with the greatest dili-gence. . . . And in case the tax-collector pretends that Zeeland can't afford to provide the money, see to it that he negotiates with the Diet to lend the 10,000 guilden. . . .
>
> We urge you to employ all your diligence to get 5,000 guilden, or whatever you can, and use this money for [York's] jour-ney from Malines. . . .

Concerning the money from the Hanseatic tax-collector, Sigmund Gossenbrot's agent recently sent us a letter addressed to the
collector in which he asked him to pay us the money, so we ask you
with all urgency to send someone to the collector to get it. . . .

About the 20,000 guilden that our curator in Ermberg
was supposed to get from George Gossenbrot in Antwerp and
Malines . . . he is coming here to Worms in two or three days, and
we'll negotiate this deal with him. . . .

You say you are still waiting for some 2,000 guilden from the
Dutch. We shall write herewith to our dear son the Archduke
Philip, so that from now on he can take over and see that the pay-
ment is made without delay. . . .

As you will need all this money for York's expedition, we
seriously entreat you to let all other matters go.

The loan from George Gossenbrot was so large that Maximilian seems to
have left his wife, Bianca Maria, and her court servants as a human pledge
for it. Albrecht was asked to proceed to Hertzogenbosch with the tax-
collector's money, "redeem" Bianca Maria from the Gossenbrot loan, and
take her in great secrecy to the Duke of Cleves, who would then accompany her to Cologne. Meanwhile, out of "all that remains of the money
after the release of our dear wife", Albrecht was to give the Duke of York
1,000 guilden directly and distribute the rest to "our chamberlain . . . and
the other gentlemen round Malines who have further orders to deal with
it." Presumably Bianca Maria understood what these dealings were that
required her to be passed from hand to hand across Germany. It is harder
to imagine that she would have been happy, no matter how charming the
prince she was assisting.

On April 3rd came a sudden scare: news of "the *descente* of the
English in Zeeland," evidently to destroy the force that was assembling for
the invasion. Henry had planned this in the first week of March, spending
almost £500 "for the victualling, waging, and rigging forth of five [of]
the king's ships." Philip sent desperate messages to Albrecht, who was in
Holland, and set a watch in the coastal towns to see that no men-at-arms
were concealed there. The third part of his strategy was to check on the
continuing validity of the Treaty of Senlis with France, and to talk to
French envoys "to see what remains to be done". Philip, in York's cause,
was on the very brink of war with England, but he dared not start without watching his back. As it happened, the English attack was no more

than a show of defiance and a proof that Henry knew what was up. The ships and their soldiers seemed to fade very quickly into the mists of the *plat pays* and the flat sea, even as Philip was summoning his nobles to be ready "at any moment" to resist them.

At length Philip and Albrecht got a small fleet together, some fourteen ships, among the low sandbars at Vlissingen in Zeeland. By June 27th Philip, obedient to his father, had ordered stocks of gunpowder from his master of artillery and had summoned his chief gunkeeper to see him. A force of mercenaries was assembled: 6,000 of them, said Maximilian in the *Weisskunig,* "1,500 of them footsoldiers, the rest sailors", and he promised to top it up with 800 more. The receivergeneral of Zeeland and the *burghermeisters* of various local towns were pumped for funds. There were disappointments: Maximilian's huntmaster raised only 400 "serfs" for the enterprise, having promised 1,500, and in June Albrecht told Maximilian that not only the "conscripted peasants", but the crews, too, were refusing to stay with the ships. A Milanese envoy, writing to Ludovico Sforza in midMay on rosetinted information that had been "heard" from somewhere, thought the number of troops was closer to 10,000, supplemented by "a number of ships with many troops sent by the King of Scotland".

The men themselves were a mixed crew of Flemings, Germans, Dutchmen and the yeomen recruited from England, armed with the usual assortment of bills, bows, swords, lances and pikes. Many were troops discharged from Maximilian's recent war with the Duke of Guelders, and still owed pay. Vergil described them as criminals and scavengers. A betterclass contingent went also, however, and Molinet mentioned "nobles" in Richard's company. Roderick de Lalaing, one of Philip and Maximilian's best captains, of bastard noble blood from Hainault, was on board, besides other *compaignons de la garde forts experimentez de la guerre*. De Puebla, gathering snippets in London, heard that there were two Spanish captains, Diego el Coxo ("the Lame") and Don "Fulano" ("Soandso") de Guevara. Both were officers of Philip's household and also seasoned fighters; Diego's jousting motto was "Out of the Reckoning," while Pedro (the "Soandso") was a squire of the carvery, acquainted with knifework. Of Richard's closer circle, Keating was there with George Neville, the most eminent of his exilesupporters, and Richard Harliston, who had served Edward IV in several naval commands.

The fleet hung around for a while at Vlissingen, awaiting a favourable wind. Ferdinand and Isabella were "astonished" that the ships had been assembled at all, "because we had always written to the King of the Romans and to our ambassadors at his court to prevent such a thing." They had also written to the Duke of Milan, Maximilian's father-in-law, since they had heard he might be a good man to put a stop to it, and they trusted that he had written to his son-in-law, "though we do not know exactly what his opinion was." Of course, Ferdinand and Isabella explained, Maximilian really wanted to free himself of York, and that was why he had pushed him off to the "island" where he was now preparing to embark. But he had not managed to do so yet. "He was in such a poor state," they went on, "and had so few soldiers, that he did not sail. In fact, all our subjects who are in Flanders . . . believe the whole fleet will soon vanish away for want of money and men. If the King of the Romans does not help any more, the whole affair seems like nothing to us."

Molinet made it all sound more hopeful. Despite the disaster in England, and despite the "subtle spirits" who continued to attack him, Richard had not given up the enterprise. He had got his ships, men and guns together "and finally went to sea in the hope of conquering England, full of trust and great confidence in his supporters and his friends." At Worms, the Scottish ambassadors picked up talk of "certain victory", apparently coming from the prince himself. Zurita caught an echo in a boast from Maximilian: "He was going to try to overthrow [Henry] with a powerful army and, with just one battle, win the war." Where was that powerful army to come from? A Yarmouth sailor, talking later to some of the "Dutchmen", was told that "they trusted on one man should help them with many men", hopeful and vague as ever.

In England meanwhile John Kendal, almost the only conspirator left standing, was getting ready. At the priory of Milborne, in Bedfordshire, he was having jackets made for his attendants. They were parti-coloured green and red, with a narrow section like a scarf on both front and back on which to place a red rose. But Kendal also had a tunic made for each jacket, in the same colours, "and ordered that each of his men should carry it in the bow of his saddle . . . and this was done with no other intent than to place a white rose on each jacket." For Henry, or for Richard: as the news came from the coast they would decide, snapping the right livery from the saddle-bow. Commines had seen the same instant switch of badges at Guisnes in 1470, when he found the lieutenant of Calais and his men, within a quarter of an hour of the arrival of the news that Edward IV had fled into exile, already wearing the ragged-staff badge of the Earl of Warwick, Edward's rival, on their hats. "This was the first time," he wrote, "that I had ever seen or considered such an instance of the instability of human affairs."

Kendal's men, in their reversible jackets, sounded less like soldiers than like the liveried retainers kept up and down England, against the law, to stake claims and rough up debtors on some lord's behalf. Nor did Kendal seem to be using them to swell the invasion force. Instead, the fighters-for-Richard, now on board the ships that rode in the sea off Zee-land, had come from elsewhere. Among them was Maurice Seles, the London goldsmith. For some reason, despite the clearing-out of the London conspirators, Seles had gone to Plantagenet in Flanders, abandoning his work with the purest metal to assay a young man who was perhaps all artifice, as far as he knew; and who, when tested, was more than likely to break.

The fleet sailed out of Vlissingen on July 2nd, a Friday. The sun was at the mid-point of Cancer, a good time for journeys by water; the day was hot, and the voyage was a short one by Richard's standards. Vergil said the young man did not know which part of England he was aiming for, drifting where the wind took him. But they made progress and, the next day, dropped anchor in the Downs off Deal, in Kent. The pebble shore was shelving and open to the sea, inviting for invasion. Caesar was said to have landed there, if that gave any encouragement.

It is unclear how much the would-be King of England knew of the people on shore. Judging by those who were captured, few of his recruits were Kentings. The county had a reputation for rebelliousness and a tendency to be Yorkist; but Richard, prudently, did not assume that they would welcome him. André said the Kentings were feeling chastened because, not long before, many of them had fallen for a story put about by charlatans that Christ and his apostles had returned to earth. The deceivers had been punished, and the Kentings rendered unreceptive to saviours. This new one, therefore, stayed at a safe distance. Molinet reported that Richard sent about three hundred foot-soldiers, in small boats, "to spread the message and do a bit of pillaging"; Vergil said he allowed one small party to go, then another, to test the feelings of the local people.

Many of those he sent were English yeomen and labourers: a sensible strategy, as if they had come to rescue their country rather than invade it.

These soldiers, by Molinet's account, got a little way inland and
planted three standards of the White Rose in "the villages", probably not
much more than fishermen's huts behind a bank of stones. As soon as the
standards were displayed, a man-at-arms, very well accoutred, rode up to
the soldiers and asked whose men they were.

"The Duke of York's," they told him.

The man on the horse was ecstatic. "We ask for no other lord in the
world!" he cried. "We wish to live and die with him! Make him disembark with his company! We will do him all the honour, help and favour
we possibly can, with our hearts, our bodies and our goods." Meanwhile,
since they must be thirsty, he would order up a couple of jugs of beer for
them.

The soldiers, overjoyed, felt victory was theirs already, and sent word
to Richard of their wonderful good fortune. But the prince and his noble
advisers, "fearing that he was being tricked" and suspicious of the slow
deliberations on shore, refused to disembark. This proved wise. As soon
as the man-at-arms had gone a little distance, riding into the sandhills
behind the beach, armed troops "rained down" on the foot-soldiers from
all sides. The invaders put up a fight, but in a short time were hopelessly
outnumbered. Around 150 were killed on the beach, riddled with
arrows and "mutilated by slicing swords" as they tried to regain their
boats. English sources thought most of them had died by drowning. Only
one casualty, Thomas Grigge, "sore hurt", was mentioned on the other
side. The London Chronicle summed it up with understated accuracy:
"They could have no comfort of the country."

Those of the landing troops who had not been killed were captured
and taken to London, stumbling in chains like robbers or roped like
horses in harness, with the wounded drawn in carts. A royal letter mentions 163 rebels sent "from the sea side" at Sandwich, some by sea and
some by road. The sheriff of Kent, John Petch, brought a crowd of
mostly Dutchmen and Germans to London Bridge on July 12th, where
they were handed over to be conveyed to Newgate or the Tower. On July
18th a commission was set up at the White Hall to interrogate the
English-speaking rebels and pass sentence on them. Hugh Standish, a
notary, was paid 40 shillings for his labour and diligence in taking down

"in various books", long since lost, the rebels' depositions and confessions. However lowly, these men might have first-hand knowledge of the feigned boy, his plans and the nature of his network in the entrails of England.

Eight captains were also captured, according to de Puebla, though only six—Mountford, Richard White, John Corbet, John Belt (a truly "diabolical" name, André thought), Quintin, a Spaniard, and Genyn, a Frenchman—were named in the chronicles. In Norfolk, up the coast, the Pastons heard of them when the bailiff of Yarmouth told Sir John that a Yarmouth man, Robert Albon, had met the "English captains of the king's rebels" at Canterbury. The captains had planned to take "a town of strength, for they would have had Sandwich, and the country had not resisted them." Albon talked to "Captain" Belt, a yeoman from Guild-ford, and found him still defiant: "he wist well that he [Albon] was but a dead man, and for as much as he wist that he was of Yarmouth, he showed him that they will have Yarmouth, or they shall die for it."

Nine particular prisoners, those closest to the boy's counsel, were sent to Henry at Fotheringhay for special interrogations. By September 4th, the king had sent them back to London to be beheaded. Not all, however, were executed. Sir Thomas Lovell, who was in charge, "respited" some, and sent Henry a list of the reasons why. One who escaped was Captain Mountford, spared perhaps for his "good and commendable" service to the king not many years before—though he alone was named in Henry's subsequent letter about the invasion, as if the king felt his treachery more keenly than that of the rest. Another was Captain Corbet, who died in the Tower "of God's Visitation and the occasion of the great hurts and wounds which he Received in time of his first taking." He had refused to let plasters be put upon his wounds. His martyrdom, like Belt's defiance, showed how fiercely the cause of Richard burned in some hearts; but not in enough.

The forty-odd English labourers and yeomen who had come to join Richard, and had been taken, were all drawn and hanged. ("The animals got their veins squeezed for their trouble," André said.) The bodies of four particular Flemings were left hanged in chains at Wapping on the Thames, on the "wash" or ooze where pirates were routinely executed. At every full sea, the water flowed over them. Others were left "for sea-marks or light-houses" on the coasts of Norfolk, Essex, Sussex and Kent, mouldering towards Flanders.

The richer and better-connected survived, since they had stayed on board with their prince. Among those declared traitors after the invasion were Neville, Keating, Harliston, John Heron, Edward Skelton, John Brampton and Taylor the younger, the established inner circle. All had long since left the country. They were attainted "by what name soever or names they or any of them be called", standard form in such indictments, but especially apt for the servants of a counterfeit master. Other absentee traitors came from York, Chester, Cumberland and Lincoln, from one end to the other of the country. Presumably some took the chance to drop the cause, while others fled with their prince.

The king exulted in this victory, ordering beacons to be built on the Kentish shore as both warning and celebration. He also sent Sir Richard Guildford to commend the Kentings for their actions. Those actions, he insisted, had been quite spontaneous. Not a single royal soldier had been called upon to intervene. Henry himself had been at Worcester on the 4th and was still there on the 9th, unperturbed and trusting in his subjects. The invaders, he told Philip's councillors in a furiously sarcastic letter written that day,

> intended to do us all the damage and displeasure they could well do, little as that was. But, thanks be to God, it was not in their power or capability. They were roughly rebuffed [*rudement Reboutez*] by the villagers of the sea-coast of Kent by themselves, who made great efforts to defend it. And while we were hunting at one end of our Kingdom, a great part of these men were killed and many of them were drowned when they tried to get back to their ships, and their principal captains, like Mountford and others, were taken. And we advise you that if they had all wanted to disembark and wait for the arrival and attack of the said villagers, scarcely one of them would have got away, and you can be very sure there would have been no need to call on other people besides the said villagers to defeat them.

That hunting image was nicely done: the debonair king riding in the distant woods, while the invaders were hunted and slaughtered on the shore. The verb "to defeat," *défaire*, applied both to beating enemies and to ceremonially butchering the animals killed in the chase. Had Henry not been so angry, this was almost sport.

The Spanish ambassador faithfully repeated the king's story, with extra details that may have come from Henry too. All the villagers, he wrote, said that "the king should come"—proof that there was no sign of anyone resembling a king there already—and that "that fellow should go back to his father and his mother, who are living and are known in France." "They hold it as fact," de Puebla went on, "as in pure truth it is, that this business is like that of the other Duke of Clarence whom they crowned as a king in Ireland, and afterward it was found that he was a barber's son . . . The doctor grieves greatly for these madnesses [*locuras*], for so they are judged by those who take any notice of them."

As usual, Henry told the story he wished Spain to hear. The real picture was not quite so clear. Henry was still deeply worried by the pathetic young man who had been told to go home to his mother. In April he had tried to forestall the invasion, and from Worcester on July 5th and 6th letters had been sent out to every port in England, alerting them to keep watch. Moreover, the Kentings—having wavered at first, Vergil said—had in fact needed something of a nudge to start fighting the invader. The lord chancellor, already usefully stationed in the county and in constant touch with the king, seems to have ensured that they did so. The town accounts of New Romney, southward from Deal down the coast, mention payment for beer "given to the men of Lydd, when they went forth upon the expedition of our Lord the King when our enemies were in the Downs." The Canterbury accounts list payment for drink for three hundred armed men going off "to fight Peter Warbeck and his men, enemies of our lord the King of England". Canterbury later received a letter from the king, praising the city and its citizens for their "resistance".

The Exchequer rolls also show a certain amount of scrambling, some of it after the event, to make the Kent and Sussex coasts secure. At some point that July, Stephen Bull, Henry's top naval captain, was sent to Sandwich. William Fourness, the clerk of the king's ordnance, endeavoured to supply him "in all goodly haste" by sea, packing a small craft with iron and lead shot and crossbow strings, while chests of bows and arrows went by road. (Henry, ever economical, had exhorted Fourness to buy these supplies "at as little price so the stuff be good and able as ye can.") At around the same time Nicholas Haynes, Henry's chief messenger between Worcester and the southeast, rode with royal letters to the chief churchmen of Sussex and all along the sea-coast, searching for stragglers left behind.

Most Englishmen were unmoved by and uninterested in this would-be king who was hovering round their shores, but many were also waiting to see how events turned out. London, though Yorkist by inclination, seems to have generally found the Flanders plots mysterious. When the invading ships appeared, the London Chronicle reported at first that they just contained "divers rebels of the king". Only later did it report that the captured rebels "affirmed to be their head captain the second son of King Edward iiijth, which was in one of the said Ships." London seemed not to have heard of this possibility before, as if the conspirators of Charing Cross and Holborn had never left their tiny fervent circles. The news of Edward's son caused no frisson on the Thames; on July 24th the city heard that "the Captain of the said persons", whoever he was, was in Ireland with the residue of his men.

One Star Chamber document provides a picture of a party of Londoners on invasion day, out hunting bucks that Saturday in the fields beyond Aldgate. The mayor sent an officer to tell them to get ready "to array [themselves] towards the same Perkin to resist him." The Londoners, relaxed, supped that evening in Holborn with no preparations made. They would probably have fought this Perkin, had he shown up. But since he made no appearance on that long summer evening, they enjoyed themselves and discounted him. The ships rode at anchor, soldiers drowned in the sea, and five Londoners followed the bounding deer on an otherwise ordinary day.

Matters looked very different from the other side. Defeat had been total. Molinet, probably receiving his information from a Yorkist source at Malines, did not doubt that Richard's force had fallen into a trap set by Henry. The impressive armour and equipment of the defenders showed they were not unprepared. Possibly the king's progress north had been a trap in itself, luring Richard across. If so, it had worked, and the magnitude of the defeat had not gone unobserved by the owner of the standards. Molinet was keen to stress how Richard and his men, bobbing on the sea, had watched the armed troops burst into view and set about the slaughter. It was over very quickly; and then "Richard, seeing this calamity, slipped away."

Although his fleet did not seem to be chased, it scattered and disintegrated. At least two ships were blown off course. Sir John Paston heard of "an hoy of Dordrecht" (a small passenger vessel, used for short hauls) brought into Wallrens, in Normandy, "with eight horses, with many saddles and bridles." The surviving crew, mostly "Dutchmen", included eight or nine Englishmen, who disappeared into the back country. The ship itself was seized for the king, and the Dutchmen imprisoned. As for the ships with the rebels and their prince still on them, "they be forth out of Camber westward; whither they be, they cannot say."

Vergil thought the spurned invader fled back to "Aunt Margaret" for one last council of war. De Puebla, however, was certain that he could not show his face at her court now, "since that whole land is destroyed by his sojourn there", and his backers across the Channel had no idea where he was. Maximilian was so impatient to hear his news that he insisted that any dispatches sent to Malines (to Margaret, always the first destination) should be forwarded immediately to Worms, where he was holding the Diet. From there, his view heavily obscured by misinformation, he tried to follow his prince's progress.

On July 11th, a week after the invasion, Maximilian knew that "the Prince of York was already at sea on his way to his country", and expressed the hope that "should he establish his right to the kingdom of England, he will be one of the colleagues and confederates of the league with his Majesty." On July 17th, he heard from Malines "that they are of the opinion that the Duke of York . . . has reached England, and been received by some of his adherents, whereat his Majesty rejoiced greatly." Two days later, Maximilian was hoping aloud that York, having won England, would "immediately start a war against the King of France, as the duke has most certainly promised us."

From that point, the news became harder to follow. On July 25th, three weeks after Richard had sailed, Ludovico Bruno reported to the assembled ambassadors that there had been a hitch:

> The Duke of York, the kinsman of his Highness, had arrived with his fleet in the neighbourhood of London; and, not having found the population well disposed towards him at the spot where he was most anxious to land and attack the hostile army, he had removed to another part of the island; though it is hoped that his affairs will prosper.

Wilfully, the King of the Romans clung on to him; just as wilfully, his "new King of England" stoked the dream that victory remained within his grasp. He had made straight for London, Henry's very heart; and though "a hostile army" waited for him, he was "most anxious" to take it on. On August 16th, Maximilian was "still waiting for the result of the

Duke of York's expedition, which will be known in a few days." Eventually, however, the bold invader had to admit defeat. Maximilian's account in the *Weisskunig* may reflect the tale he was told. "The New King [Henry VII, in this case] awaited there with a great number of men, and when they went ashore he accepted battle with them, as he had about three times as many men as they had, and he killed nearly all of them." The implication was that Richard had gone ashore and bravely challenged Henry in person: an echo of the lie Maximilian had heard and repeated in late July. But he had not won.

At the time of the invasion, a secret message was sent from Maximilian to Henry. It has not survived, but it was clearly not polite. Henry's letter of July 9th described how the letters had arrived,

> brought to us by a person who said he was [the King of the Romans'] shieldbearer. We found them extremely strange [*fort etranges*] and would never have believed they had been written by him, had they not been signed with his hand, sealed with his seal and countersigned by Lalaing, his secretary. [The letters] requested us to make reply to the various things [he demanded] by the same carrier, and though it displeases us to make answer in the way we are doing, this matter so closely touches our honour that we feel we have to do it.

Maximilian's message no doubt contained the same cocksure defiance that was being heard from both him and his prince in the days before the fleet sailed. It was not heard again.

By August 16th, the King of the Romans was already resigned to the thought that York "might be defeated". The Milanese, the Florentines and especially the Spaniards were nagging him constantly to agree that Henry should be admitted to the Holy League against France. Maximilian explained that he was delaying because, if York succeeded, he should be the one admitted to it. Only if York failed would he agree that Henry should join. The outcome, he insisted, was still uncertain. But by September 5th, as the Venetian ambassadors reported, he knew the worst.

> Having audience of his Majesty the King of the Romans, the Neapolitan ambassador read to him in our presence an extract from letters written by a colleague of his, also a Neapolitan, and accredited to the King of England, whereby he informed him how

the Duke of York was in Ireland with but a few troops, and that
the King [of England] had made great preparations, meaning to
send in pursuit of him. . . . His Majesty listened without making
reply.

The attack on Deal was the moment when Richard of York had at last
been put in serious play, and it had failed. He was shown to lack substance not so much in himself—though a braver man might have tried to
rescue his troops—as in the loyalty, or even the interest, he could command in England. This changed the picture. It was now much clearer in
Europe, as it had been clear from the start to those not determined to cause
trouble, that Henry was the established king in England, to whom all
requests should be directed and all negotiators sent. Pitting claimants
against him, whether false or true, would henceforth be even riskier than it
had been before.

Yet Richard of York was still at large. He had not been caught, and
preserved his value as an irritant to Henry who could, at any moment,
become dangerous again. Many months later, Ferdinand and Isabella
instructed de Puebla to give Henry a little lecture on how easily kingdoms
were lost and won, and how risky a war might therefore be with "him
who calls himself the Duke of York". "In feats of arms," the Spanish
sovereigns wrote, "no one must ever place his hopes in an abundance of
power or soldiers, for it often turns out that smaller forces triumph over
larger ones . . . the stronger one is, the more one has to justify one's cause
and have God on one's side." They urged Henry "not to stake his good
authority and his fortune on an adventure".

Publicly, Henry would never have agreed that the balance was so precarious. Yet he was prey to just those nerves. Bosworth, after all, had been
close-run, and at Stoke two of his "battles" had refused to engage until
they saw what the issue would be. In the Parliament of October 1495 an
act was passed, evidently the fruit of long anxiety, "that no person going
with the king to the wars shall be attaint of treason". Henry remembered
how, after Bosworth, he had backdated his reign by a day to make
Richard III's supporters traitors, though they had been fighting for their
anointed king. He had been aware ever since that this might happen to
him. His power, too, might be overturned in one battle in a matter of
hours. The act referred to him as his subjects' prince and sovereign lord
"for the time being", a rare admission of fragility, and spoke tremulously

of "what fortune ever fall by chance in the same battle against the mind and weal of the prince". To fight, he said sometime later—still thinking specifically of fighting this boy—was "to set the trial . . . upon an unlike- lihood." This did not sound like a man who had sent his flimsy enemy packing.

Maximilian, though with yet more feinting and circumspection, went on backing his *Prinzen von York*. On September 19th, he admitted that he had been induced by "the pope, the sovereigns of Spain and others of the league," as well as the Duke of Milan, to include Henry's name in the league. With that, he officially gave up his idea of funding an invasion to recover the right of his protégé in England. On September 21st in Worms a document was drawn up stating Maximilian's readiness, in principle, to agree that Henry should join the league by Christmas. The notary then put in, after the words "everything included in this agree- ment to be observed", a weasel clause that allowed for exceptions. Maxi- milian scrawled his own, in Latin, in the margin: "Except for what we may wish to be done to the same King of England in the cause of the illustrious Prince Richard, Duke of York, if divisions and disputes arise between them." Again, he had trouble with the name of his protégé, crossing out both the "Richard" part and the "Duke" part and then re- writing them. The very next day, he invoked higher powers to protect him by writing to the pope on Richard's behalf.

His son Philip seemed to abandon the cause completely. He officially dropped "Monsieur d'York" as soon as he had failed in Kent, and entered into proper talks to renew trade with England. Five clauses of the new trade treaty of February 1496, the *Magnus Intercursus*, were concerned with ending favours to fugitives and rebels, including assistance for inva- sions. Another promised that Margaret, cited by name, would give them no more help or hospitality in any of the towns or palaces in her territory, and would lose those properties if she persisted.

Margaret, therefore, moved away and fell silent, in order not to dam- age Philip's interests. Although Henry was quite aware, Zurita said, that the *mala voluntad* of Philip and Maximilian was by no means exhausted, their armed support was no longer publicly behind the cause of Richard, Duke of York. From now on their efforts on his behalf, like Margaret's, had to become surreptitious. Both men's secret payments for him before the invasion had been distinguished by the phrase *a son bon plaisir*, as if he were some hidden game or indulgence. They now had to leave him, the falcon trained and sheltered so carefully for so long, to flutter and possibly to fall in his own wildly altering element, the air.

He had become a wanderer again. A rational observer—Erasmus, say, whose path had crossed his in Brabant—might have wondered what impelled him. He himself, talking two years later, did not place the blame on anyone in his circle: not Maximilian, not Margaret, not John Atwater or John Taylor, or anyone else in the tattered retinue that was left to him. He followed after Fortune. She grasped his hand.

CHAPTER FIVE

The Pavilions of Love and the Tents of War

In March 1471 Edward IV, England's great lover, had also tried to reclaim his kingdom. He sailed from Vlissingen in Zeeland with a force of Englishmen, Flemings and Dutchmen, putting an end to his three months of exile at the court of Burgundy. On the 12th he anchored off the coast near Cromer, in Norfolk. He sent some men ashore, including Robert Chamberlain and Gilbert Debenham, to find out whether the country was well disposed towards him. It was not, and he sailed on. Storms blew up the next day and he was forced to land at Holderness on the Humber, with the rest of his fleet grounded and scattered up and down the coast. He lodged in a village while his force regrouped, but the people would not come to him.

The love Edward sought as he progressed disconsolately through eastern England was not the kind with which he was freely associated—snatched fumbles behind the arras or romps with the merriest, the wiliest and the holiest harlots in the realm, the last of whom "no man could get out of the church to any place lightly, but if it were to his bed." He sought political supporters, men who would form a party and sustain his quarrel with arms. The language was often close to that used for chamber-love. Royal and noble allies "loved together" and called each other "bed-fellows", sometimes sealing their amity by sleeping together between sheets as they did with their paramours and wives. It was in this spirit that the Earl of Kildare expressed his fury that anyone should think he had "lain with" the French lad in Ireland. In June 1500, Henry VII's own report of an embassy to Burgundy spoke repeatedly of "loving offers", "right loving audience" and love itself. The word was commonly con-nected less with women than with ties of political interest and, if called for, blood.

Edward found, as he travelled, that England loved King Henry rather than himself. Yet he persevered, and lulled the country into quiet-ness. The young man who claimed to be his son did not show the same persistence. Rebuffed in Kent, he did not sail further north to try his luck in the places where chalk cliffs gave way to easier sands and gravels. He seems to have been meant to. "English Edward" had been sent, after all, to proselytise for him in the coastal towns, and his captains had revealed that Yarmouth, in Norfolk, was a target. But Richard had obviously aban-doned that further effort, even if, for a few frantic days, Yarmouth still expected "the sight of the ships". There may never have been a firm idea of softening the country village by village as Edward had done. Instead, once spurned, Richard made for the open sea.

Henry followed him. As in 1492, the king knew exactly what his movements were. By July 23rd four ships were being victualled at the western ports of Plymouth and Fowey on Henry's orders, to be at sea for six weeks with 470 men on board. In the days that followed, dozens of crossbowmen, horses and soldiers in brand-new uniforms were sent across to Ireland. Henry, as Maximilian learned, was chasing his protégé hard, "and hoped speedily to get possession of him". As an extra layer of precaution, he made a general inquisition in England and especially in London to find out the names, ages and "faculties" of all Irish men, women and children living there, in case they needed to be watched. Edward Poynings and William Hatcliffe had already been sent, in Octo-ber 1494, to reduce Ireland to proper obedience, including reversing the legal immunity for rebels; by December, £4,266 3s. 4d., a vast sum, had been disbursed for their operations. In all these ways, Henry tried to make sure that the feigned lad would find no favour there.

The patrolling ships from Fowey and Plymouth did not, however, intercept him. He sailed on, battling storms that were forcing other ships off the sea round Ireland, and reached his old friends in mid-July. They were not as numerous as they had been before. Poynings and Hatcliffe had done a good job, and various men suspected of supporting Richard—the dean of Limerick, the dean of Kilkenny, the mayor of Dublin—had recently been arrested and interrogated. Nonetheless, lords in both the north and the south had openly declared for him early that summer. They included two great Gaelic chiefs, O'Neill of Clandeboy and Hugh O'Donnell of Tyrconnell, who commanded the whole northwest and the outer isles towards Scotland; Shane Burke in Galway, described by one of Henry's officers as "the greatest succour that Perkin had while he was in the land save only the earl of Desmond"; and Lord Barry of Munster, in the southwest. The city of Cork, still fired by Atwater, also came out for him. His first ally remained Desmond. Henry had tried hard with him, appointing Richard Hatton in December 1494 to negotiate, receive his oath of fealty, deliver to him a pardon under the great seal and put his firstborn son in ward as surety for his allegiance. All this had worked with Kildare, but it failed with Desmond, and the pardon seems to have stayed in Hatton's pocket.

Just before the Deal invasion, but apparently without co-ordination, the earl determined to make a show of force for Richard in southern Ireland. He marched his troops overland to attack Waterford, the principal southeastern port, from the west. After some weeks, Richard's fleet arrived from Kent to reinforce him. The errant prince had begun luckily. As he sailed past Youghal, forty miles from Waterford to the southeast, he attacked the port and a ship docked there, the *Christopher* of Plymouth, carrying sixty tons of iron from Spain and forced into harbour by the bad weather. The ship was seized, and the iron and other goods in her sold to various local merchants. Thanks to this piece of piracy, Richard got cash and an extra ship. Once joined up with Desmond, he could muster eleven vessels and an army of 2,400 men.

The choice of Waterford was a mistake, for this was the only place in Ireland that had remained consistently loyal to Henry during Simnel's rebellion. The city's motto proclaimed it, *Urbs intacta manet*, like some haughty spinster who would open neither her gates nor her thighs to a stranger. Nevertheless, Desmond and Richard tried a joint attack, the earl's army from the land and Richard's ships from the river. He himself was not with them. He had disembarked at Passage, at the mouth of the river, and apparently sent out from there his command that Waterford should surrender. Once again, as at Deal, the cautious invader con-ducted his rough courtship from a distance.

But the citizens resisted. A siege started that went on for eleven days, "hot of every side", while the town's cannon pounded at the ships. The roaring detonations and the cries of the dying could be heard far outside the city, as far as the timid prince was. After one sortie, the citizens returned with a large band of prisoners, lopped off their heads and fas-tened them on stakes. This seemed to turn the tide. The besiegers, "in dread of this cruelty," became disheartened, and on August 3rd the siege was lifted. They departed before dawn, continuing the siege for a while at Ballycasheen, and the next morning left there too, "with dishonour and great loss of their people, and the said Perkin in person fain to take ship-ping at Passage, and to make sail out of the haven." His ships picked him up as they retreated.

He had probably never heard artillery fired in war before, and cer-tainly not that close. The four small cannon taken to Deal had never been used, and in any case the fusillade at Waterford was being aimed at his ships, from the other side. The terrible noise of artillery amazed people. Different sizes of guns were called howlers and clangers, vividly suggest-ing how they sounded, and Hell was imagined to be full of gunfire. "Then came the awful sound of the cannon, the big drums, trumpets, clarions, cries of men and beasts, worse than had ever been heard before," wrote Molinet of the siege of Arras in 1492; "thunder, tempest, lightning had never been heard like that."

Four of Richard's ships, including the stolen *Christopher*, were cap-tured. One was reported smashed by gun-stones, either real stones or chunks of iron, and the crew killed. The others were sold for derisory sums, showing how small they were. One vessel, *la Mare*, was swapped for six pieces of woollen cloth to the value of £40. Richard himself slid away—so good at sliding away by now—under Desmond's protection to Cork and his friend John Atwater. Although Atwater and his son had been summoned before the Irish Parliament in 1493 and condemned the next year, John was now mayor again. He helped his prince for a while, but Richard needed to move on. Some said he was shipwrecked in Ireland, possibly that autumn as he proceeded up the coast, and had to flee across the mountains in disguise so that Henry's men would not know him. Geronymo Zurita, who promoted that story, had him drifting as a vagabond "among the islands of that sea". Whatever happened, it added to the drama of the story he would tell to the next potential friend.

For almost three months he wandered, keeping safely west of the English Pale and heading north towards Ulster. No one really knew where he had gone. Henry heard "rumours" from Waterford about "the earl of Desmond's and Perkin Warbeck's journey in August", with more from Brother John and other spies about their movements in Munster "and elsewhere". The king still gave out that he was in hot pursuit, but the quarry had disappeared. Desmond, as Henry thought, was probably with him for the first stage, with Burke and O'Donnell taking over to protect him as he moved through their lands.

The gorgeous prince of Malines was now among the *sylvestres homines*, as Polydore Vergil called them: with the wild men of the woods. Here chieftains in greasy homespun plaids continually fought each other, while the common people crouched in smoky hovels over peat fires, eating the clotted blood of their cattle with butter to sustain themselves. O'Donnell had once defeated his great enemy O'Neill by driving wild mares through his camp; the corpse of a Scottish captain, killed in the mêlée, was propped against a tree by O'Neill's men and plied with drink and women in case these could revive him. Around Lammas, or harvest time, in 1495 O'Donnell was fully engaged in raiding, drowning and burning in the northern parts of Connaught, whether or not he had a fugitive prince with him.

It is easy to see Prince Richard in those months in the guise of King Sweeney, fleeing across the bogs and mountains, numbing his fierce hunger with watercress and wild apples as he lamented the loss of the affection of his people. The lover shut out from love traditionally roamed disconsolate in the greenwoods and wild places, living on acorns and stream-water, with his bed among the brambles that tangled in his hair. Yet Richard Plantagenet may still have managed to live softly, moving from castle to castle and preserving some segment of his retinue and his soldiers. Henry had heard that remnants of his Deal force were still with him, and these men may have defended their prince quite capably as he wandered. John Wise, sent by the king to spy on them as far as Munster, was forced to flee without his horses "and so he lost them", because he had got too close.

Those in Prince Richard's entourage in Ireland were lovers of long standing. Most of them had been with him in France and at Malines, and had joined him for the invasion. With the exception of George Neville, Anthony de la Forsa and "gentleman" Edward Skelton, they were a group with almost no social standing and few resources to contribute to the cause. At least some of their money had come from theft. Besides selling the iron from the *Christopher* and the relics from Keating's priory, they had profited from the sleight of hand of another crooked priest, William Lounde. This cleric—a Yorkshireman, originally from Doncaster—was said to have absconded with "certain money and jewels to a good substance" from the house of Ralph, Lord Hastings, whose chaplain and steward he had been for some years. The stolen treasure had gone to Richard's cause and, possibly in gratitude, Richard had made him his private chaplain and one of his principal advisers.

This venal and unimpressive group had the virtue, at least, of fairly long service together. Their adventures bound them together in a way that seemed to go beyond self-interest, for self-interest would surely have caused them to bail out long ago. Yet the essence of liege-love was also to fight for a cause; and not one of these men was a fighter. Richard of York's hopes were now directed towards a man who was.

The young King of Scotland, James IV, had been roughly propelled to power in 1488 by a clique of nobles who had first opposed and then killed his father, James III. From the earliest days of his reign he had been warmly receptive to taking up a quarrel with Henry Tudor. England remained "the auld enemy", never to be trusted. Henry supported James's own rebels, that faction in Scotland that continued to regret the rebellion that had destroyed his father. There were also old scores to settle, such as the English occupation of the frontier town of Berwick and the ownership of wild tracts of land in Northumberland. Low-level border raiding and cattle-stealing were constant, and to move from these incursions to invasion or war proper was, as Henry knew, a constant possibility.

James also had his own ambitions. As he emerged from his minority, intelligent, curious and highly charged, he wanted to prove that he could take decisions and forge policies for himself. Much more than this, he wanted to cut a figure in the world and ensure that his cold, poor, marginal country was noticed in the councils of Europe. A marriage could help, perhaps with Maximilian's daughter or a princess of Spain. Strategic alliances could help too, and would be especially welcome if they unsettled the King of England. The most alluring, if distant, prospect, to James as to Maximilian, was Henry's replacement with a new king who would be amenable and grateful.

Among the first acts of his reign James had been happy to give safe-conducts to, and then receive, a crowd of exiled Yorkists from Margaret's court. They were, in fact, his first foreign visitors. The safe-conducts said that James did not mind how many came or of what condition, and implied the more the merrier. They could stay for a year, "or longer if the king wills it". It is not clear how long these Yorkists stayed or what they did, besides sparking a teenage king's ardent imagination. But from then on James appeared to be shadowing the new Yorkist hope.

By 1491 his interest was shifting, or being shifted, subtly to France, where Charles was on the brink of war with Henry. A French herald was in Scotland for some weeks in the spring, and in April James paid £50 Scots to George Neville, "the English knight that was banished". In July, when Monypeny came to escort the Scottish ambassadors to France, tapestries were hung for his reception and he was given a purple robe; when he left, on the 16th, he was paid £250. The ambassadors—chiefly Patrick Hepburn, Earl of Bothwell, a favourite councillor of the king's—stayed until November, receiving frequent letters of instruction from home. By February 1492 James was showing reluctance to ratify the seven-year truce he had made recently with England, and on the 23rd he made his first payment, of £72, to "the Dean of York", an agent associated in subsequent accounts only with service to Richard. Rowland Robinson was also receiving regular payments from James for bringing the letters from Margaret in which, most probably, she was arguing Richard's cause. When, in March, letters came from Richard himself in Ireland, these were immediately described as "from King Edward's son". By now, James did not need persuading.

By July 1493, Henry VII was aware of frequent sailings of rebels between Scotland and Flanders. Besides the seven-year truce, which had now been ratified, he suggested the possibility of an English marriage, and agreed to pay 1,000 marks for damage done by the English in the border lands. But James was not won over. Aware, it seems, of the Yorkist conspiracies growing in the south, he planned a distracting or reinforcing raid in the north. In November that year the border chiefs and their tribes poured into England to promote a rising for Richard. They had raided too early, perhaps impatient with waiting, and the movement faded away. James, meanwhile, bided his time. In 1494 he sent a large delegation to Flanders, including a herald and his chief admiral, Andrew Wood. By August that year, Henry had heard that James intended to help with the invasion of England; the next year, Scottish ships and men were apparently sent to Vlissingen. As the invasion neared, the Scottish ambassadors at Maximilian's court showed an excitement about it, and an eagerness to "stir up opinion for the Duke of York", that seemed to come from a higher source. And when Richard won no victory, or even a foothold, James's hand of love was still extended to him.

Another subject was also in the air. For a while there had been talk of a marriage for Richard with one of the eligible princesses of Europe. Such a strategic alliance—which, in the first instance, marriage was—would add necessary substance to him. Maximilian's daughter had been mentioned, but the thought had been taken no further: a sign, perhaps, that her father was still uncertain of the young man's credentials. But negotiations for a wedding in Scotland had probably been proceeding for some time.

The proof of that is simple enough: Richard had no sooner arrived there, than he was married. Those who dismissed his claims thought that nothing had been arranged; he had simply fallen in love (or in lust, as André preferred) with a girl when he arrived, and asked James for her. But this was not the normal practice for princes, and he was a prince. Marriages at this level did not occur without months, more often years, of careful preparation on both sides. His portrait had probably been done with this in mind; and as he left Flanders to invade England, on fairly clear instructions to continue rather than return, his thoughts may have been set more keenly on Scotland than those around him knew.

Of his love-life before then nothing is known. It is highly likely that in France or in Brabant some young woman had already "taken his belt off", as the saying was, and he hers. His sexual awakening may also have come much earlier. In Portugal, as an impressionable adolescent, he had found a court that was alive with casual liaisons and hopeless amours between the servants of the king's and queen's households. The Infante Afonso, at the age of thirteen, had already publicly declared himself in love. At riverside picnics, at late-night dancing parties, in the rustic lodging-houses where the pages and squires were billetted as the court travelled, a mysterious youth, "slim, fair and like a Frenchman", had plenty of occasions to make conquests or to be seduced. If he was silent or inarticulate, this too, as Garcia de Resende described it, was part of the game. The court divided between those sunk in the inexpressible despair of love, *cuydando* (as Pero Vaz had said he was), and those who were convulsed, *sospirando*, with moans and sighs. Either way, the lover languished until his beloved embraced him. As Richard Plantagenet grew into princeliness he became, as all young princes did, effortlessly desirable, no longer needing to sigh for the young women who would do whatever he wanted in the baths or in bed. Yet by his last year at the court of Burgundy, when he was twenty-one and old, as a prince, to be unmarried, there was evident advantage in a more settled kind of love.

His petition to his beloved, long-arranged or not, appears to have survived in a copy in the archives in Spain. The letter is unsigned, the recipient unnamed, but internal evidence strongly suggests that it was his. It was written in the mid-1490s, in Latin, and was addressed to a young woman of high nobility in Scotland. Its preservation, and its sending to Spain, implied it was of the greatest political importance, like the love-letters also preserved there between Prince Arthur and Katherine of Aragon. In contrast to those letters, however, with their stilted expressions of regard and their sense of parents hovering, this was a work of maturity, passion and independence. The use of a Latin secretary (betrayed by his fine Italian hand) to craft the phrases and then to write them out was evidence that it came from a royal secretariat. It was not the prince's own work, but it expressed a prince's desires, though couched in the abject humility that was expected of lovers.

The letter may have travelled with him from Malines—kept among his papers, or pressed in a prayer-book—ready for presentation to a young woman he did not yet know; or he may have written it, with a little help, in the wake of his first meeting with her. In the letter, he had seen her and was deeply in love; but such feelings could be anticipated by young men with strong imaginations and perhaps a few details to build on. In the romances, gallants often fell in love with fair virgins they had seen only in dreams, leaping from their disordered beds to ride out over the world in hope of finding them. If Richard had not seen her, in her portrait or in life, he had dreamed her to distraction.

Most noble lady:

It is not without reason that all men turn their eyes to you; love you; admire you; honour you. For on the one hand they contemplate your twofold virtue that always makes you shine so brightly: so that no man may have before him a sweeter example of manners. Your riches are always admired, and in second place your easy fortune, which secures to you both your nobility of birth and all that goes with that nobility. On the other hand there suddenly appears that extraordinary beauty, divine rather than earthly, which testifies—as you deserve—that you were not born as humans are, but fell from Heaven.

They look at your face, so bright and serene that it gives splendour to the cloudy sky. They look at your eyes, as brilliant as stars, which make all pain to be forgotten, and turn despair into delight. Lastly, they look at your white neck, easily outshining pearls; they admire your peerless brow, the glowing bloom of youth, the bright gold hair, and all the splendid perfection of your body; and in looking, they can only praise you; in praising, they can only love you; in loving, finally, they cannot but reverence you.

I shall be a happy man, perhaps the happiest, among the others who share this fate with me, if I may deserve at last to win your love. When I embrace in my mind all those qualities of yours, I am impelled not only to love you, worship you and honour you, but love makes me your slave. Waking or sleeping, I can find no rest, thinking myself wretched since I may not be able to please your nobility, on which alone I have wished to base all my hopes.

Most noble lady, my soul, turn your eyes upon me; most piously intercede for this man who has been called your servant from the first hour he saw you; for love is not a human thing, but rather divine. Nor should it seem beneath you to obey love; for not only human Princes, but goddesses too, have bent their necks beneath its yoke.

I beg therefore that your nobility may be willing to cleave to me, who is ready to do your will in all things as long as life remains in me. And Farewell my soul and my consolation and the greatest ornament of Scotland; Farewell and again Farewell.

Although both sender and receiver spoke English, English could not do such sentiments justice. Such letters had to be in Latin, like prayers that approached the mysteries of Heaven. The language of princes in love was required to be as mannered and beautiful as possible. At the same time, the letter was tentative, as courtesy dictated. He did not deserve her, and could only hope that she would notice him among the crowd of her admirers. To accept his love would be a burden and subjugation for her, depending completely on her kindness. The letter was written largely in the subjunctive, the mood of possibilities and dreams.

At times, the ritual self-abasement seemed to go a good deal too far. Repeatedly he emphasised her nobility, "on which alone I have wished to base all my hopes", as if he needed her high blood to reinforce his own. He feared he could not please her and was in awe of her "easy fortune", as though he himself had nothing to offer her. But this, in fact, was Richard's case. Only he, at this time and place, combined majesty and nothingness in this extraordinary way.

He either could not yet name her, or did not yet dare to; and little in this letter, save "of Scotland", and the bright gold hair, could have tied it to any young woman in particular. Even the bright gold hair was standard, preferably falling to the waist in token of virginity, and thrillingly on show. The neck was always white: as pear-blossom, as milk, as new-fallen snow, shining under the chemise or the little veil of soft white gauze that was sometimes meant to conceal it. The dint between the collar-bones and, especially, the declivity between the breasts were known to desperately arouse a man. Ideally, pale blue veins could be seen beneath that whiteness, showing where the warm blood pulsed with what might become reciprocal desire. The "bloom of youth" caught a little of that, blood rising with excitement in a pretty face. All these phrases suggested he had seen her, and at close hand; yet these were also the qualities of every beautiful girl and goddess in 1495.

The phrases of love in this letter, too, were lustrous with long use: a heavenly birth, the allurements of sweet manners, the wondering of the world, the lover enslaved. A young man with his head full of poetry could produce them almost without thinking. He knew, too—as all lovers knew—that he was taking risks. Love hurt him as though he were in real war, struck with searing arrows that could not be pulled out again. He was caught in the middle of a perilous approach, wounded by graciousness and beauty and by the torment of broken nights; but quietly, insistently, by constant looking, he was attempting to negotiate the terms of a mutual surrender. His beloved was already involuntarily enmeshed with him. She was not only his consolation, but his soul. In that divine sphere where, like Our Lady, she turned the stars of her eyes upon him and interceded for his intentions, they were already one. His identity was hers, though he may not yet have known whose identity that was.

II

PRINCE RICHARD OF ENGLAND REACHED SCOTLAND on or around November 20th, 1495. Perhaps thirty men accompanied him as he disem/ barked. One Scottish historian gave him "an opulent equipage and hon/ ourable train of foreigners", but not much opulence can have got through the rigours of Ireland. Though he doubtless put an elegant face on things, he was all but washed up. The Scottish accounts list payments for six servants of the Prince of England, who were clothed at James's expense. A more tattered train of "Englishmen who came from Ireland" were billetted in Ayr and Irvine as a drain on the king's budget. German mercenaries in Richard's train, then or later, were blamed for bringing in the pox they had contracted from prostitutes in Italy.

He was expected; perhaps because Margaret had sent word, or because Hugh O'Donnell, who was in Glasgow in July renewing old alliances, had kept the king apprised of his likely movements. James received him with great pomp at Stirling, moving across from Edinburgh the hanging tapestries, the sideboard of silver plate and the chapel gear (the vestments newly mended with gold and silk), and furnishing a large house for Richard's use in the town. William Dunbar detested gray/stone windswept Stirling, calling it "purgatory" and "hiddous hell", and de/ crying its dull company and thin beer. Lead us not into this temptation, he prayed:

> Et ne nos inducas in tentationem de Strivilling:
> Sed libera nos a malo illius.

But James liked it, and was busy rebuilding the entrance gate and plan/ ning new royal quarters on the highest part of the great rock on which the castle stood, besides laying out a large garden in the ward with ditches, fish/ponds, stands of young trees, lawns and flowers. The wolves were kept at bay. Through this work/in/progress the Prince of England rode with as many as had followed him. Every castle and palace he was to visit in Scotland showed James's enthusiasm for building and improving, an enthusiasm he also directed towards his friends.

The Scottish winter had already started: short, dim daylight hours before the torches were lit to shine on the best tapestries, the best silver, and on him. Dunbar again, still in Stirling:

> In to thir dirk and drublie dayis,
> Quhone sabill all the hevin arrayis
> With mystie vapouris, cluddis, and skyis,
> Nature all curage me denyis
> Off sangis, ballattis, and of playis.
>
> Quhone that the nycht dois lengthin houris
> With wind, with hail and havy schouris . . .
> My hairt for languor dois forloir
> For laik of symmer with his flouris.

James had taken pains with more besides the furniture. He had been in Stirling since at least the 10th of November, checking that everything was ready. For himself, to make sure that he looked as impressive as his castle, he had ordered a new jacket, shirts of holland cloth, tippets, hats and a gold-and-silk embroidered belt. Jousts were laid on in celebration, for which the king wore a white arming doublet sewn with silk. It is hard to disentangle the costs of Prince Richard's welcoming from the costs of his wedding, since the clerk who wrote up the accounts put everything together. They were all of a piece, an outpouring of a love that was already his.

The two young men were natural allies. James was twenty-two, only a few months older than his new friend: cultured, polyglot, athletic, musical, and apt to order four new hats on every feast day. (In 1489 he bought twenty-five: caps, bonnets, hats of beaver fur, hats with ear-flaps.) His five hawkers and their birds went with him almost everywhere, and he wore a gold whistle to call his dogs. His love affairs were famous and, despite prattling tongues, he kept his favourite mistress in grand and public estate. Generosity was natural to him; so, too, was wildness, in spending and enthusiasms and even in appearance. He kept a shaggy half-beard, showed a strange fascination for the manners of savages, and was so headstrong that John Ramsay, Henry VII's Scottish agent, thought he was "far out of reason". Clever as he was, James could be gulled too; it was in character that he never suspected Ramsay, in whom he confided, of being a spy for England.

Like Maximilian, he was a wanderer around his kingdom, casting off formality when he could. He would sometimes ride out unattended in the guise of a common wayfarer, lodging in the crofts of the poor and sleeping on their hard beds, in order to ask his lowliest subjects what they thought of their king. His pilgrimages to his favourite shrines, St. Duthac's in Ross and St. Ninian's in Galloway, were sometimes made on foot, though his Italian minstrels went along to serenade him. As in Maximilian's case, the wanderer and disguiser in him, the risk-taking king, seems to have warmed to Richard as to a kindred soul.

Yet he was also constant, remaining loyal, in particular, to the memory of the father he had scarcely known. It was said that a little while after the battle of Sauchieburn, when no one was sure whether the king was alive or dead, James approached Sir Andrew Wood and asked him, "Sir, are you my father?" The brooding sense of a father he could not forget, and whom others would not let him forget, would also have brought him close to Richard. Stirling, where they first met, had been James III's favourite residence, and from the top of the king's new tower a far line of trees marked the place where his father had lost the battle. A double complement of choristers and musicians sang daily in the castle chapel for the soul of the murdered man. As a pledge that his grief and his love continued, James wore an iron belt to which he added a new link every third year. When Richard of England embraced him to seal their common cause he would have felt this belt press hard against him: beneath the shimmering damasks and velvets that his friend wore as avidly as he did, uncompromising steel.

A few days after Richard's arrival, James asked him to address the assembled lords directly. This was probably at Perth, then called St. Johnstone, on December 3rd. There, according to the chroniclers, he gave perhaps the saddest of his orations: the story of his own life, presented as a desperate search for people who would help and befriend him.

He had lived so miserably abroad, he told the council, that he had found himself wishing that he had died like his brother. Sometimes he would try to tell strangers who he was, to induce them to help him, but they would only mock at his pretensions. When he began openly to declare who he was, he was "assailed with all the arrows of adverse Fortune", for it was then that his "most crafty enemy" began to bribe and corrupt his friends and spread false tales about his birth. His aunt Margaret too, and his friends among the English nobles, had been reviled and mocked when they recognised him.

After a while, he went on—tears stealing down his cheeks, sobs racking him, as the lords listened—he had tried to interest the neighbouring rulers, Philip and Maximilian, in taking up his cause. He could not bear that "the blood of princes, oppressed by weeping and misery and fear, should end by wasting away in grief." But then, in a reference perhaps to the failed invasion, he had fallen into "very serious evils". He would have lost heart completely (though he had always tried not to lose heart) if he had not thought of Scotland. It was common fame through all the world that—in Vergil's words now—"no man shipwrecked by the injuries of Fortune or expelled from his country, as I was when I was a child, has ever sought your help in vain." If the Scots could do nothing else for him, perhaps at least they could give him a place, "so I will not have to wander any more." But if they helped him to recover his father's kingdom, "I will promise in the future always to cherish friendship for the name of the Scottish people, to protect it with devotion, and you may depend especially on all the resources of my kingdom. . . . In thanking you for this bounty, [my people] will think themselves never capable of making up their debt to you."

He ended, said George Buchanan in his history of 1582, with many praises of James, "part of them true, and part of them tailored to the present design", deliberately exaggerating the sadness and the gratitude he felt. Then he fell silent, apparently overcome with tears, for James called him aside and told him to be of good cheer, comforting him. With that the sad prince withdrew, and the council debated whether or not they should help him.

The debate was for form's sake only. James had promised to help him as soon as he arrived, the decision already approved at the council of forty lords that had been held in Edinburgh in October. Yet the approval was not entirely solid on either occasion. Vergil said the wiser heads advised James not to touch this young man: the affair was just a fraud set up by Margaret, "and all these things should be considered as dreams." Even those who were keen to use James's prince to make war on England nonetheless nursed doubts about him.

The uncertainty shows up in a document from two days later, a deed of resignation drawn up in the king's chamber at Linlithgow Palace on

December 5th at around ten in the morning. There, listed first among the witnesses, was "the most excellent Richard Plantagenet, the son, *ut asseruit*, of the serene prince Edward, once the illustrious King of England." *Ut asseruit*, as he claimed. The cautious Scottish notary gave him no title of his own but "man": *excellentissimus vir*. As ever, a slight emptiness touched the magnificence. Yet his grandness impressed people, all the same; as did his tears. In the immediate aftermath of the speech to James's council, Buchanan said, the majority "whether from the imperative of the thing, or the inconstancy of their minds, or to please the king . . . commiserated with the fortune of this man." So James decided as he had already done. Vergil suggested that he took Richard up with passionate nonchalance, telling him that "whoever he was [*quisquis esset*], he should never regret coming to him."

Quisquis esset. Like so many others who dealt with this young man, James had no cast-iron evidence of who he was. For a host of reasons, he chose to believe in him. Richard looked like a prince and behaved like one, and gave him bargaining power against England and in Europe. So he took him in his arms. Once he had done that, other considerations came into play. De Puebla, the Spanish ambassador in London, mentioned the most obvious: since Richard had placed himself in his trust, James now had an obligation to "look out for" him.

As soon as the formal presentations were over, he treated Prince Richard with more and more honour, calling him "cousin" and showing him to his people as the Duke of York. A special minder was appointed for him: Master Andrew Forman, priest, protonotary and previously James's envoy to the pope. Forman's diplomatic career showed him to be subtle, haughty and insistent on proper respect from his fellow ambassadors. By 1498 Raimondo Soncino thought him "a man of considerable influence", and a few years later he was made Bishop of Moray. This figure, in his solemn black, was now constantly at Richard's side. He had lighter moods, playing with James at cards and "catch", a sort of tennis, and may well have played them with his charge, too. But his principal tasks were to attend him and protect him.

In Edinburgh James gave Richard lodgings at the Black Friars, about half a mile west of Holyroodhouse, where Parliament sometimes met and where Henry VI had stayed in his exile. His horses were kept there for some weeks, and he was there with James for a priest's first Mass at the end of January. But mostly, in those early months, James took him round the country with him. Their movements can be tracked from the king's use of the great seal: December 3rd, Perth; December 6th, Cupar, where they offered together at Mass on St. Nicholas's day; December 8th, Dundee; December 11th, the monastery of Abirbrothock; December 14th, Perth again; December 22nd, Dunfermline. They were at Linlith-gow together for Christmas, in the newly fortified red-stone palace at the edge of the loch. For Candlemas they were at Edinburgh, processing round the church with their blessed and lighted candles. To walk beside each other in church, or to hold each other's hand as they went to make offering, was a strong sign of confederation and love. On Easter Day in Stirling, having taken the Sacrament privately in their own chapels, they walked together at the High Mass to make offering, shining with new fin-ery and grace. In June they were at Perth, hawking in the hills and down-ing the salty whey provided by Goldie, a local woman, to refresh them in the chase. They were friends, no matter what anyone else thought.

This friendship was not cheap. Since Richard had nothing, James topped up his wardrobe with gowns, coats, hats, hose and underwear, and gave him a pension of £112 Scots a month. (The Scottish pound being worth around one-third of the English one, this generosity was somewhat less than it may have seemed in England.) A general subsidy was raised "for the sustentation of the Duke of York", with Wood appointed to col-lect it in the districts north of the Forth. Prince Richard's horses, between thirty and sixty of them for his closest followers and himself, were stabled, ferried and fed on chalders of oats and barley at the king's expense.

The Englishmen who had followed him, filling the taverns and lodging houses of Edinburgh and Ayr, were paid for too: £26 here, £40 there, more than £100 in May alone. They did not always behave them-selves (a number ended up in prison), and there was plenty of mutual antipathy to go round. Still James paid for these dregs of Richard's forces, or made others do so. Certain towns received letters from the king "directing" Richard's men to be lodged there at the burgh's expense, while some of his subjects had their arms twisted more directly. Sir Dun-can Forrester of Skippnick, the king's comptroller, persuaded Katherine Murray and Annes Glass to take in "the Duke of York's folks", promis-ing them, so they said, 13 crowns and £3 10s. respectively. (For his part, he claimed he had promised them no more than the 20 shillings he had paid them.) Aberdeen in July 1496 had to raise 5s. 4d. a day to keep eight of the Duke of York's people for a month, and this in a town with so little ready cash that when a subscription had been raised to repair the parish church, three years earlier, people had paid their share in lambskins and fish.

James himself was as poor as his kingdom. John Ramsay told Henry VII, only half in jest, that at one point the king had barely more than £100 left in the world. "My kingdom does not overflow with silver and gold," James had told Pope Innocent, through Forman, in 1490, excusing himself from helping with the pope's crusade. In 1493 he found himself so short of funds that he was forced to pawn his gold locket, his French saddle and his copy of Gower's "Confessio Amantis", with its moral tales of high courtly love. Yet James found money for Richard, to the point of impoverishing himself. He even gave him his Mass offerings when they were together in church: usually 14 shillings, just a little less, as rank decreed, than his own. The pension should have covered that, as it should have covered Richard's clothes. But rather than passing cash through a servant, as the pension was paid, the offerings and money pres-ents were placed directly in Richard's hand by James; more evidence of love.

The greatest pledge of James's commitment, however, was to give him another's love. Almost as soon as Richard arrived in Scotland he was betrothed and married to Lady Katherine Gordon, the daughter of George, Earl of Huntly, the most powerful lord in Scotland below the king himself.

James III had depended on Huntly, his ally against various trouble-makers and, after 1478, his justiciary north of the Forth, a post to which he was reappointed ten years later. In the ructions that led to the murder of the king, Huntly's loyalties were hard to judge; but in 1491 he was made James IV's lieutenant north of the Esk, and from then on was firmly in his favour. His father, the first earl, had been high chancellor of Scotland; his tomb described him as "a noble and powerful lord" and so his son, too, saw himself. From the centre of his domain, the tower-house castle of Strathbogie in the Grampians, he commanded on every side views as sweeping as his ambitions. He was at least sixty when Richard came to Scotland, and on his third marriage. Katherine seems to have been his sec-ond daughter by his latest wife.

Huntly emerges from the records of the Lords of Council as an almost terrifying figure, and the whole family as violent and litigious. In

1496–97 alone the earl was involved in three lawsuits over land. In May 1497 his nephew Alexander Seton tried to serve a writ against his own father, Huntly's brother, alleging that he was "not of composed mind, a fool and a natural idiot." (He was made to renounce it.) Seven months later, James himself brought a case against Huntly for failing to ensure the good behaviour of the Innes brothers. Huntly had to pay the king the full amount of the surety, 1,000 marks, and immediately claimed the sum back from Alexander Innes. The Gordon clan seemed to feel that they could wink at infractions, and trample on their neighbours, because they were so far from the king's eye. When Alexander Seton's idiocy writ came up, Huntly was given forty days to declare his interest in the case, "the distance of his dwelling place being considered." He probably did not hurry himself to appear.

Huntly's most famous son-in-law was to say, later, that Huntly had believed him to be Richard, Duke of York. The aged earl was in James's privy council, and had therefore heard Richard's heart-rending account of his life. Yet marriage was essentially a business and financial contract made without emotion, especially by brides' fathers, and there was little in a marriage to Prince Richard of England to secure—let alone advance—Katherine's position. Her husband-to-be was an exile and a wanderer. His kingdom was a dream, and his only income was the money James allowed him or which Katherine, in her dowry, could bring to him. He in turn offered nothing but his titles (on paper) and himself, the perfect image of a prince. From Huntly's point of view there was nothing solid to be gained from this alliance and everything to lose, from his daughter's "shame-faced chastity" to his own reputation. A few years before, his son Alexander had written to Henry VII, in the heavy burr of his Scottish spelling, fretting about ties of honour and "neyr teynderness of blude" to the murdered king, whose cause he still favoured. To form such ties with an impostor would have been intolerable both to the son and to the father. Huntly may have acquiesced, as the king's council did, mostly because it was the king who asked; and because he could not prove that this princely young man was other than the person he said he was.

Of Katherine herself very little is known except that she was young, a virgin, and beautiful. She was born around 1474, a year or so later than Prince Richard; and she was so lovely, as all attested, that Henry VII fell for her himself when their paths crossed. Robert Fabyan twice mentioned her beauty and fairness, as well as how "goodly" she appeared. "A modest and graceful look and singularly beautiful", was how blind Bernard André described her, no doubt on good information. The graceful look of the time was well documented: a long neck, slender arms, a neat waist, high round breasts. André also said she blushed easily, confirming how fair-skinned and young she was. Her accent would have been as strong as her half-brother's, from the Highland hills close to Aberdeen where the family lived. Pedro de Ayala, the Spanish ambassador, was enchanted by Scottish girls: courteous in the extreme, very bold "though mostly honest", gracious, handsome and with the most becoming headdresses in the world. That outsider's view may well have been Richard's first impression, too.

Around the time of his arrival, probably in early November 1495, James paid £108 17s. 6d.—almost as much as Richard's pension for a month—for fifteen and a quarter ells of crimson satin brocaded with gold, and fifteen ells of velvet, to be delivered to "My Lady Huntly in Edinburgh". This "stuff", the only purchase the king ever made for the Huntlys, was almost certainly for the gown Katherine wore when she first met Prince Richard. The lengths of material suggest that she was about the same height as the young man to whom she did reverence, as he to her. The bright dark red (James's favourite colour) would have been the perfect foil for the gold of her hair and the ivory of her skin. At that moment, she was perhaps more lovely than she had ever been.

Katherine was probably not a princess of Scotland, but she came close enough. As Huntly's daughter by his third wife, Elizabeth Hay, she had no Stuart blood in her. But she was descended from two daughters of Robert II, and her father's second wife had been Arabella Stuart, the sister of James II. James called her father "cousin" when he wrote to him, and in general Scottish parlance Katherine too was called James's "tender cousin", acknowledging the closeness of blood by marriage. Henry VII was to treat her, without quibble, as someone of near-consanguinity to James; *illustris domina*, "noble lady", was how he addressed her in André's writings. In short, she was the closest and noblest woman of marriageable age whom James could offer to his friend.

There was also, of course, something in it for him. Vergil thought James arranged the marriage so that Richard, when he recovered his kingdom, would be all the more indebted to him. He did so, too, to make him more substantial, both as Henry's enemy and as his own friend: "confirming him in this affinity in the hope of better fortune", in George

Buchanan's words. Treaties held no security, but a marriage was binding, and usually lasted unless death cut it short. It tied James to Richard almost as deeply as it would tie Katherine. The power of the bond was well understood by all those, from Henry to Isabella to the various envoys and agents, who laboured to make James ignore it. He could never do so, for from January 1496 he considered himself bound to Richard, *quisquis esset*, by ties of blood and sacrament.

The couple were betrothed almost instantly. For a very short time, per-haps, they went through the rituals of courtship that seemed to stifle, but in fact stoked high, the feelings of both sides. Invigilated meetings would be held in cold rooms and cold gardens (far south, in London, the frost lay thick as glass that winter), after which they might "commune aside", the chaperone still present but the words unheard, the young man some-times kneeling bare-headed as courtesy required. At public functions he would find occasion to linger close to her, encouraging her to look and smile at him and, if possible, reaching to touch her. The ceremonies for Richard's arrival in Scotland meant music and dancing; there was his chance.

> O Lord God / how glad then I was
> So for to dance / with my sweet lady
> By her proper hand / soft as any silk
> With due obeisance / I did her then take
> Her skin was white / as whale's bone or milk
> My thought was ravished / . . . I might not aslake
> My burning heart . . .
> For the fire kindled / and waxed more and more
> The dancing blew it . . .

As dancing tends to.

Katherine scarcely knew the young man who now smiled at her and, in the dance, took her hand. Books of instruction for young women insisted that she ought to know him well before she committed heart and body to him, but she was not allowed the chance. Over the days, trust-ingly as became a woman, she hoped to find out more. Since 1491, when her elder sister Margaret had married the Earl of Bothwell, James's envoy that year to France, she may have heard whispers of this hidden Yorkist prince. But, in all likelihood, she knew no more about him than he had told her father: his miraculous escape, his miserable exile and his desertion by his friends. She knew, too, that young men had a habit of deceiving girls with words. They used tears less often but those, too, softened and beguiled girls' hearts.

She was young, with no experience of a man paying serious court to her, and this one was presented to her as her husband-to-be, without contention. In the first instance she thought less, perhaps, of who he was than of his closeness and his maleness. The "stuffing of the codpiece" was something young women were known to notice, for all their bashfulness, and the striped hose Richard wore from his first days in Scotland, the codpiece aggressively large and fastened with buttons, were designed precisely to show a man from waist to toe, leaving nothing to the imagination. From there, as Stephen Hawes wrote, a young girl's thoughts might well turn to the still-mysterious deeds they were to do together:

> Otherwhile ye think full privily
> What the man is and what he can do
> Of chamber work as nature will agree
> Though by experience ye know nothing thereto
> Yet oft ye muse and think what it may be
> Nature provoketh of her strong degree

Betrothal itself was marked in the romances by no particular ceremonial, but with the first kiss. The lover kissed his betrothed on the lips once, then twice: the first kiss tentative and polite, the second bolder, confirming his right to be there and to touch her in this way. Modesty required that in public young women should open their mouths only a little, dimpling rather than smiling. It was understood, from the merest hint of a smile, that they wanted more than this. The favourite symbol of nascent sexual love was the red rosebud, the petals not tight-folded but ready to unclose, as soft lips pressed open. Within them, if he dared, the lover might touch her tongue, sugared and swelling gently under his own. Such a kiss was a private act, usually reserved by princes for the chamber and the closet, as was the taking of the Sacrament. To kiss properly in public was a deliberate demonstration of the intimacy to follow.

It sometimes followed very quickly, as soon as the Mass of betrothal had been sung. Ferdinand and Isabella, their betrothal sealed and the Mass said, immediately went to bed together. In 1490 Prince Afonso of Portugal, betrothed but not yet married to their daughter Isabella, stole in

to make love to her night after night in the monastery where she was staying, scandalising the monks by choosing such a place but not, it seems, by
the act itself. (The wall of the monastery church, just beside their room,
crashed to the ground as if shaken by their passion.) Once a young man
and a young woman were solemnly contracted to marry, all parties to the
contract willed their bodily union and, in some cases, assisted it. The
chaperone would slip from the girl's bed, allowing the young man to take
her place, or the couple would simply find each other, understanding that
their love was sealed and permitted. In a famous poem by Guillaume de
Machaut the lover, approaching his beloved to kiss her, found a leaf across
her mouth. Her chaperone gently took the leaf away.

In Richard and Katherine's case, the season of Advent intervened
before they could sanctify their vows in marriage. Advent was a period of
penitence and fish-fasts when marriages could not be solemnised and
when the absence of meat, so churchmen hoped, dampened down desire.
But young desire is not easily dampened, and it seems that they did not
wait. A child was born to them the following September, too early for a
January wedding. In some unguarded room, with the tacit approval of
those who had brought them together, they probably made love a matter
of days after they had first seen each other.

The actual wedding took place on or around the octave of Epiphany
in mid-January, presumably in Edinburgh, where the king then was.
Richard wore a "spousing gown" of fourteen and a half yards of white
damask, costing £28. His six servants were also in damask robes and his
two trumpeters in gowns of tawny cloth, with camlet doublets and red
hose. No concession was made to the bitter cold except tippets, or short
capes, for the king and the prince, of taffeta and fur. Katherine, like
Richard, was robed in white, her hair loose on her shoulders. Both wore
wedding crowns. These, with the white robes, proclaimed them as virgins
and maidens, words applied equally to her and to him, whatever the truth
was.

The bridal couple, having reverenced each other, stood first at the
door of the church and made the dowry offering, laid out on a gold or silver tray. After this Huntly gave Katherine away to her husband-to-be,
who took her right hand in his. By this "hand-fastening", in the presence
of witnesses, the first sacramental seal was set on the marriage. After this,
inside the church with the guests standing around them, the priest asked
the couple and the assembled company whether the marriage might law-

fully go forward. The questions to be asked were set out in the order of service; they concerned only consanguinity and prior contract, the most common rocks on which marriages foundered. No mention was made of doubtful or false identity, and clearly no one raised it. To most of those who stood there, the identity of this crowned and shimmering young man was not uncertain.

When the priest had "diligently" made his inquiries, he asked the bridegroom "by name", Richard, whether he would protect and keep his wife. He answered, *Volo*: "I will." Katherine was asked whether she would take this man for her lawful husband, "to serve him faithfully in all things", and replied, in turn, *Volo*. Her father then gave her again to Richard, who presented her with a marriage gift. The ring and the bridal offering were placed on a dish or on the Mass-book to be blessed and sprinkled with holy water: one ring only, as was customary, for Katherine, "and may she who wears it be armed with the virtue of heavenly protection and may it be to her eternal salvation . . . may she remain, O Lord, in your peace, and live and grow and grow old and bear children in long length of days."

Richard then took the ring and placed it lightly on each finger of her left hand. As the priest led him, he said after him: *In nomine patris*.

"In nomine patris."

Moving the ring from the thumb to the second finger: *Et filii*.

"Et filii."

To the third finger: *Et spiritus sancti amen*.

"Et spiritus sancti amen."

There he left it, on the finger from which a vein ran directly to the heart. He then said, after the priest, "With this ring I thee wed": *De isto anulo te sponso*. Lastly, he gave Katherine the gold pieces from the dish: *Et de isto auro te honoro*, "And with this gold I honour thee." They bowed their heads as the priest declared them blessed by God, who had made the world out of nothing. Then, her right hand in his, they walked to the high altar for the Mass of their marriage.

The Epistle was from Corinthians ("Know you not that your body is the temple of the Holy Ghost, and you are not your own?"). The Gospel was from Matthew ("They shall be no more twain, but one flesh"). Prayers asked that their bodies and hearts should be conjoined and sanctified in the delights of love, as Adam and Eve had been coupled by God's grace in the garden. After the *Sanctus*, bride and groom prostrated them selves as a golden canopy was spread over them. They did not rise until the moment when the priest pronounced the *Pax Domini:* at which point Richard received from the priest the pax, a silver tablet engraved with an image of the Crucifixion, kissed it and gave it to Katherine, "kissing her and no other, and neither kissing anyone else." They now belonged exclusively to each other, "knit together fleshly", living in truth and faith to the other as parts of one body and one soul. Churchmen taught that the foundation of married love lay in that moment, their kiss in the presence of Christ. Poets took it further. When a girl "sweetly gave me the pax between two pillars of the church," the act plainly symbolised a sublimation that was no longer surreptitious, but fully lawful.

Katherine was now his wife. She was also the Duchess of York, sister-in-law of the Queen of England, niece of Margaret of York, daughter-in-law of the most serene Edward, late king. She shared her husband's name and all it meant, if it meant anything. A cloth of estate was hers, and the right to have her train carried by a baroness in her own house. She could dream, if she wanted to, of processions and coronations in England. Among the crowd of guests, there were probably not many who thought that outcome likely, even if the young man's claim was true. And somewhere outside, no doubt scribbling a report to Henry, was at least one man, John Ramsay, who believed this "boy" had simply hoodwinked her.

In love, the state in which they were, the possibilities of deception were manifest. Everyone knew that love "obfusked, endulled and ravished" all those it touched, men as well as women. The poet François Villon described how, in dalliance with his love and leaning close to her, she could make him believe that cinders were flour, old iron glass, a felt hat a mortar:

> Heaven, a brass pot
> The clouds, a calf-skin
> A cabbage stalk, a turnip
> Morning, evening . . .

The trusting lover also believed that roses grew on nettle-stalks, that leeks gave honey, that curlews dried clothes on stands in the meadows and that, in the woods, whiting armed with bows went hunting the deer.

Love's world appeared to be a garden of delight, but not if you looked closely. Venus, who ran the only tavern there, offered arousing hippocras spiked with gall. If you plucked an apple from the shining boughs of the trees, it fell apart as gray ash. Under the leaves of the pretty flowers in the borders, adders lurked, and tiny pricking serpents coiled around their stings. In the garden strolled characters of exquisite looks and courtesy whose names, Fair Semblant and Fair Seeming, gave warning that nothing could be trusted. Still the lover was taken in, entranced and half-drunk, and lured towards destruction.

A baron's daughter fell for a vagrant juggler once, a man who had changed himself into an angel and had conjured "a well good steed" from an old horse bone and a saddle cloth. He pricked and pranced so alluringly before her bower that, though she had disdained all lovers, she took him to her bed. The dawn broke, the birds sang: still twined around her angel-lord, she called for her maidservants.

> "Where be ye my merry maidens
> That ye come not me to?
> The jolly windows of my bower
> Look that you undo
> That I may see;
>
> For I have in mine arms
> A duke or else an earl."
> But when she lookéd him upon
> He was a blear-eyed churl—
> "Alas," she said.

Robert Fabyan and Bernard André both assumed that something similar had happened in Katherine's case. The mawmet from Flanders had married her "to her confusion", a phrase carrying strong implications that she had been tricked, seduced and left ruined. But this never seemed to be her reading of it, then or later. However little she knew of Richard, she, like James, had decided to believe. She trusted him, as she had shown in that moment when she had let him take her hand. The churchmen taught in any case that, inside marriage, it was right that some love-blindness should remain. "Every woman should love and fear her husband so highly," said the *Secreta*, "that she should find no man fairer, wiser or stronger than he; and if any man does appear fairer, wiser and stronger, she should not find him so."

From her husband's point of view, the marriage may have seemed very different. James obviously meant it to bolster him, to give him confidence and express his own support, but he may have gone uncomfortably far. Contemporaries describing this young man's career considered his marriage as the extraordinary peak of his deception, and possibly it was: a climb too high, to a place where the world was different and unsettling.

By this time, Richard of England had bound himself with many sorts of obligations to Margaret, Maximilian and Philip. He had been liberal in his promises of how far he would get and what he would do for his friends once he got there. This was part of the game of high politics; papers signed but not acted on, breezy undertakings given. Each side understood the limits of any commitment that was made, including the recision of all that had been promised. Marriage, by contrast, was a pledge without reservation. As the love-letter had acknowledged, his soul was now enfolded with another's, and his life was not his own.

If that life was a lie, it was hardly possible to admit it to the young woman with whom he was increasingly in love, as she with him. He could not do so without destroying her as well as himself, for the greater part of her honour now stemmed from his. He was her husband and her lord; he could not break that. As much as Margaret's maternal bullying, or James's fierce encouragement, or any convictions on his own account, it may have been Katherine's devotion to him, and his to her, that bound him to pursue the claim of Richard, Duke of York. This may have been what he meant—if anything he said at that point was sincere—when he confessed two years later that he had been prevented, sometime around the autumn of 1495, from letting the whole thing go, as he had longed to.

If he was not Richard, marriage made him more vulnerable than he had ever been. He was so close to someone else that their flesh was supposed to contain one heart, hers and his together, each laid open equally to the secrets of the other. In love, he could not pretend with her. As he could lawfully undress her (unpinning her headdress to loosen her hair, unfastening her bodice, lifting her kirtle over her hips), so she could uncover him: robe, surcoat, shirt, points. One by one, under her hands, all princely trappings could fall away. He could not conceal himself, any more than he could conceal the eager hardness of his gear as she embraced him.

Yet at that moment, too, there was no escaping love's deception. Inside the drawn curtains, in the busy and tender darkness, Venus taught

them to work by touch alone, uncumbered by the knowledge or the etiquette of daylight. At the height of pleasure both partners closed their
eyes, the better to lose themselves in the rapture of their bodies. He could
deceive her then as completely as he abandoned himself to her, and she,
crying out in love, would not have cared. He was hers, and she his—
whoever he was.

III

HE HAD BEEN MARRIED in white damask. Once the ceremony was over
he fought in white damask, or was at least apparelled in it, in a tight-
fitting arming jacket stuffed with horsehair and halved or quartered with
purple. His attendants would have laced him into it, hard. He also put on
thick white arming hose and prepared to take part in the wedding tournament. It is unclear whether he ever did so. His six servants were also given
arming jackets, of cheaper stuff decorated with wide ribbons, and may
have had a go in his place. New bridegrooms were sometimes excused
from fighting, in order to conserve their energy and preserve their bodies
for the jousts of love. James fought, in an arming doublet of costly crimson satin, and hurt himself; more than two weeks later his "sore hand"
was still bound up in a bandage of double-thick silk, a mitten of white
kersey and a taffeta sling.

The difference between them was telling. James was devoted to tournaments, often inviting all his lords, earls and barons, as well as champi-
ons from Europe, to come to his court and prove themselves by jousting,
fighting with battle-axes, fighting with two-handed swords, and cross-
bow-shooting. In the welcome-jousts for Richard at Stirling, perhaps
lacking other challengers, James paid for an unnamed "person" to dress
up in damask and break spears against him. Pedro de Ayala, the Spanish
ambassador, found him so prone to dash into dangerous situations "that at
times I had to drag him back at all costs and restrain him myself to get
him out of them." At his own wedding, in 1503, James fought disguised
as the Wild Knight with an escort of savages, highlanders and borderers,
laying about him with such frenzy and disregard for bloodshed that spectators were amazed to see afterwards, tugging his helm from his sweat-
slicked hair, the king himself.

James was eager to cement his new friendship not just with a marriage, but with war against England on Richard's behalf. Almost as soon as Richard arrived, written orders for weapons-showings were sent to sheriffs round the kingdom. In February 1496, a tax of spear-silver was levied from barons, clergy and burghers to pay for a campaign. In June, couriers were sent to summon the host to meet James at Lauder. He himself supervised the collection of artillery from his forts and castles. By then, such loud war noises had reached England that Henry's Scottish fool, Harry the Scot, was being fitted out in "habilaments of war" to pour mockery on James's efforts.

John Ramsay's reports to Henry of September 1496 made clear that it was James, not the "boy", who was pushing for an invasion of England. James insisted on it, despite the truce concluded with Henry and despite visits, in 1495 and 1496, from English envoys led by Richard Fox, Bishop of Durham, to offer him Henry's little daughter Margaret in marriage. The rewards for threatening Henry were increasing; there was no reason to stop now. James also insisted on fighting despite some uncertainty, exaggerated by Ramsay, among his own lords. He would "in no wise be inclined to ye good of peace nor amity," wrote Henry's spy. His "young adventurousness" was likely to put all his people and the "boy", too, in jeopardy. "This simple willfulness," Ramsay concluded, "can not be removed out of ye King's mind for nae persuasion nor mean."

Foreign envoys, too, were drawn in as sympathisers. Early that September, Alexander Monypeny, Richard's old captain-of-the-honour-guard from Paris, arrived in Scotland as ambassador from the King of France. His brief, according to Ramsay, was to understand the king's mind and to work out whether James or Henry was to blame for the drift towards war. James seized on him, took him before his council and explained "how it was all moved on the part of England." As a result Monypeny became, to Ramsay's disgust, "but right soft in ye solicitation of this peace." According to a member of Henry's council, the arrival of the French envoy immediately caused the Scots to abandon their vague "arrangement" with the Bishop of Durham. Monypeny told Ramsay himself that it was no wonder the Scottish king was stirred to unkindness. Such encouragement was hardly needed, and especially not from Monypeny, who had also found his young prince again and was constantly in his company. "He and the boy," wrote Ramsay crossly, "are every day in council."

Henry did not underestimate the danger from Scotland and, espe-

cially, he did not want the other members of the Holy League to belittle
it. In May 1496 his envoy to Maximilian, Christopher Urswick, had told
the Venetian envoy Contarini in private that Henry

> was compelled to be much on the watch against the youth who
> says he is the son of King Edward and went lately to Scotland,
> whose king received him with many promises; the which king is
> linked by an indissoluble understanding and league to the King of
> France, and although the poorest king in Christendom, yet all his
> subjects are bound to serve him in person and at their own
> expense, during three weeks in the course of every year, on any
> expedition he may undertake; and for that period he can bring
> 50,000 men into the field.

Contarini's brother, then in England, had reported that Henry was "in
dread" of being expelled from his kingdom by the Duke of York. Dread
was not the word Henry would have wanted at all: he preferred a sense of
general suspicion, watchfulness in the face of danger. The truth was perhaps midway between them.

Ramsay claimed to have done his best to persuade the Scottish
nobles away from war. He had given James's brother, the Duke of Ross,
a crossbow, evidently a present from Henry, and had "communed at
length" with him, as a result of which the duke said he would not march
against the King of England. But Ross was a bending reed, helping at the
same time to get letters from Richard to Margaret, and James was
intractable, hell-bent on invasion.

Only two offers might have dissuaded him: peace with England on
his own terms, or a proper marriage with a Spanish princess in exchange
for a truce with Henry. As late as August, a Scottish envoy was still offering "perpetual peace with England and perfect safety for Henry from
York" if James could be given a princess of Spain. The possibility was
kept dangling before him by Ferdinand and Isabella, but no daughter
materialised. ("We have no daughter to give to the King of Scots, as you
well know," the Spanish sovereigns wrote to de Puebla, "but we must not
deprive him of his hope. On the contrary, we must amuse him as long as
possible.") James, however, knew he was being duped, not least because
he had intercepted the Spanish ambassadors' letters of instruction before
they arrived. An embarrassing showdown seems to have occurred in the
new garden at Stirling. "We are very sorry about what you say the King of

Scotland tried to do in the castle garden, especially since our ambassadors were there," wrote Ferdinand and Isabella, blushing to think of it. They remained unblushing about their own deceptions.

Since James felt that both Spain and England were playing with him—warming the wax, as the saying went, without setting it alight—he would play with France, their great enemy, and he would go to war. When Ayala arrived from Spain late that summer, with a brief to do all he could to persuade James to marry Henry's daughter, it was already too late. With his brand-new ally, or without him, James wanted to fight almost for the sake of fighting.

If love resembled war, the rituals of warfare were often close to those of love. Young men "did battle in love" and "embraced each other to joust"; the strokes were given and received on "targes", or breastplates, that covered only lightly the target of the heart. Tournaments often started with beguiling displays of beauty, only to end in blood and death. At the jousts in 1494 for little Henry, Duke of York, four young women in white satin gowns, riding on white palfreys, led in the four defending knights by laces of white and blue silk; before the famous tournament of Anthony Woodville against the Bastard of Burgundy in 1465, the Bastard accepted the challenge by honouring and touching a "flower of souvenance" concealed in a young woman's handkerchief. Yet, as in love, these delicate rules of engagement were a cover for violent compulsion. In the Woodville tournament, the Bastard was unhorsed when Woodville's pike crashed into the nostrils of his mount, and Woodville came within an ace of cleaving his opponent's skull through the eye-piece of his helmet. At the jousts of 1494 the best bouts were fought "furiously", and a combatant who moved away from the sword-strokes, either out of fright or short-sightedness, "was not praised for the voiding". "Good stripes" and "good strokes" were what spectators hoped for: shards of spears flying into the viewing stands, or the sword, often still in the gauntlet, smashed out of the hand. This was probably how James had hurt himself at Richard's wedding, with the sheer force of steel on steel, or pommel on glove, in the brawl of sword-fighting that followed the tilts.

From tournament to real war was often a small step for those who starred in both proceedings. The urge to do something warlike often came on, like love, in the spring. Jean Molinet described how shortly after Easter in 1489 "some young gentlemen of Hainault . . . wishing for honour and wanting to perform some exploit of prowess that would be famous in time to come" attempted to seize the castle of Arras from the French. In the same season the young Duke of Saxony seized the town of Arscot and then took, and burned to the ground, the castle of Luine. "It was a night in May," wrote Molinet, "when gentle companions in war are wont to challenge their enemies and to plant the May boughs, that the duke of Saxony rode out, flowering in prowess and in knightly deeds of arms." May boughs were symbols of a young man's arousal, in love as much as war; and it was under the hawthorn that William Dunbar dreamed of fields of young women dressed in green, the colour of new passion, playing dangerously with bows and guns.

Most sieges and wars began, as courtships did, as elaborate set-pieces, with challenges sent out by heralds and trumpeters and painstaking preparation of weapons, tents and battle clothes. Henry VII, gathering forces in 1492 for his "noble voyage" into France, ordered cloth-of-gold, precious stones and rich pearls for the garnishing of helmets and head-pieces, together with several sets of white armour, for a total cost of more than £4,000. If war soon showed itself as brutal and chaotic as ever, it was also ritual and spectacle. Sir John Paston in 1474 wrote that he would be very sorry to miss the French king and his great host if they came near Calais; a year later, he intended "to ride into Flanders to purvey me of horse and harness [armour], and percase I shall see the siege at Neuss ere I come again, if I have time . . . I think that I should be sick but if I see it."

This appeared to be James's view: sick if he did not see war. Richard's attitude, on past and future evidence, was exactly the reverse. He had presumably read the same books as James and, indeed, as Henry: Livy's *History of Rome*, the siege of Troy in various versions, the feats of arms of Alexander, the war commentaries of Caesar. Henry's son Arthur, then aged ten, was being coached from them in that very year. They were part of any prince's education and essential, too, for pseudo-princes. From these histories he could learn tactics, strategy, orders of battle, the laying of sieges and the management of men. From works like Christine de Pisan's *Fayttes of Armes and Chyvalrye* and the *Secreta*, Alexander's own rule-book, he could draw precise lessons in how to behave on the field: not to risk his own person, not to follow the enemy when it fled, to camp near water and, before battle, always to check that Leo was in the ascendant and Mercury in mid-heaven. Richard probably read all this, and picked up a little: the lesson, for example, that he should not land at Deal himself, but should send some troops ahead of him.

What he may never have received was physical instruction in war. Little Prince Richard fought with sticks and a two-handed sword and the next year disappeared into the Tower, his military education over. The child Piers in Tournai would have seen, at most, archery and crossbow competitions in which the rival bands gave themselves names such as "Joy" and "Good Loving". The boy in Portugal waited on a knight who may have trained him, or may have preferred to use him as decoration. Pages at the Portuguese court were not allowed swords of their own, and the favourite game for young men, besides girl-chasing, was tilting at each other with *canas*, or untipped lances made of reeds. ("A pretty dangerous game," Dr. Münzer thought.) The new-fledged prince may never have seen, or only touched in admiration, the costly white armour that Taylor the elder apparently brought for him when he arrived in Ireland.

Since then he had seen plenty of ceremonial warfare, sometimes of a semi-comic kind. On All Saints' Day in 1494, on Maximilian's return to Antwerp, jousts had been demanded by Claude de Vauldrey, who declared himself the servant of "the beautiful giantess with the blonde wig, the biggest wig in the world", and who claimed he had been inspired by Mars and Pallas telling him in a dream, on twelve successive Tuesday nights, to do this for Jesus. Sire Claude could not sit at table, or kiss a woman, until he had proved how brave he was. These jousts, which Richard would have watched from the best seats, were fought for nothing but two rings, though each was worth at least 10,000 *écus*. Like any prince, he had also done his share of hunting and hawking: good experience, many said, for deploying forces, discovering terrain, use of scouts, surprising the enemy, encounter and pursuit. Perhaps so, if you were not thinking more keenly of the bright arc of a falcon's flight, or the dewy greenness of the morning woods, or the girl you would rapturously unmake when it was over, perhaps on that very bed of grass from which the deer had risen. Little about Prince Richard, as he hawked in the mountains, suggested Edward IV's military prowess, James's bravery or Henry's gift for tactics. He was a prince for chambers and gardens.

Yet he seems to have come to Scotland prepared to fight. His servants included one Laurence the armourer, a Frenchman who can only have been assigned to make, and fit, armour especially for him. Laurence was at Richard's wedding, arrayed by James in a tawny gown, a velvet doublet and black hose, and was given an arming jacket for the tourney, in which he may have seen some action. In any event, his services had been judged necessary as the White Rose left Flanders.

So too had those of Roderick de Lalaing, Richard's old troop commander and, in Molinet's opinion, one of his "chief managers". Soon after his arrival James bought a small ship for him for £60, on which he sailed to and fro fetching men and munitions from Flanders. De Lalaing was from the line that had produced Jacques de Lalaing, praised by Georges Chastellain as the greatest jouster of his age. The whole family, Commines said, was remarkable for its courage, bravely serving generations of Burgundian princes, as well as producing a series of mercenary leaders and captains for the recent wars in Flanders. In 1491 Roderick, as a member of the Order of the Golden Fleece, fought with distinction in the lists held at Malines when Philip joined the order. There, among knights assuming the mottoes "It's done", "Noiseless", "Knock-out" and "Waiting for it", he took the motto *Riflez, Ranconnez:* roughly, "Lay them waste and make them pay".

De Lalaing was a typical international fighter, and a man after James's heart. He could fight in jousts, he could fight wars; it did not matter, though it helped, as in Scotland, if someone provided his armour and equipment. Although he was rough and illiterate, signing his pay-warrants with a wild "Z", James clearly liked him, giving him fancy clothes and calling him "Rodego", like a Spaniard. With Richard, de Lalaing got on much less well. The artificial world of the jousts, with its gilded mottoes and disguises and made-up names, happened to be one the captain excelled in: but he did so as a tough skilled fighter and not, like Margaret's protégé, as a bridegroom prettily parading in his white-and-purple fighting jacket.

By the summer, real war was approaching fast. Ramsay reckoned that the Scottish people, as opposed to their king, had no wish to fight; and if it came to war, he told Henry, "I doubt not . . . your Grace shall have ye best day-work of your enemies that any king of England had this C years." Aberdeen, certainly, preferred not to help with the "fortifying and supplying of the prince of England, Richard Duke of York", but obtained a licence for its citizens to stay home instead, joyfully announcing it through the streets with the ringing of the hand-bell. Some of the

Buchanans had to be pardoned later "for their inobedience and contemp-tion done to the king's highness" in not joining his war-force. But the prospect of a jab at England seems to have been broadly popular, even if the cause still made some Scots uneasy.

James worked his war-makers hard all through July, August and September. Since his men were bound to serve him, the army itself, as Ayala pointed out, did not cost the king a *maravedi;* but the equipment did. The accounts bristle with payments to wheelwrights, cartwrights, armourers and fletchers. Tallow and tar were bought for the wheels and axles, special carts for hauling the serpentines, chains for harnessing the draft horses. De Lalaing brought a contribution from Margaret of "lx of Alemans . . . and sundry pleasant things for the war, both for man and horse", conveyed in "twa little ships", as Ramsay reported. Deliver-ies were taken of arrows, stone cannonballs, gunpowder, saltpetre and sharp-edged "diamonds" to be fired from guns.

James, like many kings of his time, had a weakness for artillery. Ramsay sniffed that the king had "but little, that is to say twa great *curtalds* that were sent out of France, x falcons or little serpentines, xxx cart guns with iron chambers", but Ayala thought James's French guns were very good and "modern". Frequent royal visits were made to the gun-house in Edinburgh to chat with the Flemish or German gun experts, Hans and Henric (as armourers were French, so gunners were German), and to admire the pieces. James's favourite was Mons, later known as Mons Meg, a mighty cannon that was almost too heavy to shift. She was not used for the 1496 campaign, though she was there, and was doubtless shown to Richard as the king's pride. She was wheeled out a year later for a back-up invasion, minstrels playing before her as she rumbled along the street, but broke down before she reached the outskirts of the city. As she lay there at St. Leonard's, like a wounded whale, it took seven wrights two and a half days and thirteen stone of iron to make a new cradle for her, and eight ells of brightly painted canvas "to be Mons's cloth to cover her". The tenderness reflected the way James felt about her, his wonderful big gun, although she had not yet struck terror in any Englishman.

The main war-preparation for Prince Richard, typically enough, was his beautiful battle-banner: double red taffeta faced with single blue taffeta, on which a yard of single white taffeta was worked into a rose. Two ounces of gold foil and three leaves of a book of silver were used to pick out the centre of the rose and perhaps the rays of the sun behind.

More gold ornamented the taffeta ground. Each colour of the banner had its own virtues in war display: gold for the sun, "very clear and re-splendishing, virtuous and comforting", a colour to be carried only by a prince; red for fire, the most noble of the elements, symbolising a prince's eminence and majesty; blue for air, "receptive of the luminous influ-ences"; white or silver for water, cleanliness, innocence, the robes of Christ. The banner appeared incongruously among the lead, gun-shot, cart-chains and powder-horns, but it was meant to be a war-cry too, marking the position of the prince in the middle of the battle, where he was meant to be. Richard also had a battle-standard, four yards of linen cloth worked with half a book of gold foil, which may have displayed the Yorkist sun that was now to rise over England.

James, too, to judge by the accounts, was preoccupied with matters more decorative than carts and gun-stones. In the July accounts, where twenty-six entries covered artillery, twenty-seven had to do with the mak-ing or ornamenting of pavilions. Ayala mentioned this obsession: when James prepared for war, he wrote, he had thousands of tents made. For the 1496 campaign they covered the meadows at Restalrig, northeast of Edinburgh towards the Forth, where the soaked lengths of canvas were laid out to dry and the finished pavilions assembled. The king himself had several tents of different sizes for bedroom, council chamber, chapel and "ousting closet", or privy. On all these, as on Prince Richard's pavil-ions, the vanes were gilded and ornamented with pennants and the flaps held back with ropes of silk. There was so much sewing to be done, with bright blue thread, that children were recruited and given "drinksilver" for their efforts. At night, like the guns, the pavilions had men appointed to watch them.

Any army on the move, especially in uncertain weather, needed cover. Some kings were unfussy about it. Henry VII kept his tents for years in a house in Holborn for which, in 1495, four years' rent was owing, and his tent expenses were largely for patching up the tattered stock. Others took portable palaces with them. Charles the Bold on his Swiss campaign of 1476 had carried his jewels, tabernacles, reliquaries, archives, coffers full of carpets and Flanders lace, his solid-gold chair and three hundred complete dinner services of silver plate. His tents far out-shone James's, boasting glass windows in frames of gold. Yet James's emphasis on pavilions reflected, once again, how closely tournament and war resembled each other for those who promoted them. Every tournament field was lined with such tents, gilded and embroidered with the colours of the challenger, just as James and Richard laid out theirs.

These tents meant war; and yet, in the stories of Arthur and else-where, their other meaning was sport and delight. They were places of snatched passion, together with pantries, cellars, gardens, woods, attics, wardrobes and stables. It was in a pavilion outside a city that Sir Gawain and the Lady Ettard took supper together; a bed was made up for them, and there, over two days and nights, "she granted him to fulfill all his desire." Sir Lancelot narrowly escaped death when a knight, returning to the pavilion of red silk where he expected to find his mistress, found Lancelot in the bed instead. The pavilions of pleasure set up by Edward IV when he went hunting were presumed to be precisely that, furnished and cushioned with women.

Inside these pavilions, the language of war and the language of love were often the same. To "have ado with" was both to make war and to make love. A man's sexual organs were his "weapon", his "gear" and his "harness"; he came to bed, both partners hoped, with his *bonne epée d'armes* hard and ready in his hand. "Mercy" was shown both by the warrior, spar-ing his victim, and by the girl, admitting the aching lover to her body. The act of love itself was a "raid" or "sweet combat" after which, as after real battle, the combatants were exhausted. Love, like war, addled a man's wits until his lust was sated, but speedy success in either was a triumph. Henry VII's court poets in 1486 delighted to yoke together, in frames of full-blown red roses, his victory at Bosworth and his victory in the bedcham-ber, planting Prince Arthur almost at once in the belly of his queen.

Both love and war were young men's games. And appropriately enough, James and Richard—cousins in love, partners in war—camped in the pavilions before they set off in earnest. At the end of August, two or three weeks before the march towards England began, they were al-ready sleeping under canvas. The canvas was overlaid with silk, embroi-dered with their arms, and Richard's banner with the White Rose floated beside his door; but it still meant dewy-cold mornings, pallet beds and trips to the ousting closet across the grass. September was late for northern campaigns. "Ye inconvenience of ye season," Ramsay called this; and he was watching him.

Please your Grace anent the matter that Master Wyatt laid to me I have been busy about it, and my lord of Buchan takes apon him ye

fulfilling of it, if it be possible; and thinks best now in this lang
night within his tent to enterprise ye matter; for he has nae watch
but the King's appointed to be about him; and they have ordained
the Englishmen and strangers to be at an other quarter lodged but
a few about him.

The evenings were already drawing in: "this lang night". The civilian
English advisers, on whom Prince Richard relied quite heavily, were
sleeping elsewhere; around him were "the King's appointed", Scottish
men-at-arms. The tent, for all its grandeur, smelled of tanned sheepskins.
The Prince of England slept alone, or essentially alone, like a knight
before his induction.

The "matter" that Ramsay mentioned to Henry, and about which
he and Buchan had been so busy, was almost certainly his murder.
Everything pointed to that: the setting within the tent, the advisability of
darkness, the need to overpower his guard. The Earl of Buchan, James
Stewart, was another Scot happy to linger round the court and work
against James. Although he did not report direct to Henry, in this
instance the English king offered a reward for his services. ("I presented
my Lord your letter," wrote Ramsay, "of the which he was full glad and
well contented.") In the end, however, the deed was not attempted, or not
done. The murder of Prince Richard might have scotched the invasion
plans, dismantling the fair pavilions all over the meadows of Restalrig,
but not necessarily. James, once fired with a project, was difficult to turn
round, and the killing of his cousin would have been another pretext for
war. Besides, he had spent £110 on a new cloak for this: his favourite velvet cramoisy, lined and bordered with crimson satin, fit for any sort of
jousting, and the colour of fresh-spilled blood.

IV

THE ARMY MARCHED for England on September 17th. Three days
before, James and Richard commended their cause at High Mass in
Holyrood, then full of their guns, on the Feast of the Exaltation of the
Holy Cross. At the sight of that blessed wood, ran the Sequence of the
Mass, "kings believe, enemies retreat, and one man drives out a thou-
sand." *Reges credunt, hostes cedunt.* At the Offertory, the priest prayed that

the sign of the Holy Cross would protect them from "all the wiles of the enemy".

James paid for Richard's offering again: 14 shillings. He paid too for candles to burn on the altar of Our Lady and for a trental of Masses—thirty over the year, with daily recitation of *Placebo* and *Dirige*—to be sung before her altar and that of St. Triduan, the local patron. These were Masses both of intercession and of requiem for the souls of the departed. The two young men (bellies aching as they inspected the ordnance afterward, for this was a bread-and-water fasting day) expected hard fighting and deaths: or at least James did. Richard, always sunny, seemed to be thinking mostly of the people who would flock to him. Vergil said that the young man assured James "that great reinforcements were coming from England, and that many nobles would come over to him when they heard he was raising his standard." The king apparently believed him. Similar dazzling reports had reached Maximilian since the beginning of the year, "informing him that his affairs were prospering and that, through the disturbances imminent in England, he hoped for victory." In September, Richard seems to have told his European backers that he and James were taking the field against Henry with thirty thousand men, at least seven times the true number. But he was forgiven. Just before they left Edinburgh for the invasion James gave him a present of £36, spontaneous and unexplained.

In truth, even his inner circle was not secure. Ramsay observed that one of the boy's chief counsellors, George Neville, was wavering. Neville was the wavering sort. Pardoned after Bosworth, he was knighted by Henry for fighting for him at Stoke against Lincoln and Simnel, but soon drifted Yorkist again. "What ye think best me to do I shall gladly follow your mind," he wrote to an associate some years later, half-helping another Yorkist claimant, but unsure. In September 1496 he was both advising Richard and talking to Ramsay, agreeing that he would "quit him" of the boy if James and Henry came to terms. But Ramsay could hardly follow the contortions of his loyalty. Neville seemed to be not only in a "new consort" with the boy, but also keen to do Henry pleasure, "and I answered him that ye cared not for his pleasure or displeasure." So much for one of Richard's longest-serving friends.

His firmest support no longer came from his advisers, but from James, in his pushing and full-hearted way. Yet their interests were not always complementary. This much could be seen from the focus of the war. James wanted a raid on Northumberland, and never considered any-thing else, for he was doing all the planning; but Richard's support, such as it was, lay at the western end of the border. Ramsay noted the arrival on August 28th of a man from Carlisle who had been sent, so Ramsay was told secretly, by the brother of Lord Dacre, Henry's loyal lieutenant of the West Marches. Henry's spy believed there was a connection between the new recruit and the Skeltons of Cumbria, "for Michael Skelton that is here had ye conveyance of him." Edward Skelton was by then full-time in Richard's service; and Neville, too, had Carlisle connections. When the new recruit arrived, Richard welcomed him and took him at once to James as a token of the great rush of support he knew would come. But in many ways the king was not fighting this war for him.

Like Maximilian before him, James had managed to extract from Richard a high and material price for his support. On September 2nd, Ramsay wrote, the king had gathered his chief advisers in the council chamber and summoned "the boy" before him. The etiquette of the meet-ing was suggestive: not two allies holding a war council together, but the king in his council ordering Richard to attend. Ramsay always insisted on this contrast: the king and the boy, active and passive, powerful and pow-erless, though they were almost the same age and dressed in much the same fashionable splendour. James then demanded of his friend, as ex-pected, the castle and town of Berwick on the border, currently held by the English and well stocked with English guns; the restoration to Scot-land of seven border "sheriffdoms", unidentified tracts of the debatable lands between the kingdoms; and 100,000 marks, or just under £70,000 English, "for the listing of the king's army, and for charges made upon him and his company." All this was to be given to James, of course, when Richard was crowned king, the money to be paid within five years of his entry into his kingdom.

Ramsay reported that the boy did not agree to this immediately. He asked for a delay until the morning and then, with his advisers Neville, John Heron and William Lounde, went before James's council for more "lang communing". In the end he granted about half of what James wanted, refusing to surrender the sheriffdoms and reducing the sum of money to 50,000 marks, to be paid within two years. The agreement was then drawn up in writing.

In Flanders in 1495, ten weeks of deliberation had preceded the sign-ing away of England in Richard's name. Yet it was almost certainly Margaret and Maximilian who wrangled then, while their protégé sat silently by. In Scotland, the debate depended on him; and he resisted, at least in part, the demand to give his kingdom away. The bits in question were wild, far-flung and already half-Scots, but he clung to most of them, as well as cutting the colossal sum that James demanded. As his dependent in every way, he was in no position to bargain. But he tried, arguing for a night and a day, as if responsibility and the claim to a birthright meant something real to him. Perhaps they did, or perhaps he had grown sufficiently into the role to understand that they should. Whatever the truth, he was acting now like a man who cared for England.

On his coming to Scotland he had given a love-letter to a girl he did not yet know. On his coming to England he bore a proclamation addressed to a people he did not know either. Whoever he was, he had never engaged with them. At best, they had forgotten him; at worst, they dismissed him as a French or Flemish trickster. All this he knew. The proclamation, elegantly written and inordinately long, was intended to persuade them of his sincerity and urge them to join his cause. From a distance he looked lovingly, sadly and hopefully on England, as he had gazed on the unknown young woman with her white neck and her eyes like stars.

The voice behind the proclamation seemed to be his own, rather than that of any of the rag-tag people round him. It ran on for almost two thousand words, all of them shouted by common criers at the gates of a handful of English border towns. It is impossible to know how this torrent sounded in the ears of those who heard it in the early autumn of 1496. But it shows, more clearly than anything, the weight that sat on this young man's shoulders, whether or not it belonged there.

> Richard by the grace of God King of England & of France Lord of Ireland prince of wales. To all those that these our present letters shall see hear or Read & to every of them greeting
>
> & whereas we in our tender age Escaped by god's might out of the tower of London / and were secretly conveyed over the sea into other divers Countries / there Remaining certain years as unknown; The which season it happened one Henry son to Edmond Tydder Earl of Richmond created / son to Owen Tydder of low birth in the Country of wales / to come from france & Entered into this our Realm / and by Subtle false means to obtain the

Crown of the same unto us of Right appertaining: Which Henry
is our Extreme & mortal Enemy. . . .

The usurper-king had tried to destroy him in every way he knew, but he
had "graciously" escaped, and was now with "the right high and mighty
prince our dearest cousin the King of Scots":

> which without any gift or other thing by him desired or demanded
> to the prejudice or hurt of us or our Crown or Realm / hath full
> Lovingly and Kindly retained us . . . ascertaining you how the
> mind and intent of the foresaid noble prince our dearest Cousin is
> if that he may see our subjects and natural liege people according
> to Right & the duty of their allegiance resort lovingly unto us with
> such power as by their puissance shall move, be able of likelihood
> to distress & subdue our enemies he is fully set & determined to
> Return home again quietly with his people into his own Land,
> without doing or suffering to be done any hurt or prejudice unto
> our Realm or to the inhabitants of the same.

After that necessary reassurance, there followed a catalogue of Henry's
crimes. He had cruelly murdered "our Cousin the Lord Fitzwater Sir
William Stanley Sir Robert Chamberlain Sir Simon Mountford Sir
Robert Radcliffe, William Daubeney Humphrey Stafford and many
other besides such as have dearly bought their lives." He also kept "our
Right entirely well-beloved Cousin Edward son and heir to our uncle
Duke of Clarence" and others in prison, preventing them from helping
the true heir, himself. But for all his cruel wiles, the usurper was beginning to panic. He had sent his treasure abroad, and was preparing to
escape:

> And if he should be so suffered to depart as god defend it should
> be to the greatest hurt jeopardy & peril of the whole Realm that
> could be thought or imagined; Wherefore we desire & pray you . . .
> as ye intend the surety of yourself and the Common weal of our
> land your native ground to put you in your most effectual devoirs
> with all diligence to the uttermost of your powers to stop and let
> his passage out of this our Realm; ascertaining you that what per-
> son or persons shall fortune to take or distress him shall have for his
> or their true acquittal in that behalf after their Estate and degrees /

so as the most low and simplest of degree that shall happen to take
or distress him shall have for his labour one thousand pounds in
money / and houses and lands to the yearly value of one hundred
marks to him and his heirs for Ever

Richard moved on to the pitiful state of England: the "great and execrable
offences daily committed & done by our foresaid great enemy and his
adherents" against the Church, "to the high displeasure of almighty
god", besides "the manifold treasons, abominable murders, manslaughters, robberies, extortions the daily pilling of the people by dismes, taxes
tallages, benevolences, and other unlawful impositions." He, however,
came as a saviour, putting himself "Effectually in our devoir / not as a
stepdame / but as the very true mother of the Child / languishing or
standing in peril to Redress, and subdue the foresaid mischief and misrule." He would govern benevolently, "dreading god & having tender zeal
& affection to indifferent ministrations of Justice and the public weal of
the land." Good laws and customs would be enforced and preserved,
wrongs righted "according to Right law and good Conscience", trade
promoted, and all grievous exactions "utterly . . . fordone and laid apart &
never from henceforth to be Called upon but in such causes as our noble
progenitors, Kings of England, have of old time been accustomed to have
the aid succour & help of their subjects and true liegemen." He was not
so unworldly as to forgo grievous exactions altogether.

Lastly, Richard promised to pardon all those who had "imagined,
compassed or wrought privily or apparently since the reign of our foresaid
enemy, or before anything against us"; unless they had imagined his
death. By these gentle means, he hoped his enemies would be persuaded to
embrace his cause. Yet for those who did not, punishment would be
severe. Everything depended on the side his listeners chose.

And over this we let you wit / that upon our foresaid Enemy / his
adherents & partakers, with all other such as will take their false
quarrel and stand in their defence against us with their bodies and
goods / we shall come and enter upon them as their heavy Lord
and take and repute them and every of them as our Traitors and
Rebels / and see them punished according; and upon all other our
subjects / that according to right and the duty of their liegance
will aid, succour & comfort us with their powers with their lives or

goods / or victual our host for Ready money; we shall come and enter upon them Lovingly as their natural liege lord & see they have Justice to them equally ministered upon their causes,

wherefore we will and desire you & every of you that incontinent upon the hearing of this our proclamation ye according to the duty of your allegiance arready yourselves in your best defensible Array and give your personal attendance upon us where we shall then fortune to be; And in your so doing ye shall find us your Right especial & singular good lord / And so to see you Recompensed and Rewarded as by your service unto us shall be deserved.

RR

RR: Ricardus Rex. The first "R" was his monogram again, exactly as he had drawn it in January 1495. Although the original proclamation does not survive, the early-seventeenth-century copyist was careful to record that final flourish. In fact, Richard had improved on it, for the final left-to-right horizontal no longer petered out inconsequentially: it became the second, smaller "R", placed to the bottom right and ending with a graceful flourish towards the left. The monogram was instantly recognisable, and it was consistent. He had evidently been practising it, as he kept practising everything to do with being a king.

He had not been crowned, but he anticipated it. When he spoke of "our Realm", "our subjects", "our land", "our crown", he did not argue his right to the throne, but wrote as if he already sat there. Such pre emptive talk of kingship had been heard only once before in England's long history of seized crowns, when Henry Tudor had written that way after his landing in Wales in 1485. Yet Richard's letter carried this palpable distinction; that he was apart, both physically and mentally, from the land he loved and longed to relieve. One little slip, the phrase "our land your native ground" suggested, maybe more than he meant to, the distance between himself and the people he claimed as his.

Nor did he really know the state of his country. The picture of England that he painted, ground down by Henry's taxes, was to be truer the following year than it was in 1496, when Henry was only just beginning to levy the enormous sums that were to finance his war with Scotland: oppressions justified, of course, by his rival's presence there. As it was, Richard's listeners may well have wondered what "abominable murders, manslaughters, robberies [and] extortions" he was thinking of. Once more, as in the love-letter, these were standard phrases. The misery, like the beauty, was heavily overstated so that the lover might rise to the occasion: either to worship, or to rescue, the object he loved.

The most striking image in the proclamation was of himself saving England, "not as a stepdame / but as the very true mother of the Child / languishing or standing in peril to Redress." "Very" and "true" were the same word; he could not emphasise the fact enough, nor the depth of his involvement. A true father could have intervened just as effectively, but fathers did not languish, pining for pity and love, and they did not feel a mother's passionate compulsion, driven by emotion rather than strength, to run into danger to save her child. This, Richard was saying, was how he felt. Henry had no regard or care for England, beating it like an evil stepmother, blackening it with "Injuries and wrongs". He, on the other hand, though he would not hesitate to punish as a "heavy Lord" those who fought against him, meant mostly to "come and enter upon them Lovingly", as he hoped they would resort lovingly to him.

Few love-letters are entirely true, and certainly this one was not. King Richard did not hesitate to peddle false stories of nobles and treasure sent abroad on Henry's orders, and of the quavering king's intention to flee before him. The largest lie came early, with the assertion that James had asked for "no gift or other thing" that would be prejudicial to England. A few sentences later came something between a lie and a pious hope: the claim that James, once he saw "our subjects and natural liege people" returning to their allegiance, would go back home quietly, making no more trouble.

The proclamation went first; the army followed. The men marched southeast from Edinburgh across the wide, bare Lammermuir Hills towards the border, marked by the west-east course of the Tweed. James had gone ahead with his force and was waiting at Ellem Kirk, at the confluence of the Whiteadder and the Blackadder, for Richard to join him. He was anxious to get on, for he did not intend the expedition to take long. Despite the lengthy preparations, workmen had been recruited from the streets of Edinburgh—143 carters at a shilling a day, paid in advance, and 76 men with spades and mattocks to clear the way for the guns through "peats and mires"—for two weeks' service only. A quick border raid, not a war, seemed to be what James imagined. The king would start matters off, and when he saw England rising for his friend he would leave him to continue.

A special cart was needed for Richard's stuff, with an Englishman, John of Chamer, in charge of it. Richard's own army numbered about 1,400 "of all manner of nations", Ramsay wrote, but not notably from England. De Lalaing was there with his brother and his band of Germans. The appearance of the "Alemans" can be judged from an etching of the same year by Dürer: swaggering men in padded clothes rather than armour, equipped with swords and halberds but also with fashionable hats, trailing long feathers, slung across their backs. "Rugged men of the mountains", Vergil called the Germans who fought at Stoke, but Dürer's had found refinement somewhere.

A force like this posed problems of its own. Mercenaries were professional fighters, bound to the man who had hired them only by their pay and by hopes of plunder. A prince was ill-advised, wrote Christine de Pisan, to fight with great numbers "of strange soldiers that he knoweth not". They caused nothing but noise, tumult and dissension. If the weather turned bad, or if the pay was late, they would often take to pillage to seize back what they felt was owed them. (Germans, Molinet said, always wanted to be paid a month in advance.) They were not easily controlled, and they felt nothing for the land and people on which they practised their well-honed techniques. Like "hungry cats" and "ravening lions", they were fearless and merciless in action, and once their job was done the survivors would move on—the Germans with their drums, the Flemings with their beer-thirst, the Swiss with their blood-freezing war-cries—to terrorise, for pay, some other place.

The march south was difficult, and the weather cold; under his finery, James was wearing socks and thick black mittens. The army took two days to straggle across the Tweed, helped by local coble-men. One of the closed carts got stuck in the river, and was left to stand in the water all night while the rest of the force pushed on. With his beautiful standard and banner, gleaming with gold thread, Prince Richard was now in England. But his subjects did not appear to notice. No supporters came to him along the stony roads. Before the invasion Ramsay had thought that men from Northumberland were gathering "shrewdly" and "secretly" to him, making covert arrangements with Scotsmen, "and every day through them their vagabonds escape, coming to Perkin." A lot of letters had come, too, and Rowland Robinson had ridden to the border in July to stir up interest. But once Prince Richard was there in person—in a place where the wool on the sheep was so scraggly and thin that it was exempted from customs duty—the picture looked far different. As he rode past the isolated hamlets and the bleak hillsides, the response to him was complete indifference; or, worse, fear and hatred of the Scottish-German rabble who came with him. Some of James's cavalry, sent ahead to see if the English were arming, reported that everything was quiet. The people had retreated to the high stone towers of their lords, expecting, on frequent experience of visitations from Scotland, that all they owned would be destroyed.

Kings on the move customarily marked their way with little acts of pity and largesse. On the Scottish leg of the march, James's almoner had ridden with the army to hand out pennies to the sick and poor. The king's accounts for other years show payments to "a travelling man by the road", to "a boy that broke his leg and lay still there", and to "a poor bairn that took the king by the hand". In England, Henry VII paid generously for small gifts he was given on the road—new bread, cherries, a glass of rose-water—and paid too for crops that were damaged by his progress, or reaping that was interrupted. In these tiny exchanges, the king bound himself to his subjects by accessibility and kindness. He demonstrated the benevolence that was expected of princes and, for that, they thanked him.

Prince Richard knew about benevolence in the abstract. It was in his portrait, the expected expression of gentleness, and in his proclamation, with all that talk of tenderness and love. But now he was bringing "his people" not kindness, but war. As the Scottish army realised that no support was coming for this prince, they turned to the casual pillage that normally characterised their trips across the border. Richard's mercenaries joined in. The grand campaign became another routine raid. "[The king] laid waste the fields," wrote Vergil, "pillaged and then burnt the houses and villages. The natives who resisted he cruelly killed . . . having widely devastated the countryside of Northumberland, he would have gone even further, but his troops were so laden with spoils that they refused to follow him." James allowed this, since he had promised to go home peacefully only if the men of Northumberland came over to Richard's side. His henchmen had marched south wearing black hoods and jackets, like Death. They stayed to deal it out to the English who had so sorely disappointed him.

His friend did not stay. Barely two days into the march, hardly further than the English side of the Tweed, Richard left the force and returned to

Edinburgh. By all accounts, he and James had a bitterly angry exchange of words. Richard, in tears, asked James "humbly" to stop savaging his country and his people. Lordship was worth nothing to him, he said, if it was obtained "by so piteously spilling the blood and destroying with sword and flames the land of [my] fathers." Vergil added that he cried out: "Oh my cruel heart, that I am not moved by the destruction of my people!" The word was *meorum:* more simply, "mine". But they were not his. James retorted: "It seems to me, Sir, that you are meddling in another man's business and not your own."

The remark was devastating, and the "Sir," if spoken, made it worse. Chroniclers could not resist thinking that James said more; perhaps he did. He added, in Vergil's words, "that though Peter called England his country and the English his countrymen, no one had rushed forward to lend him their aid." Buchanan said he pointed out that the English, far from recognising Richard as a king, did not even recognise him as an Englishman.

"By mutual consent", according to Buchanan, Richard rode away. Somehow he knew where he was going, eventually splashing through the ford where the Tweed met the Till just east of Coldstream, the first town of size on the Scottish side of the river. James dispatched Andrew Forman to go after him and give him a present of £74 8s., the equivalent of two-thirds of his monthly pension. It looked like a peace offering, and so it may have been. The king seems to have been immediately sorry, on one level; but he stayed four more days in England to sack, burn and lay siege to Heton Castle, until the approach of an English force from Newcastle induced him to go home. De Lalaing, the proper soldier, stayed with him; the Burgundian captain was given another two horses "to the raid" to make his presence felt. The king's treasurer seems to have tried to cover up Richard's precipitate departure, deleting it without explanation from the accounts for the middle of the raid and inserting it later, so that the prince came home when the guns did. But the truth, as everyone knew, was otherwise.

What had actually happened on the ground by the time Richard left was little enough in the annals of warfare. By Henry's own estimate, the troops had marched four miles into England and "cast down three or four little towers". Within that range, to be sure, they had "done . . . great cruelty to man, woman and child," besides "burning, and other outrageous deeds", but it is hard to imagine, in that wild and open border country, that many people could be found to be hurt or many buildings to be burned. A solitary complaint survives from Chapletown of Esilmont, about the "wrongous spoilation, awaytaking and withholding", under cover of the raid, of eighty-seven gelded rams worth 4 shillings each. The undoubted violence was on a tiny scale; but it was more than enough to turn Prince Richard's stomach.

It is possible that he had never been so close to real war before. At Deal he had been out at sea, watching men killed but not seeing in any detail how they died. At Waterford he had stayed well away from the business of fighting. His most prolonged exposure to blood would have been the regular bleedings, essential to health, on which both Margaret and James insisted. These were done most propitiously in the spring, when the sun was in Aries. A little vein in the arm was opened with leeches to take away repletion of blood and aggregations of humours from the head, the liver and the heart. Nothing spilled, but the black unmoving slugs swelled in contentment until they were rubbed off with salt and the tiny puncture bound, perhaps with a poultice of mallows to help it heal. This done, people often lay for a while in bed in a darkened room, the windows closed "that no air come in to hurt us", staying still and quiet. Only so much blood coursed in the body, containing its inner heat and spirit; age and sorrows dried and slowed it, and once lost it was not remade. The thought of losing blood, and the sight of others losing it, may well have upset Richard as much as the feeling that the blood belonged to his people. Any of this would have been incomprehensible to James, who was so fascinated by blood that he sometimes paid his servants to let him bleed them or pull their teeth.

Violence, too, was known to upset people physically. The book of the heart, laid open to impressions, began to flutter and fold at the sight of it. William Caxton's *Dialogues* included instructions for wrapping in blankets a young girl seized with uncontrollable shaking after seeing two men fighting. In 1465, at the battle of Monthléry, Philippe de Commines related how the young Duke of Berry, then nineteen, tried to stop the fighting because "he had seen so many men wounded that he wished these things had never been started." His listeners were astounded at him. Berry was so inexperienced in war that some said he had never yet put on armour, and wore only a lightweight brigandine of satin covered with gilt pins. It is likely that Prince Richard too had gone to war still decked with fancies and fashions and, like Berry, was shocked by what he saw: shocked into pity.

In books, and in time of peace, the pity and mercy of princes was much admired and recommended. But in the heat of war, pity was itself pitiable. In Richard's case it was perhaps an act too, another piece of artistry to add to the confection of a king. "That glorious sighing," Hall called his appeal to James; "ridiculous mercy and foolish compassion." For Vergil, this was the finest performance of the young man's menda-cious career: "well worth noting", as he sarcastically remarked. Rather than stay, and expose his own fakery by his failure to win England over, he gave the excuse that he loved his country too much to carry on. Yet he may have meant it, for all the chroniclers mocked. All these incidents—the hesitation over Berwick, the "languishing" of the proclamation, and now the tears in Northumberland—may have been signs of an involve-ment that had grown deep enough to hurt him.

Nonetheless, the appearance was awful. When a new knight went first to battle or to the tournament, feeling his courage unsteady, he was told to remember whose son he was. To those still comparing this prince with King Edward—a comparison he had moved slightly away from now, emerging more and more in his own right as Richard—there was a disturbing difference. Edward had loved war as James did, inspecting his guns almost daily and naming two of them, ironically as it might seem now, after his sons ("Edward and Richard Bombardel"). He had also been notably courageous, fighting eight or nine battles in England by Commines's count, "in which he had always been present himself, and had fought constantly on foot, which redounded much to his honour." That manly blood appeared to have turned in Richard to milk and water. It was true that the Black Prince, victor of Poitiers, had sired an-other Richard who had been delicate, effete and soft-fingered, while Henry V, the great hero of Agincourt, had fathered a poor silly saint in farmer's boots. Perhaps it could be argued that sons often turned out con-trary to their fathers. Yet it was keenly disappointing, especially if this son was supposed to win back England.

The king's army came back home, walking the guns over the hills. A month later, men were still clearing up wheels and a cart "that the Englishmen left behind them by the gate [road]" at Haddington, sorry souvenirs. The dismal failure of the Great Invasion did not leave James's friendship with Prince Richard undamaged. Although the king had used Richard's claim largely as a pretext, he did not want vicarious humiliation. Vergil wrote that James, "having manifestly proved the man's vanity and impudence", paid less and less attention to him, "since the facts in no way corresponded with his false statements and promises."

There is some sign of this. After the raid, the accounts fell largely silent about Prince Richard, as if he was no longer a visitor at court or even an occasional companion. His one surviving letter from Scotland, written that October, was drafted in Edinburgh on a day when James and his court were in Stirling. For some months, possibly because Katherine's dowry was sustaining him, his pension seems to have gone unpaid. When it reappeared, the next May, the treasurer did not call him the Duke of York or the Prince of England any more; his servants were given his pension for "their master". At each point of payment, "York" was written in the margin in a different, paler ink. It seemed like discourtesy, but— since marginalia were so rare in the Scottish accounts—it may only have been a quick way for James, who reviewed them, to check that payment had been made. The sense survives, though, of a prince now pushed to one side. The Spanish sovereigns, responding on March 28th 1497 to information sent by Ayala, said that "since he proved himself by running away, and didn't stop running" during the invasion of England, "the King of Scotland keeps him now almost as a prisoner." Now that James had no further reason to protect him, they went on, it was quite likely that he would soon hand him over, or at least keep him in such complete security that he was no longer a nuisance. Perhaps then this *liviandad*, this frivolity, could be forgotten.

The failure of the invasion and the change of heart in James—overstated but still tangible—did not stop Henry mobilising his army for a huge offensive against Scotland. War was officially declared on September 25th. The king obtained a grant of £120,000 from Parliament and raised, in loans from his subjects, more than £50,000. In all, about £300,000 was gathered in and 44,000 men mobilised for a spring march northwards. James could have war if he wanted it; or he could give up the feigned lad, and have peace. James's response was to busy himself on the border that winter and spring, checking his forts and preparing men and supplies for the enormous onslaught that threatened from the south; but these efforts now appeared to have little or nothing to do with Prince Richard of England. James was going to fight on his own account.

Since the raid Richard's supporters had been steadily leaving Scot-land, and James was often glad to pay to see the back of them. By the end of September, as Ramsay had predicted, George Neville had gone. De Lalaing, with a farewell present of 100 marks, left on October 7th. Monypeny left on the 19th, taking a gift of £90 in silver and £28 for the two French heralds who accompanied him. "O'Donnell's man" had taken news of the fiasco to Ireland, to spread among the friends there. James gave Rowland Robinson £200 for the "red [paying-off] of the Englishmen to the sea, like as is contained in an indenture made betwixt the King's good grace and the Duke of York." Whether this was made preemptively, or after the raid, they had agreed, on paper and formally, that the enterprise of getting England back was over for the time being.

The Prince of England may not have minded as much as some sup-posed. His soldiers may have left him, James may have been disen-chanted, but he still had, in Katherine, one believer without reservation. Perhaps this was enough to allow him to live out of the public eye for a while, in a tiny ambit of disinterested love. He had been a wanderer, in whatever version of his life was true, for more than a decade, far away from and out of touch with whatever family had once been his. Now he had the makings of a new family, a household of dependents with ties far closer than disaffected merchants and mercenaries.

Besides Katherine there was also, by now, a baby son who bore his features and, in some form, the name he said was his. Both Bernard André and Andrea Trevisano, the Venetian envoy, thought that by the time Richard left Scotland he had children; Trevisano's word was *fioli*, suggesting these were sons. But the firmest evidence came from Maximil-ian, who received news of York's "one-year-old son" in October 1497. It is highly likely, then, that the birth of this child explained the mysterious payments made to Richard "at the king's command" in September 1496: the first just before he left for the war, the second as he "came home" from Northumberland. The birth of a first child was often a moment when kings gave presents to their friends. Perhaps, too, the squeamishness Richard felt at the violence to women and children in England was spurred not only by his "tender zeal" for his subjects, but by his longing to be with his own wife and newborn baby at home.

Babies, though mostly women's work, were still held, kissed and adored by their fathers, no matter how exalted. Edward IV, on his return from exile in 1471, had kissed his "sweet babies", according to a contemporary song, and carried his newborn son in his arms. A man far from home, informed of the birth of a child, was presumed immediately to love him as strongly as though he had seen him. A child—asleep in the cradle with his shock of new dark hair, nuzzling his own tiny fist, softly grasping a finger—extended a father's claim and blood far into the future. Prince Richard founded his own argument on being Edward's son, continuing his features, his character and his presence. An heir of his own now deepened and strengthened, as Katherine's love had done, his own cause and his own person as he had portrayed them to the world. Whoever he was, his little son now touched his face in utter trust and love. This too, like marriage, may have frightened Richard as much as it thrilled him. But he could not, as in Northumberland, mount his horse and ride away, nor would he want to. Like Edward from his exile, he had come home. He was never described as being there at any other point in his career.

V

RICHARD STAYED TEN MORE MONTHS in Scotland, living on James's hospitality. Once his pension resumed it was paid regularly, around the 10th of every month. Yet the king could barely afford to keep him. Ramsay said that James had already turned his chains, plate and "cupboards" into money to finance the raid of September, and fifty-four links of his great chain were sold off the next July and August. The loss of chain, in a prince just as dandified as Richard, underlined how expensive in every way their friendship had become.

They seem to have been together very seldom now. James was living openly with his favourite mistress, Margaret Drummond; Richard was with Katherine. From the payments for stabling his horses, it is clear that the couple were living from early 1497 at the royal hunting lodge at Falkland, in Fife, at the base of the Lomond Hills. Falkland was nearer to Katherine's family and, in its rural quietness, closer to what she was used to. She and Richard lived there with their own attendants, for Andrew Forman seemed to be back with the king, at least for the time being. James himself, though he liked Falkland, hardly ever visited. In April he passed by on his way to St. Andrews, sending a present of "apple oranges" by messenger, and he heard Mass at the palace chapel on the way back. The chapel was dedicated to St. Thomas, the doubting disciple, though in the end Thomas had decided to believe.

Falkland was a hidden place, remote from the bustle of court and government. James had rebuilt the west and south ranges, but the palace still had narrow old-fashioned windows, and its scale was small. Water came from an aqueduct laid across the meadows. New gardens with a lawn had been made at the palace, an orchard of pear trees planted and a park laid out where horses and cattle were pastured. To the north, or west across the orchard that was misted with white blossom in the spring, the view was of deep forest. To the south, the moor-topped Lomonds rose like a wall. There was wonderful hawking there; and little else perhaps, save loving Katherine and watching their tiny son learn to smile and crawl, that Richard felt inclined to do. Yet he may have been staying mostly because he did not know where else to go.

His backers in Europe still kept his argument going, but with increasing difficulty. Margaret, as ever, remained the most committed. The Spanish sovereigns did not doubt, all through 1496, that she was still his chief support in Flanders—despite the new trade pact with England that forbade her to assist him. They ordered Francisco de Rojas, their ambassador there, "to try to stop the old duchess favouring York and annoying the king of England." It is not known whether he tried. In October 1495 Margaret, through her council, had endeavoured to raise 2,000 Rhenish florins from Casius Hacquenay and other Antwerp lenders to pay for more artillery and supplies for her White Rose. This was presumably the shipment that de Lalaing brought in September, though there may have been others.

Even when that help came, the moment was unexpectedly painful. Ramsay happened to observe it:

> I stood by when ye King received [de Lalaing] in presence of Perkin; and thus he said in French. "Sir, I am coming here according to my promise, to do your Highness service, and for none other man's sake am I come here, for and I had not had your letters of warrant I had been arrested in Flanders, and put to great trouble for Perkin's sake"; and he come not near Perkin; and then came Perkin to him, and he saluted him and asked how his Aunt did; and he said "Well"; and he inquired if he had any letters from her to him, and he said he durst bring none, but he had to ye King.

De Lalaing would not have called the young man "Perkin", but his other discourtesies sounded plausible enough. He avoided him as if he had the plague and, when pushed by Richard's courtesy to say something to him, choked out a single word. Any contact with this young man now had to be at arm's length. It meant, as de Lalaing said, that Margaret no longer dared send him letters directly—although from that January, as Maximilian told Philip, he had been leaving her to carry on all necessary correspondence with him.

The letters de Lalaing brought to James were undoubtedly about Richard's business. But Margaret's White Rose still needed and sought her love and direction privately, for himself. This particular correspondence had always been so vital, to him and to her, that his reports on the Deal invasion had been sent to her rather than to Maximilian, as precedence preferred. The studied distance of his most ardent supporter would have been hard to endure. After that rebuff, he seems to have had nothing more to say to the Burgundian captain.

He wrote to her, though carefully and through several intermediate hands. In April 1496 a letter was sent to Margaret at Binche by the hand of a servant of the Duke of Ross, James's brother, via the duke's factor at Middelburg. The same servant, Davy Rattrie, an Aberdeen man who generally took salmon and trout to Middelburg and chasubles and chalices back, carried letters to her in April 1497 and again in September. These last were "White Rose letters", perhaps with a slight tang of fish. If Rattrie carried letters back, they were not recorded. But at Binche, sometime between the autumn of 1496 and the summer of 1497, a room below the chapel was renamed "Richard's room", redecorated with a traverse screen and eight feet of leaded glass, and fitted with a special wooden stand where Margaret placed "the candle of virgin wax that was sent to Madame from Rome". Margaret had never been to Rome, but expressed her devotion to the Holy City by using a guide book to pray the seven stations of the churches there. The holy candle, which enhanced those prayers and the indulgences they earned, was apparently lit now, as if in a shrine, for Richard's sake.

Maximilian, meanwhile, was persisting doggedly, but against the wishes of almost all the other princes of Europe. The "York exception", which he had written in September 1495 into his agreement to let Henry into the Holy League, had naturally been pounced on, though both Maximilian and the Spanish sovereigns had tried to keep it out of any copy of the treaty that Henry might see. Henry of course knew of it, and refused to join under that condition, and by December the other league members were again beseeching Maximilian to remove the clause. Henry also sent Lord Egremont ("not a man of much repute, only ten horses with him," as Contarini, the Venetian ambassador, mocked in his letter home) to Nördlingen to remonstrate directly. On the Feast of the Epiphany, January 6th, 1496, Ludovico Bruno read out Maximilian's reply to the Holy League ambassadors assembled before him. It contained, first,

a justification, purporting that the King of the Romans having no league or relationship with the King of England, the Duke of York, whom he firmly believes to be the son of King Edward, came to him; and that he considered it his duty not to abandon the duke, nor to fail in affording him all just and fitting favour.

A second clause purporting that, should the King of England approve, the King of the Romans offered to negotiate a ten-year truce or peace between him and the said Duke of York;

And thirdly, a paragraph to the effect that, should the King of England be admitted into the league, he was to be bound to attack the King of France next Easter with a strong and powerful fleet.

The ambassadors, especially those of Spain, told Bruno candidly that he could not send Egremont away with such an answer, "in the first place, because all the paragraphs about the Duke of York would only irritate the King of England." The meeting broke up with an apparent promise that Maximilian would concur; but the only solid things Egremont carried back to England were a gold cup and a hundred florins.

During the meeting, Contarini had publicly remarked how desirable it would be if Maximilian were to "drop the business of the Duke of York." The King of the Romans would not consider it. He explained that he could not abandon him for honour's sake, because he had received him at his court and shown him favour. But he did what he could to immobilise him, within honour's bounds. In January 1496 he told Philip what he had told the ambassadors: that he wanted Margaret to "press York so much [*pratique et faire tant avec Monsieur d'York*]" that he would conclude a truce with Henry, "for ten years, or as many years as possible". He had worked out a pension for Richard, too: 20,000 gold florins a year, which he would "do his utmost" to get the members of the Holy League to pay, assigned as follows:

The pope:	5,000 gold florins
Himself:	5,000 gold florins
The King of Spain:	5,000 gold florins
"The Venetians":	5,000 gold florins

Et demeura tousiours ledit d'York en son cuvertur, "And the said York will stay under wraps for good."

At this stage, however, there seemed no need for such a scheme. In February Maximilian received glowing letters from York, newly married, full of hope for the future. What a shame it would be, Maximilian told Contarini, if he were to abandon him now! What a pity if the diplomatic effort to bring Henry into the league impeded the duke's success! Especially since "were the Duke of York to obtain the crown, the King of the Romans and the league might avail themselves of England against the King of France as if the island were their own."

Contarini, as before, said he thought it would be better if Maximilian "left York alone and ended his friendship with him." Maximilian answered only that he would get a second opinion from his ambassadors as to how well things were truly going with him. If he ever asked, he seemed satisfied. When, in April, Henry sent Sir Christopher Urswick to Augsburg to try and reason with Maximilian, Urswick found a court full of people who supported York and Margaret, especially Bruno, who held particular influence over Maximilian. Urswick added that Maximilian continued to be ill-disposed towards Henry, "and keeps up communication with the King of Scotland about the person who is there." The contact was carefully indirect, but it persisted. Maximilian had no intention of giving up his protégé, not least because, as he told Contarini, "the fear that the King of England has of the Duke of York gave greater hope of obtaining what was required from him." When Urswick was sent home, at the end of May, the York escape-clause remained in the treaty.

Before he dismissed the English envoy, Maximilian discussed with the league's ambassadors the possibility of negotiating "some form of agreement" between England, Scotland and the Duke of York. He offered to take charge of those talks himself, Zurita said, and had in mind either peace, or a three-year truce. But all the momentum was now on Henry's side. The King of England joined the league that very month on his own terms of neutrality, without the obligation to go to war with France. As Maximilian gave in, he tried to insist once again on his old exception in the case of "the illustrious prince the Duke of York". Henry seems to have chosen to overlook that condition, as if he knew that Maximilian would not pursue it.

Still the emperor tried, as far as he could, to delay the ratification of Henry's entry by the other powers. "He has always made difficulties," explained an Italian envoy in January 1497, "owing to his feelings for Richard, the son of King Edward." The envoy was writing to the Duke of Ferrara, who, thanks to Maximilian's "feelings", had no reason to query the claim of Edward's son to England. Ludovico Sforza, too, was kept neutral, though he begged Maximilian in November for "more pre-cise information about the Duke of York, and about how the King of the Romans can support him in a way in which the whole league could co-operate." The question was awkward, but the prince was by no means dismissed. Although the great powers of Europe, save France, were now ranged on Henry's side, and the claims advanced by the young man in Scotland looked increasingly hopeless, the name of Richard, Duke of York, remained his in every country—England apart.

Ambassadors thronged the court of Scotland while Richard was there. They did not want to make alliances with him, as a prince might hope. They wanted to buy him. Ayala, the Spanish ambassador, was working to detach him from James by providing ships on which he could seek refuge, and presumably a pension, in Spain. Maximilian's plans for a pen-sion, in exchange for keeping quiet, had probably been transmitted to him. France offered cash down. Shortly before the invasion of September 1496, Monypeny volunteered to pay James 100,000 crowns for him. Henry, believing this was the only purpose of his journey, had threatened to delay the ambassador a year in England, but Monypeny got past him and made his bid. The object of the bid later told Henry that he had been offered, privately and directly, an ample safe-conduct and a pension of 12,000 francs a year. Ramsay said he could not think what the purpose might be in taking the boy to France, but Charles, James and Henry all knew; Charles could use the threat of him to stop Henry siding with his enemies in the league. James, however, refused the offer.

Pensions and friendship were one thing; but an exiled prince also needed strong public allies, men who could provide money and soldiers and, if necessary, a new base. These were much harder to find. Richard had by now exhausted his welcome in most of the countries of Europe, including the one he called his own. There, the executions and proceedings of 1495 had destroyed what little had existed of a coherent Yorkist party. In general, the English had no interest in him. They wanted peace, law and good government, and believed they enjoyed it under Henry. Richard of York's brief moment had passed.

Ireland, too, had lost its Yorkist flavour. The Earl of Kildare had gone for good, reinstated as Henry's deputy in Ireland in August 1496 with an extra sweetener of almost £500 and an undertaking, in particular, to defend the island against any further rebellion by Richard's main ally, the Earl of Desmond. Anyone found indulging in treasonous activities was also to be sent to Henry. Despite that, Richard seems to have written again from Scotland to Desmond, begging him for help to recover "his right in England". It is not quite clear at what point he wrote, but Desmond (already pardoned in April 1493 and potentially re-pardoned, if he proved himself amenable, in December 1494) had definitively defected in March 1496 and bound himself to Henry. That summer, Henry sent John Ramsay a copy of Desmond's bond to prove to James, and presumably to "the boy", that the boy's support was fading. Desmond had promised to be a "faithful and true liegeman" to "the king my sovereign lord Henry" and never again to help, receive "nor . . . suffer to be received . . . within any town or place being under my power" any of Henry's rebels. This time—though James, in Ramsay's words, "will scarcely believe it"—the earl appeared to mean it.

The search had to go on, therefore, for help from another quarter. Much of Richard's energy after the September raid may have gone into dictating letters to those he hoped would be, or had remained, his friends. Hence his letter from Edinburgh on October 17th to Bernard de la Forsa, a former ambassador of both Edward IV's and Richard III's, now living in Fuenterrabia in Spain. It may well have been typical of others he sent, written in the royal style ("Right trusty and our right entirely well-beloved") and sealed, as a king, with the signet Margaret had given him. The purpose of the letter, though well buried, was to wonder about "the good heart and mind that our most dear Cousin the King of Spain beareth towards us." He had not yet tried Spain.

And Spain had not yet tried him, or not with any consistency. Ferdinand and Isabella still publicly mocked him and privately hedged, wondering both how to use him and how to remove him from the picture so that England and Scotland could make peace. If they were to marry their daughter to Henry's son, as years of negotiations anticipated, they wanted England to be utterly secure both from Scotsmen and from Yorkist claimants. In August 1495 they had wondered whether they should get James into the Holy League, "to be more certain that he won't help him of Ireland", but events had overtaken them. When York fled to Ireland, they exulted that Maximilian had got rid of "the joke" at last; but when it appeared that the joke had perhaps been set at large to find support, and threaten Henry, from elsewhere, they found him less amusing.

Soon after he had devised it (and having extracted a written promise that de Rojas would not divulge it to Henry), Maximilian showed his "York exception" to the Spanish ambassador. Ferdinand and Isabella took it surprisingly well. Maximilian could not have done anything else, they told de Puebla in London. It would not have been honest of him to behave otherwise, "because York has lived in his palace and under his protection." ("York" again now, not "him of Ireland", and the *burla* forgotten.) Henry should understand this, and should join the league despite the clause. Even more generously, they offered to be guarantors between Henry and Maximilian for whatever they agreed about York, though Henry was not to be told this. At the end of January 1496, they reassured Henry through de Puebla that Maximilian had inserted the escape-clause only to keep York in his debt and to allay his suspicions. He was playing him along, as perhaps he always had.

In June 1496, the Milanese ambassador in Venice picked up a rumour that the Spanish rulers were going to mediate between the Duke of York and the King of England. For six months their letters had given this impression, of a balance between ruler and would-be ruler in which they themselves would make the vital difference. But there was also another scheme afoot. Since late 1495 Ferdinand and Isabella had been under great pressure from Henry to get hold of York themselves and hand him over. The Spanish sovereigns, spurred on by de Puebla, then began to be intrigued by a further refinement of that thought: that they would get York and keep him, thereby both removing a nuisance and driving Henry to the bargaining table.

The idea first surfaced in the autumn of 1495, when neither they nor de Puebla knew where York had gone. His disappearance made him all the more dangerous. "As for what you say, that you wish this York might come into our hands," they told the ambassador, "since we've made an agreement with the King of England to help him, it's certain that if we got hold of York we would help [the king] all we could, please God. And if it's true what they say, that York is captured, then it's all over."

In the next paragraph of their letter (for the Spanish sovereigns, as so often, seemed to be maturing their thinking as they dictated), a less unselfish plan was taking shape. They had it deleted afterwards, but they had toyed with it all the same:

> As it would be a very great disadvantage to the King of England
> in his negotiations with us, and a great security for us to make him
> fulfill all his promises, we should very much like, if possible, that
> our servants should take *him* prisoner, or that others should take
> him and deliver him to us. But . . . we are of the opinion that it is
> best only to cut him off from all assistance, and for the King of
> England to get him into his hands by his own exertions.

In January 1496 a rumour came, passed on from de Puebla, that York was actually in Spain. No, said Ferdinand and Isabella, he had not come, as though he would have arrived in great state and would not have been missed. At the end of March, replying to de Puebla's letter of January 21st, which had just arrived, they were "astonished" that the ambassador had no news of him and that, if "he" had gone to Scotland, their ambassadors to Scotland had sent them none, "because making sure that the King of Scotland doesn't help him or do anything for him is one of the things they're there for." The complaint was strengthened later: this was the main news that Ferdinand and Isabella wanted. Nothing the ambassadors wrote has survived, but gradually, as James showed his friend increasing favour, the tone in Spain changed. By April, Ferdinand and Isabella were consistently calling James's guest "the Duke of York", and were treading more carefully in the marriage negotiations with Henry "until we see where the affairs of the King of Scotland will stop." And at this point too the old idea, to get York into their hands, began to gleam again.

They clearly wrote about it to de Puebla, for on June 13th he thanked them for a letter they had sent him, "[which] gave me great pleasure, because . . . do not doubt this, you would have absolute control of

things here, if you had in your hands him who calls himself the son of
King Edward." He then showed the letter to Henry:

> And when the King of England had understood your Highnesses'
> secret instructions, and everything in your letter, he said that by the
> faith of his heart you showed in this your prudence and greatness
> and the love you had for him, and that if your Highnesses could
> quickly conclude that matter, there would be no delay or alterca-
> tion in these matters [of the marriage]; that otherwise he might
> indeed get more heavily involved in a war, having such a problem
> in the kingdom of Scotland, and he implored me that he wanted
> both matters concluded soon and in secret. And [he said] I might
> rest assured that if your Highnesses can do what you say in the one
> business and in the other business, he will do whatever you desire.

De Puebla said he was writing immediately to tell them this. "Above all, I
beseech your Highnesses to get him who calls himself Edward's son into
your royal hands. He is the entire obstacle. If you can have this person,
and take him away from France, that is the complete remedy for the present troubles." In a postscript, he kept pushing. "This is the whole thing
. . . once you have him of York in your royal hands, know for certain,
from what I can understand and from what they tell me, that they will
absolutely do your Highnesses' will *in omnibus et per omnia.*"

How the capture was to happen was either never discussed or has not
survived. The only hint appeared in a letter to de Puebla of April 14th:
"We shall not try to get him to come to Spain, but if we can get him in
our hands, we will try to do so for all the good reasons you say. There is no
more to be said on this matter." The Spanish sovereigns did not, however,
warm to the next part of the scheme as Henry envisaged it, that they
should send "him of York" as a prisoner to England. "If we had him in
our power," they told de Puebla, "he would not be a person to be kept by
us, but the King of England would request us to deliver him into his
hands—a thing which we would not do for any consideration whatso-
ever."

During these months Pedro de Ayala too—whose relations with de
Puebla were famously poisonous, though they were meant to be working
in secret concert for the marriage and the peace—was trying to persuade
Richard to leave Scotland for Spain. Ayala was a charmer, a dancer, a
hunter and player of cards with James; "not learned", Vergil said of him,

but clever and exceedingly discreet. He would have encountered the Prince of England on the dance-floor or out hawking, and would have befriended him in his easy and laughing way. He had arrived just before the raid on England and had gone along, unusually for an ambassador, to observe at first hand not only James's wild foolhardiness, which he reported, but the timidity and distress of his friend. His surviving dispatches, packed with information and colour but relatively rare, never mention the young man, and it is hard to tell what he thought of him. His sovereigns, however, were displeased with Ayala for "so easily believing what the Scots tell him."

Ayala, in fact, was playing a double game they would have approved of. Zurita said the ambassador had been given a commission to ensure that the King of Scotland delivered "this false duke" up to Ferdinand, and that the King of England "should never have him". He was therefore working on James to persuade him to drop his prince; but James, to lull any suspicions, was to keep paying Richard his pension as usual. At the same time, Zurita said,

> [Ayala] gave him of York to understand, as if in great secrecy, that peace was inevitably going to be concluded between the Kings of Scotland and England, to put him in suspicion and fear. Distrust of this peace put him in such terror that he determined to leave [Scotland] to go to Ireland, where he would put himself in a Spanish boat that had carried fish, and sail from there to seek a safe-conduct from the Catholic king.

Whether or not the full particulars of this scheme were laid out by October, Ayala was already mentioning Spain to Richard. The ambassador was also writing back to Spain that he had some hope of getting the Duke of York, and Ferdinand and Isabella were urging him "to accomplish this in every respect." ("Write to us particularly about all this," they begged de Puebla, "and tell us what must be done.") They hoped to achieve this "secret thing" before making any public announcement of the marriage of Katherine and Arthur; it was that important.

At this point, Richard wrote to Bernard de la Forsa. It was only prudent to check, from some knowledgeable source, what his fate was likely to be when he got to Spain. De la Forsa was the best man to know, for as Edward's envoy to the Spanish court he had often been instructed to talk freely to Ferdinand and Isabella, trying by his discretion and "by all means of policy" to draw what was necessary out of them. Ferdinand was perhaps particularly mentioned in the letter because Isabella had been tried before, to no effect. She may have been more sceptical; certainly, when she wrote to de Puebla on her own account in July 1496, she dismissed the Scottish nuisance as "that boy", a term never used for him when she and Ferdinand wrote jointly. Both sovereigns had told de Puebla, though, that they had read "his" letter and had spurned it equally.

Yet Richard's inquiry about Ferdinand's state of mind was almost forgotten in his letter. Instead, he did his utmost to recruit a new friend, a suddenly remembered and obvious one, in a landscape that was now almost barren of supporters. The theme of love occurred repeatedly, as if repetition could bind the wise old diplomat to the tenuous claim of a young man he did not know. The loving counsellor, if he showed Richard the same love he had shown his father, would in turn be rewarded even more lovingly. Richard would be his "good lord", his pledged and dependable protector. He asked de la Forsa to "exhort move and stir our lovers and friends" to advise him what best to do. Lastly, he signed himself "your friend Richard of England", in a hand so expansive, so boldly and informally assuming friendship on the other side, that the words "your friend" squeezed "of England" almost off the edge of the page. The letter was then folded several times, very small, and tied with a ribbon on which the royal seal was set.

There is no sign that de la Forsa answered. He may not have been inclined to for, despite his Yorkist service, he had worked more recently for Henry too. Like his son Anthony, who was apparently still at Richard's side, he was happy to serve both the White Rose and the Red. He was paid a regular annuity of £40, topped up by larger rewards, in the late 1480s and early 1490s. The work of "our trusty and well-beloved Bernard de la Forsa", as Henry too called him, was never specified, nor his exact standing in relation to the king. But he was certainly paid on occasion for spying for Henry in Brittany and later in Spain, invaluable work. It is possible that Richard did not know—and certain that Anthony, himself so recently in Henry's pay, would not tell him—that Bernard's love was likely to be much more constrained than the love that was poured out on him.

Richard's letter ended up somehow at the Spanish court, either sent on directly or intercepted before it had reached its destination. His letters

seemed to have a habit of ending up there, and perhaps not simply because the Spanish sovereigns wished to read them and laugh. Their secretary Almazan endorsed this one as he had endorsed the one to Isabella,
but with different words. This letter was now "from the Duke of York",
their own possible pensioner, puppet and prince.

The greatest pressure on James to drop Richard, however, was coming from England. By the summer of 1497 Henry had spent at least
£60,000, an almost unconscionable sum, equipping an army and a navy
for war. Robert Clifford's registers of expenditure, as master of the ordnance, show how frenetically busy he now was opposing the young man
he had once supported. It was Clifford's job to draw up contracts with the
twenty-two ships, from ports all over England and from abroad, that were
destined for Berwick with timber, cannon, serpentines, carts, "crows
of iron", barrels of gunpowder, gun-shot and gun-stones, axes and pad-
locks, hogsheads of vinegar, and all the gear of war. There they were to
wait "until such time as the king's grace shall come thither". Ordnance
and artillery were brought too from the palace at Kenilworth, from the
Tower and from Calais, emptying the forts elsewhere. Some pieces had
aggressively Tudor names: Windsor, the Rose, the Greyhound. One May
afternoon in 1497, on the Tower walls, Clifford arranged a demonstration
of the guns for Henry, but it was James and his prince who were meant to
hear them firing.

By June 1497 the fleet had sailed north, one-third of the king's forces
were committed against Scotland and another third were making their
way to Newcastle, where Lord Daubeney was to command them. Henry
had also stepped up his own diplomacy, continuing to offer James the
hand of his six-year-old daughter Margaret as well as peace, but James
had to relinquish his guest first. Revelling in the attention, he went on
refusing. On grounds of honour and the bond of blood by marriage,
Vergil said, he could not deliver the young man up to death. Yet the pres-
sures from both directions, England and Spain—with the pope, equally
anxious to see Europe united against France, adding his weight—were so
intense that James was bound to yield eventually. Vergil thought the king
had in any case understood "that Peter was not Richard the son of
Edward"; but if he did, James never said so. De Puebla was probably
closer when he said later that it was Henry's mobilisation, the sight of
"the ears of the wolf", that finally cooled James's appetite for war. By that

June, the question was not whether to divest himself of Prince Richard, but how to do so as fast as honour would allow.

His friend may have sensed this for some time. Though Richard made a good show of buoyant determination, he cannot have missed the indications that his days in Scotland were numbered. There is some sign too that James hoped he would leave earlier, just after the failed invasion. The ship in which Richard eventually sailed was bought by the king that same October, with some difficulty, from a couple of "Frenchmen", actually Bretons, Guy Foulcart and Jean Peidzoun. The *Cuckoo*, as she was called, was not a large vessel; she cost something over £100 Scots, or perhaps 40 "pounds English," as Ramsay would have put it. After a bit- ter spat in court over the silver owed for her, James ordered Peidzoun to furnish her in the Duke of York's service. From the end of 1496, there- fore, the ship that was to take Richard away from Scotland was already in dock, being patched up in all the ways necessary to transform a merchant vessel into a craft for a prince.

Yet her name remained, and the cuckoo was a bird associated every- where with foolishness. In Sebastian Brant's "Ship of Fools", idiots held cuckoos on their wrists when they went hawking, and the cutaway fash- ions of Malines and Leyden, as favoured by presumptuous peasants, were said to have a cuckoo embroidered on the (extra-wide) sleeves. The cuckoo was also famous as an interloper, muscling its way into the nests of other birds demanding to be fed, though its plumage showed clearly that it must be an impostor. The connotation of foolish generosity to a mas- querading prince was difficult to miss, as was the echo of that prince's empty claims: for the boaster was like a cuckoo, said *The King's Book*, "that can sing no song but of himself." The name may well have con- tributed to Henry's later remark that his enemy had been "set full poorly to the sea by the king of Scots."

They parted in the first week of July 1497. The farewells were ap- parently said in Edinburgh, with little of the ceremony that had greeted Prince Richard's arrival nineteen months before. Vergil said that James, summoning the young man before his court, reminded him of his kind- ness to him and pointed out, too, that nothing he had done for him had borne any fruit in England. He had tried his best, but his friend had made too many "empty promises" of the favour he would find across the border. From now on, he would have to pursue his claim himself. That claim, James believed, was still important, but he would have to bide a better time somewhere else. Having said this and more, Vergil wrote, the king ordered him to leave.

This does not ring true. James was dismissing Richard with honour and as his friend, with the wife he had given him still lovingly beside him. But the moment was no easier for that. Richard's reply was apparently an impressive example of dissembled politeness, concealing the devastation he felt inside. He said he was deeply grateful and would not forget. "Having understood the king's wishes," said Buchanan, "he was utterly cast down by this. . . . But having accepted so many benefits without being able to repay them, and not wishing to seem ungrateful, he accepted the king's orders with equanimity." He left Scotland, Buchanan went on, "laying down nothing of his simulated greatness of soul."

Their belongings were loaded onto two carts and, in slow convoy, they made their way west to Ayr. James had arranged to pay for Richard's board and lodging in his "chamber" in the town, the word still implying his princeliness, since only men of standing ate in their rooms and not in the common tavern. His meals and incidental expenses there, for perhaps one night, came to £10 16s., extravagant to the last. Andrew Forman remained in attendance on him. Ayr—a brewing town as well as a port, smelling of fish and beer, loud with seagulls—was full of the prince's men; James paid to lodge them too, and for the hire of other horses to take thirty of these men to the sea.

James himself was not there. Some of his horses were in the town, and men were paid for walking them, but on July 9th he was at King-horn in Fife, on the other side of the country. As always, he had done his best for Richard, even paying him the July instalment of his pension early, on June 27th. Katherine was given a last present from him of three and a half yards of tawny Rouen cloth for a sea-gown, and two and a half yards of black Lille cloth for a cloak: sensible, unluxurious travelling clothes. His last present to Richard was to pick up the tab, through Forman, for the "quitting out" of the prince's brown horse, which was left behind in Ayr to cover £14 in debts.

The company that sailed from Ayr was not a war-party. Richard was transporting himself and his family away, as if his whole claim to kingship-in-exile was now contained in the timbers of one small ship. The *Cuckoo* was provisioned with a good Scottish diet of oatmeal, bis-cuit, six stones of cheese, a hogshead of herring, twenty-three sides of mutton, seventeen carcasses of salt beef, twelve large dried cod, beer for the men and four pipes of wine for the nobility. Cider, a rarity in Scotland, seems to have been laid on especially for English tastes. The equipment, however, was spartan: five drinking vessels, some barrels of water, a cauldron for cooking, coals and peat for the fire, a hundred candles for light.

Most strikingly, however, the *Cuckoo* contained no weapons and no soldiers. She was just a merchant ship, as she had been before. They had even left Laurence the armourer behind. Protection was provided by two renowned sea-captains, Andrew and Robert Barton, in their own ships (Andrew had also provided the cider, biscuit and beer). Guy Foulcart, the previous owner of the *Cuckoo*, was still in charge of her. If thirty horses had gone towards the sea at Ayr, there were presumably thirty men with Prince Richard, but they were probably attendants and the small, established circle of advisers. The number of his supporters had not grown since his arrival in Scotland, except for the beautiful young woman in the tawny sea-gown and the little boy, wide-eyed, squirming or asleep, held tight in his nurse's arms.

His family's presence on the small and unarmed craft suggested that they were sailing for some unknown safe-haven. But as far as James was concerned, his friend was heading directly for the land he claimed was his. The agreement between James and Foulcart was that the captain should "only [*dumtaxat*] restore the Duke of York to the shores of England". In effect, any landing of Richard in England would be, as James well knew, an act of war and probably an act of suicide. But the western parts of England were restless, and it seems that James and Richard had devised a two-pronged plan: Richard would attack from the southwest, James from the north. As yet the plan was ill-formed, and there was little hope of proper co-ordination; but as the Prince of England sailed, James's guns and pavilions were being assembled again and the troops and masons recruited. Robert Barton knew all about it, telling the Breton pirates who subsequently captured his escort ship that he was in the middle of "making war on England". Certainly Richard let James know when he arrived in Cornwall, as if this was expected, and as he left Scotland he seemed to announce that England was his destination. His parting words may be paraphrased in Adam Abell's vernacular history: he was passing with Katherine to England "to win his father's crown as he alleged."

There was also, by Zurita's account, that counter-offer from Ayala, that "the duke" could be smuggled by fishing boat to Spain if he crossed

to Ireland first. Whether Spain meant a trap, or the royal pawn's treatment
he had found everywhere else, was still unclear, since Ferdinand and Isabella had never entirely opened their minds to de Puebla on the subject.
But at the solemn leavetaking of Richard and James, the last embrace of
silk against steel, it is likely that both friends were keeping certain options
secret.

To the very end there had been hard bargaining. By sending Richard
away with a modicum of honour, James had avoided being made to give
him up to Henry. The King of England, of course, had wanted him
badly. He emphasised in his instructions to Bishop Fox, who was given
a new commission to negotiate on July 5th, that the surrender of Perkin
in person was the most important thing. If the Scottish king would not
"make delivery unto us of Perkin Warbeck" (and Henry knew he would
not), then Fox was to suggest that James and Henry should meet in Newcastle and talk about it, in the hope that "more fast love and affection
should grow betwixt us." Henry wanted pledges from James, at least, that
he would send an embassy to him and that "other things concerning the
said Perkin Warbeck be performed and accomplished." The pledges
were to take human form: two men of good estate and condition, such as
two earls or their sons and heirs, or two barons, would be sent to England
and kept there until Perkin was given up.

As usual, Fox had a second book of instructions to "keep secretly
unto yourself". He was to try to get Perkin "by all wise means to you possible". But if the talks seemed likely to break down altogether, he was to
ask the Scottish spokesmen "to send to their prince for further understanding of his mind in this behalf." The essential was to keep James talking
and not to risk war, since despite all Henry's preparations—including,
that July, the setting of £60 worth of new jewels in his helmet and his
sword—"our subjects [are] sore wearied, and also the issue of battle is full
uncertain." But these feverish schemes were moot as soon as Fox arrived
in Scotland on July 10th, for James no longer had the young man with
him.

In his instructions to Fox, Henry expressed amazement that James
could cling so fast to his protégé, "since he is not the person that he surmised to be when he obtained his safe-conduct of our said cousin, as it is
well known through all these parts of the world." It could not hurt his
honour, surely, to give up a man who had deceived him. Ferdinand and
Isabella, too, thought that ever since the failed raid James "was less in-

commoded about doing what our brother the King of England wanted in the case of the one who is in Scotland." To James, however, Richard was the same, without another name or lineage than the one he had always claimed. Despite his disappointment in him, and the necessity now of dropping him, he never seemed to alter that opinion. It was, of course, difficult to do so, for Katherine's honour and Huntly's as well as his own. Richard was his cousin: tied to him by marriage, tied to him by blood, taken in as an exile and a supplicant, fought for, loved.

Yet James's best efforts had not come near to winning him England, and the obvious symbolism of the failed invasion was not lost on Henry. At the end of the *Roman de la Rose* a great assault threw down the walls of the rose garden, and the lover, forcing his staff through the narrow gate, at last plucked the blushing rosebud from among her agitated leaves. Not many months after the feigned lad left Scotland, Johannes Opicius, one of Henry's court poets, produced his own version of this scene. The rose garden was England, bright with Henry's red roses of virtue, honour and vigour, swelling and propagating with the king's seed. The Beaufort greyhound and portcullis guarded the gate against intruders. Who, Opicius wrote, would be mad enough, *quis demens*, to want to sully these scarlet blooms and make their perfumed brightness fade away in sorrow? Only a false, base, foolish duke, *dux perperus*, who rushed in to rape the rose and then, rebuffed, could do no more than scatter his sterile seed on the ground.

CHAPTER SIX

King Perkin

From Ayr, the ships sailed south. They were hardly a royal flotilla: the *Cuckoo*, escorted by two pirate craft, rocking through the blue-gray waters of the Irish Sea. In the low airless cabins where the king-to-be and his queen-to-be took refuge with their attendants, there was probably little appetite for the cold salted beef that was served to their table. And by the rocking flare of the night candles, carefully watched by some servant, there were probably few plans made of any lasting consequence.

The enterprise—"the great abusion", as Henry called it, or "our Righteous quarrel", as Richard did—had now been playing on the stage of Europe for almost six years. Three or four rulers were still behind Richard and several were staying neutral, as if his claims and Henry Tudor's could be given equal weight. He had done that much. But he could not win over, or even much interest, the country that now lay dimly to the east in the heaped-up hills of Cumbria: his country, as he kept saying.

Time and again—in Margaret's letter to Isabella, in his own proclamation, in his exhortations to his followers before each attempted invasion—he had hoped and expected that the lords of England would join him. They would not. Lord Fitzwater was the only English peer who had backed him, and bastard George Neville the only representative of the great houses. The gentry and merchant classes, too, much preferred security and prosperity to the rash dreams he offered, whether true or false. His English supporters had been overwhelmingly the unlettered and poor: yeomen and labourers at Deal, escaped vagabonds in Northumberland. Robert Fabyan—no sympathetic eye—concluded that his followers everywhere had been "lewd", low-class and dishonest, and his chief advisers, too.

His enemies noted that he appealed particularly to the simpleminded and barbarians. More often than not they came from the west, bordering on the great ocean, or from lands of impenetrable bog and forest. You could argue that even James and Huntly, his noblest supporters in Scotland, had a streak of savagery in them, the natural attribute of rulers over wild places. James in the Isles, speaking Gaelic, in his thick travelling clothes and with the taste of herring on his fingers and his beard, was not so easy to distinguish from his subjects.

The essence of barbarians was that, like wild beasts, they preferred to retreat and hide themselves in forests or in caves. The king's rebels and enemies, according to warrants issued for them, often fled to such secret places to nourish their malice unobserved. So Bernard André made Perkin, too, a cave-dweller. He called him Cacus, after the base fire-breathing villain of ancient Rome who crept out of his cavern to steal the cattle of Hercules. (Hercules, of course, eventually killed Cacus, but André did not get that far with his story.) Although Cacus boasted and threatened wildly, shooting great flames from his mouth, Hercules/Henry made him run away, "nimbly without torch or lantern", and hide himself in his cave again. This timorous monster, André explained, was "by nature a great robber, who had never done anything else but rob"; and the cave where he hid, with other ruffians and cattle-stealers, was "in Ireland among the savages".

To Henry, this explained why the feigned lad so often went to Ireland. Though he had been fêted and embraced there in cosmopolitan places and by Anglo-Irish lords, the core of his success, as both the king and Polydore Vergil believed, was the primitive credulity of *les Irlandais sauvages* outside the English Pale. It was perhaps not his claims that had lured these men at all, but only his clothes: as Edward Brampton said, "that little bit of brocade". Neither speaking nor understanding English, the savage Irish could hardly judge him otherwise. People had seized on his "birthmarks" too in Ireland, just as they emphasised the marks of their chiefs ("Red Hand", "Large-eared", "the Freckled") and took these for signs of election. They also noted, perhaps more keenly than others would have done, the heavy rains and "English sweat" that preceded Richard's coming, the star that shone the Christmas he was with them, and the comet that blazed for two months as he left again.

Though intelligent men soon dropped this folly, the *sylvestres homines* of the bogs and wild places continued to run after the false Plantagenet, and would doubtless do so again if he returned. Henry's officers, sent, in Vergil's words, to cleanse the country of the contamination Peter had left wherever he stayed, found that the filth was lasting. It seemed that he had learned two years earlier, however, that the wild Irish could not make up an army for him. Their organised troops were largely of two kinds, common foot-soldiers, called kernes, and armed retainers, known as gallowglasses: the gallowglasses grim brutes, the kernes light-armed with javelins and darts. Some wore primitive brigandines stuck with nails, but their custom was to fight "naked", without armour, as they had fought for Simnel at Stoke with astonishing bravery and futility.

In the late summer of 1497, nevertheless, the would-be king was back in Ireland. It is possible—since hints of a second child coloured these weeks—that some family crisis, rather than strategy, drove him west rather than to England. But he also may have meant to raise troops there. He was spotted on July 25th in the south, "in the wild Irishrie", as Henry put it, having probably spent the best part of three weeks at sea. John Atwater at Cork welcomed him with his old faithfulness, as did Barry of Munster, and the people of Cork, "some out of affection, others for desire of change", flocked round him as they had done before, but no other friends remained. In August 1496 Henry had issued a general pardon to all the boy's supporters in Ireland, Barry and Atwater explicitly excepted, and the next month Kildare (now Henry's lieutenant in Ireland) had arrived to root out rebels. O'Donnell and O'Neill, the two northeastern chiefs who had helped Richard in his wanderings, had sent letters to the earl as soon as he landed, saying they would be ruled by him. Shane Burke submitted too, offering to go to England and seek the king's grace in person. All took a bizarre form of the oath of loyalty, since they could barely speak or understand English. Their appeals to Kildare had been written by their priests in best church Latin, and they themselves could not sign them in letters of the alphabet.

It seems that Richard may have been enticed to Ireland by Sir James Ormond, who had commanded Henry's forces against him in 1491 and 1492. Ormond had grown warmer to Richard as he had become resentful of the newly empowered Kildare. He kept an army of kernes and gallow/glasses whom Henry Wyatt blamed, in 1496, for wasting and "desolat/ing" much of the country. Conceivably, their wildness might have been harnessed for Richard's cause. But on July 17th, nine days or so before his prince landed, Ormond was killed in an ambush in the fields outside Kilkenny, a typically Irish blood/feud settled in mud and grass. Ormond had quarreled with Sir Piers Butler ("Piers the Red", as the Gaelic/Irish called him), and when Butler had given his allegiance to Kildare, as he later explained, Ormond "showed openly that wheresoever he might find me he would kill me, and over this took goods and cattle from such as he knew were towards me." When the two men met, by chance Butler said, they fought together "so long til God had wrought his will upon him." Butler told Ormond's brother, who held office at the English court, that the dead man, "upon his comfort and special desire moved, caused Perkin Warbeck to come lately into this land for the destruction of the subjects and possessions here of our Sovereign lord, like as his High/ness shall understand within brief time by the report of such as were privy unto the counsel of the said Perkin."

So the close counsellors, once again, were betraying their prince, and the man who may have invited him was dead. It was a dreadful time to come in any case, with "very great, grievous famine throughout all Ire/land", as the Annals of Ulster reported. In Meath, five ounces of wheat now cost as much as a peck in good times, and a cow in calf would buy no more than "a slender bundle of oats". Amid this scarcity, there was no hunger for a prince of York. Ireland was now almost totally hostile ground. The mayor of Waterford, getting wind of the wanderer, wrote to Henry on August 1st, sending the letter with such dispatch that the king received it at Woodstock by the morning of the 5th. The mayor said he knew that Perkin intended to head for Cornwall, a clue that he had only interrupted his journey thither to find strength, or draw breath, in

Ireland. Henry urged Waterford to go after him immediately, offering 1,000 marks "in money counted" to anyone who could take him and send him over.

The king was still not entirely sure that his enemy was not in Scot/land, and was briefing ambassadors until mid/August that "the individ/ual who styles himself Duke of York" was with James on the border, making trouble. But the Irish rumour gradually hardened. Waterford, though it sent "four great ships at [its] own charges" to chase Perkin, lost him; but Desmond and Kildare pursued him themselves, old friendship and sacred oaths now laid aside. They would have caught him, too, so Henry told Gilbert Talbot, "if he and his wife had not secretly stolen away." A rumour reached England that Richard had fled incognito and that his wife had been taken prisoner, but it faded again. Atwater smug/gled Richard and Katherine out of Cork by night in a small boat and dropped them at Leprous Island, near Kinsale. There, in that "little sea/port," the Spanish ships, probably contracted by Ayala, were waiting.

Zurita said that Ayala had told York and his party the exact place where they had to be to catch those ships, and the exact day. What was still unclear, at least to the crews, was where they were to go. Until the very moment of sailing, Richard may have kept the Spanish option open. But Cornwall seems to have been his first intention, and for good reason. The Cornishmen had risen in rebellion a few months before, protesting against the burden of taxes levied for Henry's war on Scotland. Behind that griev/ance lurked broader discontent with the king and his advisers, one possi/bly to be exploited by rivals for his throne. Under their leaders, Thomas Flamanck, a lawyer, and Michael Joseph an Gof, a blacksmith, some fif/teen thousand of the "poor commons" of Cornwall—joined by those of Devon, Somerset and Wiltshire to the east, and abetted by gentry and clergy—had marched on London. On June 16th, the king's army had defeated them without much trouble at Blackheath, outside the city. The leaders were executed, with Joseph's bloody quarters sent back to Corn/wall. But the Cornishmen, embittered and humiliated, waited only for another man to lead their cause. In June they had recruited James Tou/chet, Lord Audeley, to add the necessary cachet of nobility. Now they had another, better candidate in view. Richard of York was sent for, Zurita said, "because they did not have a principal person to strengthen their rebellion . . . and they offered him help to take the kingdom of England, as rightfully his." The message reached him either in Scotland or in Ireland, and he accepted.

It was not clear—as it had not been clear since the fiasco at Deal—who exactly was impelling him on the courses he took now. His royal sponsors in Europe had withdrawn, at least publicly. None of his lower-class advisers could force him on a path he did not want to take. There were, however, private obligations: commitments to Margaret, promises made to James, more personal pledges to Katherine, from which he may have felt he could not draw back. He may also have wanted the throne of England because he believed it was his. For better or worse, he was now his own royal sponsor, and he was returning to rescue England.

He had promised to do so in Northumberland, but nobody had listened. Now he would make the same promises again, assured of an audience that was ready to take up arms for him. The chance that he had found, at last, a crowd of supporters in England outweighed the attractions of retiring to Tortosa or Barcelona. Although it meant dicing with war and death, he behaved as though he had a duty to himself and to England. Molinet thought only extreme indoctrination ("nursing", as he expressed it) could have caused him to pitch himself against Henry's power like this. No one else at the time sought to offer an explanation.

The Cornishmen, at least, wanted to see a prince and had asked him to lead them. The names of those who "moved and stirred him by divers messages and writings" have survived in their attainders. No lords or knights invited him, only three "gentlemen": John Nankevell of St. Mawgan, Walter Tripcony of St. Columb, Humphrey Calwodley of Helland. Beyond these came yeomen from Polwhele, St. Crowan, St. Gwinnear and St. Teath, and three Devon men: John Gill of Stamford Spiney, Robert Sturridge of Ashburton, Thomas Hart of Barnstaple. Another Cornish supporter, John Tresinny, emerges from the now crumpled and worm-eaten petition of John Whalley of Padstow, who was set upon by Tresinny as he came home from church, beaten and "sore wounded" and then made to watch as his assailant robbed his house of goods "to the value of fifty pounds and better", all "upon trust of the landing of Perkin Warbeck," to whose cause, presumably, Tresinny meant to make a contribution. As with those who gathered to him in Ireland, it was hard to picture the golden prince responding to their humble or brutal approaches. But he did so, as though he had only been waiting to be asked.

II

THE IMMEDIATE SEQUEL was high drama. He told the story himself to de Puebla after everything had failed. The Spanish ambassador took the precaution of checking the story, since nothing was automatically to be believed that came from this strange young man. Having had it confirmed, he wrote to Ferdinand and Isabella.

> On the subject of Perkin I don't know whether I wrote to your Highnesses in another letter about what the Biscayans did, in addition to taking him from the domain of Ireland to Cornwall. While they were crossing over, the Biscayan ship which was taking Perkin met the fleet of the King of England, and the fleet captured the ship. The English captain called to the Biscayan master and to those who seemed best to him on the ship, and told them that they already knew about the friendship of your Highnesses with the King of England . . . and the betrothal of the Prince of Wales with the daughter of your Highnesses. . . . And for that reason he required of them that if they had Perkin hidden anywhere they should say so and show him, because those Englishmen did not know him. And if they did so, they would be acting like loyal subjects of your Highnesses and the king would give them 2,000 nobles as well as other favours; and for that purpose he gave them a letter, signed and sealed by the King of England, which the said fleet was carrying.
>
> Despite this, [the sailors] swore blind that they did not know and had not heard of such a man—and he was hidden in the bows of the ship in a barrel. Perkin told me this himself, and so did the man who came here to get letters from your Highnesses about the pardon of these Biscayans, who were present on the ship during all that, and your Highnesses may hold this for truth.

Two phrases rose out of the tale. First, "those Englishmen did not know him". They had been sent in search of Perkin, but had no idea what he looked like. England knew little of him except that this foreign "child" had been trying for years to invade. If they had found him in the barrel, it would have seemed appropriate enough: packed in like salt herring or butter, or some other stuff that Flemings shipped.

Yet the sailors "swore blind that they did not know and had not heard of such a man." That may well have been true. They had never heard of Perkin, only of the Duke of York, and him they were not asked for. Two thousand nobles were promised them, but they kept up their denials. Their contract with Ayala, of course, made denial easier. But in their own minds they were not concealing Perkin, for they had no such person on board. Instead they had a prince, even if at that moment he was swaying in an upright coffin, his knees pressed under his chin, almost fainting from the reek of the wine-soaked wood around him.

This was stirring stuff, but it was also an omen of his future. So far he had largely dodged Perkin, but with each encounter that person (that "nickname", as he had put it) became a more insistent presence in his life. The Biscayan captain had been shown letters patent, sealed with the royal seal, demanding Perkin's arrest. On the high seas, as on the land before him, there was a growing legal record in which his actions and his supporters were accredited to Peter Warbeck, born in Tournai. When he landed, unless he swept all before him, Perkin would not be kept at bay for long.

September 7th was the day of his landing. It was not a grand affair. Although the attainders said he came with "a great multitude and number", Raimondo Soncino thought they amounted to eighty savage Irishmen. His ships were unimpressive, too. Henry, probably well informed as always, called them "two small ships and a Breton pinnace"; Soncino knew they were fishing boats. They beached on the startlingly bright sand of Whitesand Bay at Sennen, near Land's End, to establish Richard's cause with another group of rough and half-civilised people.

Cornwall in the 1490s was not impoverished: its people were farmers, fishermen and miners, and the eastern counties had rich Devon as a market. Tin-working had industrialised Cornwall earlier than the rest of England, and the metal, though not precious, was highly prized. In Bodmin and Launceston, you could find rich merchants and impressive buildings. But this was not how the county was seen from the soft southeast or from civilised Europe. The Cornish, to those eyes, were dirt-poor, "the poorest people in England", according to the Venetian ambassador. Bodmin was "a village". Another Venetian called it "a very wild place, which no human being ever visits, in the midst of a barbarous race." Fifty years after Prince Richard landed, the Cornishmen were still described as going barelegged and barefoot, drinking foul muddy ale and heating their hovels with fir cones. At Blackheath they had fought, as the savage Irish did, with little more than raw courage: raw courage and enormous arrows, the length of a tailor's yard, which Londoners collected with wonder as the weapons of wild men. Those taken prisoner were sold to the authorities for one or two shillings each, all a Cornishman was worth.

Most tellingly, many of these people could speak only Cornish, and did not care to do otherwise. English was known to be essential for anyone who wished to progress, or for gentlemen, but these were not the men who followed Richard, Duke of York. As so often, his supporters could barely string together three words of English, let alone distinguish the subtleties of native or well-bred speech from what had been learned by rote by a foreigner. Many would have had no notion what this young prince was saying to them. They merely looked at him.

The Cornish showed their primitive nature by working underground, tapping for silver and tin. Earth smeared the miners' faces black, as smoke tanned the skins of the smelters. Richard Carew, describing his native county at the start of the seventeenth century, wondered how such skills "could couch in so base a cabin as their (otherwise) thickclouded brains." From Falmouth and Fowey the Cornish also worked as pirates, sending out fishing boats to attack Spanish and Italian ships, for preference, with their cargoes of wine and silks. Although the sea-lanes were busy, a man arriving at Land's End—as Richard Plantagenet did on his half-pirate ship—was still struck, and even dismayed, by the immensity of the western sea by which the Cornish lived.

Their faith, like that of the Irish, was fervent Christianity infused with superstition. Their land swarmed not only with home-grown saints, whose chapels and holy wells were half-hidden in glades and rocks, but with beings who moved the leaves, turned the stones and, if a man was a fool, tormented him. The world contained, to the Cornish, a parallel half-seen kingdom of mysterious foundlings and spirit-people engaged in trickery and enchantment. Some may have seen glimmerings of all this in the new prince, bright-haired and slightly unsteady after days of sailing, as his new supporters knelt to him in the white sand.

In the folk-tales of Cornwall, there were already heroes whose lustre he could borrow. The *Life of St. Meriasek* (*Beunans Meriasek*), written around 1497 to be performed at Camborne, featured the bold and pious Duke of Cornwall whose appearance, even in rumour, struck terror into the tyrant Teudar. The duke lambasted Teudar for his lack of a royal claim "on the side of mother or father"; that "dirty hound", with his "caitiff knights", had no right to rule in the country. He therefore gathered the Cornishmen against him. A messenger raced to tell his enemy the news:

> Hail Teudar, Emperor of Grace!
> A duke is here in the kingdom
> Risen surely against thee.
> And with him right truly a great host.
> Thy death he will see
> He doth boast certainly.
>
> *Teudar.* Out on him, the false dirt!
> I defy him day and night!

After much challenging and counter-challenging (the duke threatening to turn Teudar into "hash" and "broth") they fought with enormous, ear-shattering guns, and Teudar was driven from the country. Or so the dramatisation went.

Arthurian echoes could be heard too in the Meriasek play. The Duke of Cornwall particularly mentioned that his chief seat was Tintagel, Arthur's castle. The Cornishmen's reverence for Arthur, the king who would come again, not only coloured this stage-duke but told in favour of any personable prince who arrived, as if shipwrecked, on their shores. At Sennen, where Richard landed, fishermen still dragged up on their hooks pieces of doors and windows from the lost, drowned land of Lyonesse. The region between Bodmin and Exeter, through which he was to march with his men, was Arthur's country: his rocky throne could be seen on the high moors, ready for his return.

Yet Richard did not fill the king-longing that Arthur represented. Tudor loyalists could point out that there was an Arthur, Duke of Cornwall on the scene already: Henry's son, deliberately named after him. If the new arrival was any figure from Cornish legend, he was much closer—in wandering, love and perhaps dissimulation—to Tristan, who had never come to much good at all. He was their leader for the moment, the man to poke Henry Tudor in the eye; but the Cornish rebellion had already lost much of its momentum. The great landowners in the west were Henry's men, and the churchmen and gentry were uninterested this time. All that remained was the primitive unrest of simple men who sought some outlet, somehow. As much as anyone else who had embraced him, their first cause was their own.

If Richard had doubts, he did not show them. He came to Corn-wall, wrote Gutierre Gomez de Fuensalida, *con boz de Rey*, "with the voice of a king". He so roused and impassioned the people, Vergil said, and promised them so much, that they immediately embraced him as their leader. At Penzance, he raised his standards and was received with adula-tion. Immediately after that—according to the local story—he captured St. Michael's Mount, the holiest place in Cornwall.

There he left Katherine with their son, almost on his first birthday. It is possible that by now there were two sons, the second even more vulnera-ble and helpless than the first. The small family was placed in the great archangel's protection. Andrea Trevisano thought that Katherine and the children were left at "a place by the sea called Perin", presumably Penryn, along the coast, and Henry seemed to think she was entrusted from the beginning to the sanctuary of St. Buryan, on the road from Sennen to Penzance. But this was not yet a moment for guiltily retreating, as sanctu-ary implied. On the contrary, everything seemed possible, including seiz-ing the sea-circled shrine of the first warrior of Heaven.

The Mount was "a strong place and a mighty", wrote William Warkworth in his chronicle, "and cannot be got if it be well victualled with a few men to keep it, for twenty men may keep it against all the world." Yet Richard did not find it difficult to capture. The garrison there was small, with few weapons; it was manned by three priests, a receiver and a master of works, all Yorkist by inclination. It therefore made sense for the young man who claimed to be Edward's son to seek favour and blessing in this place, as well as the high symbolism of making it his first foothold in England.

In the event he and Katherine had merely to appear, crossing the causeway or the sea, and climb, like any pilgrims, the "fourteen times sixty steps" William of Worcester had counted, nineteen years before, to the top. The priests could confirm that they had thereby remitted one-third of the time due in Purgatory as penance for their sins. Prayers could be said before the reliquaries of the Virgin's milk and the Virgin's girdle in her chapel; September 8th, as it happened, was the day of her Nativity. But the most urgent pleas for intercession were made at another altar before the

silver-gilt statue of St. Michael, protector in battles and trampler of dragons. This particular St. Michael was dressed more for hawking than for
fighting, in a cloth-of-gold coat, a bonnet of tinsel satin and a chain of
gold, like any prince. Somewhere, you might presume and hope, he also
had a sword of fire, and could draw himself up in vengeance to the flaming height of the sky.

Richard, having left the most precious things he possessed in the
world, marched on towards the east. By local accounts his ships sailed
north to St. Ives, the nearest safe anchorage by sea. He was said to have
proclaimed himself king there, but it was off the path of his march; it
merely seemed that a king had come, with "four ships of war", as they
appeared in that poor fishing village. Wherever he went now, men flocked
to him. Fra Zoan Antonio de Carbonariis, a Milanese friar who happened
to be in the West Country, reported that, barely off the ship, the Duke of
York already had eight thousand peasants brandishing arms at his side. He
was full of confidence, Vergil said, and in his joy he had decided, for once,
to be methodical. He was going to proceed from one fortified place to the
next, moving by careful and defensible steps across the south of England.
The fact that his force was quite undisciplined—*tutta via male in ordine*, as
Soncino put it—did not discourage him.

On the news of his appearance Henry had ordered Piers Edgecombe, the sheriff of Cornwall, to muster the county against him. Edgecombe was said to have raised twenty thousand men; but when the force
drew near Bodmin they found the would-be king in possession of Castle
Canyke, an ancient hill-fort southeast of the town, and his troops blocking
the roads to the west. Castle Canyke also had spiritual power, as the natural focus of the paths of the saints across Cornwall. Edgecombe's men,
defying their captain's repeated orders, would not go on, but fled home.
They may have been afraid, or they may have begun to sympathise with
the cause of the invader. News of Richard's victory was greeted in Bodmin with trumpets, bonfires and acclamations. He entered the town as
king indeed: king almost by right of battle, since Edgecombe's forces had
turned back, stumbling over the purple moors, merely at the sight of him.

There was no coronation. That glorious culmination would have to
wait for his arrival in Westminster, where he would sit in the throne that
Edward had assumed and be anointed with the special, sanctified oil of
the Yorkist kings. Instead, he was proclaimed king—as the local story had

it—in a house behind St. Petroc's church. Heralds and trumpeters cried him aloud as Richard IV, "second son of Edward late king", undoubted heir to the crown of England. He now had three thousand followers thronging the hilly streets of Bodmin, one and a half times the population of the town itself. He would have thanked God for them in one, or perhaps all, of Bodmin's three impressive churches: the priory church of the Augustinians, where he was probably staying; the large and beautiful church of the Franciscans, with a hall attached to it accounted as fine as the one at Westminster; or St. Petroc's, the finest and largest parish church in Cornwall, built only twenty years before of golden Pentewan stone and furnished with brand-new oak benches costing almost £200. There, members of the town's forty guilds would have prayed with him. This was perhaps not so poor a place to begin being King of England.

Richard IV assumed majesty, wrote Davies Gilbert in his *Parochial History of Cornwall*,

> with such boon grace and affable deportment, that immediately he won the affections and admiration of all who made addresses unto him. . . . And, moreover, besides his magisterial port and mien, being an incomparable counterfeit, natural crafty, liar and dissembler, *Qui nescit dissimulare, nescit regnare*, as the old proverb saith; so that in short time he grew to be so popular and formidable about Bodmin that no power durst oppose him there.

"About Bodmin" was a pitifully small compass, a *regniculum*, in Gilbert's words. Within that span, however, the people seemed to have in Richard IV a king as good as any other: better, indeed, since he loathed Henry's taxes and had promised not to repeat them. Perhaps his claim had cloudiness and mystery in it; but all kings to some degree lied, dissimulated and made improbable promises to their subjects. *Qui nescit dissimulare, nescit regnare*. As a king, he was perhaps a dissembler; if a dissembler, he made a perfect king.

He did not stay with them long, only a day or so, before moving on to subdue the rest of his kingdom. He crossed the Tamar at Launceston and entered Devon. As he rode across Dartmoor, with its crags and tors and deep ravines, his irresistibility stayed with him. He made sure his troops paid for the food they were given in the tiny settlements they passed through, proof of his royal magnanimity and kindness. Devon men flocked to join him, and the sheriff of Devon, ordered to prevent his march to Exeter, found his forces, like Edgecombe's, too terrified to fight the king who approached them.

At the walls of Exeter, the first substantial town they had come to in England proper, close to eight thousand men camped under Richard's standards. Those standards showed the escaping child and the red lion, a symbol in prophecy of political salvation. His own standard of the White Rose, so briefly aired in Northumberland, may have been borne before him as he rode, now a king, now in battle armour, through the strange moors and red-earth hills of a landscape he had never seen before.

Yet he had another identity in this country. As he rode eastwards that identity kept pace with him and also loped before him, competing for attention. Along the roads and in the villages, Henry's officers had distributed "placards"—official licences, signed by the king himself under the signet or privy seal, like the one produced by the English captain to show to the Biscayans. The placards offered a reward for the taking of Perkin, alive. This "reward and benefit" was proclaimed in the ports too, so that people would be alert to catch Perkin if he tried to escape by sea. Henry was offering 1,000 marks, or £667, for him, the same sum he had promised to the citizens of Waterford just a little before. Whoever caught him would also have all their offences forgiven, "first and last", but nonetheless his price was falling. It was now much less than the reward offered to the Biscayans, and many times lower than the 100,000 crowns the French had wanted to buy him for in Scotland. But Perkin, the boatman's son, could not command what a prince could.

Meanwhile he was being sought on all sides, fast and hard. Henry, keeping court at his hunting-palace at Woodstock, had word of him by September 10th, three days after his landing. "So," André had him say, with a sarcastic smile, "this prince of knaves is troubling us again." He wanted, André said, to try "gentle methods" first, to avoid bloodshed; Soncino said that Henry offered the Duke of York "a full pardon" as soon as he landed. But if the king had that thought, it soon passed. His natural caution impelled him to act as though the threat was serious; and he could not be sure that it would not be. He later paid Simon Digby, the constable of the Tower, for bringing in forty gunners and other troops to defend the Tower against "Peter Osebek and his adherents", as though they might well reach London.

Before September 12th the king had sent Giles, Lord Daubeney, his chamberlain and lieutenant of Calais, to "arready our subjects for the subduing of him" by land, and Lord Willoughby de Broke, the steward of the household, "to take the said Perkin, if he return again to the sea." On the 12th itself he sent letters to Gilbert Talbot, Lord Darby and Lord Strange, among others, ordering them immediately to get men organised; Talbot was to bring "six score tall [strong] men on horseback defensibly arrayed," and was to meet Henry at Woodstock on the 24th. By the 17th word had got as far as Knaresborough, in North Yorkshire, where Sir Henry Wentworth mobilised his colleagues to march against Perkin. These, in turn, spread the word to others.

King Richard, too, would have heard of the forces quickly massing against him. As early as the 12th he had probably had Katherine transfer, ied from the Mount, which had no privilege of sanctuary, to St. Buryan, eight miles to the west. In itself, this was an admission of uncertain hopes. St. Buryan was a strange and dismal place, virtually abandoned by its clergy. It was hardly safe, despite its privilege, and hardly comfortable. Katherine presumably stayed in one of the handful of prebendaries' houses beside the church: a building of surpassing ugliness, new-built of great blocks of brownish granite, on a bleak plateau with views of noth, ing except the sky. Across the new rood-screen in the church, strange crea, tures fought each other: black demons devouring blue-and-gold birds, hounds with gold collars pulling down gold-antlered deer, a speckled uni, corn engaging with a writhing winged dragon whose jaws were open to seize its throat. There Katherine waited, with a few servants and a few priests, to hear what would become of her husband.

At this point, Henry was not sure that he would need to go himself to defeat him "and all other that will take his part if any such be". He almost disdained to, confidently expecting that his rival would run away or find no supporters. André insisted that the king never wanted to fight him, just to save the country from the evil he represented. To take on this lying rascal with arms would do him too much honour, especially since he would soon destroy himself. On September 15th, in a letter to the pope, Henry announced that his enemy "would soon fall into his hands." Soncino picked up that mood, writing on the 16th from London that "everyone thinks that this will be the final ruin of the Cornishmen and the end of the Duke of York . . . it was considered impossible for him to escape from [the king's] hands, and it was thought that the affair would be settled within a month . . . he cannot possibly escape."

The duke seemed still to be hoping, Soncino said, for "some stroke" from Scotland, but his detour to Ireland had ruined the chance of a double-pronged attack. James had launched his own raid more than a month before, taking advantage of Henry's distraction with the Cornishmen's first march on London. There had probably been every intention that they should strike together, one last throw on Richard's behalf. But Richard, for whatever reason, had delayed, and James grew tired of waiting. In August he attacked Norham Castle, just over the border with England. Henry sent forces under the Earl of Surrey to cross the Tweed at Ayton; headstrong as ever, James challenged Surrey to single combat with Berwick as the prize, but was soberly waved aside.

As the English prepared to fight properly, in the constant rain and cold of a Scottish August, James gave the order to stop fighting and brought his artillery home. On September 22nd Rowland Robinson arrived, with the news that Richard had landed in Cornwall; but by then the momentum in Scotland was all towards peace. Ominously, Robinson did not bother to return to the master who had sent him. Richard was on his own and perhaps, as the days wore on, he knew he was. "The Duke of York," Soncino added, "like a desperate man, does not want to drag this out at length."

That psychological insight may have come from Henry. Having watched him so long, he already knew the young man he was pursuing, and how hard he found it to persist in violent action. He knew, too, what the odds were. Some Spanish envoys later maintained that Henry had reacted with great fear and distress to Perkin's landing, but other foreign visitors, less eager to see weakness in him, noticed only a determined calm that covered intense activity. It was at this moment, at Woodstock in September, that Soncino was ushered into the "wonderful presence" of Henry beside his throne, utterly confident and blazing with jewels. "Everything favours the king," Soncino reported, "especially an immense treasure." ("I am informed that he has upwards of six million in gold," he wrote in another letter, "and never spends anything.") "All the nobles of the realm," he went on, "know the royal wisdom and either fear him or bear him an extraordinary affection, and not a man of any consideration joins the Duke of York." The core of his rival's weakness, as always, was that noblemen would not join him, few gentlemen were interested, and his chief supporters were the half-civilised and poor. "The state of the realm," said Soncino, rather unnecessarily, "is in the hands of the nobles and not of the people." The king of the wild people stood no chance.

III

ON ST. LAMBERT'S DAY, September 17th, which was a Sunday, King Richard IV arrived at the gates of Exeter. His herald shouted his proclamation at the city walls, commanding Exeter to surrender by the duty of its allegiance. The new king also promised, Francis Bacon said, that he would "make them another London, if they would be the first town that should acknowledge him."

The city clerk briefly recorded that "one Perkin Warbeck, calling himself king" had come through the country as far as their gates. They had no intention of admitting him. In Northumberland, his proclamation had been met with indifference and silence. Here in Devon they mocked it, laughed at his pretended title, and sent him back defiance by his own messenger. Then they locked the city gates against him.

Exeter, like Waterford, seemed a bad choice for a siege: the most important town in the West Country, entirely walled, protected by the river on the west, and moreover a town with loyalty to prove, since its citizens had let the Cornish rebels pass through some months before. A new gun, with a store of four hundred gun-stones, was installed on the roof of the Guildhall, and Edward Courtenay, Earl of Devon, was already in the city with his son preparing to resist attack. Courtenay came from a line of faithful Lancastrians who, as early as 1483 during Buckingham's rebellion, had proclaimed Henry king in Exeter and in Bodmin. He himself had been restored to his earldom by Henry. At first he and his men, mustered at Okehampton, had been meant to oppose Perkin there. But, fearing that he was up against a multitude, Courtenay withdrew east to protect Exeter. Once there, he managed to augment his force with other local gentry: Sir Edmund Carew, Sir Thomas Fulford, Sir Piers Edgecombe (anxious to redeem himself), Sir John Halwell, Sir John Croker. Their retainers and indentured troops came with them. This company, though gathered slowly, made in the end several thousand men.

Meanwhile Henry, still no further west than Woodstock, had sent money to Exeter: 1,000 marks, dispatched with Sir Richard Empson on

September 10th. He had also sent Courtenay full instructions, dictated on September 16th "at viii of the clock in the night", very late for him, and dispatched, as a matter of extreme urgency, by a night messenger. His local commissioners in Devon had told him what was happening, and news had been transmitted regularly by his "posts" along the roads. By these means, he knew every step and flutter of Perkin's kingly progress; and he knew, too, that Exeter might be a target. His letters, however, came too late, reaching Exeter on the day the siege started.

Henry was not certain that Exeter would be attacked. He thought it likely that Perkin would march past; in which case, while taking care not to leave the city undefended, Courtenay was to harass Perkin's rearguard, stop food getting to his force and keep them in a state of constant fear. While the Earl of Devon prodded the rebels from the west, Daubeney would approach from the east, Henry wrote, "with . . . such an army royal of people so furnished with artilleries and ordnances for the field as shall be able to defend any prince Christian with God's favour." And Perkin would not escape; for if he slipped through this trap, Henry had ordered his ships, "be they at Saint Ives, Penzance or in other place," to be "taken, bouged [holed] or burned."

Unaware of these plans, and no doubt bolder for his unawareness, King Richard on September 17th surrounded Exeter on the north and east sides and tried, for about two hours in the early afternoon, to take it. Henry described him arriving with his company at about one in the afternoon and "inrang[ing] themselves in the manner of a battle, by the space of two hours": a clumsy, inexperienced performance. Since the morning had been set aside for hearing Mass and observing the proprieties of Sunday, the siege took place in the part of the day when melancholy had mastery, rather than the choler of the morning. No textbook would have advised it.

Exeter, meanwhile, got its priorities straight. The second and third items in the siege expenses, after the gunpowder, were 40 shillings for "two hogsheads of wine carried and sent to the north and east gates of the city", and 8 shillings for *duobus barrels de beer* "sent to the gates in the same way". The disproportion of wine and beer showed how many gentry and nobles were now among the city's defenders. After this Exeter quickly moved its guns to the gates, brought in a dozen "men called gunners", evidently never employed before, to fire them, and invested in five hundred pounds of lead to make pellets, seven sheaves of arrows, a few big gun-stones (apparently chipped into shape on the spot, at night) and, at the north gate, various lengths of iron piping.

However improvised those defenses were, King Richard could do little against them. Of the five principal engines recommended for besieging towns, he had none, and no guns. Instead he used rocks, fire and battering rams. He tried to burn the north gate, but the townsmen piled up a fiercer blaze on their side, flinging on piles of wood, and beat him back. Undeterred, he tried again at the east gate. When that failed, he attempted to get his troops in by ladders over the walls. His force gave up after a while, but then, regrouping on September 18th, broke in through the east gate and poured into the High Street.

The alarm bells rang, the signal for the defenders to mobilise. Courtenay rushed out of the Blackfriars, where he was staying, and took an arrow in the arm; "but he was therewith so little dismayed," wrote Richard Hooker, a mayor of Exeter in the next century, "that both he and his son, the Lord William Courtenay, did more eagerly follow upon them." The earl ran to the east gate, where the fighting was handtohand, "hot and fiery", and found the enemy swarming in the High Street as far as Castle Lane, "yet they were driven back and with force compelled out of the gate." Exeter also let its artillery loose on them, charged not only with gunstones but with shards of glass, old iron and musket balls.

Richard's men had hardly got far; Castle Lane was only just inside the east gate. But they had had enough, and Courtenay, writing to Henry by return on the same day, admitted that he and his men were too tired to follow them. Instead, they had come to an arrangement:

. . . when Perkin and his company had well assayed and felt our Guns, they were fain to desire us to have licence to gather their company together, and so to depart and leave your City, and put us to no more trouble; which because we be not able to recounter them [engage them in battle], and that our company were weary and some hurt, therefore it was granted unto them that they should depart, and not to approach the City in no wise. And so the said Perkin and his company be departed from us this day about eleven of the Clock in the forenoon, and by twelve were out of sight, and which way they would hold I cannot yet ascertain your Grace; But as it was said amongst them they would to Cullompton this night, and thanked be God, there is none of your true subjects about this business slain, but divers be hurt. And doubt not again, one of yours hurt, there is twenty of theirs hurt and many slain. And now I understand certainly that Perkin is to Cullompton, and many of his company departed from him, and more will as I [see] well, and trust verily that your Grace shall have good tidings of him shortly.

Hooker never mentioned Richard among the besiegers in Exeter. He thought little of him in any case, a poor figment of Margaret's "malicious mind" who had been brought to "confusion" by her. Yet if "Perkynge" or "Parkyns" had been spotted there, Hooker might have included it among the other tales of the siege that he had gathered. It is probable that the new king stayed outside, directing the siege, rather than braving the terrors inside. Yet he had changed, all the same. He was attacking his own subjects with flame and sword, as he had shrunk from doing almost exactly a year before. When the siege failed, some sources said he decided to starve them out. The Northumberland softness had gone now; he was their heavy lord, as he had threatened he could be.

And he might have taken Exeter if he had persevered. For all their defiance, the townsmen had been terrified at first, letting messengers down on ropes over the unmolested walls to appeal to King Henry for help. Courtenay was far from confident, but was hanging on in the hope that Daubeney would soon arrive. Meanwhile, the king himself was about to come westward, though very slowly. On September 20th, still at Woodstock, he told the Bishop of Bath and Wells that "we with our host royal shall not be far, with the mercy of our Lord, for the final conclusion of the matter." ("We trust soon to hear good tidings of the said Perkin," he added, as if it hardly mattered whether he stirred or not.) It was not until September 30th that the city fathers of Wells were to see "our most serene prince and lord Henry the Seventh" coming through the town with ten thousand armed men "against a certain Perkin Warbeck, rebel, and other rebels of the said king."

At the news of his approach, and the worse news of Daubeney's, King Richard first asked Courtenay for the truce, of six hours, and then moved away towards the northeast and Taunton. His forces were beginning to be badly outmatched. Although he had started his siege with about eight thousand men, he had lost (by Courtenay's count) hundreds of men dead or injured in the fighting. Around five hundred, dead and injured, was the figure most agreed on; Henry thought it was certainly "above three or four hundred." The Exeter receiver boasted that the city had lost no men at all.

In striking contrast to Richard's forces, Daubeney's "army royal", as Henry had described it, was packed with nobles and guns. Courtenay's force, headed by lords, was heavily provisioned with gentlemen and local worthies. Henry, taking evident pleasure in the repetition, called it several times a company of "nobles" with their retinues, well-equipped men serving their worthy masters. However confused or slow Courtenay seemed at times, he, like Daubeney, was in constant touch with the king himself. The lines of command were clear, the weapons organised, the discipline generally tight. This was the sort of force Richard had watched from the sea off Deal, suddenly overwhelming and slaughtering his men.

By contrast, his own men were even poorer than on that occasion. He was without mercenary troops and military captains. Astonishingly, he was now his own commander. (Hence, perhaps, the elaborately polite and almost apologetic request to Courtenay: "they were fain to desire us to have licence to gather their company together, and so to depart . . . and put us to no more trouble.") Courtenay, watching them leave Exeter, had seen them straggle across the landscape for an hour with no clear idea where they were going. These men had no armour, no weapons save swords, billing hooks, pitchforks and bows, and no social standing. Among all Perkin's troops, Henry sniffed, "on Monday last, the eighteenth day of September, there was not one gentleman."

These "poor commons" were becoming disheartened. Discouraging numbers had been killed, and the bridges had already been cut on the straight roads in front of them. They were probably not being paid, for there is every sign that the enterprise was running out of money. Henry had sent messengers among them, Soncino said, promising them pardons if they laid down their arms. God seemed to be on that king's side anyway, because all the Cornishmen who had eaten grain harvested since the June rebellion, or who had drunk beer brewed with this year's barley, had died as quickly as if they had taken poison, felled by papal excommunications. If Henry's men did not get them at Exeter, or at whatever place was next on King Richard's list, they would be sickened by the curse that had soured their bread and fermented in their beer.

By the night of the 18th, having marched, or perhaps walked slowly, all day, they reached the village of Nynehead Flory, four miles west of

Taunton. There John Wikes, the fifty-four-year-old lord of the manor of Nynehead, appears to have given Richard a bed for the night; he was later fined 100 marks, one of the stiffest fines levied on rebel sympathisers in the west. Richard's men camped in the yard and the fields and, the next day, moved on to Taunton. But the force was disintegrating. Henry knew as much; the letters he sent to London said that Perkin had "fled" from Exeter to Taunton, already panicking and retreating, though to the east, nonsensically, straight into the path of the king.

Gradually, then in increasing numbers, men began to desert his army and go home. Their king kept trying to encourage them. He was going to coin money, he told them, and give cash to everyone. He was in close touch (*avia grande intelligenza*, in Soncino's words) with certain lords of the realm, who would soon help. If the bridges ahead were cut, he would simply track to the right and find another way. He was taking them all to Somerset because it was easier to get recruits there, and then they would march on London to see him crowned.

At Taunton, at least in the local memory, he threw the town into consternation by seizing the castle and seeming determined to make a stand there. The castle, on the west side of town, was little more than a fortified house; it was not defensible, and nor was the unwalled town around it. The owner, Bishop Thomas Langton of the Kendal circle, was in the middle of repairing it, so the place could only be camped in. Langton had finished, two years before, a new crenellated gateway decorated with an escutcheon placed between roses and charged with a Cross carrying, as roses, the five wounds of Jesus and the inscription *Laus tibi Christi*, "Praise to you, O Christ". The date 1495, the moment of the dissolution of Richard's previous hopes in England, was carved underneath and in other places here and there.

The new king may have attempted to contact Langton, one of those "great men of the realm" he had such hopes of, but the bishop could not be blamed if he ignored him. Richard tried to dig himself in by other means. It was here, by Soncino's report, that he published certain "apostolic bulls" confirming that he was Edward's son. Almost certainly, these had been nowhere near Rome; and even if they had, the papal envoy of eight years before could have told him that the English thought most papal bulls were fakes.

For much of St. Matthew's Day, September 21st, Richard reviewed his troops in the fields at Taunton, encouraging them for the confrontation to come. Henry had sent Daubeney to issue a challenge to him and set a day for the battle, which the king supposed would be at Glastonbury. Daubeney now awaited an answer. Courtenay in Exeter had meant to engage him formally also, but had been too tired. All this was fascinating in itself. Challenges were not issued to rebels, but to equals or near-equals, as James IV had challenged the Earl of Surrey, representing Henry, at Norham earlier that year. Honour was involved here, and Henry, through Daubeney, apparently did not hesitate to match his honour against this young man. Trevisano had also suggested that if the "war" did not end in a battle, it would do so "by agreement". Such terms suggested that, for all Henry said and wrote, he did not yet know for certain with whom he was dealing. At Glastonbury, Arthur's holy place, the seal of royal legitimacy would be set at last on one of them.

His opponent, having made no answer yet to Daubeney, issued his orders and took a muster roll, noting exactly who was there and who was not. His forces, according to Fabyan, were "minished & somedeal decreased"; he noticed this "as a man comfortless", but still went up and down the lines with a dissembled show of confidence. For the last time, he smiled on them. Then, around midnight, he fled for the coast.

At that moment, Daubeney's army was perhaps twenty miles away. King Richard could neither see nor hear it but, in the pitch-dark, he could imagine it. "The night," Thomas More wrote, "is by itself discomfortable and full of fear." To an army waiting for battle, no part of the landscape of the dark could be trusted. More told the story of an army encamped near Belgrade that saw, by the glimmering of the moon, the Turks' whole force "coming on softly and soberly in a long range all in good order." By day, that force turned out to be "a fair long hedge standing even stone still." Commines related how an army bristling with weapons had loomed up at night once before the Burgundians: when dawn came, they saw it was a field full of thistles.

It is easy to believe that night fears may have got hold of Richard. Henry had recommended, after all, that he and his force should be kept harried, sleepless and hungry, "watching and waking by means of scries [attacks] and near approaches as those horsemen may well and wisely do . . . that they shall be half discomfited without any stroke." It is easier to believe that he fled because he could not face what was coming, by day or night. Zurita said that Richard knew he was surrounded, and had already heard that James in Scotland was suing for peace. Far away in Lon-don, the citizens and ambassadors knew that Henry was about to take him and that he could never get away. The young deer had in its heart a piece of bone that stopped it, when the hounds went baying after it and it crashed exhausted through the woods, from dying of fear. Men did not have such things.

When Richard fled, he took little with him. Sixty horsemen were said to have left Taunton when he did, but he seems to have lost them on the way. Many were probably captured. John Heron, Edward Skelton and Nicholas Astley—"the most worthy of his council," as the London Chronicle sneered—kept him company, but William Lounde, his chap-lain, galloped back with a few others towards London, throwing himelf on the 26th into sanctuary at St. Martin's le Grand. "And thus," said the chronicler, "his disciples fled from their feigned Master." Richard's chests were abandoned and seized by Henry's men, leaving Soncino to worry that many people might be compromised by the documents and letters inside them. But there had been no time for sifting or selective destruction. The imperative was unhampered speed.

It is not clear which sea he was aiming for at first—any sea, Henry thought—but he made at last for Southampton Water. This was eighty miles away, much further than the nearest coast, but it offered the sanctu-ary of Beaulieu in case of desperate need. The route was hard, often trackless: to Ilchester, through the moors, over the Sherborne Heights, through the Forest of Blackmoor, across Cranborne Chase. What was most in his mind, perhaps, was the thought of taking ship for Flanders. Possibly the ships that Henry had destroyed, or ordered to be destroyed, had been meant to sail from Penzance along the coast to find him if he sent word. They could have taken Katherine and the babies too; but there were now, very probably, no ships. There were no troops, either. He left behind his ragtag army and, at least in intention, the country he had kept insisting belonged to him.

He also left his kingship behind. For twelve days, as Richard IV, he had dazzled his lowly followers in the West Country with the elegance and manners that had charmed the rest of Europe. If only in the eyes of these strange, swarthy, tin-scrabbling people, he was at last a king. They had knelt in reverence to him, expecting favours and healing in the touch of his hand and benediction in the sweetness of his smile. No longer. According to the London Chronicle, the remnants of his army were "amazed and disconsolate" to find him gone. Vergil said they feared at first that he had been killed; but when they realised he had abandoned them, they fled too. By the third hour of the day, Soncino wrote, not one of them was left in Taunton. They did not yet understand, until Henry told them later, that "they had been worshipping a low-born foreigner as their king."

Only the Cornish were ever said to have worshipped or adored him, as if he were a false god. He was their *idolum aut simulacrum*, wrote Henry's clerks. It was in the nature of most idols, not being Christian, that they could bring only disappointment. When his followers failed to find King Richard after Taunton, about six hundred of them, led by a man called James the Rover, turned their fury on one of Henry's commissioners and tore him limb from limb in Taunton's market place. Fabyan said this happened "in the time of the rage of this Perkin", as if he had maddened and infected whole parts of the country. William Parron, Henry's astrologer, agreed. Perkin had sickened people with his poison, especially the men of Cornwall, turning their stomachs like the bad bread and the bad beer. The king, by contrast, brought them both death and cleansing, or, as Soncino neatly described it, "holy oil".

His enemy had now to be hunted down. "Good number of well-horsed men," wrote Henry as soon as he knew, "been after him from every quarter." The London Chronicle said that Daubeney "sent towards the seas side CC Spears to Stop him from the Sea, and to Search the Country if they might take him"; Fabyan made it five hundred. But ex-king Richard, riding so fast that his pursuers could not catch him, reached Southampton Water in less than two days. Whatever plans he had made for fleeing, he found no ship there. He was forced to double back to Beaulieu and take sanctuary on the 22nd, as he may have always intended.

When he arrived, he was apparently in disguise. He had fled *incognito*, Trevisano wrote, and the abbot merely "thought" that the young man was in the party of fugitives who banged in desperation on his door. Once admitted, he put on in any case the habit of the monks themselves—most probably the black habit of the *conversus*, rather than the black and white of a fully fledged Cistercian. So dressed he was obliged, like all sanctuary men, to attend at least some of the offices of compline, matins, prime, terce and evensong, as well as daily Mass. In his short time at Beaulieu his persona was that of a rather-too-graceful and uncertain lay-brother, telling his beads with the rest, his dark cowl hiding the emotions on his face.

It is not hard to imagine what those were: fear, misery and shame. There was nothing more dishonourable than to flee the field of battle ("foul flight", as Vergil called it), except to do so before the battle had started. Trevisano said that the Duke of York had "not wished to accept" the challenge from Daubeney to fight, but no official refusal was recorded. He merely abandoned what would have been the field. To flee by night was "the most shameful manner", Christine de Pisan said, "because it is called running away." Henry was keen to emphasise both Perkin's panic ("he took no leave nor licence of them") and the sorry hour when he had bolted, just as, the year before, he had noted that James IV fled "about midnight" from his approaching army.

Failing hearts and desertion of forces happened often enough, it was true. Earl Rivers, a paragon of courage, had left the retinue of Charles the Bold just before a battle against the Swiss, and Charles had mocked that "the Queen of England's brother" was scared. (Rivers denied it, and claimed to have been tipped off by an Italian astrologer.) The Duke of Buckingham in 1483, finding that he could not trust the little band of men he was reduced to, slipped on a disguise and left them. Henry too, before Bosworth, had deserted his troops for a while and seemed to lose his nerve, wandering away in the dark assailed by fears of Richard III's "host innumerable" and his own uncertain reinforcements. But he recovered and went back to his men, "heavy for the sudden loss of their captain", to explain that he had left them "of set purpose to receive some good news of certain his secret friends." Sudden secret news, or new wiles to hurt the enemy in another place, were the textbook methods of running away and yet preserving some honour. King Richard IV had not had time for that subtlety of conduct.

Of course, the situation had been desperate, with the odds over-whelming and his army crumbling around him. Vergil thought he had perhaps feared he was betrayed; or that *vecordia animi*, frenzy of soul— a sort of wild distress that Bernard André, too, attributed to him—had overtaken him; or that, "most likely", he knew his men were incapable of fighting Henry's. He had also not expected the fight to come upon him so fast. In other words, Vergil rather gently excused him. Yet some of the poorest members of his "lousy army", unarmed and unlettered, had not fled as he had done but had waited, leaderless, at Taunton Castle to see if he returned. His actions made him less than they were. Cowardice was in itself a mark of baseness, for in the end it was virtue, not appearance, that proved a man's true worth.

September 22nd found the King of the Cornishmen cowering in sanctuary with a bankrupt mercer, a bankrupt merchant and a scrivener "of like authority & dishonesty", as Fabyan thought. These second-rate and venal characters were seen as reflecting the prince they thought they served. His status, in the monks' eyes, was no higher than theirs, for they were all rebels and wanted men. The beautiful robes and polished armour had been put away. There was also little treasure left. Henry's men later found the grand sum of ten crowns, or £5, at the sanctuary. Either the English, wrote Soncino, or the others who had supported "Perichino" had allowed him to come to want: *lo havenano lassato venire in miseria*. Five pounds would hire five carts for three days, or pay 100 soldiers for two days at the king's rate. It would also buy you a pardon from a Grey Friar or eight coat-armours, should you qualify to wear one. The King of the Cornishmen could not pay an army, or win a throne, with that.

On entering chartered sanctuary, as well as handing in his weapons and paying 2s. 4d. for his fee, he had to give the clerk 4d. to enter his name in the register. One wonders what name he gave. He was nobody in particular, nobody to notice. In fact, he might as well have been Perkin.

IV

EVERYTHING IN NATURE was laid out in order. The concentric circles of the universe moved as God had planned them. In the beautiful machine of the world itself all things were arranged in threes, the perfect number. North Pole, Centre, South Pole; Europe, Asia, Africa; past, present, future; line, surface, body; beginning, middle, end. Inside the three lay the power of four, as in air, water, earth and fire; the humours phlegmatic, sanguine, choleric and melancholic; childhood, green youth, maturity, crabbed age; spring, summer, autumn, winter. Containing both was the mystical seven: planets, sciences, sacraments, deadly sins, stairs in Purgatory by which the penitent stumbled to Heaven.

The pattern did not vary. None of the tricks and devices of Fortune affected in the least the movement of God's grand design. Within that design, all things had their fixed limit and their natural course. A fire could throw its heat only a certain distance, and no more. The sound of artillery could be heard for so many miles and no further. A stone, cast upward, could only fall to the ground again.

The earth, suspended at the centre of this ordered creation, went through its days and seasons as the sun, in its course, moved around it. Winter's frosts, with the peasant warming his cold legs by the fire, gave way to the verdant cloak of spring enamelled with numberless flowers. The lord went hawking among the May boughs, and lovers lay together. As the sun climbed higher, the wheat grew and ripened until by searing August the cutters were in the fields, their tunics hitched round their waists. The progression was sometimes delayed or surprised by freak weather, but it was never reversed. Winter did not follow the May games, any more than ripe wheat could suddenly rise from the snow.

All things came not only in their season, but in their place. Everything in the world, wrote the author of *The Treatise on the Ball Game*,

is inclined by a certain innate and constant desire to move to the place assigned to it by nature for the preservation of the universe . . . each having its own inclinations and desires by which they are kept to their own places. . . . Furthermore . . . each of these moves by natural inclination towards the habitation of that element that holds dominion over it: earthly things towards earth, watery things towards water, airy things towards air, and fiery things towards the fire.

The ideal of beauty was perfect tidiness in accordance with God's scheme. The perfect landscape had about it nothing wild, no "loathliness" of mossy ruins or upstart weeds. The demolished towers and scattered stones of the House of York, as Molinet had described them, were a horror-picture, awry and "counterfeit" in the word's most disturbing sense. Instead, the ideal scene was a garden with sanded paths "in compass", lawns soft and short as carpets, and carefully clipped trees within an enclosing wall. In the world's best gardens, according to John Mandeville, the songbirds and peacocks were mechanical, singing and flying only to order. The centrepiece of such a garden was often a fountain from which water was trained to run, with crystal clearness, over raked and ordered stones. Alternatively, it might be an arbour as perfectly circular as creation, or a temple in which the number of sides, the number of columns and the number of steps to be ascended symbolised the fixed gradations of earthly life or the life to come. Here, in bliss, the poet could set his dreams:

> The gravel gold, the water pure as glass,
> The bankés round, the well environing,
> And softé as velvet the youngé grass
> That thereupon lustily came springing
> The suite of trees about encompassing
> Their shadow cast, closing the well around
> And all the herbés growing on the ground.

Within this garden all flowers were in their order, beginning with the rose; all trees in their order, beginning with the oak; all birds subservient, and by degree, to the eagle, which was the king of birds. Above in his heaven shone the sun, emperor and chief of the seven planets, with his hair arranged neatly in rays of gold, highest of all metals.

There was no part of life that had not been minutely divided, subdivided and placed in ascending rank of importance. *The King's Book* listed seven sorts of meekness and seven ornaments of obedience. No prayer was simpler or more often said than the *Pater Noster*: but this had "seven notes, that are the seven biddings that purchase the seven gifts of the Holy Ghost, that destroy the seven capital wickednesses of heart and set and nourish the seven virtues by which a man comes to the seven blessednesses."

Such lists were not merely aids to salvation, but reflected the organising and prioritising principles of God Himself. Heaven was the most hierarchical of kingdoms. In a treatise owned by Edward IV on the nine orders of angels, the highest-ranking seraphim did nothing but worship God in devotion and love like fire; the cherubim plumbed the secrets of God; the thrones relayed His majesty to the subordinate angels; dominions, principalities and powers cared for the world in general, protecting it against the Devil, and the lowest orders of archangels and angels acted as messengers and helpers to ordinary men and women. All knew their place and duties, linked each to each in perfect harmony and unfeigned obedience.

The well-governed earthly kingdom modelled itself on this. Each king commanded, in descending order, barons, seneschals, esquires, secretaries, messengers and servants, all minutely aware of their duties and their place. The heralds who recorded the public festivities of Henry's court took their greatest pleasure from this "fair order". They noted eagerly the proper precedence of men and horses, the required salutations and firing of artillery, attendants "well-appointed", lords "honestly accompanied" and the perfect manners of all concerned. Any glimpse of chaos, a thrilling subversion of everything normal, was carefully organised at the king's command. Henry's Lord of Misrule, one Ringley, was paid £5 each Christmas season for the careful anarchy he planned.

Outside the court, the same strict rules of social order were expected to prevail. By wearing the clothes of their station and holding the tools of their trade, people could be known for what they were, without deception. By this means, with any luck, they would not get above themselves. Pages, before they left their chambers in the morning, were enjoined to see that every item of clothing "be so sitting / As to your degree seemeth according." It was pure bad manners, when walking in the street, to look so proud that men stared after you and wondered what you might be. Rather, men and women were urged at every moment—as they opened a door, began a conversation, took water to wash—to make their rank obvious and acknowledge who their betters were. Due reverence and obedience, no person desiring more than was his or hers by kind, kept the world in tranquil governance and peace. Peter Idley explained the ideal to his son:

> . . . an order would be had
> Among each degree and each estate
> To ken a tapster from a lady, a lord from a lad.
> Then shall truth and falsehood fall at debate,
> And right shall judge and set aside flattery and guile
> And falsehood for ever be put in exile.

It might be argued that such a passion for social order implied that the order was crumbling, undermined by ambition or presumption. Most contemporaries claimed it was. Low people in trumped-up clothes, with trailing sleeves or fur trimmings, were symbolic of a more dangerous blurring of the lines. The ways to advancement were marked out, and men on the make, more curious and better-educated than in times past, were increasingly seeking them. Through the Church, the law, the universities and the grammar schools, the sons of ambitious gentry and tradesmen could climb into the professions or find a place at court. At the lowest level the foundling or the peasant boy, entering a song-school, could start on the first rung of a respected life. From what Henry knew so far, some wild version of those presumptions had propelled Perkin towards him, up a ladder whose highest part was hidden in sun-touched clouds.

Yet men and women, by and large, did not move from the rank their birth had given them. The Cornishmen who had marched on London that summer did not wish to be more than peasants and artisans, but merely to register their anger. The bumptious Flemish merchants who caused such grief to Charles the Bold and Maximilian ("villeins", as Georges Chastellain called them) wanted mostly to have their privileges guaranteed, not to overturn the order of the world. Families remained for generations in the labouring, merchant or gentry classes, without trying to cross the divide between their estate and the level above. They grew rich, or poor, inside the confines of that class. The wandering son, leaving home to find an education or see where his wits could take him, was much rarer than the son who followed—though not without hopes that he could do better at it—the path laid out before him by his father.

The foundation of social order still lay in blood, pedigree and land. Those with shaky pedigrees, including, occasionally, kings, tried hard to improve them by marriage, legal argument and imaginative genealogies. Land, in practice, counted for most of a man's standing: a lot, a little, none at all or, in the king's case, the whole land itself. Yet property could not ennoble anyone without that line of blood. The Pastons, wealthy country gentry with lands, local offices and contacts at court, understood themselves to be socially far below the noble families, the Mowbrays and the Howards, in their part of Norfolk. The Howards were related to kings by marriage and had royal preferments passing through their hands. The Pastons could merely hope that some of those offices and annuities might end up with them.

Henry himself had in some ways disturbed this picture. As an only son, with no extended family, he had no claque of nobles round him and did not naturally look to them for counsel. England's nobility had in any case grown weak from fighting and treason, and some of the greatest houses—Buckingham, Warwick, Northumberland—had heirs who were minors and under the king's control. Henry made few peers to swell their numbers: just five in a reign of twenty-two years, of which one was the faithful Giles Daubeney who had chased Perkin into submission. His intimates, insofar as he wished to have any, were men of lower rank and blood who held power purely by his grace. His council was weighted less with bishops and nobles than with lawyers, many of them sprung from the lesser gentry or, worse, trade, who could now outbid the peers for Henry's favour. If that favour was the central fountain in the garden of England, the new men were like plumbers brought in to lay alternative pipes from the fountainhead, briskly bypassing the old.

Richard IV, in the brief time he had addressed the world, had considered this an abomination. In his proclamation of 1496, repeated at the walls of Exeter, he had excoriated Henry for promoting and confiding in these new men:

> and putting apart all well disposed nobles / he hath none in favour & trust about his person / but bishop Fox, Smith, Bray, Lovell, Oliver King, Sir Charles Somerset, David Owen, Rysley, Sir James Turberville, Tyler, Robert Litton, Guildford, Chomondley, Empson, James Hobart, John Cutte, Garth, Hansey, Wyatt, and such others Caitiffs & villains of simple birth which by subtle inventions & pilling of the people have been the principal finders / occasioners & counsellors of the misrule and mischief now reigning in England.

"Oliver King" was the bishop of Bath and Wells, but Richard thought nothing of him; nor yet Fox, a mere manor-born boy, who had hounded him in Scotland. Somerset was captain of the king's guard, Turberville the marshal of the household, but Richard did not rate them either, especially not bastard Somerset, whom he had already called "villain" to his face in Flanders. Sir William Tyler and Sir Richard Chomondley were stripped of their "Sirs" for consorting with Henry and his crew.

The men Richard named were a mixture of those he loathed for private reasons and those he thought egregious examples of Henry's disordered governance. Tyler was the captain of Berwick, a natural enemy in Scotland, and Wyatt had tried to have him assassinated there. The rest were Henry's tame churls. Rysley and Bray were associates from pre-Bosworth days, Bray recently favoured with high office in Wales, where he held no lands and was no one's good lord. Hobart and Lovell were members of the new wave of lawyers-in-high-favour, as was Empson, the son of a sieve-maker. Owen, a Welsh hanger-on, was the king's chief carver, Litton one of his treasurers of war and Wardrobe. While these men were kept "in favour about his person", Richard complained, Henry had sent certain nobles forcibly abroad. He had also debased the best stock of the kingdom by marrying "divers Ladies of the blood Royal"—Richard's blood—to "certain his kinsmen & friends of simple and low degree". Meanwhile, since they had no other way to build their fortunes, the king's favourites pillaged the people. Richard explicitly offered an end to all that. His reign would mark a return to proper order: rule with the help of prudent and experienced "great lords of our blood", from whom favour and good governance would flow down as they should.

His proclamation showed a deep reverence for rank and the preservation of social order. It could not have been otherwise. People had to be treated "after their estate and degrees". The reward he offered for the taking of Henry, £1,000, was what the "lowest of degree" would get; further up the ladder, he implied, the prizes would be stupendous. His will of 1495 had made the same point, so standard and incontrovertible, that though Fortune might batter both paupers and kings, in the end "the deserving man" would obtain what was his "in the scale of honours". By "the deserving man"—a phrase not necessarily his, but endorsed by him—he seemed to mean the deserts of birth and blood, not those of ingenuity, talent or hard work. He was talking of himself, the prince, getting his kingdom back, not of some ordinary striver finding success. Richard had never been a friend of social climbing.

By the autumn of 1497 those words seemed rich indeed. By then, according to Henry's best sources, the would-be king stood exposed as a boatman's brat from Tournai. This was not merely effrontery and folly, as Henry described it to others in exasperated disbelief; it came close to sacrilege. On one occasion, Henry was said to have ordered one of his falconers to kill a prize bird "because he feared not to match with an eagle". The falcon might be the fairest of fliers, hovering in his airy tower as a symbol of high breeding and nobility, but the eagle was the king. Another story ran that Henry had ordered all the mastiffs in England hanged, because they dared to take on lions. The mastiff was the second among dogs after the greyhound; but the lion, maned and clawed with gold, was royal.

Perkin had committed a deeper outrage than these. He was not merely a little below kingship but, by Henry's lights, unutterably far removed. He was no falcon, but perhaps a sparrow; no mastiff, but a prick-eared farmyard cur that ranked, according to *The King's Book*, eleven steps lower. As Bernard André put it, voicing the universal view:

> It seems to me to be against nature
> To endeavour to put in possession
> A poor man of ignoble birth
> In royal place; it is a great oppression.

Of course, it could not get far. In this world of exquisitely measured hier-archies, gentility and baseness could be discerned at once. Nobility, according to Reason in the *Roman de la Rose*, could not enter any base heart; courtesy and generosity could not coexist with a man who licked his knife. There was no concealing the fundamental nature either of ob-jects, or of living things. The knight Beaumains, who had come as a nameless stranger to Arthur's court and was set to work as a kitchen-knave and ladle-washer, was thought to be "villein-born or fostered in some abbey", but at last revealed his nobility in his beautiful hands. Conversely, as Friend put it in the *Roman*, "If anyone wanted to cover a dung-heap with silken cloths . . . it would undoubtedly be the same foul-smelling dung-heap that it had been before. And if any man says . . . it appears fairer on the outside, I would say that such deception comes from the eyes' disordered vision."

In Perkin's case too, Henry insisted, people were not fooled. They knew of what stock he was, scorning him for it, while Henry himself held him *de si petite estime et valeur* that he was hardly worth bothering with. In fact, *le Roi ne fait estime nulle de lui*. It was the same, he felt sure, at Maximilian's court: people of standing could immediately see through him. The delivery of Perkin, he told James IV through Bishop Fox in 1497, was "of no price nor value" in itself; he desired it only as recom-pense for wrongs done and honour slighted, "not for any estimation that we take of him", for he took none.

A little while after transmitting those remarks to James, Henry had been presented at Sheen with one of his finest books, *L'imaginacion de vraye noblesse*. He paid £23 for it, delighting in its quality and, no doubt, its content. The timing and the theme may not have been coincidental, since this was a book completely concerned, though in a muddled way, with the authentic virtues of princes and the dangers of social climbers. Quintin Poulet, who transcribed it for him, was also Henry's librarian. Although the text had first been written in Hainault fifty years before, Poulet had subtly updated it with references to the "treacheries and deri-sions" that were taking place on the borders of England, and with the *mauvais garsons felons et orguilleux | pleins de sedicions*, the pride-filled evil boys, who were being set up daily to destroy princes. Such charlatans, however, could not possibly succeed, since virtuous knights would never serve them, rendering them limbless and broken. At one point the knight-narrator of the book came face-to-face with this hapless type, a pleasant young man in a long robe of cloth-of-gold, not unlike himself; but the young man's arms were severed, and floated disturbingly in the air beside him in their fashionable detachable sleeves.

More subtle and pervasive undermining was also going on. "Good rich bloodlines" were being overlooked in favour of men with small estates and meagre virtues: *garsons, varlets et menues gens*, little people, with whom men of noble stock wisely had nothing to do. Poulet, of course, was treading on dangerous ground here, with a dedicatee whose own line-age was cloudy and whose favourites were sometimes not noble. Perhaps, in some cases, pedigree did not matter much. "The times are such today that people don't look for good manners or virtues . . . but like fools they look only at the line they're descended from, saying 'He's noble on his father's side but not his mother's,' or 'He lacks a half or a quarter,' and thus . . . nobility is chopped in pieces, as a butcher chops meat in the mar-ket." In the end, however, it could not be denied that nobility of blood was "beautiful," both in itself and in the lordships, clothes, houses and retainers that went with it. The ideal and unshakable prince possessed both gentility and virtue, in direct opposition to the *garson* at the margins of his kingdom: without honour, conscience, chivalry or pity, despicable in everything.

In that year, of course, the *garson* had argued back in kind. His proclamation threw in Henry's face his father's mere creation as Earl of Richmond, his grandfather's "low birth" and the "simple and low degree" of his advisers. So the insults were traded, but hardly in equal measure. The king had too good a story to exploit, and the scorn he expressed, both in public and in private, was picked up by all those around him. Nothing remotely connected the spawn of a boatman, load-ing and unloading goods on a filthy river, to the majesty of kingship. Var-ious documents described Perkin, almost gratuitously, as *vir infimi status*, a man of the lowest degree; he was called so even when set beside Michael Joseph, the Cornish blacksmith. Vergil called him "most vile", *ignobilis-simus*, obscure and poor from his very beginnings, fit only—as Simnel had been—to wash the dirty cooking pots in the royal kitchens. John Skelton called him dung, with or without the silken cloths to cover him. It was in that spirit that mud and night-soil had been thrown at his shield in Antwerp, shit to shit. Bernard André used of him not only the words *miser* and *servus* but *misellus* and *servulus*, a snivelling and worthless little servant boy.

The word "boy", Henry's and John Ramsay's favourite appellation for him, was strong mockery in itself. At best, it meant a page or a servant; more usually, it meant a low-class knave whose vileness was matched only by his weakness. "He can't hurt me," said Henry, more than once; "he wouldn't know how." When Grand Amour fought the fifteen-foot seven-headed giant in Hawes's "Pastime of Pleasure", "he struck at me with many strokes rude / and called me boy and gave me many a mock." Grand Amour whacked the giant's heads off; but that was in a story.

The snivelling boy was now in Beaulieu, with his pretensions apparently at an end. From the windows he could see the gleam of the inlet that led out to the sea. At high tide the water came almost to the abbey, leaving seaweed along the banks and letting the masts of ships ride above the trees; but there was no escape that way. The country he had galloped through, though perhaps scarcely seeing it in his desperate wish to leave, was already showing signs of autumn: the fields harvested, apples reddening on the heavy trees, dry leaves turning yellow in the woods. It was almost Michaelmas, when the great archangel himself—having somehow failed to heed his intercessions—began to tint the land with fire. Autumn was the falling of things, the season of coldness, dryness and contagion, in which men declined into melancholy and fear of scarcity in winter. It was also the season when boys went fruit-stealing in other men's orchards, as he had three times tried.

Nothing changed the natural order. Within the walls where he was confined, the day was divided into regular periods of prayer, the scarcely varying hum and chant of men praising God. The monks prayed at the east end of the abbey church, he and the other sanctuary men at the west end, keeping their separate worlds. Lay servants swept the floors or fetched the wood in bundles on their shoulders, while labourers worked the garden. Outside the walls, soldiers guarded, messengers reported and the king, though now on his way westward and no longer enthroned in Westminster, ruled in his own land.

Henry's whole court was on the road: the councillors, the knights, the household officers, the sewers and squires, the grooms and pages, the yeomen of the chamber and the yeomen of the guard, the Office of the Butlery, Pantry and Scullery and the man responsible for spices and sauces, with thirteen carriages of furnishings, clothes, papers, reliquaries and jewels. Some of the army, with guns, accompanied. The king's rule was working as smoothly as kingship had ever worked in England: officers doing his bidding, the nobles peaceable, the people, or most of them, consenting and deferring to his firm benevolence with no desire for change. As Raimondo Soncino wrote on September 16th, "[In England] nothing revolutionary occurs, except what may be compared to the generation of aerial bodies": first the Simnel bubble, blown in Ireland, broken in England, and now the bubble of the young man whom Soncino still referred to as the Duke of York, drifting towards the inexorable crushing majesty of the king. Soon, the ambassador knew, he would be "smoke", nothing more.

The social hierarchy was as it had been the week, the month and the year before. Only for the fugitive in Beaulieu had the world turned upside down. His adoring subjects were lost to him, and his three tattered counsellors had begun to edge away. There remained in loyal attendance only the guardian he had always had, from the lowest order of the angels. In one of Margaret's most impressive books, the soul of the knight Tondal, grieving in Hell, had turned to his guardian angel with the words "Goodly sir". "You call me that now," his angel replied; "but I have always been with you, and you never once deigned to call me by that name."

V

IT BELONGS TO HENRY to finish this part of the story. On October 7th, at Taunton, the king dictated a general letter to "all his friends and well-wishers" across the Channel. He sent it to Richard Nanfan and the other officers at Calais for translation into French and wider distribution; it survives, in French, in a copy in Courtrai. On October 17th, Waterford got a slightly different and updated version sent from Exeter. Henry had never rewarded the officers of Waterford for the intelligence they had passed on about Perkin or the chase they had attempted, as they plaintively reminded him. But he kept them abreast of the news, at least.

. . . When [Perkin and his accomplices] perceived they might not get to the sea, and that they were had in a quick chase and pursuit, they were compelled to address themselves unto our monastery Beaulieu to the which of chance and of fortune it happened some of our menial servants to repair, and some we sent thither purposely. The said Perkin, Heron, Skelton and Ashley [*sic*], seeing our said servants there, and remembering that all the country was warned to make watch and give attendance, that they should not avoid or escape by sea, made instances unto our said servants to sue unto us for them. The said Perkin desiring to be sure of his life, and he would come unto us and show what he is; and over that do unto us such service as should content us. And so, by agreement between our said servants and them, they [   ] them to depart from Beaulieu, and to put themselves in our grace and pity ["mercy" deleted]. The abbot and convent hearing thereof demanded of them why and for what cause they would depart, whereunto they gave answer in the presence of the said abbot and convent and of many other, that, without any manner of constraint, they would come unto us of their free wills in trust of our grace and pardon aforesaid.

Henry had no obvious reason not to tell his friends and well-wishers the truth. Nonetheless, this was neither the whole nor the straight story. Polydore Vergil summed up some of it: Henry could not get Perkin into his hands by force, so he did so by subterfuge. The evidence shows that force was applied too, though not by the king directly. As far as he was concerned, the process was heavy—artificially so—with negotiation and free will. He was generous, too, offering not only to pardon Perkin but to forget everything he had done. His agents at Beaulieu were always "servants" or "menials", suggesting pages, grooms or cook's boys; they were not "soldiers". The dirty work was left to others, and was certainly not revealed in correspondence.

Henry had a long record of taking people forcibly from sanctuary. In 1486, Humphrey Stafford had been removed from Culham, near Oxford, by a man called John Savage and sixty "helpers". Stafford tried to argue in court that his privilege should have been respected, but the judges, after some difficulty, concluded that it could not be pleaded in cases of treason. So the law stood. Henry had sent 140 horsemen to pluck out Robert Chamberlain in 1491, besides rewarding the mayor and bailiff of Hartlepool "and his servant" for their help. Thomas Bagnall's friends, in sanctuary in St. Martin's le Grand in 1494, had been extracted by armed officers. Although Humphrey Savage and Gilbert Debenham were left untouched in Westminster Abbey, staying there at least until 1499, they were in effect the king's prisoners, fed and watered at his expense: and somewhat indifferently, as the abbey kitchener complained in 1495, as the king had not expressly mentioned "meat and drink" in his orders, and the treasurer would not pay him for them.

The privilege of sanctuary had also been amended, a few years ear-lier, to allow the king to put royal soldiers round the holy place when a traitor was inside. (Although Perkin could not be a traitor by Henry's def-inition, his counsellors were, and in any case the technicality of Perkin's foreignness was often forgotten, then and later.) So Henry sent his men to Beaulieu. His letter of October 7th said that, *par fortune*, some of his ser-vants already "found themselves around" the abbey when Perkin appeared. Their numbers were speedily increased until Beaulieu was encircled by squadrons of cavalry, reinforced by boats on the sea, "so that he would have no hope of escape". One particular shipman, Robert Symonds from Barnstaple in Devon, was paid £10 10s. for apparently plying the southwest coast in his "balinger", looking for Perkin's ships in order to destroy them, and keeping an eye on the inlets round Beaulieu in case the fugitive tried to slip away.

In cases of treason, the king could also legally appoint "keepers" to "look to" a fugitive within the sanctuary itself. So he made sure, as he said in his letter, that his men got inside Beaulieu too. By the end the place was crowded with outsiders, many of them his officers. The account he sent de Puebla on September 30th shows how the stand-off stood. "We signify to you that we are informed of where Perkin is," wrote Henry:

> and furthermore he is in such a place that he may be held there at our request and guarded by our servants and will come to us as soon as possible. We therefore wanted to tell you this fact, for we do not doubt that you will be truly glad to hear it.

De Puebla was asked to pass the news on to the Venetian and Milanese ambassadors, who had been sending scare stories home, to emphasise how certain of the outcome Henry was and how glad they themselves should be. The phrase *non dubitamus*, "we don't doubt", occurred three times in the last sentence. His men were there in force, inside and out, to press Perkin to give in.

It was important, however, for Henry to emphasise that all the moves towards surrender had come from Perkin's side. The feigned lad and his counsellors, "seeing our said servants there", "made instances" to the king's men, and eventually to the king himself. According to Henry, Perkin himself said, more or less, that he would do anything to be sure of his life; "showing what he was" would be only the start of it. Once the "agreement" was made with Henry's officers, the fugitives insisted they wanted to leave: "without any manner of constraint", of their own "free will", seeking the mercy of the king.

That the young man wanted to surrender in the end is not unlikely. He had little choice, less hope and no resources. That he agreed quite so readily and fully to turn himself in is doubtful. It was probably not co-incidence that Henry switched from "he" to "they" for the scene of the explanations to the abbot and the leaving of Beaulieu: the feigned boy led and persuaded by his counsellors. Soncino heard what seemed like the full story from Richmond Herald, who, with some of the king's council (hardly "servants"), had gone to Beaulieu:

> and came to the following arrangement [*compositione*] with John [Heron] and his fellows, that John should go to his Majesty and either bring back a pardon for himself and his companions, or should be put back into sanctuary, while in the meantime the two companions should stay behind and guard the boy [*il garcione*] so that he should not escape, despite the fact that all around the fran-chise, especially on the sea side, there were so many royal guards that not one of them could get away from the place.
>
> John, having sworn to the king that he had never known Perkin except as Richard, second son of King Edward, returned with a pardon, and offered the young man the chance to be par-doned too if he would go to the king's presence. The boy agreed to go, and renounced the franchise into the abbot's hands.

It seems he had not wanted to bargain until then. If he had ever been offered, on landing in Cornwall, the full royal pardon that Soncino talked of, he had rejected it. He had wanted to fight, at least at first, and now he wanted to escape: badly enough to need Nicholas Astley and Edward Skelton, counsellors-now-turned-keepers, to prevent him, over and above the soldiers the king had posted. But John Heron arranged to go to the king. As early as the 25th "a man that came from Perkin" arrived at Woodstock: ostensibly not pushed, but petitioning. The role of Heron, not his prince, as chief negotiator may explain why his prince later exposed him as a man who had lied to the king, thereby dropping him in trouble and treating him as someone who was no longer his friend.

When the fugitives decided at last to leave Beaulieu, the abbot, by Henry's account, went through the motions of asking them why and potentially dissuading them. He is very unlikely to have done so, since it was the abbot, on Richmond's evidence, who had first tipped off the king about them, despite the duty of attendant clergy to defend the privilege of sanctuary. The scene was in Henry's letter to stress how willing, even eager, Perkin was to go. But if his decision had truly been voluntary, there would have been no need for the extra help that Henry recruited.

The king's privy-purse accounts suggest that no one was sent to Beaulieu until, on September 30th, he sent one Bradshaw, a man who was often employed to make arrests. London heard on October 1st, however, that Perkin had been taken "within the sanctuary of Beaulieu", well before Bradshaw arrived. It was done by the mayor of Southampton, the nearest town to Beaulieu, "and other divers persons", who acted, as in Stafford's case and Chamberlain's, on the king's behalf. They were put down for £482 16s. 8d., a huge amount, for "costs expenses and rewards to others for causes and business concerning Piers Osbeck"—the name Henry had now announced that Perkin ought to have. The payment was recorded on two separate sheets of parchment and in a separate book, as were all the expenses surrounding the boy's capture. This triplicate record, undated and presumably kept apart because the action was happening at some distance from king, court and Heron's pen, showed the huge importance in Henry's mind of getting Perkin out. All were signed with the royal monogram later, one set twice over at the bottom and the top. Their separate status also suggests that some of these payments, if not all, were meant to be kept secret.

The town accounts show that the men of Southampton had been observing Perkin for a while, as might have been expected. On September 20th, when Perkin was still at Taunton, John Elmes was paid 5 shillings "for riding to Master Dawtrey and to Master Controller to have tidings of Perkin", while Oliver Sherde was paid the same "for riding to spy on Perkin's ill demeanour". That remark suggested that Perkin was seen as a threat to Southampton, or that he already looked like a man about to flee for the south coast. A last payment on the 20th went to a man from Lymington who brought news of "masts by the stream", possibly a glimpse of strange ships approaching to spirit the boy away.

Southampton's role in his capture, and the large sum it apparently earned for it, did not appear in its own accounts: with one exception. At the end of September, the town got a new mayor. By that time the old one, John Godfrey, had earned himself a reward of £40 from Henry "for the taking of Perkin Warbeck". The reward was listed proudly at the top ("in primis") of Godfrey's list of his own receipts as mayor—a list that also included money from sales of old pewter and a brass pot, fines from a cobbler for making defective shoes and from a baker for making bad bread, forfeits for violent misbehaviour and "the killing of a cow great with calf". Quite how, amid all this, he had captured Perkin is not clear. There was a story in Southampton that at the end of September the fugitive was not at Beaulieu but at Bugle Hall in Bugle Street, near the west gate, a fine house that belonged to the abbot and was under his protection. No other source suggests that. Perhaps Godfrey put him there, having seized him; for it is fairly clear, Henry's story notwithstanding, that Godfrey and his men went in and got him in the king's name, and handed him over to the king's officers.

The actual leaving of Beaulieu seems to have occurred on about October 3rd, two weeks after the four men had sought refuge. The sixteenth-century copyist of Henry's letter to Waterford left a blank for the verb that described how the "servants" made Perkin leave sanctuary. It is not clear whether Henry left a blank too. The letter of October 7th merely said that the fugitives resolved among themselves to leave. Bernard André, in an account written for Henry and read around the court, produced a scene that wavered just on the edge of violent extraction. "He was led out trembling, jocularly hissed at [exsibilatus] by the king's servants, with wonderful deridings and insults thrown at his ridiculous head."

According to André, surrender had been on Perkin's mind as soon as he had despaired at Taunton. This *ganeo*—this ruffian and brothel-seeker—had realised then that Henry's power and virtue irresistibly assured him of God's favour. His own cause, he now knew, was useless and hopeless. His unwarlike and effeminate soul shook with terror, and what strength he had deserted him. In a frenzy of shame and crying, he told his men he would have paid them that day, "but I've got nothing left, not a single coin, and I don't know where to get any or what to do with myself." He told them that he was really the servant of a converted Jew, but begged them to forgive him. "Please pardon me and be nice to me, and make every effort to save yourselves, for I myself don't know where to turn or where to flee. But wherever it will be, I will certainly surrender to this most gracious king rather than die." So saying, racked with weeping and exposed by his own cowardice, he had made for Beaulieu and sought the king's clemency. Henry, the most merciful of kings, had granted it. And the *ganeo* was led out of sanctuary, still trembling, as though he had never stopped.

Dramatically, from Henry's point of view, this was the right and satisfactory ending. The idol and painted puppet was revealed for what he was. André's marginal notes, allowing the king easily to find the place he wanted, read at this point "Perkin's surrender", "Perkin's frenzy", "Perkin expresses his misery", "Perkin is mocked". The word *exsibilatus* meant "hissed off the stage"—and so, perhaps, it happened. But there was a twist in the final scene. Richmond, who was in the party that escorted Perkin back to Henry at Taunton, reported that the young man "put aside the habit in which he had disguised himself in this place and, clothing himself again in gold, set out with some of the king's men."

A man who clothed himself in gold was not surrendering. In the most extraordinary way, he was going to Henry on even terms. The wearing of clothofgold was forbidden to anyone below the rank of duke; so he was meeting the king as Richard, Duke of York. No one seems to have suggested that he should not do this. He was, by Richmond's account, "governed" by his three companions and obedient to their advice, but this particular action was his own. Without their help, he put on his prince's clothes. Clothofgold was heavy, and not especially suitable for a ride of eighty miles. If a king's robes were all he had (the clothes he had fled in, not pausing to find others), he could doubtless have borrowed some more suitable for a boatman's son, and for the circumstances. He did not do so.

Not only Richmond recorded this scene. An echo of it seemed to reach the king's own accounts. The strangest payment in the triplicate Perkin expenses of the autumn of 1497 was one "to the Duke of York for certain considerations". One version, much damaged, seems to read "for certain considerations and messengers". The official Duke of York, the king's son Henry, was six years old and in Woodstock or London "in our nursery" with his sisters. It is hard to see what secret "considerations" could have concerned a six-year-old, or what messengers he might have wanted to send. It was not his birthday while Henry was away. He was not of an age to be given money directly, and was not paid in his own name for several more years. These particular expenses, in any case, were incurred away from the court, somewhere in the West Country or around Southampton, on the road. The amount in question, £7, was almost exactly the same as Henry was to pay for Katherine's travelling expenses from Exeter to London. Although the entry sat cheek-by-jowl with those relating to "Piers Osbeck", another character remained disconcertingly on the scene.

They went back more or less the way he had fled, but more slowly now, through the October woods and fields. Richmond rode beside him. He had taken down pages of instructions about this "lad": how he was held in derision by anyone of consequence, was no kin to anyone of standing. The appearance was contrary and unsettling. In the party of sergeants and officers he was the golden-robed and golden-haired exception, the captive prince. Richmond talked to him a little and found him *ingenioso*, in Soncino's translation, clever in a witty sort of way, as well as *ben parlante*, well-spoken. The words suggested, as the clothes did, that Richard, Duke of York had not given himself up. Not quite. Not yet.

CHAPTER SEVEN

Confession

Kneel down. Make the sign of the Cross: Father, Son and Holy Ghost. Begin:

Benedicite.

Dominus vobiscum.

He had done this so often in his life. The common people made do with confession once a year before the Easter Sacrament; but princes, as always, were different. Confession, for them, was much more frequent and more or less a public act. An official confessor (in his case, William Lounde) was part of his household. Ambassadors would notice how often and with how much devotion a prince confessed; and people would especially take note when, holding hands with some former enemy, a prince walked to church to repent and be reconciled with him. Louis XI confessed every week before touching for the king's evil, a necessary precaution. His confession, said Chastellain, was an "exterior sign" that was beautiful to see.

Yet the process of cleansing was meant to go deep. A man should show his sins to the priest, William Dunbar said, as he laid out a grievous wound to the surgeon, allowing it to be agonisingly probed and cleaned. *The King's Book* said the sinner should spill out his mind and heart like water from a pot, "and when the water is out there is no colour seen, no sweetness of milk nor smelling of wine nor no savour of honey; no more shall they withhold within them, after they have shriven of their sin, no manner colour of shrewdness that they have used. . . ." With this sweet vomit, like the recommended vomits of spring, he was to shake himself out and be cleansed utterly.

The priest's own questions were meant to be exhaustive. The grades and lists were gone through in order: the seven deadly sins (how often?), the Ten Commandments (how badly broken?), the five bodily wits (luring to sin by looking, feeling, touching, especially of money and women), the seven spiritual works of mercy, the seven corporal works of mercy, the seven gifts of the Holy Ghost, the seven sacraments (how often cheated of the reverence owed to them?), the eight beatitudes. Of each infraction the penitent was to say where, how, when, with whom, how many times, and whether in speaking, consent, will or deed; ending after each, with knocking of the breast, "whereof I cry God mercy."

This young man's confessions, very probably, had seldom been so rigorous in recent years. Once he had knelt and gone through the formalities, there might follow a soothing conversation in which the gravity of his sins was dismissed and the penance lightly imposed, for he was a prince. More than that, his confessor was his dependent and perhaps, at times, his debtor. To say *Confiteor* alone might be enough to obtain forgiveness, especially with the dramatic *mea culpa*s it contained. In sanctuary, however, without Lounde, a new sort of confession was required. A fugitive was assumed not to seek sanctuary unless he had sinned, and could not be granted it unless he was penitent. He had therefore knelt down in Beaulieu with a hooded "ghostly father" who was unknown to him, bent on proving, with desperate intensity, how sorry he was.

Cordis contritio, oris confessio, operis satisfactio: contrition of heart, open confession, reparation. All three were needed, and the first, the most essential, was not necessarily contrived in his case. There may have been much to be sorry for. The list began with Pride, the first of the seven deadly sins, by which Lucifer, the Prince of Hell, had desired to govern all Heaven and make himself equal to God. "False usurpation" was Satan's particular sin, so grotesquely arrogant and presumptuous that few had tried to imitate it. But Perkin had, if he was Perkin; and in that moment when, robed with gold, he had gone towards the king, he had epitomised it. Robert Fabyan's favourite word for him was "ungracious", implying not ingratitude but the sharp removal, for pride, of God's grace from him. He too was bound to fall in flaming shards from Heaven, but not before other particular and subsidiary sins had been laid to his charge.

His new confessor could list them, if he had the right manual to hand. Hypocrisy, the blindness by which a man could neither see himself, nor know himself. Vainglory of the world, especially in fair tales and quaint words, well polished and coloured. False goodness, arrogance and vaunting ("facing and bracing", in the common phrase); self-exaltation ("the devil's own frying-pan, where he maketh his fritters"); rebellion. These were the first, second, tenth, twelfth and thirteenth branches of the sin of Pride, almost the whole tree. After these offences came the twelfth branch of Envy, drawing others to sin; the second branch of Wrath, hatred and conspiration; the sixth branch, homicide; and the ninth, clamour, cracking and fraud. He had clambered too to the first branch of Sloth, dolorous cogitations and desire not to leave sin; and to the third branch, inconstancy, pusillanimity and curiosity. Of Covetousness he had assayed the thirteenth branch, fraud and being double, and the seven-teenth, forswearing and false witness. All this, and he could still parade himself as though God favoured him.

Henry imputed only three sins to him: great abusion (deception), presumption, and folly. Bernard André, who himself accused Perkin mostly of boasting and robbing, said the king rebuked him directly with the deaths of his worthier followers and the slaughter of his people, as he might justly have done. But Henry generally played the outrage down. Perkin may have been as presumptuous as Lucifer, but he was also, always, a boy playing the fool.

What had he himself confessed to so far? Any of the above, perhaps, vaguely and in general. André had imagined, at Taunton, a full exposure of his heart:

Fear and dread of conscience are now so overwhelming me that I am going to open my mind to you, open it completely to the light of truth, though I've kept it hidden from you right until this moment. The truth is, I am not Edward's son as I told you, nor worthy to be of such stock or great blood at all. . . .

But the young man's real list may still not have included the taking of another name and "the May-games of a higher life", as Buchanan called them. That sin was anyway so rare that the manuals of confession did not include it. The words "imposture" and "impostor" were not yet in use, and no single word summed up that notion in the mind of the monk who now confessed him. Either he had not committed such a sin, being truly Richard, or the sin had so consumed his life that it was almost past explaining; or somehow, in one of the ceaseless bargains with God that men and women made every day, he had justified it before Him in a way that stilled the subject in his mind. Perhaps, after all, he did not need to mention it in so many words.

Yet nothing could be hidden from God. God knew what he was. Each daily Mass began with the *Judica me*, a virtual plea to be closely watched: "Judge me, O God, and discern my cause," the words Henry had sung as he knelt, fresh from exile, on the beach at Milford Haven. God also knew him from his beginnings, flesh and bone and marrow of the bone, as he had been woven in the womb of his mother; He knew the action while his mind still pondered it, and the words of his mouth when his tongue had not yet formed them. The almost frightening truth was there, among the psalms of David in his psalter: *O Lord, you have tried me and known me.*

> *Domine, probasti me, et cognovisti me:*
> *Tu cognovisti sessionem meam et resurrectionem meam.*
> *Intellexisti cogitationes meas de longe . . .*
> *Non est occultatum os meum a te, quod fecisti in occulto;*
> *Imperfectum meum viderunt oculi tui, et in libro tuo omnes*
> *   scribentur.*

All-seeing God saw him, and recorded him. Every particle of what he did or what he was was written in the book that would be opened at the moment of judgment. All silences, too, confessed themselves to Him, and were written down as words and deeds were. Again, there was no denying them.

The point of confession, then, was not to reveal himself to God, who already knew him in every way, but to reveal the self to the self, which could not bear to admit what it was. The act often sprang from struggling and coercion, the sinner clinging to the spiritual darkness in which he had learned to be comfortable. He feared to see himself exposed in the light; but others could see him, besides God. Confessions of any kind, to ordinary men as well as to priests, were sometimes merely an admission of something the confessor already knew and could insist upon. They did not disclose a secret, but marked the end of resistance. Manuals of confession noted that simple people often felt so much awe and fear, when unburdening themselves to others, that they would "say 'Yes sir' unto that that a man them demandeth, be it truth or lying."

Such a confession was not accounted valid by the churchmen. True confession had to spring from a free heart, not out of dread but from love of Christ. Yet the sinner having said that "Yes sir" and heard the *Ego te absolvo*, the words of absolution, the same feeling often followed: joy-ous lightness and relief. From the branches of the apple tree of Penance, as one of Margaret's books described it, four fruits were gathered for the body: clearness, lightness, subtlety, impassibility. He would shine; he would be as light as thought, and would feel as if he could pass, like the risen Jesus, through locked doors. Most of all, the grace of Jesus would reform his human body to the figure of clearness, like His own. As all sin was a wandering from God's loving fatherhood, so penance restored the bond of recognition. The stained and spotted conscience was wiped as clear as glass; and God, leaning down, received the penitent again as His child. God was his father, he God's true son, as undeniably as Jesus was.

> He is the mirror clear and bright
> Without spot both day and night
> In the which a man by grace
> May behold his own face.

Kneel down. Begin. *Benedicite*.

II

AT TAUNTON, his chief confessor waited for him. Henry was not in the half-repaired castle but in the Augustinian priory in comfort, as became a king. His excitement was intense. He had been tormented by this *garçon* for six years; now was the endgame. Eagerness to see him, despite his pro-fessed indifference, pervaded the letters that Henry had sent to foreign princes, mayors and army captains. "We have received your writing by the which we conceive how there is word that Perkin is landed," he wrote to the Bishop of Bath and Wells on September 20th, 1497. "Truth it is that he is so landed." The drama was spun out with delight. "It is the chief thing we desire," he wrote to Edward Courtenay on September 16th, "to have him brought unto us alive." Perkin must not escape them, "not in any wise". He wanted no limp or broken body, but the creature in all its moving fascination: one reason why, though some in his council had advised him to kill Perkin when he was seized at Beaulieu, Henry had not considered it.

The cost of this young man was worth bearing in mind, too. Henry was to pay a total of £3,621 11s. 6d. for travelling to "the parts of the west" and back to apprehend him; without thinking—or not without horror—of the money he had sent in advance to fight him, or the thousands of pounds dispatched to Ireland to keep the country safe from him, or the treasure he had laid out to oppose him in Scotland. He had never spent, and was never again to spend, so much money resisting anyone. Now he would see the cause. In the accounts of John Heron, his keeper of the privy purse (and no relation to Perkin's counsellor), the heading "Tuesday" for October 5th was superscribed with the words "This day came Perkin Warbeck." Heron had not noted a news event since the crying of the peace with France five years before, and did not do so again until four years later, when Katherine of Aragon came at last to marry Prince Arthur. At the end of the entries for the day before came one for £9, corrected from £7 13s. 4d., for Henry's losses at cards. The king had never lost so much in a single night, as far as is recorded. He can seldom have been so wildly, prodigally happy.

The details of Perkin's arrival in Taunton came from Richmond Herald, who told them to Soncino later in London. His report suggests that the young man was ushered at once into a room already filled, in expectation of him, with noblemen, councillors and the king, to whom he made his formal surrender. But it is likely that other, less public, conversations took place first. Henry's own phrase, "immediately after his first coming", suggested a two-stage proceeding. Not least, he wanted the first sight of him, as kings always saw before anyone else any curious object that was brought to their courts. When Henry wrote to de Puebla after Perkin's capture, in a note so excited that even the address was ridiculously overdone, he told him that his prisoner "will be brought with us on our return, which we think will be very shortly; then you will be able to see [him]." This was clearly a man who was still thrilled to see him himself.

Besides, a public meeting without preparation was something that Henry's native caution would not have allowed. Whatever had been ar-ranged in Beaulieu—and most people called it an arrangement, as though the two sides dealt on even terms—his captive was well known for his charm and trickery. Above all, Henry had never heard him say, confessing it with his own mouth, that he was Perkin. He needed to. His letter to his "friends" stressed that Perkin had promised "to show us what he is". This was the young man's principal exchange for his life. Henry would give him everything; he would give Henry something the king professed to have known for four years, his name, now publicly acknowledged. To be sure this was done, and to avoid any sort of unexpected difficulty, the king was well advised to take a brief first stock of the feigned boy himself, in private.

In effect, they took stock of each other. What the young man saw was a slender man of forty-one, taller than himself, with a pleasant but sallow face, lively blue eyes, greyish-brown hair that fell limply to his shoulders, and a few widely spaced black teeth. All these, though, would have been subsidiary to the grandeur of his kingship, the robes and jewels, and the calculated stillness. Henry was especially good, Polydore Vergil wrote, at maintaining his royal dignity, and everything pertaining to it, at all times and in all places. On most days in the West Country he displayed the divine power of his unction by healing the sick (the cure hastened by an angel coin, worth 6s. 8d., slipped into the sufferer's hand by an aide). His captive, too, now depended on that royal grace and gen-erosity, though it was far from certain that he deserved it.

What Henry saw before him was a tired, childlike young man with perfect manners, dressed in gold. He had a strange eye, its dullness per-haps more obvious for the strain he had been under. Dressed up as he was, he was capable of the same royal attitudes as Henry, perhaps incapable of changing them. The king in his majesty faced the boy, at least at first, in his. This artificial confrontation cannot have lasted long.

The substance of their private encounter emerges from the finer details of Soncino's report, crumbs too small for a fully staged surrender. Perkin "told the king" that Skelton and Astley believed he was the Duke of York, but that Heron, despite what he had said to Henry, knew he was not. Maximilian, the King of Scotland and Katherine's father "had all been taken in". Margaret "knew everything". Although the King of

France had long ago "been put right as to the truth of the matter" (Rich-mond's words, not Perkin's), Alexander Monypeny had still tried to per-suade his old charge to go to France with a broad safe-conduct and a large pension. All this was allegedly Perkin confessing to Henry, directly and without intermediaries. According to Henry he also confessed his name to be Piers Osbeck, the first thing Henry wanted. The French version said he "declared and understood" that, as if persuading himself, as much as Henry, of the person he was now bound to be.

André's account, most unusually, made no attempt to reconstruct or embroider their conversation. "It is very difficult for me to relate what words our most modest king addressed at first to this most worthless trifler," he wrote, "since this conversation took place between them alone [*singulari*]." However, he knew "this one thing": that Henry was truly pained by, and presumably blamed Perkin for, the deaths he had caused in England, and that Perkin, seeing the king's great clemency, "told him everything".

Did matters really go so smoothly? Naturally everyone said so, taking their lead from the highest source: "of his free will . . . openly shown", Henry wrote, Perkin had confessed to the whole charade. The king con-trolled the story, but what he said cannot be contradicted by anything in the records. Andrea Trevisano, whose reports were generally accurate, said that when Perkin mentioned the men who had "instigated" him, "the king wanted to know who these were, and he showed great kindness to Perkin," *feva bona compagnia a ditto Perichino*. There was almost the sound of laughter in this, and pleasant conversation. It was not the last time Tre-visano used the phrase to describe how the king and his prisoner got on together. No torturers' services appear to have been paid for. He had already been mentally softened up, it is supposed, in Beaulieu, and had been brought back to Taunton, the scene—as Henry pointed out—of his despair. His confession was now understood as the price of his life; and, at twenty-three or twenty-four, he wanted to live. His wife and baby son were, or soon would be, under Henry's control. The king held all those cards. Richmond did not infer that the information Perkin gave was forced from him in any other way. On the contrary he seemed astonish-ingly, even frantically, talkative. He was falling over himself to "do such service as shall content us", in Henry's words: as though he was laying down, with relief, a burden he no longer wanted to carry.

The Perkin of Taunton, and later of Exeter, was also busily assign-ing blame to others. He evidently gave the impression to Richmond that

Heron, Skelton and Astley "governed" him; he told Henry "at whose instance he took upon himself this abusion and folly". Soncino said he fingered the English and the Irish, but Trevisano said he laid the blame on certain people of Cornwall. The official confession, when it appeared, made much of the way he had been forced into the imposture. It was natural, of course, for young princes to be managed and governed by others—and to be led astray by them, too. Richard Plantagenet had often made use of the counsel of older advisers, such as Monypeny in France and Huc de Melun in Flanders; behind the scenes he had been helped by more shadowy figures, such as George Neville and Taylor the younger. But Henry, to this point, had held him completely responsible for his claims and his actions, once Margaret had set him in motion, and he in turn had given the impression that he was. In Taunton he became, by his own admission, a puppet cynically set in play by others.

In these early conversations or interrogations—evidently more the former than the latter—he seems also to have let slip his own description of what he was. He was not a deceiver but, in Soncino's translation of Richmond, a "substitute" (*suppositio*), ready to replace a prince and able to do so naturally. He did not play the part of Richard, but stood in for him, as one preacher or jouster might replace another in the pulpit or the lists and provide, for the audience, a spectacle just as satisfactory. In short, he had simply filled, with his own qualities of grace and princeliness, the gap that Richard had left behind.

After that first meeting came the set-piece, his formal public surrender. The audience that witnessed this was still elite and select. Richmond, who reported it but was not invited, said it was made only in front of "princes"; Henry told Waterford that it took place before "the lords of the council and other nobles", presumably the twenty-three lords or earls and the one real prince, Arthur, aged eleven, who were travelling with the king. In some chamber of the priory these great men were assembled, and Perkin was brought in. Although he did not come freely, but "at our will and commandment", as Henry put it in another place, he was apparently not bound or chained. He had to be shown to be confessing not for dread, but because he wanted to.

Before the king, Richmond said, he knelt down and asked for mercy. Requests of this sort were properly made with the hands joined and upraised, as at the Sacring of the Mass. He did not, however, throw himself at the king's feet and beg pardon, as Robert Clifford had done. There was a sense of greater dignity and restraint. Trevisano used the verb *inchinarsi:* he did not kneel to Henry, but bowed to him. This, in fact, fitted more naturally with what followed.

The king—to stay with Richmond's account—bade him rise, kindly and magnanimously. He said, "We have heard that you call yourself Richard, son of King Edward. In this place are some who were companions of that lord; look and see if you recognise them."

The gentleness had an edge. Richmond and Soncino translated Henry's "you" as *tu,* the form of address for children, servants and fools. The king pointed already to the social chasm between the prince and the claimant: "that lord", and *tu.*

The young man replied that he did not know anyone among the men who faced him.

No other outcome could have been expected. Had the question been put the other way—did any of them know him?—it would have received the same response, for the same reasons. No one's interests were served by an affirmative answer. You could argue on both sides that the task of recognition was either impossible, since he was a stranger, or made difficult by the lapse of time, fourteen years, since they could have seen each other. But neither strangeness nor the lapse of time was the chief reason for the young man's statement and the council's silence. They knew, and he knew, that he had to be Perkin now. He said what had to be said, and the council, silently, accepted it. They did not know him, golden robes or not, just as he did not know them, and no one present at the meeting ever hinted otherwise.

Yet recognition could have been possible, in principle. Some thirty-five of Henry's regular councillors had also been councillors to Edward IV, attending him sometimes when the little duke was present, and certainly knowing the look of the father well enough. Some of those who were there in Taunton might well have recognised him, if he had been the prince. On the other side, three men were in the room whom the young man should have known instantly, if he had been Richard. They had been fetched specially, presumably for this; their names are mentioned consecutively in the accounts for September 26th, the moment Henry knew he had his quarry in his hands.

One was Thomas Grey, Marquis of Dorset, Richard of York's half-brother and his companion, before he fled away, in sanctuary at Westminster in 1483. Although he was twenty-two years older, Dorset had perhaps been as close to Richard as the difference in age allowed. When Edward IV had created him marquis in 1475 he had wished especially to elevate him as a companion for his sons, joining them "perpetually by love as much as by blood". The second companion of old was John, Earl of Arundell, Richard's cousin, a contemporary of the little prince who had recently married Dorset's daughter. The third associate was far less prominent, and not a gentleman. This was John Rodon, the servant who had turned down Richard's sheets, brought him his watered-down wine and laid out his clothes.

Henry's production of these old companions might have seemed risky on his part. In fact, he was fairly sure of all of them. After several years of wavering loyalty, Dorset in 1492 had made an indenture with Henry, "whereby it is agreed that if the said marquis find sureties and demean himself loyally, his highness will admit him to favour, and grant him letters of pardon." The sureties were for £10,000, an enormous sum; fifty-five people, among them three bishops, undertook to guarantee them. Almost all Dorset's lands were put in trust, save two manors in Essex, on the income of which he was supposed to live. Dorset also gave up his son to be a ward of the king. What exactly he had done is unclear; what he promised not to do, on pain of disinheriting his son and forfeiting his lands, was treason and misprision contrary to his allegiance. If Dorset heard of such treason, he was to disclose it to Henry in writing, "and the parts be proved and the plotters convicted".

This pre-emptive strike appears to have worked on him. He never supported the newfound prince in Flanders, and in March 1495, at the height of Henry's reprisals against the conspirators, Dorset could be found not only shooting at the butts with the king, but also daring to beat him. Sometime in 1496 or 1497 a lighter arrangement to ensure his loyalty seems to have been put in place: Henry persuaded nine lords and knights of the West Country, including Edward Courtenay and his son, to put up new bonds for Dorset's allegiance. By this time he was in any case in his mid-forties, past the age of dangerous tendencies. In the late summer of 1497 he was actively on the king's side, fighting the Cornishmen and their butterfly with his own body and those of his men. So, too, was Arundell. There was little risk in showing either man this prisoner, even close up and still dressed as a prince.

With Rodon, too, Henry had not been incautious. He had made him a royal sergeant-at-arms, with wages of 12d. a day and a livery of vesture, immediately after Bosworth, and had granted him "the rule and keeping of the place called Broken Wharf" in the city of London, with all profits going to his pocket. In 1491 Rodon had been appointed joint keeper of the great park at Windsor. In 1497 this still seemed to be his job; he was the king's servant now, and had nothing to gain by jeopardising that.

The young man who claimed to be Richard could not, in any case, recognise any of them. He seems to have said so very quickly, as if he barely glanced at the faces before him. He immediately added, Richmond said, that "he was not Richard, nor had he ever come to England except that time, and he had been induced by the English and the Irish to commit this fraud and to learn English. For two years now he had longed to escape from these troubles, but Fortune had not allowed him."

This was apparently his true confession, made with the mouth as well as the heart. For what it is worth, this was the form his spoken confessions were always to take: not who he was, but who he was not. Henry said his captive declared before the council that he was Piers Osbeck; but Richmond, Soncino and the Venetian ambassador merely reported that he said he was not Richard. In truth, this was all that Henry required of him. The young man had once boasted to Maximilian that he could prove he was Richard to all the princes of the great houses, and to Henry himself, "if the opportunity were only given him", by the birthmarks on his body. Here was his opportunity. But there was no mention of birthmarks once he got to Taunton. That fire had gone out of him.

At this point, the performance seems to have ended. Though Perkin had been taken from Beaulieu "in trust" of Henry's pardon, he had not explicitly received one. A request for mercy made formally and kneeling required some sort of answer; but Henry merely showed him mercy by not killing him, and by courteously allowing him to stand. He did not go further. Perkin's three "councillors" were officially pardoned, and their pardons appeared in the patent rolls a few weeks later. Perkin himself was not given that grace. As a foreigner, of course, he could not be pardoned of his offences, since he did not owe this king a subject's spontaneous respect. Instead, he was "pardoned of his life" with no paper record needed, like a prisoner of war.

He was then removed by the guards, and the lords of the council dispersed. One of them, or the king himself, briefed Richmond on what had happened. Rodon, who had come a long way, prepared to go home again.

As he went, bumping in the saddle over rutted roads, ducking under low trees, he would have held in his mind the image of the young man who had not known him; as well as the image, buried for many years, of the fair-haired and beautiful little boy whom the young man had once said he was.

III

AFTER THE FIRST SET-PIECE, another followed. According to Bernard André, Perkin was faced with Katherine and was made to confess to her, in Henry's presence, that he was not a prince but a deceiver.

The king's interest in Katherine long predated her arrival in England. Her family was not unknown to Henry, for her half-brother Alexander had been in secret correspondence with him four or five years before her marriage. After it, secret missives from John Ramsay in Scotland may have told the king how lovely she was. Henry was a keen appreciator of the fairer sex, hoping aloud that Katherine of Aragon's ladies would be good-looking, and once remarking to the Earl of Oxford, who had boasted how handsome Norfolk women were, that "he would see them sure." His privy-purse expenses contain an extraordinary payment of £30 in September 1493 to "the young damoiselle that danceth", and another, of £12, to a little dancing maiden in January 1497. He had always mentioned Katherine in his letters whenever he had an excuse; from their leaving of Scotland until their separation in Cornwall, it was always "Perkin and his wife" he was pursuing. Now that the pursuit was over, he was gallantly prepared to pay court to her.

It took some time for Katherine to be fetched from west Cornwall. Although Henry knew as early as September 16th that she was at St. Buryan, it was not until the morning of October 7th that the king's delegation—Daubeney, Courtenay and the Earl of Shrewsbury, the master of the household—turned up at the sanctuary to take her away. They appear to have set out after Perkin's surrender, as Daubeney already knew all about "how he gave himself up to the king and is with his Grace at present". The very size and weight of the delegation, considerably more impressive than the one that had fetched Katherine's husband, showed how much importance Henry attached to her.

In his letter of September 16th, the king had made it clear that he meant to extract her despite the privilege of sanctuary. "It is thought unto us," he wrote, "that ye should in anywise do the wife of Perkin being in Saint Buryans to be taken by sea or by land out thereof and to be safely kept in ward or sent unto us." Like her husband, Katherine needed persuading. "She was so much talked to," wrote Daubeney to his colleagues back in Calais, *l'on a telement parle,* "that she was content to renounce the privileges of sanctuary and surrender herself to the king's grace." Daubeney's original words have not survived; the French translation suggested a hands-off, delicate operation. As a result of it, "at her own desire she has come to this town in my company."

"This town" was apparently Marazion, opposite St. Michael's Mount, and it was either there or at the Mount itself that Katherine was lodged for a while. Daubeney, though not entirely in the king's good graces (Henry had thought him "very slack" in dealing with the first Cornish rising in June), was now deliberately delaying sending her to the king. By the 7th, the day Katherine was taken, Henry knew Daubeney had her; he mentioned the vital news in the postscript of his letter "to his friends". The journey could be done, therefore, in well under twenty-four hours by a fast rider, and in three or four days by a sedate one. But ten days later, when the king sent his update from Exeter to Waterford, he had still not seen Katherine, although he had issued orders the day before for her to be properly looked after. "We trust she shall shortly come unto us to this our city of Exeter," he added, "as she is in dole." There, almost certainly, was the reason Daubeney had not brought her: a reason the king had not known on the 7th. Katherine was not simply in distress—grieving, one might suppose, for the capture of her husband and the implosion of her dreams—but in formal mourning, which required her to be shuttered in a house or a room for several days without disturbance. She may well have been mourning the loss of a second child, perhaps miscarried or stillborn after their arduous journeys between Scotland, Ireland and England. And meanwhile her little firstborn still sought her arms and wept for her.

Although she was a prisoner, she had therefore to be dealt with very gently. Henry did so, showing also by his courtesy how close to royalty she was presumed to be. Once protocol allowed, Katherine was honourably brought from the Mount, André said, with all the respect due to her nobility. A troop of the king's horsemen "escorted" her. Henry also had

a full travelling outfit made for her: a satin dress decorated with velvet ribbons, a riding cloak and hat, gloves, a kirtle, hose and shoes. Everything
was black. The king took her mourning seriously, and wished her to
know that he did.

Katherine arrived in Exeter around October 18th, the day new
horses and saddles were ordered for her journey onwards. Henry was not
disappointed when he saw her. As he wrote in his frisky letter to de
Puebla on October 23rd, the capture of Perkin and his wife "did not
deceive us in any respect at all", a neat joke. Vergil said the king fell
for Katherine at once, judging her "more meet to be the prize of a
commander-in-chief" than of a common soldier. Hall added that he "began then a little to fantasy her person," and the evidence suggests that this
was so. For the moment, though, he was a father to her, showing her every
solicitousness and giving her money, clothes, sober matrons to escort her
"because she was but a young woman," and even "night kerchers" for her
periods. In providing the most elementary things for her, the "necessary"
things, the king emphasised how utterly her husband had failed her.

There was barely time for Katherine to pause in Exeter; on the Saturday before the Feast of Sts. Simon and Jude, October 28th, she was
apparently at Sheen. At some point, somehow (André placed it in
Taunton, though it could not have been), Henry supposedly engineered a
meeting with her, her husband and himself. No record survives of this
except André's: a scene written not for history, but for Henry, in a small
plain volume to be perused in the king's spare time. It was for entertainment like this that Henry paid André his 10 marks a year, ordering it to
be put "into his hand" so the blind man could feel it, and gave him his
occasional rewards. The importance of the scene his poet had painted was
not that it had happened this way, but that Henry liked to think it had. In
André's account of the history of Perkin, this was the longest chapter.

Perkin had confessed; Henry, with great clemency and forbearance,
had merely chastised him. The two were alone, Perkin limp and dazzled
with the king's mercy, when the door opened.

Then his wife, with a modest and graceful look and singularly
beautiful, was brought into the king's presence in an untouched
state, with great blushing and breaking into tears. To her this most
kind king offered this most humane prayer:

"Most noble lady, I grieve too, and it pains me very much, second only to the slaughter of so many of my subjects, that you have been deceived by such a sorry fellow. For the nobility of your blood, the excellence of your manners and your whole body, beauty and dignity were crying out for another man of far greater superiority. But because it has pleased God that you should be reduced to this miserable condition by the perfidy and wickedness of this lying scoundrel here, you should suffer this with equanimity; and because the remainder of your life will not be lacking in many possibilities, for my part I exhort and advise you to bear your fate with an even mind. . . ."

Henry's first theme was rank and blood: Katherine's nobility, her excellence of manners, compared with the *homuncio* (a little insect, a man scarcely worth the name of a man) and the *nebulo* (idle liar) who stood before her. His second theme was sex. She came in "untouched", not simply because she had been courteously treated by his officers—and it was a marvel they had not touched her, beautiful as she was—but because she was, in a sense, beginning again after marriage with a man who had not counted. His lustful fumblings had left no mark on her. Her "whole body" had "cried out" for something and someone better, and now she could make the comparison herself. On the one hand stood Henry, forceful, kingly and compassionate; on the other, defeated and silent, "this lying scoundrel here". That dreadful association was now almost over, and a life full of new possibilities of "worthiness" and "honesty" lay ahead of her. She should not concern herself further about this man, "your husband hitherto".

All through this speech, Katherine knelt on the ground crying. She was "soaked through with a fountain of tears". Because she could not move for grief, Henry had to order her, though gently, to stand. When she had done so, "he ordered her husband to repeat to her the same things he had said to the king."

There followed, at first, silence. "Partly out of fear and partly out of shame", Perkin could not bring himself to say anything. At last "he openly confessed that he was not who he had said he was, and asked for forgiveness; he had been badly advised, he grieved for her abduction, and he begged the king that she might be sent back to her family." So this was all their marriage was: an "abduction", or a rape. André had implied this before, saying that Perkin in Scotland had wanted only "a woman to copulate with". Now, pathetically, the wastrel tried to undo the damage by having Katherine sent home again.

His wife broke out in fresh tears, convulsed with a storm of loathing for him. "So after you seduced me as you wanted," she sobbed,

> with all your false stories, why did you carry me away from the hearths of my ancestors, from home and parents and friends, and into enemy hands? Oh wretched me! How many days of grieving, how many worries will this give my most noble parents! Oh that you had never come to our shores! Oh misery . . . I see nothing before me now but death, since my chastity is lost. Alas for me! Why don't my parents send someone here to punish you? Most wicked man, are these the sceptres you were promising we would have? Most accursed man, is this the honour of a king to which you boasted that our glorious line would come? And as for me, hopeless and destitute, what can I hope for? Whom can I trust? With what can I ease my pain? I see no other hope ahead. . . .

Except in one man. Beside her stood "this most powerful and merciful king, who has promised not to desert me. I place all my faith, hope and safety in that royal promise." Here at last was a true, dependable prince, not a false one. Katherine turned definitively to Henry, while he bathed her in royal *consolatio, mansuetudo ac benignitas*, tenderness and kindness. "I would say more," she whispered, "but the force of pain and tears chokes off my words."

In reality, both she and her husband would have known that some sort of confession would be drawn from him if he were captured. He knew already what his "nickname" was, and the shape of the story that went with it. Katherine would not necessarily have believed it even if she heard him say it, but that would not have made it any easier to hear. His confession—in any form—meant that the great adventure had ended and that her prince had consented to be filth, dragging her too into filth alongside him. She may well have been as angry and heartbroken as André painted her, and her husband as silently miserable, and Henry, ardently admiring her in the new black satin gown with the black ribbons, as full of clement satisfaction as a king could justly be.

He had decided very early, some time before he saw her, to send Katherine as a lady-in-waiting to the household of his queen, the sister of Richard, Duke of York. There was little else he could do with her, if he wished to treat her with honour and yet not send her home; and he did not dare, at this point, to allow her out of the country and out of his control. It was extraordinary, on the face of it, to send her to Elizabeth, for if Katherine still believed in her husband's claim at all—or, worse, possessed some proof of it—she might work against Henry through the queen herself, rekindling Elizabeth's love for a brother she had supposed was dead. But Henry seemed confident that there was no danger in it. Perkin had confessed—perhaps indeed, in some form, to Katherine too—and that play was over.

There remained the question of the marriage. When André wrote his scene, he supposed that this marked, in effect, its natural and formal end. The record supported him in one respect. From the moment of her capture, Katherine was no longer Perkin's wife in any official document produced by Henry's officers. She was "My Lady Katherine Huntly", or "the daughter of the Earl of Huntly", as if she was unmarried or, at any rate, alone. In that state, she could begin to be rescued from her terrible humiliation. In effect, André implied, she had divorced him.

Canon law would strongly have supported her. She had married a man who, by his own admission, was not who he had claimed to be. This constituted an "error of persons", a rare occurrence that usually involved a pouting harlot playing the virgin, or a layman posing as an officiating priest. Tricks of this sort immediately dissolved the bond of matrimony—a bond that could not be broken if a husband merely beat or imprisoned his wife. If Prince Richard was no prince, Katherine's marriage could be annulled as if the white-robed bridegroom of her wedding day, called "by name" to take her hand, had never stood beside her.

To establish this fact, in the neutral and holy words of the Church, would have been hugely useful for Henry. Divorce would not only have freed Katherine, but would have dissolved the bond of blood that still tied his captive to the trouble-making King of Scots. Yet it was never mentioned or applied for. Perhaps Katherine refused to agree to it, or perhaps Henry was finally unsure of the grounds on which he would request one. The sending of Katherine to Elizabeth may well have been posited on the easy assumption that her marriage to Richard of York, like Richard of York himself, was dead and buried. But this, too, was still not proved and certain. Richard's ghost had not yet been laid, but had merely been brought indoors.

IV

IN ANDRÉ'S ACCOUNT of the scene with Katherine, Henry gave no name to her husband. He was in any case *levissimus*, the lightest and least of men. He himself, when attempting to explain matters to Katherine, admitted only "that he was not who he had said he was". He did not identify himself as Perkin, grandly Latinised by André as "Pirquinus". He was as anonymous as his shame suggested he would want to be.

Yet his name, and his lineage too, were now established. Shortly after his surrender, a "confession and pedigree" was published containing the facts, as Henry had determined them and Perkin had apparently confirmed them, of his early life. Henry, writing two days after Perkin's surrender, gave the gist in his letter to his friends; ten days later, he sent this version to Waterford. His captive,

> humbly submitting himself unto us, hath of his free will openly showed . . . his name to be Piers Osbeck, whence he hath been named Perkin Warbeck, and to be none Englishman born, but born of Tournai and son to John [   ] sometime while he lived comptroller of the said Tournai with many other circumstances too long to write, declaring by whose means he took upon him this presumption and folly. And so now this great abusion which hath long continued is now openly known by his own confession. We write this news unto you, for we be undoubtedly [   ] that calling to mind the great abusion that divers folks have been in by reason of the said Perkin and the great business and charges that we and our realm have been put unto in that behalf, you would be glad to hear the certainty of the same, which we affirm unto you for assured truth.

Henry never claimed to be surprised by this news. The confession had been under construction for more than four years, ever since he had told Gilbert Talbot that he knew the feigned lad was Perkin Warbeck of Tournai. From that time on, the bare outline had been continually added to. By October 1497 there was probably a document in existence, waiting only to be confirmed, perhaps improved on, and signed. The "certainty" was kept under cover until then.

This confession was to become, as a later historian said, the chief document of this young man's history; but it became so only because he had failed to convince England that he was Richard, Duke of York. Had he succeeded, this story might never have seen the light of day. That did not mean, however, that it was not true. The sheer intensity of detail sug-gested, on the contrary, that it had to be.

First it is to be known that I was born in the Town of Tournai, and my father's name is called John Osbek, which said John Os-bek was comptroller of the town of Tournai. And my mother's name is Kateryn de Faro. And one of my Grandsires upon my father's side was called Deryk Osbek, which died; after whose death my grandmother was married unto the withinnamed Peter Flam; and that other of my grandsires was called Peter Flam, which was Receiver of the foresaid town of Tournai and Dean of the Boatmen that be upon the water or River of the Scheldt. And my Grandsire upon my mother's side was called Peter Faro, the which had in his keeping the keys of the Gate of Saint Johns, within the abovenamed Town of Tournai, Also I had an Uncle named Master John Stalyn dwelling in the parish of Saint Pyas within the same Town, which had married my father's Sister, whose name was Joan or Jane, with whom I dwelled a certain sea-son; and afterwards I was led by my mother to Antwerp for to learn flemish in an house of a cousin of mine, officer of the said Town, called John Steinbeck, with whom I was the Space of half a year. And after that I returned again unto Tournai by reason of the wars that were in Flanders. And within a year following I was sent with a Merchant of the said Town of Tournai named Berlo, and his master's name Alex., to the Mart of Antwerp, whereas I fell sick, which sickness continued upon me five months; and the said Berlo set me to board in a Skinner's house, that dwelled beside the house of the English nation. And by him I was brought from thence to the Barrow mart [Bergen-op-Zoom], and lodged at the Sign of the old man, where I abode the space of two months. And after this the said Berlo set me with a merchant in Middelburg to service for to learn the language, whose name was John Strewe, with whom I dwelled from Christmas unto Easter; and then I went into Portugal in the Company of Sir Edward Brampton's wife in a Ship which was called the Queen's Ship.

The last part of the confession, a little more than half of it, went on to describe his service in Portugal, his waylaying by the Yorkists in Cork, his multiple denials, his eventual persuasion, his training in English, his forcing into the character of Richard, his invitation to France. It ended: "And thence I went into France, and from thence into Flanders, and from Flanders into Ireland, And from Ireland into Scotland, and so into England."

The confession was evidently drafted as a legal document, or pieced together from several depositions; Soncino spoke of Perkin "deposing" to the king in Exeter, though about more recent matters. "The said town of Tournai", "the withinnamed Peter Flam", "the water or River of the Scheldt" were all stranded legalisms that added, together with the fractured English, to the stiffness of the piece. Fabyan claimed it was intended to make this ungracious person "notarily known what a man he was". It is impossible to say how much had been discovered by detective work beforehand, and how much may have come from Henry's suddenly talkative prisoner. One curious phrase in the Irish section, "they threped upon me"—that is, they insisted—was a northern or lowland Scots expression, possibly picked up by him in Scotland. But his contribution may not have been particularly necessary. The confession was largely ready and was drawn up quickly, for Soncino and André both talked about it in the same breath as his surrender.

The version Soncino saw, however, was in French. A copy of this survives in Courtrai, in Belgium; it was apparently sent across via Calais in the same packet as Henry's letter of October 7th, another clue to how fast the confession was disseminated. The Courtrai copyist did not say it had been translated from English, as he said Henry's letter had. He viewed this as the original, and possibly it was. No stray legalisms grace this version; Piers's aunt is plain Jehane, not "Joan or Jane", the Scheldt is neither a water nor a river, just the Scheldt, and the whole thing displays greater fluency and pace. It contains, too, the most bizarre spellings of the English and Irish names (Brampton becomes "Sir Edward Brixton"), as if it was taken down by a Frenchman from dictation. The French itself had little Picard touches: *ung mien cousin* for "a cousin of mine", *che* for "ce", *Franche* for France, *wicquet*, the proper local usage, for the little wooden wicket gate by the river at St. Jean. This was surely a boatman's son from Tournai talking.

He did not begin, as in the English version, by saying where he was born, but simply with the name of his father, "living on the Scheldt". After this came a simplification of the mind-numbing crowd of grand-parents. Deryk Osbek was not mentioned, nor his grandmother's second marriage. The French version read simply: "One of my grandfathers was Pierart Flan, receiver of the said town and dean of the boatmen." There was no need, as in the English version, to explain what the boatmen did. His readers knew.

They would also have known that there were several things wrong with this account. The confession called Piers's father "comptroller" of Tournai, a grand-sounding office that did not actually exist there. Perhaps this meant to imply that he collected some of the many tolls payable, in cash or kind, for bringing a boat up or down the Scheldt, but it would have meant nothing at home. It is possible, since none of the Setubal wit-nesses thought Jehan was anything but a boatman into the mid-1490s, that the new job was made up by his presumed son, to make his father sound a little more exalted. It is more likely, since Piers would have been out of touch with home for years, that his father's new job was made up for him by someone else.

The confession also stated that Pierart Flan was the town "receiver", but this too was untrue. Town records show the post existed; there were, in fact, two receivers in Tournai, "the one in charge of the coffer" and "a companion", with their own clerks and sergeants. But since they were seen as employees of the town government, they were forbidden by law to combine this office with the rather political post of being dean of a guild, which Flan was. As the rule expressed it, a dean's job was to protect the common people; he could not also be the man who took their rent and distrained on them for debt. Again, as with "comptroller", this showed either embellishment or ignorance.

A smaller point, but one that would also have been noticed in Tour-nai, was the question of the keeping of the *wicquet* at St. Jean. The confes-sion made Pierre Farou, Piers's maternal grandfather, the keeper of the keys, but this was wrong, as years of watch-lists testify; Flan was the keeper of the *wicquet*. The *wicquet* itself was described as in *la porte St. Jan*, but there was no gate there, as war-weary Tournaisiens were only too aware: only the frail wooden wicket, fortified with a mound of mud and stones. A *wicquet*-keeper got 20 *sous* less than a gatekeeper, for doing only half his job.

On a more private level, Flan was called Piers's grandfather, a serious slip if taken literally. He was clearly not that. The English confession had made him his step-grandfather, which was bizarre enough. If Piers's grandmother had really married Flan, it would have been a strange marriage indeed, between a woman who was probably in her seventies and a contemporary of her sons. Elsewhere this versatile man—fairly well known in town as the dean of the boatmen's guild—was more plausibly described as Piers's godfather and his guardian, neither of them roles that a grandfather, or even a step-grandfather, usually played.

Yet if there were mistakes in this family story, as there were, they seemed fairly small in a background that was given in such detail. Confusion, forgetfulness and wandering could account for all of them. Most vitally, these were real people. They lived, or had lived, in Tournai. You could find them in the town records if you cared to look, in assembly debates and court papers. You could visit the *wicquet* by the Scheldt, find Pierart Flan jangling his keys in a self-important way, and shake him by the hand. If Jehan Werbecque still lived (the confession assumed he did, but it was uncertain) you could have seen him too, handling goods or checking sacks on a boat that rocked and strained out on the river, and you could have asked him, half-joking, when he last had word of Piers. The sheer detail of these unimportant lives seemed to prove conclusively that Jehan's son, whatever his minor stumblings, had finally confessed the truth.

The most interesting part of the French confession came as a separate appendix. Both Soncino and Jean Molinet mentioned this, marvelling that the confession gave the names of schoolmasters and neighbours as well as "godmothers and godfathers". Its omission from the English version may have been deliberate, or may simply have reflected lack of interest among the London chroniclers who copied down the rest of it. Here the evidentiary detail, already overwhelming, became even more so.

Here follow the names of my neighbours living in the Parish of St. Jean, and also my schoolmasters.

First Jehan Pernet [Josbert, in the Tournai version], Pierart Pernet, Nicholas du Bos, Jehan Carlier, Michel de Grandmont, Jehan Capelier, Jehan de Genet, Guillem Rucq, Thieri Micquelet, Jerome Capelier, and Michael de la Chapelle.

The first of my teachers: Master Jehan Badoul. And afterward Master Baulde Muguet [Maquet], cantor of Notre Dame de

Tournai, who taught me to play the manicordium. Also I had another master who taught me my grammar and he was called Master Guilhem. And he lived in a house called Les Bons Enfants.

That was the end. But if you wanted more, you could go to Tournai and catch Jehan Capelier or Guillem Rucq in the street, as Henry's agents had probably done, and ask them about the boy. Henry said he had made inquiries of "those who have been brought up with him". In case you distrusted that, here were their names. They were flesh and blood; they lived in the parish of St. Jean, right by the river; and they knew him. He had been their playmate, their friend, the boy they saw out of the window. If you had suggested to any of them that he was a prince, they would have laughed.

So Tournai was his place, appropriately ambiguous, an island of Frenchness on the western edge of Flanders. The Scheldt on which it stood marked the border between French Picardy and the Burgundian lands. The city was under the jurisdiction of the King of France and owed him allegiance, but the Dukes of Burgundy also made bids, sometimes roughly, for Tournai's loyalty. In its own mind the city was independent, "fair, free and entertaining all comers", as Commines described it. ("Incorrigible and ill-conditioned people" was Henry VIII's sourer view.) The Tournaisiens were mostly French-speaking, with French administration and French names, but their parentage and their blood were often Flemish; so they commonly had Flemish names too, just as Rogier de la Pasture, Tournai's most famous son, was also Rogier van der Weyden. Piers's father, though he was a Fleming whose name was properly Weerbecke, was therefore spelled as a Frenchman, Jehan Werbecque, in the town records.

Tournai, though several notches down from Antwerp or Bruges, was a bustling and impressive city. Its craftsmen produced tapestries, carpets, copperware and statuary that were famous all over Europe; its guilds were vigorous and frequently troublesome, and in good times the river was busy with commerce. Its great cathedral proclaimed its confidence and the wealth of many of its merchants. Yet for much of the latter half of the century Tournai's fortunes had been mixed. Constant sniping and full-scale wars between France and Burgundy interrupted trade, diminished taxes and cut food supplies. Twice, in 1451 and 1477, town officers made agonised representations to the King of France. That of 1477 shows how the situation stood, painted blackly to be sure, when Piers was supposedly three or four:

> [May it please you to know] that the merchants of this town always used to go to Antwerp and elsewhere to buy everything that's used in this town, but [ever since the king's men-at-arms came to Tournai] they have not been able to do so. When it pleased the king to declare war, all communication stopped.
>
> This town has now been at war for about half a year, and we are running out of everything that might feed the tradesmen and the people and the men-at-arms. There is great and extreme scarcity. . . .
>
> The common people can't earn money and don't know what to live on, and those who used to be rich get nothing now in revenues. . . .
>
> Some merchants of the town got as far as Lens with cattle and other provisions, but they couldn't get closer [to Tournai] because of the men-at-arms in Artois, and the cattle died. . . .
>
> Lots of people want to leave, and would abandon the town if they could get safe passage.
>
> So the town will lose people, and that will mean ruin and desolation.
>
> The chiefs and the deputies are in great perplexity and don't see what, by themselves, they can possibly do about it. . . .

The officers added later that year that they had never been so low, *tant au bas*.

Long debates took place over whether the city should be neutral between France and Burgundy, which might have made it more secure. But Tournai, though polite to Burgundy, clung to France, and suffered. In 1477, German men-at-arms in the service of Maximilian, then Duke of Austria, forced their way into town and insisted on taking over watch duty, though the terrified citizens "do not think they know the proper watch-cry." Tournai closed its gates but, in some confusion, kept the famous *wicquet* open. In May 1478 the town officers reported that there was only two months' grain left, and no wine, salt or salt bacon; the next month, the straw roofs of all the thatched houses at the edge of town, where Piers lived, were torn off in case of attack by fire. Men-at-arms were seen just outside, on horseback, menacing to come in.

By then, though "with no skill or experience in war", as they protested, the townsmen found themselves caught up in local fighting, helping to provision the French army at the siege of Condé, a few miles upriver, and also trying to supply the army round Mortaigne. Pierre Farou lost his boat (for he was a boatman too, as almost all Piers's relations were) to some men-at-arms at Condé, who returned it in such a battered state that it was seized by the town officers as an unfit craft. Not until 1484 did the town officers talk of war as something "in the past", and in that year there were still men-at-arms camping in the suburbs and demanding, in no uncertain terms, food and fodder for their horses. It made little sense for a child and his mother to travel to Oudenaarde, let alone to Antwerp, in years when merchants from Tournai were routinely beaten by raiders on the roads; or for a child to retreat, as Piers said he retreated, from Antwerp or Oudenaarde to Tournai in order to be safe.

But Tournai was apparently his home, and not, perhaps, strange territory to nourish a dissembler. The whole region, with its huge vistas and shifting lights, was good country for tricksters: a place where in 1477 two merchants had mistaken, in broad daylight, a shimmering field of hop-poles for an advancing army of France. The city itself, whether or not beset by war, made a speciality of illusions of one kind or another. Its painters, carvers and gilders produced masterpieces of imagery and statuary, capturing with every delicacy of line and colour the appearance of princes or of angels. Its weavers wove landscapes of fantasy, of love and war or of deep woodland scenes enmeshed and planted with every imaginable green leaf and flower, which were rolled up as "counterfeit Arras" and sent to the King of England. Henry had such "pieces of verdure" hanging in his palaces, where he could go hunting in dreams.

Tournai produced actors, too. The rhetoricians, who were treated as "workers" with their own guild, put on *jeux de personnages* and held public-speaking competitions, in French or Flemish, with other towns. Passion plays, performed by *canteurs de geste* in the street, were so wildly popular that in 1446 the town banned them, ordering people to go instead to church and hear their salvation properly explained by theologians. Some years earlier, a similar ban had been imposed on plays about the mystery of the Blessed Sacrament *par histoires, figures, imaginations ou experi-*

ences par personnages. The streets also saw mummers and players "with their faces disguised, covered and unknown", who had to be banned in the war years, together with their outsize knives and sticks and the singing of defamatory songs.

By contrast with other towns in France, Tournai seemed overrun with players. In 1462 a troupe called "The Monastery of Sleepers" went off to perform in the festival at Valenciennes, and in 1472 "a band of companions called the Joyful Hearts" put on "An Abridged Version of the History and Destruction of Troy" as a Christmas show in the assembly hall. The surviving records of town deliberations are haunted by a character called the Prince of Love, the lead player of the "Rhetoricians of the Mount of Love", who held a feast each August together with his companions. Every year he would go before the town assembly to ask for "pennies", like a beggar or a poet, for the sets and lanterns for his show. The good *prevots* and *jurés* of Tournai, though stretched by war, always humoured him. They found the money somewhere, and never called him anything but the Prince of Love, as though this was his only personality. In 1472 a princess came, ideally for him. She said she was Catherine of France, a natural daughter of the king, captured by the Burgundians and kept for seven months in Quesnoy; the townsmen innocently believed her, and gave her 100 *écus* "for the honour of the king." You could live thus in Tournai, masked, *princiant* or weaving stories, if this was your talent and your inclination.

Jehan Werbecque's world, however, was far removed from this. He was described in the town records as a boatman or *pireman*: both a docker, working on the quays at Caufours, the boatmen's quarter, and the owner of his own boat, shipping goods up and down the Scheldt. The river was not wide or fast at Tournai, but it was murky and sinewy with currents, and so tidal that in 1477 the bodies of Frenchmen, drowned downriver by Burgundians, floated as far as the centre of the city. Jehan's expertise on the water was important, especially since the objects that Tournai exported were often precious and fragile. Nonetheless, boatmen ranked low in the town's hierarchy of trades. The top guilds were those of the cloth-merchants, weavers, dyers, fullers, cutters and tailors, with the boatmen in the bottom half of the regulations and processions, alongside the fishermen and rope-makers.

In 1474 Jehan was described as *fils de bourgeois né en bourgeoisie*, on the strength of which, in that year, he was claiming bourgeois or freeman status for himself. Most people in Tournai had this standing. As part of the drive to stop people leaving, or to bring them in, you could usually buy a *droit de bourgeoisie* for 20 *sous tournois*, with an extra 5 *sous* for the sergeant and the clerk. To be a bourgeois protected you from high-handed treatment under the law, especially arbitrary arrest by local lords; saved you from many seigneurial tolls and taxes; and guaranteed you a place in "the Valley", the local hospital, if you fell seriously ill. In the great scheme of things, however, it did not mean you were anyone in particular. The least squire who wore his master's livery in Tournai was recognised as "a person of authority" from an outer and higher world. Those who were not bourgeois were very poor, temporary residents, or *forains*, outsiders, who had no rights to speak of.

Jehan's father, Deryk (as the English confession had him), had been a boat-carpenter from Beveren, near Oudenaarde. The nearby hamlet of Weerbecke was where the family sprang from, and they affected "van Weerbecke" or "de Werbecque" at times, which gave a touch of class. According to the French confession, Perkin's cousin Jehan Steinbeck still lived in Oudenaarde and held office there; and it was here, not to Antwerp (as in the English confession), that his mother took him to learn Flemish. The town, on the Scheldt about twenty miles north-northeast of Tournai, was a Flemish place, and the Weerbeckes were Flemish-speakers, but Frenchified Tournai was the place to go to advance in life. Grandfather Deryk had purchased his own *droit de bourgeoisie* in Tournai in 1429. He also bought the house, on the river at Caufours, where the family was to live for the next seventy years.

His son Jehan had a more chequered history. As a young man he moved back to Beveren and became a bourgeois there, presumably in the boat business. Early in 1462 he was involved in a tavern brawl, wounding a man called Weyne with a beer-mug. (Beer, and who was allowed to sell it, was a subject of much passion around Oudenaarde at the time.) Jehan petitioned the Duke of Burgundy to pardon him; it was only "a little wound", though it had bled, which had increased his punishment, and it was Lent in any case, "the holy time . . . of the holy Passion of our holy saviour Jesus Christ", an apt moment for mercy. The duke and his council agreed, and just before Easter pardoned him of the "corporal" part of his punishment. Jehan was heavily fined and, as part of the arrangement, took himself away as a banished man to Tournai. As it happened, he was pardoned not long after the duke had received the first ambassadors sent to him by the new King of England, Edward IV. As Philip the Good, at Valenciennes, was plying the English ambassadors with banquets, silver-ware and their own choice of women in bath-houses "equipped with everything for the work of Venus", beer-stained Jehan, probably taking his own boat slowly upriver, was leaving Beveren in disgrace. The two worlds could scarcely be imagined to touch and yet, for a moment, they had done so; as, it seemed, they were to do again.

Once back in Tournai, Jehan settled down a little, living in his father's house and pursuing the boat business with his brother Noel. Noel was a *wantier*, a rigging-and-ropes man, who like his brother gave his trade in Flemish. After twelve years, Jehan became a bourgeois of the town. It was a long time to wait, but he had arrived in Tournai under a cloud, having forfeited his *bourgeoisie* in Beveren and, as a banished man, all the property he could not take with him. He was probably about forty by this time, and his behaviour had not improved. In February 1476 he and Noel were caught up in a series of quayside fights which, by all accounts, Jehan started. He hit Bernard du Havron, another boatman, with his fist, was punched back, tried to hit him with a *hef* (a sort of forked stick) and then joined in with Noel, who was laying about him with a sword. Swords, though allowed to bourgeois, were not commonly worn around town, attesting again to the family's violent streak. Pierart Flan, who was work-ing beside the Werbecque brothers, got into the fight too, beating du Havron with a pitchfork.

These infractions brought down the wrath of the magistrates. Jehan had to go on pilgrimage to Cologne as his punishment. Noel was sent on pilgrimage to Rouen, and Flan and du Havron, more important figures in the town, were fined 100 *sous*. Jehan's sentence, only one step away from perpetual banishment again, took immediate effect. Anyone under such a sentence, if found to be still in the town, was thrown in prison "and treated so badly that they will feel they have to leave." Cologne, where Jehan was tasked to make his penitent prayers before the relics of the Magi in the cathedral (and to bring back proofs afterwards), was two hundred miles away. The journey would have taken him from home for months, leaving his wife and, presumably, his baby son to live somehow without him. Women could take over many enterprises, but less easily the steering of a boat.

Jehan's offence sounded like typical boatmen's brawling, the sort of thing for which Southampton's galleymen were often up in court. Low

class meant low behaviour, naturally enough. The culprits were probably well watered at the many quayside taverns offering black beer, strong
beer, fermented beer, *goudale*, or "ordinary" beer, and *blanche forte*, "called
Oudenaarde", the best of the local brews. The instruments they used were
mostly the tools of their trade: sticks and forks to pick up bales or to pluck
stuff out of the river. In Jehan's case his offences, though far apart, suggested that he took readily to violence. Middle age had not calmed him.
He sowed his wild oats, too, and two illegitimate sons, Colin and Innocent, were fostered with other families outside town, though Jehan sent
money for their keep. He was apparently never an officer in the boatmen's
guild or a particular contributor to town efforts, and may have remained
to the end of his life a rough-edged character ready with his fists.

At Setubal the royal herald Tanjar, who claimed to be a native of
Tournai, said Jehan was a rich man; not just a river pilot, but the master
(*señor*) of "a boat that comes and goes between Flanders and other places
by river". Yet Jehan was not rich by town standards. The only reference
explicitly to Perkin in a Tournai chronology, drawn up some time after his
death, said that his parents were poor and implied that they were
unknown. The boatmen's wealth lay in their boats, not in their property
on shore. The larger boats, like Jehan's, were *nefs*, flat-bottomed vessels
that could take whole shipments of wheat, wine or men. The smaller
craft, called *bacquets* and *pieches de bos*—literally, buckets and bits of
wood—were for shorter trips and lighter loads, or for ferrying people from
their homes when the Scheldt flooded. Many boatmen had two or three
bacquets, darting between the slow *nefs* and crowding the narrow river. The
loss of a large boat—as Farou lost his at Condé—might mean the end of
a family's livelihood. The place where they were moored was secondary.

This was just as well. Caufours was a rough industrial place on the
northeast side of town, outside the walls, stinking with the coal-fired lime-
kilns from which it drew its name and with the effluent that flowed
through from the tanning works at Marvis, just to the north. Wash-water
from cod-gutting and fish-salting was tipped illegally into the Scheldt at
night. Soot-covered vines grew in people's gardens, pigs rooted there, and
sheep were dipped in the river among the boats. (Fishing was absolutely
forbidden, by day or night and with any sort of tackle, including eel-
baskets, fish-hoops and pails, by town regulations of 1449 and 1466.) In
1468, the floor of the little gray-white church of St. Jean, with its neatly

budded spire and buttresses, was mud, with no paving. The parish was lumped in with richer St. Brice, next door, for elected supervisors and for watch duty. Caufours was *dela Escaut*, on the wrong side of the river, ranked at the bottom of the tax⁄ and watch⁄lists as the poorest part of town. From the quay there, where a small boy might stand and dream with his forbidden fishing tackle hidden in his hand, the town and the great five⁄spired cathedral rose to the southwest on a little hill that pro⁄ claimed their separateness and their importance.

Pierart Flan had made money in Caufours. He was evidently among the more important residents, though well down the pecking order of town officials. The guilds made up the fourth layer of government, under the *prevots et jurés*, the *maieurs et echevins* and the *eswardeurs*, or supervisors; there were seventy⁄two guild deans and sub⁄deans, of which Flan was one. Between his guild duties, with a full meeting of the four colleges every Tuesday "at the sound of the bell", and his *wicquet*⁄watch, he was also run⁄ ning what was probably the town's most successful boat business. When the boatmen were mobilised in May 1479 to take provisions to the siege of Condé, Flan claimed, over four sheets of paper delivered to the receiver, to have spent £162 17s. *tournois* on the boat, the victuals and the journey. He was also put in charge of the sappers sent by the town "in the service of the king our lord"; in the name of all the boatmen, he demanded payment for the boat⁄hire and everything else.

The Werbecques' circle was therefore the highest of their poor parish and their relatively lowly trade. The list of neighbours and friends in the appendix to the French confession contained some who had "de" before their names, as well as Nicholas Dubos from the family of the dean of the harness⁄makers (a "notable man" in the town records). It also included Jehan Carlier, otherwise known as "the armed goat", who in 1479 was made to stand in the pillory, with a mitre on his head and two distaffs on his belt, for having made a bigamous marriage and falsified the papers.

A house "on the Scheldt at Caufours", as Jehan's was described in the town records, was probably one of the better ones, right by the water and with the *nefs* and *bacquets* moored in front of it, as the houses there were shown in a map of a century later. The Pont de l'Arcq that crossed the Scheldt here (not "the St. Jean bridge", as Brampton called it) was an obvious landmark, and could have been Jehan's toll⁄point later, if he ever had one. Yet a regulation of 1473, around the time Jehan's son Piers was presumed to have been born, gave a vivid picture of the scene outside the room where his cradle rocked.

> [Item, it is ordered] That no person from now on keep taverns or brothels or hostelries on the quay [*werp*] of the Scheldt at Cau, fours, from the little bridge that crosses the quay towards the *wicquet* up to the rue Rifflart, to avoid the dangers of fire . . . to the wool workers in the vicinity.

For that son's birth there is no evidence, other than the confession and the evidence at Setubal. Births were not normally recorded, any more than marriages were. The date of Jehan's marriage was itself a nineteenth-century guess, based mostly on Perkin's age when he was captured in 1497. Since he was then twenty-three or so, Jehan was assumed to have married Nicaise Farou—the "Kateryn de Faro" of the confession—in 1473, the year before he took up his *bourgeoisie* in Tournai. The arrival of a child in the first year of marriage was usual and expected.

It may have happened that way. Marriage and *bourgeoisie* would have gone well together, doubly respectable, at least for a short spell. Pierre Farou, Nicaise's father, was in the right trade and of slightly higher standing. The Farou family had been settled in Tournai since the twelfth century, and were French-speakers. They were also relatively new in the boat business; they had previously been fullers, a job considered rather better-class in Tournai. But Jehan was old for a first marriage, if it was his first, and Nicaise was clearly much younger, since many years later she was still having children. There is no proof, in fact, that she was the woman Jehan married in 1473; only that she was his wife in 1497, when the confession was redacted.

The confession mentioned no children, other than Piers. A "letter home" that accompanied it mentioned several more: Jehanne, who died around 1486 of the plague; Thiroyan, a younger brother, who died with Jehanne; and a second daughter, born in 1486 as her siblings were buried. This daughter was probably the second Jehanne, known as Jenette, who lived on for many years and, in the next century, made a good marriage to a lawyer in a prosperous parish. There are indications, too, of another son, possibly born as late as the mid-1490s. But in the early 1490s, when Jehan was allegedly quoted in the Setubal testimony, Piers—by then a teenager—was said to be his only legitimate son.

According to the confession, this child had had a strangely unsettled early life. A boy born in Caufours was expected to be a boatman, without much argument or alternative. The quarter showed its dedication to the business in the little boatmen's chapel on the quayside, where the *piremen* themselves had charge of the ornaments and the vessels of the altar. To whom could the family *nef* be passed on, if not to the eldest or only son?

But rather than staying at his father's side, learning the trade, the Piers of the confession was shuttled round to relations in Tournai and in Oudenaarde and, at about the age of ten, was "sent" to Antwerp with a merchant called Berlo. (In the French confession, he simply "went to the fair" with Berlo, an interesting outing for a small boy.) The foray with Berlo was never described as a formal apprenticeship. The boy's first proper master seemed to be John Strewe at Middelburg, who perhaps contracted him to make leather purses in his haberdasher's shop, a craft that took two years to learn. Piers was still too young, however, to make a contract for himself, and Berlo presumably signed the papers for him. It was odd in itself that he took up a trade so far from any of his family, who would normally have inducted him into the workshop of his new master. But he had been left to fend largely for himself, in sickness and in health, ever since he had been taken to Antwerp.

Up to this point, according to the main text of both confessions, he was barely educated. The only subject he appeared to have learned in his wanderings was Flemish with cousin Jehan—a language he could have learned just as well from his Flemish-speaking father at home. As a result, he could presumably read and write to a fair standard in two languages, and could add up bills. Such an education would not have been unusual for a boy of his class: Tournaisiens who wished their children to prosper took care to have them trained in the city's second language. What was unusual was how much the boy was sent away, as though he was not wanted at home.

The appendix to the French confession, however, presented a quite different picture. Piers was not sent away, but kept in Tournai, and no expense was spared to educate him. Jehan had ambitions for his only son that went far beyond the daily grind on the river. The first indication of special care was mentioned in the English confession, where he was sent, still very young, to live with his uncle and aunt Stalyn in the parish of St. Pyat. He was moved out of rough Caufours to the other side of the river, up the little hill, to the wealthier streets just east of the cathedral. This may have been done because he was a delicate child, in need of better air; later on in the confession, he was ill for five months when he went to Antwerp. The move may also have reflected some sort of trouble at home since his father had been sent away.

If Jehan had wished to educate his son, he could have sent him to school in Caufours. The monks of the Cross, *les Croizières*, had just set up a school at St. Jean that was highly regarded, so much so that the cathedral schoolmasters complained of it as a "novelty", and tried to get the town to close it down. The monks' new church, with the school attached, loomed impressively across the road from the church of St. Jean itself, beside the main town graveyard and the "profane place" where unknown bodies were buried. But, according to the French appendix, Piers did not go there. He was instructed first by a graduate priest and then at the cathedral choir school. Brampton at Setubal also gave this story— a musical training (though Brampton talked of it as an apprenticeship with an organist) that lasted some years. Piers was deliberately placed on the ladder to a better, higher life: tuition in music, service in the church, perhaps university. Lessons in the cathedral were supplemented by classes at Les Bons Enfants, the Good Children School, the best in Tournai, founded in 1255 by Bishop Walter de Marvis specifically for the cathedral choristers. Here, at the feet of Master Guilhem, Piers learned his Latin grammar.

It is hard to believe that Jehan Werbecque cared a bean for either grammar or polyphony. The low-key commercial wanderings of both the English and French confessions sounded far more plausible for a boy of Piers's background, with such a father. For some reason, perhaps because he did not seem cut out for dock-work, Piers took the path that was painted in the chapel of the Blessed Sacrament in the church of St. Jacques, on the good side of the river, where sweet-faced angels made music on trumpets, citharas, manicordiums and little organs, against the blue vaults of a Heaven spangled with gold stars.

Yet his training in music was not, perhaps, as strange as it appeared. The family's most famous member in those years was Gaspar van Weerbecke, born in Oudenaarde, a celebrated priest-musician who spent much of his career in Italy, working especially for the Sforzas of Milan. In his time, Gaspar ranked with Jospin and Dupré as a composer of motets and Masses on themes from popular songs. One Mass was called *N'as tu pas?* ("Haven't you?"), another *Et trop penser* ("To think too much"). He wrote settings of the Lamentations, the *Stabat Mater* and verses from the Song of Songs. From time to time he came back north to recruit boys for the Duke of Milan's chapel, travelling as far as England in search of the purest voices. In 1472 Gaspar was in Bruges, the next year in Burgundy; in 1490 he was back in Oudenaarde, where his hometown celebrated and gave him wine. A little after this he returned for good, and was listed in 1496–97 among the musicians in Archduke Philip's chapel. All this had begun in the church of St. Walburga in Oudenaarde, much less grand than the cathedral at Tournai, where Gaspar had been a chorister. His story formed a link—indeed, a second link after Jehan's pardon—between the Dukes of Burgundy and the family at Caufours. And there were others. Oudenaarde was one of Margaret's dower properties, to which she would have paid attention; and in the late 1470s the ducal chapel was run by the Bishop of Tournai. It is not implausible that at some point, for some reason, these connections touched Piers's life. Certainly Gaspar's story proved that a leap from the banks of the Scheldt to a palace was not impossible, through music.

So Piers, if this version of his life was true, learned singing and Latin in the huge cathedral piled up like a fortress in the middle of town, and in the Good Children School close by. The cathedral, built in the grandest Romanesque style, was already several centuries old. Both buildings were surrounded by market stalls selling cloth, meat, bread, knives and cheese from as far away as "England and Cornwall". Women hawking leeks and onions plied their trade as the choristers filed past, their market hours set by the chiming of the bell as Christ's Body was raised at the high altar. From time to time, the town officials tried to ban commerce on "the Little Hill", so close to the cathedral, but they failed. This was no rarefied academy; although within the vast cathedral, in the forest of pillars and vaulting that rose a hundred feet above the heads of the worshippers, the racket of the world was hushed by the solemnity of God.

Piers's days at school would have been largely taken up with music of one kind or another. The appendix said he was taught the manicordium: in French, this meant the clavichords or some sort of keyboard instrument, possibly the organ that Brampton had mentioned. The strings of such instruments were sometimes wrapped in cloth to muffle the sound, especially in church, of small boys practising. Or perhaps he learned the monochord proper, a single-stringed instrument played with bridge and plectrum, which was used to instill the principles of harmony in small children and to accompany singing. Master Muguet or Maquet, his teacher, would have been in charge, as cantor, of the choir and all the music. (Since Muguet was not cantor before 1480, Piers would not have gone to the cathedral until he was seven, at the earliest.) The little chorister would have worn a robe supplied by the cathedral and would have taken his turn, as all the choirboys did, to serve at daily Mass in local great houses. The boys would stand four or five to the lectern that held the single book of music, small heads close, just behind the priest as he did his holy work at the altar. On Saturdays they sang the *Salve Regina*, a special devotion newly instituted in the cathedral, before "the Virgin Mary Our Lady of Tournai", as she was always called. To the silver Virgin, as tall as they were, flanked by blazing banks of candles and with a golden crown containing a jewel that shone at night like a star, they made the prayer for her mercy in their valley of exile and tears.

> *Salve regina, mater misericordiae,*
> *Via dulcedo et spes nostra salve.*
> *Ad te clamamus exules filii Evae,*
> *Ad te suspiramus gementes et flentes*
> *In hac lacrymarum valle.*

At Corpus Christi, and at the Feasts of St. Barnabas and St. John the Baptist in June, much play was made with crowns of red roses that were worn by the priests or placed on the Blessed Sacrament in procession. This would have been Piers's first contact with the higher significance of roses, carried reverentially (though their velvet petals still fell, making a crimson-pink mosaic underfoot) to be placed on the high altar. Once a year too, on the Feast of the Holy Innocents at the end of December, the choirboys would deck themselves as little priests, dance in the sanctuary and pretend to say Mass. Then, on a special stage on the cathedral porch, they would dress up one of the priests or minor canons as the Bishop of Fools, in full pontificals, and take him on a wild and jeering progress round every tavern in town. Such observances were seen elsewhere, but the show of the small counterfeit priests sometimes lasted as long as a week in Tournai, performed so boisterously that in 1462, just for that year, the town banned the foolish bishops, "or abbots, or anyone else like them". They were causing, it was said, great *excès et desrisions:* the very accusation Henry VII was to level against the madcap counterfeit boy who had been, perhaps, one of them. At the end of the days of dressing-up the mock robes were put away, the daily round of Masses and classes reverently resumed, and the unbroken voices rang again in the high dark vaulting, innocents and angels.

It was from this regime, Brampton said, that Piers ran away. A fine education, like rich food, was known to sometimes turn boys wilful. Music, especially organ music and polyphony, could also have dangerous effects, leading to vanity, pride and lasciviousness of heart. The Setubal testimonies made Piers fourteen or fifteen when, no longer an angelic choirboy in the Good Children School, he fled from Tournai and the "organist" who was teaching him. He became a runaway, the very definition of a bad child; and so, some would say, he remained.

The confession took great care to give a plausible chronology for Piers's life until he sailed for Portugal. But the fact remained that there were two distinct versions of his life, and they could not be reconciled. Either Piers had spent those years roving around the markets of Flanders, or he had learned the organ in Tournai. If the latter was true, as most of the evidence suggested, there seemed no reason for a different story.

In any event, neither story made sense of what had happened. This, as contemporaries pointed out, was an abusion that had lasted a very long time, played without mistakes. "The greatest persons in the world," as Molinet said, had been deceived by this young man and had heaped honours on him. Not least, he had taken a princess of Scotland as his wife. His English, his manners and his knowledge of the Yorkist court seemed exceptional. Even now, when he was a captive, ambassadors could not help seeing him as the noble young man they had imagined. Was this really a Flemish boatman's boy, indifferently trained, who had flitted from master to master before ending up in Ireland with no idea "what I should do and say"?

Francis Bacon, writing in the 1620s, best expressed the general bewilderment. "This youth was such a mercurial," he wrote, "as the like hath seldom been known . . . [and] one of the strangest examples of a personation, that ever was in elder or later times." Yet with the confession, he went on,

> the king did himself no right: for as there was a laboured tale of
> particulars, of Perkin's father and mother, and grandsire and

grandmother, and uncles and cousins, by names and surnames, and from what places he travelled up and down; so there was little or nothing to purpose of anything concerning his designs, or any practices that had been held with him; nor the duchess of Burgundy herself, that all the world did take knowledge of as the person that had put life and being into the whole business, so much as named or pointed at, [but utterly passed over in silence]. So that men missing of what they looked for looked about for they knew not what, and were in more doubt than before. But the king chose rather not to satisfy, than to kindle coals. . . .

The king's manner of showing things by pieces, and dark-lights, hath so muffled it, that it hath left it almost as a mystery to this day.

Nonetheless, some tried to explain it. Perkin himself, to begin with, must have been an extraordinary child. Vergil started this, and later chroniclers enhanced it; he was so marvellous that, even in Tournai with a boatman for a father, people might well have assumed he was royal. It sounded like the old story of the weaver's son with his prince's soul, mismatched by the stars. Bacon added, for good measure, dark powers of intoxication and enchantment.

The musical version of Perkin's childhood explained the mismatch slightly better. Tournai was his place, but the little chorister had naturally grown restless there, educated beyond the town's drab horizons and the salty dockers' talk. According to Geronymo Zurita, he confessed to Henry not only his name and his base birth but also "how he had longed that in his upbringing, and in the disposition of his person, he should correspond to the blood and nobility that he pretended to be of." This was why, despite "the sort of man he was, so dirty [soez] and of vile condition", he nonetheless sustained his character "for so much time, and with such great industry and talent." Pressure from others had not done this; everything came from inside, from his own motivation to be more than he was.

The theory plausibly fitted his character as Brampton had described it: the moço posturing and pestering to be taken to Portugal, the boy dressing in his silks in Ireland. He was always too restless to settle in one place, and also too hungry for the admiration of others. Vergil thought Perkin had responded so readily to Margaret's teaching because "it's the nature of that sort of man, coming from that background, to strive for the praises of those better than himself." In the end, he wrote, he drove himself to destruction because he despised his birth. Molinet's conclusion was similar. Perkin had been pushed, but the prime factor had been his own *outrecuidance*, his overweening conceit, which had turned him into the gorgeous prince he had observed in Flanders.

Yet even that, surely, could not account for what he had become. No piece of evidence offered up by Henry and his spies could explain it. Contemporaries, therefore, put these explanations aside. Ambassadors ignored them, as did the rulers they worked for. More gallingly for Henry, his own historians did so. Both Vergil and André, under the king's nose, clung to the story that Margaret had trained Perkin for years before his appearance. They preserved "born in Tournai," his baseness and his name; but if those things were true, the most intensive princely training, they believed, must have followed them. André even added, for good measure, his story that Perkin had been Brampton's servant at the Yorkist court itself. To a man, they refused to touch the allegation that he had merely been kidnapped and trained in Ireland. The masquerade, they were convinced, had started long before, with the boy already under Margaret's wing when he was sent to Portugal. The record suggests that Henry, too, thought this was the real story. And if this vital part of the young man's life had been rewritten, as it seemed, it raised the question of what else had been invented, and why.

When Simnel had been captured and exposed, nothing more was made of him than that he was an artisan's son, trained by a priest. By contrast, the Perkin information was overwhelming. Henry clearly felt he needed it because he could produce no real York, living or dead, to make his case impregnable. It seemed unnecessary, all the same, to argue quite so much; especially since, having argued so much, he seemed not even to have convinced himself.

V

THE KING WAS NEVER SATISFIED with the Perkin story. Although he had the main outlines early, he followed up through 1494 with almost obsessive spy-work and, as he claimed, interviews and depositions in

London. The envoys sent to Flanders between 1493 and 1495 hinted first
at the boy's base birth, then at a bourgeois family in Tournai, without apparently providing names either for him or for them. They also brought
no written proofs: just "assurances by mouth alone", Molinet said. No
mention of Perkin or the Werbecques reached Molinet until more than
two years later, when the French confession arrived at the court of Burgundy.

Right up to that point Henry kept looking, always groping further
and gathering more. In the summer of 1495 the king subjected to interro-
gation anyone useful he could find among the captives from the Deal invasion. Two men who worked for him during those years—his astrologer,
William Parron, and Richard Nanfan, then deputy-lieutenant of Calais
—later admitted they had feared he would kill them if they failed to sort
out the rumours that Edward's son was alive. "I had likely to be put to a
great plunge for my troth," said Nanfan, thinking of the gallows. Parron
thought he might lose his head.

Henry's anxiety to find more and better details, or indeed a whole
new line of evidence, was well known in Europe. Other kings, wishing
either for his friendship or to have him in their debt, did their best to help
him. None helped more than the French, who needed particularly to have
him on their side as the Holy League formed against them. From at least
1494 Henry's research was assisted by Louis Malet, Seigneur de Graville
and Admiral of the French fleet, who was then also Governor of
Picardy. Commines said that Malet was Charles VIII's favourite among
his closest advisers, acting as his chamberlain and gentleman of the bedchamber, and he had undoubtedly known Plantagenet during his sojourn
in Paris. In December 1494, Richmond Herald's secret instructions for
his trip to France included the note to thank Charles especially for "such
services as [the admiral] has done . . . and will do for us" at "our express
charge and commandment", and the request that Malet should keep
doing Henry's service and pleasure in any way he could.

Charles himself helped too. After Richmond had "put him right as
to the truth of the matter", as Soncino said, and after Henry had written
to tell him "that it was quite clear that Perkin was a bourgeois of Tournai," he made himself useful. By the beginning of 1496, Charles was providing Picard spies for Henry to send into Scotland. He also sent him
evidence from a Portuguese herald, sealed by himself and his council, to

prove, in Ferdinand and Isabella's words, "that the so-called Duke of York was the son of a barber, and offering to send over his father and mother, etc." His offer sounded exactly what Henry needed. Tournai was technically a French city, from which only Charles had the power to extract the Werbecques, as his subjects, to send them to England. De Puebla had noted that the Kentings at Deal knew that "his" father and mother lived in France. Charles's Portuguese herald was plausibly Tanjar, who also gave evidence at Setubal; and *barbero*, as Ferdinand and Isabella had it, may well have been a slip for *barquero*. But Henry was not interested. He "did not like the proofs and testimonies that [the French king] sent of who *he* is," de Puebla said. This came more than three years after Henry had started delving. He did not like the Tournai story, at least in Charles's version, and wanted something else.

The French, in any case, were not to be trusted. When they wanted Henry as their friend, the young man was a barber's or a boatman's son; when they wanted to put pressure on him, attempting to frustrate any alliances with Spain or the Scots, he was still the Duke of York. When John Ramsay met Alexander Monypeny in September 1496 in Scotland, they talked about the "boy". Monypeny remarked, in Ramsay's words, that "great inquisition had been made to understand of Perkin's birth both by the admiral and him." The ambassador implied that they had not come up with much, so Ramsay privately showed him "the writing" drawn up by Meautis, Henry's French secretary, which presumably contained what Henry had gleaned of the boy's background so far. It must have been much the same as the evidence Charles had offered. But Monypeny looked at it, "and he plainly said he never understood it but rather trowed [believed] ye contrary."

Monypeny's part in the delving, after his stint as Plantagenet's minder in Paris, was curious in itself. His failure to credit Henry's story, which by now had been known at Charles's court for more than two years, was less so. Since he had come to offer good money for James's guest, he could not possibly say he was a nobody. To confirm that he thought "rather the contrary", he sought out and kept daily company with his former charge at the Scottish court, as if he still believed him to be Richard, Duke of York. There is no knowing what Monypeny truly made of Ramsay's "boy"; but he was enmeshed, as everyone else was, in a diplomatic game played out at the highest level.

Ramsay, realising Henry's keen interest in all this, said he would tell him more when he came home. The thrust of his letter, however, was that the king's story was proving hard to sell. Nor was it being mentioned openly at James's court. It was still no more than a background rumour, a rustle of papers exchanged in anterooms, and Henry was doing nothing to push it forward.

But help was also offered from other quarters. In April 1496, when Ferdinand and Isabella got wind that Charles had sent "some *dicho*" (literally, some witticism) to Henry attesting to the young man's identity, they were profoundly annoyed. If the King of England wanted anything of this sort, they told de Puebla, *they* could do much better, sending Henry the statements of "lots of people who know him". They promised this on April 14th, exactly eleven days before the depositions were taken down in Setubal. But they knew all about those already, warmly recommending what Rui de Sousa had said. They also offered, "if it will be any use to the king", to send him the young man's father and mother, "who, they tell us, are in Portugal and are our subjects." De Sousa had seen this father and mother, they went on (this thought interpolated in the draft, and trailing down the margin). The next moment they thought better of both remarks, and the secretary crossed them out with a couple of light lines, sloping this way and that, as if the thought had hardly been serious in the first place. There were certainly no parents in Portugal, but there could have been if it had been diplomatically useful to find them.

Ferdinand and Isabella offered in the same letter to try everything, *todas las vias*, to make Henry's lot easier. The testimony from Setubal should have been especially useful to him: circumstantial, consistent, and tying the boy firmly to one family whose name and address were given. Yet the Spanish sovereigns were in no hurry to send the evidence to him, as if, in some odd way, they thought it might be unwelcome. "You should try this on the King of England as though it came from you," they told de Puebla, "and tell us what he says in reply." In January 1497, nine months after the evidence had been taken, Henry was obviously asking about it, but they were still fussing round. "We haven't sent the testimony about York with this letter," they explained to de Puebla,

because the copy we have has been authenticated by only one notary, and it's in Castilian, and it seems embarrassing to us to send such a thing in a language that they don't understand over there. We are sending off immediately to get it translated into Latin and signed by three notaries, and when it comes back we will send it to you at once and with great care.

Looking at the document, it is hard to see why they were so worried. Fernan Peres Mexia, the notary, had written it out with exceptional regularity and neatness over two and a half sides of paper; in a spidery hand and in Spanish, to be sure, but with only one tiny deletion and two small blots. Evidently it had been copied out properly from rough notes taken at the interviews. As for authentication, that could hardly have been more splendid: a four-step pyramid of Mexia's name and title crowned with a cross and big crossed keys, signifying "notary apostolic", which took up almost a quarter of the page. Had Ferdinand and Isabella sent it to de Puebla, he could easily have seen to the translation.

Nonetheless in March 1498, five months after Perkin had allegedly confessed to Henry, they were writing as though they had kept the document to themselves right up to the last moment. "We give great thanks to God for having shown the truth so clearly," they wrote to Sancho de Londoño,

> which truth we always believed and took for just such a certainty as we now see, because here in the parts of Portugal where he was [still "he"; no need to say who] we got so much assurance of who he was, as now has appeared by his own confession, and with this same certainty we affirm it both by word and in our letters where he was and what was said about him; and because news has come that Fernando Perez [with our letters] has been lost at sea, we ask you to go into England and tell the king all this on our behalf, and find out if there is anything we can do for him, because we will do it most willingly. . . .

Fernando Perez de Ayala, who had been sent to check on his relative in Scotland, had been drowned that month on his way to England. He may well have had the Setubal evidence with him but, if so, it was very late. Of course the Spanish sovereigns had always wished to be useful to Henry, as they kept saying; but perhaps, as long as the marriage negotiations for Katherine and Arthur dragged on, not too useful. If they had still wanted, from time to time, to frighten Henry with the thought of York, it was not helpful to their case to send proof that "he was the son of a boatman before, from Tournai which is in Flanders."

Once the boy was in custody, however, Ferdinand and Isabella happily took credit for knowing who he was all along. In their letter to Londoño, for the first time, they called the nuisance "Periquin", and said how pleased they were to hear he had been captured. The French were pleased too, and had also thought the deception obvious, though they much enjoyed boasting, Soncino said, that they had kept this imaginary enemy going against Henry for years. Both parties could have kept York in play even longer, had it suited them. For this reason, Henry seemed to feel he could not trust any evidence they offered him. He could only trust his own.

Accordingly, the king went on adding to the details he had of the Werbecques. In 1496 and 1497 payments to anonymous Frenchmen and women were made regularly, probably for such information. In the late summer of 1497, only days before the boy's surrender, Breton spies were still providing titbits about the family. On August 16th one brought letters from "John Lenesque's wife", possibly a Tournai contact; another arrived on September 20th with "word of the death of John Perkin". No other such entry, payment for news of a death, appears in John Heron's accounts, but this added another crumb to Henry's precious store. His letter of October 7th placed Perkin's father confidently in the past tense, *sometime while he lived comptroller*. Heron's transposition of "Perkin" to become his assumed father's surname (rather as, in the patent rolls, Walter Herford, baker, became "Walter Baker") neatly caught the only reason why this man was important. In several minds, not just Heron's, Jehan Werbecque was indeed "John Perkin".

His name caused Henry a strange amount of trouble. In 1493–94 the king had it right ("a boatman named Werbec"), but constant worrying with the story later made him doubtful. The letter of October 17th 1497 to Waterford, after mentioning that Perkin Warbeck should properly be Piers Osbeck, apparently left a blank after "son to John", as if Henry was not sure he could assume the father was "Osbeck" just because the son now was.

The king attributed the change of name to Perkin's own information, "freely and openly shown". But if Perkin said that, he was lying, for the name was only Werbecque or Weerbecke in Tournai or the country roundabout. Osbeck was unknown. Henry was lying too, for he had been trying out "Osbeck" at least since the summer of 1495, when it had appeared in his letter of thanks to Canterbury. The punctilious city clerk, who had called the invader Peter or Perkyn Warbecke before, now corrected himself: he was "named Peter Osbek". Henry's source may well have been Spanish or Portuguese, some witness who had a romance-speaker's trouble with saying the name. (Gaspar van Weerbecke's name gave such grief to his Italian employers that they called him simply "Gaspar".) But whatever its origin, this was not a simple change of spelling, as Henry confirmed by mentioning it at all. It was a conscious change of name from something true to something false.

Why this was done is a mystery. Names often mattered little in this world, jobs or rank being more important: so men and women were called, quite simply, "the ambassador of France", "the herald", "the silk-woman", "the mayor's son". As for the names themselves, people sometimes boasted several. Pardons were issued to offenders "by what name or names soever [they] be called", or with a list of aliases and addresses. The identity of men and women was not fixed about one name, and Henry may have believed the change was of no consequence. Fabyan's flung-out remark that Brampton had called the youth "Petyr Osbek or otherwise Styenbek" suggested that Londoners, at least, did not care what this "unhappy imp" was called.

Yet Henry had made great efforts to fix this boy's identity, and now appeared to be undermining them. To English ears and tongues "Osbeck" was trickier than "Warbeck"—a name by now well established in the copious legal records of the commissions set up to deal with the conspiracies. By February 1494, and probably months earlier, "Peter Warbeck, born in Tournai" was already the leader of the plots against Henry. Now the name was in question again, assuming peculiar forms. The confusion was plain in London, where on October 12th 1497 the council learned from Henry's letter that Peter Warbeck, as they had always called him, had now confessed "that he himself was that same person, Peter Warboys". If the king or his captive were trying to protect the family, or lay a false trail, this was effort wasted, for the Werbecques and their circle were too clearly identified for that. Yet someone chose to muddy the waters.

It is probable that Henry's captive did not volunteer the name

Osbeck at all. There was no reason why this garble should have reached his ears before he was taken prisoner. He had never heard it, but agreed to it, since he was bound to do whatever Henry wanted. He may also have agreed to "Piers", rather than volunteered it, since the name was English and unknown in Tournai. Like Osbeck, it may have come from Portuguese evidence. Together, they made yet another identity for him.

"Perkin", of course, was a baby name, not a proper name bestowed at baptism or usable in law unless he was actually a child. It became attached to him, Vergil said, with all its connotations of littleness, feebleness and silliness, "when his folly had made him an object of contempt". Had he accepted it he would have colluded in the insult, rather as if James IV had acknowledged himself as the "Jemmy" that Skelton mocked. It may be significant that the only time he is known to have used it, in telling his sea-story to de Puebla, the other characters in the story did not know who Perkin was.

In any event, when he came—obligingly or not—to sign his name, he used the version that Henry and he had now agreed between them. In October, at Exeter, he apparently wrote "per Pero Osbek" at the bottom of a copy of the confession, in French, that Richmond later showed Raimondo Soncino in London. ("He says it's Perkin's writing," said Soncino, betraying a smidgen of doubt.) The confession took up a single sheet of paper, with the main text written in a different hand. As for his signature, a trace of class still hovered in that *per:* the suggestion of clerical training that had seemed to show through, almost three years before, in *Rychard d'engleterre manu propria.* The same hand wrote, but this time apparently in very large letters, as Soncino reproduced it in his dispatch to the Duke of Milan. The writer was making a statement, as he was by embracing the false name "Osbeck" at all, though few of those who saw it could have guessed what that statement was.

But "Piers Osbeck" did not catch on. It survived for only three or four months in official use before giving way, inevitably, to the Peter or Perkin Warbeck everyone already knew. "Osbeck" featured especially in the documents recording the collection of fines for the rebellion in the West Country, as if it was most closely attached to that time and that place. It appeared as Osebeck, Oxebeche and Osebethe. Fabyan, remembering how the name had first emerged in London, revealed it as a gift to doggerel-artists. "And shortly after," the chronicler wrote, "were made of him sundry Roundells & songs to his shame & derision, whereof one I intend to express In the end of this mayor's time." He forgot to do so, but they could be imagined.

Londoners may not have been the only ones who played around with his name. The French version of the confession, and the letter Perkin allegedly wrote home later, produced a new hybrid, "Wesbecque". Molinet, who saw this version, naturally picked it up. Again, it was an apparently senseless change of name from the easy and established version. The person who did this may have been the same French clerk, taking down from dictation, who had also produced "Sir Edward Brixton"; or it may have been the young man, clever and not yet bereft of tricks, who was supposed to have written these documents himself. It is quite likely that "Wesbecque" was a play on words by someone who knew Flemish as well as French: with the Flemish *wezen*, to be or to be real, and *weze*, the word for an orphan. For those who could understand him, this was Orphan Perkin speaking.

"Perkin", too, had been used very little before the young man arrived in Cornwall. Henry himself seemed deliberately to avoid it. With his own officers, he almost always called him the *garçon* or the "feigned lad". With ambassadors, even the favoured de Puebla, he did not use "Perkin" until the autumn of 1497, preferring "the boy who says he is the son of King Edward", or "he who calls himself Plantagenet". By repeating the claim his foe was making, Henry gave some substance to the threat against him. This may have been why, as late as September 15th, 1497, the king apparently referred to him as the Duke of York, and certainly offered no alternative, in a letter he wrote to the pope. But it is equally possible that, in his careful heart, he did not yet feel he knew enough to call him "Perkin" publicly.

As soon as he thought he could use the name, foreign envoys could help his case by spreading "Perkin" round Europe. But habits of deference, or hedging, took a while to break. Both the Milanese and Venetian ambassadors tried out "Pirichino" before the young man's capture, Soncino on September 8th and Trevisano on the 17th, but both, on subsequent information that made more of his strength, made him *il ducha di Jorch* again. "At least," wrote Soncino at the end of 1497, reflecting on Perkin's defeat, "there is no one else of the royal blood at home and abroad who might cause war and mischief." *No one else*, from a man who had seen and read the confession, signed by Perkin's hand—and had seen him too, in his humiliation.

Henry seemed similarly reluctant to publicise the other details he knew. He could have published a report of Perkin's origins, attested by competent authorities, at least three years before he did. The rulers of both France and Spain implicitly urged him to do so by offering their own versions, and Vergil said that Henry took great pains to get the story out as soon as he knew it, in 1493. But this was not so. All the king did in fact, Bacon said, was to spread the details "by court fames," or palace rumours, "which commonly print better than printed proclamations." He seemed to be waiting for his rival to confirm them himself.

Even then, Henry used the vital document with circumspection. Soncino, when he was shown the French confession, said that many similar sheets, all signed, had been made to be sent "so I take it" to various places. André said that Henry had it printed, in one of the first such uses of the presses, and distributed "to strike fear into the wicked in a public way". But Vergil, despite his earlier remarks, mentioned no confession of any kind, oral or written. No originals survive, and no master-copy, with or without "per Pero Osbek" to authenticate it. The wholesale disappearance of the confession documents stands in striking contrast to the survival in triplicate of the expenses for Perkin's capture.

London at least saw a copy of the confession as soon as Henry returned there in November 1497, for that is when it appears in the London Chronicle. The city council may have heard it earlier, on October 12th, when the mayor, John Tate, read out to them a letter from the king "and other letters from various other persons declaring that Peter Warboys had come to our lord the king of his own accord and confessed . . . that he was born in Tournay in the parts of Germany." There may later have been multiple and printed copies in London, handed out in the street as Perkin passed, or there may have been no more than that original, sent to the mayor and aldermen and copied out by the chronicler, as royal missives often were. Fabyan said that Henry publicised the confession in London to avoid "the further harm of his subjects," as if the nuisance was not yet crushed, or as if, in this Yorkist-leaning city, the sight of Perkin was dangerous without it. But there is no contemporary evidence that Henry's captive read the confession publicly at any stage. Only at the end did he seem, in some way, to paraphrase and acknowledge part of what it said of him.

The London Chronicle asserted that, for similar reasons of prudence and security, copies were sent into "all places of England and elsewhere". But no town besides London hinted at receiving one. The French version, sent through Calais, may have been more widely distributed. Jean Molinet saw it at the court of Burgundy, for his bizarre spelling of the names of the Yorkist plotters in Ireland ("Jehan Water, Stimen Pomouni, Jehan Taillant, Hurbert Baurd") exactly follows it, as does the order in which they appear. He saw Henry's letter of October 7th too, reproducing much of its detail and phrasing in his chronicle. Again, however, no original of the French confession survives, and no ambassador seems to have sent a copy home. For the most part, despite all the labours, it seems to have been ignored.

Molinet's first use of the revealed name, Pierquin Wesbecque, came right at the start of his 293rd chapter, like a great cry of relief. But his last words on the young man called him not Perkin but the White Rose, as if he still more naturally thought of him that way.

VI

A DEEPER DIFFICULTY also haunted the confession, of family and blood. Henry had made no physical connection between his captive and the Werbecques of Tournai. The father and mother of the confession seemed tied by the lightest of bonds to their son. They played almost no part in his upbringing; he was with them for a while, but was constantly farmed out and soon gone for good. Henry's greatest problem with the evidence he was offered was to fit his prisoner to this family.

There was clearly some reason to connect the young man to the Werbecques. It would seem preposterous, otherwise, to have picked them out, although a king could deal with people of that class in any way he chose. The route of inquiry, too, may have seemed clear enough. Henry's agents, asking their questions and distributing their rewards, had tracked the boy back from Ireland, to Portugal, to Bruges, to Middelburg, to Tournai, possibly on Brampton's evidence. There they found Jehan Werbecque, whose teenage son was said to be missing. He was therefore the boy's father, this was the family, and all other details could be fitted neatly—or not so neatly—round this fundamental fact.

Yet this "fact" was never proven save by the king's own word, the word of his captive given in custody, and the corroboration of people who wished to be in Henry's good graces. The story had never needed to be true if others would co-operate, and they did so. Contemporary chroniclers raised no questions; they were interested not in the parentage of the lad, but in his training. Only much later did the notion of a mismatch, so clearly suggested by Henry's behaviour at the time, cross the minds of writers on the subject. Some surmised that the Werbecques had played foster-parents to a fugitive prince, though surely no prince, no matter how destitute or dejected, would have sought out shelter with a thug in Caufours. Some thought that Jehan had gone for a spell to England, where Edward IV had fallen for his wife and fathered her son. The tale had currency round Tournai itself, and in 1850 Kervyn de Lettenhove, the most eminent historian of Flanders, called this "tradition" "not improbable". In fact, nothing supported it save the English name "Piers" and the care that was possibly lavished on his education. But the story played to the strong impression that these were not quite the parents, and this was not quite their son.

Henry never confirmed the point as contemporaries expected, by linking his rival visibly and physically to the people who were meant to be his parents. This was the easiest way to scotch his claims and, at the same time, humiliate him: the boy going home to mother, as the Kentings had mocked that he should. Both Charles VIII and the Spanish sovereigns, by offering to send his parents, confirmed that this was the acknowledged way to deal with impostors. Charles seemed to have the Werbecques specifically in mind. But Henry rejected or ignored his offer, "not wanting it," de Puebla said. He did so despite the fact that, if he had talked to Brampton or heard anything of what was said in Setubal, he would have gathered that Jehan Werbecque was desperate to see his son again and know he was alive.

The story came from the herald Tanjar, who had returned to Tournai—his native town, or so he claimed—sometime in the early 1490s. He was in the house of one of his relations, he told his questioners, when the boy's father had suddenly turned up. The father had apparently heard that Tanjar had come from Portugal and had seen his son there. So he asked, Was this true? Had he seen him?

The herald said he didn't know him. Then he asked: "Who did he go with?"

His father said, "He went with the wife of Duarte Brandon, in a ship with her notary."

The herald said that he had seen a boy arrive over there in Portugal, the one who had since gone to Ireland, and that they had raised him up as a king, saying he was the son of King Edward.

The father said: "That's my son."

"What distinguishing marks did he have?" asked the herald.

The father said he had a mark on his face under his eye, and he was a bit of a fool, and he had an upper lip that was raised up a bit and thin legs, and that when he left there he was fourteen going on fifteen.

The herald said that he had all those marks.

Then his father, weeping, said, "That is my son, who got him mixed up in this, ah me, they will kill him." For he had no other son. . . .

Coincidences like this were the stuff of legends. Tristan's father, Rual, having looked for his missing foster-son the world over, came after almost four years to Denmark, where he "fell in with" the two pilgrims who had first met Tristan in Cornwall. He asked them whether they had seen his son; they asked him what Tristan looked like; his father described him, "and they told him how long it was since they had seen just such a boy . . . all his peculiarities of face, hair, speech, behaviour, body and clothes; and . . . Rual saw at once that the descriptions tallied." In much the same way Jehan Werbecque, still searching for his son after four years or longer, fell in with a foreigner by chance and discovered, weeping, that this stranger had the very news he wanted.

If this tale was true, father and son seem to have kept in touch before the boy left. Jehan knew the details of the ship Piers had sailed on and who had accompanied him. Brampton's evidence at Setubal claimed that they had also been in contact afterwards, with Piers attempting to send news back to him through Brampton's other servants. Yet Tanjar also implied that this was no ordinary boy. For some extraordinary reason, his father, like Rui de Sousa, immediately identified him with the young man hailed as a king in Ireland. By his kingship he knew him, before anything else.

Other parts of Tanjar's evidence sounded more authentic. Jehan's list of his son's distinguishing marks was almost incoherent, mixing tiny signs with general observations, as a grieving father might well do. The boy's "thin legs" showed his delicateness, the reason perhaps why Jehan had had to indulge in different dreams for him, his precious only son. Whatever those hopes were, the boy, "a bit of a fool", had run away from them. There was tenderness as well as rebuke in that remark. Such a father, searching through Tournai with tears and petitions for news of his vanished son, and able—as fathers were presumed to be—to bring the boy to repentant obedience, could surely have been put to Henry's service while he lived. He never was.

For several years no approach was made either to Nicaise Werbecque, who had been identified as Perkin's mother. She was absent, even strangely so, from the Setubal testimonies, where only Jehan had charge of the boy or any eagerness to find him. Of course, it was only the young man's father who had ever been of interest to Henry; but typically in such cases (Tristan apart) both parents grieved and searched. By contrast, the news that Piers sent back to Tournai was directed only to his father. No mother was ever mentioned or invoked. The fugitive that Brampton's wife took in seemed desperate not only to travel but also to acquire a family, as if he had never had one. He wanted to live with them, Brampton said, "like one of his sons", and it was because Brampton would not "take him for his son" that he wanted to leave again. In the French version of the confession he spoke of his mother in the past tense, as though she had died. In both versions, his "certain season" with his aunt and uncle, when very young, might have suggested the same.

In the English confession, however, his mother emerged as the more important parent in Piers's life. It was she who had "led him" away from home to learn Flemish, his necessary bilingual education; his father had had no particular charge of him. On October 13th, 1497, therefore, the omission was rectified, and Perkin wrote to her from custody in Exeter.

Ma mere, tant humblement comme faire je puis, me recommande a vous.

Mother, as humbly as I may, I commend myself to you. And may it please you to know that by fortune, under the colour of an invented thing [*une chose controuvee*], certain Englishmen made me take upon myself that I was the son of King Edward of England, called his second son, Richard Duke of York. I now find myself in such trouble that if you are not in this hour my good mother, I am compelled to be in great danger and inconvenience, because of the name which, at their instance, I have taken upon myself and the enterprise which I have carried out.

And so that you may understand and know clearly that I am your son and none other, may it please you to remember how, when I parted from you with Berlo to go to Antwerp, you wept as you said "God be with you," and how my father went with me as far as the Porte de Marvis. And also the last letter you wrote to me at Middelburg by your hand, [saying] that you had been delivered of a daughter, and also that my brother Thiroyan and my sister Jehanne had died of the plague at the time of the procession of Tournai. And how my father, you and I were going to live at Lannoy outside the town; and you remember the beautiful pig-place [*Porquiere*].

The King of England now holds me in his power, to whom I have declared the truth of the affair, very humbly imploring him that his pleasure may be to pardon me of the offence which I have done to him, since I am not his native subject at all, and what I did was at the instigation and wishes of his own subjects. But I have as yet received no good reply from him, nor have I hope of one, at which my heart is very sad. However, Mother, I beg and pray you to have pity upon me and purchase my deliverance. Commend me to my godfather Pierart Flan, to Master Jehan Stalyn my uncle, to my comrade Guilhem Rucq, and to Jehan Bordeau. I hear that my father has departed this life, God keep his soul, which is heavy news to me. And may you be with God. Written at Exeter, the 13th day of October, by the hand of your humble son,

Pierrequin Wezbecq.

Mother I pray you to send me a little money so that my guards may be kinder to me for my giving them something. Commend me to my Aunt Stalyn, and to all my good neighbours.

To Mademoiselle Catherine Wezbecq, my mother, living at St. Jean on the Scheldt.

The letter was very like the confession: so like it, that the source was certainly the same. The French version of the confession had the same spelling and something of the same style, including an overfondness for the word *pareillement*, "as well", as fact was piled on fact. The two documents, both produced in October, seem to have arrived in Flanders simultaneously in a number of copies, and survived together in the archives of Tournai and Courtrai. They were clearly sent to each town as a pair, or in a bundle alongside Henry's October letter to his "friends" and Daubeney's letter from Marazion, to authenticate each other, and they did so to striking effect. (Daubeney had begged his Calais colleagues, in a postscript, not to fail to pass on his news "as truth".) Whether the letter to Tournai was ever intended, as it claimed, for Nicaise Werbecque privately, its public life was more important. Most probably it was meant to persuade and shame Maximilian and Margaret, for it was not redacted in English and was apparently never circulated in England.

Letter and confession kept in careful step. Both gave the "trading", rather than the musical, version of his life. Once more he went to Antwerp and Middelburg, after which he naturally lost contact. Aunt Jane appeared again, together with Uncle John, and Guilhem Rucq appeared from the French appendix. The Irish kidnapping was given in much the same form: *certain Englishmen made me take upon myself that I was the son of King Edward of England.* At the same time, the letter, unlike the confession, had kept up with the news. In the confession, Perkin implied that his father was still alive; in the letter, he had heard that he was dead. The confession did not say that Pierart Flan was his godfather; the letter did, perhaps because—alongside the news of his father's death—word had come that Flan was now doing godfatherly duties as the legal guardian of Jehan Werbecque's children.

All through the letter, however, the writer also inserted private references to prove to his mother that he was her son. None of this was in the confession. He spoke as son to mother, as they might have sat talking in some window seat, he holding her hand, trying to impress on her the reality of who he was. To underline how vulnerable he was, and how much her little boy, he used the baby name he had refused to use in England. For her he was Perkin, or Pierrequin, again.

The references were tiny but convincing. He reminded her of her tears as he left for Antwerp, how his father had walked on with him through the half-dozen evil-smelling tanners' streets that lay between Caufours and the Porte de Marvis, and how she had written to him some years later with news of the birth of a daughter. He recalled deaths in the family and dreams of moving to safe Lannoy, a walled town away from the river in the lee of an impressive castle, the home of counts. Only a real son would remember dreams. *Et vouz souvenez de la belle Porquiere*: a difficult word to interpret, probably the communal field where pigs were meant to be put in the daytime, rather than being left free to roam in Tournai's gardens and streets. Possibly this was a family joke, as if a piggery could ever be *belle*. At this point you could smell the scene, bristling pigs rooting in the dung-hill, the mud of the *Tournésis* underfoot, a typically Picard idyll of a quieter country life. "Commend me to Jehan Bordeau": a name of no meaning or importance, except to his mother and to him.

The letter gained extra authenticity from its portrait of the king. He was not merciful, as he usually liked to present himself, but impervious to pity or argument. If royal officers had written this they would surely have mentioned Henry's justice and clemency, but Perkin saw no hope of it. The letter seemed credible, moreover, in everything else it said. Such remarkable detail, like the list of neighbours and teachers, could not have been invented. No one would have taken the trouble to produce such a picture of a life if it were not true.

Yet in Tournai, for which it was intended, much in the letter would have rung false. To begin with, Perkin seemed to have forgotten his own surname, his mother's name, and her address. His name was not Wezbecq, and neither was hers; this variant was as unknown in Tournai as "Osbeck" was. Second, her baptismal name was Nicaise or Caisine, not Catherine, which was what she had been called in England. In Tournai, following the French fashion, the names were attached to two different saints and hence to two separate city parishes. Her son would hardly have got it wrong. Third, she lived at St. Jean des Caufours, as everyone in Tournai called it, not at St. Jean on the Scheldt. That address, for what it was worth, seems to have come from Brampton.

The language of the letter was ordinary, unremarkable northern French, grammatically correct but with no regard for euphony or elision. It was the same as the French into which Henry's "letter to his friends" had been translated, and in which the confession had appeared. By comparison with the records of town deliberations in Tournai, where the standard elisions were naturally made, it read like the French of an Englishman. In fact, the distinctive Picard use of "ch" for "c", as in *chité* (city), *menchonge* (lie) and *Franche*, appeared more often in Henry's and Daubeney's letters, translated into French in Calais, than it did in Perkin's. A private letter to a mother, though, was surely an occasion for writing in the language of home.

Other things seemed wrong, too. Perkin mentioned that Lannoy was "outside the town", as if his mother would not know that. He also spoke of "the procession of Tournai," during which, according to the letter his mother had sent him in Middelburg, his brother and sister had died of the plague. Tournaisiens talking among themselves did not call it that: this was just *le prochession* or *le grant prochession*, when the statue of Our Lady and her glittering reliquary were carried through the streets on the feast of the Exaltation of the Holy Cross in September. The festival lasted nine days, with special food—roast game, goslings stuffed with shallots—on sale in the streets, and with thousands of people visiting. It was the high point of Tournai's year, exhaustively prepared for. Only a foreigner would call this "the procession of Tournai". Its fame raised the suspicion that it was in the letter mostly to gild its authenticity, and that, as with the directions to Lannoy, the writer was trying too hard to set a scene he did not know.

As Perkin remembered his mother's letter, the plague and the procession had coincided. Certainly plague would not have stopped it from taking place. In the summer of 1426, when terrible pestilence broke out in Tournai, preparations for "the" procession went on as usual all through August, with busy sewing of the guild liveries and banners and with no thought of cancellation. The strange and poignant scene conjured in the letter was therefore possible: Tournai in its splendour, hung with flags, bright with liveries and trumpets and deafened with bells, the Virgin's reliquary swaying past under a canopy of velvet and silk, while in the house by the Scheldt two little bodies lay in winding sheets, bunched herbs burning slowly in the fireplace to keep the contagion away. It was impossible only because, between 1484 and the end of the decade, there was no plague in Tournai.

The sister who had died was called Jehanne, the letter said. The new sister, apparently born at almost the same time, was called Jehanne too, and survived. The letter ignored her. Perkin sent her no greeting and did not ask about her; she was just "a daughter", impersonally noted. The proposed move to Lannoy, apparently mentioned in his mother's letter, featured only his parents and himself, as if the suddenly smaller family was trying to start again somewhere else. And as for that, it was surely improbable that his father, whose only life was the river, would move away from it.

Even without their high false colour of pestilence and procession, the birth and deaths in his mother's letter seemed too dramatic a combination. More plausibly, they looked like an attempt to devise a family structure that fitted the Werbecques as they were in 1497, apparently with two young children still at home. The traumas relayed to Middelburg contributed to a feeling that the frame was not quite straight, and that, for all the labour, the young man and the family did not quite connect. Perhaps it was not so impressive, after all, that he remembered his mother crying when she said goodbye to him, or the gate where his father had left him. What mother would not weep? What other road went to Antwerp? What Tournaisiens did not think sometimes, in those years of sporadic war and famine, of leaving the city and its troubles for a quieter life outside?

Those who were able to compare the stories attached to this young man, as Richard and now as Perkin, could notice that they moved in parallel. In both, at about the age of nine or ten, a weeping mother said goodbye to him. A father-figure, in Richard of York's case the man who had spared his life, gave him his instructions for the road ahead, before he was handed over to a life of permanent wandering. Two men had charge of him (in the confession, Berlo and his master Alexander), but he was never to see his family again. You could choose, as you listened and looked at him, which biography seemed the more true. There was Richard's story, with its curious lacunae and lapses of memory, based on a premise that strained credulity; or this one, Perkin's tale, minute and circumstantial, but strewn with mistakes too fundamental to be explained away by disorientation or distress.

The letter was most remarkable, however, for its lack of feeling and courtesy. This was supposed to be a son writing to his mother after fourteen years of absence, eleven of them without contact of any kind. It should have been hard to exaggerate the remorse and love he felt. But the letter began, with extraordinary curtness, "Mother". No qualifying words: no "right worshipful and reverent", no "most honoured", "right special" or "most beloved", the words that were naturally given to mothers. Nor did he ask for her blessing, a source of deep pain to any mother if it was omitted. Margaret Paston rebuked Sir John strongly when, on a rare occasion, he forgot to seek it. A son writing to his mother began with that genuflection, putting himself physically in her presence and often continuing as though he was responding to her anxious questions. Here, by way of example, was Henry VII writing to his own mother. As he himself admitted, he did not do so very often; but when he did, it was as a son was meant to.

> Madam, my most entirely well-beloved lady and mother, I recommend me unto you in the most humble and lowly wise that I can, beseeching you of your daily and continual blessings. . . . I shall be as glad to please you as your heart can desire it, and I know well, that I am as much bounden so to do, as any creature living for the great and singular motherly love and affection that it hath pleased you at all times to bear towards me. Wherefore, mine own most loving mother, in my most hearty manner I thank you. . . .

By contrast, Perkin's letter began with words ("as humbly as I may, I commend myself to you. And may it please you to know . . .") that were the standard opening to a piece of business correspondence. Addressed to a mother, they were cursory and even hurtful. Though he called her "Mother" five times, including (rather gratuitously) in the address, in truth he did not seem to feel the bond at all. The redactor of the Courtrai Codex called the letter a *rescription*, an official statement or report, just like the others that had come across to Flanders. The only character in this missive was Perkin himself, in such trouble and confusion (*tele perplexite*), put upon, broken-hearted. He was not writing to his mother to try and restore the love and due obedience between them, but to ask her to send money to release him and an extra bit of cash "so that my guards may be kinder to me". The letter portrayed him as low-class, discourteous and self-pitying; it was useful for that. It was less useful for its implication that he did not know this mother, or she him.

The mention of his father's death was also curious. It was virtually a postscript, as though he had just heard it; but he had presumably known it for at least a week, or as long as he had been in Henry's hands. The letter had been written, to this point, with no mention of the event that should have overshadowed it. His father had already featured several times with no addition of the required formula, *whom God absolve*, and even with the implication that he was still alive. Such news, in a real letter, would hardly have been tacked on after "Commend me to my friends"; it would have informed his whole approach both to his father and to his mother, who was grieving for him. He was now her chief comfort in the world, presumably also the proper organiser of her affairs, yet he had no more to say to her than "May you be with God." He would have said as much, since it was as common as "Good morning", to a stranger passing in the street. In this respect, as in his first words to his mother, there was a sense of a writer not daring to plumb—or unable to imagine—emotions that were not his own.

The letter seems in any case never to have reached her. Certainly, if it did, Nicaise Werbecque took no action that is recorded. If she was indeed his mother, and he her only son, it would have been extraordinary if she had not tried to see him, risen from the dead. Only in Hell, the churchmen said, did parents feel no compassion for their children. She would surely have tried to intercede for him and reclaim him, as mothers did constantly, even when their sons were grown. The words of "King Richard's" proclamation in Scotland bear repeating: *[We] shall put ourselves Effectually in our devoir not as a stepdame | but as the very true mother of the Child | languishing or standing in peril to Redress.* At any time after June 1494, when news of the son of a *bourgeois* from Tournai was being cried in Malines, Nicaise and Jehan could have travelled the sixty miles to find him; at any time after November 1497 she could have been brought to London to drown, with a mother's tears, any lingering doubt as to who this young man was. But there was never, at this stage or later, the least public confirmation of any connection between the Werbecques and Henry's prisoner. As he himself seems to have hinted, he may have been *Weze*beque after all: Hall's "young fond foundling", whose real name, and real parents, the best labours of Henry's spies could never quite uncover.

Henry could also have asked for official proclamations from the Tournai authorities, attesting to who the boy was. He does not seem to have bothered, and Tournai does not seem to have provided them, perhaps because a king's word was good enough, or hard to argue with. The town authorities, to all appearances, neither claimed him nor denied the association. No other place was linked to him. But throughout the Perkin episode, only silence came from the city whose name he was associating even more closely with artifice and sleight of hand.

With one exception. The city fathers had a habit, when moved or excited, of striking commemorative copper money. Coins had been struck in 1421, at a time of particular difficulty in their straddle between France and Burgundy, with the legend *Vive le Roy de Franche*. At some point after 1497 a batch of copper marks appeared in Tournai with the inscription *Vive Perkin, jetois de Tournai*: "Long live Perkin, I was from Tournai." Either Tournaisiens or Englishmen (for in 1513 the English captured the town) could have produced them. Their size and style were so like the silver *gros* minted for the White Rose in Flanders that it is possible they were copper coins of King Richard IV that had been overstamped. Appropriately, they were worthless. English visitors probably bought them as souvenirs. On the reverse, among royal flotsam and jetsam such as fleurs-de-lis and rose branches, they carried the common, constant prayer to the mother who could intercede and whose address was known: *O mater dei | Memento mei*. O Mother of God, remember me.

CHAPTER EIGHT

This World My Prison

On All Souls' Day, November 2nd 1497, the court left Exeter for London. Mass was sung that morning in remembrance of the dead who had gone before and were still imprisoned in Purgatory, hoping for release by God's mercy and by the prayers of their friends. These souls were vivid in books, not least Margaret's books, heaped naked in the dark or falling like flakes of ash into deep crevasses of flame. None was yet damned; they were punished for their sins that they might in the end be purified and walk in the shining parks of Heaven, free. You prayed, on this day in particular, that their captivity would not be long and that yours, too, would not be.

On the king's last evening in Exeter the town fathers, showing off their loyalty and possibly their relief, organised a sumptuous banquet. The king contributed, with the costs of Butlery, Scullery and Spicery rising to three times as much as usual. The town had already been presented by Henry with a black felt cap, probably from his own head, which became for them a ceremonial cap of maintenance; the sword "which he wore about his middle", which they sent away to London to be decorated; and a new set of rules for mayoral elections. In exchange they gave him a fifteenth from the city's taxpayers, tipped his officers handsomely and fed the royal commissioners with capons, cygnets, "a big fish called a gross conger" and "light bread". The River Exe must have abounded with eels: Giles Daubeney, too, was presented with one. In all, the city spent £76 6s. 6½ d. on entertaining the king. By contrast, the total spent on resisting Perkin had been £21 16s., wine and beer included.

A high point of Henry's visit was his review of the captured rebels, corralled on the green by St. Peter's church (coincidentally, the church where Taylor the elder and John Hayes had done their plotting six or seven years before). Henry observed them from a "fair large" window in the treasurer's house, where he was staying. This window had been specially installed, and half the trees on the green cut down, so that the king, stepping from his chamber, could appreciate the scene: "the commons of this shire of Devon . . . before us in great multitudes in their shirts, the foremost of them having halters about their necks, and full humbly with lamentable cries for our grace and remission, submit[ting] themselves unto us." Untruthfully, Henry told Waterford that this was happening "daily"; the piteous crowds kept coming. The ringleaders had already been hanged and quartered outside Exeter's walls. But the men who knelt and cried before him he let go, after pausing for an agonising while, simply enjoying the sight of them, and giving them a lecture on the obedience he expected in future. More surprisingly, he seemed intent on showing fairness and mercy to his chief captive, too.

That particular prisoner was not in the public eye. Though Henry had brought Perkin with him, he seems not to have been displayed at any stage in the three weeks the king remained in Exeter. He was probably being kept close, as was only to be expected. His letter to his mother, for what it was worth, implied that his guards were being rough with him and that talking to other people was discouraged. Yet he seems not to have been under arrest in the usual sense. Raimondo Soncino, when he talked to Richmond Herald, asked him a strange question: *se la vita de Perichino sea libera*, whether Perkin's life would be free. Richmond said yes, but it would be "necessary to guard him well" to stop the Cornishmen killing him. He was in custody, it seemed, for his own protection, and would probably enjoy freedom in spite of all he had done.

He was also, presumably, in mourning of some kind. If Katherine had been mourning a second child, that child had also been his, and the death perhaps only just announced to him. Besides, as Perkin, he was

Maximilian by Albrecht Dürer, 1518

(*Facing page*) James IV by Daniel Mytens, c. 1500

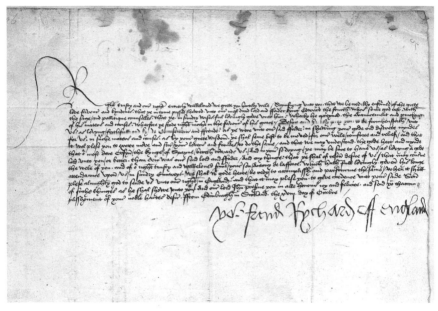

Letter of Richard of England to Bernard de la Forsa, October 17th 1496

E te veul ie monstrer et infor
mer quel estat est ordre de che
ualerie et aquoy elle doit ser
uir / et des ce que ie nome or
dre le nom declare son expo
sicion cest assauoir que ceulx
qui en sont . Doruent uiure par riegle z ordon

The limbless prince from *L'imaginacion de vraye noblesse*, 1497

Henry VII, c. 1503

ELIZABETHA · VXOR
HENRICI · VII ·

Elizabeth of York, c. 1500

a strorū criminatur et cruciat uel
destruit nō dico tm̄ plures inocen
tes. Sed etiam inocentissimos ut
plures infantes ꝫ pueri destruūt?
De filijs regis eduardi quarti.
Que quidē lex destruxit inocen
tissimos filios regis eduardi nisi
fata astrox̄ suarū natiuitatū p̄
ut cognosci potest p̄ suas natiui
tates. quox̄ quidē destructio cog
nita fuit p̄ sōmin in quarta die
per quarteriū huius hore ante
mediam noctē post natiuitatē
secundi filij ricardi habitū in
hac sentencia et forma. De ui
sione sōmij de rosa alba et sole ꝫ
luna pallidis. ▦▦ Uisio sōmij de

Richard of York's bad stars: the *De astrorum vi fatali*, 1499

Margaret's Lamentation, c. 1500

mourning the death of his father. To wear drab clothes and go unshaven were the signs required to show grief for a parent. At Exeter, bizarrely, he may have grieved in both characters, with the liturgy of All Souls more than usually sharp and raw to him. As the royal party left the city after-wards, through the east gate that still showed the marks of King Rich-ard's siege and his fire, he could reflect that the king who had ordered them was now invested with nothing, like souls when they stepped out naked from the bodies of the dead.

The journey back was as slow as the king's progress westward had been. By November 6th they were at Bridport, by the 9th at Salisbury, by the 15th at Basingstoke, still forty miles from London. All the way, the crowds gathered to gaze on Perkin. They were "eager above all", Vergil wrote, "to see Peter Warbeck, for most accounted it miraculous that a man of such humble origins should have dared to try to get so great a kingdom by trickery, and should have made so many illustrious men believe him." The chroniclers said people "wondered" at him, looking on him boldly with amazement and surprise. (When Edward IV's mistress, Jane Shore, did public penance in 1483, this "wondering" was like a rough undressing that brought blushes of shame to her cheeks.) It is not clear whether Perkin's low birth was advertised yet, with shabby clothes and a shambling horse, or whether Henry was still indulging the joke of the king's golden robes. Heron's accounts, however, contained some weeks later a payment for "Perkin's trumpet": not this time a spy, for he was constantly guarded, but probably a man on real trumpet-duty, blow-ing ironic fanfares to announce that the fake king was coming.

Vergil said the rumour reached Flanders that Perkin was led as a captive in chains. Henry's historian did not claim this himself. Instead, the king "took him in his company", and contemporary sources give the same picture. There Perkin "awaited" or "attended upon" the king, as lords did when they met the king on his progresses round the country and joined his train with their retinues. "By appointment [agreement] he came to the king," wrote the Grey Friars chronicler, "and so remained following the court"—a courtier rather than a prisoner. Prisoners did not attend upon the men who arrested them, but were "brought up", lords and common-ers alike, with no sense of volition. Henry, however, wished at every stage to stress the free will and consent of his captive. So this strange figure rode somewhere behind him, probably neither bound nor chained but civilly and without protest, and drawing crowds so great that the king's own safety was sometimes threatened by the press. Henry, despite his mood of "marvellous joy", would have sensed that he himself was not the main attraction: a peculiar sensation for a king, crowned with victory, passing through towns that had rarely seen him.

Henry had dreamed of this moment for months and years: the feigned boy at last in his hands. Again and again, in his letter to Edward Courtenay of September 16th, he had imagined how he would capture him. Courtenay's troops would trail behind him as he marched, then hem him in, jostle and exhaust him "to the intent that ye may the more assuredly annoy [him]," closing in with Daubeney's men like the jaws of a trap from the east and the west. Ordinary people, reading the royal placards and moved by the thought of reward, would "take Perkin in fleeing or going backward by sea or by land." Arriving at last at the coast, Perkin would find his ships half-sunk or blackened by fire, and know there was no escape. "Hereunto we pray you to have an especial regard," Henry had written, "for it is the thing we have greatly at heart." Now, less simply but with no less drama, he had the lad fast; and had to decide what on earth to do with him.

On November 18th the royal cortège reached Sheen, where the king rested for three days. The palace was a favourite retreat, on a broad bend of the Thames seven miles from London. Edward IV had enlarged, reglazed and beautified the palace; Henry's gardeners and builders had worked assiduously on the grounds around it, planting orchards, vines, lawns and new flower beds and erecting tennis courts and galleries for archery. Beyond were fields where men found hares and partridge nests, and from where their wives brought peascods and fresh curds to the king. Richard of York would have known this place, remembering where doors led and what was seen from windows, how the low knot-hedges could be jumped and how the river shone below the grassy banks. Henry's improvements had probably not altered the fundamental look of it. To enter Sheen, his first prison-palace, may have been a strange test of both memory and imagination for Henry's captive. Or perhaps he thought of nothing more, as he rode across the tilting yard and dismounted, his escorts uncomfortably close, than that somewhere in these buildings was the woman he had claimed as his sister, and with her his son and his wife.

By this time, if not earlier, Henry was disclaiming the importance of the West Country campaign. On November 22nd he rode to Lambeth, his prisoner attending him, and then took his barge to Westminster. As was customary when the king came over the water, the trumpets blew, but Trevisano said that Henry had no wish to enter London with his usual pomp and triumph. He had hardly gained a worthy victory, he felt, over "such poor people as these Cornishmen". No ambassadors were picked to go and meet him, and the London worthies welcomed him not in the street, in their special violet robes, but in Westminster Hall, where the aldermen and guild officers stood in rows on either side to hear the recorder greet the king "with a short proposition . . . of the good exploit of his Journey and subduing of his Rebels." After this, they got their first glimpse of "the Person Perkin". When the king went towards the palace of Westminster his captive walked freely before him, leading a courtier by the arm: as if he was graciously in charge, or as if he was dancing. He seemed to have slipped into his natural place, among the young men who led the revels and disguisings.

The aldermen and commons were astonished. Again, they "wondered", and threw curses at him, a racket that must have echoed round the king himself. This reaction was to be repeated whenever Perkin appeared. On at least two occasions—Soncino said it was "every day" when the court first returned to London—he was led on a horse through the city streets, "so that everyone may understand the past mistake". Francis Bacon said he was conveyed leisurely, not in any ignominious fashion, while the crowd jeered him tumultuously, like small birds mobbing an owl uncovered in the daylight. The mockery came from above as well as below, from people standing at the windows of overhanging upper floors that darkened and narrowed the streets. The purpose of these displays, Bacon wrote, was so that Perkin "could tell better what himself was."

On one such ride, on November 28th, he was required to lead a horse on which sat Henry's old sergeant-farrier William, the keeper of the king's mares and foals, who had joined Richard's court at Malines in 1493. William had fled after his prince's capture, "when he apperceived that all was otherwise than he before supposed", and had taken the habit of a hermit. He rode bound with ropes, still in his hermit's robe, with his feet lashed together beneath the belly of the horse. Robert Fabyan said that when this man had been brought to Henry, "[the king] commanded his said master Perkin to bring him unto the Tower for his faithful service." So his master led him there, delivered him to the Tower gardens, and then

"with such as were assigned to ride with him returned again by Can-
dlewick Street towards Westminster with much wondering & many a bitter curse."

In this strange little scene Perkin appeared as Henry's servant, the
obedient performer of a cruel joke. Yet he performed as if he was without
constraint, escorted rather than guarded; as if he was himself in charge
and free. By contrast, when Henry VI had been paraded through London
as a captive in 1465, he had worn a foolish straw hat and had been bound
with a rope that was held on either side. Nothing of this kind was
reported in Perkin's case. He rode down Cheapside, the most showy street
in London, where more than fifty goldsmiths' shops displayed gold and
silver vessels more magnificent, one Venetian wrote, than all the shops
in Milan, Rome, Venice and Florence put together, and it seems that he
might almost have lingered to admire them through the spitting uproar
around him. Soncino remarked that on these rides, when Perkin was
made "a spectacle for the world", he bore his fortune *animosamente*, with
spirit and courage.

Londoners clearly found these relaxed outings strange. Henry had
every reason to keep Perkin in strict custody, not least because—however
amenable he had appeared since his capture—he was thought very likely
to try to escape. More than this, the king had reason to kill him. By the
laws of nature, opposites did not spare each other. Fire did not pardon
water, nor the cat the mouse, nor the victor his powerless captive. Besides,
a prisoner who remained an active threat demanded to be killed for the
good of the kingdom. Henry had not hesitated to hang as "adversaries of
the king" the Flemings he had captured at Deal. In early November 1497,
while "the duke" was still in the west with Henry, Trevisano relayed a
report "that he had been taken by the king and hanged for being in his
dominions". It seemed reasonable enough. A month or so before, Soncino
had thought it "impossible" that the Duke of York would be pardoned,
despite the talk of it. When the king had badgered James IV to hand
Perkin over, this had always been understood as the preliminary to his
execution. Ferdinand and Isabella understood the same and, indeed,
expected it. This was why neither party had been prepared to let him go.

Several reasons, however, suggested that Henry should not execute
his captive and should even, perhaps, treat him kindly. He had removed
Perkin from sanctuary on the promise of his life, although an agreement
reached with a criminal was eminently breakable. Beyond that, it was the

general duty of a lord to pardon and show mercy: God's law, not nature's, the expression of his higher self. Soncino mentioned with wonder how Henry "is most clement and pardons everybody, even the common people of Cornwall, although if he wanted to do strict justice he would have to put to death more than 20,000 men."

There was a famous precedent for clemency, too, in the king's treatment of Simnel. The eleven-year-old had been placed among the mean dependents or "blackguards" of scullery and woodyard who, on royal progresses, followed after the court in a cart with the clanking kettles and pans. Vergil thought this was Perkin's natural station too, among the dirty plates. Unlike Simnel, however, Perkin was not an innocent child: he, and no one else, had been at the head of the troops who had marched against Henry. To put him in the kitchens would appear to make light of the appalling deeds he had attempted.

To treat Perkin kindly might also raise questions, now meant to be settled, about who he was. Henry knew well that esteem and status were measured by how a prisoner was kept. He himself had been treated *doulcement* as a child in Brittany, out of regard for his blood. In 1505, checking on how a new and noble Yorkist claimant, Edmund de la Pole, was being treated by the Duke of Guelders, he asked his envoy to find out "what the Duke of Guelders intends to do with the said Edmund: whether he has a liking for him, or only esteems him a little? How is the said Edmund now watched: is he kept like a prisoner in strict confinement, or does he enjoy freedom, though not complete freedom?" The questions betrayed, fairly clearly, his anxieties of eight years before.

The answer, perhaps, was to intersperse clemency with organised mockery in order to stress the king's contempt. Every so often Henry seemed to play with people who had deeply offended him, before they were put to death as they deserved. In this spirit, he disputed in April the following year with a heretic at Canterbury, converting him from his error and giving him 6s. 8d. in alms, before the man was burned alive. Henry had often said that Perkin was so insignificant that he was hardly worth troubling with. Now, crushed and beaten, he was perhaps being kept at court as a token of the king's utter confidence that no one would take him for Richard and try to adhere to him.

Yet Henry was not confident at all. In truth, he was hamstrung by uncertainty. In June 1498, more than eight months after Perkin's surrender, de Puebla reminded Ferdinand and Isabella that Henry still did not know what to do with his captive, and wanted their advice. "I besought your Highnesses many days ago," he wrote,

> to write your opinion and advice about what the lord king ought to do about the Perkin business. Your Highnesses—no doubt for some just reasons and impediments—have never to this day sent word about this nor written any other thing . . . This causes me great pain, because I am sure the lord king would do whatever your Highnesses direct.

Henry had never before admitted to Ferdinand and Isabella, on any subject, that he did not know what to do. Now that Arthur and Katherine were officially betrothed, he could be somewhat more familiar and forthright with her parents; but to admit uncertainty, implying weakness, was still not a wise course. To them, the answer to this *burla* was simple: now that the boy was definitely useless for Spain's purposes, Henry should imprison him or kill him. If the King of England dared not, it raised unwelcome questions both about him, and about the boy he seemed too nervous to touch.

At around the same time, Henry had agreed—at Pedro de Ayala's suggestion—to ask Ferdinand and Isabella to act as mediators in his dispute with Scotland. It was best to do so, wrote Cardinal Ascanio Mario Sforza to the Duke of Milan, "while the King of England has the Duke of York in his hands." Without that bargaining chip, it would be hard to push the King of Scots towards a proper peace. Henry was now to discover that he could make diplomatic play with this young man himself: another reason, if a temporary one, for keeping him alive.

On September 30th, nine days after Perkin had fled from Taunton, a treaty of peace had been concluded between England and Scotland at Ayton, on the border. It was to endure for seven years and was to be sealed, at last, by the marriage of James to Henry's daughter Margaret. But James, though he realised that Richard's cause was lost, was not prepared either to drop or to disown his friend. He had restricted the scope of Article 6 of the treaty, which bound the sovereigns to surrender each other's enemies and rebels or expel them, by introducing a clause exempting from the article anyone who had a safe-conduct. By this he meant explicitly Richard and his supporters, to whom he had given safe-conducts when they arrived in Scotland. The exemption was expressed in a forceful phrase in the ablative absolute: "the safe-conducts granted formerly, by the aforesaid princes or one of them, being not in the least revoked by the force of the present article, but remaining in their strength and effect for ever." This clause allowed James, as Henry complained, to keep in his kingdom indefinitely "and favour and aid the same rebels saying, that he doth it not . . . for he will so straitly keep him or them that they shall have no power." The king saw through that at once. Although "continual or established peace" with Scotland was proclaimed in London in December, Henry would not let the clause stand, and in February 1498 he sent Norroy King of Arms, one of his heralds, to remonstrate with James. The safe-conduct clause had to be taken out, and more besides:

> Item in the same article be left out these words *Salvis conductibus* etc. for the principal cause moving his said Cousin [James] to put in the said words . . . was for a grant of Safe conducts made by [him] to Perkin and other his adherents the king's Rebels. And forasmuch as [at] this time the said Perkin is in the king's keeping and at the commandm[ent] of his grace and shall never use the benefit of the said Safe conducts. . . . And also his adherents . . . be departed out of his said Cousin's realm. And if there [*sic*] should under the colour of their said Safe conducts resort and repair unto the same Realm again and there to have grace and succour there might grow a grudge between the king's grace and his said Cousin . . . it is thought expedient those words touching such Safe Conducts to be left out.

As Henry reminded James, he was keeping Perkin "straitly" himself, and had exposed what he was. One of the earliest showings of him after Henry's return to London took place as part of the reception of the Scottish ambassador, who could hardly have missed it. Yet the February negotiations still snagged on him. James—completely unmoved by the confession—was keeping alive the possibility that his Prince of England, somehow springing from his confinement, would one day come back. He was still his cousin, bound to him by blood and love, whoever Henry said he was. In July 1498 Ayala admitted that it was "very difficult" to conclude the peace because "the old enmity is so great". In August, Norroy had still not got his alterations.

There was pressure on Henry, too, from other quarters. Bernard André's poem "Les Douze Triomphes", written in 1497 but before

Perkin's capture, showed that despite the restoration of trade with Burgundy and the fine pledges of the Holy League, Henry did not believe that Philip and Maximilian had stopped their machinations against him. In July 1497, after all, wild letters had still been passing between Philip and Maximilian, claiming that the people of England "in great part" had taken up arms against Henry in favour of the Duke of York and James, and that "the king had fled London in terror". Whatever the source (conceivably King Richard IV, whose proclamation had so boldly predicted such events), Philip and Maximilian wanted this to happen. They exulted in it. André saw the two rulers, with Margaret, as a three-headed monster, "the three being all of one opinion, and also of the same will, living in union." They were still cooking up "evil designs", including offering large rewards for Henry's assassination; they had "never understood how to behave." And they continued to cling to the young man whom Henry had so utterly defeated.

No reaction to his capture was recorded from Margaret except what Vergil imagined: that the story, relayed to Flanders, "made her weep many tears for her prince, for whom previously she had spent many nights full of fear, waiting for news of his doings." The news of "Monsieur d'York", as she and Philip had received it, reached Maximilian at Innsbruck on October 16th. The Duke of York, he learned,

> had gone to a certain part of England called Cornwall, which had rebelled against the king, and having collected a multitude of 30,000 armed men he led his expedition towards London against King Henry. King Henry himself, while he prepared to encounter him, sent ahead a certain chief of his army who, having joined battle with them, inflicted such huge slaughter on them that the rest of the multitude was routed and fled; and in that flight were captured, among others, the Duke of York himself with his wife and one-year-old son. They were brought as prisoners to the citadel of London.

Thus his sponsors preferred to believe: that he had fought in battle and been honourably defeated, brave to the last.

Maximilian fired off a letter at once to the Council of Flanders and its president, Jean le Sauvage, asking him to go to Henry and appeal for York to be spared and released. He then explained his strategy to Philip

—belatedly, since le Sauvage was Philip's officer and not his own—in a letter, full of urgency and emotion, written from Metz on November 8th.

Right dear and well-beloved son: We have heard that our very dear and well-beloved cousin the Duke of York has recently been taken prisoner and delivered into the hands of the King of England, his enemy, and we are very much afraid that, for the reasons you know well enough, he will put him to death. And because we hold our said cousin of York in very great love and affection because he is our kinsman and our ally, we are bitterly saddened by his evil fate and his misfortune and would be very much more saddened by his death; and we are held and obliged, for the quittance of our honour and the discharge of our conscience, to help and comfort him to all our power.

We have determined that you should be a mediator in this matter with King Henry, and that to this end you should send to him Mr. Jean le Sauvage, the president of Flanders, to request him not to put our cousin of York to death and also not to do any harm or injury to his person; but to be willing to send him back to us and put him in our hands safe and sound. And in return we will leave off and renounce in perpetuity all rights, quarrels and actions that our said cousin of York and his heirs and successors may pretend, dispute or demand in the kingdom of England in whatever fashion or manner he or they may do so, and will never make or move armed warfare. . . . And we will give [the king] our letters patent of assurance such as he will wish to have them; and thus he should be satisfied and content and completely assured.

Besides this, you know that in such a task it is necessary to have some good friends and procurers to see to things and help to steer the business. So we have given power and authority to the said [president] of Flanders to promise in our name to the people who seem best to him, the most intimate servants of King Henry, a one-time payment of up to 10,000 gold florins so that they may see that King Henry lets this business take effect and reach the good conclusion that we desire and intend. If you agree to this, please send the president of Flanders to King Henry and dispatch him with good and simple instructions in these matters . . . together with all the other good means and methods you may think best for the welfare and salvation of our cousin of York. And you will be doing us a wonderful favour.

Maximilian enclosed with this letter two documents authorising le Sauvage to plead for his cousin's life. One promised to pay the 10,000 florins to any useful contact; the other, which did not mention money, was "the one he was to show to the English". Both these, and the letter to Philip, were kept in several copies. The King of the Romans recognised, however, that there might be a complication. There would need to be a secret page to le Sauvage's instructions:

> You should also adjust these instructions to tell King Henry by way of remonstrance that insofar as he says and maintains that our said cousin of York is a counterfeit person and not the son of the late King Edward, nevertheless it is the common renown of the whole of Christianity that yes, he is, and he is held to be the son of the late King Edward, and because of this if he puts him to death he will be putting to death his own brother-in-law, which would be shame, dishonour and reproach to him for ever and to his people too, because he [York] will not be able to do him any more harm from henceforth, alive or dead.

Maximilian also drafted a short personal note to le Sauvage, explaining to him directly that he wished "with all his heart" to save his cousin. He ended: *Employez vouz en ce le mieux que pourrez, car nous avons la matiere fort a coeur*: "Do the best you can in this, for we have the matter much at heart." Ten days after sending it, his sadness had not lifted. Describing York's defeat and capture to the papal legate, he closed with the remark: *Sic transit gloria mundi*.

For all the paternal pushing, or perhaps because of it, Philip did not send le Sauvage to England. (As Maximilian's envoy to Flanders had once told him, the archduke, at nineteen, could be surprisingly wilful and unhelpful.) But he sent le Sauvage's servant and Jean Courtville, his own councillor, who was in London by December 10th. Courtville was paid £20 by Henry. There is no sign that he made use of Maximilian's bills behind the king's back, but presumably he had them with him. Hard-up as he was, Maximilian seems to have had every intention of paying the sum he had promised. He was doing this for a young man not only declared, but apparently self-declared, to be a boatman's son. This "fact" was as well known across the Channel as it was in England, yet Maximilian did not believe it. He insisted, on the contrary, that the boy was

Henry's brother-in-law, challenging the king (who still had no proof that Edward's son was dead) to prove him wrong. Though his interests were no longer remotely served by this young man, he honoured him and loved him; to the point of abandoning all his own claims, and York's too, just to have him back and safe.

Another unwavering view may well have touched Henry more closely. He had sent Katherine to the queen in the apparent belief that the marriage could not long survive her husband's confession of imposture. As early as October 23rd, however, when he wrote to de Puebla, he spoke of his captives as a couple, just as he had pictured them before. He told the ambassador that he would soon see Perkin and his wife, whose capture had so delighted him. They were to be displayed in London together as joint collaborators. The king's words were the first indication that, whatever had passed between Katherine and her husband in Exeter, they remained— and insisted on remaining—married to each other.

Soncino and Trevisano saw them together on November 26th in the palace of Westminster. The occasion was the formal reception of the Scottish ambassador, who had arrived ("with 30 horses") to present his credentials to Henry. After the reception, the ambassadors accompanied the king to a smaller chamber for more favoured conversations, though still in a crowd. When Henry told Soncino that he had heard reports that the French king was planning another Italian expedition, Trevisano had to make signs to him that the French ambassador was in the room too, and close. Everyone was there. On the way out of the chamber, towards the door, Soncino found that an extra treat had been laid on for the envoys, a showing of Perkin and Katherine. "He is 23 years old," wrote Trevisano, "a noble young man [*zentil zovene*], and his wife a most beautiful woman; the king treats them well, but does not want him to sleep with his wife."

This information could hardly have come from Perkin or Katherine, who in any case apparently stayed silent. Presumably it came from court gossip. The arrangement seems to have been in place for a while, perhaps from not long after the king had returned to Sheen. They were quite naturally together, as Trevisano described them, with no visible contrast of condition between them. (Skelton later called them Jack and Jill, also implying the lack of difference.) And yet, because the king did not want it, they were not completely a couple again.

Perkin was of course under guard, and that watch did not relax at night. His minders slept with him, one on either side and probably in the same bed, as Edward, Earl of Warwick's slept with him in the Tower of London. They made sure not only that he did not escape, but that he did not find Katherine or she him. By forbidding the act of love, Henry had removed the core and reason of their marriage, the "sweet due debt of nature" that couples owed each other. Not to pay that debt, if either side desired it, was a sin against the meaning of the sacrament, and the separation of either party from the bed of the other was seen by the churchmen as a form of divorce. That was why Trevisano mentioned it, in his forthright way. He was the one envoy who, by referring to "children"—more than one, in a marriage barely twenty months old—had suggested how passionate their union was. Now he also implied that, if Henry had not forbidden it, this pretty couple would have "loved each other fleshly" as if nothing had changed between them.

Perhaps nothing had. They had not chosen to appear together in this corner of a crowded room, yet their togetherness spoke volumes. If Katherine had disowned her husband, Henry would not have put her there. Instead, she had clearly not shaken off her love for him. That he had not lost his love for her was less surprising; if their marriage had been damaged, the fault lay only with him. A line of Skelton's—"Lord, how Perkin is proud of his peahen!"—suggests how he felt, staggered by the fact that, whatever was now said of him, he still had a beautiful and noble wife and could passionately flaunt her. Skelton confirmed Soncino, too: they were a couple about the court, known as one, and evidently still in love, despite everything.

Katherine's state of mind is harder to read than her husband's. She was the highest in rank among the queen's ladies, holding fifth place among the women at court after the queen, the king's mother and the two small princesses. In the normal run of the world, a woman of her standing would never be seen with such a man. Yet, by preserving the marriage, she also preserved the duties attached to it. She was bound to obey her husband's commandment, to show him "honour and semblant of love" and to call him "lord", as all wives called their husbands. So in public, as at that busy reception for the ambassadors, he could naturally take her hand, or touch her cheek to tuck a hair away; he could slip his arm around her waist, his possession, or lean his head on her, or kiss her. She, the earl's daughter, accepted this from him, the piece of shit from Flanders.

She would only have done so because she still believed at least some of the stories he had told her.

Henry doubtless knew this. His fondness for Katherine disposed him to treat her gently; the meetings with Perkin, and even Perkin's soft treatment in general, may have stemmed in part from this regard. Yet he could not entirely trust her. Among the six servants he allowed her—the normal number for a duchess—at least some would have been spying on her. This young woman was still politically dangerous, or might be; not least because the slightest public act of love or reverence for her husband was unsettling to a king who could not yet definitively prove that his own story was correct, and her husband's wrong.

The prohibition on love-making fitted into this pattern. It was important, first, as proof that Henry had unmanned Perkin. Although the young man might flaunt Katherine around the court, he could not unlace her chemise, uncovering those beautiful breasts, or unfasten her girdle, as Henry himself seemed to dream of doing. She was out of bounds to both of them, and Henry's prisoner endured the added torment of unattainable desire. But second, the lack of sex removed the fear of more children. There is no knowing what had happened to the one-year-old son, perhaps just learning to toddle in his walking strings and to say "papa" and "mama", who had come with them as a prisoner to London. Later clues suggest that he was separated from them and sent far away, where no misguided hopes could cluster round him. Though the business of the feigned lad had been only an "abusion and folly" in Henry's eyes, he could not risk the danger of a second generation.

II

MEANWHILE, IN THE GARDENS at Sheen or in the corridors of Westminster, Henry's prisoner walked with the appearance of a free man. He could open a window, lean out, breathe the air. He could ride, not simply in shame down Cheapside but in the parks around the palaces, watching the leaves whirl down from the trees and feeling the wind in his face. "In court at liberty", was how the London chronicles described it. Fabyan added that Henry gave Perkin "many other benefits which I would ask long time to write." To him, and to all his contemporaries who mentioned it, this looked like honourable confinement as allowed to captured noblemen. If this was prison, it was little more than every man and woman knew, held fast in the corruptible body and the snares of the world, where God and Death were warders.

The guards who were assigned to him, Robert Jones and William Smith, were trusted royal servants of long standing. Jones was a sewer of the chamber, the man who supervised the laying of dishes on the king's private table and tasted his food. Smith had been a page of the chamber and later an usher, handling Henry's petty cash for him (including, once, paying the royal apothecary out of his own pocket) and receiving, in thanks for the closeness of his service, leases on crown lands and honourary offices in several northern cities. These men were not armed soldiers or sergeants, and probably carried no weapons with which to hurt their ward if he tried to escape. In the rare sightings of him at this bizarre stage of his life, his guards were never mentioned. One Venetian dispatch, however, said that he had "servants".

This sort of quasi-freedom was something Henry himself had known in exile in the 1470s, when the Duke of Brittany had kept him and his uncle at court as useful bargaining chips with England. And it was perhaps not so new to his prisoner, either. Pedro de Ayala, a good observer, thought this had been his condition in Scotland after the abortive raid, James "keeping him secure in such a way that you could be certain and sure of him . . . not making trouble." Falkland, with its high wall of hills, had perhaps been his prison, despite the honourable and happy estate he had kept there. Soncino, too, thought he had "escaped" from Scotland when he left. It seems clear that if he had gone to France or Spain he would have been kept in the same way, in silken chains.

Henry naturally tried to conceal the lightness of his punishment, pretending that he had captured and imprisoned him as harshly as reason would expect. Perkin was said to be *sub custodia* Smith and Jones and *in prisone*; in official attainders he was said to have been taken, *captus*, in the West Country "and afterwards, as the king's enemy, committed in sure and safe custody in the Tower of London, and kept there as a prisoner." Molinet certainly believed this, writing that Perkin had been kept in "miserable prison" from the outset, and Maximilian too seemed to have this picture in his head. In fact, the king had done nothing of the kind. Though Vergil said his guards had been tasked never to leave his side, Smith and Jones were hardly formidable or even, at times, attentive.

It is difficult to know how hard their job was. Their charge's frame of

mind seemed fairly changeable. His first appearances in London suggested the same high-spiritedness that he had shown on his arrival in
Taunton, the mannequin-boy of the confession once again parading
himself and enjoying the attention of the crowd. He was very chatty at
times with de Puebla, like him a scorned outsider confident in his own
intelligence. On other days, he did not wish to talk at all.

His meeting with Soncino and Trevisano on November 26th was a
case in point. The ambassadors' eagerness to see "the false duke who fared
so ill" was not reciprocated. Soncino reported that Perkin *mostra havere
ingenio pur non li parlassemo*, "did not seem to care for us to speak to him."
What he disliked, without doubt, was the name by which he was introduced to them and by which they had to address him. He could have
done little to avoid it, however, in a room crowded with dignitaries. Perhaps, in the royal fashion, he simply turned to speak to someone else, or
bowed his head to make it clear he would give no answer. What he really
wanted to do was hide, like a leopard hunted in the woods, or like the savages of Newfoundland who had fled from the explorers that very summer, leaving only a bone needle, ashes on a hearth and the fresh-cut
stumps of the trees.

Soncino could not conclude, from this brief meeting, what he felt
about Henry's captive. He had to think about it, promising to send his
views "in a few days", but no more survives than his remark that Perkin
seemed to show spirit in adversity. Trevisano's first word for him, *zentil*,
carried such a wealth of assumptions about manners, bearing, virtue and,
particularly, blood that nothing else was needed. The young man
appeared to have all of these, yet he was called Perkin: a name from which
he gracefully turned his head away. After Trevisano had seen him, he
began to call him the Duke of York again.

In those early days, looking at this strangely elegant captive was
something of a court entertainment. To the extent that he was on display,
he would have been stared at with particular keenness by people who had
known the little Prince Richard and wished to make a comparison. Several old servants of Edward IV still worked about the court, including,
most notably, Cardinal Morton in advanced but active old age. Soncino
saw a fair amount of him, enough to know that he thought Perkin's
movement "puerile" and "had no fear except that the man would escape".
Sitting with the aged cardinal, the Milanese envoy had tried unsuccessfully
to draw from him who Perkin's supporters really were. Morton did not

know: the King of Scotland, he thought, and Margaret, but no one else in particular. The English in general did not believe his claim and that, Morton implied, was good enough for him. These remarks were made before Perkin arrived at court, but there is little reason to think they would have altered when Morton saw him. People had always seen what they wished to see in him, or what they believed already.

Others besides Morton could have tested this boy against the little prince they had known. Oliver King, the Bishop of Bath and Wells, who had been secretary to Edward IV, was now in fairly regular attendance on Henry. Piers Courteys, who had delivered from the Wardrobe Prince Richard's silks and satins, continued to do so for the new set of small princes and princesses. (Courteys, who had worked occasionally with Brampton and seems to have been in sanctuary with the little prince at Westminster, had been granted a general pardon both in March 1492 and in February 1495; he was not altogether certain, therefore, that Edward's second son was dead.) Prince Richard's attorney, Andrew Dymock, was now Henry's solicitor, and had been for more than a decade. Katherine, Lady Courtenay, Richard's youngest sister, was often at court, as was his aunt Elizabeth Plantagenet, the Duchess of Suffolk, and her second son, Edmund de la Pole. No longer at court, but still alive had anyone wanted their opinions on this young man, were Elizabeth d'Arcy, Richard's nurse, and Dr. Argentine, his companion in the Tower. Above all there was Richard's eldest sister, Queen Elizabeth, keeping a separate and almost unvisitable household from which she issued on ceremonial occasions, with Katherine attending.

The queen seems to have been a gentle, passive creature. Her world, as seen in her account books, was one of frugally mended gowns, wicker baskets and works of charity. She had little money of her own (her yearly allowance was one-eighth of the king's), and what she had she often gave away. On Maundy Thursday each year she distributed new shoes to poor women, but her own shoes cost no more than 12d. each and had cheap latten buckles. Her subjects loved her, bringing her cakes, almond butter, apples and flowers, for which she paid them generously. But Ayala in 1498 thought her "beloved because she is powerless", and believed, as many did, that Henry's formidable mother kept her in subjection. Although Margaret Beaufort showed kindness to her daughter-in-law, she was undoubtedly a stronger character. A citizen of Nottingham once tried to speak to Elizabeth when she visited the city; their pleasant conver-

sation was stopped by "that strong whore", Henry's mother, and Elizabeth acquiesced.

Such a woman was not about to question her husband's version of
events. Her appearances with Henry showed her attentive and fond of his
company, and he himself was faithful and generally considerate to her.
When he was planning war against Scotland in June 1497 she had his
half-helmet garnished with jewels, for which he recompensed her; he paid
her debts, too, though he expected to be paid back later. Elizabeth most
probably accepted that her younger brother, seven years her junior, was
dead. This was, after all, the prevailing opinion. She had little reason to
think otherwise, or to question Henry's explanations. No confrontation or
repudiation was arranged. Since the young man had agreed to be Perkin,
this was unnecessary. It would have been unseemly in any case to recruit
the queen for such a purpose, and might have stirred uncertainties that
were better left untouched. Nor is there evidence of the slightest contact between them. Presumably, at times and from a distance, they saw each other.
An extraordinary link existed, of course, in Katherine, who still believed
in her husband and who was daily at Elizabeth's side. But it is likely that
the subject was considered closed and that, in the formality of their dealings with each other, there was no reason or opportunity to raise it.

He, too, may not have wished to do so. In front of the ambassadors
he had seemed ashamed; but perhaps he, like Henry, was also uncertain
how to behave. For six years, and probably a good deal longer, he had
lived as a prince. Whether or not this had been an act then, it could only
be an act now, when he had apparently admitted he was base. Yet it was
hard, as Vergil said, "to alter the natural disposition of one's mind, and
suddenly to root out the thing therein settled by daily conversation." In a
place that lived by fashion, manners and appearance, he could not put
away his elegance. So there was princeliness, but with no purpose, like a
velvet coat on a monkey. Henry had such a creature, with a small white-
whiskered face and a leather collar; he kept it on a chain, but it escaped
once (so the merry story went) and tore up his most important notebook,
the one in which the king recorded the characters and demeanours of all
those about him. Inside his now-tamed captive, ostensibly no trouble,
there may well have been flashes of a similar violence that stemmed from
complete humiliation.

For Christmas that year the court went to Sheen: Henry and Elizabeth, Henry's mother, and most of the small royal children, gathered for

the festivals in the favourite royal retreat. There was much to celebrate: the capture of Perkin, the truce with Scotland, the proxy marriage of Prince Arthur that had now bound England to Spain. "They speak of nothing here but of making good cheer," wrote Soncino on December 18th. But three days later a fire broke out in the palace, catching a beam and burning for three hours with such ferocity that the ruined areas were never rebuilt. "Great substance of Richesse"—tapestries, hangings, beds, clothes, plate and furniture—was lost. Henry himself estimated the damage at 50,000–60,000 ducats, one-tenth of his annual income. On subsequent days he paid various servants £20, large money in itself, to sift around for jewels in the rubble.

Fires in palaces were commonplace, and in this case the seasonal feasting and entertaining seemed to continue as usual in the undamaged rooms. But rumours persisted. The blaze had started in the king's apartments (though Trevisano said the queen's) at around nine o'clock at night, when fires were usually doused. From what was burned, it seemed to have been centred on the chapel and the king's Wardrobe, where his robes and furnishings were stored. This was where Perkin slept when he stayed in other palaces, locked in for the night in a dressing room stuffy with tapestries and velvets. The men who dealt with him, those he lived among, were grooms and ushers of the chamber whose tasks were to make up the fires, set the torches and candles, strew the rushes or knot-grass on the floors and help make up the beds. Accidents were likely, and the yeomen of the guard were supposed to check every quarter of the night for "an adventure of fire". Less likely, but conceivable, was a candle tilted into a curtain (who would notice?) or a still-glowing brand dropped quietly to the floor.

The account of the fire that was sent to Milan came from one of Henry's councillors, who was anxious to play it down. After several paragraphs on the happy state of the kingdom, he admitted that "It is true that a fire broke out." But it was an accident, he stressed, not malice. He said this twice. The king confirmed that he was not unduly troubled, "seeing that it was not due to malice", and let it be known that he would rebuild the chapel "all in stone and much finer than before". Construction of the new palace next door, eventually called Richmond, began as early as January 14th; the king moved on, unconcerned.

Such carefree briefings had been heard before. In fact, Henry seemed well aware that malice was a possibility. To outside eyes, the source could well have been the strange and unpredictable young man who now haunted his court. Ambassador Trevisano made the link fairly explicitly, as well as letting slip that he thought the blaze deliberate. "The Duke of York was thus with the king," read his letter of January 11th, 1498, "and an accident occurred . . . that a fire was set [*impiato*]." Possibly.

Wherever he was "with the king", at Sheen or Westminster or on the road, Henry's prisoner had no position or function save that of being Perkin. In a court of minutely organised routines and duties—in which one esquire's job was to shake the king's sheets, another's to smooth them, another's to sprinkle them with holy water—his job was to be the person he had said he was, and nothing more. That single, "homely" name placed him among the lowest servants and the court characters: with Bradshaw, who had fetched him from Beaulieu, with Dick the Fool and Pierre the French cook, or with "James" and "William" who, in 1502, were among "certain persons working upon the rich bed". Menials were ordered by these names to run errands or to saddle the horses; and in 1494, dictating his promises to Margaret in a different world, Richard of York had called Henry "Henry", *tout court*, deliberately to insult him.

This was now his level. He was always just "Perkin" to John Heron, after his first eruption into the accounts on October 5th, just as he had always been Perkin to Henry even when listed with a run of other men's surnames. ("Perkin, Heron, Skelton and Ashley", ran the king's letter of October 7th.) Heron usually wrote Perkin with a lower-case "p," or with the *per* abbreviated, as in clerks' Latin, to leave a name that was barely there at all. Those lower than "Pkin" were nameless: "a man who scared away crows" from the cornfields outside Sheen, "a woman who brought the king cakes", or the French and Breton spies.

Signs of him are very rare for the eight months he was at court. His life there can be reconstructed only from a few scattered payments in Henry's private accounts. Two grooms of the privy chamber, Hugh Denis and James Braybroke, were paid £2 "for Perkin's costs" on December 18th and March 10th respectively; Jones, one of his minders, was paid 13s. 4d. for him on May 23rd. These were small sums, appearing near the bottom of the daily list of payments: that of December 18th came after payments to Harry the king's barber, to a woman for three apples and to a poor man in alms.

Since Denis and Braybroke were not guarding Perkin, and since their usual job was to provide the king's household with dishes, books, pin-cases and tennis-balls, they were probably buying general articles of that sort for Perkin also. Braybroke was so far an intimate of the king's that he was one of the envoys sent, in 1505, to appraise the skin and breath of the young Queen of Naples as a suitable wife for him. Denis, as the groom of the close stool, was the servant who went with Henry to the privy and supervised his comfort there, laying out the water and scraps of cloth for wiping, holding back the royal robes. His involvement with Perkin, like Smith's, suggests that Henry was keeping his captive in the circle of his most intimate attendants. They also slept close to each other, Perkin among Henry's clothes, as quick to find (if you wished to find him) as a fresh shirt or a pair of gloves.

His own clothes are something of a mystery. They were paid for not through the Wardrobe, as Katherine's were (and as were the liveries of all court officers), but through Henry's privy-purse accounts, perused by the king himself. The only other clothes ordered in this way were occasional pieces of extravagant armour, cheap coats purchased for acts of charity, and the shirts and hose, in wild patchwork colours, that were bought for Dick the Fool, Henry's favourite jester. But Perkin also had his own tailor, one Jasper, who was paid £2 in February 1499. The notion of a dedi-cated tailor, like that of guards who could be taken for his servants, sug-gested that some bizarre form of princeliness still hovered round him; and Skelton, by calling him a peacock, implied this too. But the only specific payment for his clothes, 11s. 8d. for a knee-length "riding gown" in April 1498, implied it was made of rough woollen cloth, like the Kendal cloth ordered the same year to make a coat for a child.

The privy purse paid too for his "horsemeat", reckoned at 5d. a day. He rode not because his health and exercise mattered, but because he was following the ever-shifting court. Nonetheless this seemed oddly trusting, as if he would never think of suddenly cantering away. The horse and its harness may have been his own, spurred furiously from Taunton and kept since. There is no record that a horse was bought for him, only that it was fed, just as James had paid for the barley and oats in Scotland. Henry did not pay regularly for horsemeat for anyone else, although in 1492 he paid for a horse, saddle, spurs and bridle for Diego, the Spanish fool, who rode to Dover with him, hot to make war on France.

In many ways, Perkin's status—however honourable it may have seemed to the chroniclers—was close to Dick's and Diego's. At Henry's court he appeared in close association with tumblers, leapers, wrestlers, eaters of live coals and two vain bright-feathered popinjays, brought to the king in January and February, who squawked out bits of French and Dutch from their little gilded cages. He was also a freak among others kept to amuse the king: a woman with a beard, "a great Welsh child", "Alen the little Scotsman," a giantess from Flanders, and three real Indians from the land Columbus had reached. These last came a little after Perkin's time, brown-skinned and mute, dressed in beasts' skins and with peculiar straight black hair. Their brazil-wood bows and two red arrows were presented to the king. They were stared at as Perkin had been, captured monsters. *It is the chief thing we desire to have him brought unto us alive.*

Also somewhere round the court, but never mentioned in the accounts, was Lambert Simnel, his precursor. At some point in 1493–94 Henry apparently made him serve, in his capacity as kitchen-boy, at a banquet of Irish lords. The king introduced him with the words: "My masters of Ireland, you will crown apes at length." The table fell silent. Simnel, no doubt forced to do so, pledged them in a cup of wine, but no one responded; he went round with the cups, but none would be served by him. At last Lord Howth cried, "Bring me the cup if the wine be good, and I shall drink it off for the wine's sake and mine own also; and for thee, as thou art, so I will leave thee, a poor innocent." So the story went. Simnel too was a joke, but, as Howth had said, he was innocent; and for almost all the time he was invisible, burying himself in whatever lowly duties, first scullion and then falconer, he seems to have been given. Despite the possibilities of a rich comic double-act, he and Perkin were apparently never paraded together.

Despite his odd name, Simnel was also English. But Perkin was supposedly foreign, allowing an extra layer of suspicion and entertainment. Though he had been mocked as French for most of his career, at Henry's court—with his Flemish name—he was obviously a Fleming. This meant a steep social dive. The French, as everyone knew, were flatterers, lechers, fops and braggards; but Flemings were boors, drunkards, egregious overdressers and stealers of English jobs. Skelton's "Rutterkin" was Flemish, a dashing little gallant who could speak no English but babbled instead of fish smeared with butter. (Butter was freely associated with Flemings, who shipped it to England, and a Venetian observer described children in London "eating bread smeared with butter in the Flemish fashion.") Rutterkin's drinking was prodigious: "A stoup of beer up at a pluck, / Til his brain be as wise as a duck." So, too, was his pissing afterwards. Jehan Werbecque, brawling with beer-mugs in the muddy lanes of Beveren, fitted the caricature exactly.

If people laughed in their sleeves at Perkin, the foolish Flemish prince, he was far from alone. Court life spared no one. Many found it a hellhole of backbiting, gossip, social climbing and craven overwork; but, above all, a place of dissembling and false flattery. Skelton's courtiers, beneath their politeness and mock concern for newcomers, wore cloaks "lined with doubtful doubleness", and spent much of their time in sly conversation in dark corners, undercutting the plots of their so-called friends. "I hate this feigning!" cried the courtier Dissimulation to Skelton once, as he pressed his hand and wished him to "have good-day"; "Fie upon it, fie! A man cannot [know] where to become." Perkin was proba-bly in the same state of confusion. Court should have been his element, but he could never fit neatly back into that element again.

The man who so acutely observed this world was there with him, in late 1497 and 1498. Skelton was Henry's poet laureate and Prince Arthur's grammar teacher, treating both duties with immense seriousness and pride. He wore a robe of green and white, the king's colours, embroidered on the breast in gold with the name of Calliope, the muse of epic poetry. At times, he may have worn a laurel wreath in token of his several degrees in rhetoric; certainly he knew he deserved one. Both as a poet and a composer, his opinion of himself was unbounded.

In the spring of 1498, as close as it can be dated, Skelton produced a poem that was aimed with particular viciousness at someone who had offended him by trespassing on his second patch, the playing and singing of music. As with most of his poems, he did not attack his victim by name but went at him sideways, through allusion. Those allusions, as well as dozens of incidental details, make it almost certain that the man he was attacking was Perkin. Skelton was already engaged in, or had finished, a now-lost "Treatise on the Triumphs of the Red Rose", his only attempt at epic history under Calliope's wing. He knew Perkin's story and could use it, cunningly interwoven with his own expertise in music, to wreak revenge on him.

From the other side, it is certainly plausible that Henry's captive, after a few empty months at court, would have tried to find something to do and turned to music. In every version of his life, save the English confes-sion, he had been trained in it, and music-making was in any case a skill expected of princes, true or false. Henry's court was full of music:

harpers, Welsh rhymers, singers, trumpet players, small royal children stumbling over lute pieces. The court had a pair of organs (apparently last tuned in December 1493) and some "round organs" that were recast and "new furnished" in 1496. Prince Arthur also had an organ player of his own, presumably on another set. One more young man tinkering on a keyboard would not have attracted much attention. But Perkin seems to have given some sort of public recital, or to have tried to teach his skills to others, and hence brought about his own skewering by the most wounding pen at court.

> Skelton Laureate
> against.
> A comely coystrowne that curiously chanted, and currishly countered, and madly in his musics mockishly made against the ix Muses of politic poems and poets matriculate.

Ten verses eviscerated this "coystrowne"—this groom—who had turned political history upside down. In the second verse, Skelton described the deception as it appeared to him. A coarse bran horse cake had been somehow made to look like a costly loaf of sugar or a dainty "maunchet", a roll of fine white bread, as served to kings at breakfast:

> A sweet sugar loaf and sour bayard's bun
> Be somedeal like in form and shape,
> The one for a duke, the other for dung,
> A maunchet for Morel thereon to snap.
> His heart is too high to have any hap;
> But for in his gamut carp that he can,
> Lo, Jack would be a gentleman!

Skelton then moved on, raising the pitch, to link his victim to a previous ridiculous enterprise:

> With, Hey troly, loly, lo, whip here, Jack
> Alumbek sodyldum syllorum ben!
> Curiously he can both counter and knack
> Of Martin Swart and all his merry men.
> Lord, how Perkin is proud of his pea hen!
> But ask where he findeth among his monochords
> An holy water clerk a ruler of lords.

Martin Swart had been the German captain recruited by Margaret to help
Simnel; Skelton's second line was the chorus of a song about him. Like
many others then and since, he threw the pretenders together; two stupid
boys whose invasions had been fortified by German mercenaries. The
"holy-water clerk" may have been William Lounde, Perkin's "chancellor", or Perkin himself, who possibly owed to a spell of churchly training
all the skill, or non-skill, he was now showing. Skelton, on the other
hand, was a graduate on the verge of holy orders, trumping him there as
soundly as he trumped him in music. At any rate, the "he" of the poem
was now clearly Perkin, the monochord-player, the unbearable peacock
with his arm about his wife and his iridescent, angel-winged pride.

> He cannot find it in rule or in space:
> He solfyth too haute, his treble is too high;
> He braggeth of his birth, that born was full base;
> His music without measure, too sharp is his *mi* . . .

> He lumbreth on a lewd lute, *Roty bully joyse*,
> Rumble down, tumble down, hey go, now, now!
> He fumbleth in his fingering an ugly good noise,
> It seemeth the sobbing of an old sow:
> He would be made much of, and he wist how;
> Well-sped in spindles and turning of tavels,
> A bungler, a brawler, a picker of quarrels.

Skelton's victim seems to have sung in a high tenor, so high that it was
sharp, and to have accompanied himself on both the monochords and the
lute. Elsewhere he "knacked" curiously, or sang in an ornate and affected
way. But Skelton also stressed, particularly, the singer's low-born clumsi-
ness and his Flemish stupidity. *Roty bully joyse*, "Good roast boiled," was a
folk-song from Brabant, the region round Brussels and Malines. (In
another verse, Skelton got in a dig at Flemish drunkenness, describing
how the singer sang the longest notes in his counterpoint as steadily as a
man like Rutterkin would drain a flagon of beer.) Spindles and tavels
were Flemish tools, for spinning and silk-weaving. His victim should have
stuck to these and stayed in his place, both musically and in general: curb-
ing his wish to be made much of, when he was made of the muck in
which the old sow snuffled and sobbed.

There was plenty more. At times, though dripping with sarcasm,

Skelton recognised the charm of "this proud page": he looked "comely" as he played the clavichords, whistling "so sweetly, he maketh me to sweat." He implied, too, that the young man's pretensions were not over. Though "Jill" tried to hold "Jack" back, "He counteth in his countenance to check with the best. . . . Dreaming in dumps to wrangle and to wrest." Most of all, astonishingly, he remained full of arrogance and self-belief:

> Nay, jape not with him, he is no small fool,
> It is a solemn sire and a solain,
> For lords and ladies learn at his school;
> He teacheth them so wisely to solf and to fayne,
> That neither they sing well prick song nor plain:
> This Doctor Deuyas commenced in a cart,
> A master, a minstrel, a fiddler, a fart.

Yet all was not fake solemnity and refusal to engage. When mocked, he could defend himself sharply. Skelton in his last two verses described the original quarrel: his rival had "brawled" and "barked" at him first, "that meddled nothing with your work." The poet told him to get lost: "Walk and be naught!" And he ended, deliberately, on a note of Perkin-style lying and confusion, where even the time and the place were not what they were said to be.

> Now have I showed you part of your proud mind;
> Take this in worth the best is behind.
> Written at Croydon by Crowland in the Clay,
> On Candlemas even, the Kalendas of May.

In February then, or perhaps in May, this diatribe was read around the court. Perkin would have heard it. There was sometimes fun to be had in "flighting", or arguing back in kind, but his reaction may well have been the reverse: to say nothing and to stop playing. It was hard to withstand mockery as scathing as this.

His custody, meanwhile, was growing stranger. He was not confined to palaces but, by the spring, was being taken round the country by the king. April found him in Henry's train on a tour of the Medway towns in Kent. He was an exhibit of particular interest in the county that had rebuffed him two and a half years earlier. The last time Henry had toured

Kent, in 1492, he had travelled with one of his fools called "the foolish Duke of Lancaster", who had gone with him to the shrine of St. Thomas at Canterbury and had put on a performance in Sittingbourne. This time, he travelled with the foolish Duke of York.

When they reached Canterbury on the 21st, a man from Hythe brought Henry one of the standards that had been captured on that occasion: one of the three, perhaps, that Richard Plantagenet had ordered to be planted in the seaside villages when he had conquered them. Henry paid him £1 for his trouble. The standard might have been the White Rose; it might also have been the little boy escaping, so magically and boldly, from the jaws of the wolf or the enclosing tomb. Henry felt such satisfaction that day that he had the *Te Deum* sung, the hymn of victory. It is harder to imagine what his prisoner would have felt. But less than two months later he slipped his guards, and was gone.

III

HE ESCAPED ON JUNE 9TH, 1498, Trinity Sunday, one of the great feasts of the year and the very day, as it happened, of Skelton's ordination. Agostino de Spinula, a Milanese agent in England, reported that "Perichino Oxbeke", sleeping between two guards in the Wardrobe of the palace of Westminster, had climbed out of a window at midnight. (Again at midnight, the coward's hour.) The Wardrobe had been refurbished, with special attention to the better care of the king's clothes, late in 1493; along with the racks of hanging robes, a press and a "brushing table", a wooden ladder was kept to reach the higher shelves of pillows and hats. If the window was high, perhaps that ladder helped Perkin up and out.

Instantly, all hell broke loose. Messengers were sent to all the ports of England he might conceivably reach—to Poole, Weymouth, Lyme Regis, Bristol, Bridgewater, Barnstaple, Southampton, Boston, Grimsby, Lincoln, Ipswich, Yarmouth, Sandwich, Dover, Hastings—to warn town officers to watch out for him. One messenger was sent to the Abbot of Beaulieu, in case Perkin should think of going that way again. Almost two pages of Heron's accounts were taken up with payments to these couriers. In New Romney, the mandate brought that day about "Peter Warbekke" was the only mention of his name in the corporation accounts—accounts otherwise more concerned with the leasing of the Salt

Marsh and the presentation of capons to the Archbishop of Canterbury. Heron, listing the royal officers looking for him, at first wrote "Perkin seeking for Perkin", a rare slip that seemed to reflect the agitation around him.

For all this, Henry affected not to care. A letter sent on June 10th to the Earl of Oxford, whose lands extended to the east coast, played the incident down:

> Through the folly and simpleness of such as we put in trust to keep Perkin Warbeck, he is escaped from them, and albeit it is no great force where he be come, yet to the intent he might be punished after his desert, we would gladly have him again. Wherefore cousin we will and desire you to cause good and sure search to be made for him with all diligence all along our ports, creeks, and passages in those parts about you, that he in no wise pass those ways. And over this within the same ports and elsewhere that shall seem good ye make open proclamation that whosoever he be that taketh the said Perkin, he shall have for his reward an hundred pounds with our special thanks.

For those still keeping track, Perkin's price had fallen further, this time precipitously. His flight, Henry implied, was no more than an unfortunate accident; it did not concern him greatly but, almost for the sake of tidiness, he would be grateful to have him back.

Why had he done it? Contemporaries were baffled. The London chroniclers assumed that Perkin had simply forgotten all the benefits Henry had allowed him: obliviousness, combined with ingratitude, was the reason he had gone. Yet he must have known that Henry had always seemed able both to foresee his plans and to track him down. If he tried to run away, the king would simply extend a finger and haul him in again, this time probably to kill him. Unless he was pricked by some constant longing to destroy himself, as Vergil suggested, to break out of Westminster made no sense.

To run away, of course, was not out of Perkin's character. The boy of the confession had wandered around for years until he had reached Ireland. His birthplace had been a house with a boat moored just below it, ready to be steered to the northwest and the sea. He had been a typical Saturn-child and moon-child, running away from school and away from Portugal, according to Brampton; he seemed to have a horror of settling, an itch never to be tied down to one place or one master. He had run away from violence in Northumberland and from the burden of kingship at Taunton. Always, when he ran, it was towards ships that could take him away for miles beyond the horizon.

While he was at court, a mariner called Lancelot Thirkill came three times to Henry to beg money for a voyage to "the new isle", Newfoundland. The king was fascinated by this enterprise, often mentioning it to Ayala and other ambassadors, and several mariners besides Thirkill were given money to go there. Henry's warrant of 1496 to John Cabot, the head of the expedition, imagined that he would find houses, towns and castles if he explored, as Henry wished him to, "all parts, regions and coasts of the eastern, western and northern sea". Cabot had already found, according to Soncino, two very large and fertile new islands, the Seven Cities, and a sea so thick with fish that they could be taken in baskets weighted with a stone. ("He tells all this in such a way," Soncino added, "that I too feel compelled to believe him.") The mariners expected more, of course, including "an island which he called Japan, situated in the equinoctial region, where he believes that all the spices of the world have their origin, as well as the jewels." Those "other countries" were now impossibly beyond Perkin's dreams. Others were fitting out ships, as Thirkill was; he was in an anteroom or a corridor, his whole world, listening.

Yet he had also found courts comfortable and congenial, unsurprisingly. It had sometimes seemed hard to pry him from either Flanders or Scotland in favour of active promotion of his cause. A soft life, with a pension and fine clothes, suited him far better. A boatman's son from Tournai should have found Henry's court just as acceptable, with a little forbearance. He could have settled in time, becoming just as unremarkable as Simnel was and perhaps, on constant evidence of good behaviour, being allowed to be where his thoughts took him, in Katherine's arms again.

There are some signs that, by the early summer, they were beginning to edge closer. In mid-March 1498, for the first time, their names were together in Heron's accounts. The next month, perhaps not coincidentally, Katherine abandoned the black clothes she had worn since her arrest. On the last day of April Henry issued a warrant for a gown of tawny medley, the colour of the sea-gown she had worn as she left Scotland. Yet the element of competition, apparent as soon as Katherine had been captured, was also clear to see. The king made out the warrant for "our right dear and well-beloved Lady Katherine Gordon", using her

maiden name and showing again how kindly he was caring for her. He
had also made a double payment for her servants in March. In his order to
Robert Litton, the keeper of the Wardrobe, Henry enumerated, as he had
done before, not only the gown but the kirtle, of lined black worsted; the
ribbons for her girdle; and the hose of kersey lined with "a piece of single
cypress", soft white gauze—doubtless imagining each of them, and on
her body. By another warrant in the same week in April he ordered a velvet riding gown of tawny for himself, trimmed with black as her gown
was. As a final sting, Litton had been condemned by name in King
Richard's proclamation; but this "Caitiff & villain" was now procuring
Katherine's clothes.

Her husband would have felt even prouder now as he walked beside
her; and yet, perhaps, also closer to despair. It was spring, when the sap
rose in the green shoots and all living creatures sought their mates and
coupled with them. Under the soft breezes and the fine grass powdered
with flowers in a hundred thousand colours, the world itself was restless.
The courtiers were organising the royal maypole and the bringing of the
May boughs, symbols of compulsive physical love. He was in the April of
his own life as the almanacs measured it, perhaps not yet twenty-four, prey
to sensuality. His wife was beautiful; it would have been their third spring
together, but she was still in the deepest sense apart from him.

In other ways, too, his confinement may have become more difficult.
Just before the escape, he had been several times in Henry's train to the
Tower of London. The court was there from May 8th to the 19th, and
from the 23rd to the 30th. Before this Henry's captive had visited only
briefly, not going inside, to deliver his former servant William to prison
and death in November. Henry was not fond of the damp and hemmed-
in Tower, much preferring Sheen, Greenwich or Windsor where he had
wide parklands to disport in, and it was mostly at Sheen that Perkin
passed his strange semi-captivity. Now, in the joyousness of green May, he
was at the Tower, the place established in his memory or his imagination
as the most dread prison of all. Henry had made it more so, stuffing it
with heavy artillery, hand-guns, arquebuses, bombards and battle-axes,
besides bows and crossbows. Lions and leopards roared there in basement
cages, and in 1494 the privies and drains in the inner ward, so little used,
were blocked up with filth and rubbish. The Lanthorn Tower, where
Henry had his lodgings, was very probably where the princes had been
kept. Richard of York had escaped this place, God's might intervening,

and now his shadow had returned to stones and passageways haunted by the little prince who had laughed and danced in front of Death. Had that been him? If so, by what joke of God's had he been spirited away, only to be brought back again?

If all things were bound to find their particular course, perhaps his course was to be this prince; perhaps he could not avoid it. You could cage lions, Boethius said, and make them eat from the keeper's hand; but if a single drop of blood touched their jaws, they remembered their old nature and tore him apart. You could cage birds, minister to them and feed them on honey; but if a caged bird glimpsed again the green trees where he had once flown free, singing from the highest boughs, "the woods are all his sorrow calls for."

Vergil's simplest explanation for Perkin's flight was that he could not bear confinement, or tolerate his "actual distress". But he suggested also that Margaret, or "friends", might have pushed him to "further his affairs", whatever he thought those were, by wriggling free. As late as September 1497, on the brink of his capture, they had been in touch by letter, at least from him to her. Although she seemed to have fallen silent, her solicitude for him had not altered. Since she had last seen him, every single military venture had crumbled in his hands. He had proceeded from failure to failure, and had now apparently confessed that Margaret knew he was a boatman's son. Yet neither Margaret nor Maximilian was prepared to let him go.

Maximilian, always more open in his efforts and his opinions, was caught musing in May 1498 by Gutierre Gomez de Fuensalida, the Spanish ambassador to Germany. He was agonising again over his daughter's marriage prospects; almost ten years after the French king had repudiated her, she still had no husband, for her marriage to the Prince of Asturias, Ferdinand and Isabella's son, had lasted a mere six months before he died. Bluntly, half-jokingly, Maximilian ran through the possibilities among the Christian princes. "The King of Naples has no son of the right age; the King of England has already married his son to the daughter of your princes; the King of Scotland is unimportant; the Duke of York is married and is not at liberty; the King of Hungary has a wife; the King of Poland is nothing." The Duke of York was certainly not at liberty, for all Maximilian's efforts. But he remained among kings and even above some, including James.

Nor had Maximilian dropped his schemes to get him out, somehow. At that moment, he seemed to be trying to get a fleet together to rescue both his cousin of York and Edward, Earl of Warwick, the pathetic subject of so many earlier conspiracies, who was still confined in the Tower. Two months later, in July, Fuensalida reported several remarks about armed ships gathering in Flanders "to deliver the Duke of York and the Duke of Clarence [sic] who are prisoners." This was only rumour, *fama*, but Fuensalida thought he should pass it on to Ferdinand and Isabella all the same. "I also see [the King of the Romans]," he wrote,

> inclined to do everything contrary to the King of England . . . and as far as I can find out, I believe he will do what he can to set Perkin free and throw the realm into confusion, notwithstanding the marriage alliance that your Highnesses have made with England, and I believe that won't hold him back from trying everything he can do for him, if he gets the chance. I may be deceiving myself in my knowledge of this, but I don't think so; your Highnesses may take it as my fantasy . . . but if this matter was as I thought it was, putting together this with what he said about the fleet which would be ready to go and deliver Perkin, I think that if he sees he can do it, he will try it.

Maximilian himself in the *Weisskunig* admitted that for some time he had thought of raising an army and a fleet to help King Edward's son. "He seriously considered avenging these people," he wrote (himself, as usual, in the third person):

> and he plans an assault in great secrecy. He wants to go over there personally, across the sea, with a great force, and ventures to make himself king in this same kingdom, as he also has a right to this crown through his old mother [Margaret]. And he comes to some kind of agreement with the Blue King [France] that he doesn't obstruct or interfere with his plans. But when the new Red and White King [Henry] came to know this, he sent a messenger to the White King and said he wanted to be his good friend. . . . Whereupon the White King reconsidered the whole situation and meanwhile deliberated how he could get on with the Blue King. But he found the Blue King so difficult that he could not get on with him.

A cryptic note, sent to de Puebla from Brussels in June by a contact calling himself "Licenciatus et Decanus", may also have described these ill-formed plans. "A messenger sent by the little duck to the falcon," it ran, "returned a short time ago much pleased with the answer of the falcon. . . . Everything is going well now . . . and it will be concluded in favour of the cuckoo and the young eagle." These last two birds may well have stood for York and Warwick, on the point of being sprung by someone's efforts.

Little, if any, of this plotting and musing could have been apparent to Henry's captive. If Margaret had not dared to send letters to Scotland, she certainly would not have attempted to send them to Henry's court. Maximilian, too, had not dared to write directly either to York or to Henry, but had tried to intercede for his cousin at two removes. The prisoner was probably unaware that his old supporters were still backing him, in Brabant or anywhere else. An entry in the patent rolls for the end of March mentioned that Atwater and Barry in Ireland "have now of late at several times received as well letters with certain instructions from Parkyn Wosebeck, and the same hath concealed, and as yet keepeth secret from the knowledge of our sovereign lord." But this may have referred, with the usual time-lag, to the activities of the summer before. It is unlikely that he was allowed to write to anyone; or, if he was allowed to, that he would have been so foolish as to try to revive, under Henry's nose, the network round Richard, Duke of York.

Another supporter, who did not need to write, may have had some influence on him. Heron's accounts strongly suggest that Katherine was assumed to have played some part in Perkin's disappearance. She had, after all, taken part in his last escape, from the forces of Desmond and Kildare in Ireland. This time, too, she may have abetted him. After her husband's flight, her name disappeared from the accounts for almost a year. When she reappeared in April 1499—her first name omitted and replaced by a dash—her status had evidently changed. Her payments had been so curtailed that she was constrained to borrow money from the king, and her servants had been reduced from six to one, for whom payment (eleven months in arrears) was not made until the following November. To be deprived of servants was not merely a social humiliation. It also stopped intrigues. For this reason Margaret Beaufort, Henry's mother, had been deprived of "any servant or company", on Richard III's orders, for her complicity in Buckingham's rebellion in 1483. In Katherine's case, too, this may have been punishment for complicity. In the first year of the next king's reign, for unspecified reasons, she was included in a general pardon.

Yet there was little she could do to advance a plan of escape. She had no money or resources save what the king allowed her; the only hint at independent wealth comes from another entry in the warrants for the Wardrobe, some years later, when she was to have a gown "furred with mink from her own store". In May and June of 1498 she was almost as penniless as her husband. Like him, she could presumably receive no letters from supporters; and she was watched, as he was. Since they were together only under supervision, any plotting would have had to be almost unspoken. He may have sought to include her; or, as at Taunton, he may have fled without stopping to think what his actions might have meant for his wife.

The question of why he had escaped seemed unanswerable; and there was also the question of how. It was assumed by Thomas Gainsford in the seventeenth century, and the rumour may have surfaced at the time, that Perkin must have plied his guards with "a sleepy drink" to be able to climb from the bed without disturbing them. He had also to get past the king's watch, two dozen yeomen of the crown who accompanied Henry from palace to palace, "piping the watch" three times on each summer night, and his guard, some 150 to 200 strong, who lined the corridors and passages on either side wherever the king was likely to pass. These men were trained to detect "treasons, bruits or noises" that might annoy the king from any quarter of the palace, but they had somehow missed Perkin leaving. Doubtless this was another miracle or magic trick, or yet another example of how he could "graciously escape and overpass" the enemies set about him.

In fact, it may have been much easier; as easy as opening a door. Three weeks or so after his flight, two "yeomen" of London, John Kebyll and John Sherwyn, were indicted before the king for helping Perkin escape. Nothing is known of them, except that Sherwyn at the end of 1496 suffered a comprehensive burglary from his house in the City in which he lost, among other things, gold rings, a silver chain, a jacket and a russet robe trimmed with lamb's wool. The burglar was a woman, and the shaming experience may have piqued Sherwyn's interest in locks and keys. Both men were apparently ordinary Londoners, unconnected to the court. But, knowing that Perkin wanted to escape, they were said to have made "various counterfeit keys to open the locks on the prison door".

The indictment was hard to believe on several levels. It placed Perkin both in the custody of Smith and Jones and *in prisone domini Regis;* but he was known not to be in prison, and the "prison door" for which the locks were made was no such thing, just some ordinary door of the palace of Westminster. He seemed able to talk to, and deal with, these tradesmen quite freely, though his guards were meant to be beside him. Peculiarly, too, the initiative did not seem to come from him. Kebyll and Sherwyn, eager to help implement "that false proposal", were said to have produced the keys without being asked. The indictment said that traitor Perkin had escaped to wage war treasonably on Henry: a standard phrase when dealing with him, but one that meshed oddly with the king's remarks that he added up to nothing important. He could hardly wage war on his own, however inflated his conceit.

When prisoners escaped from custody, those who had charge of them—usually the sheriff of the county—were always fined. The standard fine was £5, rising to £20 for the loss of important captives. But Smith and Jones were apparently not punished for their lapse, though Henry himself had blamed the escape on their folly and simpleness. Both went on appearing in Heron's accounts, receiving payments and working for the king, as if nothing had happened. In November that year Smith was rewarded with £5 in cash; not long before, he was made a king's officer in Lancashire. Kebyll and Sherwyn seem not to have been punished either, and the indictment petered out inconsequentially. The whole thing looked like incitement or entrapment, and some contemporaries read it that way. A report sent to Venice mentioned that Henry was apprehensive of some insurrection, "and this because the king arranged with some of Perkin's servants that they should put it into his fantasy to escape out of his Majesty's hands; and thus did this youth do." Bacon said it was "believed generally" that this had happened.

De Puebla maintained that Perkin had escaped "without any opportunity having been given him to do so". He may, as so often, have been stressing—at Henry's bidding—the opposite of the truth. Heron's accounts, too, suggest the opportunity was there. On May 23rd, between the payment to Jones for Perkin and the entry for his riding gown, a payment of 4 shillings appeared for "a new lock made". No other lock-fitting was going on in those weeks, and the unusual lack of specification—whether for coffer or box, window or door—suggested that it was just for Perkin, somehow.

Henry had been kind to him for a long time. But Perkin's presence at court, where he still played the prince, was an anomaly and an embarrassment. In particular, it did not make much sense to the hard-headed Spanish sovereigns with whom Henry was still, tediously, negotiating dowry details. Fuensalida, writing to Ferdinand and Isabella from Maximilian's court, talked of "the Duke of York Pierrequin", as though a little dynastic hedging was still going on. The Milanese and Venetian ambassadors, too, kept his old name going; since this young duke was defeated anyway, and his cause lost, they saw no need for the further humiliations. Nothing more rigorous could be done to Perkin unless he deserved it; but he could be made to deserve it. Henry's strategy had always been to allow him enough rope so that, in his folly and vanity, he could hang himself. He may well have paid out a little more rope in the summer of 1498, in the almost certain knowledge that his captive, delighting in it as in new gold chains, would twine it round his neck.

The chance, then, was probably given to him. By opening the window or unlocking the door, no guard preventing him, he slipped away from the palace of Westminster. At midnight, the dark could be depended on, as could the emptiness of the fields that lay beyond the palace to the south and east. No one, for the moment, chased or stopped him. He had no shadows. In all likelihood, he also had no plan. He ran, almost certainly, not towards an objective—whether war, or Margaret, or a waiting ship—but away from something he could not endure. He ran away from being Perkin.

IV

HENRY WAS SURE that his captive would go towards the sea. Instead he fled upriver, as if the dark had disoriented him. Molinet said he spent three or four days hiding in the reed-beds on the banks of the Thames. At most he may have been a few hours there, knee-deep in the dark water. It should have been a good season for hiding: the air balmy and the trees and hedges, elder, hawthorn and eglantine, thick with leaves and blossom that glowed white and shed perfume in the dark. A hare could hide in those hedges, as in the young corn, quivering and listening like he did, appearing and disappearing with all the wiles of a moon-creature. When Dorset fled from sanctuary at Westminster in June 1483, he had managed to escape the king's troops and dogs "who sought him, after the manner of huntsmen, by a very close encirclement", by hiding in the high crops and woodland nearby. But the summer of 1498 was a hot one, the grass "sore consumed" and dry, and the crops not yet tall enough to conceal a man.

As he ran, he soon heard the king's men after him. They were picketing all the roads that led away from Westminster. Two naval captains, one of them Stephen Bull, were in charge of searching the port of London for him, and four yeomen in boats had been sent to scour the Thames. He could probably hear their shouts, and the splash of their oars in the water. Vergil imagined that their clamour pushed out of Perkin's mind whatever faint plans or resolve he had. Racing at full tilt, he managed to get seven miles in a night along the bends of the dark river, at some point crossing it by boat or swimming, and then threw himself into sanctuary in the Charterhouse at Sheen.

He was in terrible distress. Having bungled his escape, he had to cast himself once more on Henry's mercy, and it was unclear that any remained. In that light, the choice of Sheen may have been deliberate as well as desperate. The Charterhouse had Yorkist connections: the prior before last, John Ingelby, had been an executor of Elizabeth Woodville's will. But Henry, too, had a particular devotion to this house. He referred to the palace of Sheen itself as "the palace at the Charter House", and wrote enthusiastically to the pope in 1490 to tell him that the Carthusian rule "exceeds that of all other orders as regards religious perfection". Their abstinence, he wrote, their hair-shirts, their solitude and their abandonment of the world bound him to protect them, and the Jesus House of Sheen in particular, "with peculiar favour." His favour, sitting uneasily with their austerity, included the gift every year of two tuns of "our prize wines" coming into the port of London, an ancient tradition that was sometimes replaced, in his reign, with hard cash.

Henry also had a high regard for Ralph Tracy, the prior. In June 1497 he had taken delivery from him of a "table of imagery", a series of sacred paintings for private meditation, and Robert Fabyan thought that Tracy stood greatly in the king's regard. The prior was now "instanced lamentably", with "piteous motions", by a young man whose history, in his deep otherworldliness, he may not have known. He was treated, no

doubt, to a story as heartbreaking as the one that had been told by Richard Plantagenet around the courts of Europe. It had worked then, and it
worked now. Tracy agreed to intercede for him and, having placed the
wretched fugitive under firm lock and key, went to the king to implore
him to spare his life.

The Charterhouse had no place for prisoners, only another cell like
those of the monks themselves. The Carthusians were an enclosed order,
preserving silence towards each other and leaving their private rooms only
for their tiny walled gardens or for the church next door. Their whitewashed cells contained a pallet bed, a crucifix, and sometimes a vivid
painting of the Passion; a small window gave light, and a hatch in the wall
allowed the delivery of food. The new arrival may have been handed,
silently, one of the holy cards that the brothers had had printed and sent out
all over London: a heraldic shield of the five bleeding wounds of Christ,
surmounted with the crown of thorns and held by two angels against the
Cross. *Of your charity in the worship of the five wounds of Our Lord and the five
joys of Our Lady say Pater Noster and Ave.*

The monks themselves scarcely ceased praying. They lived on their
knees, "grovelling like beasts," their critics said, through day and night
alike. Their privations were considered almost foolish; but on the other
hand, they were released by them. Carthusians were never afraid, Thomas
More wrote, of "the loathness of less room and the door shut upon us, a
horror enhanced of our own fantasy." Their souls had almost escaped from
the prison of the body and the world, dwelling only on the beauty of the
kingdom to come. They remembered that kingdom as theirs and recalled
that they were royal, a king's children—as this young man, in whatever
clothes he had grabbed before he ran, falling to his knees on the doorstep,
had said he remembered too.

Before the king, Tracy argued hard. He would not leave, Fabyan
said, until he had "gotten grant for his life". Vergil said that Tracy interceded for Perkin humbly, with many prayers, so moved was he by his distress. Molinet wove a more highly coloured story out of this. His Perkin,
once out of the reeds, rode to the Charterhouse on a mule—no doubt
provided by a sympathiser—and besought the prior to hide him. "And
because Henry had announced that Perkin was not to be helped, on pain
of great punishment, the prior was extremely worried about what he
could do for him, and took it into his head to put him in the hands of the

Bishop [of Cambrai], who also helped him for many days; but then, fearing to be held in disrepute, he delivered him up to the king again."

Cambrai had not yet arrived in England, so the story was pure fantasy. Yet it was not thought odd, on its face, that eminent churchmen should scramble to help Perkin. And it was not thought odd, though it was an astonishing access of charity, that Henry, in the end, agreed to spare him. With that message, the prior returned to Sheen. Alongside him rode Bradshaw, who had fetched Perkin—with a little help—from Beaulieu, ready to strong-arm this fugitive for the second time in a year. The young man had left Beaulieu like a prince on progress and had entered London like a dancer, but no such scene was likely now. Almost certainly it was Death, with his stretched-paper smile and his belly heaving with worms, whose likeness he would dance with next.

The whole process, escape to recapture, took about four days. At some point in those four days, probably on June 13th, de Puebla sat down to write to Ferdinand and Isabella, appealing to them again for help with "the Perkin business". Perkin's escape, he wrote, made good advice even more vital.

The Spanish sovereigns, still keen to keep Henry on edge and Katherine's dowry down, were always eager to get news of *Periquin*, as de Puebla called him. The harried ambassador remarked once that he had written "so often" to them about him, implying that it was hardly possible they could want more. June 13th, however, was his lucky day. In mid-letter, within an hour of the event, Henry sent an officer of the bedchamber to tell him that Perkin had just been recaptured. "Thanks be to God!" the ambassador wrote. "No time to know what will be done with Perkin yet," he went on, rejoicing in his topicality and writing on a small, snatched scrap of paper, "because the king sent to tell me the news just as I was writing this, but I think one of two things: either he will be executed for it, or kept under very strict guard and in prison."

For two or three strange days, Perkin was held in the palace of Westminster under tight security. Execution would have suited Spain better, but the Tower, where Henry had now determined to put him, was good enough. It probably meant death fairly quickly, as other ambassadors assumed. "So the king has put him in prison, where he will end his life," wrote Trevisano. Once he was there, de Puebla could reassure his sovereigns that *Periquin* was "in safe keeping in a tower where he sees neither sun nor moon." He added, in another letter, "He is in such a secure prison that he won't be able to play any *burla* now, God willing."

Before he was committed, however, he was exhibited again. On Friday, the day after Corpus Christi, he was set "fast locked" in the stocks—and in chains, Vergil said—on a scaffolding of barrels in Westminster Hall. The hall, which was both concourse and meeting place, contained three "houses" called Paradise, Purgatory and Hell, and was crammed with people even on ordinary days. A high proportion of them, according to contemporary prejudice, were petty criminals and prostitutes. Now they swarmed round Perkin, who was "wondered again upon, as he had been oft times before."

A double meaning lay in his barrelthrone. It raised him above the crowd like a mockking, and it was made of "empty vessels" like his promises and claims. The constant escaper could not escape this time. His sentence, though, was light. Although lowclass players of tennis and bowls could expect to spend a day in the stocks, and idlers and tricksters three, he merely sat there "a good part of the forenoon", after which, it seems, he was taken back to the main palace.

On the next Monday, June 17th, he was displayed again. This time he stood on a special scaffold, made of empty barrels like the last, in front of the King's Head tavern (or "at the Standard") in Cheapside. Standing in the street, though usually in the pillory and usually at Cornhill, was the longestablished punishment for frauds and deceivers. In 1493 two men were put in the pillory for counterfeiting pardons, "and one of them feigned himself a priest, and was none." In 1496 John Gamelyn was pilloried there for changing Greek wines into "candy butts" and selling them as malmseys, "to the great hurt and jeopardy of all such persons who drank of such muddled wines." Perhaps most ingenious of all was a young man called John Camell, punished in October 1496, who had tricked people

by the mean of iv Boxes of ij Sorts, ij of them being like of fashion and quantity, in one of the which ij boxes was beads or other things to the value of xxs or iv nobles, in the match old nails and Stones; upon which Box stuffed with the beads he would have borrowed certain money, and suddenly and craftily delivered the

Box with nails and Stones in pledge for the other with the Beads;
by mean whereof he had by his own confession deceived divers
men and women.

Perkin stood on the scaffold, "to his great shame", from ten in the
morning until three in the afternoon, and was "exceedingly wondered
upon." He seemed to be simply standing there, though some kind of
restraint must have been put on him. Possibly he was tied to the Standard
itself, a giant wooden post that had been festooned in the past with various
papers from his life, true or false: with Thomas Bagnall's rhymes against
Henry, which had signalled the public start of the conspiracy, and with
the notices for the wedding jousts of Richard, Duke of York, to which
Robert Clifford had so eagerly signed up. Now Perkin was advertised
there. Nothing so marvellous was to appear again at the Standard until a
pageant was built there three years later to welcome Katherine of
Aragon, featuring God the Father enthroned in a heaven of seven gold
candlesticks and a blaze of lesser candles, surrounded by singing angels
and with a great red rose before him as tall as a man.

As Perkin stood there, according to Hall, he read his confession to
the crowd from a copy he had written out himself. No contemporary
reported this. Those who stood on public display as malefactors in the city
did not read out papers for themselves; they simply stood there, carrying or
wearing the items that accused them, while their crimes were proclaimed
by a city officer. The crier sometimes recited the list three times, crying it
properly, as ordinary folk could not do, even assuming they could read. If
Perkin's offences were proclaimed, he did not do it himself.

Nor is it likely that he had written out his confession to be read,
though he may have done, and had apparently signed copy after copy the
previous autumn with his new name in large letters. All he was required
to do was stand and listen, displaying his face, allegedly his instrument of
deception, as the others had displayed their fake pardons and their boxes
full of old nails and stones. He had plainly demonstrated, by escaping,
that he had not settled into the person he was required to be. Now he was
to be made to understand who he was. The crowd mocked him, Vergil
said, with more derision than ever. But it could not be said that he did not
deserve it.

These shows were not only for his own instruction, but also for
that of the crowd and an audience far beyond. De Puebla, writing to his

sovereigns on July 17th, was anxious to check that they had received his letters about Perkin "being put to shame for two days" and then imprisoned, "since it may be . . . that others, biased by party feeling, will write about the escape and not about what followed it." His letter betrayed that a faction still existed that had wanted Perkin to escape and would have feasted on his disappearance. Those hopes were quite dashed now.

When he had stood there long enough, he was taken down from the scaffold, put on a horse and taken "in the greatest ignominy" to the Tower. He passed along Cheapside to the Great Conduit, then to the stocks, to the Standard on Cornhill, to St. Peter's Church and Grace Church, then along Mark Lane, "cursed by everyone and laughed to scorn." City officials and Tower officers went with him: "sure guides", said Fabyan, in case he doubted where he was going. He was led through the gates, and the door was shut on him.

His adventure was over, and so, a few months later, was another. John Cabot, having persuaded his backers of his expert knowledge of the world, had sailed out over the West Sea early that summer towards the new island he was certain was there. Merchants of London and Bristol had "adventured goods and slight merchandises" (caps, laces, woollens and "other trifles") on this dream-voyage, and Henry had helped to pay for his ships and released the prisoners to man them. "Vast honour is paid to him," wrote Trevisano disapprovingly; "he dresses in silk, and these English run after him like mad people, so that he can enlist as many of them as he pleases, and a number of our own [Venetian] rogues besides." But after the smooth self-promoter sailed west, nothing more was heard of him. Vergil said he had probably found his new isle all the same, tilting his bold ships towards it with their sails trailing like seaweed, at the very bottom of the sea.

CHAPTER NINE

Bad Stars

William Parron, Henry's Italian astrologer, had been right about June 1498. He had predicted trouble at the beginning of the month—though also, to be honest, in the middle of May, the middle of August and "around the 10th or 24th day of April". His printed prognostication for 1498 had generally taken the broad and safe view. The king would be "exalted and fortunate", and disposed to ride about his kingdom. Prince Arthur "would prosper and increase his stance and honour." There would be sickness in some places but easy profit in others, and the weather would be variable but fruitful. Though readers might mock, Dr. Parron (doctor of medicine, professor of astrology) did not hesitate to point out the cases where he had been right before. "Kings shall subdue their adversaries," he wrote for 1498, "as [I] said the last year in my prognostications / whereby the Cornishmen if they had been wise might have been wary."

That was true enough, and the false god of the Cornishmen had now disappeared altogether from public view. If they were still furious with him, as seemed likely, they certainly could not get at him now. At the top of one of Henry's subsequent lists of fines, raised unsparingly by his commissioners from all who had followed or vaguely favoured King Richard, the Cornishmen were described as *infelicissimi*: ill-starred and bound to come to grief. Parron's printed booklets, popular in London, clearly did not reach the extremities of England.

The nature of their idol's new captivity can be pieced together from the indictments issued at the end of his life. The Tower had no prison cells as such, only rooms of various sizes and levels of salubriousness; so his room was called a *camera*, or chamber, like the room above it, which was used for a state prisoner who was kept in some comfort. This implied that Perkin had a certain amount of space and furniture, in theory. The ceiling was fairly high, with stone vaulting, suggesting that he was confined in the thirteenth-century wing of the Tower that stood out over the river. The room above his had a proper bed; he probably had one too, with the bedding changed, as often as anyone remembered, by two boys who worked for his old guard Smith, sometime keeper of the beds within the Tower. Since he apparently managed to write letters, he may have had a table and a chair. De Puebla was not quite right to say that he saw neither sun nor moon; there was a window, but it was small enough to be blocked with a single iron bar. Through this window, probably open to the air, small objects could be passed. He was allowed to receive letters, though they were usually read first, and he could have visitors. William Lounde, his chaplain and chancellor, seems to have come regularly to say Mass for him.

The services of Jasper were no longer required; in February 1499 he was referred to as "late Perkin's tailor", though neither man was dead. Perkin now wore basic prison clothes, hose and a shirt, with perhaps a coat of some sort. He was also fitted with *pedenae*, foot-shackles, and *cathenae*, the sort of neck-and-body chains that were put on performing animals. The Tower had two categories of prisoners, those with "liberty of the Tower" and those under close constraint, although this normally meant no more than confinement to a room. Chains such as his, as if he were some criminal in Newgate, were relatively rare.

Four men guarded him: Thomas Astwood, Walter Bluet, Thomas Strangeways and Roger Ray, known as "Long Roger". All were described as servants of Simon Digby, the constable of the Tower, but at least two of them, from the beginning, were also sympathisers with the cause of Richard, Duke of York. Long Roger had fled his job in 1494 and had been arrested by the king's officers, which suggested treason or rebellion; for some reason, he had been spared and re-employed. Astwood had been a fervent believer, spared the rope at the last minute in 1495 only because he was so young. The arrangement had possibilities, as did the fact that their charge's room was directly under the one that held Richard's cousin Edward, Earl of Warwick. For more than a year, however, these possibilities seem to have gone unexplored.

The new prisoner was brought out three times in the seventeen months he was confined there. The first time was on July 30th, about six weeks after his committal. A delegation had arrived in London from the court of Burgundy, sent by Philip to try to sort out various nagging disagreements over trade. Its second, hidden purpose (de Puebla said he had been told this was a secret) was to negotiate for Margaret. Henry, well aware that the duchess had not dropped her protégé, wanted to impose sanctions against her as agreed in the trade treaty of 1496, but Philip and Juana, his new archduchess, would not allow this. Somehow, from Henry's point of view, Margaret had to be persuaded to give up the boy, since her support continued to sustain his claim; somehow, from hers, she had to save her White Rose and get him back to Flanders.

The delegation was headed by the Bishop of Cambrai, who was then Philip's first chamberlain and leader of his council. His deputy was Jean Courtville, whom Philip had sent at his father's request the previous December; the third-ranking member was the servant of the president of Flanders, who had come on that embassy also. Cambrai, according to Erasmus—who had been his Latin secretary and was in regular touch with him—had left Brussels on July 3rd in a thoroughly bad mood, "embarrassed by a crowd of engagements, anxious about the raising of his own supplies, and somewhat angry, too, that Prince Philip, in whose name he is sent, has helped him with only 600 gold pieces." (A man of Cambrai's magnificence, Erasmus said later, really needed more when being sent on an embassy "to rich and very ostentatious people".) In short, "He expended on me plenty of complaints."

The secret business of his embassy—Erasmus, too, said there was a secret side—was broached about a week after his arrival. The bishop, de Puebla reported, asked for Perkin to be brought out "so that they could see him and talk to him, because the bishop had brought news with him." Behind the peculiar thinness of this reason was the obvious wish of the dowager duchess to find out how he was. For much of that summer she had retired to Binche, so ill that she had a new wall built in the courtyard to stop people entering the palace, and so restlessly unhappy that her whole living quarters were reorganised "so that Madame can make her bedrooms and her lodgings wherever she will please to do so." She now depended, though she must have known it was hopeless, on whatever Cambrai could do.

Maximilian, too, may have made another approach to Henry. In July the king had letters from him, ostensibly friendly, egging him on to war with France to win back the lost English lands. Maximilian offered eagerly to help such an effort, promising to perform "wonders". This drew from Henry the sarcastic remark that "he was extremely pleased to hear that, and he would be even more pleased to see the King of the Romans in the thick of a war." An ambassador had been expected from Maximilian for a long time, but he was making "infinite delays": still plotting, as Fuensalida knew, to rescue his cousin of York. Something of this may have caused his sudden amiability, a dream of delivering York from what was now almost certain death. But Henry, reasonably enough, was not to be moved by any such appeal.

Nonetheless, he showed Cambrai his prisoner. The bishop, after all, knew him well. How well, perhaps Henry too wondered; for if Maximilian's piece of gossip about Cambrai and Margaret had indeed reached London with Robert Clifford, the king may have heard it. For what it was worth, the suburban part of Tournai *dela Escaut*, including Caufours, lay within Cambrai's diocese: there, perhaps, lurked another possibility of a link between the bishop and the boy. These murmurs aside, the bishop may well have been the young man's confessor at Malines, as he was Margaret's. Molinet's made-up story, that Cambrai had helped to shelter Perkin after his escape, showed that he had no trouble in presenting the bishop as an intercessor for him and almost as a private friend. Erasmus found him both kind and distant, his moods ebbing and flowing like violent tidal water: at times generous with affection, at times "so cold that it seemed almost unnatural". His coldness stemmed from his awareness of his high nobility: and he evidently cut a fine figure in London, despite Philip's stinginess with his money.

On July 30th Henry himself conducted the bishop to the Tower. He was on his way east with the court in any case, heading for Stratford and on to East Anglia. It was a Monday morning. De Puebla was invited too, the essential Spanish witness to how closely Perkin was now guarded. What followed was another set-piece carefully arranged by the king.

Perkin was to swear solemnly to his identity in front of Cambrai, who would then understand—and lead Margaret to understand—that the game was up. The importance of the solemn oath-taking, which could not be done without due ritual, and the fact that Henry made an offering in the chapel of Our Lady in the Tower that day, suggest that the inter-view was staged after or during Mass, with the Mass-book laid open and Christ brought in as witness. If so, there was a horrible familiarity to the scene. This young man had so often sworn on Christ's Body (His Body racked on the Cross, His Body under the form of bread) to confirm what his own body was, whose flesh and whose blood. By this time, he may hardly have known.

Simon Digby, who had been paid 16s. 8d. for his services, brought Perkin in. As form required, he knelt down in his chains. Henry asked him, de Puebla said, why he had practiced such a great deception (*tan gran engaño*) on the archduke and his country. Perkin did not precisely answer the question. Instead, "he swore solemnly to God that the Duchess Ma-dame Margaret knew, as well as he himself did, that he was not the son of who he said he was."

The too-ready answer to a different question suggested words that had been practised. They had also been heard before. Soncino remarked that, among the other bits and pieces tumbling from the young man's lips in Taunton, he had said that "Madame Margaret of Burgundy knew everything": knew, in other words, that he was fake. Now, in the Tower, the words were more laborious. They could also have been clever and ambiguous, but the prisoner seemed past that. De Puebla was shocked at the sight of him. He found it hard to believe that he could have changed so much "in so few days". He thought, "as many others here believe", that he could not live much longer. In six weeks, however, it was clearly not just confinement that had altered his appearance, or the chains or the prison clothes. He was *desfigurado*; they had broken his face.

Why they had done so was easy enough to see. It was another way to emphasise the end of being Richard. He had admitted, Henry said, to being Piers Osbeck, and had written this as his name. He had proba-bly stood silently by while the story of Piers was proclaimed in public. Yet his face had still looked like Edward's to some people, and in that half-recognition, as well as in his own appreciation of his handsomeness in a glass, there was a danger that he would never put Richard away. The answer was to beat Richard out of him. "And it serves him right," said de

Puebla, recovering from his moment of queasiness and horror: *Quien tan fizo que tal pague.*

Perkin apparently said nothing more during the interview. What he had said was enough, sending a clear message to Margaret that the lie was exposed and her support of him should end. In fact, he had implied yet again that Margaret had been involved in setting him up from the beginning. When Henry had asked him *why*, his first words of answer had been her name. *She knew as well as he did*, with not a moment of doubt, though he had ostensibly come to her as suddenly as he had come to all the others. She knew, most probably, because she had made him.

This was not the story of the confession. It was Henry's old story, with Margaret as prime mover, though more delicately put than at some times in the past. The king still believed this in private, but no hint of her agency had appeared in the document her protégé had signed. It is hard to say why. Henry had no wish to spare her feelings, since he still loathed her heartily, and she him. Late in 1495 de Puebla seems to have told his sovereigns that Henry wanted to drive Margaret out of Flanders, a suggestion that almost made them feel sorry for her, "though she has always shown herself an enemy of ours." The next July the king was telling de Puebla how pernicious and central, at Maximilian's court, Margaret's supporters were. "I will never be certain of the King of the Romans," he told the ambassador, "especially while the duchess lives." Yet her very support, like that of Maximilian and James (who also went unmentioned in the confession), gave the feigned lad his credibility; and so, too, might the story of a trainee prince, dangerously close to Richard of York, fostered with her in Flanders. The adventures of Piers Osbeck, dragged round the boarding houses of Flanders and tossing on wool ships in the Irish Sea, were nothing like that.

Perkin remained silent, standing or still kneeling, in front of the king, the bishop and their attendants. Henry went on talking. "The king said to the Bishop of Cambrai and to me," wrote de Puebla, "that the pope and the King of France and the archduke and the King of the Romans and the King of Scotland had been deceived, and almost all the Christian princes except your Highnesses." The vital second part of the show was Henry's public appreciation of the shrewdness and perceptiveness of Spain, the only country not gulled. In his enthusiasm, he seemed almost to be praising the wretched young man for the scale of his deception.

De Puebla did not record any more of the interview after that, the best part, and there may not have been much to report. It is not known whether Cambrai, having seen the state of the prisoner, thought it worth-while to give him the "news" he had brought. It could only have come from Margaret, whom the young man had just repudiated. De Puebla gave no indication that they talked privately. For all his coldness, Cambrai was probably much more shocked by the prisoner's appearance than de Puebla was; for he had seen him at the height of his glory. The words he had just heard from the prisoner's mouth were plainly not his, but forced out of him, as spirits had spat out words from the foaming mouth of a young nun at Quesnoy-le-Comte seven years before, when Cambrai's dean had jammed his fingers between her teeth to exorcise her. In every way, the scene was awkward and distasteful. But visiting prisoners was one of the seven corporal acts of mercy, one in which Margaret had portrayed herself, in cloth-of-gold and ermine, tapping delicately at the barred window of a jail from which two men gratefully watched her. To try to deliver them was an even greater mercy, reflecting the delivery by Jesus of the souls bound in Hell. The bishop would probably have blessed this prisoner, at least, before leaving with that part of his mission undone. He may not have said another word to him.

Cambrai stayed until near the end of September, struggling on with his diplomatic instructions. When de Puebla talked to him in August, in the ambassador's rather scruffy suite of rooms at the Austin Friars, Cam-brai was full of "pain and passion of heart", having made no headway on any of the subjects he had been sent to discuss. De Puebla offered to help, claiming later that he had persuaded Henry to drop completely "the bold expedient he had determined on", aimed most probably at Margaret, "though he was very angry at first, and the things he said were by no means nice."

Some time later, while Cambrai was still in England, Margaret apparently wrote to Henry, apologising for what she had done and asking him "to receive her into his obedience". No letter survives; de Puebla re-ported it. The dowager duchess had probably never written to Henry be-fore, although André suggested she had sent a letter of simulated joy when he had married Elizabeth. She did so now largely because of the report that Cambrai had sent to her, though also, de Puebla suggested, because the Archduchess Juana and her chaplain had advised it. Shrewd as she was, Margaret would have realised the pointlessness of persisting with her White Rose. But an apology, with a promise of good behaviour, was also her last hope of saving him. Maximilian, when he had promised that he and York would make no more trouble, had done the same. Henry had no intention of rising to such offers, but he needed to reply somehow. He held a great council, de Puebla said,

> about what the duchess Madame Margaret wrote to him, and what he decided was that since the lady archduchess and her council so clearly rejected the measures which the ambassadors of King Henry demanded should be taken against the said duchess Madame Margaret, he must send her a gracious reply about the matter. And he did so, and the bishop is very pleased with it.

Because Henry could not isolate Margaret as completely as he wished, he was obliged, through gritted teeth, to be civil to her. He could not compel her by a trade embargo to keep her promise of good behaviour; but he had her precious White Rose in his custody and, through him, all the lever-age he wanted. He would not release him; but if she agreed to cease all efforts for him he would, perhaps, not kill him. "It doesn't seem a bad way to me," de Puebla concluded. Cambrai had achieved half of what he had come for.

The summer was not, in any case, filled only with ambassadors and trade talks. With Perkin in the Tower, Henry could at last relax in the safety of his favourable stars. William Parron had foreseen a little trouble in mid-August, but the king was so victorious that the forecast did not need to disturb him. Soncino reported that Henry, "in great peace of mind", had planned to spend the weeks until mid-September on hunting and recreation, travelling from pleasance to pleasance with a reduced court and no great state, round his quiet kingdom.

On August 1st, the day after Cambrai had seen Perkin, the king set off through East Anglia on his way to stay with the Earl of Oxford. At every stop, but especially at Bury St. Edmunds, he made several offerings, an outpouring of thanks. At the Earl of Oxford's, where great entertain-ments were laid on for him, the king seemed most impressed with the earl's dancing bear. He gave the bear-ward 4 shillings, and "one that held my lord of Oxon's bear" 6s. 8d., so delighted was he with the mangy creature that stood on its hind legs, clanking its shackles and neck-chains, and did what it was told to do.

II

AFTER CAMBRAI'S VISIT, Henry's chief prisoner was not produced again for more than a year. He did not, however, die, as de Puebla had predicted. He clung on, and in the summer of the next year allegedly began to plot to be King of England again.

The beginnings of the conspiracy, fragmentary and dim, seem to have centred on the person of Warwick, the ghost of the past twelve years. On February 6th, 1498, John Finch, a London haberdasher, entertained Thomas Astwood and Robert Cleymound, "gentlemen of London", in his house in the parish of All Hallows Honey Lane, in a warren of run-down streets and gardens not far from the Tower. Cleymound was War-wick's keeper, sleeping beside him in his chamber in the Tower. Astwood was to be Perkin's keeper in the room beneath, but that was still five months away.

Finch had a prophecy to show them, probably written—as they usually were—on a small roll of paper. "The bear," it ran, "will shortly beat his chains within the city of London." The chained bear with a ragged staff was Warwick's badge; the prophecy needed no further ex-planation. Nonetheless, Finch went on "traitorously" to say that he hoped to see in Cheapside a great crowd shouting, "A Warwick! A War-wick! A Warwick!", the earl's battle cry, and wearing their ragged-staff badges. Finch wanted Cleymound to comfort the earl with this prophecy, sending it along to him with a present of two pairs of gloves and "a pot of spice called *grenegynger*". Thus, as Finch's indictment put it, he compassed the destruction of the king.

Five months later, with Perkin now committed to the Tower too under Astwood's charge, a man called John Williams introduced Ast-wood to Warwick in the earl's chamber. Their conversation, clearly con-spiratorial, was described in their indictments for treason. "My lord," said Williams, "I have brought you hither this man who loves you well and he has lately escaped a great danger, for he was to have lost his head lately, and yet he loves you."

The account suggests a pause: Warwick looking, perhaps, and won-dering. He probably knew nothing of the plotters' executions of 1495 or, if he had known, had forgotten them.

"My lord," Williams continued, "you may be sure of me and Thomas Astwood at all times."

Warwick then "received Astwood favourably": taking his hand, embracing him. "Now," he said, "I have a special friend."

Astwood rose to the occasion: "My lord, I love you, and I will place myself in as great peril as I ever was in before to do you good and help to put you in your right, in which I hope once to see you."

Warwick thanked him. Nonetheless, almost a year passed before any-thing else was done. Cleymound and Astwood guarded their charges as they were meant to. But in the spring of 1499 a young man called Ralph Wilford, a Cambridge student and the son of a London cobbler, sud-denly proclaimed himself as Warwick. Some said he had been prompted into this by a rogue priest, others that he had been "sundry times stirred in his sleep" to say he was Clarence's son and dream he would be a king. He was hanged for those dreams, and not much else, on Shrove Tuesday, just before Lent. No rumour or insurrection sprang from this, but Henry's fears were stoked again. While Warwick and Perkin lived, there might be no end to such abusions.

The following June, warder Astwood, loitering near the Tower in the parish of All Hallows Barking ward, had a conversation with a yeo-man, or freeholder, called Thomas Pounte. He asked Pounte a peculiar question: whether, "if it were need, he could associate to himself one or two fellows of kindly disposition [*humanae conditionis*]." "For what pur-pose?" Pounte wanted to know. Astwood answered, "You shall know hereafter."

A month later, on July 6th, Pounte came back to Astwood and asked him "when the said felony was proposed". Astwood shook him off, saying that he could not attend to him just then. He seemed to be marking time and gathering information. One snippet came from Wil-liam Walker, who muttered to Astwood on June 20th that the king would leave Greenwich soon for the Wardrobe (a royal annex near St. Paul's) and would then go from place to place as his "gestes" were appointed, but would never return to London alive. Walker, a chaplain, appeared to be a colleague at Wanstead in Essex of Perkin's chaplain and chief councillor, William Lounde. Like much in this strange affair, his fragment sounded like prophecy rather than solid fact.

Pounte eventually learned the details from another source, for others were well advanced in plotting. On July 12th, in the parish of St. Mary Wolnoth in Langburne ward, Edward Dixon, a draper, laid out the plan for Edmund Carre, a broker who had dabbled in the plots of 1493–95. Dixon, with help from others, was going to snatch Warwick out of the Tower. More important, however, for he mentioned him first, he was going to get "Peter" out. (He would not have called him Peter, or thought of him as such; here, as throughout the indictments, the lawyers rather than the conspirators were speaking.) Having sprung the two prisoners, Dixon would set them at large. Nothing was planned afterwards; like Maximilian's grand plans for a rescue, the chief point was liberty. This made the plan no less treasonous, of course. Dixon said he was assured that various servants of Simon Digby would help him. Carre said he would join in and, taking "a certain book", probably a psalter or a primer, from his purse, swore on it to be true and secret.

Still nothing happened, according to the indictments, for almost three weeks more. Then suddenly, on August 2nd, the various plots came together. On that day, Warwick, Astwood and Cleymound, with others unnamed, "confederated and agreed that the earl should assume the royal dignity, and erect himself king, and falsely and traitorously depose, deprive and slay the king." This was a new and fatal dimension: not merely freedom for Warwick, but the death of Henry and the seizure of the crown. "With all their force", whatever it amounted to, the conspirators would seize the Tower, killing any who resisted them. They would then break into Henry's treasury, carry away all the jewels and money, get hold of the Tower's store of gunpowder and ignite it and, under cover of the wildly exploding fire, escape beyond the sea with Henry's treasure. At the same time, they would issue a proclamation that anyone who helped them make war on the king would receive 12d. *per diem* from the booty they had stolen.

The plot appeared at this point to be Cleymound's idea, but he easily persuaded Warwick to take part. "My lord," he told him, "you are well minded in what danger, sadness and duress you here remain; but if you will help yourself . . . you shall come out of this prison with me; I will take you out of all danger, and leave you in surety." As a hint of what he meant by telling Warwick to help himself, he gave him "an hanger", a short sword that criminals and muggers often wore on their belts, "and the earl received the hanger for such purpose." It is doubtful that he knew either how to use it, or what the "purpose" was.

So far, Cleymound had not mentioned Perkin. But another indict-ment outlined strikingly different plans. Warwick and Cleymound had apparently agreed to "take and deliver Peter Warbeck and set him at large, and create and constitute him king and governor of England"—firing the Tower for his sake, not Warwick's. This made sense, of course. If he was Richard, as these plotters were assuming with or without sincerity, then his claim was better than Warwick's, and he was naturally king. Most future indictments put the plot this way round. Some documents, however, kept the question of precedence open. The record of the king's council meeting on November 12th, for example, said that Warwick meant to help Perkin first to the crown, "if he had been King Edward's son"; and, if it turned out he was not, "to have had it for himself." Such thinking was perhaps deemed typical of the strange and rambling mind of Warwick. Not knowing a goose from a capon, he was probably equally incapable of knowing a boatman's brat from a proper prince of England. The wording also suggested, however, that King Edward's son was still a possibility in more minds than poor Warwick's.

Others, as always, were sceptical. On the same day, Pounte and William Basset, another yeoman, were in conversation elsewhere in All Hallows ward. Basset asked Pounte if he would help "Peter" and the Earl of Warwick out of the Tower of London. Pounte replied "that he would help the earl but not Peter," and asked what they would do with them once they had them out of the Tower. Basset said he would get them a ship, which Dixon, the draper, would help to fill with woollen cloths, "and so the earl would cross the sea", well buried under the bales. Perhaps in response to Pounte's opinions, he had left out Peter; or perhaps Peter was never meant to cross the sea, staying instead as king.

The same day brought other treasonous mutterings in which Peter, rather than the earl, was on the plotters' minds. Thomas Ody, another yeoman recruit, remarked to Astwood: "Will this world never mend?" Astwood seeming to stay silent, Ody went on: "By the Mass, I need money, and I care not what I do, fighting or robbing, just so I have money." Ody then swore by the Mass again: "I wish Peter Warbeck was at large, because then there would be money around, as there is not now."

That remark carried an echo of Richard IV's last apostolic promises in the West Country, that he would coin new money and hand it out far and wide. Perhaps someone had believed him.

The object of Ody's longing was present at this conversation, but only half-acknowledged, as if he was on the other side of a slightly open door. He said nothing, while others talked about him and pricked him with the thought of power. Astwood, too, continued to keep silence as Ody cursed along. Throughout the scenes of August 2nd, he was non-committal. John Walsh, a priest, also accosted him that day and asked how those in the Tower, especially "Peter", were.

Astwood replied, simply, "Well."

Walsh then said, "If I and [he] were now in Ireland, knowing him as I now know him, we would make another kind of rumour than was lately made."

"Sir John, how do you know him?" Astwood asked. The question was politely, even slyly, put. The "sir" showed deference to Walsh as a priest; the question itself, from Astwood, should have been unnecessary. He knew how he himself had known "Peter", not so long ago.

Walsh answered, "I know that Peter is the second son of King Edward IV."

Meanwhile, in the Tower, Cleymound and Warwick had allegedly decided to make contact with the prisoner in the chamber below. Why they had waited more than a year to do so, nobody can say. Possibly he had not always been there. Whatever the truth, by August he was only a few yards away from the man he had called, in 1496, "our Right entirely well-beloved Cousin Edward". On August 2nd, Cleymound, with Warwick's agree-ment, "in order to comfort the said Peter", knocked on the vault of the chamber so that he could hear them. "Perkin, be of good cheer and com-fort," Cleymound called. He also told him that he had a letter for him from Jacques, a priest "from the parts of Flanders", which he would deliver to him the next day.

Several others, too, saw him on the 2nd. Ody talked to him, and Lounde paid a visit, after which his priestly ministry took a different turn. Lounde cut the silver tags or *agglettes* from his mantle, gave some of them to his prince, and then asked warder Strangeways, presumably just outside the door, to give the others to Luke Longford, a gentleman of London. Longford, too, was apparently present, casual visits from the outside world being both easy and encouraged. He "then and there" showed the silver tags to the prisoner, comforting him with the thought that he now had a network of friends. Lounde sent another token to his charge by Astwood, a gold ducat he had bent with his teeth. The bending of a coin meant a promise made, in some extreme difficulty or sickness, to present the coin at the shrine of a saint when the trouble had passed. The plots were coalescing, gathering pace.

That night, Cleymound reported his conversations to Warwick as they lay in bed together in the Tower. Perkin, he said, had declared to him "a certain matter that maketh me right heavy", and he wanted Warwick's advice about it.

"What matter?" Warwick asked.

Cleymound said that Perkin had advised him "that he should try to get the Tower for his will from Simon Digby, if he could do it with any subtlety or craft."

"How could you get the Tower from Simon Digby?" Warwick asked.

Cleymound, according to the indictment, "told him how".

The earl then said, "Why do you want to get the Tower for yourself and your adherents?"—the saddest question, implying that he had understood nothing of what had already passed. Cleymound answered "that he, with many of his adherents, wished to do so for the earl and Peter Warbeck."

Warwick, lying beside him in the dark, agreed to the proposal and became a traitor.

Over the next two days, the indictments suggest that the earl took a little initiative of his own. He had a hole bored in the vaulting (being noble, he would not make it himself), so that he could talk to Perkin properly. But on August 4th, Cleymound suddenly bailed out. He told Warwick that the whole plot had been revealed to the king and his council by Perkin, and that "the said Peter hath accused you and me and Thomas Astwood." As a result, he was going to seek sanctuary. Warwick agreed; this seemed the best thing to do. Bolting out of the Tower, Cleymound stumbled across Thomas Ward and told him the same.

Ward was another old adherent of the cause of Richard, Duke of York, and his presence now, like Astwood's and Lounde's, was suggestive. After his service with the White Rose in Flanders, he had come back to England by 1496, when twenty-two men had given sureties for his future good behaviour. He was forbidden to indulge in any treasonable activity at home or abroad by letter, messenger or in person, and if any of his guarantors died he was to be committed to the Tower. In February 1499 the king had officially pardoned him, but he seemed to be loitering round the Tower as if it was his home. Either he could not stop intriguing, or he was in semi-custody of some sort, or he was acting as the king's agent to keep the plots simmering, as others seemed to be.

Cleymound told Ward that he was going to seek sanctuary in Colchester, probably for a long time. Ward recommended Westminster instead, presumably because he might be closer to the action if action happened, and Cleymound agreed. The conspiracy was evidently not over, and Cleymound's tale, though hinting at real danger, was rubbish. Revealingly, he asked Warwick to send a token to Ward, "that he might be the more well-affected to them". Warwick gave him an "image" of wood, presumably a saint's image; Cleymound delivered it, fervently asking Ward to help. Warwick also gave Cleymound, as he left, a cloak and a velvet jacket. He did not seem to think he would see his keeper again.

Left more or less alone, the earl communicated busily with his newfound friend in the chamber beneath his own. "Many subsequent times" he spoke to him through the hole, "saying to him 'How goes it with you? Be of good cheer.'" His tapping may not always have been heard, for sometimes the chamber below was a hive of activity. On August 4th, warder Bluet dropped in a file and a hammer (the words left in English in the indictment), so that Perkin could cut through the bar on his window and break his chains, especially the shackles on his legs. Longford, now alerted by the token of the tags from Lounde's mantle, sent Perkin a closed letter containing a long white thread, "by means of which he could receive through the said window letters from the said Luke and other traitors and could send out [news of] his false purpose by other letters to them." The long thread may be another clue that the window looked out over water; letters could not simply be dropped, but were lowered, to conspirators in boats.

The prisoner himself delivered "a certain book called ABC, otherwise called a Cross Row"—a code-book, so that people could write to him secretly—to John Audeley, an esquire of Stowey in Somerset, now living in Woolwich. Audeley was apparently the brother of Lord Audeley of the Cornish rebellion. The secret code, which featured a different character or sign for every letter, was probably much like the one that had authenticated, in sunnier days in Flanders, the great loans for men and ships that were to win the crown of England for Richard, Duke of York. The thetas, gammas, musical flats and double-crossed crosses were perhaps employed now to a humbler end, to get him out.

Meanwhile Cleymound, despite his panic, had not left the scene. He still had in hand the letter from Jacques, the priest of Flanders, which he had to deliver to Perkin, but not until he had read it first. It seemed harmless enough: "Jacques advised [him] to be of good cheer, and not do himself any harm for anything that Simon Digby might say." In other words, he was not to respond to provocation from the constable. Cleymound handed over the letter and received another from Perkin to Jacques, "to comfort him in his felonious purposes". Long Roger delivered two letters from Longford, apparently supplementing the missive with the white thread. Lastly, Astwood came by, bringing a new shackle for the moment when the prisoner should have cut through his old one, to disguise the deed.

He also brought, or Ward brought (the indictments disagree), "a certain book of prognostication" to encourage him. Since prophecy was Ward's speciality, the book was probably his own work, based on the same cryptic forecasts that he had made some years before in Flanders. Doubtless it contained more dreams of Edward's son, the king "twice buried", ruling England again. By an irony, there was now more substance to them, since by this time Richard had indeed been twice buried, once by his uncle Richard and once by Henry, in the bowels of the Tower. Had he risen now, suddenly, to take his crown, he would have looked as terrifying as the prophecies predicted: a gaunt, dead man with a battered face, clanking his chains along the night roads. In the dim light of his room, turning the pages with his manacled hands, he may have tried to summon up such images again.

Meanwhile, back in the parish of St. Mary Wollnoth, Astwood, Carre and Dixon gathered with two new recruits: Thomas Masborowe, Edward IV's old bow-maker, and William Proude, a draper. Together, they swore to be true and secret to the plan and to each other. Carre took the book out of his purse again, and all laid their hands on it to take the oath. On the same day, in the parish of St. Dunstan in the West in Farringdon Without, Strangeways (ostensibly Perkin's jailer) told another recruit, Richard Pynkney, what the plotters were up to and made him swear secrecy in the same way, on a prayer-book. Afterwards he asked Pynkney to join them. Yet nothing happened, and the days passed.

Perhaps the omens were not propitious. On August 4th, when so much else was going on, Finch—the man who had foreseen the bear shaking his chains in the street—delivered a roll of prophecy to Cley-mound, asking him to look at it with Warwick. Finch also went to Dr. Alcock, a priest in the parish of All Hallows, to ask what would happen to the earl. His nervous inquiries had already stretched over many days and ranged up and down the country. One of those who helped, besides "Rede of Bristol", "Hurt of Nottingham" and the authors of numerous other prophecies that Finch anxiously read, was the ever-useful Ward. Ward told Finch that the earl would shortly go free, and gave him cause to hope that he would soon be King of England.

So far, however, Warwick himself had done almost nothing. For most of the time he seemed bewildered. He did not understand why Cleymound wanted to seize the Tower or how he would do it, and seemed unconscious of any sympathy for him outside his prison. When he assented to the Tower plot, or to the effort to contact Perkin, he was merely agreeing with what Cleymound suggested. For himself, he mostly ap-peared to be seeking human company and friends. Although the indict-ment said that he and Perkin frequently discussed their treacherous designs, all that was recorded on Warwick's side were simple words of fel-lowship. The tokens he produced were Cleymound's idea. But when Cleymound seemed to be leaving his service Warwick gave him clothes of velvet that must have been his own, as innocently generous as when he had welcomed Astwood, and embraced him, on hearing the extraordi-nary words that he loved him.

Warwick did little; but the prisoner in the chamber below did less. He had visitors, and they talked to him, but he said nothing back that was worth recording even by those in diligent search of incriminating words. Cleymound said they had talked, and Perkin had asked him to "get the Tower", but the words were not directly reported, nor his side of any other conversation that allegedly included him. The chief actor was curiously absent from the stage. He received all kinds of objects, but in turn sent only three: his letter to Jacques of Flanders, one to Astwood (strangely, since he could surely talk to him) and his ABC, or code-book, sent to Audeley.

Nothing quite worked in this conspiracy because at its centre—the nerve-centre, as Henry hoped to prove—was a young man who was utterly demoralised. When Cleymound and Warwick spoke to him, the

words they used—"Be of good cheer and comfort"—were the kind commonly addressed to the sick and the dying. He does not seem to have
replied to them. The same sentiment, that he should keep his chin up (*esse
boni vultus*), appeared in the letter from Jacques of Flanders. The word
"cheer" meant no more than the expression of the face; people who were
not of good cheer, but had to be told to be, were in a state of deep sadness. Lounde's bending of the coin, too, suggested a prayer for recovery
from desperate affliction.

He had been in prison for fourteen months, and most of that time
alone. Katherine may have visited sometimes; it was thought unusual if
wives did not, though after his escape she may have been under more pressure to forget him. His little son, for whose birth he may have thrown
away a chance of winning England, had vanished from his life as, most
probably, from hers. But from day to day, before his room became a marketplace in early August, he could not often dispel his melancholy by
unburdening himself to other people. The black bile was allowed to work
in him unhindered. When Charles the Bold immersed himself in solitude after his defeat at Granson, drowning his grief with too-strong
wine, his doctors had to apply hot tow and cupping glasses to his side to
reduce the rush of blood to his heart. Neither wine nor cupping glasses
would have been brought to a prisoner in chains.

He may have used the hammer that was slipped to him to break his
shackles; this was not difficult, and officers struck them off prisoners all
the time. But he remained in chains, and the filing of the window bar, if
he had tried it, would have gone rather slowly. Astwood or Ward tried to
jog him on August 4th with the book of prognostication, "comforting
him by the same book to execute the more speedily and willingly his said
purpose"—to break out and seize the throne. That "more willingly",
libentius, suggested no great desire on his part.

On August 24th Astwood had to nudge him again, sending him
this time through Cleymound a Cross painted on parchment which Astwood had received from John Watson, a priest. Watson, like Astwood,
had plotted before and been pardoned. His picture, according to the
indictment, "was sent to the said Peter Warbeck for his relief and to help
him achieve the aforementioned things." Again, it did not seem to have
the desired effect. The idea that this prisoner was afire with wild schemes,
and then revealed them to the king and the council, was plainly untrue.
He hardly seemed to know what he was doing. On the day the parchment

was delivered, Astwood also received a letter from him, delivered by Jacques of Flanders, beseeching him urgently, by a private token agreed between them, to ask Lounde "to be friendly and helpful to him in the accomplishment of the matters aforesaid." Astwood went to fetch Lounde for him. Again, nothing happened afterwards.

Watson and Astwood may have erred in sending the parchment. The Cross, capitalised in the indictment, would not have been an empty symbol. The purpose of looking at this image was to feel the pain of Jesus in every detail: the nails tearing through His soft flesh, the thorns digging down almost to the bone of His skull, the lance thrusting to His heart. On His livid and contorted body the blood ran down in streams. His sinews stretched to the limit, His veins broke; His sweet face sweated with the pallor of death. To look on this image with a receptive heart was known to be "convenable . . . lacrymable and profitable", but it would hardly persuade a man to smash off his shackles and break out of jail. On the contrary, he was supposed to find his own chains light and his own pain bearable, compared with Christ's. He would kiss the picture and cry. Watson and Astwood might have done better to send their would-be king a pair of gloves and green ginger.

The continuing presence of Lounde told its own story. The two had been together, as priest-counsellor and prince-penitent, in Flanders, Ireland, Scotland and the West Country, before Lounde had fled east to sanctuary in London. His arrival there was noticed, but he received no punishment and, within a year or so, was ministering to his prince again. As with Katherine, there was no particular reason why their closeness should have been altered by the still-dubious and disbelieved official story. While Lounde was in attendance Richard could survive, if only in the compass of a room. Yet one might wonder why Lounde was allowed, with Henry's knowledge, to keep this flame alive.

Jacques, the priest "from the parts of Flanders", played a similar role. The letters he was taking to and fro were in English, and contained the sort of caring, uncryptic messages—that the prisoner should put on a brave face and take care of himself—that a mother, rather than a plotter, might write. It is quite possible that the person behind Jacques was Margaret. Her prayers had multiplied through the year, with Mass now celebrated every day in the chapel at Binche; and on St. Michael's Day that year, for the first time, a votive Mass to the great avenging archangel was sung there. She could not write to him, but messages might still pass, continuing the contact on which her White Rose had depended so heavily in his glory days. If so, she too could have kept a little breath in Richard, if anyone still wanted him to live.

Did the prisoner himself want such a thing? Despite everything, the answer was yes. Thomas Ody, after complaining to him about his lack of money, threw out a remark: "If you were known for such a man's son as you think yourself to be, I suppose many men in England would be glad to do you good."

As you think yourself to be. The word was translated as *cogitetis*, that slightly dreamy subjunctive, and the remark drew no response from him, either concurrence or denial. Yet the sense of what had been said was clear enough. In the Tower, in chains, he was still Edward's son in his own estimation; even now.

The schemes in which he was enmeshed, so evidently trembling on the point of exposure, had a trumped-up look about them. Yet the comings and goings outside the Tower were not concocted from thin air, and a much wider conspiracy appears to have lain behind them. Molinet thought that "some lords of England" were plotting that year against Henry, and from the end of July to the beginning of September the king was providentially away from London, making a slow progress to the Isle of Wight and back again.

Several other close associates of the young man who still thought of himself as Richard were outlawed at the beginning of August 1499, just before the fermentation of the plots in the Tower. John Heron, the chief adviser who had betrayed his prince at Beaulieu, was sentenced despite his pardon of 1497: the Parliament roll revealed that he had been indicted "lately . . . divers times" for misprisions, concealments and high treasons, but had failed to appear in court. Thomas Ward and James Keating, the relic-selling Irish prior, were accused of "various treasons now touching the person of the king"—that "now" showing that these were new crimes, not past ones. On the Monday after the feast of Sts. Peter and Paul, Henry Mountford, Richard's captain at Deal, was also accused of current treasons. All were outlawed at the king's suit; the names of Heron and Ward were underlined, showing their importance. Henry had shown mercy to these men before, but they had not reformed, and the shaming and imprisonment of their prince had made no difference—as it had made no difference, either, to his supporters outside England.

Another old adviser also reappeared that summer. On August 12th, John Taylor the younger was granted a general pardon. He had evidently fled to sanctuary, and now gave Beaulieu as his second address. The fact that he was pardoned when all about him were punished suggests that he had given Henry information about the flowering of new treasons around the two prisoners in the Tower. He, too, may well have been involved in them.

The plots inside the Tower itself had no such spontaneous character. They were evidently pushed by agents. All the warders were involved both in getting gear and in spreading the word. Polydore Vergil, loyal as he was to Henry, shed some doubt on their devising, and Henry, too, gave different accounts of them. At first, as he told the new King of France, Louis XII, at some point that autumn, he supposed that the plots "were led and organised by certain servants of the captain of the castle and great tower of London to get out of that place the son of the Duke of Clarence and Perkin Warbeck who were there for their deserved punishment." Later, when he had looked into the matter properly, he found that the truth was this:

> that this past summer, when the king was in his Isle of Wight which is beyond the sea, the son of Clarence and Perkin Warbeck, who had more freedom than they should have done in view of their offences, laid out their whole project to the point of executing and accomplishing it.

The blame had clearly shifted from the "servants of the captain of the castle" towards the young men they were guarding. Yet it is far from clear that the Tower officers were always doing what Henry wanted. As it turned out, the king was to punish all of them severely. If they had been put in place to steer his enemies to their deaths, they had not escaped deeper involvement. Had Perkin's demoralisation been less complete, it is easy to believe that the old charm might have begun to work again on Astwood, Cleymound and the others, as most early historians thought it had.

Real plots, then, were still forming around these two young men, to which Henry was adding impetus of his own. The removal of Warwick and Perkin had become a political imperative. As long as uncertainty persisted as to how dangerous the young men in the Tower were or what they intended, the Spanish marriage hung in the balance and Henry's enemies remained insubordinate. The king had grown visibly worn as he pondered what to do. On March 26th that year, around the time of the Wilford conspiracy, Pedro de Ayala reported that Henry had aged twenty years in two weeks. In the end, the king sought his answer where the plotters had done: in prophecies and in the stars.

In midMarch, although it was officially a felony to do so, Henry had ordered a Welsh priest to tell his fortune. ("In Wales there are many who tell fortunes," Ayala explained to his sovereigns, "in the same way that people in Galicia tell fortunes from certain signs on the back of a man.") The priest came highly recommended, having foretold the deaths of both King Edward and King Richard. He told Henry, horrifyingly, that his life would be in danger for the whole year. He then added, in a sentence more ominous than Ayala made it sound, that there were "two parties of very different political creeds in his kingdom". In other words, the Yorkist faction would keep causing trouble. "Many other unpleasant things" were also imparted by the priest. Henry swore him to secrecy; and when he chatted, as a Welshman would, those he had chatted to were thrown into prison on Henry's orders.

William Parron, too, was heavily relied on, in a way he found both flattering and terrifying. For much of 1499 he was working on two projects: his normal set of predictions for the year ahead, and a special book for the use of the king. This was the *De astrorum vi fatali* (*The Fateful Meaning of the Stars*), which was completed and privately printed for Henry in October. The main theme of the *De astrorum* was the chastisement of the just and innocent: why it occurred, how Fate had determined it, and how necessity, too, could sometimes demand it. "For those who are unlucky under the stars," Parron wrote, "the law and causation and justice say they must be beheaded or hanged, or others burned or drowned; some through ruin, some through fate, some by the sword, some snuffed out by various diseases, unless the fate of the stars at their birth dictates that by God's might it shall be otherwise."

To the "most serene and most fortunate king", his astrologer then described in detail how hopeless Warwick's stars were. In the cryptic fashion of such works the earl was not mentioned by name, but the tenor of the booklet left little doubt who this man "not of base birth" was. His fate was worth eleven pages of careful typesetting and of Henry's time. All the triple lights had been unlucky at the time of his birth, Parron wrote, set firmly in the house of death. Mars in conjunction with the sun signified the death of his father and the destruction of his property, besides, for himself, the clash of iron and combustion of fire. The positions of Saturn and Mars spelled utter destitution and prison; the movement of the moon between them meant that "no act can be profitable to him, and nothing he desires can come to pass." His fate was frequently repeated: imprisoned, shackled, troubled. He was not only unlucky in himself but also, despite his impotence, a lasting focus of unrest and rebellions in England. Until death "took him out", the evils and upheavals linked to his birth signs would constantly succeed each other.

Henry was therefore justified in keeping Warwick in prison. "A prince may imprison another prince or lord because he fears he will cause insurrection, or that insurrection will come through him, and that is with-out sin," Parron wrote; "if he detains him otherwise, he acts through evil intention." His death, too, would not necessarily be an evil act. A judge who condemned a man to death for some crime did not sin unless he rejoiced in the death. And if the man was innocent? Again, Christ was innocent, and His death the most evil act of all, yet God had ordained it for the good of mankind. Considered in that light, Christ's death was not a scandal but an act of mercy and charity. It was undoubtedly good for the country, Parron told Henry—echoing the words Caiaphas had spo-ken of Jesus—that this one man should die in order to preserve the peace.

Parron did not mention Perkin, either, by name in the *De astrorum*. But he reassured Henry that Richard of York, too, had had unlucky stars: so unlucky that he had died as a child, and had now been dead for four-teen years. For four days after Richard's birth, Parron wrote, at a quarter of an hour before midnight, a white rose had been seen falling from the sky and sinking into the Thames. With it went a pale sun, a pale moon and two arrows flaming and thundering with fire. They fell into the foggy water. All this, said Parron, was written in an almanac not only at the time of Richard's birth but in the year of his begetting, by a man "most worthy of credence". The signs confirmed the words of Jesus, he told Henry: "Bad things must come from evil constellations." No other ex-planation could be found for the pitiful fate of Edward's sons. "What but the fate of the stars presiding at their nativity," he asked, "could have destroyed such innocents?"

In previous almanacs, Parron had evidently tried to reassure Henry that Richard was dead. He had done so, he said, *sub pena capitis mei*, under

pain of death if he had been wrong. Despite that, he had failed to convince everyone, and perhaps had failed to convince the king himself at the
deepest level. In his public prognostication for the next year, 1500, Parron
complained about his reception. "When I wrote and said that [Richard,
Duke of York] had not been alive for fourteen years past," he told Henry,
"sick people said I was just fawning."

He may well have been fawning again, and could not be blamed for
it. But he had done the best that an astrologer could manage for Henry: he
had suggested that in clear conscience and for the good of the country,
with the signs agreeing and the stars abetting, the king could do what had
to be done. The servants of Simon Digby had done the rest.

III

ON NOVEMBER 12TH, before the king and his council, Chief Justice
Fineux laid out "certain treasons conspired of Edward naming himself of
Warwick [his identity, too, now wavering by association] and Perkin &
other within the Tower." The councillors determined that they "had done
treason" and deserved death. They then addressed Henry:

> It is thereupon demanded of the King's Grace what is to be done
> herein, whether process of law pass upon them, or else that nothing
> be done further upon the said treasons: All the said Councillors
> and every of them by himself adviseth councelleth and prayeth
> that not only process but execution of Justice be also had, of not
> only Perkin but also of the said Edward and other offenders.

In effect, this was their trial: indictment, arraignment and sentence *in
absentia*, in Henry's council chamber. Nonetheless, some form of broader
judicial process was put in motion. A commission of oyer and terminer,
convened on the 13th, immediately asked the sheriffs of London to pick a
jury from the city and suburbs, "by whom the truth of the foresaid matter
may be better known". Once sworn in, the jurors returned their verdict
on November 18th at the Guildhall.

Perkin, however, had already been arraigned and sentenced. Two
days before, on a Saturday—Henry's lucky day—he had appeared at the
White Hall in Westminster. The councillors had put his name first

among those who had to die, and Henry did not hesitate. The jury was not yet sworn, the proofs unproduced and unexamined; uniquely among those who were accused of plotting in the Tower, no record remains of Perkin's indictment or the evidence against him, suggesting that none was gathered. But Henry now had ample justification for hanging him with- out deliberation, as his lower-class followers had been hanged in 1495.

No record of his "trial", such as it was, survives either, except a scrawled interlined note that he appeared before the Earl of Oxford, sit- ting as lord high steward *pro tempore*, "in the same way as Edward, Earl of Warwick". Since Warwick was noble and was tried by his peers, it could not have been in quite the same way, but the old ambiguity persisted. The phrase may have meant merely that Oxford presided and that Perkin was led to the bar in chains by Digby's deputy Thomas Lovett, the lieutenant of the Tower. His judges were apparently Sir John Sygly, knight marshal, and Sir John Troubilfield, the warden of the Marshalsea. The charge was "certain treasons". It is hard to see how any definition of treason could apply in England to "Peter Warbeck, born under the obedience of the Archduke of Austria and Burgundy", his legal personality; but for as long as his career had lasted Henry's lawyers had alternated between de- scribing him as a "rebel and traitor" and making him "the king's enemy", a category all his own. Rebel or not, traitor or not, he pleaded, one as- sumes, guilty, and offered no defence.

His sentence was as the crime required, though that too was not recorded in the controlment roll, his name the only one missing among the suspects in the case. He was to be taken back to the Tower, then drawn on a hurdle through the city of London to the gallows at Tyburn. There he was to be hanged, "and cut down living to the ground and his innards torn out of his stomach and burned before his face. Then he shall be beheaded and his body divided into four parts, the head and quarters to be placed where the king wishes to put them."

He had not been arraigned alone. His old friend from Cork, John Atwater, who had been arrested in Ireland a few months before, was con- demned with him, as were Atwater's son Philip and John Taylor the elder. Taylor had been arrested, to Henry's delight, in France in July. All were summarily convicted, with no record of evidence against them, though again this was hardly necessary. Atwater, for example, had already been attainted and convicted *in absentia* of high treason in the Irish Parliament in March 1498. All, too, received the same sentence, though Taylor's was commuted to life imprisonment in the Tower. Atwater's son was pardoned. Two days later, on the 18th, the grand jury was assembled and returned its verdict, presumably in these cases.

Perkin's four warders—Astwood, Long Roger, Bluet and Strangeways—were tried before a petty jury of twelve local men at the Guildhall on St. Andrew's Eve, November 29th. For these jurors the evidence was properly laid out and presumably sifted through, for they had time. The warders were eventually found guilty "of various high treasons touching the king's person" and sentenced to drawing and hanging. Only Strangeways confessed his treason. The others "said they were not guilty of any of it", and flung themselves on the mercy of the court. Even Astwood did this, though he must have known he could hardly escape the rope a second time.

The others mentioned in the indictments, laymen and priests alike, were also indicted of high treason. (Ward, the maker of prophecies, had died in the Tower in September, apparently of natural causes.) Yet only one, Finch, was executed, and only two, Proude and Masborowe, were committed to the Tower. The rest were outlawed, with the outlawries renewed until the end of Henry's reign and, in some cases, beyond it. The king appeared to acknowledge by this that he could not bring these men to justice, but could only forfeit their goods—such as they had—and place them outside the law's protection. The priests, of course, could not be executed under their privilege; the laymen had probably run away or sought sanctuary, as Cleymound, for one, had always intended. Lounde, his invulnerability peculiar to the last, returned to his other job as rector of the parish church of St. Mary Wanstead, and was pardoned within eighteen months.

Warwick was brought to trial before his peers on November 21st. He was judged by the Earl of Oxford, sitting under a cloth of estate in the Great Hall at Westminster, and by twenty-two lords, including Daubeney, the chamberlain, and John Kendal, still prior of the Order of St. John of Jerusalem in England. The indictment said that Warwick was to be "examined and compelled to answer", but there seems to have been no examination. Judge Fineux had said, in any case, that he had confessed already. Standing at the bar with Lovett beside him, the earl was asked how he wished to plead. He replied, in the standard phrases, that he could not deny he was guilty of the treasons, that he expressly acknowledged them, and that he put himself in the king's hands. He may or may not have understood what he was saying. He was sentenced, as his new friend had been, to drawing, hanging, disembowelling, beheading and quartering. The record of his trial, exceptionally and illegally, was locked away in a special cupboard with three locks, to which three different royal officers had the keys.

Warwick's execution was almost a private affair. The sentence was commuted, in deference to his rank rather than his innocence, to simple beheading, and on November 28th, between two and three o'clock in the afternoon, the earl was led out between two guards to die on Tower Green. No crowds watched, but the effects were noted. That same day, wrote the Grey Friars chronicler, "was great floods, winds, thunder, lightnings, which did much harm and hurt in divers places and counties in England." Warwick's head and his body were placed in the coffin together—he was not, at least, to be exposed and shamed—and the next day were conveyed by water to Bisham Abbey in Berkshire. Henry's privy-purse accounts show that he paid £12 18s. 2d., in four separate bills, for Warwick's burial there beside his ancestors. The king's conscience was bothering him, but at least the Spanish marriage, "made in blood," as Katherine of Aragon later described it, could go forward unimpeded.

The rest of the blood had been shed five days earlier, at Tyburn. In contrast to Warwick's execution, and the summary references to the executions of 1495, this was an extraordinary event that took up more than a page of the London Chronicle. The chronicler went solemnly into Latin (as, for the death of Charles VIII the previous year, he had gone showily into French) to flag the two deaths in the margin. "*Comes de Warwyk*" was followed by "*Obitus Petri Warbeck.* The death of Perkin."

A huge crowd had gathered and a special scaffold had been erected, once more to raise him up above the crowd. It was a Saturday, exactly a week since he had been sentenced. The interval can probably be explained by Henry's wish to keep the stars on his side. The feast was that of St. Clement, the first pope, the day that marked the start of winter and on which—appropriately enough—boys went round in elaborate disguises, giving mock-blessings to households and demanding fruit and money. Some of these urchins were probably in the crowd, with gaudy robes and nut-stained faces, pausing for a moment in their begging and nuisance-making. In the Gospel reading for the day, *Nihil opertum*, Christ told his disciples that there was nothing covered that would not be revealed; words spoken in darkness or whispered in closets would now be shouted from the rooftops. This final certainty, proclaimed from the scaffold, was what the crowd was waiting for.

Perkin and Atwater had been drawn on hurdles from the Tower. The London Chronicle said so, and this had been their sentence, though Molinet thought they had walked the distance led by the halters around their necks. If so, this would have been a commutation of their sentence; but it was probably not so. They were pulled behind horses through streets that were covered, as an Italian visitor described them, with a vast amount of mud, churned up by cattle and rain, that smelled awful and never went away. November added a mulch of fallen leaves, especially in the open fields round Tyburn, and more dead leaves, in their last gold livery, drifted in the wide sky above their heads.

When they arrived at the scaffold, Perkin climbed the small ladder to the stage. Since his wrists were bound, it was difficult for him to do so. A guard pushed him up, and the executioner put the halter on him. He probably wore, apart from this, the simple knee-length white shirt that was the usual garb of the condemned man. After three miles of muddy roads and vituperation, there was probably not much white left about it, nor brightness in his hair. His face would still have shown traces of the beating of the previous year; the late November cold would have turned his legs blue and stiffened his hands. "Some said and still believed he was King Edward's son," wrote Molinet, "but he didn't look much like him on his last day."

Some slim chance remained of a miracle. A few years before, a labourer, unjustly sentenced to hang, had called on Blessed King Henry, the king's step-uncle, to save him. The murdered Henry VI had appeared as the man swung in the noose, supporting him in his "most sweet embrace" and putting his soft, dead hand between the prisoner's neck and the rope. Another man, a cupbearer, had been saved in the same way: King Henry appearing, tall and thin in his blue velvet coat, to relieve the pressure of the noose, while Our Lady, in a white cloak, tenderly held the hanged man's feet and supported him. Both men, though cut down as dead after a while, revived and were pardoned. In more prosaic fashion, an officer might ride through the crowd, waving a piece of paper in which the king declared a change of heart. Wild optimism of this sort had always been a feature of this young man's career. But there had been too much optimism and too much mercy, and both were now at an end.

Standing before the people, the rope around his neck, he made some sort of confession to them. Hall, writing fifty years later, said he recited the version he had read at the Standard in Cheapside: the whole lot, with the cousins and uncles and aunts and the Portuguese knight with one eye. Even allowing for the fact that he had probably not read it there, or anywhere else, this would seem inhuman. He could not have held it to read it, and few would have heard him if he had. In any case, it was unnecessary. The final confession needed to be, above all, a negation, not an affirmation: he was not Richard.

In the London Chronicle "he showed to the people . . . that he was a stranger born according unto his former confession . . . and . . . never the person that he was named for, that is to say the second son of King Edward the iiijth." It seems, this time, that he spoke himself, for there is no indication that anyone spoke for him. He said, Fabyan wrote—and the alderman was almost certainly in the crowd to hear him—"that he never was the person which he was named nor anything of that blood, but a stranger born likewise as before he had showed." Only astrologer Parron, who does not seem to have heard him, suggested that he gave more details: "he said he was not English, but a Picard from Tournai, by the name of Peter, the son of the late Peter de Orbeth."

Perkin also added "that he named himself to be the second son of King Edward by the mean of the said John Atwater there present and other as before time he had truly showed." The handing-off of blame seemed exceptionally mean-spirited, as Atwater prepared to follow him on the scaffold, but Zurita said that Atwater seconded Perkin's words and admitted they were true. If Atwater took the blame, those "other" could be absolved of it, most obviously Margaret. Ever since her protégé's capture, and up to this point, her plain promotion of his cause had been publicly passed over. In the end, it was better that way.

The confession on the scaffold, whatever the actual words, was vital both to Henry and to him. For pressing diplomatic and domestic reasons, Perkin had to confess again at the very point of death, with his soul's salvation in the balance. Only then would his supporters believe the official story was true. "He took it upon his death to be true," said the London chronicler; conclusive, incontrovertible words. Parron explained that Perkin's "free" confession, "at the point of death, in public", was the one thing that could cure his sick followers from the poison of his base words and deceptions. Silence, as preserved at their executions by the conspirators of 1495, would have left a question mark. The imperative for Henry was that no question remained.

For this reason, the king made sure that both de Puebla and Ayala (probably standing together, their mutual loathing palpable) "heard the confessions" on the scaffold. That they witnessed the deaths was less important, though de Puebla seems to have been much affected by them, writing to his sovereigns later that "I must forbear importuning you on the subject, as I have written at great length and in many ways about the execution of Perkin and the son of the Duke of Clarence." Henry also apparently briefed the two ambassadors, telling them that Perkin's execution was justified "because the Duchess Margaret of Burgundy and the King of the Romans would not stop believing that Perkin was the true and legitimate son of King Edward, and Duke of York; and the duchess had given him so much authority and credit, that it had to be done."

The briefings had limited success. After the executions, de Puebla told his sovereigns that "no drop of doubtful royal blood" now remained in the kingdom; *dudosa*, perhaps, but *sangre real* all the same. Molinet, too, could not help but describe the double executions as Henry's attempt to remove all traces of the rival line. To do the job thoroughly, he wrote, the king had to kill Warwick too, as well as the young man who had "gone on saying" that he was Edward's son.

Henry's captive therefore had to confess on the scaffold that he was not Richard. Nevertheless, it is hardly possible to think it was a lie. The moment, as the whole crowd knew, was too dreadful for lying, and the consequences for his soul too great. Since his sentencing, he had been given a few precious days to think hard about what lay ahead of him. The great blessing—the only blessing—of a criminal's death was that the hour was known and could be prepared for. "If thou wilt learn good and evil," said *The King's Book*,

> go from home, go out of thyself, that is go out of this world, and learn to die; depart thy soul from thy body by thinking; send thine heart into that other world, that is unto Heaven or into Hell or into Purgatory, and there thou shalt see what is good and what is evil.

Half in that other world, for a man condemned to die was adjudged dead already, he would have made a proper private confession before leaving the Tower. In that state of grace he may also have received the Sacrament, although in the case of the condemned this was controversial and often withheld (as it was withheld, too, if every last sin was not confessed). At the least he would have been given holy water and holy bread, a quasi-sacrament with which he could sublimate, to some degree, every Christian's longing for the sight and honeyed taste of Jesus before he died. As far as possible, he had cleansed and prepared his soul for leaving the body. It would have to pay the penalty for past sins in any case, but these absolutions made it as ready for God's preliminary sentence as an earthly man could manage. At public executions, the condemned tended either to keep silent or to burst out with some defiant truth, clearing their consciences. The last thing they did was to speak falsehoods. It is almost unthinkable that Henry would have forced such a thing on Perkin, or that he would have agreed to do it.

Yet Henry still had some leverage over him. He had possession of his wife and, presumably, control of his son, and he also had the power to commute or soften his sentence, as he had done for Warwick. These considerations, combined with the utter collapse of his own schemes and the schemes of others, could have induced the prisoner on the scaffold to seek a last bargain. He had always been sickened by the shedding of blood, both his own and other people's. Young, and not brave—how easy to say that—he confronted the thought of being cut down from the gibbet alive, butchered and eviscerated, with his bloody entrails burned before his eyes. All that stood between a man's hands rooting in his ripped belly, and merciful oblivion at the end of a rope, was the statement that he was not Edward's son, or anything to do with him. The torments of Hell, believed in but not seen, may have faded before that calculation.

It is just possible, therefore, that he lied on the scaffold. It seemed evident to the crowd and the chroniclers, however, that he could only be telling the truth. The third possibility, also aired at the time, was that he no longer knew what the truth was. Vergil was the first to suggest that if he had lied in his career as Richard, he had come to believe in the lie. "Having twisted falsehood into truth, truth into falsehood," he wrote, "he fell at last on the scaffold, the victim of his own deceit." A century later, Francis Bacon continued the thought. "With long and continued counterfeiting," he asserted, "and with oft telling a lie, [he] was turned by habit almost into the thing he seemed to be; and from a liar to a believer." In his own later Latin translation, Bacon dropped the "almost": *quae fingeret simul et crederet*, "what he feigned, he believed." It is also possible that, in this state of deep confusion about who he was, the young man on the scaffold simply did what others asked, or what they had come to expect of him.

At the end of his confession, he asked God and the king "and all other that he had offended unto" for forgiveness for what he had done. The plea for absolution might have cleansed his soul again, to some degree, if that were necessary. He then prepared to die. The way men died was not usually recorded in the London chronicles, any more than the details of their deaths. But this event, before an immense crowd, was clearly a performance worth describing.

Whatever the public may have been expecting, what Perkin gave them was the attitude their spiritual manuals ceaselessly recommended. The priest would urge the dying man, as a final act of imagination, to "wrap himself" in the Cross that was held up before him. True meekness came when the sinner, at last, knew himself for the wretch he was, "nought and foul as a knave", and, having acknowledged that, tried to become like Christ.

Perkin, or Peter, or Richard, or however they thought of him, gave them this last impersonation. He took his death "meekly", said the London Chronicle, "patiently", said Fabyan: like Jesus, surrendering completely. The death of the gibbet was the closest in form to Christ's; in some meditations on the Crucifixion, He had even climbed a little ladder to position himself against the Cross. Then, "having been so courteous, noble, free and benign", He gave himself up to His executioners. *In manus tuas, Domine, commendo spiritum meum*, Christ's last prayer on the Cross, was traditionally the prayer of those on the scaffold or without much time. The first three words alone had become a shorthand for hanging, the last gasp of the condemned man:

And that *in manus tuas* check
Shall break thy neck.

When the ladder was taken away, his neck suddenly took the weight of his body. "It finds out what your buttocks weigh," as François Villon said. A man long in prison, thin and starved, did not strain the rope much. Men usually died within an hour, but it was seldom quick. There was time to feel the noose tightening, the eyes fogging over, life leaving. Some men still prayed and beat their breasts as they swung there. You could struggle, or you could hang there quietly, as the crowd watched and listened for your death to come. Apparently, he died that way.

Epilogue: Absence

THE WHITE SHIRT covered carrion and dung. That was all the body was, a coming feast for the worms of the earth. The carcass of a hanged man in particular was held for nothing; people squeamishly avoided it. When you cut it down it fell like a sack, and you saw the naked arse or the drawers stained with the frightened shit of the dying. "Drivelling and spurging" were the usual results of hanging. A corpse did not bleed, so they said. But when the head was lopped off there was often blood enough to dip a rag or a kerchief in it, if you thought it would do you good. Some kept those scraps for precious relics, as other misguided people took up the ashes of heretics in little pots and bowls.

Perkin's body was cut down dead, a surprise and a disappointment. ("They gave him such grace," Molinet wrote.) In the end his death had not been a traitor's, merely that of a common criminal, hanged high for men to see. His stillpulsing guts were not grilled on the fire, but his head was cut quickly from the flopping bag of the rest of him. That was put in a cart for the Austin Friars to take charge of, burying it somewhere with other gallowsbirds on the west side of the nave of their church in Bread Street. At least, it was assumed to be there and not cast away; but when the chronicler John Stow visited the church a century later, writing down the names on ninety tombs, he found no record of him. The names of those executed for treason were generally marked there, yet his, perhaps unsurprisingly, was not. Book, bell and censer, *Placebo* and *Dirige*—the obsequies accorded, in poems, even to pet sparrows—were evidently for gotten. The writer of the London Chronicle, so assiduous at asking God's mercy for the souls of those hanged or burned or beheaded, also neglected to do so in his case.

The head was jammed on a pole, the fair hair falling over the face, and placed on London Bridge. (If heads were not put out of reach, mad women sometimes washed their cheeks and combed their hair, as one had done for Owen Tudor.) Weather and the birds worked on it. The eyes went first, dug out by crows, or by the kites and hawks that walked quite tamely in the London streets. Villon described the faces of hanged men pecked like soft fruit on a garden wall, until they were as full of holes as thimbles. The flesh sank closer to the skull, blackening, and sagged round the empty sockets of the eyes. The hair was the last to go, an improbable wig, wispier but still bright when the morning sun rose over the river. Those who knew Tournai and the letter to his mother and all that side of his history—if it was his history—would know that in Tournai the heads of criminals were put only on the Porte de Marvis, where his father, if he was his father, had said goodbye to him. The grinning heads had stared down at him, the crying child, bound for the same end. "And so," wrote Molinet, "the White Rose, who had caused so much trouble to the Red Rose . . . was hung and dried in the sun."

The buried body bloated and began to liquefy, breeding worms in its own slime. Within nine days it was bones and ash—ash rather than dust, *cinis* rather than *pulvis*, as the priests said on Ash Wednesday—as if life had consumed it like a fire. All things ended that way, even the stars that went shooting through the sky in summer. A century later Bacon constantly likened Perkin, a comet and mercurial, to such blazing stars. "Whereof it happeth," wrote Caxton,

> oft they that sail by the sea or they that go by land have many times founden and seen them all shining and burning fall unto earth; and when they come whence it is fallen, they find none other thing but a little ashes or like thing, or like some leaf of a tree rotten, that were wet. Then apperceive them well, and believe, that it is no star . . .

In the case of men and women you might find buckles and coins in the debris, or charred ends of velvet and tarnished scraps of cloth-of-gold, all whitened with flesh-powder among the bones. But there was no distinction otherwise between the beggar and the king. Though one had crouched in a hut and one had brought lands and seas to his subjection, each lay for a while with the roof of his new habitation pressed against his face and his own ribs as vaulting above him, before dissolving into the earth. Great Alexander lay like this beside the poorest man, equal. Both were dirt, born of it and returned to it. So Perkin lay, and blew away, not differently from kings.

England was comfortable without him. Although Molinet thought his imprisonment astonished the country, causing several "great persons" and "barons" to revolt against Henry, the reaction both to that and to his death was very quiet. (Molinet, still confused about his subject, could not have it both ways; if this young man was exposed as "Pierquin Wesbecque", his treatment could not be outrageous or lead to disorder.) The great pestilence that followed in 1500, killing thirty thousand Londoners by Vergil's estimate, was loosely linked by some to Warwick's death, but not to Perkin's. The earl's death, the killing of an innocent, had truly scandalised all those who knew of it. Perkin's, long overdue by almost every reckoning, had not.

The game was over, and could be treated with proper contempt. Henry had once offered £1,000 for the capture of Perkin alive; but at some point in 1499 the king had himself acquitted and utterly released from "all manner writings, bills, obligations or promises" that he had made on that subject. In the end, the capture of Perkin had been worth no more than the £40 paid to Mayor Godfrey of Southampton. William Parron's prognostication for the next year was appropriately decorated by the printer, Wynkyn de Worde, with a woodcut of a squint-eyed king being delicately but decisively trampled by the Virgin Mary.

Around the same time a strange little poem appeared, suggesting that the Virgin's preferences might have been different. But the scene had been too confusing and uncertain, both for her and for everyone else.

> In a glorious garden green
> Saw I sitting a comely queen
> Among the flowers that freshé been.
> She gathered a flower and sat between.
> The lily-white rose me thought I saw,
> The lily-white rose me thought I saw,
> And ever she sang:

> This day day dawes
> This gentle day day dawes
> This gentle day dawes
> And I must home gone.
> The gentle day dawes
> This day day dawes
> This gentle day dawes
> And we must home gone.
>
> In that garden be flowers of hue,
> The gillyflower gent that she well knew
> The fleur-de-lis she did on rue [take pity on]
> And said, "The White Rose is most true
> This garden to rule by rightwise law."
> The lily-white rose me thought I saw.

But after those brief glimpses—on a ship off Kent, in John Wikes's house at Nynehead Flory, on a horse in the Strand—there was no confirmation, but rather the reverse, and nothing more to see.

At the beginning of the new year and the new century, de Puebla summed up with a sweeping historical perspective:

> This kingdom is at present so situated as has not been seen for the past 500 years till now . . . because there were always brambles and thorns of quality that gave the English a reason not to remain peacefully in obedience to their king, because there were various heirs of the kingdom and of such quality that the matter could be disputed between the two sides. Now it has pleased God that all should be thoroughly and duly purged and cleansed. . . .

On this reading, the matter had been finely balanced to the end. Henry had faced not upstarts and impostors, but a clash of legitimate claims of *calidad*. The image of the tangling briar, like Molinet's rose-bush and Bacon's later metaphor of a "winding ivy of a Plantagenet", suggested that Henry's enemy had sprung, though in some disordered way, from genuine royal stock. Yet Spain could now feel confident that the scare was over, and Henry was in charge.

The king himself, however, did not feel safe once Perkin was gone. He could not forget. Tiny acts of piety suggested that his conscience pricked him: payment for some of William Stanley's debts in 1499, and for the burial of Gilbert Debenham, who had apparently died still in sanctuary, in September 1500. In March 1497 he had also made a gift of £33 6s. 6d. to Lord Fitzwater's widow. Charity vied with deep suspicion in his mind. Ayala remarked in April 1500 that "the sentiments of the king towards a great number of his people are not very friendly, partly on account of their dealings with King Richard [III] and partly on account of Perkin."

In particular—feeling, as Vergil said, an aging man's crabbed avariciousness as well as distaste for disloyalty—he seemed to become obsessed with collecting every last fine from those who had favoured his rival in the West Country. The first finecollecting commission, set up in September 1498 (and covering both the 1497 rebellions under the general heading of "contempt"), had brought in about £1,500 from Devon and Cornwall by August 1499. The second, covering Hampshire, Wiltshire, Somerset and Dorset, was set up in March 1500; a third, for the same counties (Henry being dissatisfied with the second), was set up the next August. These two commissions, after backbreaking months of work, assessed 4,541 people to pay more than £14,000. Henry endorsed the rolls of fines with memoranda in his own hand, noting who had to answer for the money and when the first payments were due. His men swept "most ruthlessly" through the West Country, Vergil wrote, sparing none at all. Long after the shining impression of King Richard had passed through, yeomen and labourers were made to repent for the error of following him. Not all of them understood why. "For why 'tis hard", remarked one Cornishman in 1500, "to know who is rightwise king."

In 1504, seven years after the event, Parliament attainted for treason the Cornishmen who had invited Prince Richard to lead them in their rebellion. It proceeded too, at the king's behest, against five of the Tower plotters of 1499, three of whom—Astwood, Bluet and Finch—had been executed long before. Warwick, "the late earl", was also attainted. Henry needed to tidy up unfinished business beyond the grave, making sure the heirs felt their fathers' disgrace. Around the same time some of the 1495 attainders were reversed, but other hangerson remained conspicuously unforgiven. At the beginning of the new king's reign in 1509, a general pardon specifically excepted John Taylor the elder, "in ward in the Tower".

The attainders of 1504 included Edmund de la Pole, Earl of Suffolk, the focus of a new conspiracy. The de la Poles, nephews of Edward IV and therefore legitimate claimants, had kept quiet as long as Richard of York had been in any sense politically alive. Suffolk seemed comfort-ably in favour with Henry, aggrieved only that he had been demoted to "earl" on assuming his father's dukedom. In 1494, when little Henry was made Duke of York, Suffolk had been the star challenger in the "jousts of peace", his Yorkist ambitions apparently reduced to the favours on his hel-met. But he had fled the country in the summer of 1499—that summer of wide and vague conspiracy—and, though fetched back and apparently restored to grace, fled again two years later, in August 1501.

Before leaving England he dined secretly with Dorset, the Earl of Essex (a Yorkist by inclination) and William Courtenay, the son of the Earl of Devon, who had married Edward IV's daughter Katherine. Dorset and Courtenay might have been considered safe king's men, espe-cially since the autumn of 1497 when they had both fought Perkin, defeated him and seen him close and scorned. But clearly they were not safe, and neither was Courtenay senior, the victor of Exeter, who seemed to give Suffolk his blessing as he left. Something, possibly the executions of 1499, had troubled their loyalty and caused Yorkist feelings to resurface. George Neville also joined the reconstituted cause, though since 1498 he had been pardoned three times over for his previous misdeeds. So did Stanley's son Thomas, after serving years in jail for his part in the previous conspiracy. Dorset's son Thomas, implicated as ever in his father's waverings, had been pre-emptively imprisoned in the Tower before being moved to the castle of Calais, "and should have been put to death if [the king] had lived longer."

Another conspirator also remained, still young and beautiful and still at court. Molinet recorded her at St. Omer in June 1500, six months after her husband's death, when Henry and Elizabeth crossed the Channel to avoid the plague in London and to renew the alliance with Philip. Katherine was fifth-ranked among the fifty English noblewomen, "beauti-fully adorned", who accompanied the queen to church. As the festivities continued, sweetened with strawberries, cream, spice-cakes and seven horseloads of cherries, she was kissed by Philip and let him dance with her, as he danced with all the queen's chief ladies. Presumably he knew who she was, as Molinet did: the chronicler called her *la veuve de Pierquin Wesebecq*, as if widowhood was now her first acknowledged status. It was not, or not officially, at Henry's court. There she was "Lady Gordon", her marriage unacknowledged, or "the White Rose", a name that may have wounded as much as it flattered her. Katherine herself wore black until her death, enlivened with only the tiniest touches of colour: brass spangles sewn on her bodice, a headband of crimson velvet, a tawny kirtle glimpsed as she turned. In 1509–10 the new king, Henry VIII, included "Katherine Gordon, widow" in his general pardon, but whose widow she was went unsaid.

She had still not remarried; possibly because the old king had not wanted it, or possibly because she herself had no desire to. This evidently surprised Bernard André, at least. At the end of his great scene of Perkin's confession to Katherine, he had confidently written what he thought would happen next. "For a while, grieving, she lost her faith in men as marriage partners in Christ, but eventually she married —— and ——, men of outstanding soundness, trust and probity"—so unlike her last. Yet when André wrote, continuing to improve his text until 1502, he had to leave blanks in the manuscript. The inevitable new marriage had not happened, and Katherine's severe disappointment in men was perhaps not the only explanation. Indeed, it may have been no explanation at all.

At court she passed her days largely as she had done before, waiting on the queen until Elizabeth's death in childbirth in 1503. She was held in proper honour, and was present in 1502 at the betrothal of Margaret and James IV by right of her blood connection to the Scottish king. The money for her servant was paid regularly again as soon as her husband had been executed, and her own allowance was changed in 1508–9 to an annuity of £40 a year. The royal Wardrobe continued to provide her with gowns, kirtles, stockings, shoes and body sheets. At times of formal mourning, for Prince Arthur in 1502 and for the queen a year later, she was once again dressed in black at the king's expense. On the last day of the funeral ceremonies for Elizabeth, Katherine, in her black, laid the fourth of thirty-seven palls on her coffin, one for each year of the queen's age. As she did so, she may still have believed that she knelt to a sister as well as a queen.

By then her home was England, and she became a denizen in 1510. The same year, she was granted—apparently at the late king's behest—large estates at Fyfield, in Berkshire. Both the denization and the grant of lands carried the condition that she could not leave England, for Scotland or for any other country, without royal licence. As far as the estates went this was standard practice, emphasising that the crown would not subsidise her unless she stayed and cared for her properties. It was not, how-ever, a standard part of becoming a citizen of England. For more than economic reasons, Katherine had to be kept close. She was so far an exile from her own country that in 1510, bizarrely, a beautiful woman claiming to be her turned up in Scotland and, until she confessed the fraud, was kindly received by the late earl's friends.

The shadow of her little son may also have passed across the picture. He had seemed to disappear as soon as they reached London, but a rumour surfaced later in Wales that a child of Perkin's had been brought up there. The Perkins family of Rhos-y-gelli traced their descent to the son of "Peter Osbeck of Tournai", and the Perkins family of Reynoldston, at the very tip of Gower, also claimed him as an ancestor. This story, though perhaps pure fantasy, gained a strange strength in coming from Wales, where Richard—or Perkin—had never been and was scarcely known. Katherine, having obtained permission, settled briefly in Swansea, eight miles from Reynoldston, later in her life. The child's name was apparently Richard, to which was added the patronymic "Perkins": a little Yorkist ghost, grounded in the valleys of Wales.

Whatever his deeper fears were, Henry's fondness for Katherine had not faded. This too was a reason for retaining her at court, especially once Elizabeth had gone. In Scotland, Adam Abell repeated in his chronicle what may have been the local gossip: "[She] oftenmost remains in com-pany of King Harry and some [thought] that they were married." Physi-cally, however, the king had little to offer her. Though not far past forty, he had aged fast, and his ill health seemed directly connected to the grief her husband had caused him. He fell sick in the month after Perkin's execu-tion, and lay so ill for a while at Wanstead that his death and the succes-sion were murmured of. From 1501 he began to build his tomb. Each spring found him weak, with a variety of illnesses for which he craved exemptions from the Lenten fast. He employed more and more doctors, and consulted schools of medical practice in Germany and Italy. Each day he heard sermons and increased his devotions, hoping for healing that way. William Parron left his service under a cloud, having foretold that the queen would live to eighty. That death too, of a wife he had loved deeply in his undemonstrative way, aged and weakened the king. His interest in quintessentia, the hidden fifth element after earth, air, water and fire, may have been an attempt to find an elixir, distilled from good wine or the blood of sanguine young men, to preserve the living body from rot-ting and to restore its youthful vigour. The blood of sanguine young men had not, until then, been propitious for him.

In these sufferings Katherine was sometimes with him, though the documents cannot prove whether she was his paramour or simply his friend. On December 10th, 1508, after she had been absent from the ac-counts for almost two years, she was paid 20 shillings for "stuff bought for the king", the sort of entry that Elizabeth of York had earned in years past. Near that entry was one for money lost by the king at cards; perhaps they played together. But Henry was already gravely ill, no longer able to ride, and organising, through his private chaplain, increasing numbers of daily Masses and offerings for his soul. He was probably suffering from consumption. Within weeks he was so frail that he could not swallow the Sacrament but was reduced, weeping and praying, to looking at Christ's Body in the monstrance that was brought to his bedside. On March 25th, 1509, the Feast of the Annunciation, Katherine was paid 18s. 8d. for "four painted cloths for the King's grace": holy pictures, often of Christ coming in judgment, that were stretched before the eyes of the dying. The king had strength enough, the same day, to get £2 from Heron as "play-ing money". But he lived less than a month longer.

His will, made on the last day of March, seemed to carry a final echo of his struggle with Katherine's husband. He implored Our Lady, "whom in all my necessities I have made my continual refuge", that "the ancient and ghostly enemy nor none other evil or damnable esprite, have no power to invade me." The horror of a horned devil diving into his throat to seize his soul—as had happened in some cases—seemed juxta-posed with Perkin's ghostly shadow diving at Kent and Cornwall, fearful memories and imaginings laid equally before the Virgin for her help.

Katherine's compassion for him may still have seemed unthinkable. Henry had hanged her husband and kept her, in effect, in confinement, honourable as it was. But he was the only help and protection she had, and they were both alone. The welfare of her son, too, may have depended on his protection and his amenable kindness. She may therefore have allowed him to show affection to her, however far that went. Her husband had not been executed without provocation, and perhaps she herself was not untouched, in the end, by the doubts surrounding him. She knew the stories and the "nickname" and would have heard, especially, of her husband's confession at the point of death. To take a man on trust, and to love him, was not the same as being certain who he was.

By the last years of Henry's life, the rumours and tales surrounding the deaths of the princes had taken more coherent form. According to Fabyan and Vergil, the children had definitely been killed in the Tower on Richard III's orders. Molinet, too, reported that they had been smothered between two quilts five weeks into their imprisonment and their bodies bundled into some secret place. Both Fabyan and Vergil thought, or hinted, that the murderer had been James Tyrell, who in 1502 had himself been confined to the Tower for helping Edmund de la Pole. Vergil said he knew no details of the deaths, only that Tyrell, though forced and unhappy, had done the deed "thoroughly" when Robert Brackenbury, the constable of the Tower, had shown himself reluctant. Tyrell, he said, could have spared the boys or rescued them, producing the sort of scene that the contrived Duke of York (*Ricardus Dux adulterinus*, as he called him) had once reduced his listeners to tears by describing. He had chosen instead to kill them, preferring—for unfathomable reasons—to back a claimant further down the Yorkist list.

Thomas More, in his *History of King Richard the Third* of 1514, embroidered the story greatly, and said that Tyrell had confessed to the murder before his execution. No one mentioned a confession before More did; none survived, and Henry appeared to make no use of the information. But More's account soon became the accepted story of what had happened to Richard, Duke of York.

The actual murders, More said, had been performed by Miles Forest, one of the princes' warders, "fleshed in murder before", and by John Dighton, "a big broad square strong knave". They had smothered the boys as they slept with feather-beds and pillows forced hard into their mouths, and had then laid them naked on the bed for Tyrell to see. After this they had buried the bodies at the foot of a staircase, "meetly deep in the ground under a great heap of stones". Later, however, on King Richard's orders, they were transferred to some more fitting and secret place "because they were a king's sons". A priest in Brackenbury's service buried them, and died without revealing where they were.

Forest, too, had died by the early 1490s—More said he had "piece-meal rotted away", apt punishment for such a crime—but Dighton still lived when the confession was allegedly taken, and was left at liberty. Tyrell was not punished for the murders, but for treason, and his attainder of

1504 made no mention of his part in killing the princes. There may have been no confession at all, but a hardening flurry of London rumour. Sir Richard Nanfan said that Henry had been hearing whispers about Tyrell for a while and, typically, had refused to believe them. He had pardoned him in the year after Bosworth and employed him as a royal steward and receiver, first in Wales and then, "in consideration of his services", at Guisnes, outside Calais, giving him the chance to start again. The sub-poena under which he had been placed in 1486, obliging him to reveal Richard III's actions in the case of the Countess of Oxford, apparently involved no broader inquiries. Even if the story of the murders was true, and he had confessed to them, the information was now of little use to the king. There were still no bodies and, in any case, the young man who had claimed to be Richard no longer required refutation.

More claimed that the details he gave came from several different sources, as well as from what Tyrell had revealed. He had heard the story "of them that much knew and little cause had to lie", and "by such men and by such means, as me thinketh it were hard but it should be true." Others, he admitted, remained uncertain about what had happened to the boys:

> [Their] death and final infortune hath nevertheless so far come in question, that some remain yet in doubt, whether they were in [King Richard's] days destroyed or no. Not for that only that Perkin Warbeck, by many folks' malice, and more folks' folly, so long space abusing the world, was as well with princes as the poorer people, reputed and taken for the younger of those two, but for that also that all things were in late days so covertly demeaned, one thing pretended and another meant, that there was nothing so plain and openly proved, but that yet for the common custom of close and covert dealing, men had it ever inwardly suspect, as many well counterfeited jewels make the true mistrusted.

More hoped to look at all this in detail, especially if he could find time to write "that history of Perkin in any compendious process by itself". He never managed to. His story of the deaths of the princes, however, use-fully consolidated general fears and suppositions that had existed for thirty years. In any event, there were no more feigned lads or well counter-feited jewels. Tyrell was buried close to the last of them, on the west side of the nave of the church of the Austin Friars.

II

As THE YEARS SLID AWAY from the November of Perkin's hanging, not only Henry's subjects, but foreign rulers too, gave up the game of irritating the increasingly impressive King of England. James IV was the first to give in, though he did not do so lightly.

For much of the spring and early summer of 1499 the peace talks had dragged on with England, still snagging on the safe-conduct clause. Andrew Forman, Richard's attendant, was now the chief negotiator on the Scottish side. Though James was not persuaded to drop his prince for any of the reasons Henry put forward, he seemed to understand at last that Richard was never coming back. Article 6 of Ayton was stripped of the offending clause, and a new Article 5 cancelled all existing safe-conducts, including Richard's. Unable to protect his friend any more, James ratified the treaty on June 20th at Stirling, where he had first received him. Three more years passed before the Treaty of Perpetual Peace, drawn up on Henry's side in a document overgrown with red roses, marked the end of James's dalliance with Richard of England. The next year, 1503, saw him married at last to Henry's daughter Margaret.

He was now not only Henry's son-in-law, but ostensibly his firm ally. James seemed to prove as much in 1504, when he wrote to the Duke of Guelders to upbraid him for sheltering Suffolk, the new Yorkist claimant, as if he himself had never done such a thing. He poured scorn on the idea that because Suffolk had trusted Guelders, Guelders could not give him up. The duke had already done enough for him; were it not for his help, Suffolk would have "wandered over the world in disguise", without friends, or would "long ago have fallen into the power of the king". As for restoring Suffolk in England, he wrote,

> if you or [Maximilian] entertained such a notion . . . the enterprise might lead to greater difficulties, and be remembered for ages. Beware. This Edmund [Suffolk] will deceive you by too much promising of friends . . . You have sustained no small charges ever since he came to you, and you will not be able to bear them longer, for the heavy expenses of war. Pray excuse me, Illustrious Cousin, if I do not deal gently with you now. You treat kindly a rebel of England, an exile from the greater part of Christendom, to the disgust of your friends and to the complication of your own affairs, at

a time when you ought to be conciliating princes rather than exasperating them.

James urged the duke to be quickly rid of his "hateful guest" with his importunity and his "pretended power". This was surely bitter experience talking, especially that "too much promising of friends". Yet Suffolk's claim was legitimate, all the same; and so, James continued to believe, Prince Richard's had been. Deception in promises, and deception in a person, were not the same. For honour's sake and to save his face, but perhaps not only for that, he kept the old story going.

In 1503, writing to the Duchess of Brittany to try to avoid paying compensation to Guy Foulcart, the Breton captain who had been contracted to take Richard to England, James called Foulcart's charge "the Duke of York" three times, as straightforwardly as when he had been helping him. James's officers, too, continued to use the name, knowing or admitting no alternative. To the end of his life, in 1502 or so, the Earl of Huntly, Katherine's father, showed no animosity towards the sovereign who, out of willful headiness, had supposedly lost him his daughter to some chimera out of Europe. Her husband's confession apparently made no more impression on Huntly than it had done on James. Legend preserved a final act of piety: that James had Richard's body brought from London and interred at Cambuskenneth Abbey, just outside Stirling, where his own father and mother were buried, laying him in the vault he had prepared for himself.

Maximilian, that pusher of dreams, also did not forget his cousin of York. In January 1499, writing to the Estates General of the Netherlands, he insisted that his costly promotion of York, "his kinsman", had been for their own good. "Had there not been deception and betrayal by people in whom [I] trusted," he told them, "he would have been King of England, which would have brought great security and peace to Archduke Philip and this country, and might have helped it with financial aid [*Hilfsgelder*] too." When Henry sent ambassadors that summer to try and renew the friendship "damaged by the favour shown to Perkin", they were treated to poor presents and unloving words; and for a year after the death of Maximilian's cousin, in November, there was no official contact.

Sir Robert Curzon, meeting the King of the Romans soon after the execution, reported his grief and anger. When he told him of "the murders and tyrannies of H.," Maximilian burst out that "if [he] might have one of King Edward's blood in his hands, he would help him to recover the crown of England and be revenged upon H., or else he would spend as much money as his whole lands were in value for a whole year." Suffolk, when he first met Maximilian, also took care to stir him with the "murders", and said he had been threatened too. But this new claimant, though undoubtedly of Edward's blood, did not appeal to Maximilian as the old one had. The King of the Romans thought him "but a light person", and kept Suffolk cooling his heels round various imperial towns while he prevaricated, or went hunting. In the end, after toying with helping him, he banished him from his territories. When the English envoys tried to discover where Suffolk was going, Maximilian answered that "he knew not, but to seek his fortune," as if he hardly cared.

It had not been this way with his cousin of York. At the moment of the hanging, as Henry knew, Maximilian still believed as firmly as ever in his Prince of England. A decade later, however—now Henry's great friend, and honoured with the Order of the Garter—the emperor began to let doubts show as he supervised the writing of the *Weisskunig*. The young boy had come to him in 1493 and had said he was Edward's son, but the White King was unsure, and had helped him just a little. He himself believed him to be Edward's son, but the English "thought only that he was a feigned son and not King Edward's real son." Later he had helped this "other king of England" more, but the English had still not wanted to believe in him. In the end, the young son of King Edward "went to war against the New King of England. But he lost the battle, and he was captured." The White King thought for some time of mobilising his forces to help him after his defeat, but in the end made friends instead with the Red and White King, Henry, "who because of his wise rule is called the English Solomon." As for the young man, he had "died in prison". He had not been strung up like a felon, but had lingered forgotten in some dungeon or had been killed secretly, as kings and nobles often were. Had he been Edward's son, then? In his gloss to his own text, Maximilian pondered. Without sure knowledge of "the crime committed against him by his uncle Richard" after his father's death, "even the White King himself couldn't really know whether it was him or not."

From Flanders came silence. Philip, allied to Henry through his own Spanish marriage and more civil trade relations, had long ago taken the path of sobriety. But one last squawk came in 1505 or so from Paul Zachtlevant, a Pomeranian merchant living in Amsterdam, who had lent money to Richard, Duke of York for his expedition to Deal. In his office he had papers signed and sealed in the duke's name, now worthless. His debtor had tried to pay back some of it, requesting the customs officers of Edinburgh in 1496 to grant Zachtlevant a waiver of duties on 1,612 woollen cloths. Obviously this remission, "at the request of Richard, Duke of York", had not gone far enough.

Zachtlevant told Thomas Killingworth, Suffolk's steward, that he had two strategies to get his money back. First, he would send someone to Henry with "copies of such writings and duties as the duke of York oweth me under notary's signs, desiring him whereas he hath lent his goods unto the duke of York, which was the right king of England [Killingworth then struck out that phrase], and that, seeing that he is dead without paying, that it would please King H. to pay him the same money." If he would not, as seemed certain, then Zachtlevant would get a certificate of authority, signed and sealed by Suffolk, and would show it to the King of Denmark and the Duke of Pomerania, who were friends of his. The king and the duke would then distrain upon the English merchants in their lands to pay his money back. The purpose of the certificate was to prove that his debtor had been the man he said he was. "Ye know well the abusion King H. hath made against the duke of York that he was a counterfeit," Killingworth told Suffolk (revealing, incidentally, what Suffolk's own view was of the young man who would have been his cousin, and whom he had probably seen at Henry's court). "[Zachtlevant] desireth therefore to have your certificate that it is untrue."

Neither the certificate nor Zachtlevant's money seems to have appeared. There was no interest in Europe in posthumously authenticating Richard, Duke of York, even assuming that it could be done. Yet the official story of Perkin, too, still found little purchase there. A hundred miles from the credit-houses of Amsterdam, on the quayside at Tournai, the Werbecque family lived apparently untouched by their notoriety. The town chroniclers did not know or care who they were, and made no effort to flesh out the reports that had come from England. There were signs, though, of greater prosperity in this household now.

In December 1498, shortly before her marriage to Jehan de la Croix, Nicaise sold the house on the Scheldt at Caufours. She went along to sign the deed of sale with Pierart Flan and Adrien Carlier, described as *tuteurs et curateurs de ses enfants, Pierrechon et Jenette Werbecque*, the guardians of her children after the death of their father. Presumably the house was sold to raise money to support the children, and because Nicaise would shortly be living in another.

"Jenette", or Jehanne as she was called when she grew, was certainly a child. She had been born in 1486, according to the "letter home", and still had her baby name. Pierrechon was evidently a child too, or he would not have been called one and would have had no need of guardians. Legal documents were precise about such things and precise, too, about not using diminutive names for men and women who were grown. Despite Henry's constant belittling of him as a "boy", Perkin had always been "Peter" in legal documents in England from 1494, and probably earlier. Child nicknames occurred only in apprentice contracts, where a child was spoken for by his relations (and sometimes, adult or not, kept his nickname as long as the apprenticeship lasted), or in instances like this, where a child was still in care. By the age of twenty-one a young man had put off childish things, becoming a "son" of the household and being called Pierre or Pierart, like a man.

Absence might have provided an explanation. Perhaps he was "Pierrechon" because the family no longer knew him, and had forgotten how old he was. He was still imagined as a slim and unbiddable boy in need of Flan's strong hand; a boy whose age had frozen sometime after they had last seen him, and who had never grown up. The letter to Nicaise, if it had ever reached her, would have confirmed this impression. "Pierrequin", after all, had written it, and its whole tone had been that of a child remembering simple things, begging for money, fearing the strap. He had not explained that he was then twenty-three, now twenty-four, married, and a father. So the family instinctively provided a guardian for him, as it did for his twelve-year-old sister. Though Nicaise could not save him, she could give him the comfort of Flan and Carlier signing the paperwork.

Yet the scene evoked in the document seemed simpler than that. A widow went to the office of the *maieur et echevins* of St. Brice to sell the family house, accompanied by the guardians of her children. Since children usually attended such occasions, they went with her, standing solemnly beside her as the deed was signed. The deed of sale gave no hint of complications in this picture. The lives of the Werbecques, unperturbed by anything that had happened outside Tournai, continued as usual. If Nicaise had known that her son was in the custody of the King

of England, she would hardly have arranged guardians for him in Tournai, just as she would not have stayed indifferent to his fate. By doing
both, she strongly suggested that the Pierrechon of the deed of sale was
not the young man in the Tower. It is possible that he was a much
younger brother, named after a son who had gone missing and was presumed dead. Tanjar at Setubal, allegedly recording a conversation of
around 1492, had said that there was no other son save "Piris", the teenager who had disappeared, but one had perhaps been born in the intervening years. It is also possible that there was no blood connection
between these boys: that one was a son of the family, and one had never
been.

Whatever the truth, Pierrechon did not reappear in Nicaise's will of
1509. Jehanne, now married, was the residuary legatee and apparently the
only child, though Nicaise left money to Jehan's two illegitimate sons,
Colin and Innocent. She also left money to the church of St. Jean des
Caufours, where she wished to be buried, to the hospital at Marvis and to
the hospital of Le Plancque at St. Jean, where she asked to have a perpetual Mass sung for her soul in the chapel. The will has vanished now; but
it seems that she made no mention of the soul of her first husband, or of
his only legitimate son.

Insofar as prayers were said for the mysterious young man who had been
attributed to the Werbecque family, they were said elsewhere in Flanders.
Margaret had ceased to push his cause since her apology of 1498, at least
in public, though Henry was quite correctly convinced that in private she
had not changed. Her support for Suffolk later proved how incorrigible
she was. She may well have kept in touch with her White Rose before he
died, through Jacques of Flanders and others. Just before his execution a
priest-servant of Anthony de Berghes, the Abbot of Flanders and Cambrai's brother, turned up in London. This was perhaps a last vicarious
visitation. The next year, almost three times the usual sum was spent to
burn candles in Margaret's chapel at Binche.

By now there were other substitute children in her life. In November
1498 the Archduchess Juana had given birth to a daughter, Philip's first
child. At the baptism, held with great pomp in Brussels on the last day of
November, Margaret, who was one of the godmothers, carried the baby
in her arms for Cambrai to plunge in the water. The last scene Molinet

recorded was of Margaret riding home in a special "throne chair" borne by two strong men, torches and trumpets blazing round her, still carrying the baby.

The chair showed her advancing age. She was growing weak and had been ill for much of the year, with her Masses and devotions multiplying. Yet she had not ceased her semi-secret acts of charity. In July 1499 she undertook to pay for the upbringing of "a little English child" from the revenues of her estates at Rupelmonde. The child was put to nurse with the family of Pieter van Tiemple, from his name a Fleming of some substance. Van Tiemple was given, along with the little bundle, £144 *tournois* "to be used to the profit" of the child. There is no knowing where this child had come from, or what was supposed to happen to him next. Yet the money to be spent on him, though a large sum, was considerably less than Margaret had spent on the last child she had taken under her wing.

That child had come into her life more than twenty years before, in the autumn of 1478: the first year after Charles's death, and the year when Mary, her beloved stepdaughter, gave birth to her first child, a son. Sometime after September a little boy called Jehan le Sage, "good little John", was taken into her palace at Binche, her favourite country retreat in the hills of Hainault, to live there at her expense and to be educated by a priest. He was then "about five", the same age as Richard, Duke of York. Jehan appeared to be an orphan and his name a nickname: the same name, as it happens, as Edward IV's favourite jester, who had accompanied Margaret on her wedding-journey to Burgundy ten years earlier to soothe the distress of a long voyage. He was also, perhaps, an especially bright or well-mannered child who was thought likely to benefit from Margaret's close attention. Although she helped other children, and provided scholarships, Jehan was the only one whose upbringing and teaching she personally supervised. Yet this was done at a distance and out of the public eye, a long way from Brussels or Malines, with Margaret often absent, and with the priest officially in charge of him.

Every year, for seven years, Margaret gave the priest £24 *tournois* for Jehan's keep and his instruction; he did not seem to have his meals counted in with the other palace residents'. She also paid up to £12 a year for his "clothes, gear and other essentials". For one precious year, 1479, when he was about six, his clothes and gear were itemised in the accounts. The list was then struck out, as though these details were not to be publicly recorded. He had a robe of costly scarlet cloth for Easter, a "jacket of vesture" to wear underneath it, two shirts of fine linen, two doublets, a bonnet and a hat, three pairs of shoes. He was a very small boy; less than two ells of cloth made up his robe. His doublets were striped and laced with silk, and the "bonnet and hat", usually worn together, turned him into a little nobleman. The insignia on his jacket was not improbably the one worn by Margaret's escorts the next year in England, the white rose.

That same year he was given, as presents, a rosary and a pair of skates. In his sharp shining shoes perhaps, skidding on the ice, he broke his leg, and the surgeon of Binche was paid £8 to mend it. The surgeon, Master Colart Fedorq, was not otherwise called on in twenty-seven years of accounts, and his fee for this treatment was probably a quarter of his annual salary. But little Jehan was, in effect, Margaret's child, and was cared for accordingly.

He may never have known, and may never have thought to ask, what his real background was. It is not impossible that he was a child from Tournai whose violent father was sporadically absent and whose mother had died. Rescued, perhaps, from a home where he had already been beaten, he had been passed on through the Cambrai diocese or through relatives to Margaret. It is also not impossible that he was a love-child of Edward IV's, sent out as his namesake had been to comfort a childless sis-ter. Edward's warrants for the summer of 1478 show a fair amount of secret business going on with "Flanders": a voyage by the *Falcon* "from London to the parts of Flanders and from thence unto London again", and the sending of "certain secret persons . . . to bring us knowledge of certain matters . . . Whereof we have the perfectness to our great pleas-ure." The possibilities can only be raised and left, but there they are.

Jehan's education may not have been especially high-flown. The teacher who had nominal charge of him, Sire Pierre de Montigny, was from a family closely related by marriage to the de Lalaings, the highest blood of Hainault and longtime fighters and councillors in the service of the Dukes of Burgundy. The de Montignys, too, had been councillors and ambassadors, with several made ducal chamberlains and knights of the Order of the Golden Fleece. Sire Pierre was of noble stock, therefore, but also an ordinary non-graduate priest. Evidently, from the rosary, he was teaching Jehan his prayers and some of the Latin that went with them. The boy would have learned reading and writing, but not necessar-ily any language other than the French his teacher spoke. On the other hand, education of this intensity may have included many subjects, for he was evidently in some ways an experimental child. So his days passed, in peculiar isolation with his tutor in the palace, picking up the ways of court and church as he picked up his grammar, until at the end of 1485 he and Father de Montigny vanished from the accounts.

The timing of his disappearance, as Margaret realised the apparent finality of the destruction of the House of York, was suggestive, but may have been merely coincidence. The boy was twelve now, old enough for higher schooling or service somewhere. It may also have been coincidence that the room in which Jehan lived, the only one at Binche designated for a child alone (all other designated rooms being shared by Margaret's "girls", or her "gentlemen", or allotted to important officers and visitors), was the same one, under the chapel and with the tennis court outside, that was later called "Richard's room".

If the young man who tormented Henry was not Richard—and nothing definitively proved, or so far proves, that he was not—he may have been Margaret's surrogate son. Either story seems likelier, on the evidence found so far, than the tale of commercial wandering and random kidnapping that was hung on him in 1497. The inexplicable factors, as Henry too noted, were his rival's own persistence and the enduring loyalty of the greatest names that backed him. Both he, and they, seemed to feel themselves under an obligation which had not been invented and which the confession did not change. We may never know what it was.

In 1512, well after Henry's death and more than a decade after the death of her first love, Katherine felt herself free again to take a succession of husbands. Her second was James Strangeways, an usher of the chamber, who died six years later. Her third, Matthew Cradock, whom she married almost instantly, was the Earl of Worcester's deputy in South Wales, a sea-captain, a grandfather and the owner of large estates in Glamorgan. In 1531 he too died. Cradock had built a great tomb for them both in Swansea, but Katherine did not lie there. She married Christopher Ashton, another gentleman usher, living with him at her own manor of Fyfield. Almost the only image of her comes from those years: she was remembered often riding a white gelding, Ashton's gift to her, round the parish, always in her widow's black.

No children came from these marriages. But she was now a woman of substance, with wide landed interests and an array of gifts from her husbands. Cradock's will listed the jewellery and plate she had owned at the time she married him, some of it given to her by the first two men whose hands she had taken. Among the jewels were two hearts of gold, one with a fleur-de-lis of diamonds "and a pearl hanging by him, which was a noch [brooch] of Our Lady". There was also a separate fleur-de-lis of diamonds, "with three pearls hanging by him". The fleur-de-lis, highest of flowers, was a royal symbol and a favourite device of Edward IV's; for his meeting with the French king at Picquigny, cheekily, Edward had worn a large fleur-de-lis of precious stones in his hat. The symbol could not in fact be worn or bestowed by anyone who was not royal. The fleur-de-lis of diamonds, the stone of betrothal, had therefore probably been given to Katherine by the man she had first married; the heart of gold, with the royal lily repeated, had perhaps been placed by him round her neck on their wedding day. The face of that impoverished and wandering prince may have passed in remembrance as Katherine touched them. *The lily-white rose me thought I saw.*

Her subsequent husbands, Strangeways and Cradock, had been members of the Tudor establishment, Cradock becoming constable of Caerphilly six months after Bosworth. Yet Cradock was said locally, in South Wales, to be "warm against" Henry VII and "on the side of the one whom he believed to be the true heir of the crown—the one who is nicknamed Perkin Warbeck." That sympathy may have drawn him and Katherine together, or may more plausibly have grown once Cradock had married her. It is hard to say otherwise why this far-away Welsh captain should have been on Richard's side.

On October 12th 1537, two days before her death, Katherine made her will at Fyfield. She described herself as "wife unto Christopher Ashton of Fyfield in the County of Berks Esquire, sometime wife unto James Strangeways, late of Fyfield aforesaid esquire . . . and also late wife unto my dear and well-beloved husband Sir Matthew Cradock of Cardiff in Wales." Ashton, her "most entirely beloved husband", was thanked for "his loving licence and gentle sufferance" in allowing her to make a will at all.

Women never having much of their own to give away, her own gifts were small: her white gelding, a black silk gown, a kirtle of black worsted. But the first bequest, after 40 shillings for her executor, was to her "cousin" Margaret Keymes, who was to be given "such of my apparel as shall be thought meet for her by the discretion of my husband and my said executor." Margaret was the daughter of Cicely, Edward IV's second surviving daughter, who had taken Thomas Keymes or Kyme as her second husband. This marriage, to "an obscure man of no reputation", as Vergil called him, had made Cicely an outcast among the royals. Evidently, at some point, Katherine had befriended her and her daughter. The term "cousin", though, suggested either a blood tie or that general cousinage of royals that Richard Plantagenet had claimed, in 1493, with half the crowned heads of Europe. Katherine's claim to be cousin to Margaret could have come only through her first husband, assuming that he had been the prince he said he was. It was perhaps a tiny signal that she still believed in him.

The suggestive mention of cousin Margaret, however, hardly made up for the aching absence of Katherine's first husband from the rest of the document. There was supposed to be no love like a woman's for that first partner, to whom her unschooled heart had been given and with whom she had first felt a man's weight, urgency and desire, shockingly physical and real. In nature, some birds of the air never took another mate after the death of their first; the type of the faithful widow was the turtle dove, sobbing low and soft in the woods and flying only to barren trees in never-settled grief. Tradition said that Katherine felt this way; "in all fortunes," Bacon wrote, she "entirely loved" him. Yet Katherine could not call him either "Richard" or "Perkin" in her will, and to call him "my first husband" was also impossible if she could not name him. So she did not mention him, as though he had never been part of her life.

Yet his name was vital. More than anything, men and women wished to be held in such remembrance. Since their souls could not help themselves, they hoped to depend on the constant recollection of family and friends. In that hope they had their names carved on tombs, set in glass, painted on rood-screens, engraved on chalices or specified as a permanent part of the prayers that were said in chantries. At family graces, before meat, the *De Profundis* was said particularly for them, and the priest intoned their names as he washed his hands at the *Lavabo* of the Mass. Their names, "rehearsed openly" by the living, immediately and directly succoured their souls struggling in Purgatory. Katherine herself had bequeathed a penny, on the day of her burial and at her month's mind, to five hundred of the "impotent and poorest" folk in Berkshire, "through whose devout prayers it may please God to mitigate my pains that my Soul the sooner may attain to the fruition of his godhead."

With Strangeways, Katherine had also founded a perpetual chantry in the monastery of St. Mary Overy in Southwark—a place, incidentally, where special prayers had been instituted years before for the family of Edward IV. In her will she mentioned the regime she had established there, "with one priest therein daily to sing Mass for the souls of my father the Earl of Huntly and Gordon, and my lady and mother his wife, my soul, my said husbands' souls, James Strangeways his father and mother and all Christian souls." These were all the people of importance in her life, save one. He was included, of course, in "all Christian souls", but not among "my said husbands", since he had not been previously mentioned. He was numbered, in effect, with the forgotten dead in the churchyard, in sunken or unmarked graves, who had no kin or friends to pray for them. The phrase covered him as adequately as "all other that he had offended unto" had covered Katherine in his plea for absolution on the scaffold. In that sad, vague way they were equal in their treatment of each other.

There remained one other will in which he might have been mentioned. In October 1503 Margaret, by then very ill, drew up hers. Her French still showed that she was English, and her chief anxiety remained the "return and restitution of our marriage money, amounting to 115,000 écus d'or more or less." Despite all Richard had tried to do for her, she was now owed more than when he and she had drawn up the protocols in 1494. Margaret asked that the money, if recovered, should be paid to Philip, who would then assign it to various charitable causes. "Among other things," £30 tournois was to go each year for devotions in the chapel of Our Lady at Binche. Every day, "towards evening," the Angelus was to be sung there before Our Lady's image, and every Thursday a Mass was to be sung in honour of the Blessed Sacrament: "which foundations we are making principally for the salvation and remedy of the souls of our late lord and husband, of our very dear daughter Dame Mary of Burgundy, of ourselves and of those souls to whom we feel bound."

A cui nous sentons tenue. The binding had gone very deep; and yet at this moment, exposed before posterity and before God, Margaret went no further with her list of names. It is possible, in the case of her White Rose, that she felt she could not do so. She left him wrapped with others, in a vague embrace of love.

Sometime in 1499 she had commissioned a copy of a popular paint-ing, *The Lamentation on the Road to the Sepulchre*, to hang in the palace at Binche. She herself, her face familiar from other portraits, appeared in it as Mary Magdalene weeping at the pierced feet of Christ deposed from the Cross. She wore a robe of cloth-of-gold trimmed at the neck and sleeves with pearls, a cloak of crimson velvet lined with gray fur and a rich belt (the *balteus* Bernard André had mentioned, wantonly removed for her beloved) set with enamel daisies surrounded with pearls, her flowers and her stones. Fixed to the belt was a White Rose for which, you might imag-ine, she also wept.

The rose, though she had always claimed it, was never so prominent in any other portrait of her. Her body seemed contorted deliberately to show it and to make it catch the eye. She appeared, in short, not merely as the Magdalene, with high-braced breasts and straggling hair that fell louchely on her neck, but as the matriarch of the House of York. Mary Magdalene had recognised Jesus when no one else had done so, anointing His feet with ointment and drying them with her hair in token of rever-ence for who He was, and had been mocked for it as a woman of sluttish reputation. At the Crucifixion, her grief was second only to the grief of Jesus's mother; when He rose again three days later, she was the first to know Him and call Him "Lord". So Margaret pictured herself. A nun from the order of Black Sisters in Binche stood behind her with a new jar of ointment, ready for the reanointing. In death she again acknowledged him, openly showing her love and contrition of heart.

Her White Rose was now wandering again. At the moment of death he had felt himself breathed and lifted out of his body, which at once appeared so horrible to him that he could not believe it had been his. He saw the earth too, little, dark, bare and naked, with its riches and honours "all but child's play in the street . . . wind and a dream." Almost immedi-ately, certainly in less than half an hour, he found himself before the heav-enly tribunal, between God and the Devil, accounting for his sins. Bristling Satan made the case that, though vested with the stole of immortality by his true father, he had accepted instead the black garment of perpetual death: "he hath left thy livery and hath taken mine." His

angel defended him, assuring the Divine Judge that his life had been vir/
tuous in some ways, but there was no escaping punishment.

The charge/sheet against him was mostly pride and lying, though to
what degree he had lied or been presumptuous was still uncertain to
almost all those he had left behind. On the gravity of his sins depended
whether he wandered in Hell or in Purgatory. Hell was permanent, allot/
ted to those who had not shown true contrition for their sins; he had
shown contrition, but perhaps it had not been true. Purgatory was tempo/
rary, God's mercy intervening after years of punishment to pluck out the
purified soul; but for his soul now, naked and crying, God's grace could
not be counted on.

Long ago, when he had first come to his body, God had set his print
and figure in him. As he stood at the tribunal, you could not see that
resemblance any more. Gradually, through his life, his sins had appeared
as blemishes on his face until it was the Devil he conformed to. As he
entered Purgatory, his angel held up a mirror to show him his own filth
and deformation and the horns and claws he had tried to pretend he did
not have. After that single horrifying glance his soul plunged down into
horror itself, whimpering and screaming.

In the pitch/dark, the devils attacked him. He saw only the gleam of
their claws and their white fangs. Since his chief sin was pride, he was
hung on iron hooks on a slowly revolving wheel that was basted and
pushed by demons. Where was his pride now? they screeched at him.
Where was his vanity? Why didn't he dance? He fell down, and red/hot
grappling hooks rolled him over the coals. A pitchfork pierced him, flung
him into the fire and roasted him; his soul/flesh dripped from the bones, yet
he did not die. He could still scream, and his screams rose with those of his
neighbour/souls, loose/haired women and elbowing men, trampling and
tearing him in their own panic. He became liquid, and was passed
through an iron sieve as cooks strained a sauce through canvas, falling at
last into a great bowl of carrion and sulphur. That smell was all about
him, the farting reek of terrified souls, his own stink. At no point was there
quiet or the cessation of pain. All was howling, darkness and his own
continually repeated dissolution: in flames, on anvils, in the foaming jaws
of devil/dogs and in the guts of demons, who shat him out again.

After many years, depending on the sins he had committed and the
prayers that were said for him on earth, his angel would take him out of
the fire. Together they rose towards the pure ether of which his angel was

made. The air was gradually brighter and softer, like ointment on his raw wounds. Light, and growing lighter, he passed through the firmament silvered and soaring with larks that sang "Jesu", a song he had not heard before. The light grew brighter, almost too bright, and dappled with the rainbow-wings of uncountable angels. He stood in the clearness of Heaven Imperial, seven times brighter and fairer than the sun. It astonished and almost frightened him. Before him rose the jasper walls of the heavenly city, shining like glass, and the golden streets in which white-robed souls lived on white manna and sweet unending praise. Everything blazed with light. All was perfect clarity, all veils lifted, at last.

He was close to the judgment throne of God, so close that he would have to stop, hanging back on the hand of his angel, to keep the distance that reverence required. He knelt down. Only two things could happen now, at the moment of his final judging. Jesus would turn His back on him, ending the possibility that he would ever gaze on those sweet eyes that had loved him, leaving him only with the words "I tell you, I know you not." Or He would look on him, smiling, and call him by the name He had always known him by, confessing it as He had promised before His father and all the angels, face to face.

APPENDIX

The Setubal Testimonies, April 25th, 1496

IN THE TOWN OF SETUBAL in the kingdom of Portugal, the 25th of April 1496, in the presence of me, Fernan Peres Mexia, apostolic notary and [notary of] the witnesses recorded below, on behalf of Don Alonso de Silva, Knight-Commander of Calatrava:

First to be interrogated and questioned was Rui de Sousa, knight of the household of our Lord King of Portugal. In my presence, Don Alonso asked the said Rui de Sousa if he had known the Duke of York, son of King Edward, when he was in England. To which he answered that he had seen him and that he was a very noble little boy and that he had seen him singing with his mother and one of his sisters and that he sang very well and that he was very pretty and the most beautiful creature he had ever seen, and he also saw him playing very well at sticks and with a two-handed sword. And then he heard it said that they had put him and his brother too, the Prince of Wales, in a fortress where a body of water passed by, and that they bled them, and they died from the forced bleeding.

Then Alonso asked the said Rui de Sousa who the person was who now called himself the Duke of York; Rui de Sousa said that a youth had come to Portugal with the wife of Duarte Brandon, a Portuguese knight, and he had seen him walking in the Court of Portugal behind a *fidalgo* who was called Pero Vaz da Cunha, who treated him as his page, and when they had the celebrations for the Lord Prince of Portugal [Pero Vaz] dressed him up, and he saw him in a doublet of brocade and a long gown of silk. And after that he knew nothing more until now, when he'd heard what people were saying about him.

Don Alonso then asked him if he resembled in his person the Duke of York he had seen in England; he said no, because the other one was very beautiful.

Then in my presence and that of the witnesses Don Alonso, Knight Commander of the Order of Calatrava, asked Duarte Brandon, a Portuguese who was brought up in England in the household of King Edward, if he knew who this person was whom they now called the Duke of York.

He said it was the worst evil in the world that he and his brother the Prince of Wales had been killed, and the one who they now said [was him] was a youth from a city called Tournai and his father was a boatman who was called Bernal Uberque and he lived below the St. Jean bridge and [the boy] was called Piris. And his father had placed him in the said city of Tournai with an organist to teach him the craft for a certain number of years, and the boy had run away.

And the boy came to a place called Middelburg where his [Brandon's] wife had fled from the plague that was in Bruges. In Middelburg he found a position with a craftsman who lived opposite the place where his wife was staying. The craftsman sold needles and purses, and the boy got to know some of the French boys who were in his wife's service.

And when the said Duarte Brandon sent for his wife to take her into Portugal, [the youth] found out and told her boys that he wanted to go with them to Portugal and that he would live with the son of Duarte Brandon. So he went on board ship with [Brandon's] wife and came with her to Lisbon. And his wife asked him [Brandon] if he wanted to take him for the household and he answered no, that he had other French boys in service and didn't want any more, but he would place him with a *fidalgo*. And he gave him to Pero Vaz da Cunha. And he, in the season, attended the celebrations of the Lord Prince of Portugal and clothed [the youth] in a doublet with sleeves of brocade and a gown of silk and other things, and he was with him at the celebrations and in them.

A few days after that one of [Brandon's] boys was being sent in a ship to Flanders and the said boy told him that he wanted to go with him;

he wasn't staying in that country since Duarte Brandon did not want to take him in as his son, but when he had agreed to go with Brandon's boy the ship sailed and he was left behind. Then he came across another ship that was ready to leave, and asked where it was going. They told him, to Flanders; he asked them if they would take him; they said yes, but they had to go to Ireland first; he said it didn't bother him.

So he folded up all his clothes and put on other old ones and boarded the ship, and he went with them. And when he arrived in Ireland and disembarked as they told him, he had taken off his jacket and dressed himself in that doublet with the sleeves of brocade and the robe of silk. And since those are wild people they ran after him because of that little bit of brocade, and some started to say that he was one of those of Lancaster and others that he was King Edward's son, and so people started to join him until little by little matters got as they are now.

In addition his boy, the one who had agreed to go with the boy on the ship, told him [Brandon] how he had talked to the boy's father in Tournai and given him news of him and told him how he had agreed to go in the ship with him and that he had stayed behind because he hadn't come in time before the ship left.

And on the 28th of the said month, in my presence and that of the witnesses recorded below, Alonso de Silva questioned and interrogated Tanjar, a herald of the Lord King of Portugal, asking whether he knew who the person was who now called himself the Duke of York.

The herald said he had known him here in Portugal and that he had seen him living with a *fidalgo* called Pero Vaz da Cunha, and that he had never taken him for a local because it was plain to see that he was a foreigner. And he knew that he had come with the wife of Duarte Brandon.

When that herald was going into Flanders once, he was in Tournai (of which he was a native) and he was in the house of one of his relations where he was staying, when the boy's father turned up. Since people had told him that [the herald] had come from Portugal and had seen his son there, he asked him [if he had].

The herald said he didn't know him. Then he asked: "Who did he go with?"

The father said he went with the wife of Duarte Brandon, in a ship with her notary.

The herald said that he had seen a youth arrive over there in Portugal, the one who had since gone to Ireland, and that they had raised him up as a king, saying he was the son of King Edward.

The father said: "That's my son."

"What distinguishing marks did he have?" asked the herald.

The father said he had a mark on his face under his eye, and he was a bit of a fool, and he had an upper lip that was raised up a bit and thin legs, and that when he left there he was fourteen going on fifteen.

The herald said that he had all those marks.

Then his father, weeping, said, "That is my son, who got him mixed up in this, ah me, they will kill him." For his father had no other [son], and by that mark that he had on his face and another that he had on his breast they said that he was the Duke of York.

And his father is a boatman, the master of a boat that comes and goes between Flanders and other places by river and he is rich and he is called John Osbeque, and the boy is Piris, which is Pedro in Flemish.

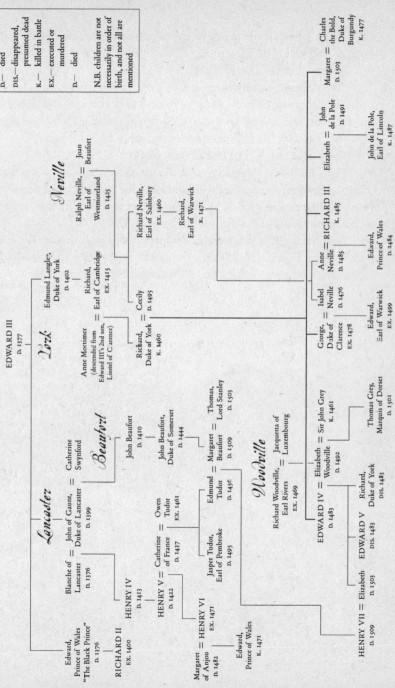

Family Tree of the Houses of York and Lancaster

NOTES

Principal abbreviations

For publications, here and throughout the notes, the place of publication is London unless otherwise stated.

ADC   *Acts of the Lords of Council in Civil Cases,* ed. George Nelson & Henry Patton (Edinburgh, 1918)

ADN   Archives Départementales du Nord (Lille)

AGS   Archivo General de Simancas

AH   *The Anglica Historia of Polydore Vergil,* ed. & tr. Denys Hay, Camden Series, vol. 74 (1950)

AN   Archives Nationales du Royaume, Brussels

ASM   Archivio di Stato di Milano

BL   British Library, London

BN   Bibliothèque Nationale, Paris

CC   Courtrai Codex

CCA   Canterbury Cathedral Archives

CCR   *Calendar of Close Rolls*

CDRS   *Calendar of Documents relating to Scotland,* ed. Joseph Bain, 4 vols. (Edinburgh, 1881–88)

CPR   *Calendar of Patent Rolls*

CSPM   *Calendar of State Papers and Manuscripts existing in the archives and collections of Milan,* ed. Allen B. Hinds (1912), vol. 1

CSPS   *Calendar of Letters, Dispatches & State Papers ... preserved in the archives at Simancas and elsewhere,* ed. G. A. Bergenroth et al., 13 vols. (1862–1954), vol. 1, *Henry VII, 1485–1509*

CSPV   Calendar of State Papers and Manuscripts relating to English Affairs existing in the archives of Venice and in other Libraries of Northern Italy (1202–1674), ed. Rawdon Brown, Bentinck et al., 38 vols. (1864–1947), vol. 1, 1202–1509

DRO   Devon Record Office, Exeter

EETS   Early English Text Society

EH   Excerpta Historica, or Illustrations of English History, ed. Samuel Bentley (1831)

EHR   English Historical Review

GC   The Great Chronicle of London, ed. A. H. Thomas and I. D. Thornley (1938)

HHSA   Haus-, Hof- und Staatsarchivs, Österreichisches Staatsarchiv, Vienna

HRHS   The Historia Regis Henrici Septimi of Bernard André, in Memorials of Henry VII, ed. James Gairdner, Rolls Series 10 (1858)

JCCC   Journal of the Court of Common Council (Corporation of London, Guild-hall)

LC   Chronicles of London (Vitellius A XVI), ed. C. L. Kingsford (Oxford, 1905)

L&P   Letters and Papers Illustrative of the Reigns of Richard III and Henry VII, ed. James Gairdner, 2 vols., Rolls Series 24 (1861 and 1863)

PI   La Politica Internacional de Isabel la Catolica, ed. Luis Suarez Fernandez, 5 vols. (Valladolid, 1965–72)

PRO   Public Record Office, Kew, London

RMS   Registrum Magni Sigilli Regum Scotorum 1424–1513, ed. James Balfour Paul (Edinburgh, 1884)

Rot. Parl.   Rolls of Parliament, comprising Petitions, Pleas, & Proceedings of Parliament, 6 Edward I –19 Henry VII, 1278–1503, 6 vols. (1767–77)

SCRO   Southampton City Record Office

SRO   Scottish Record Office, Edinburgh

SS   Sächsisches Hauptstaatsarchiv, Dresden

TA   Accounts of the Lord High Treasurer of Scotland, ed. Thomas Dickson et al. (Scottish Records Series, 1877), 13 vols. (Edinburgh, 1877–1978), vol. 1, 1473–1498

TLA   Tiroler Landesarchiv, Innsbruck

Introduction

GAIRDNER'S ACCOUNT: *The Story of Perkin Warbeck,* appended to *The History of the Life and Reign of Richard III,* 2nd edition (1898); *L&P,* prefaces to vols. 1 and 2. The sharp-eyed will detect, however, that even he had doubts.

JOHN FORD'S PLAY: *The Chronicle History of Perkin Warbeck, A Strange Truth* (first printed 1634). For the High Romantic view of this story, see also *The Fortunes of Perkin Warbeck: A Romance,* by Mary Shelley (1827), in which the hero is at least partly modelled on Percy Shelley himself. Friedrich Schiller, too, wrote an outline for a play called "Warbeck".

"WHETHER I NAME [HIM]": Thomas Gainsford, *The True and Wonderful History of Perkin Warbeck, calling himself Richard IV* (1618). Harleian Miscellany, vol. 6 (1745), p. 526.

Prologue: Presence

EMPIRE WEATHER: Gerhard Benecke, *Maximilian I (1459–1519): An analytical biography* (1982), pp. 161, 167.
LONDON INCIDENTS: *LC*, pp. 199–200.

PRINCIANT: Georges Chastellain, "Advertissement au Duc Charles", *Oeuvres,* ed. Baron Kervyn de Lettenhove, 8 vols. (Brussels, 1863–66), vol. 7, p. 312; Jean Molinet, *Chroniques,* ed. J.-A. Buchon, 5 vols. (Paris, 1828), vol. 5, p. 49.
PAINTERS' TRICKS: *The Strasburg Manuscript: A Medieval Painters' Handbook,* tr. Viola & Rosamund Borradaile (1966), *passim.* IVORY: p. 65.
"A CURIOUS PIECE": Francis Bacon, *The History of the Reign of King Henry the Seventh,* in *Works,* ed. J. Spedding, 10 vols. (1858), vol. 6, p. 134.
EFFINGERE: HRHS, p. 66.
MARGARET'S WEDDING PAGEANTS: J. de Barante, *Histoire des ducs de Bourgogne,* 10 vols. (Brussels, 1835–36), vol. 10, pp. 240–41.
CHARLES VIII'S IMAGE: Molinet, *Chroniques,* vol. 5, p. 85.
AINS JUNGEN KNABEN: Maximilian I, *Der Weisskunig: Eine Erzehlung von den Thaten.* Facsimile of the 1775 edition (Weinheim, 1985), p. 218, n (a). "THE CHILD": PRO, E404/81/3, warrant of Dec. 6th, 1491. "IMP": *GC,* p. 285.
"BUTTERFLY": *HRHS,* p. 71; *The Book of Vices and Virtues (The King's Book),* EETS Old Series 217 (1942), p. 60.
HIS CLOTHES: *TA,* pp. 263 (Richard), 227 (James). NEW UNDERWEAR: p. 259.
COURTLY ABUSION: John Skelton, "Magnificence", ls. 835–41.
PHYSIOGNOMY, NESHNESS, ETC.: *Three Prose Versions of the Secreta secretorum,* ed. Robert Steele, EETS Extra Series 74 (1898), pp. 219–22, *passim;* Antonio Scaino da Salo, *Trattato del Giuoco della Palla,* tr. W. W. Kershaw (1951), pp. 194–95.
CURLS: Sebastian Brant, *The Ship of Fools,* tr. Edwin Zeydel (Columbia, 1944), pp. 68–69; *Vices & Virtues,* pp. 179–80.
"REALLY GOOD-LOOKING": Molinet, *Chroniques,* vol. 5, p. 15. ZENTIL: *I Diarii de M. S. Sanuto,* 54 vols. (Venice, 1879–1903), vol. 1, col. 842. *FORMA NON INELEGANTI: AH,* pp. 62–63; "OF VISAGE BEAUTIFUL": Edward Hall, *Chronicle, containing the History of England . . .* collated editions of 1548 and 1550 (1809), p. 462. BACON ON HIM: *Henry VII,* p. 133 and n.
LOUIS XI'S NOSE: Philippe de Commines, *Mémoires,* ed. Mlle. du Pont (Paris, 1847), vol. 3, *Preuves,* no. xxxiv, p. 340.
RICHMOND'S PERCEPTIONS: *CSPM,* pp. 323, 330. BACON'S: *Henry VII,* p. 192.
THE DISCOLOURED EYE: For medical opinions, see the correspondence between Marie Morris and Dr. Peter Watson in *The Ricardian Bulletin* (June 1994, p. 30, Sept. 1994, p. 43). Thanks to Bill Hampton for alerting me to this. I am also grateful for the opinion of Dr. Mohammed El-Ashry of Moorfields Hospital.
JUDGING BY EYES: *The Kalendar & Compost of Shepherds,* from Guy Marchant's original of 1493, ed. G. C. Heseltine (1930), p. 154; *Secreta,* pp. 230, 232–33. Guillaume Deguileville, *Le pélérinage de la vie humaine,* ed. J. J. Sturzinger (Roxburghe Club, 1893), p. xliv.

POLITICAL SIGNIFICANCE OF MISMATCHED EYES: See the Bishop of Lincoln's sermon in John Gough Nichols, *Grants, etc, from the Crown during the Reign of Edward V,* Camden Society (1854), pp. liv–lv.

"BONET ON SIDE": William Dunbar, "The Dance of the Sevin Deidly Synnis," ls. 16–17.

IMAGES IN MIRRORS: David Hockney, *Secret Knowledge* (2001), p. 72 and *passim*. COUN-TERFEITS IN THE GLASS: Brant, *Ship of Fools,* p. 58.

CAXTON/COUNTERFEIT: *Caxton's Eneydos of 1490,* ed. W. T. Cully & F. J. Furnivall, EETS Extra Series lvii (1890), pp. 49, 110.

COUNTERFEIT COUNTENANCE: Skelton, "Magnificence," esp. ls. 410–44. BARNYARD SHIT: "Against a Comely Coystrone," l. 10.

"SO COUNTERFEIT A MAJESTY": Hall, *Chronicle,* p. 462.

"HIS RIGHT CLEARNESS": *Vices & Virtues,* p. 80; Deguileville, *Pélérinage,* pp. vi, ix–x, 20.

ST. BERNARD ON THE SOUL: *The Tretyse of Love,* ed. John H. Fisher, EETS Original Series, 223, 1951 (for 1945), p. 8.

"FOR OF THE BODY": Deguileville, *Pélérinage,* p. xxvii.

"DEAR DARLING": Hall, *Chronicle,* p. 486.

PRESSURE OF TIME: *Stonor Letters & Papers,* ed. C. L. Kingsford, 2 vols., Camden Society 3rd Series, 30 (1919), *passim; The Chronicles of the White Rose of York* (1845), p. 208; Guillaume de Lorris and Jean de Meun, *The Romance of the Rose (Roman de la rose),* tr. Frances Horgan (Oxford, 1994), p. 8. Almost every Paston letter is also written "in haste".

1. Into Adventure

RICHARD PLANTAGENET'S STORY: See his letter to Isabella of Aug. 25th, 1493, BL MS Egerton 616/3; Frederick Madden, "Documents relating to Perkin Warbeck, with Remarks on his History", *Archaeologia,* vol. 27 (1838), App. II, pp. 199–200. REPEAT-ING THE STORY: *AH,* p. 65.

PIERS OSBECK'S CONFESSION: *LC,* pp. 219–22; *GC,* pp. 284–86; Hall, *Chronicle,* pp. 488–89. All quotations in this work are from the London Chronicle.

SETUBAL TESTIMONIES: See Appendix. See also *PI,* vol. 4, pp. 526–29. This full tran-scription of the Spanish State Papers is used in preference to Bergenroth's *CSPS,* though both are usually cited. Many thanks to C.S.L. Davies for alerting me to the Spanish version, and to the Setubal testimonies in particular.

IMPELLED HIM TO WANDER: *AH,* p. 63. "LAND-LOPER": Bacon, *Henry VII,* p. 133.

MANDEVILLE/*WANDERLUST: The Voiage and Travayle of Syr John Maundeville Knight* . . . ed. Jules Bramont (1928), pp. 142–43.

GALÉES VAGANS: Chastellain, "Le Temple de Bocace", *Oeuvres,* vol. 7, p. 92.

DEPRESSED BRUGES: *The Cely Papers: Selections from Correspondence and Memoranda of the Cely Family, Merchants of the Staple, 1475–88,* ed. H. E. Madden, Royal Historical Society III, 1 (1900), p. 171.

RICHMOND'S VOYAGE: James Gairdner, *Memorials of Henry VII*, Rolls Series 10 (1858), pp. 328–33.

ANDRÉ/BRAMPTON: Ibid., pp. 65, 72 ("a Jew called Edward").

"*ALIAS* OF PORTINGALE": *CPR HVII*, vol. 1, p. 274.

BRAMPTON'S CAREER: Cecil Roth, *Essays and Portraits in Anglo-Jewish History* (Philadelphia, 1962), pp. 69–81; Marques de São Paio, "A Portuguese Adventurer in the Wars of the Roses", tr. (in the Barton Library of the Richard III Society) from the *Anāis da Academia Portuguesa da Historia,* 2nd series, vol. 6 (Lisbon, 1955), pp. 4–8.

BRAMPTON'S MANORS: *CPR EIV/EV/RIII,* p. 416.

SERVICES UNSPECIFIED: Ibid., p. 366; *CCR EIV/EV/RIII,* pp. 312, 320. £100 A YEAR: Ibid., p. 370; *CPR EIV/EV/RIII,* p. 481.

FACILITATOR IN LISBON: Gairdner, *Memorials,* pp. 364–65.

BACK IN GRACE: *CPR HVII,* vol. 1, p. 274.

PERO VAZ'S FAMILY: Rui de Pina, *Crónica de el-Rei D. João II,* ed. Alberto Martins de Carvalho (Coimbra, 1950), p. 88 and n. xix (pp. 291–92).

DA CUNHAS JOUSTING: Gairdner, *Memorials,* pp. 346, 349.

MASTER ALVARO: *The Voyages of Cadamosto,* ed. R. Crone, Hakluyt Society, 2nd Series, lxxx (1937), p. 141.

"SARDINES": Elaine Sanceau, *The Perfect Prince: A Life of João II* (Porto, 1959), p. 274.

BISAGUDO/VISAGUDO: Garcia de Resende, *Crónica de D. João II e Miscêlanea,* ed. Joaquim Veríssimo Serrão (Lisbon, 1973), p. 354.

PERO VAZ'S POEM: "Vylancete de Pero Vaz" in Garcia de Resende, *Cancioneiro Geral,* f. 200f. Many thanks to Adelino Soares de Mello for his translation. "HOW TO SUCCEED": Ibid., f. 19f–20b. *NAM POSSO VYUER COMYGUO:* Ibid., ff. 109e, 211f.

THE MANY-BRANCHED TREE: Molinet, *Chroniques,* vol. 5, pp. 238–40.

ROUNDNESS OF THE WORLD: *Kalendar of Shepherds,* p. 119. FLY ON THE APPLE: *William Caxton's The Mirror of the World,* EETS Extra Series cx (1913), pp. 51–53.

LEONE'S TALE: *Le Historie della Vita e dei Fatti di Cristoforo Colombo, per D. Fernando Colombo suo figlio,* ed. Ronaldo Caddeo (Milan, 1930), pp. 68–69.

CANARIANS' SIGHTINGS: Washington Irving, *A History of the Life and Voyages of Christopher Columbus,* vol. 1 (1828), pp. 47–48.

MEN "WITH VERY BIG FACES": *Fernando Colombo,* p. 67. PIECES OF WOOD, HOLLOW CANES: Ibid., p. 66 and n.

COLUMBUS'S JOTTINGS: *Ymago Mundi de Pierre d'Ailly [avec] notes marginales de Christophe Colomb,* ed. Edmond Buron, 3 vols. (Paris, 1930), *passim,* esp. pp. 167–69, 207, 235.

BEHAIM'S GLOBE: Ian Arthurson, *The Perkin Warbeck Conspiracy* (Stroud, 1994), p. 38; E. G. Ravenstein, *Martin Behaim, his life and his globe* (1908), *passim.* Exact replicas of this globe are made by Greaves & Thomas of Richmond, Surrey.

BEHAIM/MAXIMILIAN: Sanceau, *Perfect Prince,* pp. 380–81.

"1,200 BRIDGES": Mandeville, *Voiage,* pp. 162–63. THE BEAST IN THE FRUIT: Ibid., p. 192.

THE GREAT WHITE KING: Sanceau, *Perfect Prince,* pp. 218, 225.

AENEAS IN THE UNDERWORLD: *Eneydos,* p. 120. DISBELIEVING IN MARVELS: *Mirror of the World,* pp. 50–51, 105.

"NO OTHER COUNTRY BUT SPAIN": Gairdner, *Memorials*, p. 255. "NO OTHER WORLD BUT ENGLAND": *A Relation, or rather a true account, of the Island of England . . .*, tr. Charlotte Augusta Sneyd, Camden Society 37 (1847), p. 35.

AZERBAIJAN: Mandeville, *Voiage*, p. 189.

COLUMBUS'S SOUTHERN BREAST: *Ymago Mundi*, pp. 167, 459–61. HIS DECEPTIONS: *The Voyages of Christopher Columbus, being the Journals of his First and Third, and the letters covering his first and last voyages*, tr. & ed. Cecil Jane (1930) pp. 139–46, *passim; CSPS*, p. 44.

TOURNAI'S EGYPTIANS: Amaury de la Grange, "Extraits analytiques des registres des Consaux de la ville de Tournai, 1431–1476", *Mémoires de la Société Historique et Littéraire de Tournai*, vol. 23 (Tournai, 1893), pp. 2, 97; H. Vandenbroeck, *Extraits analytiques des anciens registres de la ville de Tournai*, 1385–1422 (Tournai, 1861), vol. 1, pp. 236–38; vol. 2, pp. 376–77.

THE ELEPHANT: *Voyages of Cadamosto*, pp. 72–73.

DR. MÜNZER'S REPORT: [in Latin] "Itinerarium hispanicum Hieronymi Monetarii, 1494–1495", ed. Ludwig Pfandl, *Revue Hispanique*, vol. 48 (New York and Paris, 1920), pp. 50, 83–84, 87. [In Latin and Portuguese] Basílio de Vasconcelos, "Itinerário do Dr Jerónimo Münzer", part 1, *O Instituto*, vol. 80, no. 5 (Coimbra, 1930); part 2, ibid., vol. 83, no. 2 (1932), pp. 546, 554–56, 562. Many thanks to Adelino Soares de Mello for his labours in finding this.

APPROACHES TO THE GREAT KHAN: Mandeville, *Voiage*, pp. 196–97.

PRESTER JOHN: *Voyages of Cadamosto*, pp. 126–28; Mandeville, *Voiage*, pp. 195–98, 212–15. HIS DIPLOMACY: P. E. Russell, *Henry the Navigator: A Life* (2000), pp. 125–26.

BEMOY'S STORY: *Voyages of Cadamosto*, pp. 128–30; Resende, *Crónica*, pp. 112–18; Rui de Pina, *Crónica*, pp. 90–91, 93–96.

NOTIONS OF THE SENEGAL: *Voyages of Cadamosto*, pp. 138–39.

PERO VAZ'S EXPEDITION: Ibid., p. 141; Resende, *Crónica*, pp. 116–18; Rui de Pina, *Crónica*, pp. 95–96.

ROUTE TO THE SENEGAL: Duarte Pacheco Pereira, *Esmeraldo de situ orbis*, tr. & ed. George H. T. Kimble, Hakluyt Society, 2nd Series, no. 79 (1937), pp. 68–82.

CONGO EXPLORERS: Ravenstein, *Behaim*, pp. 22–23.

WORM-EATEN SHIPS: Münzer, *Itinerário*, part 2, p. 155. CLOTH PUTREFYING: Ibid., p. 157.

SUN-HAT AND GLOVES: Resende, *Crónica*, p. 267.

FERDINAND AND ISABELLA'S RECOMMENDATION: *CSPS*, p. 92; *PI*, vol. 4, p. 522. For the afterthought, see AGS Patronato Real, leg. 52 f.

RESENDE/DE SOUSA: *Crónica*, pp. 42, 248. DE SOUSA AT TORDESILLAS: Geronymo Zurita, *Historia del Rey Don Hernando el Catholico*, vol. 5 (Saragossa, 1610), ff. 35v–37r. IN ENGLAND: Rui de Pina, *Crónica*, p. 22.

THE *RAINHA*: Münzer, *Itinerário*, part 1, pp. 552, 558–59.

RICH GERMANS: Ibid., part 1, p. 564.

"LIKE AN ENGLISH CHILD": Sanceau, *Perfect Prince*, p. 172.

DE SOUSA AND HIS NEPHEW: Resende, *Cancioneiro*, ff. 159e, 160e.

SUMPTUARY LAWS: Rui de Pina, *Crónica*, pp. 72–73, 116–17; Sanceau, *Perfect Prince*, pp. 278, 321–22.

DE SOUSA AS PLAY-MAKER: Resende, *Cancioneiro*, f. 36b; *Crónica*, p. 187.

WOODVILLE IN LISBON: Rui de Pina, *Crónica*, pp. 70–71; Sanceau, *Perfect Prince*, pp. 296–97. BRAMPTON/WOODVILLE: Nichols, *Grants of Edward V*, pp. 105, 107.

HENRY'S PAYMENT TO HIM: PRO E 405/76, mem. 2v. TO THE SCOTSMAN: PRO E 404/80/80. PAYMENTS FOR OTHER TRIPS TO PORTUGAL: E 404/80/71, 80; Rev. William Campbell, *Materials for a History of the Reign of Henry VII*, 2 vols. (1877), vol. 2, pp. 44, 346.

VISITS OF PORTUGUESE MESSENGERS AND AMBASSADORS: PRO E 404/80/73, 80, 333, 345; E 405/78, mem. 23r.

RICHMOND'S AUGUST TRIP: PRO E 404/80/37. HIS LATER ONE: James Gairdner, *Memorials of Henry VII*, Rolls Series 10 (1858), pp. 328, 356–64.

CARLISLE HERALD: PRO E 36/130, mem. 46v.

DE SOUSA AT BEJA: Gairdner, *Memorials*, pp. 360–61.

BEHAIM AS EMISSARY: Ravenstein, *Behaim*, pp. 43–45 and App. x, p. 113.

FOGAÇA'S QUESTIONS: Resende, *Cancioneiro*, f. 89d.

BRANCA ROSA: Resende, *Miscélanea*, p. 354.

THE DREAM SHIPS: Rui de Pina, *Crónica*, pp. 128–29; A. H. de Oliveira Marques, *Daily Life in Portugal in the Late Middle Ages*, tr. S. S. Wyatt (Madison, 1971), pp. 264–65. Thanks to Ian Arthurson for alerting me to this work.

LETTERS TO DESMOND AND KILDARE: Bacon, *Henry VII*, p. 137; Sir James Ware, *The Antiquities and History of Ireland* (1654, printed 1705), p. 22.

THE ELDER DUKE OF YORK IN IRELAND: See D. B. Quinn in *A New History of Ireland II, Medieval Ireland, 1169–1534*, ed. Art Cosgrave, pp. 564–66; Agnes Conway, *Henry VII's Relations with Scotland and Ireland, 1485–1498* (Cambridge, 1932), pp. 133–34.

MENO'S BUSINESS: *CPR HVII*, vol. 2, p. 84.

FRENCH VERSION OF THE CONFESSION: CC 111, f. 188r, v.

"GALA CLOTHES": *A Journal of the first Voyage of Vasco da Gama, 1497–1499*, ed. E. G. Ravenstein, Hakluyt Society (1898), p. 5.

LANCELOT'S QUEST: Thomas Malory, *Morte Darthur* (Oxford, 1996), p. 371. WHITE HART AND HOUNDS: Ibid., pp. 54–55. ARTHUR'S FIRST ADVENTURE: Ibid., pp. 6–12.

GREEN AND RED CLOTH: e.g. PRO E 404/81/3, warrant of December 8th, 1491; Conway, *Relations*, pp. 51, 244.

SILK IN THE ROYAL WARDROBE: Nicholas Harris Nicolas, *Privy Purse Expenses of Elizabeth of York and Wardrobe Accounts of Edward the Fourth* (1830), *passim*.

TRISTAN IN CORNWALL: Gottfried von Strassburg, *Tristan*, tr. A. T. Hatto (Harmondsworth, 1967), esp. pp. 71, 74–77, 82–83, 97.

THE FALSE BALDWIN: L'Abbé A. J. Namèche, *Cours d'Histoire Nationale*, part 1, vol. 2 (Louvain, 1853), pp. 429–34.

2. Imagined Princes

IMAGINATION: See esp. Gianfrancesco Pico della Mirandola, *On the Imagination* (1500), tr. & ed. Harry Caplan. Cornell Studies in English, xvi (Yale, 1930), esp. pp. 31–33, 51. SPIDERS' WEBS: *Secreta*, p. 98.

RICHARD'S BIRTHDAY: Cora Scofield, *The Life and Reign of Edward IV*, 2 vols. (1923), vol. 2, p. 60 and n.

THE CRADLE: John Leland, *De Rebus Britannicis Collectanea*, 6 vols. (1774), vol. 4, p. 183; Kay Stanisland, "Royal Entry into the World", in *England in the Fifteenth Century*, Proceedings of the Harlaxton Symposium, 1986, ed. Daniel Williams (1987), p. 310.

THE NURSE: Nicolas, *Privy Purse*, p. 75.

BAPTISM: Leland, *Collectanea*, vol. 4, pp. 180-81; Stanisland, "Royal Entry", pp. 302-4.

JOHN GILES: *CPR EIV/EV/RIII*, p. 592; *CCR EIV/EV/RIII*, p. 1.

RICHARD'S ROOMS AND SERVANTS: Scofield, *Edward IV*, vol. 2, p. 204; Gairdner, *Richard III*, p. 341; Michael Hicks, "The Changing Role of the Wydevilles in Yorkist Politics to 1483", in *Patronage, Pedigree and Power in Later Medieval England*, ed. Charles Ross (Gloucester, 1979), p. 79.

FIREWOOD: *The Household of Edward IV: The Black Book and Ordinance of 1478*, ed. A. R. Myers (Manchester, 1959), pp. 223 and 268n.

EDWARD IV'S RULES: *Letters of the Kings of England*, ed. James Orchard Halliwell Phillipps, 2 vols. (1846), vol. 1, pp. 136-43.

ARMS AND FLOWERS: BL MS Royal 14 E 1, 14 E VI, 14 E II (5), etc.; Janet Backhouse, "Founders of the Royal Library: Edward IV and Henry VII as collectors of illuminated manuscripts", in *England in the Fifteenth Century* (Harlaxton), p. 39.

"MOST SKILFUL": John Rous, *Historia regum Angliae*, ed. T. Hearne (Oxford, 1745), p. 212; see also Dominic Mancini, *The Usurpation of Richard III*, tr. C.A.J. Armstrong (1936), p. 115.

"MOST SWEET AND BEAUTIFUL CHILDREN": *Ingulph's Chronicle of the Abbey of Croyland*, tr. & ed. Henry T. Riley (1908), p. 482.

PRINCELY EXERCISES: *Game and Playe of the Chesse, 1474: Cassoles, tr. Ferron, tr. & printed Caxton*, British Chess Magazine Classic Reprints (1968), p. 33; Mancini, *Usurpation*, p. 85.

EDWARD IV TO HIS FATHER: *EH*, pp. 8-9 (1454).

THE TWO SONS: *Secreta*, pp. 99-100. EDWARD'S COPY: Scofield, *Edward IV*, vol. 2, p. 453.

"GLORY GLIDING AWAY": Campbell, *Materials*, vol. 2, p. 58.

RICHARD'S INVESTITURE: *EH*, pp. 242-43; *CCR EIV*, p. 9. EARL MARSHAL: *CPR EIV/EV/RIII*, pp. 75, 358. LIEUTENANT OF IRELAND: Ibid., p. 153 (and see p. 118).

WITNESSING ACTS: Ibid., pp. 108, 230.

GARTER REGALIA: Nicolas, *Privy Purse*, pp. 136, 161.

EXTRA TITLES: *CPR EIV/EV/RIII*, p. 15; *CCR EIV*, mem. 1071; PRO C53/197, mem. 11.

PRE-CONTRACTING CHILDREN: Thomas Rymer, *Foedera, conventiones, literae ... & acta publica inter reges Angliae et alios ...*, 20 vols. (1704-32), vol. 12, pp. 110, 128-29, 147. "NUBILE YEARS": Ibid., pp. 142-45.

"HIGH AND MIGHTY": *Rot. Parl.*, vol. 6, pp. 168-70.

MARRIAGE JOUSTS: BL MS Harley 69, ff. 1r-2r. THE MARRIAGE ITSELF: W. H. Black, *The Wedding of Anne Mowbray and Richard Duke of York* (Roxburghe Club, 1840), pp. 27-40.

HENRY, DUKE OF YORK: *L&P*, vol. 1, pp. 392–93; *The Paston Letters, 1422–1509*, ed. James Gairdner, 6 vols. (1904), vol. 6, no. 1058.

"HEIRS OF HIS BODY": *Rot. Parl.*, vol. 6, p. 206.

A PRAYER OF THE PRIMER: *Horae Eboracenses, The Prymer or Hours of the Blessed Virgin Mary . . . with other devotions*, ed. Canon Wordsworth, Surtees Society, vol. 132 (1920 for 1919), p. 73. Henry VII said he had recited this prayer from childhood: *The Will of Henry VII*, printed by T. Payne (1775), p. 2.

ANNE MOWBRAY'S DEATH: Scofield, *Edward IV*, vol. 2, pp. 322–23. LANDS PASSING TO RICHARD: *Rot. Parl.*, vol. 6, p. 206.

RICHARD'S FRAILTY: Thomas More, *The History of King Richard the Third* (with Grafton's continuation), ed. S. W. Singer (1821), pp. 51–52, 53. ANOTHER TWELVE YEARS: *CPR EIV/EV/RIII*, p. 210.

THE LITTLE LIEUTENANT: Nicolas, *Privy Purse*, pp. 155, 156, 160.

EDWARD'S DOCTORS: Myers, *Household*, p. 76. HIS ILLNESS: Scofield, *Edward IV*, vol. 2, p. 365; Commines, *Mémoires*, book 6, ch. viii; Mancini, *Usurpation*, pp. 71–73.

EDWARD'S BURIAL: *L&P*, vol. 1, pp. 3–10. THE COAT OF MAIL: Scofield, *Edward IV*, vol. 2, pp. 367–68n.

EDWARD'S WILL: *EH*, p. 371. See also, on plans for Richard, Mancini, *Usurpation*, p. 73.

RUSSELL'S SPEECH: Nichols, *Grants of Edward V*, p. xlvi.

CORONATION DATE: *Croyland*, p. 486; Mancini, *Usurpation*, n. 70.

PREPARATIONS FOR ROBES: Gairdner, *Richard III*, pp. 101–2; Doctor Milles, "Observations on the Wardrobe Accounts for 1483", *Archaeologia*, vol. 1 (1779), p. 368.

EDWARD'S LETTERS: Rymer, *Foedera*, vol. 12, pp. 185–86.

RICHARD'S ROLE: Mancini, *Usurpation*, p. 109; Molinet, *Chroniques*, vol. 4, pp. 401–2.

ELIZABETH'S PANIC, RICHARD'S EXTRACTION: More, *Richard III*, pp. 30, 50–63.

THE HOWARDS' BARGES: Mancini, *Usurpation*, p. 150 and n. 72. THAMES COVERED WITH BOATS: More, *Richard III*, p. 31.

"THOUSANDS" OF ARMED MEN: Letter of Simon Stallworth to Sir William Stonor, *EH*, pp. 16–17; *Stonor Letters*, pp. 159–60. For the sense of panic, see also the note in *Cely Papers*, no. 114 (pp. 132–33).

"MERRY": *Stonor Letters*, p. 160.

EDWARD'S MISERY: Mancini, *Usurpation*, pp. 113–15; More, *Richard III*, p. 130; Molinet, *Chroniques*, vol. 4, pp. 401–3.

"SHOOTING AND PLAYING": *GC*, p. 209.

YORKIST BOWS AND ARROWS: "Narratives of the arrival of Louis de Bruges, Seigneur de la Gruthuyse, in England, and of his Creation as Earl of Winchester, in 1472." Letter from Frederick Madden to Hudson Gurney in *Archaeologia*, vol. xxvi (1836), p. 278.

DR. SHAW'S SERMON: Gairdner, *Richard III*, p. 79.

ARGUMENTS ENSHRINED IN LAW: *Rot. Parl.*, vol. 6, pp. 240–42. For a discussion of Dr. Shaw's arguments, see R. H. Hemholz, "The Sons of Edward IV: A canonical assessment of the claim that they were illegitimate", in *Richard III: Loyalty, Lordship and Law*, ed. P. W. Hammond (1986), pp. 91–103; Scofield, *Edward IV*, vol. 2, pp. 212–13.

EDWARD IV A BASTARD: See Clarence's attainder, *Rot. Parl.*, vol. 6, p. 194; Mancini, *Usurpation*, p. 75 and n. 12; Commines, *Mémoires*, book 4, ch. viii.

TRANSFER OF RICHARD'S TITLES: *CPR EIV/EV/RIII*, pp. 358, 363, 388, 403; *CCR EIV/EV/RIII*, p. 317; Rymer, *Foedera*, vol. 12, p. 190. "EDWARD THE BASTARD": *CPR EIV/EV/RIII*, pp. 375, 495. Thanks to Peter Hammond for help with the legalities at this point.

GALMOLE'S NEW POST: *CPR EIV/EV/RIII*, p. 461.

THE CHANTRY'S PRAYERS: Ibid., p. 259.

NORFOLK AT THE CORONATION: *EH*, p. 380. ROBES ALTERED: Milles, "Wardrobe Accounts," p. 368.

DAY BY DAY "MORE RARELY": Mancini, *Usurpation*, p. 113.

RICHARD'S DEATH: *CPR HVII*, vol. 1, p. 308. PROVISION FOR IT: *CCR EIV/EV/RIII*, p. 171 (1479).

1485 ACT OF ATTAINDER: P. W. Hammond & W. J. White, "The Sons of Edward IV: A re-examination of the evidence on their deaths and on the bones in Westminster Abbey", in *Loyalty, Lordship and Law*, p. 109.

THE PRINCES IN THE TOWER: The best modern account of the controversy is A. J. Pollard, *Richard III and the Princes in the Tower* (Stroud, 1991). See also Hammond & White, "Sons of Edward IV", esp. pp. 104–12.

MEN BREAKING INTO TEARS: Mancini, *Usurpation*, p. 115.

THE CHANCELLOR OF FRANCE: *L&P*, vol. 1, p. xxv.

"SOME UNKNOWN MANNER": *Croyland*, p. 491.

BRISTOL RUMOURS: Robert Ricart, *The Maire of Bristowe is Kalendar*, ed. Lucy Toulmin Smith, Camden Society 230 (1872), p. 46.

CASTILIAN VISITOR: Anthony Goodman & Angus Mackay, "A Castilian Report on English Affairs, 1486", *EHR*, vol. 88 (1973), p. 92 and n.

FRENCH RUMOUR: Hammond & White, "Sons of Edward IV", p. 108. RUI DE SOUSA: *PI*, vol. 4, p. 526. FABYAN'S THEORIES: *GC*, pp. 209, 212, 213; Gairdner, *Richard III*, pp. 118–28.

"EVERYONE" THOUGHT SO: Letter of August 25th, 1493 in BN Fonds Espagnol 318, f. 83; A. Morel-Fatio, "Marguerite d'York et Perkin Warbeck", *Mélanges d'histoire offerts à Charles Bemont* (Paris, 1913), p. 414. Thanks to Christine Weightman for this reference.

BRAMPTON'S OPINIONS: *PI*, vol. 4, p. 527.

BUCKINGHAM HINTS: *Croyland*, p. 487; Molinet, *Chroniques*, vol. 2, p. 403; Richard Firth Green, "Historical Notes of a London Citizen, 1483–1488", *EHR*, vol. 96 (1981), p. 588; Commines, *Mémoires*, book 6, ch. viii; *L&P*, vol. 2, pp. xv–xvi. REBELLIONS: *Croyland*, pp. 490–91.

THE BONES: For the original report of the forensic evidence, see Lawrence Turner & Professor Wright, *Archaeologia* lxxxiv (1934), pp. 1–26. The fullest analysis of these findings is by Hammond & White, "Sons of Edward IV", pp. 112–47.

RICHARD'S NEW APPOINTMENTS: *CPR EIV/EV/RIII*, pp. 484, 514. HIS WARRANT: Pamela Tudor-Craig, *Richard III* (catalogue of the National Portrait Gallery exhibition, 1973), pp. 54–55, 98.

CONSPIRACY TO FREE THE PRINCES: Michael Hicks, "Unweaving the Web: The plot of July 1483 against Richard III and its wider significance", *The Ricardian*, vol. xi, no. 114 (1991), pp. 106–9.

BRACKENBURY'S APPOINTMENT: Rymer, *Foedera*, vol. 12, p. 219.

"FALSE AND CONTRIVED INVENTIONS": Hammond & White, "Sons of Edward IV", p. 108.

VON POPPLAU: Livia Visser-Fuchs, review of *Reisenbeschreibung Niclas von Popplau*, *The Ricardian*, vol. xi, no. 145 (1999), p. 529.

TYRELL'S REWARD: Rosemary Horrox & P. W. Hammond, eds., *British Library Harleian Manuscript 433*, 4 vols. (Richard III Society, 1979-83), vol. 3, nos. 2050, 2063. The services in Flanders (2050) and the reward are not explicitly connected, but the entries for both are in mid-January 1484.

WARWICK RUMOURS: Scofield, *Edward IV*, vol. 2, p. 8.

BAYARD: Skelton, "Philip Sparrow", ls. 655-59.

"SOME SECRET LAND": *AH*, p. 13 n.

ELIZABETH WOODVILLE'S "ACCOMMODATION": Pollard, *Princes*, pp. 132-33, though he suggests that this was an "insurance policy" and proves that Elizabeth thought her sons were dead.

HER SMUGGLING OF RICHARD: More, *Richard III*, pp. 42-43, 49-50, 60.

TROOPS ROUND THE SANCTUARY: *L&P*, vol. 2, p. xv.

1490 RUMOURS: *GC*, p. 244.

"GOD'S MIGHT": In his proclamation of September 1496: BL MS Harleian 283, f. 123r; Bacon, *Henry VII* (in Spedding's edition), App. II, p. 252.

STANDARDS: *CSPM*, p. 326.

PARRON'S MOCKERY: C.A.J. Armstrong, "An Italian Astrologer at the Court of Henry VII", in *England, France and Burgundy in the Fifteenth Century* (1983), p. 174; William Parron, *Anni MD pronosticon* (Bodleian, Oxford), sig. b, ir.

CHARLES THE BOLD: Georges Chastellain & Jean Molinet, *Recollection des merveilleuses advenues en nostre temps*, in M. de Barante, *Ducs de Bourgogne*, vol. 10, no. lxxix, p. 195.

PROPHECIES OF RICHARD: Gairdner, *Memorials*, p. 66; *Three Books of Polydore Vergil's English History*, ed. Henry Ellis (Camden Society, 1844), p. 167.

WARD'S LATER PROPHECIES: See pp. 480-81 and 482 of this book.

YORKIST PROPHECIES: Alison Allan, "Yorkist Propaganda: pedigree, prophecy and the 'British History' in the reign of Edward IV", in Ross, *Patronage*, pp. 182-84.

THE DEAD MAN: Arthurson, *Perkin Warbeck*, p. 61; C. W. Previté-Orton, "An Elizabethan Prophecy", *History*, vol. 2, Apr. 1917-Jan. 1918, pp. 210-11.

FILZ D'ANGLETERRE: de Barante, *Ducs de Bourgogne*, vol. 10, no. cxxiii, p. 218.

"FIRST MOVER": BL MS Add 46435, f. 137r.

EL PRIMER INVENTOR: Zurita, *Historia* (see Notes, p. 536), vol. 5, p. 170.

TAYLOR THE ELDER'S CAPTURE: *CSPV*, p. 285.

THE "STRANGE CHILD": *Rot. Parl.*, vol. 6, p. 194.

TAYLOR THE ELDER'S JOBS: *CPR EIV/EV/RIII*, pp. 129, 521.

TAYLOR THE YOUNGER'S CAREER: Ibid., pp. 236, 261, 355, 544; *CPR HVII*, vol. 1, p. 258; Campbell, *Materials*, vol. 1, pp. 200-201.

WARWICK WITH HENRY'S MOTHER: PRO E 404/79/337 (warrant of Feb. 24th); Campbell, *Materials*, vol. 1, p. 311.

HIS SHOES: Nicolas, *Privy Purse*, pp. 157, 158-59.

A GOOSE FROM A CAPON: *AH,* p. 115 n.

1499 SIGHTINGS: See Ch. 9, *passim,* and notes.

RUMOURS AFTER BOSWORTH: "A Castilian Report" (see Notes, p. 540), pp. 93, 96–97.

SPIES IN THE PORTS: Campbell, *Materials,* vol. 1, pp. 29–31.

STAFFORD'S PLOT: C. H. Williams, "The Rebellion of Humphrey Stafford in 1486", *EHR* xliii (1928), pp. 181–89.

SIMNEL: Michael J. Bennett, *Lambert Simnel and the Battle of Stoke* (Gloucester, 1987). Gordon Smith in *The Ricardian,* vol. x, no. 135 (Dec. 1996), pp. 498–536, argues— ingeniously, but on slender evidence—that the boy in Dublin may have been Edward V, and Simnel a substitute.

MAKE A PRIEST OF HIM: *CSPM,* p. 325.

WARWICK IN ST. PAUL'S: *AH,* p. 19. THE SECOND DISPLAY: "Notes of a London Citizen" (see Notes, p. 540), p. 589.

MOLINET ON WARWICK AND YORK: *Chroniques,* vol. 3, pp. 152–56.

HENRY ON LINCOLN: *AH,* pp. 26–27. "COMPASSINGS, CONSPIRACIES": J. R. Lander, *Government and Community, England 1450–1509* (1980), p. 334.

HENRY TO THE POPE: *CSPV,* p. 165.

IRISH OATHS OF ALLEGIANCE: *CPR HVII,* vol. 1, p. 225.

ACTIONS AGAINST ELIZABETH WOODVILLE: PRO E 404/78/179; Campbell, *Materials,* vol. 2, p. 148. SHE WAS PAID AN ANNUITY INSTEAD: PRO E 405/78, mem. 4r; E 404/79/130; Campbell, *Materials,* vol. 2, pp. 225, 379.

REVERSAL OF THE BASTARDISATION: *Rot. Parl.,* vol. 6, p. 289; Campbell, *Materials,* vol. 1, pp. 122–23.

"CONTRIVED AND FORGED TALES": *L&P,* vol. 2, App. IV (1486); *CPR HVII,* vol. 1, p. 108.

THE NORTHERN REBELLION: Michael J. Bennett, "Henry VII and the Northern Rising of 1489", *EHR* no. 105 (1990), pp. 34–55.

CHAMBERLAIN'S PLOT: *Rot. Parl.,* p. 455; *GC,* p. 244; *LC,* p. 195. HIS LOYALTY: *CCR EIV/EV/RIII,* p. 401; *CPR HVII,* vol. 1, pp. 104, 106.

BISHOP OF DURHAM: Barrie Williams, "Richard III's Other Palatinate: John Shirwood, Bishop of Durham", *The Ricardian,* vol. ix, no. 115 (Dec. 1991), pp. 166–69.

HENRY'S LETTER: *L&P,* vol. 1, pp. 98–99.

CHAMBERLAIN'S EXTRACTION: PRO E 404/80/373. PARDONS OF HIS SONS: *CPR HVII,* vol. 1, p. 345.

THE DUKE OF YORK RUMOUR: *GC,* p. 244 (a marginalium adds "*Initium Perkin*"); Ware, *Antiquities,* p. 16; Samuel de Carteret, *Chronique* (1585), in George Syvret, *Chroniques des îles de Jersey, Guernsey, Auregny et Sark* (Guernsey, 1832), p. 23. Thanks to C.S.L. Davies for this reference.

RAISED FROM THE DEAD: *AH,* p. 57.

MARGARET'S DUTIES: Christine Weightman, *Margaret of York, Duchess of Burgundy 1446–1503* (Gloucester, 1989), esp. chs. 3–5, *passim.*

"FALLEN FROM THE ROYAL SUMMIT": BN Fonds Espagnol 318, f. 83; Morel-Fatio, "Marguerite d'York" (see Notes, p. 540), p. 415.

JUNO AND AENEAS: *HRHS,* esp. pp. 65–69, 309, 315–21.

"SPITE NEVER DIES": Ibid., p. 65. VERGIL'S SIMILAR THOUGHT: *AH,* p. 17.

"MADE A MAN": *AH*, p. 62 n. "PRETTY PERKIN": Hall, *Chronicle*, p. 466. "IDEALLY SHAPED": Weightman, *Margaret of York*, pp. 64–65 and n.

RARELY TOGETHER: Herman Vander Linden, *Itinéraires de Charles Duc de Bourgogne, Marguerite d'York et Marie de Bourgogne (1467–1477)*, Académie Royale de Belgique: Commission Royale d'Histoire (Brussels, 1936), pp. 49–58. SURPRISE SUPPER: ADN inv. S. 51, B3434.

CHARLES'S WARS: Commines, *Mémoires*, book 5, ch. ix.

MARGARET'S PRAYERS: Weightman, *Margaret of York*, p. 65; Wim Blockmans, "The Devotions of a Lonely Duchess" in *Margaret of York, Simon Marmion and the Visions of Tondal* (Malibu, Calif., 1992), pp. 29–46.

ST. JOSSE-TEN-NOODE: Ibid., pp. 49–50; Weightman, *Margaret of York*, p. 65. Thanks to Christine Weightman for extra information about this palace. SIR JOHN PASTON'S REPORT: *Paston Letters*, vol. 4, no. 826 (February 3rd, 1473).

FRENCH RUMOURS: *CSPM*, p. 124 and n.

PHILIP'S CHRISTENING: Weightman, *Margaret of York*, pp. 131–32.

THE MALINES RECEIVER'S CHILD: AN CC11613, 18th register, f. 11v.

MARGARET/CHARLES V: Luc Hommel, *Marguerite d'York ou la duchesse Junon* (Paris, 1960), pp. 303, 333.

MARGARET'S ROLE: *AH*, p. 63; *HRHS*, p. 68.

THE SNOW-CHILD: *Les cent nouvelles nouvelles*, ed. Le Roux de Lincy (Paris, 1841), pp. 152–57.

FRION: C.S.L. Davies & Mark Ballard, "Etienne Frion: Burgundian Agent, English Royal Secretary and 'Principal Counsellor' to Perkin Warbeck", *Bulletin of the Institute of Historical Research*, vol. lxii (1989), *passim; HRHS*, p. 65; *CPR HVII*, vol. 1, pp. 17, 118; Rymer, *Foedera*, vol. xii, p. 347. HIS COMPLAINT: Campbell, *Materials*, vol. 2, p. 60.

ANDRÉ ON CO-PLOTTERS: *HRHS*, pp. 65–66. THE BOY TRAINED IN ENGLAND: Ibid., p. 72. FRION AS AGENT: Davies & Ballard, "Frion", pp. 257–58.

FRION'S DEPARTURE: Campbell, *Materials*, vol. 2, p. 505; *CSPV*, p. 183.

CHARLES VIII/JAMES IV: John Lesley, *The History of Scotland from the death of King James I . . . to the year [1561]* (Edinburgh, 1830), p. 63.

MARGARET TO THE POPE: *L&P*, vol. 1, App. A, p. 396. JOASH: II Kings, Ch. 11, vv. 1–4.

MOLINET ON MARGARET'S NEPHEWS: de Barante, *Ducs de Bourgogne*, vol. 10, no. cxiii, pp. 213–14.

"THE SON OF CLARENCE": Weightman, *Margaret of York*, p. 158.

MARGARET/BRAMPTON: Davies & Ballard, "Frion", p. 255.

CHARLES THE BOLD/PORTUGAL: Chastellain, *Chronique, 1464, 1466–68, 1470*, in *Oeuvres*, vol. 5, p. 453.

DELEGATION TO SCOTLAND: *RMS*, nos. 1738, 1798. The entries for James's reign start at no. 1731, and no. 1738 is the first use of the great seal other than for appointments of his officers. See also Patrick Fraser Tytler, *History of Scotland* (Edinburgh, 1831), vol. 4, pp. 371–72.

THE LETTER TO JAMES: *TA*, p. 99.

THE ENGLISH HERALD: Ibid., p. 130.

ROBINSON: Bennett, *Lambert Simnel*, pp. 103, 108, 125.

ACTIVELY SPREADING THE RUMOUR: Bacon, *Henry VII*, p. 132.

SECRET RYE SHIPMENTS: Blockmans, "Devotions", pp. 34–35; AN CC 11613, 19th register, f. 15v.

HENRY'S WAR PREPARATIONS: *CPR HVII*, vol. 1, p. 253 (and see pp. 369, 393–96); PRO E 404/79 and /80, *passim*.

CHARLES/SCOTLAND: Arthurson, *Perkin Warbeck*, p. 13; Alfred Spont, "La Marine Française sous Charles VIII", *Revue des questions historiques*, no. 55 (1894), pp. 419–20.

MONSIEUR GEORGE D'ANNEBAR: BN Français 32511, f. 413v.

SEPTEMBER EXPEDITION: Arthurson, *Perkin Warbeck*, pp. 15–22; Spont, "Marine", pp. 418–19.

HAYES'S JOBS: *CPR EIV/EV/RIII*, p. 134; *CPR HVII*, vol. 1, pp. 21, 45; Campbell, *Materials*, vol. 1, pp. 400, 445, 459. HIS CONTACTS: Arthurson, *Perkin Warbeck*, p. 16.

TAYLOR TO HAYES: A. F. Pollard, *The Reign of Henry VII from Contemporary Sources: vol. 1, Narrative Extracts* (1913), pp. 82–83; *Rot. Parl.*, vol. 6, pp. 454–55.

JOHN OF GLOUCESTER: Campbell, *Materials*, p. 328.

HENRY ON THE ABUSION: Halliwell, *Letters*, vol. 1, p. 172; BL MS Add. 46454, f. 6r.

"MULTIPLYING": *EH*, p. 122. For other odd doings, probably alchemical, see Ibid., pp. 117, 118, 120.

TREATISE ON ALCHEMY: MS Selden Supra 77, ff. 1r–123r, esp. 16r–21r.

KILDARE TO ORMOND: *L&P*, vol. 2, pp. 55–56. "G. E. OF K": Ibid.; Conway, *Relations*, p. 44.

EGGS IN KENT: Caxton, *Eneydos*, p. 2.

THE DUMB WOMAN: John Pinkerton, *The History of Scotland from the Accession of the House of Stuart to that of Mary*, 2 vols. (1797), p. 25.

LONG WORDS: Stephen Hawes, *The Pastime of Pleasure*, Percy Society 60 (1845), *passim*; R. T. Davies, *Medieval English Lyrics* (1963), no. 104.

A PAGE'S MANNERS: *Caxton's Book of Courtesy, The Babees Book*, etc., ed. F. J. Furnivall, EETS Extra Series iii (1868), *passim*.

LOUIS XI'S *VARLET*: Commines, *Mémoires*, book 4, ch. vii.

KILDARE'S BAD BEHAVIOUR: *Calendar of the Carew Manuscripts . . .* , ed. J. S. Brewer & William Bullen (1871), vol. 5, *Book of Howth*, pp. 179–80.

DESMOND'S CLOTHES: *L&P*, vol. 1, pp. 69, 73–74. For the wildness of Irish manners even within the Pale, see *Analecta Hibernica* no. 10 (July 1941), pp. 96–97.

"THEY CALLED HIM RICHARD": Zurita, *Historia*, vol. 5, p. 20.

"HOW VERY PLEASING": Quintin Poulet, *L'imaginacion de vraye noblesse* (1496), BL Royal 19 CVIII, f. 17v (pencil foliation).

PRINCES ENTERING TOWNS: See e.g. Commines, *Mémoires*, book 4, ch. vi.

DESMOND'S OATH: Conway, *Relations*, p. 223.

HENRY'S WHITE ARMOUR: BL MS Add. 7079, f. 5r.

MENO CONVEYING HIM: PRO E 404/81/3, warrant of Dec. 6th, 1491.

ARRIVING AS RICHARD: Ware, *Antiquities*, p. 22.

"OBLIGED ALMOST TO FORGET MYSELF": *AH*, pp. 84–85. PROMPTING: Ibid., p. 85n.

THOMAS LANGFORD: Campbell, *Materials*, vol. 1, p. 307.

THE EFFORT OF REMEMBERING: *The Cordyal, tr. Anthony Woodville, Earl Rivers*, ed. Dr. J. A. Mulders (Nijmegen, n.d.), pp. 1–6; More/Grafton, *Richard III*, pp. 159, 221; François Villon, "Le Lais", xxxvi; Dunbar, "On his heid-ake," ls. 8–10.

PRINTING ON THE HEART: *Vices & Virtues* (see Notes, p. 531), p. 40; Eric Jager, *The Book of the Heart* (Chicago, 2000), ch. 3 and *passim*.

HENRY TO FERDINAND: *CSPS*, p. 353.

"PHILIP SPARROW": esp. ls. 210–26.

MEMORY AND IMAGINATION: Pico della Mirandola, *Imagination*, pp. 34–35, n. 6.

CHASTELLAIN DREAMING: "Le temple de Bocace", in *Oeuvres*, vol. 7, pp. 76–77.

IMAGES OF HELL: Rivers, *Cordyal*, p. 6.

ANDRÉ ON DETAILS: *HRHS*, p. 66. "A CHILD OF THE HOUSE OF YORK": *AH*, p. 63.

BLUEMANTLE'S REPORT: See Notes, p. 539 ("Yorkist bows and arrows").

THE GOLD VIRGIN: Scofield, *Edward IV*, vol. 1, p. 483; PRO E 404/76/4/130.

THE LION: Ibid., 16. BEDROOM TAPESTRIES: PRO E 404/76/5/49.

RIVERS AS ST. ANTHONY: Black, *Wedding* (see Notes, p. 538), p. 33.

TAYLOR'S DUTIES: Myers, *Household*, p. 117.

CHARLES'S NIGHT THOUGHTS: Commines, *Mémoires*, book 2, ch. ix.

FAULTS OF HOUNDS: Myers, *Household*, p. 121.

FRION'S LETTER: Davies & Ballard, "Frion", pp. 258–59.

ANDRÉ ON THE BOY'S MEMORIES: *HRHS*, p. 72.

BRAMPTON'S STORIES: Roth, *Portraits*, pp. 69–83, *passim;* Marques de São Paio, "Brandão", pp. 6–9.

BLACK VELVET, ETC.: PRO E 404/76/4, nos. 39, 101, 107, 130.

TECHNIQUES OF IMAGINING: Pseudo-Bonaventure, *The Mirror of the Blessed Life of Jesu Christ*, tr. Nicholas Love, ed. L. F. Powell (Oxford, 1908), esp. pp. 12, 24, 93, 101, 154, 200, 271–78, 256.

LETTER TO ISABELLA: See Notes, p. 534.

LETTER TO SCOTLAND: *TA*, p. 199.

RICHARD'S AGE: *GC*, p. 206; Mancini, *Usurpation*, p. 97.

THE STORY IN EUROPE: P. W. Hammond & Maaike Lulofs, "Richard III: Dutch Sources", *The Ricardian*, vol. iii, no. 46 (1974), pp. 12–13; Livia Visser-Fuchs, "The Divisie-chronicle" (of Cornelius Aurelius), *The Ricardian*, vol. ix, no. 118 (Sept. 1992), pp. 319–21; Molinet, *Chroniques*, vol. 2, pp. 402–3.

CHRISTOPHER COLYNS: *CPR EIV/EV/RIII*, p. 481; *CPR HVII*, vol. 1, p. 142; *L&P*, vol. 1, pp. 5, 8.

POVERTY OF EXILES: *Chronicles of the White Rose*, pp. 19–20n., 30; Commines, *Mémoires*, book 3, chs. iv, v, and book 5, ch. xx (Henry). "A THOUSAND DEADLY DANGERS": Rymer, *Foedera*, vol. xii, p. 295.

SPEECH TO THE COURT OF SCOTLAND: *AH*, pp. 84–85. Unlike André, Vergil has very few set speeches in his history. This is the only one in his account of Perkin.

VERGIL ASKING FOR HELP: SRO SP1/1/182; *Epistolae Jacobi Quarti . . .*, ed. Thomas Rudmann (Edinburgh, 1722), vol. 1, pp. 139–41.

"A LOYAL HOUSEHOLD SERVANT": *AH*, p. 65n.

3. Evidence of Things Seen

HENRY TO THE POPE: *CSPV,* pp. 208–9.

EDWARD'S SON: *AH,* p. 57.

APOTHECARY'S BILLS: PRO E 405/78, mem. 48r.

ISMAY: PRO E 404/81/3, warrants of Dec. 7th and 8th.

GARTH AND ORMOND: *Analecta hibernica* no. 10 (1941), pp. 34–35, 55; *CPR HVII,* vol. 1, p. 367; *CCR HVII,* vol. 1, p. 168.

THE *MARGARET OF BARNSTAPLE:* PRO E 404/81/1, warrant of Feb 13th; *Analecta Hibernica,* pp. 55–56. SPIES: e.g. PRO E 404/81/3, warrant of Nov. 30th.

HENRY TO LUDOVICO SFORZA: *CSPV,* p. 211; *CSPM,* p. 283.

CHARLES'S WAR STRATEGY: BN Français 25717, pp. 119, 122–25; LETTER OF SEPT. 30TH, ibid., p. 133.

ITALIAN MERCHANT: Arthurson, *Perkin Warbeck,* p. 24; Spont, "Marine," p. 432 and n.; BN Français 15541, 9 (microfilm 8253), f. 158r.

HONFLEUR'S DEFENCES: BN Français 32511 (microfilm 1653), f. 408r.

THE RECEPTION: Ibid., f. 423r. "WELL USED TO ENGLISH WAYS": BN Français 15541, f. 133r.

"IN HEAVEN": *AH,* p. 64n.

D'AUBIGNY'S PENSION: BN Français 32511, ff. 408v, 421r.

MONYPENY SENIOR'S CAREER: *CSPM,* pp. 182, 186–87; Scofield, *Edward IV,* vol. 2, pp. 97, 102.

COMMINES/CHARLES VIII: *Mémoires,* book 8, ch. xvii.

CHARLES'S CHAMBERS: Yvonne Labande-Mailfert, *Charles VIII et son milieu (1470–1498)* (Paris, 1975), p. 145.

TO AUGSBURG: *CSPM,* p. 291.

THE TINY COURT: Hall, *Chronicle,* p. 463.

FRION'S SERVICE: Davies & Ballard, "Frion", p. 251 and n. Bacon thought he stayed longer: *Henry VII,* p. 138.

"MADE HIMSELF BE CALLED . . .": Apparent postscript to a letter from Giles, Lord Daubeney to Calais, Oct. 7th, 1497: CC 111, f. 188r.

CHARLES TO JAMES: Lesley, *History of Scotland,* p. 63.

"TRUE OR PLAUSIBLE": *CSPS,* p. 10.

PRINCELY BY APPEARANCE: Chastellain, "Les hauts faits du duc de Bourgogne", *Oeuvres,* vol. 7, p. 220.

CHARLES THE BOLD: Chastellain, *Chronique, 1464, 1466–68, 1470,* in *Oeuvres,* vol. 5, p. 368.

LOUIS XI'S DRESS-SENSE: Commines, *Mémoires,* book 2, ch. viii.

SONCINO/HENRY: *CSPM,* p. 322. TREVISANO: *CSPV,* p. 263.

HENRY'S JEWEL BILL: *EH,* p. 131. PACKING THEM: Ibid., pp. 104, 121. PUTTING THEM ON HIMSELF: Francis Grose & Thomas Astle, *The Antiquarian Repertory,* 4 vols. (1807–9), vol. 1, p. 328.

"THE MERCHANT OF THE RUBY": Madden, "Documents", pp. 207, 208.

PHILIP THE GOOD'S HAT: Chastellain, *Chronique, 1461–64,* in *Oeuvres,* vol. 4, p. 447.

RUBIES: Mandeville, *Voiage,* pp. 157–58, 178, 214; Madame A. de Barrera, *Gems and Jewels*

(Paris, 1860), pp. 242–43; Deguileville, *Pélérinage*, pp. xxii, 27. AT THE SPANISH COURT: Gairdner, *Memorials*, pp. 341, 343, 347.

CHARLES'S COURT: Labande-Mailfert, *Charles VIII*, esp. pp. 141–49.
"COUSIN," DUKE OF YORK: BN Français 25717, p. 133; Spont, "Marine," p. 433.
ETAPLES CODICIL: Rymer, *Foedera*, vol. xii, p. 508.
LEAVING PARIS: Hall, *Chronicle*, p. 463; Bacon, *Henry VII*, p. 138. THE ESCAPE-WAYS: Labande-Mailfert, *Charles VIII*, p. 142. THE GABERDINE: Ibid., p. 146.

DUNBAR'S ROSES: "The Goldyn Targe", ls. 22–36.
"CELESTIAL CLEARNESS": "Le temple de Bocace", *Oeuvres*, vol. 7, p. 81; Lydgate, *The Temple of Glass*, ed. J. Schick, EETS Extra Series lx (1891), ls. 20–29.
ANDRÉ/HOMER: *HRHS*, pp. 3, 6.
CHARLES VIII'S EYES: Labande-Mailfert, *Charles VIII*, p. 155. CAXTON'S: George D. Painter, *William Caxton: A Quincentenary Biography of England's First Printer* (1976), p. 187. THOMAS BETSON'S: *Stonor Letters*, p. 43. HENRY'S: Halliwell, *Letters*, vol. 1, p. 183.
EDWARD IV'S REPAIRS: Scofield, *Edward IV*, vol. 2, p. 430. WINDOWS AND LIGHT: see e.g. Hawes, *Pastime of Pleasure*, pp. 17, 57.
"THROUGH THE GLASS WINDOW": BL Harleian 7578, f. 110.
"BARKED LEATHER": "A Tale of Froward Maymond," l. 30.
CHARLES'S HAWKS: Labande-Mailfert, *Charles VIII*, pp. 144–45.
NIGHT LIGHTING: *FH*, p. 235; Sydney Anglo, "The Court Festivals of Henry VII", *Bulletin of the John Rylands Library* 43 (1960–61), pp. 23, 24 n.
WINDOWS AT BINCHE: AN CC 8852, ff. 45v, 47v, 51v. AT MALINES: Weightman, *Margaret of York*, p. 124; Hommel, *Marguerite d'York*, p. 325.
"ENVIED PICTURES": "The Garland of Laurel," ls. 1157–61.
MARGARET'S BOOKS: Weightman, *Margaret of York*, pp. 203–12; Thomas Kren, "The Library of Margaret of York and the Burgundian Court", in *The Visions of Tondal*, ed. Thomas Kren & Roger S. Wieck (Malibu, Calif., 1990), pp. 9–18; Pierre Cockshaw, "Remarks on the Character and Content of the Library of Margaret of York", in Thomas Kren, ed., *Margaret of York, Simon Marmion and the Visions of Tondal* (Malibu, Calif., 1992), pp. 57–62; Nigel Morgan, "Texts of Devotion and Religious Instruction Associated with Margaret of York", ibid., pp. 63–76, and other essays, *passim*.
JESUS VISITING: *La dialogue de la duchesse de Bourgogne a Jesu Christ*, BL MS Add. 7970, esp. ff. 1r, 5r, 12r–17r, 20r,v, 71v–72r, 105r, 118r–119r; and see Plate 5. THE LANCE-WOUND: *Tretyse of Love* (see Notes, p. 534), pp. 118–20.

MARGARET TO ISABELLA: see Notes, p. 540.
"SCARCELY OF SOUND MIND": *AH*, p. 65.
SENDING SEALS: Molinet, *Chroniques*, vol. 5, p. 48.
BETSON'S TOKENS: *Stonor Letters*, vol. 2, pp. 6, 47. See also *Paston Letters*, vol. 5, nos. 860, 923.
FOLLOWING HIS MOVEMENTS: *AH*, p. 65n.
"MY MOST BELOVED": *HRHS*, p. 68. "NEWLY CROPEN": Hall, *Chronicle*, p. 463.
COLDHARBOUR REDECORATED: Nicolas, *Privy Purse*, pp. 126, 141–45, 241.

THE VISIT IN "1481": P. Génard, "Marguerite d'York, duchesse de Bourgogne, et la rose blanche (1495)", *Bulletin de la Commission Royale d'Histoire*, 4th Series, ii (Brussels, 1875), pp. 11–12; BL MS Fasc. 295 (a), p. 1.

HASTINGS HOURS: BL MS Add. 54782; Pamela Tudor-Craig, "The Hours of Edward V and Lord Hastings, British Library Manuscript Add. 54782" in *England in the Fifteenth Century*, Proceedings of the 1986 Harlaxton Symposium (1987), pp. 363–69; Tudor-Craig, *Richard III*, p. 9.

CEREMONIES FOR MARGARET: Weightman, *Margaret of York*, p. 134; Nicolas, *Privy Purse*, pp. 141–45, 163–66.

SIR GALAHAD/LANCELOT: Malory, *Morte Darthur*, p. 388.

COLUMBUS/CIPANGO: Cave, *Voyages*, pp. 141, 145.

TROIS ENSEIGNES: Gairdner, *Richard III/Perkin Warbeck* (see Notes, p. 532), p. 282; Heinrich Ulmann, *Kaiser Maximilian I*, 2 vols. (Stuttgart, 1884), vol. 1, p. 263 and n. Thanks to Professor Leopold Auer of the Österreichisches Staatsarchiv in Vienna for his efforts to find this document, which seems to have vanished without trace.

TANJAR ON THE MARKS: *PI*, vol. 4, pp. 528–29.

CHARLES THE BOLD'S MARKS: Pierre Frédérix, *La mort de Charles le Téméraire* (Paris, 1966), pp. 216–17.

CHARLES THE BOLD ADVISING: *EH*, p. 230.

THE QUEEN OF NAPLES: Gairdner, *Memorials*, pp. 230, 233. FERDINAND: Ibid., p. 278.

HENRY'S WART: *The Most Pleasant Song of Lady Bessy*, ed. J. O. Halliwell, Camden Society no. 69 (1847), p. 29.

EDWARD'S FAMILIARITY: Mancini, *Usurpation*, pp. 79–81.

LAMENT FOR EDWARD: Anne F. Sutton & Livia Visser-Fuchs, "Laments for the Death of Edward IV . . ." in *The Ricardian*, vol. ix, no. 145 (June 1999), p. 517.

CHAMBERLAIN AND DEBENHAM: *Chronicles of the White Rose*, pp. 37, 42.

THOMAS WARD: C. L. Kingsford, *English Historical Literature* (Oxford, 1913), p. 184n; Margaret Condon, "The Kaleidoscope of Treason: Fragments from the Bosworth story", *The Ricardian*, vol. vii, no. 92 (March 1986), *passim*.

CHARLES THE BOLD LIKE HIS FATHER: Chastellain, "Les hauts faits du duc de Bourgogne", *Oeuvres*, vol. 7, pp. 228–29.

DR. SHAW'S OBSERVATIONS: More, *Richard III*, pp. 102–3; Vergil, *Three Books*, p. 184.

EDWARD'S PORTRAIT: See Plate 3; Frederick Hepburn, *Portraits of the Later Plantagenets* (Woodbridge, 1986), pp. 60–61 and Plate 49.

ELIZABETH'S HAIR: Leland, *Collectanea*, vol. 4, pp. 219–20.

"OF INVINCIBLE COURAGE": Commines, *Mémoires*, book 3, ch. v. GONE TO SEED: Ibid., book 4, ch. x.

"BY GOD'S BLESSED LADY": More, *Richard III*, p. 16. THE ANGELUS: *Calendar of Papal Letters*, vol. 13, part 1, pp. 90–91.

"SOMEWHAT LIKE THE DUKE OF CLARENCE": Molinet, *Chroniques*, vol. 5, p. 79.

EDWARD'S BASTARDS: Charles Ross, "Rumour, Propaganda and Popular Opinion during the Wars of the Roses," in *Patronage, the Crown and the Provinces in Later Medieval England*, ed. Ralph A. Griffiths (Gloucester, 1981), p. 28 and n; *The Chronicles of Calais . . . to the year 1540*, ed. J. G. Nichols, Camden Series, 35 (1846), p. 41.

HARLISTON'S CONDUCT: de Carteret, *Chronique* (see Notes, p. 542). HIS CAREER: G. R.

Balleine, *A History of the Island of Jersey* (1950), pp. 91–97; Campbell, *Materials*, vol. 2, p. 30. HIS PARDON: *CPR HVII*, vol. 1, p. 141.

CLIFFORD AT THE JOUSTS: Black, *Wedding*, pp. 28, 35, 37, 40.

IUVENE VISO: *AH*, p. 69. "BY HIS FACE": Hall, *Chronicle*, p. 465. "GESTURE AND MAN-NERS": John Stow, *The Annales, or General Chronicle of England . . . unto the end of this present year 1614* (1615), p. 478.

THE LADY IN CALAIS: *L&P*, vol. 1, p. 235.

ISABELLA/MARGARET: *PI*, vol. 4, pp. 400–401; *CSPS*, p. 61.

"NOBODY HAD SEEN HIM DEAD": *Weisskunig*, p. 218 n. (g).

BODIES IN ST. PAUL'S: Weightman, *Margaret of York*, p. 96.

"EXHIBIT HIS PRESENCE": *L&P*, vol. 2, p. 177.

DR. ARGENTINE/HENRY: PRO 36/130, ff. 16v, 24v; E 404/80/38.

TYRELL UNDER SUBPOENA: Campbell, *Materials*, vol. 1, p. 270.

LYNEHAM'S INVESTIGATION: PRO E 405/79, mem. IV.

ENVOYS' INSTRUCTIONS: *AH*, pp. 69–71 and n.

SOMERSET'S OFFER: Molinet, *Chroniques*, vol. 5, p. 49. THE PRINCES' FUNERAL: Ibid., vol. 2, pp. 402–3.

LETTERS OF MARQUE: Douglas R. Bisson, *The Merchant Adventurers of England: The Company and the Crown, 1474–1564* (Newark, N.J., 1993), p. 73; Christine de Pisan, *The Book of Fayttes of Arms and Chyvalrye*, ed. A.T.P. Byles, EETS Original Series clxxxix (1932), pp. 252–53.

MERCHANT ADVENTURERS LEAVING: Bisson, *Merchant Adventurers*, p. 73.

THEIR HOUSE: P. Génard, *Anvers à travers les âges*, 2 vols. (Brussels, 1888), vol. 2, p. 399.

RICHARD'S ESCUTCHEON: Molinet, *Chroniques*, vol. 5, pp. 15–16.

DE MELUN: J. S. Brewer and R. H. Brodie, *Letters and Papers, Foreign and Domestic, of the Reign of Henry VIII*, vol. 1, part i, no. 1793 (p. 815); Molinet, *Chroniques*, vol. 4, pp. 167–69.

THE THIRTY HALBERDIERS: Hall, *Chronicle*, p. 463. Molinet mentions only twenty archers: *Chroniques*, vol. 5, p. 15.

"FAIR WHITE ROSE": "Gregory's Chronicle" in *Historical Collections of a London Citizen in the Fifteenth Century*, ed. James Gairdner, Camden Society New Series 17 (1876), p. 215.

RICHARD AS "THE WHITE ROSE": Molinet, *Chroniques*, vol. 5, pp. 16, 49, 121; Hammond, "Richard III, Dutch Sources," p. 13; Livia Visser-Fuchs, "English Events in Caspar Weinreich's Danzig Chronicle, 1461–1495," *The Ricardian*, vol. vii, no. 95 (Dec. 1986), p. 318. ABELL'S CHRONICLE: *Roit or Queill of Tyme*, National Library of Scotland, MS 1746, p. 111; *CSPM*, p. 318.

WHITE ROSE LETTERS: *The Ledger of Andrew Halyburton, 1492–1503* (Edinburgh, 1867), pp. lix, 215.

HENRY'S ROSES: Benjamin Thomson, "The Iconography of Henry VII," in *The Reign of Henry VII*, Proceedings of the 1993 Harlaxton Symposium (Stamford, 1995), pp. 3–5, 10, 112.

BUCKHOUNDS: PRO E 404/80/125. TUDOR GARDEN: BL MS Cotton Vespasian iv, f. 16r.

. . .

MAXIMILIAN THE POLYGLOT: *Weisskunig,* pp. 117–21; Waas, *Legendary Character,* pp. 113–14.

HENRY VII AND FRENCH: *CSPS,* p. 178 (letter of Pedro de Ayala of July 1498); Bacon, *Henry VII,* p. 243.

CAXTON'S FAULT: *The Prologues and Epilogues of William Caxton,* ed. W.J.B. Crotch, EETS Original Series clxxvi (1928 for 1927), p. 5.

BROUGHT UP IN ENGLAND: *HRHS,* ps 66, 72. ALREADY SPEAKING ENGLISH: *AH,* p. 63.

CAXTON'S FLEMISH: *Dialogues in French and English* by William Caxton, ed. Henry Bradley, EETS Extra Series lxxix (1900), p. vi.

"WELL-SPOKEN": *CSPM,* p. 330.

RICHMOND AND THE GARTER JOB: Gairdner, *Memorials,* p. xli. He signed his salary receipt in French, after someone else had written the acknowledgment for him in English: see PRO E36/130, f. 158Ar.

RICHARD'S LETTER: Madden, "Documents", pp. 182–84; BL MS Egerton 616/6.

YORKIST CHANCERY: Compare the signet letter of Edward IV in Charles Ross, *Edward IV* (1974), plate 6, facing p. 113.

HIS HANDWRITING: Madden thought it "bold and thoroughly English": "Documents", p. 184. MAXIMILIAN'S HANDWRITING: *Weisskunig,* p. 62; G. Elwood Waas, *The Legendary Character of the Emperor Maximilian* (New York, 1941), pp. 34, 109. JAMES IV'S: *TA,* pp. 271, 311.

GREETING THE CAPTAIN: see Ch. 5, p. 300; *Original Letters Illustrative of English History,* ed. Henry Ellis, 3 vols., Series 1, vol. 1 (1825), p. 30.

THE MISTAKE: CC 111, f. 188r.

BRASCHA'S CONVERSATION: *CSPM,* pp. 292–93; ASM Borgogna Cartella 521.

MAXIMILIAN'S LAND PROBLEMS: Benecke, *Maximilian* (see Notes, p. 533), pp. 17, 31–39, 122–23.

"SITTING BETWEEN TWO CHAIRS": Visser-Fuchs, "Caspar Weinreich" (see Notes, p. 549), p. 311.

KLINGKHAMER: Rosl Philpot, "Maximilian and England", PhD thesis, University of London (1975), p. 165; E. M. Lichnowsky, *Geschichte des Hauses Habsburg,* 8 vols. (Vienna, 1836–44), vol. 8, no. 2000.

THE VIENNA MEETING: Staatsarchiv Nürnberg, Fürstentum Brandenburg-Ansbach, Reichstagsakten, nr 5, p. 271; J. F. Böhmer, *Regesta Imperii XIV: Ausgewählte Regesten des Kaiserreiches unter Maximilian I,* compiled by Hermann Wiesflecker with Manfred Holleger, Kurt Riedl, Ingeborg Wiesflecker-Friedhuber & others (Vienna/Cologne/Weimar, 1989–98), vol. 1, part i (*Maximilian, 1493–1495*), no. 136.

FREDERICK'S FUNERAL: Molinet, *Chroniques,* vol. 4, pp. 393–96; S. F. Hahn, *Collectio Monumentorum,* vol. 1 (Brunswick, 1724), pp. 784–85; Hermann Wiesflecker, *Kaiser Maximilian I,* 4 vols. (Munich, 1973–81), vol. 2, pp. 353–54.

ORAISON TRÈS DEVOTE: Chastellain, *Chronique 1461–64,* in *Oeuvres,* vol. 4, p. 58.

EDWARD'S SON/BIANCA MARIA: Philpot, "Maximilian", p. 165 and n.; *Regesta Imperii XIV,* vol. 1, part ii (*Oesterreich, Reich und Europa, 1493–1496*), nos. 2911, 2912.

WITNESSING GRANTS: *Regesta Imperii XIV,* vol. 1, part i, nos. 185, 485.

THE MASS OF MAXIMILIAN AND BIANCA MARIA: Ibid., nos. 477, 478.

MAXIMILIAN ON NOBILITY: *Weisskunig*, p. 59. ON FAIR HAIR: Ibid., p. 113.

RICHARD ON SHOW IN ANTWERP, ETC.: Molinet, *Chroniques*, vol. 5, pp. 8–16, *passim;* Hommel, *Marguerite d'York*, pp. 217–18. *Regesta Imperii XIV*, vol. 1, part i, no. 1059.

HENRY "ASTONISHED": Molinet, *Chroniques*, vol. 5, pp. 46–47.

"A FACE OF TRUTH": *AH*, p. 67.

POYNINGS AND WARHAM: Ibid., pp. 69–71n. GARTER HERALD: Molinet, *Chroniques*, vol. 5, p. 47.

SOMERSET'S JOB: *Dictionary of National Biography*, under "Somerset", vol. 53, p. 230; PRO E 405/79, mem. 7r.

THE RECEPTION SCENE: Molinet, *Chroniques*, vol. 5, pp. 49–50. "TERRIFIED": *AH*, p. 71.

MARGARET'S STUDY: Hommel, *Marguerite d'York*, p. 159.

CLIFFORD/MARGARET: *AH*, pp. 68–69.

RICHARD'S MONEY: BL MS Facs. 295 (c), and Plate 7; Charles Cocheteux, "Une monnaie attribuée à Perkin Warbeck", *Bulletins de la Société Historique et Littéraire de Tournai*, vol. 4 (1856), pp. 63–68. (For specimens in England, see p. 66n.)

MANI, TECKEL, PHARES: Almost the same version occurs in Brant, *Ship of Fools*, printed in the same year, p. 286.

RICHARD'S SEAL: Gairdner, *Richard III/Perkin Warbeck*, p. 290; Madden, "Documents", p. 200. Gairdner adds, neatly: "Thus art was not wanting to sustain the dignity of fictitious royalty."

MARGUERITE D'ENGLETERRE: Weightman, *Margaret of York*, pp. 183, 217; ADN B2150 no. 70387.

EDWARD'S GENEALOGY: Anne F. Sutton & Livia Visser-Fuchs with P. W. Hammond, *The Reburial of Richard of York, 21–30 July 1476* (Richard III Society, 1996), Plate iv, p. 30.

EDWARD'S *DE FACTO* CLAIM: C.A.J. Armstrong, "The Inauguration Ceremonies of the Yorkist Kings and their Title to the Throne", *Transactions of the Royal Historical Society*, 4th Series, xxx (1948), *passim*.

CHARLES THE BOLD'S CLAIMS: *CSPM*, p. 216; Scofield, *Edward IV*, vol. 2, p. 24. For a good account of the precariousness of both Yorkist and Lancastrian claims, see *L&P*, vol. 1, pp. x–xiii.

STOKE BLESSINGS: *AH*, pp. 21, 27.

IMAGE ON THE TOMB: *Will of Henry VII* (see Notes, p. 539), pp. 35–36.

RICHARD III ON HENRY'S CLAIM: *Chronicles of the White Rose*, p. 280.

BEAUFORT DOUBTS: J. D. Mackie, *The Earlier Tudors* (Oxford, 1952), p. 41 and n.; *L&P*, vol. 2, p. xxx and n.

HENRY TO THE POPE: *CSPV*, pp. 208–9.

ST. CADWALLADER: *HRHS*, p. 9. THE CHAMPION'S REGALIA: Campbell, *Materials*, vol. 1, pp. 3–18.

"THAT TROJAN BLOOD": *HRHS*, p. 68.

WINCHESTER AS CAMELOT: Malory, *Morte Darthur*, p. 48. HENRY'S GREYHOUND: PRO E 101/415/3, f. 26v. HIS OATH: *CSPS*, pp. 111, 164.

MERLIN'S PROPHECIES: David Rees, *The Son of Prophecy: Henry Tudor's Road to Bosworth* (Ruthin, 1997), pp. 99–102.

WELSH HARPERS AND RHYMERS: *EH*, pp. 88, 89, 101, 111, 124, 130.

HENRY VI AND THE "LAD": Vergil, *Three Books*, p. 135.

HER CLAIM MIGHT NOT STAND: Bacon, *Henry VII*, p. 30.

ENTAIL OF THE CROWN: *L&P*, vol. 2, pp. xxx–xxxi. PAPAL ANATHEMA: Rymer, *Foedera*, vol. 12, pp. 294, 297–98.

"RECOVERY OF OUR REALM": Ibid., p. 278; Campbell, *Materials*, vol. 1, *passim*.

JOHN SWIT: *CSPV*, p. 164; *L&P*, vol. 1, pp. 94–95.

HENRY AS DUKE OF YORK: *L&P*, vol. 1, pp. 388–404; *Calendar of the Charter Rolls*, vol. 6, *5 Henry VI–8 Henry VIII* (1927), p. 271; *LC*, p. 202.

"WHO ILLICITLY OCCUPIES ENGLAND": Margaret to the pope, *L&P*, p. 396.

MAXIMILIAN TO THE POPE: *CSPV*, vol. 4, pp. 482–83.

MARGARET TO MORTON: *CSPM*, p. 328.

HENRY SEIZING THE CROWN: Richard's Proclamation, Bacon, *Henry VII*, App. II, p. 252.

MARGARET'S DOWRY: Weightman, *Margaret of York*, pp. 118–21, 137.

THE PROTOCOLS: P. Génard, "Marguerite d'York," pp. 9–22; BL MS Facs 295 (a); Stadsarchief Antwerpen, ff. 134r–138v. Plate 8 shows the first page of the draft.

"NO MORE EXCUSES": Hommel, *Marguerite d'York*, p. 325.

RICHARD'S WILL: HHSA RR Bu KK, f. 31a, translated in Diana Kleyn, *Richard of England* (Oxford, 1990), App. III, pp. 193–94. (Kleyn argues, without equivocation, that the pretender was Richard, Duke of York.) Reproduced as the frontispiece to Jean-Didier Chastelain, *L'Imposture de Perkin Warbeck* (Brussels, 1952).

THE FIRST DRAFT: *Regesta Imperii XIV*, vol. 1, part i, no. 1137. SIGNED IN LATIN: Ibid., no. 1299.

4. Fortune's Smile

DÜRER'S FORTUNA: "The Little Fortune"; "Nemesis (The Great Fortune)"; "Fortune in a Niche"; "Promenade".

EDWARD AND FORTUNE: "Lament of the Soul of Edward IV", third stanza. In most editions of Skelton, and in Sutton & Visser-Fuchs, *Laments* (see Notes, p. 548), p. 514.

"A BALL OF FORTUNE": Bacon, *Henry VII*, p. 163. "FORTUNE HAD NOT ALLOWED HIM": *CSPM*, p. 330.

HENRY/OUR LADY: *Will*, p. 2; Bacon, *Henry VII*, p. 59; *AH*, pp. 21, 27.

LUCKY SATURDAYS: Bacon, *Henry VII*, p. 32; *HRHS*, p. 67.

HENRY'S SHIPS: Ian Arthurson, "The King's Voyage into Scotland: The war that never was", in *England in the Fifteenth Century*, ed. D. Williams (Woodbridge, 1987), p. 7. Another was called the *Bonaventure*: PRO E 404/81/3, warrant of Dec. 2nd 1493.

GAMBLING AND TENNIS: *EH*, pp. 90–102 *passim*. TENNIS AND LIFE: da Salo, *Giuoco della Palla* (see Notes, p. 533), pp. 4–5.

TOTUM NIHIL: Dunbar, "To the king", l. 74.

"PERFECTLY SECURE": *CSPM*, p. 331. THE SUM LOST: *EH*, p. 114; PRO E 101/414/16, f. 11.

"SLIPPERY AND LUBRIC": Caxton, *Eneydos*, p. 320.

SICKNESS AND HAILSTONES: *LC*, pp. 216–17.

LITTLE CROSSES: Molinet, *Chroniques,* vol. 5, pp. 145–48; Waas, *Legendary Character,* p. 100.

COMET AND WATERS: *Chronicles of the White Rose,* pp. 132–36.

COMMINES ON THE WARS: *Mémoires,* book 5, ch. xx.

"QUEASY" AND "ALL QUAVERING": *Paston Letters,* vol. 5, nos. 774, 841, 900.

SWEATING SICKNESS: *AH,* pp. 7–9.

HENRY'S GOVERNANCE: The standard general accounts are S. B. Chrimes, *Henry VII* (1972) and R. L. Storey, *The Reign of Henry VII* (1968). Bacon's account, though not the most accurate, remains the best-written and, in some ways, the most perceptive.

UNCERTAINTY IN 1503: *L&P,* vol. 1, pp. 231–39 *passim.*

ROAD-GUIDES: *EH,* p. 114; PRO E 101/414/6, ff. 35v, 39v.

NEWS-LAGS AND FLYING TALES: C.A.J. Armstrong, "Some Examples of the Distribution and Speed of News in England at the time of the Wars of the Roses", *England, France and Burgundy* (see Notes, p. 541), *passim; Paston Letters,* vol. 5, nos. 830, 835.

SPANISH POSTAL PROBLEMS: e.g. *PI,* vol. 4, pp. 410, 464; *CSPS,* pp. 67, 74.

"LETTERS ABOUT RUMOURS": Conway, *Relations,* p. 175.

HENRY'S CAUTION: *CSPM,* p. 331; *AH,* p. 11; *L&P,* vol. 1, p. 234.

"BLAZING AND THUNDERING": Bacon, *Henry VII,* p. 139.

CONSPIRACIES BLOSSOMING: *AH,* p. 65. ENGLAND SPLIT ASUNDER: Ibid., p. 67.

NETWORKS OF CONSPIRATORS: Arthurson, *Perkin Warbeck,* ch. 8, *passim,* esp. pp. 87–92 for Yorkist loyalties. Dr. Arthurson's impressively thorough study of the conspiracy is recommended for readers who prefer, or wish to compare, the official version of this story.

OLD COURT SERVANTS: Ibid.; *LC,* pp. 203, 204, 221, 227–28.

THE YEOMAN OF THE CHAMBER: *GC,* p. 246; *LC,* p. 196.

ELIZABETH D'ARCY: W. E. Hampton, "Sir James Tyrell: with some notes on the Austin Friars London . . . ," *The Ricardian,* vol. iv, no. 63 (Dec. 1978), p. 19. Thanks to Bill Hampton for this. TYRELL'S CIRCLE: See p. 185 of this book and Madden, "Documents", pp. 208–9.

DEBENHAM'S PARDON: Ibid., vol. 1, p. 380. HIS POSTS: *CPR HVII,* vol. 1, p. 341. HIS LOYALTIES AND INTERESTS: Arthurson, *Perkin Warbeck,* pp. 91–92; Francis Pierrepont Barnard, *Edward IV's French Expedition of 1475: The Leaders and their Badges* (Oxford, 1925), pp. 99–101.

CONSPIRING WHITES: *Rot. Parl.,* vol. 6, p. 455.

CUMBRIAN CONSPIRATORS: Campbell, *Materials,* vol. 1, pp. 2, 249, 615.

LUMLEY AND ROBINSON: PRO *36ᵗʰ Report of the Deputy Keeper* (1875), App. I, p. 20. Thanks to Bill Hampton for this reference.

THWAITES: See *The Coronation of Richard III: The Extant Documents,* ed. Anne F. Sutton & P. W. Hammond (Gloucester, 1983), p. 405. Thanks to Livia Visser-Fuchs for this reference. THWAITES AT MARGARET'S FAREWELL: Nicolas, *Privy Purse,* p. 165.

CECILY: C.A.J. Armstrong, "The Piety of Cecily Neville: A Study in Late Medieval Culture", in *England, France and Burgundy,* pp. 135–56.

THE BERKHAMSTED NETWORK: W. E. Hampton, "The White Rose under the First Tudors," part 1, *The Ricardian,* vol. vii, no. 97 (June 1987), pp. 414–17.

CECILY'S WILL: *Wills from Doctors' Commons,* ed. John Gough Nichols & John Bruce, Camden Society no. 83 (1863), pp. 1–8.

LESSY'S BOND: *CCR HVII*, nos. 790, 825. IN CECILY'S WILL: *Doctors' Commons*, pp. 3–4, 8.

CLERICAL CONSPIRATORS: *LC*, p. 203; *AH*, p. 73; *HRHS*, p. 69; *GC*, p. 257.

MONEY SENT TO FLANDERS: *HRHS*, p. 69.

TAYLOR'S SECRET SIGNS: Pollard, *Henry VII*, vol. 1, p. 83; *Rot. Parl.*, vol. 6, p. 455. SECRET TOKENS: PRO KB 8/2, 3 and ch. 9, *passim*.

FOLDING LETTERS: See Richard's to Bernard de la Forsa (Plate 11; BL MS Egerton 616/6), evidently folded, first horizontally and then twice vertically, until it was about two inches square; also Commines, *Mémoires*, book 3, ch. ii.

"A FOOT IN TWO SHOES": *CSPM*, p. 177.

DEBENHAM AND SAVAGE: W.A.J. Archbold, "Sir William Stanley and Perkin War-beck", *EHR* vol. xix, no. lv (1899), p. 533; *Rot. Parl.*, vol. 6, p. 504; PRO KB 9/956, nos. 7, 8, 17, 19, 23, 24.

THE SERGEANT-FARRIER: *CPR HVII*, vol. 1, pp. 137–38, 422; PRO E 404/81/1, warrant of Jan. 3rd, 1492.

LETTER TO HARLAKENDEN: Arthurson, *Perkin Warbeck*, p. 66; PRO KB 9/51/8. HIS STANDING: *Kentish Visitations of Archbishop William Warham and his Deputies, 1511–1512*, ed. K. L. Wood-Legh (Kent Archaeological Society, 1984), p. 118.

CLIFFORD AND FITZWATER: PRO KB 9/934/5, nos. 4, 5.

FITZWATER'S WARNING: *Chronicles of the White Rose*, p. 26 and n. AT HENRY'S CORONATION: Campbell, *Materials*, vol. 1, p. 92.

CLIFFORD AT THE JOUSTS: Black, *Wedding*, pp. 27, 37, 40. VERGIL ON HIM: *AH*, p. 72 and n. AT ELIZABETH'S CORONATION: Leland, *Collectanea*, vol. 4, pp. 214–15, 221. CHAMBERLAIN OF BERWICK: *CPR HVII*, vol. 1, p. 85 (March 15th, 1486).

CLIFFORD IN BRITTANY: PRO E36/130, ff. 22v, 130v.

EMBASSY WITH RICHMOND: Gairdner, *Memorials*, pp. 369–71.

CLIFFORD AND STANLEY: Archbold, "Stanley", pp. 530–31.

STANLEY'S CAREER: *DNB* under Stanley, p. 812; Gairdner, *Richard III/Perkin Warbeck*, pp. 227–28, 238; Campbell, *Materials*, vol. 2, p. 69; PRO E 404/79/164. RENTS AND FEES: *LC*, pp. 204–5. HIS PETITION TO HENRY: Campbell, *Materials*, vol. 1, pp. 138–39.

HENRY "RELAXING A LITTLE HIS AFFECTION": *AH*, p. 77.

THE GIRDLE-CLASP: PRO E 154/2/5, p. 26.

BULKELEY: M. R. Hicks, "Sir William Stanley of Holt: Politics and Family Allegiance in the later Fifteenth Century", *Welsh History Review* 14 (1988–89), p. 16.

"IF HE KNEW FOR SURE": *AH*, p. 75.

CLIFFORD'S WIFE: PRO E 404/80/127.

WITNESS TO THE PROTOCOLS: Génard, "Marguerite d'York," p. 22; BL MS Facs 295 (a), p. 9.

"BY SUCH FAVOUR": *GC*, p. 256.

TWELFTH NIGHT: Ibid., pp. 251–52. THE MONSTER: "Douze triomphes" in Gairdner, *Memorials*, pp. 309, 320.

THOMAS LANGTON: *L&P*, vol. 1, p. 392.

THE KENDAL CELL: Madden, "Documents", pp. 173–77, 205–9.

KEATING'S PARDON: Campbell, *Materials*, vol. 2, p. 397; *CPR HVII*, vol. 1, p. 263.

TYRELL'S REMARKS: Madden, "Documents", pp. 208–9.

KENDAL'S CAREER IN RHODES: *CSPV*, pp. 153, 167, 169.

DE VIGNOLLES'S TESTIMONY: Madden, "Documents", pp. 173–77; BL MS Cotton Caligula D vi.

KENDAL'S LETTERS: *L&P*, vol. ii, Apps. x–xiv.

HIS OFFICIAL APPEARANCES (AND MISSTEPS): *CPR HVII*, vol. 1, p. 368; C. G. Bayne and W. H. Dunham, *Select Cases in the Council of Henry VII*, Selden Society, vol. 75 (1958), pp. xxxi, 29; Madden, "Documents", p. 172 n.

MANY MORE "GREAT MEN": *HRHS*, p. 69; Molinet, *Chroniques*, vol. 5, p. 48; *CSPM*, p. 328.

MERCHANT SUPPORTERS: *Rot. Parl.*, vol. 6, p. 504. JOHN HERON: *LC*, p. 217; *GC*, p. 281. OTHER LONDON MERCHANTS: *CPR HVII*, vol. 2, pp. 16–24 *passim*, 39, 47.

BONDS FOR ALLEGIANCE: J. R. Lander, *Crown and Nobility, 1450–1509* (1976), pp. 281–85, *passim;* *CCR HVII 1485–1500*, nos. 612, 686 (Hayes), 687 (de Lysa and Barley), 734, 737 (Hastings); Hampton, "White Rose" (see Notes, p. 553), p. 416.

A "GENERAL DECISION": *AH*, p. 69.

THE LETTER OF CREDIT: Hall, *Chronicle*, p. 465.

THE BAGNALL GROUP: PRO KB9/78/8.

THE ST. ANDREW'S PLOT: Archbold, "Stanley", pp. 532–33; PRO KB9/956/9, 15. DONE VERY SUBTLY: *AH*, p. 69.

RANGE OF SUPPORTERS: Arthurson, *Perkin Warbeck,* App. B, pp. 220–21; PRO KB9/52.

RICHARD'S CAPTAINS: Archbold, "Stanley", p. 534.

MOUNTFORD'S SERVICE: PRO E 405/78, mem. 53r; E 36/130, f. 58v; E 404/80/369; E 404/81/62. HIS FATHER'S STANDING: Barnard, *French Expedition* (see Notes, p. 553), pp. 123–25. AT LITTLE HENRY'S INAUGURATION: *L&P*, vol. 1, p. 404. THE KENDAL INDULGENCE: Painter, *Quincentenary* (see Notes, p. 547), p. 105.

CORBET'S FATHER: *GC*, p. 260.

VERGIL ON LABOURER-RECRUITS: *AH*, p. 81.

WEST COUNTRY POSTS: PRO E 101/414/6, *passim;* C.A.J. Armstrong, "Speed of News" (see Notes, p. 553), pp. 120–21; *EH*, p. 113.

THE EARL OF OXFORD/JOHN PASTON: *Paston Letters*, vol. 6, no. 1012 (1487).

HENRY'S SPIES: PRO E 101/414/6, E 101/414/16, *passim;* BL MS Add. 7099, ff. 3r, 18r. SPIES IN IRELAND: *L&P*, vol. 2, p. 298; *Analecta Hibernica*, pp. 35, 54. IN GENERAL: Ian Arthurson, "Espionage and Intelligence from the Wars of the Roses to the Reformation", *Nottingham Medieval Studies* XXXV (1991), pp. 134–54.

HERALDS AS SPIES: e.g. PRO E 404/82 (warrant to Rouge Dragon of April 24th, 1496), and other warrants *passim;* E 36/130 *passim.* GUILHEM: E 101/414/6, f. 20v. TRUMPETERS: Arthurson, "Espionage", pp. 144–45.

SPYING IN CALAIS: Arthurson, "Espionage", p. 145; Arthurson, *Perkin Warbeck,* pp. 135, 148; BL MS Add. 46454, ff. 3r, 7r, 8r.

INSTRUCTIONS TO WILTSHIRE: *L&P*, vol. 1, pp. 220–24.

"NO SPY SO GOOD": Commines, *Mémoires,* book 3, ch. viii.

DE PUEBLA'S LODGINGS: *PI*, vol. 4, p. 551 (*CSPS*, p. 102).

HENRY OUTDOORS: *PI*, vol. 4, p. 598; *L&P*, vol. 1, pp. 350–64 (interview with the Provost of Cassel, 1508). "OPENING HIS HEART": *CSPS*, p. 186.

WARHAM STAYING: PRO E 404/81/2, warrant of July 5th, 1493; E 404/81/3, warrant of Nov. 9th for extra pay owing.

"ENDEAVOUR BY ALL PROPER MEANS": Madden, "Documents," pp. 179–80.

SECRET NOTES TO RICHMOND: Ibid., pp. 200–204, esp. p. 204; BL Cotton Caligula D vi, ff. 18r–25r *passim*, esp. ff. 20v–21r, 25r.

FRANÇOIS DU PON: PRO E 404/79/22; E 404/81/1, warrant of March 27th, 1492; E 404/81/3, warrants of Nov. 19th, 1493, and Feb. 1st, 1494. JOHN STOLDES: E 404/81/3, two identical warrants of December 9th, 1493. HORSES: E 404/81/2, warrant of July 23rd, 1493.

THE GALVANISING MOMENT: *AH*, p. 69.

"AN INVENTION WOULD HAVE TROUBLED NOBODY": A point also made by Gairdner, *Richard III/Perkin Warbeck*, p. 314.

"HELD IT FOR A CERTAINTY": *AH*, pp. 65, 67.

MARGINALIA IN ANDRÉ: BL Cotton Domitian xviii, ff. 210v, 211v.

WRITING TO "FRIENDS": *AH*, p. 69n. THE BOY'S OWN FRIENDS: Ibid., p. 63.

HENRY/TOURNAI: Campbell, *Materials*, vol. 2, p. 30; PRO E 405/76 mem. 3r; PRO E 404/81/3, warrant of July 4th, 1492.

LETTER TO TALBOT: Halliwell, *Letters*, vol. 1, p. 172; BL MS Add. 46454, f. 6r.

"THE SON OF A BOATMAN": Madden, "Documents", p. 202; BL Cotton Caligula D vi, f. 18v.

"SURMISED US FALSELY": BL MS Harleian 283, f. 123v; Bacon, *Henry VII*, pp. 252–53.

EDMUND DE LA POLE'S COMPLAINT: *L&P*, vol. 1, p. 184.

"A CERTAIN FRENCH SPY": PRO E 405/78, mem. 64r.

BRAMPTON RETURNING: Cecil Roth, "Perkin Warbeck and his Jewish Master" (1920), pp. 156–57.

HIS PARDON: Ibid., p. 161; *CPR HVII*, vol. 1, p. 274.

BRAMPTON'S EXEMPTIONS: PRO E 404/83, warrant of Nov. 22nd, 1499.

THE *ANNE OF FOWEY*: PRO E 405/78, mem. 29v; Spont, "Marine", p. 418 n. 6; Campbell, *Materials*, vol. 1, p. 329.

MENO'S REWARDS: *CPR HVII*, vol. 2, pp. 14, 44 (denization), 84. HIS POSITIONS AND JOBS: Conway, *Relations*, pp. 167, 183. AS A SPY: PRO E 101/414/6, ff. 13r, 23v, 31v, 38v, etc.

HERON'S SLIP OF PAPER: PRO E 101/687/10.

CRUMBS FROM BRETONS: see Ch. 7, p. 404.

THE PAIR OF SCISSORS: Wilhelm Busch, *England under the Tudors*, vol. 1, *King Henry VII*, tr. Alice Todd (1865), p. 91.

MARGARET'S *YNPORTUNIDAD*: *PI*, vol. 4, p. 404.

"NOT VERY GOOD SENSE": "Douze triomphes" in Gairdner, *Memorials*, p. 316.

PHILIP'S CHAIN: Weightman, *Margaret of York*, p. 131.

KILDARE'S PARDON: *CPR HVII*, vol. 1, pp. 423, 425. HIS LETTER: *L&P*, vol. 2, pp. 55–56.

PHILIP WITH RICHARD: Molinet, *Chroniques*, vol. 5, pp. 4–5, 7–8, 11–12.

MARGARET'S CHESS SETS: Hommel, *Marguerite d'York*, p. 160.

COMMINES ON BURGUNDIANS: *Mémoires*, book 1, ch. ii.

MISERIES OF BRUGES: Octave Delpierre, *Précis analytique des documents . . . des archives de la*

Flandre-Occidentale à Bruges (Bruges, 1840), vol. 1, *Comptes du territoire du Franc,* pp. 145–47.

WARHAM AND POYNINGS'S EMBASSY: *AH,* pp. 68–71 and n.; William Camden, *Remains Concerning Britain,* ed. R. D. Dunn (Toronto, 1984), pp. 247, 451.

BREAKING OFF TRADE: *Tudor Royal Proclamations,* vol. 1, *The Early Tudors (1485–1553),* ed. Paul L. Hughes and James F. Larkin (New Haven, Conn., and London, 1964), p. 35.

"OUR GREAT VOYAGE": PRO E 404/81/2 and various warrants of Sept. 1493.

ANTI-HANSA RIOTS: *LC,* p. 198.

THE COUNTER-EMBARGO: Philpot, *Maximilian,* p. 203; ADN B 2151, f. 115r; *LC,* p. 200.

ECONOMIC EFFECTS OF THE EMBARGO: T. H. Lloyd, *The English Wool Trade in the Middle Ages* (Cambridge, 1977), p. 283.

GARTER'S VISIT: Molinet, *Chroniques,* vol. 5, p. 47; PRO E 404/81/3, warrant of July 5th.

"NO DECEIT MORE DEEP": Vergil, *Three Books,* p. 198.

MOLINET'S EPITHETS: *Chroniques,* vol. 5, p. 80 (all but one from 1497, after seeing the con-fession). Hall also uses the metaphor of a cheating merchant "which had falsely feigned his name and stock", attributing it to Poynings and Warham in their embassy: *Chronicle,* p. 466.

"A STOCKFISH BONE": "As a Midsummer Rose," ls. 12–13.

TRINKETS FROM FLANDERS: H. S. Cobb, *The Overseas Trade of London: Exchequer Customs Accounts 1480–1* (London Record Society, 1990), pp. 20–25 and *passim.*

32,755 YEARS: Eamon Duffy, *The Stripping of the Altars: Traditional Religion in England, c. 1400–1580* (1992), p. 214.

VERGIL'S APPRECIATION: *AH,* pp. 67, 68n., 69.

DE MELUN ON THE STAFF: ADN B 2155, f. 64r; *Compte rendu des séances de la Commission Royale d'Histoire,* vol. 11, part ii (Brussels, 1846), p. 680.

GERYON: *HRHS,* pp. 318–19.

HENRY TO PHILIP: *L&P,* vol. 2, pp. 58–59.

MAXIMILIAN'S FIRST MEETING: Philpot, *Maximilian,* p. 165; Maximilian, *Weisskunig,* p. 218 and n. (b); *CSPV,* p. 227; *Regesta Imperii XIV,* vol. 1, part i, no. 136.

THE "COMPROMISE": *Regesta Imperii XIV,* vol. 1, part i, no. 176.

HIS OBLIGATION: Zurita, *Historia,* vol. 5, f. 87v.

HENRY ON MAXIMILIAN: Madden, "Documents", pp. 202, 204; BL Cotton Caligula D vi, ff. 19v, 25r; *CSPS,* p. 457.

MAXIMILIAN'S "SECRET KNOWLEDGE": *Weisskunig,* pp. 55, 64–65; Waas, *Legendary Character,* pp. 109–10.

FREDERICK'S TREASURE: *CSPV,* pp. 225–26.

ENQUIRIES OF HIS OWN: Gairdner, *Richard III/Perkin Warbeck,* pp. 282–83. HIS NOTE: TLA Maximiliana IVa, 101, 4. Stück (f. 142).

MAXIMILIAN ON RICHARD'S HISTORY: *CSPV,* vol. 4, pp. 482–83; Zurita, *Historia,* vol. 5, f. 59v.

MARGARET AND THE BISHOP OF CAMBRAI: *CSPM,* p. 292; ASM Borgogna Cartella 521 (Feb. 11th, 1495).

BRASCHA AT WORK: *CSPM,* pp. 279–80, 281; Lichnowsky, *Hauses Habsburg* (see Notes, p. 550), vol. 8, nos. 1939, 1946.

CHARLES AND MARGARET'S MARRIAGE: Vander Linden, *Itinéraires* (see Notes, p. 543), pp. 49–58.

HENRI DE BERGHES: Weightman, *Margaret of York*, p. 198; L'Abbé A.-J. Namèche, *Cours d'Histoire Nationale*, part 4, vol. 8 (Louvain, 1869), p. 143 n.

MAXIMILIAN HUNTING: Benecke, *Maximilian*, pp. 19, 122, 123; Waas, *Legendary Character*, pp. 32, 49, 105–7, 112; Molinet, *Chroniques*, vol. 5, p. 60.

UMBZOTLER: Benecke, *Maximilian*, p. 32.

THE HUNTING PARTY: Molinet, *Chroniques*, vol. 5, p. 9.

"EXACTLY AS HE LIKES": *Regesta Imperii XIV*, vol. 1, part i, no. 2122; *CSPV*, p. 221.

LUDOVICO BRUNO: *CSPV*, pp. 221, 237; Ulmann, *Maximilian* (see Notes, p. 548), vol. 1, p. 411.

"GOING TO WIN ENGLAND": *CSPV*, pp. 221, 232. NATURELLI: Ibid., p. 219.

IMPATIENCE WITH MAXIMILIAN: Waas, *Legendary Character*, pp. 26–27, 33, 63 (Machiavelli's).

HIS NEW COINS: *Tudor Royal Proclamations*, p. 42 (1498). HENRY'S SIGH: *CSPS*, p. 457.

FERDINAND AND ISABELLA OFFERING MEDIATION: *PI*, vol. 5, pp. 306, 373 (*CSPS*, pp. 53, 57, 67).

AUTORIDAD: Zurita, *Historia*, vol. 5, f. 20r.

THE BIGGEST *BURLA*: *CSPS*, p. 93.

LETTER OF JULY 20TH, 1495: *PI*, vol. 4, pp. 400–401 (*CSPS*, p. 61). Identical protests, *PI*, vol. 4, p. 519 (and others).

"THE ONLY PRINCES HE TRUSTED": *CSPS*, p. 190 (1498).

UP TO THEIR NECKS: *PI*, vol. 4, p. 486 (*CSPS*, p. 85).

"IF THE KING OF THE ROMANS CLINGS ON": *PI*, vol. 4, p. 398 (*CSPS*, p. 59).

"WE WERE RATHER DISPLEASED": *Correspondencia de Guiterre Gomez de Fuensalida*, pub. for the Duke of Berwick and Alba (Madrid, 1907), p. 3.

YORK'S CIPHER CODE: *CSPS*, Bergenroth's preface, p. lxxxv.

THE DUKE OF MILAN'S QUANDARY: *CSPM*, p. 327; *CSPS*, p. 130.

"BY THE FAITH OF HIS HEART": *PI*, vol. 4, p. 598. "ALTHOUGH HE ARGUED": Zurita, *Historia*, vol. 5, f. 90v.

WORRIES ABOUT HENRY'S SECURITY: *CSPS*, p. 21.

INDEMNITIES OWED TO SCOTLAND: PRO E 404/81/2, warrant of July 6th, 1493.

WARD AND BAKER: Ibid., warrant of July 9th.

TROOPS TO THE COASTS: *AH*, p. 69. SHIPS TO THE SEA: Conway, *Relations*, App. iv, pp. 148–49; PRO E 404 81/2, warrants of June 26th and July 4th. "SAILINGS TO AND FRO": Conway, *Relations*, p. 41.

"JUST LIKE THE OTHER ONE": Madden, "Documents", p. 202.

WARNINGS TO THE PORTS: Arthurson, *Perkin Warbeck*, p. 80; BL MS Add. 29617, f. 103r.

"IT APPEARS EACH DAY": BL Cotton Caligula D vi, f. 21r.

SAVAGE AND DEBENHAM FLEEING: PRO E 404/81/2, warrant of April 20th, 1493; E 405/79, mem. 4r.

JOHN AP HOWELL: PRO KB9/956/24; *CPR HVII*, vol. 1, p. 422.

MONKS OF THE ABBEY: PRO KB 9/956/7, 8.

"ALL NECESSARY ACTS": PRO E 405/79, mem. 4r.

"FOUR MEN": *LC*, p. 198; *GC*, p. 246.

STEELYARD REBELS: *LC*, pp. 198–99.

BAGNALL'S CAPTURE: PRO KB 9/78 (his statement, no. 19; the dean and chapter's, no. 21); *LC*, p. 199; *GC*, p. 250.

FEB. 26TH HANGINGS: *LC*, p. 199. BULKELEY: PRO E 404/81/3, warrants of Feb. 3rd and 24th.

ARRESTS AND ATTAINDERS: *Rot. Parl.*, vol. 6, p. 504; Hampton, "White Rose" (see Notes, p. 553), p. 416.

WISHING A MAN GOOD DAY: a mistake made by John Colard, who paid his respects to the traitor Stafford in Bromsgrove market: Campbell, *Materials,* vol. 1, pp. 434–35.

ANTHONY DE LA FORSA: E 404/81/3, warrant of April 21st, 1494; PRO E 405/78, mem. 53r.

THE INFILTRATION: Molinet, *Chroniques,* vol. 5, pp. 47–48; *AH,* pp. 71–73. HENRY'S ·LETTERS: PRO DL 28/2/2 (not foliated): signet letter of Oct. 22nd, 1494.

"IT SHOULD NOT BE HE": *GC*, p. 256.

THE COURIER: *EH*, p. 100.

VERGIL ON CLIFFORD: *AH*, pp. 73–74 and n. NANFAN: *L&P*, vol. 1, p. 235. CLIF-FORD'S FRIENDS INTERCEDING: *GC*, p. 256.

VERGIL ON BARLEY: *AH*, p. 73. IN SCOTLAND: *TA*, pp. 358, 365. HIS PARDON: *CPR HVII*, vol. 2, p. 134 (July 1498); *Rot. Parl.*, vol. 6, p. 554.

CLIFFORD'S ARREST (AND REWARD): *EH*, pp. 100, 101. HIS PARDON: *CPR HVII*, vol. 2, p. 13.

HENRY/STANLEY: *AH*, pp. 75–77.

NANFAN ON HENRY: Gairdner, *Richard III/Perkin Warbeck*, pp. 287–88.

CONSPIRATORS WAITING: Hall, *Chronicle*, p. 467.

STANLEY ON THE COMMISSIONS: PRO KB 9/956; KB 9/78/20.

MELANCHOLY: Hall, *Chronicle*, p. 469.

HELPING WITH MONEY: Molinet, *Chroniques,* vol. 5, p. 48; *HRHS*, p. 69. THE BRIGANDINES: PRO E 154/2/5, p. 15.

"REBELLION": *CPR HVII*, vol. 2, p. 16.

EVIDENCE OF THE SEALS: Molinet, *Chroniques,* vol. 5, p. 48.

ARRAIGNMENTS AND EXECUTIONS: *LC*, pp. 203–4.

RICH MERCHANTS FLEEING: Molinet, *Chroniques,* vol. 5, p. 48.

PROCEEDINGS AGAINST STANLEY: Archbold, "Stanley", p. 531; PRO KB 9/78/24–34.

OPENLY ADMITTED HIS OFFENSE: *AH*, p. 75.

BAFFLEMENT ABOUT HIM: *LC*, pp. 204–5; *GC*, p. 258; *HRHS*, p. 69.

BURIAL FEES: *EH*, pp. 101, 102. THE SEARCH OF HOLT: PRO E 154/2/5 *passim.*

FITZWATER: BL MS Add. 7079; *LC*, p. 212; Hall, *Chronicle*, p. 467.

CLERGY FINES AND PARDONS: Hampton, "White Rose," pp. 416–17. LESSY: *CPR · HVII*, vol. 2, p. 16. WORSELEY BOUND: *CCR HVII*, nos. 795, 863, 965, 1144. HIS ACCOUNTS: Guildhall Library MS 25, 166/6–9.

DYING OF SHAME: *GC*, p. 257.

CRESSENER AND ASTWOOD: *LC*, p. 204. DEBENHAM AND SAVAGE: PRO E 405/79 mems. 4r, 10v.

TREASONOUS RHYMES: *AH*, pp. 77n., 79.

KENDAL'S PARDON: *CPR HVII*, vol. 2, p. 49. BOND FOR LOYALTY: *CCR HVII*, no. 792.

CLIFFORD'S APPOINTMENTS AND HIS PAY: E 404/82, warrant of May 13th, 1496; E 405/79, mem. 23r; *CPR HVII*, vol. 2, p. 37.

NEWS AT MALINES: ADN B 2151, ff. 113v, 114r, v.

DEVASTATED: *AH*, p. 81.

"HE DETERMINED": Hall, *Chronicle*, p. 471.

FEBRUARY 22ND: PRO KB 9/51/7.

MANAGEMENT OF THE "SECRET AFFAIRS": ADN B 2153, nos. 70619, 70620, 70621, 70622, 70623, etc. THE SECRET CODE: Arthurson, *Perkin Warbeck*, p. 103; ADN B 2153, nos. 70610, 70619, 70621.

"NOT INVOLVED": *CSPV*, pp. 219, 221. "IN SMALL NUMBERS": *Weisskunig*, p. 218 and n.

THE TYROLERS' LOAN: Gairdner, *Richard III/Perkin Warbeck*, p. 282 and n.; TLA Maximiliana 1. 38, ff. 162, 163.

A MORE VALID CLAIM: Philpot, *Maximilian*, p. 167.

MARGARET PROVISIONING THE FLEET: *Regesta Imperii XIV*, vol. 1, part i, no. 1482.

DANIEL BEAUVIURE: Madden, "Documents", p. 208.

KEATING'S RELIC-SELLING: Conway, *Relations*, pp. 210-11; Ware, *Antiquities*, p. 28.

ZACHTLEVANT LOAN: *L&P*, vol. 1, pp. 264-65.

THE CANNON REQUEST: HHSA Maximiliana 4, ff. 229r-231v; Wiesflecker, *Maximilian*, p. 62.

LETTERS IN VENICE: Commines, *Mémoires*, ed. Mlle. du Pont (see Notes, p. 533), vol. 3, *Preuves*, pp. 413-14.

INSTRUCTIONS TO ALBRECHT: SS HAS Loc. 8497, ff. 69r-75r. BIANCA MARIA AS A PLEDGE: Ibid., ff. 72 r, v, 74r. The papal nuncio told Francis I of France that Maximilian had a habit of doing this: Waas, *Legendary Character*, p. 61.

THE SCARE OF APRIL: Arthurson, *Perkin Warbeck*, p. 110; ADN B 2151, ff. 122r, 125r, 126r. HENRY'S FLEET: *EH*, p. 101.

PHILIP ORDERING THE GUNS: ADN B 2151, f. 140v.

THE MERCENARIES: *Weisskunig*, p. 218. PUMPING THE ZEELANDERS: ADN B 2151, f. 68v. THE HUNT-MASTER: *Regesta Imperii XIV*, vol. 1, part i, no. 1482.

PEASANTS REFUSING TO STAY: Ibid.; SS HAS Loc 8497, f. 71v.

TROOPS FROM SCOTLAND: *CSPV*, p. 219. FROM GUELDERS: *Regesta Imperii XIV*, vol. 1, part i, no. 1482.

WEAPONS: *Rot. Parl.*, vol. 6, p. 504.

THE SOLDIERS: *AH*, p. 81; Molinet, *Chroniques*, vol. 5, p. 50; *CSPS*, pp. 58-59.

DE GUEVARAS: Zurita, *Historia*, vol. 5, f. 134r; *Compte rendu des séances de la Commission Royale d'Histoire*, vol. 11, part ii (1846), p. 687; Molinet, *Chroniques*, vol. 4, p. 161.

FERDINAND AND ISABELLA'S VIEW: *PI*, vol. 4, p. 404 (*CSPS*, p. 63).

RICHARD'S CONFIDENCE: Molinet, *Chroniques*, vol. 5, p. 50; *CSPV*, p. 220; Zurita, *Historia*, vol. 5, f. 59v.

YARMOUTH SAILOR: *Paston Letters*, vol. 6, no. 1059.

KENDAL'S JACKETS: Madden, "Documents", p. 208.

WARWICK BADGES: Commines, *Mémoires*, book 3, ch. vi.

· · · ·

RICHARD DRIFTING: *AH*, p. 81; *HRHS*, p. 67.

KENTINGS CHASTENED: *HRHS*, pp. 66–67.

THE INVASION: Molinet, *Chroniques*, vol. 5, pp. 50–51.

THOMAS GRIGGE: Arthurson, *Perkin Warbeck*, p. 113; PRO E 404/82/46, warrant of Oct. 28th, 1496.

"NO COMFORT OF THE COUNTRY": *LC*, p. 205.

THE PRISONERS: *HRHS*, p. 67; *LC*, pp. 206–7; PRO E 404/82, warrant of Nov. 14th, 1495.

THE COMMISSION: E404/79, mem. 7v. For the names of those arraigned, see Arthurson, *Perkin Warbeck*, App. B, pp. 220–21.

CAPTAIN BELT: "Douze triomphes" in Gairdner, *Memorials*, p. 322; *Paston Letters*, vol. 6, no. 1059.

LOVELL IN CHARGE: PRO E 404/81/4, warrant of Aug. 17th.

MOUNTFORD'S SERVICE: PRO E404/81/1, warrant of Jan. 27th, 1492. HIS SUBSE-QUENT TREATMENT: see Ch. 9, p. 484.

CORBET'S DEATH: *LC*, p. 206; *GC*, p. 260.

"THE ANIMALS": "Douze triomphes", in Gairdner, *Memorials*, p. 322. THE SEASIDE GIB-BETS: *GC*, p. 260; Bacon, *Henry VII*, p. 157.

THE BILL OF ATTAINDER: *Rot. Parl.*, vol. 6, p. 504.

HENRY TO PHILIP: HHSA Maximiliana 4, f. 267 r, v.

DE PUEBLA'S ACCOUNT: *PI*, vol. 4, p. 397 (*CSPS*, p. 59).

LETTERS TO THE PORTS: BL MS Add. 7099, f. 27r.

KENTINGS' RESPONSE: Arthurson, *Perkin Warbeck*, p. 112; BL MS Add. 29617, f. 128r; *AH*, pp. 82 n., 83; CCA F/A 2, ff. 258v, 265v; *Historical Manuscripts Commission*, vol. 5, 5th report (1876), p. 548; *HMC*, 9th report (1888), p. 146; *LC*, pp. 205–6.

SECURING THE COASTS: PRO E 405/79, mem. 7r, v; E 404/81/4, warrant of July 25th.

LONDON REACTIONS: *LC*, pp. 204, 206; PRO STAC/1/2/30.

"RICHARD, SEEING THIS": Molinet, *Chroniques*, vol. 5, p. 52. THE HOY OF DOR-DRECHT: *Paston Letters*, vol. 6, no. 1060.

RICHARD'S MOVEMENTS: *AH*, p. 83; *PI*, vol. 4, p. 398; *LC*, p. 206.

THE INVASION/MAXIMILIAN: *CSPV*, pp. 221–22; Chastelain, *L'Imposture* (see Notes, p. 552), p. 50; *Regesta Imperii XIV*, vol. 1, part i, nos. 2122, 2136.

"THE NEW KING": Maximilian, *Weisskunig*, p. 218, in which he tangles up the Kentish invasion with the later West Country campaign to an almost indecipherable degree.

SECRET MESSAGE: Philpot, *Maximilian*, p. 168; HHSA Maximiliana 4, f. 267r.

"MIGHT BE DEFEATED": *CSPV*, p. 222. SEPTEMBER 5TH: Ibid., p. 223.

FERDINAND AND ISABELLA'S LECTURE: *PI*, vol. 5, p. 171 (*CSPS*, p. 140).

STOKE REFUSAL: J. D. Mackie, *The Earlier Tudors, 1495–1558* (Oxford, 1952), pp. 7–8, 73.

ACT OF OCTOBER: *The Statutes*, Revised Edition, vol. 1, *Henry III to James II, AD 1255–6–1685* (1870), pp. 363–64.

"TO SET THE TRIAL . . .": Lorraine C. Attreed, "A new source for Perkin Warbeck's invasion of 1497", *Medieval Studies*, vol. 48 (1986), p. 520.

MAXIMILIAN, SEPTEMBER 19TH: *CSPV*, pp. 223–24. THE WEASEL CLAUSE: HHSA RR Bu GG, f. 1a; HHSA RR Bu JJ, ff. 208, 209.

MAGNUS INTERCURSUS: Rymer, *Foedera,* vol. 12, pp. 578-82 (Margaret, p. 580); PRO E 405/79, mem. 8r.

A SON BON PLAISIR: ADN B 2151, ff. 286r, 288r, 289r, etc.

5. The Pavilions of Love and the Tents of War

EDWARD'S JOURNEY: *Chronicles of the White Rose,* pp. 36-45.

HIS HARLOTS: Hall, *Chronicle,* p. 363.

EMBASSY TO BURGUNDY: *LC,* pp. 227-28.

"THE SIGHT OF THE SHIPS": *Paston Letters,* vol. 6, no. 1060. Vergil also thought an invasion of the west of England "a possibility": *AH,* p. 83.

HENRY FOLLOWING HIM: BL MS Add. 7099, ff. 28r-29r; PRO E 101/414/6, ff. 2r, 6r; E 404/81/3, warrant of Aug. 17th, which mentions "setting forth our armies by land and sea"; *EH,* pp. 103-4; *CSPV,* p. 223.

THE IRISH INQUISITION: *LC,* p. 207. QUESTIONING OF SUPPORTERS: Ware, *Antiquities,* pp. 24, 26.

SHANE BURKE: Conway, *Relations,* App. xliii, p. 234.

HATTON/DESMOND: Rymer, *Foedera,* vol. xii, p. 567; *CPR HVII,* vol. 2, p. 27; Conway, *Relations,* p. 81.

THE *CHRISTOPHER:* CPR HVII, vol. 2, p. 42.

SIEGE OF WATERFORD: *Carew MS, Book of Howth,* p. 472; R. H. Ryland, *The History, Typography and Antiquities of the County and City of Waterford* . . . (1824), pp. 30-32 (which wrongly dates the siege to 1497). The *Book of Howth* numbers Desmond's forces at 24,000, undoubtedly too large.

GUNFIRE: *Kalendar of Shepherds,* p. 90; Molinet, *Chroniques,* vol. 4, pp. 339-40.

SELLING THE SHIPS: See Hatcliffe's Accounts in *L&P,* vol. 2, pp. 299-300.

ATWATER SUMMONED: Ware, *Antiquities,* p. 24.

SHIPWRECKED AND WANDERING: Often attributed to 1497, but correctly 1495: see Gairdner, *Richard III/Perkin Warbeck,* pp. 320-23; Zurita, *Historia,* vol. 5, ff. 133b, 134.

SYLVESTRES HOMINES: AH, pp. 65, 79-81.

O'DONNELL AND O'NEILL: *Book of Howth,* pp. 180-81.

"CLOTTED BLOOD": Rev. C. B. Gibson, *The History of the County and City of Cork,* 2 vols., vol. 1 (Cork, 1861), p. 102.

O'DONNELL'S RAIDS IN CONNAUGHT: *Annals of Ulster, otherwise Annals of Senat: A Chronicle of Irish Affairs AD 431-1131: 1155-1541,* vol. 3, 1379-1541, ed. B. Mac Carthy (Dublin, 1895), pp. 391-93.

A FEW TROOPS: *CSPV,* p. 223; Zurita, *Historia,* vol. 5, f. 134.

JOHN WISE: See Hatcliffe's Accounts in *L&P,* vol. 2, p. 310.

LOUNDE ABSCONDING: *LC,* p. 21. HIS BACKGROUND: *CPR HVII,* vol. 2, p. 237.

JAMES'S OWN AMBITIONS: Norman Macdougall, *James IV* (Edinburgh, 1989), pp. 118-19.

HIS EARLY INTEREST IN RICHARD: Tytler, *History of Scotland* (see Notes, p. 543), vol. 4, pp. 371-73.

RELUCTANT TO RATIFY: Bacon, *Henry VII,* p. 137 n.

YORKIST DELEGATION: see p. 91 and note.

Scots/French: Tytler, *History*, vol. 4, pp. 372–73; *TA*, pp. 176, 179–80, 181, 182. George Neville: Ibid., p. 176. The dean of York: Ibid., p. 185.

Northern raid: Tytler, *History*, vol. 4, pp. 374–75; Spedding note in Bacon, *Henry VII*, p. 148.

The Flanders delegation: *TA*, p. 233.

"stirring up opinion": *Regesta Imperii XIV*, vol. 1, part i, no. 1906.

"Scottish help": *CSPV*, pp. 219, 220.

Maximilian's daughter: *CSPM*, p. 291.

Infante Afonso: Sanceau, *Perfect Prince* (see Notes, p. 543), p. 287. *CUYDANDO/ SOSPIRANDO:* Resende, *Cancioneiro Geral*, ff. 1–15b.

simply fallen in love: Lesley, *History of Scotland* (see Notes, p. 544), p. 64; Ware, *Antiquities*, p. 31. André says he took advantage of James's kindness to get himself a wife: *HRHS*, p. 70.

The love-letter: *CSPS*, pp. 78–79; BL MS Fasc 295 (b).

"an opulent equipage": Pinkerton, *History of Scotland* (see Notes, p. 544), vol. 2, p. 26.

Payments for his servants: *TA*, pp. 263–64, 274, 276.

The pox (called the "grantgore"): Ibid., pp. 356, 361.

O'Donnell: Conway, *Relations*, p. 86; Macdougall, *James IV*, p. 117.

Stirling reception: *TA*, pp. 263–64, 267. Vestments mended: Ibid., p. 229.

Dunbar on Stirling: "The Dregy of Dunbar", ls. 13, 19, 94, 97–98.

Works there: *TA*, esp. pp. 277, 279–81, 283, 286, 291, 297, etc. The garden: Ibid., pp. 276, 361, 364, 367.

Dunbar: "Meditatioun in Wyntyir", ls. 1–7, 9–10.

James's clothes: *TA*, p. 256. His character: *CSPS*, pp. 169–70; *PI*, vol. 5, pp. 258–59 (Ayala's description). His hats: *TA*, pp. 145–46. "Far out of reason": Ellis, *Letters*, vol. i (see Notes, p. 550), p. 27.

Ramsay: Conway, *Relations*, pp. 12, 20, 21, 25; Mairead McKerracher, "John Ramsay of Balmain: Tudor Agent?" *The Ricardian*, vol. iv, no. 61 (June 1978), *passim*. Ramsay was in Henry's pay from 1488 onwards, and his payments feature frequently in the warrants for issues: PRO E 404/78/79/80/81. Autograph receipt of payment: PRO E 36/131, f. 395r.

Riding incognito: Robert Lindsay of Pittscotie, *The Historie and Chronicles of Scotland*, ed. Ae. J. G. Mackay, Scottish Text Society Publications, 1st Series 42 (Edinburgh, 1899), pp. 71, 82.

"Are you my father?": I. A. Taylor, *The Life of James IV* (1913), pp. 54–55.

Masses for his father: Taylor, *James IV*, p. 58. The iron belt: Ibid., p. 60; *TA*, vol. 3, p. 250.

Richard's speech: *AH*, pp. 85–87; George Buchanan, *Rerum Scotiarum Historia*, apud A. Arbuthnetum (1582), ff. 146–47.

Agreeing to help him: *AH*, pp. 86n., 87; Macdougall, *James IV*, p. 121.

Linlithgow deed: David Dunlop, "The Masked Comedian: Perkin Warbeck's Adventures in Scotland and England from 1495 to 1497", *Scottish Historical Review*, vol. lxx, 2, no. 190 (Oct. 1991), pp. 100–101. Many thanks to Wendy Moorhen for a copy of this, and to David Dunlop for a copy of the original deed (Perth & Kinross Archive MS 78/9).

QUISQUIS ESSET: *AH*, p. 86 (twice). AN OBLIGATION TO "LOOK OUT FOR HIM": *PI*, vol. 5, p. 171 (*CSPS*, p. 140).

FORMAN AS RICHARD'S MINDER: *TA*, pp. 299, 344, 345 (and cxl, clii). HIS CAREER: *CSPV*, pp. 188, 199; *CSPM*, p. 343. PLAYING CATCH AND CARDS: *TA*, pp. 172, 386.

RICHARD'S LODGINGS: *Exchequer Rolls of Scotland*, ed. George Burnett, Scottish Records Series (Edinburgh, 1888), pp. 153–54; *L&P*, vol. 2, p. 329.

ROUND THE COUNTRY: *RMS*, entries for Nov. 1495 to July 1496 *passim; TA*, pp. cxxviii–ix, cxxxi, 259, 268. CANDLEMAS IN EDINBURGH: *TA*, p. 268; EASTER IN STIRLING: Ibid., p. 259; JUNE IN PERTH: Ibid., p. 276; *Exchequer Rolls*, pp. 153–54.

RICHARD'S CLOTHES: *TA*, pp. 256, 259, 263. HIS PENSION: Ibid., pp. 335, 340, 342.

MONEY RAISED FOR HIM: *Exchequer Rolls*, pp. lvi–lvii, 15–16, 49; *Register of the Privy Seal of Scotland*, vol. 1, 1488–1529, ed. M. Livingstone (Edinburgh, 1908), nos. 311, 405.

FOLLOWERS PAID FOR: *TA*, pp. 274, 276–77, 280, 303–4. BAD BEHAVIOUR: *ADC*, vol. 2, pp. 68–69.

DUNCAN FORRESTER: *ADC*, vol. 2, p. 361.

ABERDEEN: *Extracts from the Council Register of the Burgh of Aberdeen, 1398–1570*, ed. John Stuart (Aberdeen, for the Spalding Club, 1844), p. 57. The two relevant entries, for July and Sept. 1496, are misdated by Stuart to 1495. Thanks to Judith Cripps, the Aberdeen city archivist, for help on this point.

LAMBSKINS AND FISH: *Halyburton's Ledger* (see Notes, p. 549), p. lxx.

JAMES'S POVERTY: Ellis, *Letters*, vol. 1, p. 29; *CSPV*, p. 188. 1493 FUNDS SHORTAGE: Macdougall, *James IV*, p. 113.

HUNTLY: *Debrett's Peerage* under Huntly, p. 676 and n. HIS LAWSUITS: *ADC*, vol. 2, pp. 46–47, 73, 103–4; *RMS*, no. 2036. HIS WIVES: Wendy A. Moorhen, "Lady Katherine Gordon: A Genealogical Puzzle", *The Ricardian*, vol. xi, no. 139 (Dec. 1997), pp. 194–96. I am grateful to Wendy Moorhen for many helpful discussions on aspects of Katherine's family and history.

HUNTLY BELIEVING IN RICHARD: *CSPM*, p. 331.

ALEXANDER'S LETTER: Pinkerton, *History*, vol. 2, App. 1 (no pagination); McKerracher, "John Ramsay", pp. 6–7.

KATHERINE'S YOUTH: Ralph Holinshed, *Chronicles of England, Scotland and Ireland*, 6 vols. (1808), vol. 4, p. 511; Richard Grafton, *Chronicle*, 2 vols. (1809), vol. 2, p. 203. HER BEAUTY: Fabyan, *GC*, pp. 262, 283 (a very rare compliment from him); *HRHS*, p. 73; *CSPV*, p. 266 (*bellissima donna* in the original: Sanuto, *Diarii*, vol. 1, col. 842).

AYALA ON SCOTTISH GIRLS: *CSPS*, p. 210; *PI*, vol. 5, p. 263.

THE GOWN: *TA*, p. 224; SRO E 21/3, f. 18r. The dating is difficult, but 1495 is the most likely year and the betrothal by far the most likely occasion. See Wendy Moorhen, "Four Weddings and a Conspiracy: the Life, Times and Loves of Lady Katherine Gordon", part 1, *The Ricardian*, vol. xii, no. 156 (March 2002), pp. 402–3.

KATHERINE'S PEDIGREE: Moorhen, "Genealogical Puzzle", *passim.* HUNTLY AS JAMES'S COUSIN: Ibid., p. 83. "TENDER COUSIN": Lesley, *History*, pp. 64, 66–67.

JAMES AND THE MARRIAGE: *AH*, pp. 87, 103; Buchanan, *Rerum Scotiarum*, f. 146v; Lesley, *History*, pp. 64, 66.

. . .

WINTER OF 1495-96: *LC,* p. 208.

DANCING: Hawes, *Pastime of Pleasure,* p. 63. For a curious, presumably invented, scene of Richard and Katherine courting, see Gainsford, *Perkin Warbeck* (see Notes, p. 532), p. 530.

"STUFFING OF THE CODPIECE": *Peter Idley's Instructions to his Son,* ed. Charlotte d'Evelyn (Boston, 1935), Book II B, ls. 419-20.

CHAMBER WORK: Hawes, *Pastime of Pleasure,* pp. 150-51.

FERDINAND AND ISABELLA: Münzer, *Itinerário* (see Notes, p. 536), p. 126.

AFONSO AND ISABELLA: Resende, *Crónica,* p. 169.

GUILLAUME DE MACHAUT: cited in Huizinga, *Middle Ages,* p. 119.

THEIR CHILD: See pp. 298-99 and notes.

WEDDING EXPENSES: *TA,* pp. 263-64. THE CEREMONY: *The Sarum Missal, edited from three early Manuscripts,* by J. Wickham Legg (Oxford, 1916), pp. 413-18. "KNIT TOGETHER FLESHLY": *Vices & Virtues,* p. 245.

THE FOUNDATION OF LOVE: *Secreta,* p. 191. GIVING THE PAX: Huizinga, *Middle Ages,* p. 120.

PRIVILEGES OF A DUCHESS: *The Book of Precedence,* ed. F. J. Furnivall, EETS Extra Series viii (1869), pp. 13, 26.

"OBFUSKED, ENDULLED . . .": Caxton, *Eneydos,* p. 41.

VILLON'S DELUSIONS: "Le Testament", lxviii.

ROSES ON NETTLES: Davies, *Medieval Lyrics,* no. 125.

THE BARON'S DAUGHTER: Ibid., no. 175. FABYAN ON THE MARRIAGE: *GC,* p. 262.

LOVE-BLINDNESS: *Secreta,* pp. 192-93.

HE HAD BEEN PREVENTED: He dated this, in Oct. 1497, as "for quite two years": *CSPM,* p. 329.

WEDDING JOUSTS: *TA,* p. 263. JAMES'S SORE HAND: Ibid., p. 257.

INVITATIONS TO FIGHT: Pittscotie, *Historie,* pp. 231-32. BREAKING SPEARS AGAINST HIM: SRO E 21/3, f. 81r.

AYALA ON JAMES'S DARING: *PI,* vol. 5, pp. 259-60.

THE WILD KNIGHT: Taylor, *James IV,* p. 197.

WEAPONS-SHOWINGS: *TA,* p. 267. SPEAR-SILVER: Ibid., pp. 312, 324. MUSTER AT LAUDER: Ibid., p. 269.

HARRY THE SCOT: *EH,* p. 108.

RAMSAY ON JAMES: Ellis, *Letters,* vol. 1, pp. 24, 29.

MONYPENY IN SCOTLAND: Ibid., pp. 27-28.

THE SCOTS ABANDONING THEIR "ARRANGEMENT": *CSPM,* p. 305.

URSWICK TO CONTARINI: *CSPV,* p. 241.

"IN DREAD" OF BEING EXPELLED: Ibid., p. 245.

ROSS'S CROSSBOW: Ellis, *Letters,* vol. 1, pp. 23-24. WHITE ROSE LETTERS ON ROSS'S ACCOUNT: *Halyburton's Ledger,* pp. 153, 215.

"PERFECT SAFETY FROM YORK": *PI,* vol. 4, p. 608 (*CSPS,* p. 116).

"NO DAUGHTER": *PI,* vol. 4, p. 536 (*CSPS,* p. 97).

JAMES INTERCEPTING: *PI,* vol. 4, p. 535. THE GARDEN INCIDENT: Ibid., p. 521 (*CSPS,* p. 91).

. . .

JOUSTS OF 1494: *LC*, p. 202; *L&P*, vol. 1, p. 399.

ANTHONY WOODVILLE AND THE BASTARD OF BURGUNDY: *EH*, pp. 177–93. THE TOURNAMENT: *Chronicles of the White Rose*, p. 19n.

GENTLEMEN OF HAINAULT: Molinet, *Chroniques*, vol. 4, p. 6. DUKE OF SAXONY: Ibid., p. 10.

HENRY'S WAR-GEAR: *EH*, p. 90.

SIR JOHN PASTON: *Paston Letters*, vol. 5, no. 861.

WAR BOOKS, AND ARTHUR'S TRAINING: Ian Arthurson, "The King's Voyage into Scotland: The war that never was", in *England in the Fifteenth Century* (see Notes, p. 538), p. 2.

ARCHERS IN TOURNAI: La Grange, "Extraits" (see Notes, p. 536), p. 249.

AT THE PORTUGUESE COURT: Sanceau, *Perfect Prince*, pp. 277, 336.

THE BEAUTIFUL GIANTESS: Molinet, *Chroniques*, vol. 5, pp. 19–24.

LAURENCE THE ARMOURER: *TA*, pp. 264, 269.

RODERICK DE LALAING: Commines, *Mémoires*, book 1, ch. ii. GOLDEN FLEECE JOUSTS: Molinet, *Chroniques*, vol. 4, pp. 160–61. ON PHILIP'S PAYROLL: ADN B2153, nos. 70642, 70669; *Compte rendu des séances de la Commission Royale d'Histoire*, vol. 11, part ii (1846), p. 712. PAID FOR BY JAMES: *TA*, pp. 274, 292–93. HIS SHIP: *TA*, p. 274.

"YE BEST DAY-WORK": Ellis, *Letters*, vol. 1, p. 24.

ABERDEEN EXCUSED: *Extracts from the Council Register* (see Notes, p. 564), p. 57.

BUCHANANS PARDONED: *Privy Seal* (see Notes, p. 564), no. 202.

NOT "A *MARAVEDI*": *PI*, vol. 5, p. 262.

WAR PREPARATIONS: *TA*, esp. pp. 280–98. MARGARET'S CONTRIBUTION: Ellis, *Letters*, vol. 1, p. 30.

RAMSAY ON THE GUNS: Ibid., p. 31. AYALA: *PI*, vol. 5, p. 264 (*CSPS*, p. 210). HANS AND HENRIC: *TA*, pp. 236, 284, 289, 300, etc.

MONS: Ibid., pp. 347–49, 351, 359.

RICHARD'S BANNER: Ibid., pp. 293, 294. SYMBOLISM OF THE COLOURS: Christine de Pisan, *Fayttes of Armes*, pp. 289–90.

AYALA ON TENTS: *PI*, vol. 5, p. 264 (*CSPS*, p. 174).

PAVILION EXPENSES: *TA*, esp. pp. 283, 285. THE OUSTING CLOSET: Ibid., p. 294. DRINKSILVER: Ibid., p. 288.

HENRY'S TENTS: PRO E 404/80/444; E 404/81/4; E 405/79, mem. 35v.

CHARLES THE BOLD'S: Commines, *Mémoires*, book 5, ch. ii.

SIR GAWAIN/LADY ETTARD: *Morte Darthur*, p. 78.

HENRY'S DOUBLE VICTORY: See Peter Carmeliano, BL MS Add 33736, ff. 1–3; Johannes Opicius, BL Cotton MS Vespasian B iv, f. 3.

"INCONVENIENCE OF THE SEASON": Ellis, *Letters*, vol. 1, p. 26; RAMSAY WATCHING: Ibid., p. 23. BUCHAN: Conway, *Relations*, p. 27.

THE VELVET CLOAK: *TA*, pp. 260–61.

HOLYROOD FULL OF GUNS: *TA*, pp. 282, 289, 295–96. MASSES AND OFFERINGS: Ibid., p. 296.

RICHARD'S BOASTS: *AH*, pp. 87, 105; *CSPV*, p. 232; *CSPM*, p. 308.

JAMES'S PRESENT: *TA*, p. 297.

NEVILLE'S WAVERING: *L&P*, vol. 1, pp. 277–78; Ellis, *Letters*, vol. 1, p. 28.

THE MAN FROM CARLISLE: Ibid., pp. 23–24.

BERWICK NEGOTIATIONS: Ibid., p. 26. BERWICK FULL OF GUNS: PRO E 404/82.

PROCLAMATION: See Notes, p. 541. HIS IMPROVED MONOGRAM: Plate 7 (BL MS Harleian 283, f. 124v).

HENRY TUDOR'S PROCLAMATION: Rosemary Horrox, "Henry Tudor's Letters to England during Richard III's Reign", *The Ricardian*, vol. vi, no. 80 (March 1983), p. 156.

THE CAMPAIGN: *TA*, pp. 296–300, *passim; AH*, pp. 87–89.

VERGIL'S "RUGGED MEN": *AH*, p. 25. MERCENARIES: Christine de Pisan, *Fayttes of Armes*, pp. 26, 50; Molinet, *Chroniques*, esp. vol. 4, ch. ccxliii *passim*, cclix, ccxli.

NORTHUMBERLAND MEN GATHERING: Ellis, *Letters*, vol. 1, p. 24. ROBINSON TO THE BORDER: *TA*, p. 281.

WOOL EXEMPTED: *CPR HVII*, vol. 1, p. 269.

THE KING'S ALMONER: *TA*, p. 199; Taylor, *James IV*, p. 138.

HENRY'S ALMS: *EH*, pp. 94, 99 and *passim*. NEW BREAD, ROSEWATER: PRO E 101/414/6, ff. 5r, 6r. CROPS AND REAPING: *EH*, pp. 91, 92.

RICHARD'S PROTEST: *AH*, pp. 88 and n., 89; Buchanan, *Rerum Scotiarum*, f. 147r.

COVERING UP HIS DEPARTURE: *TA*, pp. 299n., 300. Such an adjustment is almost unique in the Scottish accounts.

HENRY ON THE RAID: *Tudor Royal Proclamations* (see Notes, p. 557), p. 38; Rymer, *Foedera*, vol. 12, p. 647.

THE SOLITARY COMPLAINT: *ADC*, vol. 2, p. 116.

BLEEDINGS: *Kalendar of Shepherds*, pp. 105–7, 161; *Secreta*, pp. 243–44; *Tretyse of Love* (see Notes, p. 534), p. 54.

JAMES LETTING BLOOD: *TA*, p. 176.

THE GIRL TREMBLING: Caxton, *Dialogues* (see Notes, p. 550), p. 35.

DUKE OF BERRY: Commines, *Mémoires*, book 1, ch. v and vi.

"THAT GLORIOUS SIGHING": Hall, *Chronicle*, p. 476. Buchanan said he went to James with his expression "adjusted to compassion": *Rerum Scotiarum*, f. 147r.

REMEMBER WHOSE SON HE WAS: *Vices & Virtues* (see Notes, p. 533), p. 99.

EDWARD IV AND ARTILLERY: *CSPM*, p. 194. "EDWARD AND RICHARD BOM-BARDEL": *Chronicles of the White Rose*, p. lxxxviii. HIS COURAGE: Ibid., p. 65; Commines, *Mémoires*, book 6, ch. i.

THE LITTER OF WAR: *TA*, p. 302.

"THE MAN'S FOOLISH IMPUDENCE": *AH*, p. 89.

PAYMENTS FOR "THEIR MASTER": *TA*, pp. 335, 340.

"YORK" IN THE MARGIN: SRO E 21/4, ff. 62v, 67v, 70r.

"DIDN'T STOP RUNNING": *PI*, vol. 5, pp. 171–72 (*CSPS*, p. 140).

HENRY'S WAR MONEY: Arthurson, "King's Voyage", p. 11 and n.

SUPPORTERS LEAVING: *TA*, pp. 301, 303.

CHILDREN: *HRHS*, p. 70; *CSPV*, p. 264 (Sanuto, *Diarii*, vol. 1, col. 806).

THE ONE-YEAR-OLD SON: *Regesta Imperii XIV*, vol. 2, part i (*Maximilian, 1496–1498*), no. 5512; Biblioteca Nazionale Marciana (Venice) MSS Lat. XIV/99 (4278), f. 117r.

PAYMENT WHEN HE CAME HOME: *TA*, p. 300. Edward IV gave a present of a silver cup on the birth of the first child of his favourite Medici creditor: Scofield, *Edward IV*, vol. 2, p. 425.

EDWARD KISSING HIS BABIES: *Political Poems and Songs relating to English History, composed during the period from the Accession of Edward III to that of Richard III*, ed. Thomas Wright (Rolls Series 14, 1861), vol. 2, p. 274.

JAMES CASHING HIS CHAINS: Ellis, *Letters*, vol. 1, p. 29; *TA*, p. 314. The fifty-four links, coined into unicorns, produced £571 Scots.

RICHARD AT FALKLAND: *Exchequer Rolls*, pp. 39, 40, 45.

FORMAN WITH THE KING: *TA*, p. 324.

JAMES PASSING BY: Ibid., pp. 331–33.

THE PALACE: Helen Douglas-Irvine, ed. R. S. Rait, *Royal Palaces of Scotland* (1911), pp. 218–31.

"TRY TO STOP THE OLD DUCHESS": *PI*, vol. 4, p. 523 (*CSPS*, pp. 92–93).

MARGARET RAISING MONEY: Philpot, *Maximilian*, p. 168; *Regesta Imperii XIV*, vol. 1, part ii, no. 3589.

THE RECEPTION SCENE: Ellis, *Letters*, vol. 1, p. 30.

LEAVING HER TO CARRY ON: Philpot, *Maximilian*, p. 169.

WRITING TO HER: Arthurson, "Espionage" (see Notes, p. 555), p. 147; Dixon, *TA*, p. cxxxviii; *Halyburton's Ledger*, pp. lix, 153, 215.

"RICHARD'S ROOM": AN CC 8857, f. 39v. The two mentions of this room are the only occurrence of the name "Richard" in the Binche accounts.

MARGARET AND ROME: Walter Cahn, "Margaret of York's Guide to the Pilgrimage Churches of Rome," in Kren, *Margaret of York, Simon Marmion* . . . (see Notes, p. 547), pp. 89–98.

EGREMONT'S NEGOTIATIONS: *CSPV*, pp. 225–28.

MAXIMILIAN'S PENSION SCHEME: HHSA Maximiliana 5 f 20v.

MAXIMILIAN TO CONTARINI: *CSPV*, p. 232; *Regesta Imperii XIV*, vol. 2, part i, no. 3782.

URSWICK'S MISSION: *CSPV*, pp. 237–44, *passim*. YORK'S SUPPORTERS: *PI*, vol. 4, p. 596 (*CSPS*, p. 110).

"HIS FEELINGS FOR RICHARD": John S. C. Bridge, *A History of France from the Death of Louis XI*, vol. 2, *Charles VIII* (1924), p. 312. SFORZA SEEKING INFORMATION: *Regesta Imperii XIV*, vol. 2, part ii, no. 7605; *CSPS*, pp. 130–31.

AYALA'S SCHEME: See pp. 308–9.

MONYPENY'S OFFER: Ellis, *Letters*, vol. 1, pp. 27–28. HENRY'S ATTEMPT TO STOP HIM: *PI*, vol. 4, p. 598 (*CSPS*, p. 111). "12,000 FRANCS A YEAR": *CSPM*, p. 329.

KILDARE'S REWARDS: *EH*, p. 109. HIS UNDERTAKING: Conway, *Relations*, App. xlii, pp. 230–31.

WRITING TO DESMOND: BL Cotton Titus Fxiii, f. 76v; BL MS Add. 11595, f. 4r, v (both references to a letter that is now lost); Ware, *Antiquities*, p. 31.

DESMOND'S PARDONS: *CPR HVII*, vol. 1, p. 423; Ibid., vol. 2, p. 27. HIS BOND: Conway, *Relations*, p. 223. SHOWN TO JAMES: Ellis, *Letters*, vol. 1, p. 24.

LETTER TO DE LA FORSA: See plate 11 and pp. 144–45; BL MS Egerton 616/6.

GETTING JAMES INTO THE HOLY LEAGUE: *PI*, vol. 4, p. 416 (*CSPS*, p. 69).

FERDINAND AND ISABELLA/MAXIMILIAN: *PI*, vol. 4, pp. 464, 479 (*CSPS*, pp. 73, 81 and n.).

"MEDIATING BETWEEN HENRY AND YORK": *CSPM*, p. 298.

GETTING HOLD OF YORK: *PI*, vol. 4, p. 464 (*CSPS*, p. 73n.).

YORK "IN SPAIN": *PI*, vol. 4, p. 487. NO NEWS FROM SCOTLAND: Ibid., p. 508. "UNTIL WE SEE": Ibid., p. 538 (*CSPS*, p. 98). "THE DUKE": See esp. *PI*, vol. 4, pp. 538, 539, 610.

DE PUEBLA, JUNE 13TH: *PI*, vol. 4, pp. 552–54 (*CSPS*, p. 103).

"WE SHALL NOT TRY": *PI*, vol. 4, p. 522 (*CSPS*, pp. 91–92). In the draft, this sentence is crammed in as an afterthought down the margin of the page: AGS Patronato Real, leg. 52, f. 357v.

AYALA/DE PUEBLA: See Garrett Mattingly, "The Reputation of Doctor de Puebla", *EHR* lv (1940), esp. pp. 30–34. AYALA'S CHARACTER: Ibid., p. 30; *AH*, p. 101.

"SO EASILY BELIEVING": *PI*, vol. 5, p. 173 (*CSPS*, p. 141).

AYALA/YORK: Zurita, *Historia*, vol. 5, ff. 133b, 134; Busch, *England under the Tudors* (see Notes, p. 556), pp. 113–14.

SOME HOPE OF GETTING THE DUKE: *PI*, vol. 5, p. 148 (*CSPS*, p. 135). THE "SECRET THING": *PI*, vol. 5, p. 172.

DE LA FORSA'S INSTRUCTIONS: *L&P*, vol. 1, pp. 23–24, 48–51; Rymer, *Foedera*, vol. 12, pp. 193–99, 198, 200.

"THAT BOY": *CSPS*, p. 109.

DE LA FORSA/HENRY: PRO E 404/80/372; E 404/81/3, warrant of Dec. 9th, 1491; E 404/80/441; E 405/78, mems. 17r, 23r, v, 32r; E 36/130, f. 80v; Campbell, *Materials*, vol. 2, p. 563.

CLIFFORD'S REGISTERS: PRO E 36/8, *passim*. For war preparations, see also PRO E 405/79, mem. 22r et seq.; *CPR HVII*, vol. 2, pp. 90–93; Arthurson, "King's Voyage", esp. pp. 11–12 and Appendix.

HE COULD NOT DELIVER HIM TO DEATH: *AH*, p. 103. "PETER WAS NOT RICHARD": Ibid.

"THE EARS OF THE WOLF": *PI*, vol. 5, p. 304; *CSPS*, p. 190.

BUYING THE *CUCKOO*: *TA*, pp. 301–2, 303; *Privy Seal*, no. 99.

CUCKOO LORE: Brant, *Ship of Fools*, esp. pp. 78, 157, 269; *Vices & Virtues*, p. 17.

"SET FULL POORLY": Ellis, *Letters*, vol. 1, p. 32.

THE FAREWELL: *AH*, pp. 103–5 and n.; Buchanan, *Rerum Scotiarum*, f. 147v. PROVISIONS: *TA*, pp. 343–45; *Exchequer Rolls*, no. 310.

JAMES AT KINGHORN: *TA*, p. 344.

PAYING HIS PENSION EARLY: Ibid., p. 342. KATHERINE'S CLOTHES: Ibid., p. 343.

LAURENCE LEFT BEHIND: Ibid., pp. 347, 360.

JAMES/FOULCART: *L&P*, vol. 2, pp. 185–87.

BARTON "MAKING WAR": Chastelain, *L'Imposture* (see Notes, p. 552), p. 84 n.

"TO WIN HIS FATHER'S CROWN": Abell, *Queill of Tyme* (see Notes, p. 549), p. 111.

HENRY TO FOX: *L&P*, vol. 1, pp. 104–11; PRO SP 58/1/22. NEW JEWELS: *EH*, pp. 112–13.

JAMES "LESS INCOMMODED": *PI*, vol. 5, p. 171.

THE RAPE OF THE ROSE GARDEN: *Jo. Orpicii Carmin. ad Henr. VII* (The *Dialogus*), BL Cotton MS Vespasian B iv, f. 16r.

6. King Perkin

FABYAN ON HIS FOLLOWERS: *GC*, p. 282.

HENRY'S ENEMIES HIDING: *CPR HVII*, vol. 1, p. 179; Ibid., vol. 2, p. 159.

PERKIN/CACUS: "Douze triomphes" in Gairdner, *Memorials*, pp. 320–21.

BIRTHMARKS AND SIGNS: *Annals of Ulster* (see Notes, p. 562), esp. pp. 335, 357, 359; *New History of Ireland*, vol. 2, p. 688; Ware, *Antiquities*, pp. 18, 24.

IRISH NOT MAKING AN ARMY: *AH*, pp. 25, 85. CONTAMINATION: Ibid., p. 78.

SPOTTED IN THE SOUTH: Pollard, *Henry VII*, vol. 1, p. 156. THREE WEEKS AT SEA: Kildare's voyage from England, in the late summer of the year before, took three weeks: Conway, *Relations*, App. xliii, p. 232.

CORK'S WELCOME: Ware, *Antiquities*, p. 35.

THE GENERAL PARDON: *CPR HVII*, vol. 2, p. 76.

KILDARE AND THE CHIEFS: Conway, *Relations*, pp. 94–97, and App. xliii, pp. 230–31, 233–35.

"DESOLATING" THE COUNTRY: *L&P*, vol. 2, p. 67.

ORMOND/BUTLER: Ibid., pp. xli–xlii, 67; Conway, *Relations*, p. 111. "PIERS THE RED": *Annals of Ulster*, p. 419.

FAMINE: *Annals of Ulster*, p. 423; Ware, *Antiquities*, p. 24.

WATERFORD/HENRY: Pollard, *Henry VII*, vol. 1, p. 156; Carew MS, vol. 632, f. 251r.

STILL IN SCOTLAND: *CSPV*, p. 260.

WATERFORD LOSING HIM: Ryland, *Waterford* (see Notes, p. 562), p. 38.

HENRY TO TALBOT: Pollard, *Henry VII*, vol. 1, p. 163.

FLED INCOGNITO: *CSPV*, p. 261.

SPANISH SHIPS: Zurita, *Historia*, vol. 5, f. 134.

THE CORNISH REVOLT: For its extent, see Ian Arthurson, "The Rising of 1497: A Revolt of the Peasantry?", in Joel Rosenthal & Colin Richmond, eds., *People, Politics and Community in the Later Middle Ages* (Gloucester, 1987), pp. 1–18.

"A PRINCIPAL PERSON": Zurita, *Historia*, vol. 5, f. 133b.

"NURSING": Molinet, *Chroniques*, vol. 5, p. 78.

CORNISHMEN ASKING HIM: *Rot. Parl.*, vol. 6, pp. 544–45.

TRESINNY: Arthurson, *Perkin Warbeck*, p. 168; PRO SC8/345 C2.

DRAMA ON THE SEA: *PI*, vol. 5, pp. 297–98 (*CSPS*, p. 186).

MEN WITH HIM: *CSPM*, pp. 325, 327; *Rot. Parl.*, vol. 6, p. 545. HIS SHIPS: Pollard, *Henry VII*, vol. 1, p. 163.

CORNWALL'S POVERTY: M. John Hatcher, *Rural Economy and Society in the Duchy of Cornwall, 1300–1500* (Cambridge, 1970), esp. pp. 148–73; *AH*, p. 93; *CSPV*, no. 869.

FIFTY YEARS LATER: Andrew Borde, *The First Book of the Introduction of Knowledge* (1542), ed F. J. Furnivall, EETS Extra Series 10 (1870), pp. 122–25.

LONDONERS/CORNISHMEN: *LC*, pp. 213–15.

SPEAKING ENGLISH: Borde, *First Book*, p. 123.

"SO BASE A CABIN": Richard Carew, *Survey of Cornwall*, 1602 (Redruth, 2000), p. 24.

MERIASEK PLAY: *The Life of St. Meriasek, Bishop and Confessor*, ed. & tr. Whitley Stokes (1872), esp. ls. 1040–44, 2300–2308, 2372–74. TINTAGEL: Ibid., ls. 2212–15.

RELICS OF LYONESSE: Carew, *Survey*, p. 13.

ARTHUR'S COUNTRY: A. L. Rowse, *Tudor Cornwall: Portrait of a Society* (1941), p. 29; L. E. Elliott-Binns, *Medieval Cornwall* (1955), pp. 416–19.

HENRY'S MEN: See Rowse, *Tudor Cornwall*, chs. v and vi *passim*.

CON BOZ DE REY: Fuensalida, *Correspondencia* (see Notes, p. 558), p. 149.

THE EARLY CAMPAIGN IN THE WEST COUNTRY: *AH*, pp. 104n., 105–6; Davies Gilbert, *The Parochial History of Cornwall* (4 vols., 1838), vol. 2, pp. 187–89; *CSPM* (Fra Zoan's report), pp. 325–27; ASM AD Cartella 567 (Sept. 30th).

PENRYN: Sanuto, *Diarii*, vol. 1, col. 187; *CSPV*, p. 264.

ST. BURYAN: Attreed, "New Source" (see Notes, p. 601), p. 521.

KATHERINE AT THE MOUNT: *AH*, p. 109; *HRHS*, p. 72; Zurita, *Historia*, vol. 5, f. 134. Exeter thought she was left there too: DRO ECR book 51, f. 328v. For the bad connotations of taking sanctuary, see More, *Richard III*, pp. 37–47.

THE MOUNT: Warkworth's *Chronicle*, in *Chronicles of the White Rose*, p. 138; John Leland's itinerary of 1538 in Gilbert, *Parochial History*, vol. 4, p. 287; WILLIAM OF WORCESTER'S VISIT: Ibid., App. vi, pp. 232–33.

ST. MICHAEL'S STATUE: J. R. Fletcher, *A Short History of St. Michael's Mount* (St. Michael's Mount, 1951), p. 53.

ST. IVES: Attreed, "New Source", p. 521; John Hobson Matthews, *A History of the Parishes of St. Ives, Lelant, Towednack and Zennor* (1892), p. 47.

ST. PETROC'S: "Receipts and Expenses in the Building of Bodmin Church, 1469–1472", *Camden Miscellany* VII, New Series 14 (1875), pp. 1–49 (last article).

HENRY'S PLACARDS: Attreed, "New Source," pp. 517, 521. OFFENCES FORGIVEN: Pollard, *Henry VII*, vol. 1, p. 169.

"THIS PRINCE OF KNAVES": *HRHS*, p. 71.

A PARDON: *CSPM*, p. 325.

PAYMENT TO DIGBY: PRO E 405/79, mem. 431.

HENRY MOBILISING: Ellis, *Letters*, vol. 1, pp. 32–33; *L&P*, vol. 1, p. 112; Pollard, *Henry VII*, vol. 1, p. 163.

HENRY TO THE POPE: *CSPM*, p. 327.

ROBINSON TO SCOTLAND: *TA*, p. 360. NOT RETURNING: Ibid., p. 371.

HENRY'S DISTRESS: *CSPS*, p. 162 (Londoño and the Prior of Santa Cruz); Fuensalida, *Correspondencia*, pp. 148–49.

SONCINO/HENRY: *CSPM*, p. 322. "SIX MILLION IN GOLD": *CSPV*, p. 261. "ALL THE NOBLES": *CSPM*, p. 325.

"ANOTHER LONDON": Bacon, *Henry VII*, p. 190.

CITY CLERK: DRO ECR book 55, f. 66r.

EXETER'S DEFENCES: Edward Freeman, *Exeter* (1887), p. 94.

COURTENAY: Attreed, "New Source", p. 515.

1,000 MARKS: Nicholas Orme, *The Cap and the Sword: Exeter and the Rebellions of 1497* (Exeter, 1997), p. 11. Thanks to Professor Orme for a copy of this.

HENRY TO COURTENAY: Attreed, "New Source", *passim*, esp. pp. 519-22.

"INRANGING THEMSELVES": Ellis, *Letters*, vol. 1, p. 34.

EXETER PREPARING: DRO Exeter Receiver's Accounts, years 12-13 Henry VII, mem. 31; Orme, *Cap and Sword*, p. 14.

THE ATTACK: Hooker's account, DRO ECR book 51, ff. 329r, v; Alexander Jenkins, *Civil and Ecclesiastical History of the City of Exeter* (1841), pp. 91-92; *AH*, pp. 105-7.

COURTENAY TO HENRY: Ellis, *Letters*, vol. 1, pp. 36-37.

HOOKER ON PERKIN: DRO ECR book 51, f. 325v.

"WE OURSELVES SHALL NOT BE FAR": Ellis, *Letters*, vol. 1, p. 35.

ARRIVING IN WELLS: Arthurson, "Rising of 1497" (see Notes, p. 570), pp. 1-2.

LOSSES AT EXETER: Pollard, *Henry VII*, vol. 1, pp. 167, 168 (Henry's estimate); DRO ECR book 55, f. 66r; *LC*, p. 217.

PERKIN'S MEN: *CSPM*, p. 327; *GC*, p. 281; JCCC (JOR 10), f. 98v; Zurita, *Historia*, vol. 5, p. 134. "NOT ONE GENTLEMAN": Pollard, *Henry VII*, vol. 1, p. 168.

BRIDGES CUT, MEN NOT PAID: *CSPM*, pp. 328, 331; Gairdner, *Memorials*, p. 72.

PARDONS: *CSPM*, p. 328. Fra Zoan added that, seeing the state of Perkin's forces, Henry "dismissed all his army [of 20,000 men] except 6,000 men, with whom he himself is going into Cornwall."

GOD ON HENRY'S SIDE: *CSPV*, pp. 261-62.

NYNEHEAD FLORY: Orme, *Cap and Sword*, p. 14; John Collinson, *Somersetshire*, vol. 3 (1791), p. 267. WYKE'S FINE: "Fines imposed on persons who assisted the rebels during the Cornish rebellion and the insurrection of Perkin Warbeck in 1497" (transcription of BL Rot. Royal 14B vii), ed. & pub. A. J. Howard (1986), p. 6. Many thanks to Bill Hampton for these sources.

"FLED" FROM EXETER: JCCC (JOR 10), f. 103r.

KING RICHARD'S PROMISES: *CSPM*, pp. 327-28; ASM AD Cartella 567 (Sept. 30th).

TAUNTON CASTLE: James Savage, *The History of Taunton* (Taunton, 1822), pp. 259-61, 404-5. CONSTERNATION: Zurita, *Historia*, vol. 5, f. 134.

APOSTOLIC BULLS: *CSPM*, p. 327. AS FAKES: *CSPV*, p. 180.

THE CHALLENGE: Sanuto, *Diarii*, vol. 1, cols. 816, 825-26; *CSPV*, p. 265; *AH*, p. 107. "AT GLASTONBURY": CC 111, f. 187v (Henry's letter of Oct. 7th). "BY AGREEMENT": *CSPV*, p. 263.

MUSTERING HIS FORCES: *LC*, p. 217; *GC*, p. 282; *AH*, p. 107.

NIGHT TERRORS: Thomas More, *A Dialogue of Comfort against Tribulation*, ed. Frank Manley (1977), pp. 110-33; Chastellain, *Chronique, 1454-1458, Oeuvres*, vol. 3, pp. 243, 248-56.

MISTAKING ARMIES: Commines, *Mémoires*, book 1, ch. xi; More, *Dialogue*, pp. 113-14.

"WATCHING AND WAKING": Henry to Courtenay, Attreed, "New Source", p. 520.

KNEW HE WAS SURROUNDED: Zurita, *Historia*, vol. 5, f. 134b; *CSPM*, p. 326.

THE PIECE OF BONE: John Cummins, *The Hound and the Hawk* (1988), p. 32.

RICHARD'S FLIGHT: Pollard, *Henry VII*, vol. 1, pp. 174-75; *CSPM*, p. 328.

"AMAZED AND DISCONSOLATE": *LC*, p. 217.

"A LOW-BORN FOREIGNER": *CSPM*, p. 331. *IDOLUM AUT SIMULACRUM:* e.g. Rymer, *Foedera*, vol. 12, p. 696; *L&P*, vol. 2, p. 336; *CPR HVII*, vol. 2, p. 159.

JAMES THE ROVER: *LC*, p. 217.

SICKENED WITH POISON: *CSPM*, p. 324. "HOLY OIL": Ibid., p. 328.

"GOOD NUMBER OF WELL-HORSED MEN": Ellis, *Letters*, vol. 1, pp. 37-38.

IN DISGUISE: Sanuto, *Diarii*, vol. 1, col. 816; *GC*, p. 282. THE ABBOT THOUGHT: *CSPM*, p. 329.

"FOUL FLIGHT": Vergil, *Three Books*, p. 227. Christine de Pisan, *Fayttes of Armes*, pp. 19, 67. "NO LEAVE NOR LICENCE": Ellis, *Letters*, vol. 1, pp. 37, 38.

EARL RIVERS: Scofield, *Edward IV*, vol. 1, p. 165.

BUCKINGHAM: Gairdner, *Richard III*, p. 138n.

HENRY BEFORE BOSWORTH: Vergil, *Three Books*, pp. 220-21, 223.

EXCUSES FOR FLEEING: Christine de Pisan, *Fayttes of Armes*, pp. 65-67.

VECORDIA ANIMI: AH, p. 107; *HRHS*, p. 71.

"OF LIKE AUTHORITY & DISHONESTY": *GC*, p. 281.

IN MISERIA: ASM AD Cartella 567 (Oct. 21st); *CSPM*, p. 33.

BEAULIEU RULES: James Fowler, *History of Beaulieu Abbey* (1911), pp. 153-67.

NATURAL ORDER: See esp. da Salo, *Giuoco della Palla* (see Notes, p. 533), pp. 35-36, 71, 198-99; Boethius, *De Consolatione Philosophiae* (Dent, 1940), pp. 109, 114. POWER OF SEVEN: *Secreta*, pp. 101-2.

"LOATHLINESS": Caxton, *Eneydos*, p. 49.

MECHANICAL BIRDS: Mandeville, *Voiage*, p. 203.

THE DREAM GARDEN: Lydgate, "A Complaint of a Lover's Life", ls. 78-84.

RANKING OF MEEKNESS, ETC.: *Vices & Virtues*, pp. 130-60, *passim*. THE *PATER NOS-TER:* Ibid., pp. 96-97, 104.

EDWARD'S ANGELS: BL MS Royal 16 G iv.

SOCIAL ORDER: e.g. Caxton, *Playe of Chesse, passim;* Lydgate, "Ballad sent to the Sheriff's Dinner", ls. 29-84. "FAIR ORDER": Leland, *Collectanea*, vol. 4, pp. 265-80 *passim*.

LORD OF MISRULE: *EH*, pp. 92, 106; Nicolas, *Privy Purse*, p. 91.

KNOWING ONE'S PLACE: e.g. Furnivall, *Book of Precedence* (see Notes, p. 565), pp. 59-64; Idley, *Instructions*, Book II A, ls. 372-78; BL MS Harleian 543, f. 118v.

WAYS TO ADVANCEMENT: Michael Bennett, "Careerism in Late Medieval England", in Rosenthal & Richmond, *People, Politics* (see Notes, p. 570), pp. 19-39, *passim;* A. J. Pollard, "The Richmondshire Community of Gentry during the Wars of the Roses", in Griffiths, *Patronage* (see Notes, p. 548), *passim*.

JUMPED-UP TOWNSMEN: Commines, *Mémoires*, book 2, ch. iii; book 5, ch. xvi.

HENRY'S NEW MEN: Margaret Condon, "Ruling Elites in the Reign of Henry VII", in Griffiths, *Patronage*, pp. 123-28, 130; Stephen Gunn, "The Courtiers of Henry VII", in *EHR*, no. 108 (Jan. 1993), p. 28 and *passim*.

FALCON AND MASTIFF: Agnes Strickland, *Lives of the Queens of England* (8 vols., 1841-66), vol. 2, p. 59n.

RANKING OF DOGS: Cummins, *Hound and Hawk*, p. 12.

"AGAINST NATURE": "Douze triomphes", in Gairdner, *Memorials*, p. 316.

NOBILITY AND BASE HEARTS: *Roman de la Rose*, p. 100.

BEAUMAINS: *Morte Darthur*, pp. 120–49.

THE DUNG-HEAP: *Roman de la Rose*, p. 137.

DE SI PETITE ESTIME: Madden, "Documents", p. 202 (twice).

"NO PRICE OR VALUE": *L&P*, vol. 1, p. 104.

L'IMAGINACION DE VRAYE NOBLESSE: BL MS Royal 19 Cviii. ITS DELIVERY: *EH,* p. 112. *MAUVAIS GARSONS:* BL MS Royal 19 Cviii, f. 47r (pencil foliation). THE ARMLESS PRINCE: See Plate 12 and Ibid., f. 32v. CHOPPING NOBILITY: Ibid., f. 17v.

VIR INFIMI STATUS: Rymer, *Foedera*, vol. xii, p. 696; *CPR HVII*, vol. 2, pp. 159, 202; *CDRS*, p. 334. *IGNOBILISSIMUS: AH*, pp. 63, 79. FIT TO WASH THE POTS: Ibid., p. 71.

MISELLUS: HRHS, p. 72.

"HE CAN'T HURT ME": Madden, "Documents", pp. 167, 180, 202 (twice).

"CALLED ME BOY": Hawes, *Pastime of Pleasure*, p. 182.

THE COURT ON THE ROAD: PRO E 101/414/14, ff. 51–71 and *passim;* PRO E 36/126, ff. 36v, 37r.

BUBBLES AND SMOKE: *CSPM*, pp. 324, 325.

TONDAL'S ANGEL: Kren & Wieck, *The Visions of Tondal* (see Notes, p. 547), p. 40.

HENRY'S LETTER OF OCT. 7TH: CC 111, f. 187r, v. OF THE 17TH: Pollard, *Henry VII,* vol. 1, pp. 173–76.

STAFFORD: Williams, "Stafford" (see Notes, p. 542), pp. 186–87.

CHAMBERLAIN: PRO E 404/80/373.

SAVAGE AND DEBENHAM: Still there in December 1498: PRO E 404/83, warrant of Dec. 17th. Savage was pardoned in June 1499 (*CPR HVII*, vol. 2, p. 175); Debenham seems to have died in custody. THEIR FOOD: E 404/81/3, warrant of April 1495.

PRIVILEGE AMENDED: Isobel D. Thornley, "The Destruction of Sanctuary", in *Tudor Studies presented to A. F. Pollard*, ed. R. W. Seton Watson (1924), pp. 199–200.

ROBERT SYMONDS: PRO E36/126, f. 37v. PREVIOUS JOBS: Campbell, *Materials,* vol. 2, pp. 297, 320; PRO E 405/78, mems. 41r, 44r; E 404/79/40.

"IN SUCH A PLACE": *CSPM*, p. 329.

THE ARRANGEMENT: ASM AD Cartella 567 (Oct. 21st) (*CSPM*, p. 330).

"A MAN THAT CAME FROM PERKIN": *EH*, p. 113.

BRADSHAW SENT: PRO E 101/141/16, f. 90v. TAKEN "WITHIN THE SANCTUARY": *LC*, p. 218.

SOUTHAMPTON'S EXPENSES: PRO E 36/126, f. 37v; EXT 6/140, 25th and 35th documents. THE CITY'S ACCOUNTS: SCRO SC5/1/24A, f. 2r.

GODFREY'S REWARD: SCRO SC5/3/1, f. 19v; *Black Book of Southampton*, ed. A. B. Wallis Chapman, vol. 2, 1414–1503 (1912), p. 62n.

BUGLE HALL: John Speed, *The History and Antiquities of Southampton* (c. 1770) (Southampton Record Society, 1909), p. 122.

THE BLANK: Carew MS, vol. 632, f. 252r.

HIS EXTRACTION: *HRHS*, p. 71. MARGINAL NOTES: BL Cotton MS Domitian A xviii, ff. 220r, v, 221r, 222r.

GOLDEN ROBES: ASM AD Cartella 567 (Oct. 21st) (*CSPM*, p. 330).

PAYMENTS TO THE DUKE OF YORK: PRO E36/126, f. 37r; EXT 6/140, 25th and 35th documents.

"IN OUR NURSERY": PRO E 405/79, mem. 41r (1497); E 404/82, warrant of July 29th, 1497; E 404/83, warrant of May 24th, 1499.

HENRY PAID IN HIS OWN NAME: The first occasion is in 1502: *EH*, p. 126; Anglo, "Court Festivals", p. 38. PAYMENTS FOR ITEMS FOR HIM: *EH*, pp. 95, 98, 105.

7. *Confession*

LOUIS XI: Commines, *Mémoires*, book 2, ch. xli; Chastellain, *Oeuvres*, vol. 4 (*Chronique, 1461–64*), p. 55. "Touching for the king's evil" was the laying of royal hands on sufferers from scrofula.

SEARCHING THE WOUND: "The Maner of Passyng to Confessioun", 3rd stanza. LIKE WATER: *Vices & Virtues*, pp. 127–28, 180–81.

PRIEST'S QUESTIONS: Duffy, *Stripping of the Altars*, pp. 58–61; Dunbar, "The Tabill of Confessioun", *passim*.

BRANCHES OF PRIDE: *Kalendar of Shepherds*, pp. 34–54; *Vices & Virtues*, pp. 11–22.

BOASTING AND ROBBING: "Douze triomphes", in Gairdner, *Memorials*, pp. 320–21. DEATHS: *HRHS*, p. 73. PERKIN CONFESSING: Ibid., p. 72.

DOMINE, PROBASTI: Psalm 138.

"YES SIR": Duffy, *Stripping of the Altars*, p. 58.

THE APPLE TREE: *Tretyse of Love*, pp. 108–9.

GOD'S CHILD: Idley, *Instructions*, book IIA, ls. 60–61. "HE IS THE MIRROR": Deguileville, *Pélérinage* (see Notes, p. 533), p. xxii.

"WE HAVE RECEIVED": Ellis, *Letters*, vol. 1, p. 34. "THE CHIEF THING": Attreed, "New Source", p. 520.

ADVISED TO KILL PERKIN: Bacon, *Henry VII*, pp. 193–94.

TOTAL EXPENSES: PRO E 36/126, f. 38v; *EH*, pp. 112–13.

"THIS DAY": PRO E101/414/16, f. 1r. ETAPLES: *EH*, p. 92 (Nov. 11th, 1492). KATHERINE OF ARAGON: Ibid., p. 126.

LOSSES AT CARDS: *EH*, p. 114; PRO E101/414/16, f. 1r.

RICHMOND'S REPORT: *CSPM*, pp. 329–31.

HENRY TO DE PUEBLA: Madden, "Documents", p. 189; BL MS Egerton 616/8.

"DECLARE WHO HE IS": CC 111, f. 187v.

HENRY'S FACE AND PRESENCE: *AH*, pp. 142–44; *CSPV*, p. 264.

HEALING THE SICK: PRO E 101/414/16, ff. 1r, 2r, v, 5v, etc.

PERKIN "TOLD THE KING": *CSPM*, p. 329.

ANDRÉ'S ACCOUNT: *HRHS*, pp. 72–73.

"GREAT KINDNESS": Sanuto, *Diarii*, vol. 1, col. 826.

BLAMING OTHERS: *CSPM*, p. 330; *CSPV*, p. 266.

"A SUBSTITUTE": ASM AD Cartella 567 (Oct. 21st).

COUNCILLORS WITH HENRY: PRO E 36/126, ff. 22r–36r.

FORMAL SURRENDER: *CSPM*, p. 330; *CSPV*, p. 266. *INCHINARSI*: Sanuto, *Diarii*, vol. 1, col. 826. THIRTY-FIVE COUNCILLORS: Condon, "Elites" (see Notes, p. 573), p. 130.

ENTRIES FOR SEPT. 26TH: PRO E 101/414/6, f. 90r.

DORSET MADE MARQUIS: Vergil, *Three Books*, p. 175; Nicols, *Grants* (see Notes, p. 534), pp. viii–x; PRO C53/197, mem. 12. HIS BONDS: *CCR HVII*, pp. 177–78, 289; Lander, *Crown & Nobility* (see Notes, p. 555), pp. 286–88. AT THE BUTTS: *EH*, p. 102.

RODON'S JOBS: *CPR HVII*, vol. 1, pp. 21, 335; ibid., vol. 2, p. 516; Campbell, *Materials*, vol. 1, pp. 11, 291.

A PARDON: *GC*, p. 283; *LC*, p. 218; *AH*, p. 111. PARDONS OF THE "COUNCILLORS": *Rot. Parl.*, vol. 6, pp. 550–51; *CPR HVII*, vol. 2, pp. 122–23 (Heron on Dec. 8th, Astley on the 9th, Skelton on the 10th).

NORFOLK WOMEN: *Paston Letters*, no. 1031 (1489).

DANCING MAIDENS: *EH*, pp. 94, 111.

KATHERINE COLLECTED: CC 111, f. 188r; *AH*, p. 109; *HRHS*, p. 72. DAUBENEY "VERY SLACK": *L&P*, vol. 1, p. 232.

PROVISION FOR KATHERINE: PRO E 36/126, ff. 37r, v; *EH*, p. 115; *L&P*, vol. 1, p. 73; PRO EXT 6/140, 25th document.

HENRY FALLING: *AH*, p. 109; Hall, *Chronicle*, p. 485.

ARRIVING AT SHEEN: *GC*, p. 283.

ANDRÉ'S PAYMENTS: Gairdner, *Memorials*, preface, p. ix; Rymer, *Foedera*, vol. xii, p. 643; *EH*, p. 109. THE VOLUME: BL MS Domitian xviii (ff. 126–228). THE KATHERINE SCENE: *HRHS*, pp. 73–75 (BL MS Domitian xviii, ff. 223v–225v).

THEIR MARRIAGE: *HRHS*, p. 70.

THE CHIEF DOCUMENT: J. Desmons, "Un tournaisien prétendant au trône d'Angleterre", in *Revue Tournaisienne*, no. 6 (1910), p. 58.

THE CONFESSION: See Notes, p. 534.

PERKIN "DEPOSING": *CPSM*, p. 331; ASM AD Cartella 567 (Oct. 21st). "NOTARILY KNOWN": *GC*, p. 284. DRAWN UP QUICKLY: It had reached London by October 12th, when a version was read by the mayor to the council: JCCC (JOR10), f. 108r.

FRENCH CONFESSION: CC 111, f. 188r, v.

"COMPTROLLER": This can be checked against two lists of town jobs: Frédéric Hennebert, "Extraits des registres aux resolutions des Consaux de la ville et cité de Tournai", in *Mémoires de la Société Historique et Littéraire de Tournai*, vol. 3 (1856), pp. 279–85, and esp. Hennebert's "Charges et offices à Tournai au XVe siècle", in *Bulletins de la Société Historique et Littéraire de Tournai*, vol. 3 (1853), pp. 63–71. The list has *leveurs, gaugeurs, coulletiers, auneurs, accateurs, revendeurs, eswars, querqueurs*, and a host of others, but no "comptroller" or French equivalent. Many thanks to Danielle De Smet for these sources.

RECEIVER: See Henri Vandenbroeck, *Extraits analytiques des anciens registres des Consaux de la ville de Tournai, 1422–1430*, vol. 2 (Tournai, 1863), pp. v, 64, 66, 111. RULE FORBIDDING A RECEIVER TO BE DEAN OF A GUILD: Ibid., pp. 100, 212.

THE *WICQUET*: Flan as keeper, see Hennebert, "Extraits", pp. 124, 225. KEEPER'S WAGE: Vandenbroeck, *Extraits*, vol. 1 (Tournai, 1861), p. 10.

GRANDFATHER/GODFATHER: Thanks to Professor Nicholas Orme for advice on this point.

FRENCH APPENDIX: CC 111, f. 188v; *CSPM*, p. 330; Molinet, *Chroniques*, vol. 5, p. 79.

"FAIR, FREE": Commines, *Mémoires*, book 5, ch. xi. "INCORRIGIBLE": Cited in A. G. Chotin, *Histoire de Tournai et du Tournésis*, vol. 2 (Tournai, 1840), p. 85n.

COMPLAINTS TO THE KING: La Grange, "Extraits" (see Notes, p. 536) pp. 151–55; Hennebert, "Extraits", pp. 110–13 (1477).

TANT AU BAS: "Extraits des Registres des Consaux de Tournai", in *Compte rendu des séances de la Commission Royale d'Histoire,* vol. 11, part 2 (Brussels, 1846), p. 349.

THE TOWN AT WAR: Ibid., *passim,* esp. pp. 343, 352, 353, 368, 372, 380–85; Hennebert, "Extraits", esp. pp. 119, 120, 138.

DE FARO AT CONDÉ: Hennebert, "Extraits", p. 140.

HOP-POLES: Chotin, *Tournai,* vol. 2, p. 67.

"PIECES OF VERDURE": PRO E 404/81/3, warrant of Nov. 13th, 1493.

RHETORICIANS AND PLAYERS: La Grange, "Extraits", pp. 94, 122–23, 145, 172, 260, 331; Vandenbroeck, *Extraits,* vol. 1, p. 68.

THE PRINCE OF LOVE: La Grange, "Extraits", pp. 157, 186, 199, 256, 295.

CATHERINE OF FRANCE: "Extraits" (*CRH*), p. 340.

PIREMAN: Gairdner, *Richard III/Perkin Warbeck,* pp. 334–35.

BODIES OF FRENCHMEN: Chotin, *Tournai,* vol. 2, p. 59 and n.

BOATMEN'S RANKING: Leo Verriest, "Les luttes sociales et le contrat d'apprentissage à Tournai jusqu'en 1424", in *Mémoires de l'Académie Royale de Belgique,* 2nd series, vol. ix, p. 16 and n.

JEHAN'S *BOURGEOISIE:* Gairdner, *Richard III/Perkin Warbeck,* p. 334; Le Comte P. A. du Chastel de la Howarderie, "Notes sur la famille de l'aventurier Perkin Warbeck", *Bulletins de la Société Historique et Littéraire de Tournai,* vol. 25 (1892), p. 411.

BOURGEOISIE, FEES AND PRIVILEGES: La Grange, "Extraits", pp. 120, 156–64; Vandenbroeck, *Extraits,* vol. 2, pp. 68–69.

BEVEREN: Desmons, "Un Tournaisien", p. 56. Although a native, and writing before the complete destruction of the Tournai archives by German bombing in World War II, Desmons could add no further details about the family.

DERYK: Chastel de la Howarderie, "Notes", p. 411.

JEHAN'S PUB BRAWL: AN Charte de l'Audience no. 813; Kervyn de Lettenhove, *Oeuvres de Chastellain* (see Notes, p. 533), vol. 4, p. 164n.

"WORK OF VENUS": Ibid., pp. 165–66.

JEHAN'S QUAYSIDE BRAWL: Gairdner, *Richard III/Perkin Warbeck,* pp. 334–35. PENALTIES: Hennebert, "Extraits", pp. 390–400, *passim;* La Grange, "Extraits", pp. 162–63.

SOUTHAMPTON'S GALLEYMEN: e.g. SCRO SC 5/3/1, f. 21v, and other instances.

BEER: Vandenbroeck, *Extraits,* vol. 1, pp. 8, 208.

COLIN AND INNOCENT: Chastel de la Howarderie, "Notes", p. 414.

TOURNAI CHRONOLOGY: The MS Givaire, cited in Chotin, *Tournai,* p. 80 n.

BACQUETS AND FLOOD RELIEF: Vandenbroeck, *Extraits,* vol. 2, pp. 72–73.

CAUFOURS: La Grange, "Extraits", pp. 132, 140, 141, 288, 302 and *passim;* Hennebert, "Extraits", p. 298.

TOURNAI GOVERNMENT: Gaston Preud'homme, "Extraits des registres des Consaux de la ville de Tournai (1455–1472)", in *Mémoires de la Société Royale d'Histoire et d'Archéologie de Tournai,* vol. 1 (Tournai, 1980), pp. 297–99. Many thanks to C.S.L. Davies for providing this, which led me to most of the other Tournai sources cited in this chapter.

FLAN AT CONDÉ: Hennebert, "Extraits", pp. 136, 179, 330–31.

DUBOIS: Ibid., p. 177. JEHAN CARLIER: Ibid., pp. 398–99.

TAVERN REGULATIONS: La Grange, "Extraits", pp. 331–32.

JEHAN'S MARRIAGE: Chastel de la Howarderie, p. 411. He gives no source.

FAROU: Gairdner, *Richard III/Perkin Warbeck*, p. 334; Paul Rolland, *Les Origines de la Commune de Tournai* (Brussels, 1931), App. III.

OTHER CHILDREN: Chastel de la Howarderie, pp. 411–12; CC 111, f. 189r.

THIROYAN: CC 111, f. 189r. The words *frere Thiroyan* have been disputed, but the reading is not in doubt in this document.

ANOTHER SON: discussed in the Epilogue, pp. 513–15.

THE BOATMEN'S CHAPEL: La Grange, "Extraits", p. 112.

APPRENTICESHIP RULES: Verriest, "Luttes sociales", pp. 33 and n., 35, 36.

CROIZIÈRES' SCHOOL: La Grange, "Extraits", pp. 296–97. THE "PROFANE PLACE": Ibid., p. 306.

LES BONS ENFANTS: Leopold Michel, "Causeries à propos de nos vieux registres paroissiaux", *Bulletins de la Société Historique et Littéraire de Tournai*, vol. 20 (1884), p. 127, n. 1.

GASPAR VAN WEERBECKE: *Biographie Nationale* (Brussels, 1938), vol. 27, cols. 151–59; *Compte rendu des séances de la Commission Royale d'Histoire*, vol. 11, part ii (1846), p. 679, where "Jaspar" ranks fifth in the archduke's chapel.

CATHEDRAL PRECINCTS: La Grange, "Extraits", pp. 60, 71, 147, 235, 345.

MUGUET AS CANTOR: Hennebert, "Extraits", p. 176.

SALVE REGINA: J. Le Maistre d'Anstaing, *Recherches sur l'histoire . . . de l'église cathédrale de Notre Dame de Tournai*, vol. 1 (Tournai, 1842), pp. 240, 242.

ROSES: E. Soil de Moriame, "La dîme des roses à Tournai au XIVe siècle", in *Annales de l'Académie Royale d'Archéologie de Belgique* lxix, 6th series, vol. 9 (1921), *passim*.

BISHOP OF FOOLS: Chotin, *Tournai*, pp. 75–76. BANNING OF THEM: La Grange, "Extraits", p. 265.

EFFECTS OF FINE EDUCATION: Idley, *Instructions*, book 1, ls. 1321–22.

"THE GREATEST PERSONS": Molinet, *Chroniques*, vol. 5, p. 80.

BACON'S OBJECTIONS: *Henry VII*, pp. 195–96 and n.

PERKIN'S QUALITIES: *AH*, pp. 63, 65 and n., 69, 111; BL Cotton Domitian xviii, ff. 210v, 211v; *GC*, p. 262; Zurita, *Historia*, vol. 5, f. 135; Buchanan, *Rerum Scotiarum*, f. 145v.

"HE HAD LONGED": Zurita, *Historia*, vol. 5, ff. 134b–135.

"THAT SORT OF MAN": *AH*, pp. 63 and n., 119.

OUTRECUIDANCE: Molinet, *Chroniques*, vol. 5, p. 80.

SIMNEL'S STORY: *HRHS*, p. 50; Bennett, *Simnel*, pp. 131–33.

"BY MOUTH ALONE": Molinet, *Chroniques*, vol. 5, p. 46.

NANFAN: *L&P*, vol. 1, p. 235. PARRON: *Anni MD Pronosticon* (Bodleian Library, Oxford), sig. a, viir.

MALET AND CHARLES: Commines, *Mémoires*, book 7, ch. viii, p. 23.

RICHMOND'S THANKS: BL Cotton Caligula dvi, f. 20r.

"QUITE CLEAR": ASM AD Cartella 567 (Oct. 21st).

CHARLES'S EVIDENCE: *PI*, vol. 4, p. 522; *CSPS*, p. 92. PICARD SPIES: PRO E 101/414/6, ff. 22v, 23v, 30r, 48r.

KENTINGS: *PI*, vol. 4, p. 397; *CSPS*, p. 59.

HENRY NOT LIKING THE PROOFS: *PI*, vol. 4, p. 597; *CSPS*, p. 111.

RAMSAY/MONYPENY: Ellis, *Letters*, vol. 1, p. 28.

"LOTS OF PEOPLE WHO KNOW HIM": *CSPS*, p. 92; *PI*, vol. 4, p. 522.

"FATHER AND MOTHER": AGS Patronato Real, leg. 52–41, f. 358r, v; not given in the printed versions, though Gairdner mentions it.

JANUARY 1497: *PI*, vol. 5, pp. 147–48; *CSPS*, p. 135. THE DOCUMENT: AGS E 367, ff. 11–21 (Mexia's authentication).

LETTER TO LONDOÑO: *PI*, vol. 5, p. 211; *CSPS*, p. 147.

FRENCH PLEASED: *CSPM*, p. 339.

ANONYMOUS FRENCHMEN: PRO E 101/414/6, *passim*. BRETON SPIES: E 101/414/6, ff. 81v, 84r, 88r. LENESQUE'S WIFE: Ibid., f. 84r.

"JOHN PERKIN": Ibid., f. 88r.

THE BLANK: Carew MS, vol. 632, f. 252r.

OSBEK/CANTERBURY: CCA F/A, f. 258v.

"OSBECK OR OTHERWISE STYENBECK": *GC*, p. 262.

"PETER WARBECK": See e.g. PRO KB 9/51, KB 9/956, KB 9/934/5 and many others.

"PETER WARBOYS": JCCC (JOR 10), f. 106r.

"OBJECT OF CONTEMPT": *AH*, p. 63. Hall said "kin" was applied to him as to "younglings of no strength nor courage for their timorous hearts and pusillanimity." *Chronicle*, p. 462. Holinshed added: "which . . . are not thought worthy of the name of a man." *Chronicles*, vol. 3, p. 504.

"JEMMY": Skelton, "Against the Scots", *passim*.

"PER PERO OSBEK": *CSPM*, p. 330; ASM AD Cartella 567 (Oct. 21st). It is not in capitals, as Hinds implies, but upper and lower case.

"ROUNDELLS & SONGS": *GC*, p. 262.

WESBECQUE: CC 111, ff. 188r, 189r; Molinet, *Chroniques*, vol. 5, pp. 78–79, 118, 120, 131. For the sense of "orphan", see Weightman, *Margaret of York*, p. 170.

HENRY TO THE POPE: *CSPM*, p. 327.

SONCINO/"PIRICHINO": *CSPM*, pp. 323–24, 325, 326. TREVISANO: Sanuto, *Diarii*, vol. 1, cols. 806, 810.

"NO ONE ELSE": *CSPM*, p. 340.

AS SOON AS HE KNEW IT: *AH*, p. 69n. COURT FAMES: Bacon, *Henry VII*, p. 144.

PRINTING THE CONFESSION: *HRHS*, p. 73.

"THE FURTHER HARM": *GC*, p. 284. PRINTED COPIES: Ibid., p. 286.

MOLINET'S SPELLINGS: Molinet, *Chroniques*, vol. 5, p. 78. FOLLOWING HENRY'S LETTER: Ibid., pp. 78–79.

HIS 293RD CHAPTER: Ibid. HIS LAST WORDS: Ibid., p. 121.

EDWARD/JEHAN'S WIFE: Le Baron Kervyn de Lettenhove, *Histoire de Flandre*, vol. 5, *Ducs de Bourgogne 1453–1500* (Brussels, 1850), p. 496.

"NOT WANTING IT": *PI*, vol. 4, p. 597; *CSPS*, p. 111. Henry liked this idea even less than he liked the French evidence, and just wanted "him".

TANJAR AND THE BOY'S FATHER: *PI*, vol. 4, pp. 528–29.

TRISTAN'S FATHER: *Tristan* (see Notes, p. 537), p. 93.

THE LETTER TO HIS MOTHER: Gairdner, *Richard III/Perkin Warbeck*, pp. 329–30; Michel,

"Causeries" (see Notes, p. 578), pp. 127–28; CC 111, ff. 188v–189r. The version given is translated from the Courtrai MS.

DAUBENEY'S P.S.: Ibid., f. 188r.

PORQUIERE: La Grange, "Extraits", p. 80.

THE PROCESSION: Ibid., p. 97; Vandenbroeck, *Extraits,* vol. 2, pp. 209–11, 214.

ADDRESSES TO MOTHERS: *Paston Letters, passim,* esp. vol. 5, nos. 759, 776, 778, 780, 901, 915, etc.; *Stonor Letters* (see Notes, p. 534), vol. 2, p. 31. MARGARET PASTON'S COM-PLAINT: *Paston Letters,* vol. 5, no. 917.

HENRY TO HIS MOTHER: Halliwell Phillipps, *Letters* (see Notes, p. 538), vol. 1, pp. 180–82.

PARENTS INTERCEDING: See e.g. Commines, *Mémoires,* book 5, ch. xv; Duffy, *Stripping of the Altars,* p. 202.

"YOUNG FOND FOUNDLING": Hall, *Chronicle,* p. 475.

TOURNAI'S COINS: Chotin, *Tournai,* vol. 2, p. 10.

"VIVE PERKIN" COINS: Cocheteux, "Une monnaie" (see Notes, p. 551), pp. 63–68; BL MS Facs 295 (c). Tournai continues to show no interest in Perkin: there is no mark of him in the city, and no mention of him in the guide-books.

8. This World My Prison

EXETER BANQUET: PRO E 36/126, f. 7r; DRO Receiver's Accounts, years 12–13, mem. 3r.

HENRY AND REBELS: Pollard, *Henry VII,* vol. 1, p. 176; DRO ECR book 51, f. 329v (Hooker).

NOT IN THE PUBLIC EYE: Hooker mentions his capture as though it happened after Henry's stay: Ibid., f. 329v.

SE LA VITA: ASM AD Cartella 567 (October 21st).

"EAGER . . . TO SEE HIM": *AH,* p. 111.

JANE SHORE: More, *Richard III,* p. 82.

PERKIN'S TRUMPET: PRO E101/14/16, f. 9v.

IN CHAINS: *AH,* p. 110 and n. "IN HIS COMPANY": Ibid., p. 111.

"AWAITED," "ATTENDED": "The Grey Friars Chronicle", in *Monumenta Franciscana,* ed. Richard Howlett, Rolls Series 4, 2 vols. (1858–82), vol. 2, p. 182; Charles Wriothesley, *A Chronicle of England during the Reigns of the Tudors, from 1485 to 1559,* ed. William Douglas Hamilton, vol. 1, Camden Society 147–48 (1875), p. 3; *GC,* p. 283.

SHEEN BUILDING AND GARDENING: *EH,* pp. 97, 101, 107, 115; PRO E 101/414/6, ff. 3r, 5r, 15r, v, 23v, 72r.

HENRY'S ENTRY, AND PERKIN'S: Sanuto, *Diarii,* vol. 1, col. 841; *GC,* p. 283; *LC,* p. 219.

PERKIN ON HORSEBACK: *CSPM,* p. 335; Bacon, *Henry VII,* p. 195.

DELIVERING WILLIAM: *GC,* p. 284; *LC,* p. 281.

HENRY VI PARADED: Visser-Fuchs, "Caspar Weinreich" (see Notes, p. 549), p. 313.

CHEAPSIDE: Sneyd, *Relation* (see Notes, p. 534), pp. 42–43.

THOUGHT LIKELY TO ESCAPE: *AH,* p. 111.

"TAKEN . . . AND HANGED": *CSPV,* p. 265.

HENRY'S MERCY: *CSPM,* p. 329.

TREATED DOULCEMENT: Commines, *Mémoires,* book 5, ch. xx.

GUELDERS/DE LA POLE: *CSPS*, p. 429.

HENRY AND THE HERETIC: *LC*, p. 222.

DE PUEBLA'S APPEAL: *PI*, vol. 5, p. 202 (*CSPS*, p. 198).

SPANISH MEDIATION IN SCOTLAND: George Ridpath, *The Border-History of England and Scotland, deduced from the earliest times to the union of the two Crowns* (1810), p. 470 and n.

SAFE-CONDUCT CLAUSE: Rymer, *Foedera*, vol. xii, p. 675; Conway, *Relations*, App. 1, pp. 242–43.

"VERY DIFFICULT": *CSPS*, p. 168. See also *CSPV*, pp. 269, 271.

PHILIP AND MAXIMILIAN: *CSPM*, p. 317; "Douze triomphes" in Gairdner, *Memorials*, p. 319.

MARGARET'S REACTION: *AH*, p. 110 n.

NEWS TO MAXIMILIAN: *Regesta Imperii XIV*, vol. 2, part ii, no. 8339; vol. 2, part i, nos. 5396, 5512; HHSA Maximiliana 7, f. 302r; Biblioteca Nazionale Marciana (Venice) MSS Lat. XIV/99 (4278), f. 117r.

MAXIMILIAN'S LETTERS: Innsbruck Urkunde 1, 8225, 8226, 8265. THE PERSONAL NOTE: HHSA Maximiliana 7, f. 366r.

SIC TRANSIT: *Regesta Imperii XIV*, vol. 2, part i, no. 5512.

PHILIP'S OFFICERS IN LONDON: *EH*, p. 115.

PERKIN AND KATHERINE ON SHOW: *CSPM*, pp. 333–34; Sanuto, *Diarii*, vol. 1, cols. 841–42.

JACK AND JILL: "Against a Comely Coystrowne", see p. 447.

"THE SWEET DUE DEBT": *Vices & Virtues*, pp. 246–47; Hawes, *Pastime of Pleasure*, p. 201.

"LORD, HOW PERKIN": "Against a Comely Coystrowne", see p. 445. A WIFE'S DUTIES: Geoffrey de la Tour Landry, *The Book of the Enseignements and Teaching that the Knight of the Tower made to his Daughters*, ed. G. B. Rawlings (1902), pp. 102, 137.

KATHERINE'S SERVANTS: PRO E 101/414/16, ff. 6v, 18v, 19r; compare PRO E 101/415/3, ff. 3v, 6v, etc.

THE CHILD'S FATE: see Epilogue, p. 506.

"IN COURT AT LIBERTY": *LC*, p. 223; *GC*, p. 287.

JONES: *CPR HVII*, vol. 1, pp. 102 (Dec. 1485), 406.

SMITH'S JOBS: Gunn, "Courtiers" (see Notes, p. 573), p. 31; Campbell, *Materials*, vol. 2, pp. 175, 179, 305–6. PAYING THE APOTHECARY: PRO E 404/81/3, warrant of May 8th, 1495.

HIS SERVANTS: *CSPV*, p. 269.

PRISONER IN SCOTLAND: *PI*, vol. 5, p. 172; *CSPS*, p. 140; *CSPM*, p. 325.

SUB CUSTODIA: PRO KB 9/416/22. "SURE AND SAFE CUSTODY": *Rot. Parl.*, vol. 6, p. 545; PRO KB 8, mem. 5.

MOLINET'S VIEW: *Chroniques*, vol. 5, p. 120. MAXIMILIAN'S: *Weisskunig*, pp. 218n. (g), 219n.

NEVER TO LEAVE PERKIN'S SIDE: *AH*, p. 111.

SAVAGES OF NEWFOUNDLAND: *CSPV*, p. 262.

SONCINO/MORTON: *CSPM*, p. 328.

COURTEYS IN SANCTUARY: *CPR HVII*, vol. 1, p. 26. HIS PARDONS: Ibid., p. 380; ibid., vol. 2, p. 13.

ANDREW DYMOCK: Ibid., vol. 1, pp. 35, 121, and vol. 2, *passim;* PRO E 405/79, mems. 7v, 64r.

DR. ARGENTINE: *CPR HVII,* vol. 2, p. 158 (grant of Dec. 1498). ELIZABETH'S WORLD: Nicolas, *Privy Purse* (see Notes, p. 537), pp. 1–106, *passim.* AYALA ON HER: *CSPS,* p. 210. IN NOTTINGHAM: Lorraine C. Attreed, "The Politics of Welcome", in *City and Spectacle in Medieval Europe,* ed. Barbara A. Hanawalt & Kathryn L. Reyerson (Minneapolis, 1994), p. 208.

ELIZABETH/HENRY: *EH,* pp. 87–130, *passim.* PAYING HER DEBTS: Ibid., p. 111.

"TO ALTER THE NATURAL DISPOSITION": Vergil, *Three Books,* p. 192.

THE MONKEY: Bacon, *Henry VII,* p. 243.

"MAKING GOOD CHEER": *CSPM,* p. 341.

THE FIRE: *LC,* pp. 222, 233; *CSPM,* p. 341; Sanuto, *Diarii,* vol. 1, col. 878. HENRY'S ESTIMATE: *CSPV,* p. 267. COURT NOT DISPLACED: PRO E 101/414/14, ff. 111–131.

FUNCTIONS OF OFFICERS: *Antiquarian Repertory* (see Notes, p. 546), pp. 297–348 *passim.* MAKING THE BED: Ibid., p. 301. There were more than seventy grooms of the chamber alone, each with a particular function: PRO E36/130, ff. 230v–232v.

"CERTAIN PERSONS": Nicolas, *Privy Purse,* p. 82.

PAYMENTS FOR PERKIN: *EH,* pp. 115, 116, 117. THE DECEMBER PAYMENT: PRO E 101/414/16, f. 9r.

DENIS: *EH,* pp. 95–117 *passim;* Gunn, "Courtiers", pp. 38, 41; PRO E 101/414/6 f 79v.

BRAYBROKE: *CPR HVII,* vol. 1, pp. 332, 378, 386, 469, 470.

CLOTHES FOR DICK: *EH,* pp. 95, 96, 106, 118.

JASPER: Ibid., p. 121.

THE RIDING GOWN: Ibid., p. 117.

DIEGO'S HORSE: Anglo, "Court Festivals" (see Notes, p. 547), p. 27.

COURT FREAKS: *EH,* pp. 87–133, *passim.* THE INDIANS: Stow, *Annales* (see Notes, p. 549), p. 485.

SIMNEL AT COURT: Michael van Cleave Alexander, *The First of the Tudors: A Study of Henry VII and his Reign* (1981), pp. 108–9.

HATRED OF FOREIGNERS: See *English Historical Documents,* vol. 5, 1485–1558, ed. C. H. Williams (1967), p. 190; Sneyd, *Relation,* pp. 20–21, 35. "RUTTERKIN": "Jolly Rutterkin", not certainly by Skelton, but plausibly so, and quoted by characters in his "Magnificence". BREAD AND BUTTER: Sneyd, *Relation,* p. 11.

DISSIMULATION: "The Bowge of Court", ls. 463–69.

SKELTON'S ROBES: "Calliope", *passim.*

"TRIUMPHS OF THE RED ROSE": cited in "The Garland of Laurel", l. 1223.

COURT ORGANS: *EH,* pp. 95, 107; Anglo, "Court Festivals", pp. 33, 34.

THE FOOLISH DUKE OF LANCASTER: *EH,* pp. 90, 91.

HYTHE STANDARD: Ibid., p. 117; PRO E101/414/16, f. 24v.

SPINULA'S REPORT: *CSPM,* p. 348.

THE WARDROBE: PRO E404/81/3, warrant of Oct. 9th, 1493; E 405/79, f. 3v.

THE PANIC: PRO E101/414/16, f. 30r, v.

NEW ROMNEY: *Historical Manuscripts Commission,* vol. 5, 5th Report (1876), p. 549.

HENRY TO OXFORD: Arthurson, *Perkin Warbeck,* p. 197.

FORGETTING THE BENEFITS: *LC*, p. 223.

HENRY KNOWING EVERYTHING: *AH*, p. 115.

LONGING TO DESTROY HIMSELF: Ibid., p. 114 n.

NEWFOUNDLAND: *EH*, pp. 113, 116, 117; Rymer, *Foedera*, vol. xii, p. 595; *CSPM*, pp. 320, 337.

LISTED TOGETHER: PRO E101/414/16, f. 19r.

THE GOWN OF TAWNY MEDLEY: PRO E 404/82, warrant of April 30th.

TO THE TOWER: PRO E 101/414/14, f. 20v. CONDITIONS THERE: *CPR HVII*, vol. 1, p. 119; PRO E 404/80/482; E 404/81/3, warrant of April 3rd, 1494; Sneyd, *Relation*, pp. 45–46.

BOETHIUS: *De Consolatione* (see Notes, p. 573), pp. 61–62.

VERGIL'S THEORIES: *AH*, pp. 114n., 115.

MAXIMILIAN'S MUSINGS: Fuensalida, *Correspondencia* (see Notes, p. 558), p. 25. HIS OTHER PLANS: Ibid., pp. 52, 56; *Weisskunig*, pp. 218–19.

"LICENCIATUS": *CSPS*, p. 150.

ATWATER AND BARRY: Madden, *Documents*, p. 190.

PAYMENTS FOR KATHERINE: *EH*, p. 115; PRO E 101/414/6, ff. 18v, 19r. HER RE-APPEARANCE: PRO E101/414/16, f. 60r.

MARGARET BEAUFORT: Gairdner, *Richard III*, p. 227.

THE GENERAL PARDON: J. S. Brewer, James Gairdner & R. H. Brodie, eds., *Letters and Papers, Foreign and Domestic, of the Reign of Henry VIII, 1509–1547*, 21 vols. (1862–1932), vol. 1, part i (1864), p. 247.

"FURRED WITH MINK": *CDRS*, no. 1688.

"A SLEEPY DRINK": Gainsford, *Perkin Warbeck* (see Notes, p. 530), p. 547.

HENRY'S GUARDS: *AH*, p. 7; Sneyd, *Relation*, p. 105.

KEBYLL AND SHERWYN'S INDICTMENT: PRO KB 9 416/22. SHERWYN'S BURGLARY: JCCC (JOR 10), f. 100r.

WARDERS FINED: PRO E 404/81/1, warrant of Feb. 4th, 1492; E 404/81/3, warrants of Aug. 28th and Nov. 7th, 1493, and many others.

SMITH'S GRANTS: *CPR HVII*, vol. 2, p. 168; Gunn, "Courtiers", pp. 31–32; *CPR HVII*, vol. 2, p. 168.

REPORT TO VENICE: *CSPV*, p. 269. "BELIEVED GENERALLY": Bacon, *Henry VII*, p. 201.

DE PUEBLA'S VERSION: *PI*, vol. 5, p. 202 (*CSPS*, p. 198).

NEW LOCK: PRO E 101/141/16, f. 27r.

"THE DUKE OF YORK PIERREQUIN": Fuensalida, *Correspondencia*, p. 52.

DORSET: Mancini, *Usurpation* (see Notes, p. 538), p. 113. SUMMER OF 1498: *LC*, p. 223.

THE HUNT FOR PERKIN: *EH*, p. 118; *AH*, p. 115.

HENRY/CHARTERHOUSE: *CSPV*, pp. 177, 183–84; PRO E 404/80/198, 328. HENRY/TRACY: *EH*, p. 112; Neil Beckett, "Henry VII and Sheen Charterhouse", in Harlaxton, *Henry VII* (see Notes, p. 549), pp. 124–25.

TRACY INTERCEDING: *LC*, p. 223; *GC*, p. 287; *AH*, p. 115.

THE HOLY CARDS: Duffy, *Stripping of the Altars*, plate 99.

"LOATHENESS OF LESS ROOM": More, *Dialogue*, p. 283.

CAMBRAI INTERCEDING: Molinet, *Chroniques,* vol. 5, p. 120.
BRADSHAW: PRO E101/414/16, f. 30v.

DE PUEBLA: *PI,* vol. 5, p. 202 (*CSPS,* pp. 152–53).
"SO THE KING": Sanuto, *Diarii,* vol. 1, col. 1023.
"IN SAFE KEEPING": *CSPS,* p. 185. NO "*BURLA* NOW": *PI,* vol. 5, p. 250.
THREE "HOUSES": *CPR HVII,* vol. 1, p. 22.
PERKIN DISPLAYED: *LC,* p. 223; *GC,* p. 287; *AH,* p. 115. THE STOCKS FOR DECEIVING
  BEGGARS: *CPR HVII,* vol. 1, p. 436.
PUNISHMENTS FOR DECEPTIONS: *LC,* pp. 198, 208, 211 (Camell).
GOD THE FATHER: Ibid., p. 245 and n.
OFFENCES PROCLAIMED: JCCC (JOR 10), ff. 31v, 48v, 78v, and others.
DE PUEBLA ON THE DISPLAY: *PI,* vol. 5, p. 250.
"CURSED BY EVERYONE": *AH,* pp. 115–17.
CABOT: *LC,* p. 224; *CSPV,* p. 262; *AH,* p. 117.

9. *Bad Stars*

PARRON'S PREDICTIONS: Bodleian Douce, fragments e, ii (parts of printed prognostica-
  tion for 1498).
INFELICISSIMI: PRO E 36/126, f. 45r (also numbered 22r).
INDICTMENTS: see note on "Conspiracies", p. 585. TOWER BEDS: *CPR HVII,* vol. 1,
  p. 390; PRO E 405/80, ff. 14v, 15v.
CHAINS: PRO KB 8/13; *Fifty-third Report of the Deputy Keeper of the Public Records* (1892),
  App. II, p. 34.
CATEGORIES OF TOWER PRISONERS: Thanks to Jeremy Ashbee, the Tower historian,
  for help on this point.
LONG ROGER: *EH,* pp. 89, 99; PRO E101/414/16, f. 52r.
A SECRET: *PI,* vol. 5, p. 328 (*CSPS,* p. 196).
ERASMUS ON CAMBRAI'S DEPARTURE: *The Epistles of Erasmus, from his earliest letters to his
  fifty-first year,* ed. & tr. Francis Morgan Nichols (1901), nos. 77, 73.
MARGARET AT BINCHE: AN CC 8858, ff. 55v, 56r.
MAXIMILIAN TO HENRY: *PI,* vol. 5, p. 251 (*CSPS,* p. 157). HIS ENVOYS AND PHILIP'S
  IN ENGLAND, JULY AND AUGUST: PRO E 101/414/16, ff. 36r, v, 43v.
TOURNAI *DELA ESCAUT:* La Grange, "Extraits" (see Notes, p. 536), pp. 149, 306; Hen-
  nebert, "Extraits" (see Notes, p. 576), p. 284.
ERASMUS ON CAMBRAI: *Epistles,* nos. 50, 53, 151, 153.
HENRY AT THE TOWER: PRO E101/414/16, ff. 36r, v.
THE INTERVIEW: *PI,* vol. 5, pp. 297–98 (*CSPS,* pp. 185–86). "MARGARET . . . KNEW
  EVERYTHING": *CSPM,* p. 329.
WANTING TO DRIVE MARGARET OUT: *PI,* vol. 4, pp. 465–66 (*CSPS,* p. 74).
MARGARET'S BAD INFLUENCE: Ibid., p. 624 (*CSPS,* p. 124).
THE YOUNG NUN: Molinet, *Chroniques,* vol. 4, pp. 151–52.
CAMBRAI/DE PUEBLA: *PI,* vol. 5, p. 302 (*CSPS,* p. 189).
MARGARET'S LETTER: Ibid., pp. 327–28 (*CSPS,* pp. 196, 198).
SIMULATED JOY: *HRHS,* p. 67.

"IT DOESN'T SEEM SUCH A BAD WAY": *PI*, vol. 5, pp. 333–34.

"PEACE OF MIND": *CSPM*, p. 348.

THE EAST ANGLIAN TOUR: *EH*, p. 119; PRO E101/141/16, f. 37r.

CONSPIRACIES IN THIS SECTION: PRO *Fifty-third Report*, App. II, pp. 30–36; *Third Report of the Deputy Keeper of the Public Records* (1842), App. II, pp. 216–18; PRO KB 8, *passim*.

WILFORD: *LC*, p. 225; *GC*, p. 289; *AH*, p. 117.

CARRE'S DABBLING: *CPR HVII*, vol. 2, p. 47.

A HANGER: this was the mugger's weapon of choice: see e.g. PRO KB 9/392/35, KB 9/1109, etc.

"TAKE AND DELIVER PETER": see also *Rot. Parl.*, vol. 6, p. 545.

KING'S COUNCIL: Bayne & Dunham, *Select Cases* (see Notes, p. 555), p. 32.

WARD'S SURETIES: Condon, "Kaleidoscope" (see Notes, p. 548), p. 209; *CPR HVII*, vol. 2, p. 156.

AUDELEY: *CPR HVII*, vol. 2, p. 392.

CHARLES THE BOLD: Commines, *Mémoires*, book 5, ch. v.

WATSON'S PARDON: *CPR HVII*, vol. 2, p. 47.

"CONVENABLE . . . LACRYMABLE": Skelton, "Upon a Dead Man's Head," preamble.

LOUNDE'S ARRIVAL "NOTICED": *GC*, p. 282; *LC*, p. 21.

MARGARET'S DEVOTIONS: AN CC 8859, ff. 43r, 61v.

"SOME LORDS OF ENGLAND": Molinet, *Chroniques*, vol. 5, p. 118.

THE ISLE OF WIGHT TOUR: *EH*, p. 122.

AUGUST OUTLAWRIES: PRO KB 29/139, mems. 50v, 53r. HERON: See also *Rot. Parl.*, vol. 6, pp. 550–51.

TAYLOR THE YOUNGER: *CPR HVII*, vol. 2, p. 188 (Aug. 24th, 1499).

VERGIL'S DOUBTS: *AH*, p. 117.

HENRY TO LOUIS XII: BL MS Add. 46455, ff. 136r–137v.

"AGING 20 YEARS": *CSPS*, p. 239.

WELSH FORTUNE-TELLER: Ibid.

DE ASTRORUM VI FATALI: MS Selden Supra 77 (Bodleian Library, Oxford), esp. ff. 16r–28v; C.A.J. Armstrong, "An Italian Astrologer at the Court of Henry VII", in *England, France and Burgundy*, pp. 160–61, 165–66.

RICHARD'S BAD STARS: MS Selden Supra 77, f. 18r, v.

PARRON'S COMPLAINT: *Anni MD Pronosticon* (Bodleian), sig. b, ir.

JUDGE FINEUX'S STATEMENT: Bayne & Dunham, *Select Cases*, p. 32.

LEGAL PROCEEDINGS AND SENTENCES: PRO *Third Report*, pp. 216, 218; PRO *53rd Report*, pp. 30–31, 33, 35; *LC*, pp. 226–27. NO RECORD: This should have appeared in the controlment roll with the others: KB 29/131, rot. 4.

"IN THE SAME WAY AS WARWICK": PRO KB 8/22; "Grey Friars Chronicle" (see Notes, p. 580) p. 182.

ATWATER ARRESTED: BL MS Add. 46455, f. 137r.

TAYLOR THE ELDER'S ARREST: See p. 65 and n.

ATWATER ATTAINTED: *CPR HVII*, vol. 2 (March 28th, 1499). HIS SON PARDONED: Ware, *Antiquities*, p. 40.

SENTENCES ON THE WARDERS: *PRO 53rd Report*, p. 35. Strangeways appears to have been spared and was pardoned the next year: *CPR HVII*, vol. 2, p. 205.

WARD'S DEATH: Condon, "Kaleidoscope", pp. 209, 210.

OUTLAWRIES: PRO KB 29/131, rot. 4.

LOUNDE: *CPR HVII*, vol. 2, p. 237. The renewals of his outlawry are crossed out in the controlment roll.

WARWICK'S TRIAL AND SENTENCE: PRO KB 8/2, mem. 3v; *Plumpton Correspondence*, ed. Thomas Stapleton, Camden Society vol. xxix (1839), p. 141. STORAGE OF THE RECORDS: *PRO 53rd Report*, p. 15; L. W. Vernon Harcourt, "The Baga de Secretis", *EHR*, vol. 23 (1908), pp. 525–29.

HIS EXECUTION: *LC*, p. 226. "GREAT FLOODS": "Grey Friars Chronicle", pp. 182–83. HENRY'S PAYMENTS: *EH*, p. 123.

"MADE IN BLOOD": Bacon, *Henry VII*, p. 204.

PERKIN'S EXECUTION: *LC*, pp. 227–28; *GC*, p. 291.

"WALKING THE DISTANCE": Molinet, *Chroniques*, vol. 5, p. 121.

MUD IN THE STREETS: Williams, *Eng. Hist. Docs* (see Notes, p. 582), p. 189.

"HE DIDN'T LOOK MUCH LIKE HIM": Molinet, *Chroniques*, vol. 5, p. 121.

MIRACLES: Knox, *The Miracles of Henry VI*, tr. Ronald Knox (Cambridge, 1923), pp. 97, 154.

PARRON'S VERSION OF THE CONFESSION: *Anni MD Pronosticon*, f. 7v.

DE PUEBLA/AYALA: Zurita, *Historia*, vol. 5, p. 170. DE PUEBLA'S REPORTS: *CSPS*, p. 249.

SANGRE REAL: *L&P*, vol. 1, pp. 113–14; BL MS Egerton 616/16. MOLINET'S THEORY: Molinet, *Chroniques*, vol. 5, p. 121.

"IF THOU WILT LEARN": *Vices & Virtues* (see Notes, p. 533), pp. 70–71.

BELIEVING IN THE LIE: *AH*, p. 119; Bacon, *Henry VII*, p. 139.

IN MANUS TUAS: Skelton, "Magnificence", ls. 2044–45; "Mankind", l. 516.

VILLON: "Quatrain of Villon doomed to die/Variant", ls. 3–4.

Epilogue: Absence

"SUCH GRACE": Molinet, *Chroniques*, vol. 5, p. 121.

STOW'S VISIT: *A Survey of London*, reprinted from the text of 1603, ed. C. L. Kingsford, vol. 1 (Oxford, 1908), pp. 178–79.

OWEN TUDOR: Eric. N. Simons, *The Reign of Edward IV* (1966), pp. 51–55.

BIRDS PECKING: "L'Epitaphe Villon", verse 3.

THE PORTE DE MARVIS: Vandenbroeck, *Extraits*, vol. 2, p. 142n.

"HUNG AND DRIED": Molinet, *Chroniques*, vol. 5, p. 121.

SHOOTING STARS: *Mirror of the World* (see Notes, p. 535), pp. 122–23.

ASTONISHED THE COUNTRY: Molinet, *Chroniques*, vol. 5, p. 118.

THE PESTILENCE: "Grey Friars Chronicle", p. 183; Wriothesley's *Chronicle*, p. 4 (see Notes, p. 580); *AH*, p. 119 n.

HENRY'S QUITTANCE: BL MS Add. 21480, f. 177v.

"The lily-white rose": Davies, *Medieval Lyrics*, no. 156.

De Puebla's summary: *L&P*, vol. 1, pp. 113–14; BL MS Egerton 616/16.

"winding ivy": Bacon, *Henry VII*, p. 202.

Henry's acts of piety: *EH*, pp. 111, 121, 124.

Ayala: *CSPS*, p. 266.

West Country fines: Arthurson, "Rising of 1497" (see Notes, p. 570), pp. 12–14; *L&P*, vol. 2, pp. 335–37; Howard, "Fines Imposed" (see Notes, p. 572), *passim*. Henry's endorsements: BL MS Royal 14B vii, *passim;* BL MS Add 21480, f. 175r. "most ruthlessly": *AH*, p. 109.

"For why 'tis hard": Ian Arthurson, "A Question of Loyalty", *The Ricardian*, vol. vii (1987), p. 408.

Attainders: *Rot. Parl.*, vol. 6, pp. 544–48. Audeley's pardon: *CPR HVII*, vol. 2, p. 392.

Attainders and heirs: Campbell, *Materials*, vol. 1, p. 459; Lander, *Crown and Nobility*, pp. 147 and n., 148.

Exemptions from the general pardon: J. S. Brewer et al., *Letters and Papers* (see Notes, p. 583), vol. 1, part i, pp. 11, 10.

Suffolk's conspiracy: W. E. Hampton, "The White Rose under the First Tudors", part ii, in *The Ricardian*, vol. vii, no. 98 (Sept. 1987), *passim*. At Henry's jousts: *LC*, pp. 201–2. Secret dinner, Hampton, "White Rose", p. 465.

Neville's pardons: *CPR HVII*, vol. 2, pp. 131 (March 23rd, 1498), 236 (July 18th, 1501), 243 (March 24th, 1501). Dorset's son: *Chronicle of Calais* (see Notes, p. 548), p. 6; Lander, *Crown and Nobility*, p. 288.

Katherine at St. Omer: Molinet, *Chroniques*, vol. 5, pp. 131–32; *Chronicle of Calais*, pp. 4, 49–51.

"the White Rose": Lesley in his *History of Scotland* (1561), p. 67, seems to have started this story, for which there is no contemporary source.

Katherine's clothes: PRO E 101/415/7, nos. 26, 81, 133, 166; Dunlop, "Masked Comedian" (see Notes, p. 563), p. 126, n. 8; *CDRS*, pp. 338, 341, 419–21, 424.

André's blanks: *HRHS*, p. 75.

At Margaret's betrothal: Leland, *Collectanea*, vol. 4, p. 259. Here she was ranked tenth among the ladies.

Katherine's servants: PRO E 101/415/3, ff. 3v, 6v, 16r, 21v, 32v, 38r, etc. Dressed in black: Brewer et al., *Letters and Papers*, vol. 2, part ii (1864), p. 11. At Elizabeth's funeral: Moorhen, "Four Weddings" (see Notes, p. 564), part ii, *The Ricardian*, vol. xii, no. 157 (June 2002), pp. 450–51.

Grant of estates: See Gairdner's notes in Busch, *England under the Tudors* (see Notes, p. 556), pp. 440–41. Citizenship: Brewer et al., *Letters and Papers*, vol. 1, part i, p. 289.

The false Katherine: Taylor, *James IV*, p. 118.

The child in Wales: Lisa Hopkins, *John Ford's Political Theatre* (Manchester, 1994), pp. 61–62; Moorhen, "Four Weddings", part i, pp. 413–14. Many thanks to Wendy Moorhen for copies of her source for this: *Limbus Patrum Morganiae et Glamorganiae* (*The Genealogies of Glamorgan*), ed. George T. Clark (1886), p. 500.

Adam Abell's gossip: *Queill of Tyme* (see Notes, p. 549), p. 112. Thanks to Wendy Moorhen for a copy of this.

Henry's health: David Thomson, "Henry VII and the uses of Italy: the Savoy Hospital and Henry VII's Posterity," in Harlaxton, *Henry VII*, p. 107; *L&P*, vol. 1, pp. 233, 239 and n.

QUINTESSENTIA: *The Book of Quinte Essence or the Fifth Being*, ed. J. G. Furnivall, EETS 16 (1866), *passim*.

KATHERINE AS COMPANION: Dunlop, "Masked Comedian", pp. 126-27.

"PLAYING MONEY": Anglo, "Court Festivals" (see Notes, p. 547), p. 44.

"DAMNABLE ESPRITE": *Will of Henry VII*, p. 30. DEVILS SEIZING THE SOUL: Rivers, *Cordyal*, p. 99.

"PRINCES KILLED": Pollard, *Princes* (see Notes, p. 540), p. 120; Vergil, *Three Books*, p. 188; Molinet, *Chroniques*, vol. 2, pp. 402-3.

MORE'S STORY: *Richard III*, pp. 126-33.

TYRELL'S ATTAINDER: Hammond & White, "Sons of Edward IV" (see Notes, p. 540), pp. 11-12.

NANFAN/HENRY/TYRELL: *L&P*, vol. 1, p. 235.

TYRELL'S OFFICES: Campbell, *Materials*, vol. 1, pp. 270, 301, 460, 503; vol. 2, pp. 251-54.

"[THEIR] DEATH": More, *Richard III*, pp. 126-27, 132.

JAMES TO GUELDERS: Ibid., vol. 1, pp. xlvii-xlviii.

JAMES TO ANNE OF BRITTANY: *L&P*, vol. 2, pp. 185-87.

OFFICERS USING THE NAME: See e.g. *Privy Seal* (see Notes, p. 564), no. 405; *ADC*, p. 361.

THE NEW TREATY: Ridpath, *Border-History*, p. 471; Rymer, *Foedera*, vol. xii, p. 274.

CAMBUSKENNETH: W. B. Cook, "Stirling Castle", *British Archaeological Association*, vol. xlv (1889), p. 234. Thanks to Bill Hampton for this reference.

MAXIMILIAN TO THE ESTATES: *Regesta Imperii XIV*, vol. 3, part i (*Maximilian, 1499-1501*), no. 9018.

"DAMAGED BY THE FAVOUR": *CSPV*, pp. 267, 280-82, 371. NO CONTACT: Philpot, *Maximilian*, p. 119.

CURZON/MAXIMILIAN/SUFFOLK: Philpot, *Maximilian*, pp. 176-83; *L&P*, vol. i, pp. 134-44, 187, 212-18.

MAXIMILIAN'S DOUBTS: *Weisskunig*, pp. 218ns. (b), (g), 219n.

ZACHTLEVANT: *L&P*, vol. 1, pp. 264-65. PAYING IT BACK: *Exchequer Rolls of Scotland*, no. 309; *TA*, p. cxxviii n.

THE DEED OF SALE: Chastel de la Howarderie, "Notes" (see Notes, p. 577), p. 411.

NICAISE'S WILL: Ibid., pp. 411-12.

THE ABBOT OF FLANDERS'S SERVANT: PRO E101/414/16, f. 4v.

CANDLES AT BINCHE: AN CC 8860, f. 60v (5 lb. of wax candles burned in 1500, cost 60s. 6d.). Compare 1499 (2 lb., 22s.: CC 8858, f. 67r) and 1501 (3lb., 31s. 6d.: CC 8861, f. 60v).

BAPTISM OF PHILIP'S SON: Molinet, *Chroniques*, vol. 5, pp. 94-98.

THE ENGLISH CHILD: AN CC 7544, 5th register, f. 9v.

JEHAN LE SAGE: AN CC 8839, f. 39v, 55r (the deleted list of clothes); CC 8840, f. 58r; CC 8841, f. 50v; CC 8842, f. 53v; CC 8843, ff. 62v-63r; CC 8844, ff. 54v-55r;

CC 8845, f. 59v; CC8846, f. 53v (last entry, for the accounting period ending Jan. 1486).

EDWARD'S JESTER: Weightman, *Margaret of York*, p. 47. EDWARD'S WARRANTS: PRO E 404/76/4, nos. 21, 130. The wording of the second is not the usual spying-talk, suggesting a different sort of business.

THE ROOM BELOW THE CHAPEL: AN CC 8839, f. 42v; CC 8857, f. 39v; CC 8852, f. 51r.

RIDING THE GELDING: A.V. Billen, *1,000 Years of Fyfield History* (Abingdon, 1955), p. 33.

CRADOCK'S WILL: Rev. John Montgomery Traherne, *Historical Notices of Sir Matthew Cradoc kt of Swansea* (Llandovery, 1840), pp. 15–23. JEWELS: Ibid., p. 16. Thanks to Wendy Moorhen for a copy of this.

EDWARD'S FLEUR-DE-LIS: Commines, *Mémoires,* book 4, ch. ix.

CRADOCK AS CONSTABLE: *CPR HVII,* vol. 1, p. 99. HIS "WARMTH": Moorhen, "Four Weddings", part ii, p. 470.

KATHERINE'S WILL: PRO probate 11/27, Dingley, Quire 10.

"AN OBSCURE MAN": Vergil, *Three Books,* p. 215.

THE TURTLE DOVE: Caxton, *Mirror of the World,* p. 102.

"IN ALL FORTUNES": Bacon, *Henry VII,* p. 193.

MARGARET'S WILL: ADN B 458, 17.919.

"THE LAMENTATION": Weightman, *Margaret of York,* pp. 184–86.

LEAVING THE BODY: Deguileville, *Pélérinage,* pp. 1–10, 52, 57. "CHILD'S PLAY": *Vices & Virtues,* pp. 141–42.

LESS THAN HALF AN HOUR: Caxton, *Mirror of the World,* p. 173.

"HE HATH LEFT THY LIVERY": Rivers, *Cordyal,* p. 42.

BRIGHTNESS OF HEAVEN: Ibid., pp. 123–25, 128; *Kalendar of Shepherds,* pp. 59–67; "Pearl", stanzas lxxxiii–xciii; Deguileville, *Pélérinage, passim.*

THE CONFRONTATION: Rivers, *Cordyal,* pp. 66–68, 75, 137–38.

ILLUSTRATIONS

Thanks to the following for their kind permission to allow the reproduction of material:

1. Chalk sketch of a portrait of "Richard, Duke of York," *c.* 1494: *Receuil d'Arras*, no. 23 (Mediathèque d'Arras).
2. Richard, Duke of York, *c.* 1480 (Dean and Chapter of Canterbury Cathedral/ Geoffrey Wheeler).
3. Edward IV, 1472 (Bayerische Staatbibliotek, Munich/Geoffrey Wheeler).
   Edward IV, *c.* 1475 (Society of Antiquaries of London).
4. Margaret of York, *c.* 1470 (Society of Antiquaries of London).
5. Margaret of York greets the risen Jesus, *c.* 1470 (British Library).
6. Signature from letter of Richard Plantagenet to Isabella, 1493 (British Library).
   Signature and monogram from Richard's "will," 1495 (Österreichisches Staats-archiv, Vienna).
   Monogram from his proclamation of 1496 (British Library).
7. Silver *gros* coin of Richard IV, 1494 and copper "Vive Perkin" jeton, after 1497 (British Library).
   His secret code, 1495 (Archives Départementales du Nord, Lille).
8. The first page of the draft protocols of December 1494 (Stadsarchief Antwerpen).
9. Maximilian by Dürer, 1518 (Albertina, Vienna/Fotomas Index, UK).
10. James IV, *c.* 1500 (Collection of the Stirlings of Keir).
11. Letter of Richard of England to Bernard de la Forsa, 1496 (British Library).
12. The limbless prince, 1497 (British Library).
13. Henry VII, *c.* 1503 (National Portrait Gallery, London).
14. Elizabeth of York, *c.* 1500 (National Portrait Gallery, London).
15. Richard of York's bad stars: the *De astrorum vi fatali,* 1499 (Bodleian Library, University of Oxford).
16. Margaret's Lamentation, *c.* 1500: *The Deposition* (detail) (John Paul Getty Museum, Los Angeles).

ACKNOWLEDGMENTS

This book has been in the making for many years, since my schooldays, and first thanks are due for kindness very long ago. First of all to my parents, who tolerated my scribbling after lights out and happily made detours to obscure parts of Ireland for "colour" for the novel which, thank God, never saw the light of day. Second, to my history teacher Angela Fleming, who encouraged my first faltering researches; to Dr. John Coates, who taught me not to believe anything I read about late-fif-teenth-century history; to Nobby Russell, yeoman-warder of the Tower; and to the many archivists and librarians who fielded my inquiries, treat-ing me as seriously as they would have done an adult researcher. I'm sorry it has taken so long to produce anything to show for it.

In the second phase of my research, thanks are due first to my hus-band and three sons, who put up with a project that made me much more antisocial (and involved more trips far afield) than my previous efforts. I know they are still mystified that settling down to a batch of documents after a day in the office is not work to Mum, but delightful relaxation; but one day they may understand.

Second thanks must go, as ever, to *The Economist,* the most tolerant of employers, where flipping from the twenty-first century to the fifteenth is made easy and even, I think, tacitly encouraged. Certain colleagues, too, deserve particular thanks. Vendeline von Bredow was my invaluable liai-son with German and Austrian archives, unlocking wonderful troves of information; Michael Reid helped with the Spanish ones, besides shedding welcome light on Dr. de Puebla's more cryptic dispatches; and Fiammetta Rocco helped with Italian. Their kindness more than compensated for the prevailing bafflement, and thanks are probably due to all who did *not* say "Wasn't there another one?" or "What about Wat Tyler?" What about Wat Tyler, indeed.

Outside the office I also found extraordinary generosity with documents and time. Everyone has been, I hope, acknowledged in the Notes, but particular thanks should go to Bill Hampton, for tirelessly searching his local libraries and archives in the West Country on my behalf; to Peter and Carolyn Hammond, for providing books and answering queries; to Anna von Pezold not only for translating from the German, but for deciphering Maximilian's scribbles; to the staff of the London Library, for their unstinting help and good humour; to Lord St. Levan at St. Michael's Mount for sending all his own notes on the subject, and for his hospitality; and to Wendy Moorhen and Christine Weightman for many e-mails and several enjoyable lunches to share information on those two crucial women, Katherine Gordon and Margaret of York. C.S.L. Davies most generously provided two documents that became the core of the book, the Setubal testimonies and the guide to surviving fifteenth-century evidence in Tournai, and my reappraisal would not have been possible without him.

Abroad, thanks must go to Professor Leopold Auer, director of the Haus-, Hof- und Staatsarchivs in Vienna; to Dr. Manfred Rupert, director of the Tiroler Landesarchiv in Innsbruck; to Frau Moses of the Sächsisches Haupstaatsarchiv in Dresden; to Jose Maria Burrieza Mateos of the Archivo General in Simancas; and to Dr. Susy Marcon at the Biblioteca Nazionale Marciana in Venice. Particular thanks for kindness well beyond the call of duty to Paul Vancolen of the Stedelijke Openbare Bibliotheek in Courtrai, who sent the relevant documents from the Courtrai Codex on his own initiative and without charge, and to Danielle De Smet of the Tournai Public Library, who came magnificently to the rescue by providing all the material I needed when the archives decided to close *à l'improviste* (as archives do). A special thanks to Dr. Inge Wiesflecker-Friedhuber at Karl-Franzens University in Graz for copying and sending without charge dozens of pages of the *Regesta Imperii*, from which a great number of good things emerged. And lastly, particular thanks to Adelino Soares de Mello in Lisbon for tirelessly seeking out rare books and documents and for translating many a knotty piece of poetry or prose. Next time, I will try to pick a subject who went no further than Swindon.

Several people, all considerably more expert on the period than I am, read the manuscript, or parts of it, before publication. Thanks to all of them—C.S.L. Davies, Peter Hammond, Wendy Moorhen, Colin Richmond, Livia Visser-Fuchs and Christine Weightman—for their time, their good advice and their eagle eyes. Any mistakes that remain are lucky to survive, and are of course my fault in the first place.

Lastly, thanks as ever to my agent, Toby Eady, for his constant solici-tousness and encouragement, and to my sterling editors on either side of the Atlantic, Dan Franklin, Joy de Menil, and Benjamin Dreyer, for deal-ing with an author who was more neurotic about this book than usual and needed dunking in cold water every so often. To take on a subject who has become unknown, and is deeply mysterious anyway, is a leap of faith indeed, especially in New York.

Index

For obvious reasons, the subject of this book cannot be included here under any of his names. The entry for Richard, Duke of York, refers to the boy who was incontrovertibly the second son of Edward IV, last seen for certain in 1483.